D1278947

ALEXANDRE DUMAS PÈRE

GARLAND REFERENCE LIBRARY
OF THE HUMANITIES
(VOL. 257)

ALEXANDRE DUMAS PÈRE
*A Bibliography of Works
Published in French, 1825–1900*

Douglas Munro
Chevalier dans l'Ordre des Arts et des Lettres

Avant-propos de
Alain Decaux
*de l'Académie Française,
Président de la Société des Amis d'Alexandre Dumas*

GARLAND PUBLISHING, INC. • NEW YORK & LONDON
1981

The author acknowledges the financial
assistance of the Scottish Arts Council in the
production of this volume.

Library of Congress Cataloging in Publication Data

Munro, Douglas.
   Alexandre Dumas père, a bibliography of works
published in French, 1825–1900.

   (Garland reference library of the humanities ;
v. 257)
   Includes indexes.
   1. Dumas, Alexandre, 1802–1870—Bibliography.
I. Title. II. Series.
Z8247.M85 [PQ2230]   016.843'7   80-8975
ISBN 0-8240-9361-5   AACR2

Printed on acid-free, 250-year-life paper
Manufactured in the United States of America

For my friend
Dugald MacArthur
Librarian-Emeritus
University of St. Andrews,
Scotland

CONTENTS

AVANT-PROPOS

C'est avec admiration que j'ai pris connaissance de l'oeuvre considérable de Douglas Munro. Voici en effet la première bibliographie complète des oeuvres d'Alexandre Dumas père. Elle couvre tous les titres édités en langue française jusqu'en 1900.

Il faut être familier d'Alexandre Dumas—c'est mon cas— pour prendre conscience de l'immensité de l'oeuvre accomplie par ce géant, le XIXe siècle français se révèle, en littérature, le temps des entreprises les plus ambitieuses qui aient été jamais. Que l'on découvre dans le même siècle des hommes comme Hugo, Balzac, Dumas, Zola, voilà qui, aujourd'hui donne quelque peu le vertige.

Recenser déjà toutes les oeuvres de Dumas présente des difficultés considerables. Mais chercher entre les multiples éditions—rançon d'un succès torrentiel—celle qui doit être retenue comme originale; découvrir, d'une édition à l'autre, les éventuelles variantes et les possibles erreurs; dépister les reproduction parfois illicites; énumérer les traductions: voilà qui n'avait jamais été fait, tant il fallait y mettre de courage et d'esprit de suite.

La bibliographie proposée par Douglas Munro est le fruit de plus de quarante années de recherches dans les principales bibliothèques du monde: Autriche, Belgique, Brésil, Bulgarie, Canada, Danemark, Espagne, Finlande, France, Grand-Bretagne, Grèce, Hongrie, Islande, Italie, Malte, Nouvelle-Zélande, Pays-Bas, Pologne, Portugal, République Démocratique Allemande, Roumanie, Suède, Suisse, Turquie, Tchécoslovaquie, U.S.A., Yougoslavie. . . . Le résultat: six à sept mille différentes éditions de Dumas définitivement proposées aux admirateurs du maître mondial de l'imaginaire.

C'est en Nouvelle-Zélande, où il est né, que Douglas Munro a rencontré Monsieur F.W. Reed. Il lui a communiqué son intérêt et son amour pour l'auteur des "Trois mousquetaires". Il vit maintenant en Ecosse où il se consacre presque exclusivement à l'étude de l'oeuvre d'Alexandre Dumas. Douglas Munro a traduit en anglais plusieurs livres de Dumas: "La bouillie de la comtesse Berthe", "Marie Stuart", "La jeunesse de Pierrot", "Capitaine Pamphile", "Histoire d'un casse-noisette", et "Les aventures de Lyderic". Je le dis avec force: Douglas Munro est aujourd'hui le plus grand expert d'Alexandre Dumas.

Pour toutes ces raisons, je salue avec chaleur et le respect la publication du travail qui est aujourd'hui proposé au public.

Alain DECAUX

INTRODUCTION

Alexandre Dumas, père, was born at Villers-Cotterets on 24 July 1802, and died in his son's house at Puys, near Dieppe, on 5 December 1870. His writing life spanned 45 years.

As will be seen, this bibliography covers his works including those published in the posthumous years to 1900. This may seem an arbitrary date, but apart from the magnificent two-volume edition of "La dame de Monsoreau", superbly illustrated with engravings by Maurice Leloir, issued by Calmann-Lévy in 1903, and the collected edition of his works (excluding those for the theatre) in 25 bound volumes and in 60 paper-bound parts published by Le Vasseur et Cie. in the early 1900s, there was very little published of any merit and calling for any comment for quite a considerable number of years subsequently until, between 1922 and 1935, Louis Conard, of Paris, issued an edition of 35 volumes which included 11 of the more familiar titles; this edition, illustrated by Fred-Money with the wood engravings done by Victor Dutertre, had variant bindings. After 1945 there were published some beautifully illustrated and bound editions mainly of several of Dumas' stories for children, notably "Le capitaine Pamphile" illustrated by André Chante and published by La Compagnie des Libraires et des Editeurs Associés in 1963. Thus it is only comparatively recently that there has been the remarkable revival of interest in his writings in all their variety. My earlier bibliography of Dumas' works translated into English to 1910 gives added emphasis to this.

My interest in Dumas has been lifelong, and the research for my two bibliographies has extended over many years. I have personally done research in all the great national and university libraries in France, Belgium and Holland. The remaining vital and detailed information has been obtained from microfilm and photostats and, of course, lengthy correspondence with the other European and North and South American libraries whether national, state, university or college. I should add here that my attempts at obtaining through the accepted channels any information from libraries in the U.S.S.R., not very surprisingly, failed miserably.

As an appendix I have included those works to which Dumas contributed prefaces. This is a field which will, perhaps, be fresh to those with only a passing interest in his works. But it is an important one and should be recorded. These works are provided with separate author and title indexes. The spurious sequels to such works as "Les trois mousquetaires" and "Le comte de Monte-Cristo" have been ignored for the very good reason that not only are they irrelevant to the purpose of this bibliography, but also because their writing is so manifestly poor compared with Dumas'; they can be regarded as mere potboilers which were produced so that their authors might benefit financially from Dumas' great popularity at the time of their publication.

So to the matter of formats, for it is well to point out that a large number of works held in Continental libraries where I have researched, or from which I have received information, were rebound copies without their original wrappers. The binders, and why I cannot understand, almost invariably 'shaved' the leaves and thus altered the original format to a greater or lesser degree. Therefore, I have considered it best to give the format of each book in its wider sense, and as with my bibliography of translations into English have not attempted a highly detailed classification with its possible misleading consequences.

It should, I think, be mentioned that Continental publishers, certainly in the first five decades of the 19th century, were notoriously carefree in their insertion, or rather non-insertion, of accents on title-pages; circumflexes were arbitrarily omitted, as was the occasional cedilla. All my entries are exact copies of title-pages.

I should add here also that individual titles of works in the editions of the 'collected theatre' have not been included in the General Index.

To my certain knowledge no bibliography has ever been published that has not contained some minor, or perhaps other, inaccuracies. There may, very possibly, be errors or omissions in this bibliography—I am thinking particularly of those 'pirated' works published in Belgium despite the 'convention littéraire franco-belge' of 1852, as well as by the offshoot publishers in Holland, Germany and Italy, which could not despite the utmost diligence be traced. However, if there are any glaring inaccuracies, or such omissions, in this bibliography, I would be infinitely obliged if I could be written to at the address given below.

Nothing I have achieved could have been done without the financial help I have received from The Leverhulme Trust, The Phoenix Trust, both in London, and The American Philosophical Society in Philadelphia. I wish to thank all these bodies for that assistance and for their great encouragement and confidence.

DOUGLAS MUNRO

22, Constable Acre
Cupar, Fife
Scotland

"ELEGIE SUR LA MORT DU GENERAL FOY"   1825

This poem comprises thirteen stanzas of, in all, 208 lines and
divided into four parts entitled : "L'Apparition", "L'Hymne", "Le
Convoi", and "Epilogue".

Original edition.
"Elégie sur la mort du général Foy". Par Alex. Dumas. Paris, Sétier,
Cour des Fontaines, N°. 7, Lemoine, Palais-Royal, sous le grand vesti-
bule, á côté de l'ancienne Bourse, 1825, 8vo., pp. 14 and 1 blank.
Paper covers. Impr. Sétier.

It was next published, in part only, in : "Journée du 30 novembre,
1825, ou Récit des derniers moments et des Funérailles du général
Foy", Paris, Mongie aîne, Aimé André, Lugan et Ponthieu, 1825, 8vo.,
pp. 111, gravures.

Its third publication, in full as in the original, was in "Couronne
poétique du général Foy" issued by J.D. Magalon, Paris, Chaumerot
jeune, 189 Palais-Royal, 1826, 8vo.; Dumas' contribution occupies
pp. 63-71.

The elegy formed the first of the "Préludes poétiques" in the album
written out by Dumas for Mélanie Waldor, occupying pp. 5-22, with the
simple title "Foy". It omits the dedication and has, instead, an
epigraph of four lines.

The original text is published in full in Charles Glinel's "Alexandre
Dumas et son oeuvre" (Reims, F. Michaud, 1884) pp. 135-141.

"LA CHASSE ET L'AMOUR"   1825

For some years Dumas and his friend de Leuven had been attempt-
ing to write something for the stage, but unsuccessfully. Rousseau
was called in to help and the outcome was this vaudeville. Dumas
has stated that the first seven scenes were his own composition, the
second seven de Leuven's, while the final eight were written by the
three together. The vaudeville was rejected by the Théâtre Gymnase
but accepted by the Théâtre de l'Ambigu-Comique.

Original edition.
"La chasse et l'amour", vaudeville en un acte. Par MM. Rousseau,
Adolphe (de Leuven) et Davy (Dumas); représenté, pour la première
fois, a Paris, sur le théâtre de l'Ambigu-Comique, le 22 septembre
1825. Paris, chez Duvernois, ... cour des Fontaines, no. 4, et
Passage de Henri IV, nos. 10, 12 et 14. Sétier, ... , cour des
Fontaines, no. 7, 1825, 8vo., pp. 40 with list of "Personnages" and
"Acteurs" on verso of title. Paper covers. Imprimerie de Sétier.

"La chasse et l'amour" vaudeville en un acte en société avec MM.
Rousseau et de Leuven Ambigu-Comique. - 22 septembre 1825. "Distri-
bution" on the title-page, pp. (35)-68. Théatre complet de Alex.
Dumas Tome 1er. Paris Calmann Lévy, éditeur ancienne maison
Michel Lévy frères, 1874. 12mo. "Théatre complet" in 25 volumes.

"CANARIS"   1826

This poem of seventeen stanzas, and comprising 112 lines, was dedicated to Casimir Delavigne; it included an epigraph of three lines of verse by Delavigne.

Original edition.
"Canaris". Dithyrambe par Alex. Dumas. Au profit des Grecs. Paris, Sanson, Palais-Royal, Galerie de Bois, no. 250, 1826, 12mo., pp. (2), 19; grey paper covers bearing a portrait of Canaris by Louis Joly, with a vignette by the same artist on the title-page. On the verso of the title-page is announced : "Les nouvelles contemporaines" par Alex. Dumas. Impr. de Sétier.

The dithyramb was published in the May, 1826, edition of "La Psyché", with a number of variants.

Its third publication was as the fourth piece in the "Préludes poétiques", pp. 37-46, again with a number of variants.

The version as published in "La Psyché" is included in Charles Glinel's "Alexandre Dumas et son oeuvre", pp. 151-155.

"L'AIGLE BLESSE"   1826

A poem of eight stanzas comprising 59 lines.

Original edition.
"L'Aigle blessé". Signed 'Alex. Dumas', in "La Psyché", Avril, 1826.

It next appeared in the "Almanach dédié aux demoiselles", 1829.

It formed the fourth piece in the "Préludes poétiques", pp. 53-58, and is there dedicated to Monsieur Arnault, père.

The poem occupies pp. 161-163 in Charles Glinel's "Alexandre Dumas et son oeuvre".

"LE SIGNE DE CROIX, ou UN CONTE D'AUTREFOIS :
TRADITION POPULAIRE". (Including "ROMANCE" or "LE
PLAISIR EST UNE ROSE".)   1826

    This poem originally comprised 333 lines, and is prefaced by six lines from Hugo's "Les deux archers". It has never been printed in its entirety, but 32 lines from it have been published under different titles.

Original edition of the extract.
As "Romance", in "La Psyché", juin, 1826.

As "Le plaisir est une rose", with five variants, in the "Chansonnier des graces", Paris, F. Louis, 1827.

The poem forms the eleventh piece in the "Préludes poétiques", under the title of "Le signe de croix", pp. 97-114.

"Romance", as published in "La Psyché", is included on pp. 163-164 of Charles Glinel's "Alexandre Dumas et son oeuvre".

"SOUVENIRS"   1826

    A poem of eighteen verses each of 4 lines.

3

Original edition.
"Souvenirs". Signed 'Alex. Dumas'. In the juillet, 1826, edition
of "La Psyché".

Next, in the "Almanach dédié aux demoiselles", 1830.

The poem formed the seventh piece of "Préludes poétiques", occupying
pp. 59-66 and dedicated "A ma soeur", with a four line epigraph from
Lamartine; the poem here included an additional six verses.

The version published in "La Psyché" is included in Charles Glinel's
"Alexandre Dumas et son oeuvre", pp. 164-166.

"LE PATRE"   1826
     A poem of nine verses each comprising 10 lines, with the excep-
tion of the third verse which has 9.

     In 1826 there was published by Vatout "Galerie du Palais-Royal",
a lithographed reproduction of the collections of the duc d'Orléans.
Dumas was asked by Vatout to contribute some verses to the work, and
from the illustrations he was shown Dumas chose a picture of a Roman
shepherd lying asleep underneath a trellis.

Original edition.
"Le pâtre". Signed 'Alex. Dumas'. "Galerie du Palais-Royal", Paris,
Vatout, 1826.

The poem was next published in "La Psyché", août, 1826.

It forms the thirteenth piece in "Préludes poétiques", pp. 121-128,
being dedicated to "Mon ami Ch. Villenave", with an epigraph not
included in the printed version.

Dumas included it in Chapter CVI of his "Mémoires", and Charles Glinel
in his "Alexandre Dumas et son oeuvre" prints it on pp. 148-150,
omitting the epigraph.

"LE POETE"   1826
     Nine verses of 10 lines each.

Original edition.
"Le poète". Signed 'Alex. Dumas'. In "La Psyché" for octobre, 1826.

The poem is the eighth piece in "Préludes poétiques", occupying pp.
67-74, and dedicated to Frédéric Soulié.

Charles Glinel in his "Alexandre Dumas et son oeuvre" reprinted the
poem, pp. 166-169.

"LE SYLPHE" (Poem)   1826
     Six regular 4 line verses.

Original edition.
In"Le chansonnier des graces", 1826; followed by :

"Almanach des dames", 1828.

"La Psyché", février, 1829.

"Annales romantiques. Receuil de morceaux choisis de littérature contemporaine". Paris Louis Janet, libraire. M DCCC XXX, 24mo., pp. 'Avis de l'éditeur' (unnumbered), verso 'Liste des vignettes' and 'Liste alphabétique de MM. les auteurs dont ce receuil contient des pièces inédites', (1)-360, followed by 'Table generale des pièces ... '; "Le sylphe" occupies pp. 16-17, signed 'Alexandre Dumas'. De l'imprimerie de Jules Didot l'ainé.

"Choix de poésies françaises. Poètes modernes", Stuttgart, Edouard Hallberger, n.d. (c 1856), page 40.

"Poétiques de l'Ecole Romantique : 1825-1840" par Edouard Fournier. Paris, Laplace, Canchez et Cie., 1880, 8vo., page 119.

Included by Charles Glinel in his "Alexandre Dumas et son oeuvre", pp. 219-220.

(The poem was set to music by César Franck with the dedication to Mme. Claire Brissaud. Paris, S. Richault; it also inspired a poem written by an admirer entitled "Le fils de la Vierge" which was printed in A. Michaux' "Souvenirs personnels sur Alexandre Dumas", Paris, Marchal et Billard, 1885.)

"NOUVELLES CONTEMPORAINES"   1826

    This work comprises three short stories. It was offered to several publishers but in every case it was refused; Dumas, however, found part of the money to meet the cost of publication himself. But in the event only four copies were sold and he gave some of the remaining copies to friends, usually with a personal inscription.

Original edition of the complete work.
"Nouvelles contemporaines", par Alex. Dumas. 'Fils d'un soldat, j'aime à choisir mes héros dans les rangs de l'armée.' (Vignette) Paris. Sanson, libraire de S.A.R. Monseigneur le duc de Montpensier, Palais-Royal, galerie de bois, n⁰ 250. 1826. 12mo., pp. - following title-page - leaf inscribed "A ma Mère. Hommage d'amour, de respect & de reconnaissance. Alex. Dumas"; leaf inscribed "Laurette", followed by pp. (1)-49, leaf inscribed "Blanche de Beaulieu, ou La Vendéenne", followed by pp. (53)-171, leaf inscribed "Marie", followed by pp. (174)-216, and an unnumbered leaf "Nouvelles contenues dans ce volume" with pagination of contents. Grey paper wrappers. Imprimerie de Sétier.
NOTE - "Laurette" was later printed, unchanged, in a miscellany "La Pervenche" under the title of "Le Rendez-vous".
    "Blanche de Beaulieu, ou La Vendéenne, rewritten and improved, was re-entitled "La rose rouge" and published in the "Revue des deux mondes" in 1831.
    "Le Salmigondis", Vol. III (1831). Sous presse les chateaux de France. Descriptions, souvenirs, anecdotes, légendes et récits sur leur origine, leur fondation et leur illustration. "La rose rouge" , par Alexandre Dumas, pp. (79)-157.
    "Le Salmigondis". Contes de toutes les couleurs. Tome 3. Paris, Fournier jeune, 1832, 8vo., pp. 439, and table of contents. "La Rose rouge", par Alexandre Dumas was included.
        "Marie", again rewritten and improved, was retitled "Le cocher

de cabriolet" and was published in "Paris, ou le Livre des Cent et Un",
1832-1834, and later in its revised form in Dumas' "Souvenirs d'Antony". In its revised form, too, it appeared under the title of
"Rose", pp. 17-24, in "Les Sensitives. Album de Salons" par MM.
Alexandre Dumas, etc., sous la direction du bibliophile Jacob. Paris,
Mme. Vve, Louis Janet, n.d. (1845), 4to., with eighteen steel engravings; "Rose" was accompanied by an engraving by W.H. Mote.

"LA NOCE ET L'ENTERREMENT"   1826

In so far as its main theme is concerned this vaudeville was
drawn from one of the adventures of "Sinbad the Sailor".

Original edition.
"La noce et l'enterrement", vaudeville en trois tableaux, Par MM.
Davy (Dumas), Lassagne et Gustave (Vulpian), représenté pour la
première fois, a Paris, sur le théatre de la Porte-Saint-Martin, le
21 novembre 1826. (Vignette) A Paris, chez Bezou, libraire, successeur de M. Fages, au magasin de pièces de théatre, boulevarde S.-
Martin, N⁰. 29, vis-a-vis la rue de Lancy. 1826. 8vo., verso of
title-page : "Personnages. Acteurs"; pp. (3)-46, and unnumbered
leaf of advertisements. Impr. E. Duverger.

"La noce et l'enterrement" vaudeville en trois tableaux en société
avec MM. Lassagne et Vulpian Porte-Saint-Martin. - 21 novembre 1826.
"Distribution" on the title-page, pp. (69)-114. Théatre complet de
Alex. Dumas. Tome 1er. Paris Calmann Lévy, éditeur ancienne maison
Michel Lévy frères, 1874. 12mo. "Théatre complet" in 25 volumes.

"LA PSYCHE" (Journal)   1826-1829

As will be seen in the rest of this bibliography Dumas liked to
own his own journals and periodicals. The first of these was "La
Psyché", a monthly journal which he founded with his friend Adolphe de
Leuven. It existed from March, 1826, to towards the end of 1829; its
format was 18mo., and each number was of 144 pages comprising both
prose and verse. The printer was M. Marle, No. 8 Rue de Pouley.

According to his "Mémoires" Dumas contributed some prose pieces,
but it is remarkable for the nineteen contributions of signed verse.
These were :

"La Nereide" and "L'Adolescent malade"	March, 1826
"L'Aigle blessé"	April, 1826
"Romance"	June, 1826
"Souvenirs"	July, 1826
"Le Pâtre"	August, 1826
"Le Poète"	October, 1826
"La Siècle et la Poésie" and "Leipsick", both in 1827.	
"Reichenau" and "Le Sylphe"	February, 1829
"Rêverie"	1829
"Les trois dons de la péri"	March, 1829
"Fragment"	April, 1829
"La Peyrouse" and "Sur la Loire"	May, 1829
"Le Mancenillier", "Les Génies" and "Misraël"	1829

"LE SIECLE ET LA POESIE"   1827
    This poem consists of 120 lines rhymed in couplets.

Original edition.
"Le Siècle et la poésie". Signed 'Alex. Dumas'. Published in the
"Mercure du XIXᵉ. Siècle", 1827, Vol. XIX, pp. 385-386.

"Le Siècle et la poésie", the final twenty-eight lines only, with the
word 'Fragment' added, appeared in "La Psyché" in 1827. These final
twenty-eight lines were published in Charles Glinel's "Alexandre Dumas
et son oeuvre".

"LEIPSICK"   1827
    This is a long poem of 225 lines in verses of irregular length.

Original edition.
"Leipsick". Signed 'Alex. Dumas'. In "La Psyché", 1827.

The poem forms the ninth piece of "Préludes poétiques", pp. 75-88,
and is there dedicated to Monsieur le baron Tain.

It was finally published, pp. 175-181, in Charles Glinel's "Alexandre
Dumas et son oeuvre".

"LE SYLPHE" (Journal)   1827-1830
    All that I can say about this periodical is that it was founded
by Dumas in collaboration with MM. Desnoyers, Dovalle and Vaillant.
It is known that the first number was issued in 1827, and Dumas himself says that it was killed by the July Revolution in 1830.

    It is known that it was printed on rose-coloured paper and thus,
apparently, more usually referred to as "Le Journal Rose" than by its
proper title.

    It may be accepted, I think, that Dumas would have contributed,
most probably verse, to the journal.

"LA PEYROUSE"   1828
    This poem consists of twelve verses each of 10 lines. In the
various printings it was signed either 'Alex.' or 'Alexandre' Dumas.

Original edition.
In "La Revue Encyclopédique", juillet,1828.

Succeeding publications of the poem were :

"La Psyché, mai, 1829.

"Hommage aux dames", Paris, Louis Janet, 1831.

"La corbeille d'or", Paris, Louis Janet, 1837.

"Paris-Londres Keepsake Français 1840-1841" .... Paris, H.-L.
Delloye, 1841, 8vo., vol. 4, pp. 76-80, with a lithograph by C. Stan-
field, R.A.

In Dumas "Mémoires", Bruxelles, Meline, Cans et Cie., 1852-1856, vol. 11, chapter 5, pp. 129-133.

Finally, it is included in Charles Glinel's "Alexandre Dumas et son oeuvre", pp. 193-196.

"REVERIE, ou LES RUINES"   1829

There are twenty verses in this poem, most of which are of 4 lines but others consist of either 5 or 6.*

Original edition.
The poem's first appearance was in the issue of "La Psyché" for janvier, 1829.

It was reprinted by Charles Glinel in his "Alexandre Dumas et son oeuvre", pp. 227-231.

* The poem must not be confused with his "Rêverie" which appeared as the fourteenth piece in "Préludes poétiques".

"REICHENAU"   1829

This poem consists of ten verses, five of which are of 10 lines each while the other five are of 6 lines each alternating with the first five verses.

Original edition.
In "La Psyché", février, 1829.

Then in "Le Keepsake Français", Paris, Giraldon Bovinet; London, Whittaker, Treacher & Arnot, 1831.

Glinel included it in his "Alexandre Dumas et son oeuvre", pp. 217-219.

"LES TROIS DONS DE LA PERI"   1829

Comprising forty-three verses of varying lengths and totalling 277 lines this poem is an imitation of Thomas Moore's "Lalla Rookh". So far as is known the poem was never completed.

Original edition.
In "La Psyché", mars, 1829.

Reprinted in Charles Glinel's "Alexandre Dumas et son oeuvre", pp. 230-238.

"LE MANCENILLIER"   1829

Twelve verses of varying lengths totalling 65 lines. It was dedicated to Mélanie Waldor.

Original edition.
In the "Préludes poétiques", being the fifth piece pp. 47-52.

Then in "La Psyché", 1829, with six variations in the text.

Reprinted in 1830 in "Almanach des Dames", and "Almanach dedié aux dames".

In the "Talisman", Paris, A. Levavasseur et T. Astoni, 1832, but seemingly much changed from the original version.

In 1833 it was published in "Hommage aux dames".

"LES GENIES"   1829

Comprises fifteen verses each of 4 lines.

Original edition.
In "La Psyché", 1829.

In "L'Almanach des dames", 1830, possibly with variants.

It forms the sixteenth piece in "Préludes Poétiques", pp. 139-146.

"FRAGMENT, ou ELLE"   1829

Eight verses each of 6 lines.

Original edition.
In "La Psyché", avril, 1829.

Reprinted in Charles Glinel's "Alexandre Dumas et son oeuvre", pp. 243-244.

"SUR LA LOIRE"   1829

The poem consists of two sections, each comprising six verses of 6 lines.

Original edition.
In "La Psyché", juin, 1829.

Reprinted in Charles Glinel's "Alexandre Dumas et son oeuvre", pp. 244-246.

"A MON AMI VICTOR HUGO APRES L'INTERDICTION
DE 'MARION DELORME'"   1829

This poem was inspired following on the interdiction of the play "Marion Delorme" and by Hugo's refusal to keep the indemnity offered to him by the Restoration Government. According to Glinel the poem comprised 98 lines, with no regularity either in the verses or the rhyming. They were, in the first place, written by Dumas on the margins of a copy of Ronsard presented by Saint-Beuve to Hugo which was ultimately owned by Spoelberch de Louvenjoul.

Original edition.
In "Le Sylphe", 20 août, 1829.

Reprinted in "Centenaire de Victor Hugo La Couronne poétique de Victor Hugo", Paris, Bibliothèque-Charpentier, Eugène Fasquelle, éditeur, 1902, 8vo., pp. (27)-31.

"A MON AMI VICTOR HUGO ... ."

A fragment consisting of the first 50 lines was published in the "Correspondence litteraire", 5 février, 1857, and was reprinted by Glinel in his "Alexandre Dumas et son oeuvre", pp. 253-255.

"MISRAEL"   1829

Sixteen verses each of 6 lines; there were variants in the several printings of the poem.

Original edition.
In "La Psyché", novembre, 1829.

In "Le Keepsake Français", 1830.

The poem occupied pp. 255-259 in "Annales Romantiques. Receuil de morceaux choisis de littérature contemporaines", Paris, chez Louis Janet, 1831, 12mo.

The version published in "La Psyché" was reprinted by Glinel in his "Alexandre Dumas et son oeuvre", pp. 247-249.

"A MON AMI SAINTE-BEUVE"   1829

Nine verses each of 6 lines, with slight variants in the different printings.

Original edition.
In the "Mercure de France au XIXe Siècle", 1829, Vol. XXV, page 53.

In the "Cabinet de lecture", 5 janvier, 1830.

In the "Almanach des muses pour l'année 1830. 66e année. (Vignette) Paris Chez Audin, libraire ... M DCCC XXX, 24mo., pp. (5)-288. "A mon ami Sainte-Beuve", pp. 85-87; signed 'M. Alex. Dumas.'

In Glinel's "Alexandre Dumas et son oeuvre", pp. 256-258.

"HENRI III ET SA COUR"   1829

This was the first serious work by Dumas to be staged, and by any standards it was an incredible piece of writing by a young man of twenty-seven whose education had not been particularly remarkable. This was the sudden flowering of near-genius and despite what has been, or may have been, said and written "Henri III et sa cour" was the true precursor of the Romantic school of writing. Dumas used for his background material Anquetil and L'Estoile. There has never been any suggestion of collaboration.

In 1829-1830 there were fifty performances of the play, a large number for those days; frequently restaged over the years it had by 1894 been performed more than one hundred and fifty times.

Original edition.
"Henri III et sa cour"; Drame historique en cinq actes et en prose, par Alexandre Dumas. Représénte sur le théatre français, par les comédiens ordinaires du roi, ie 11 février 1829. (Vignette) Paris,

10

Vezard et Cie., passage Choiseul, Nos. 44-46. 1829. 8vo., half-title
(Le Normant fils, imprimeur du roi. Rue de Seine Saint-Germain, no.
8, on verso), title, verso blank, dedication to Baron Taylor (unnumbered), verso blank, pp. (vi)-x 'un mot' signed 'Alexandre Dumas',
another half-title with 'Personnages' on verso, (13)-171, last page
blank. Green paper wrappers.

Simultaneously the same publishers offered for sale the following
pamphlet - "Indications générales pour la mise en scène de 'Henri III
et sa cour', drame historique en cinq actes en prose de M. Alexandre
Dumas", par M. Albertin, directeur de la scène près le Théatre-
Français, n.d. (1829), 8vo., pp. 39. (Bibliothèque de la Société des
Historiens du Théatre. No. 11.)

"Henri III et sa cour"; Drame historique en cinq actes et en prose,
par Alexandre Dumas. Représenté sur le théâtre francais, par les
comédiens ordinaires du roi, le 11 février 1829. Deuxième édition.
(Vignette) Paris. Vezard et Cie, passage Choiseul, NOS. 44-46. Le
Normant père, rue de Seine, NO. 8, F.S.G. 1829.

The second edition is in the same format and with the same pagination
as the first- it was again printed by Le Normant fils, imprimeur du
roi, Rue de Seine Saint-Germain, no. 8. Green paper wrappers.

"Henri III et sa cour", drame historique en 5 actes et en prose, par
Alexandre Dumas. Bruxelles, J.-B. Dupon, 1829, 18mo., pp. 110. Répertoire de la scène française, 111, 23.

"Henri III et sa cour", drame historique en cinq actes et en prose,
par Alexandre Dumas; représenté sur le théatre français, par les comédiens ordinaires du roi, le 11 février 1829. (Vignette) A Bruxelles
au bureau du répertoire, chez Ode et Woton, rue des Pierres, ... ,
1829, 32mo., pp. 117. Buff wrappers. Répertoire dramatiques de la
scène française. 3e année - XIIe livraison.

"Henri III et sa cour"; Drame historique en cinq actes et en prose.
Par Alexandre Dumas. Représentée (sic) sur le théatre français, par
les comédiens ordinaires du roi, le 11 février 1829. (Vignette)
Genève, Lador, libraire-éditeur, rue de l'hotel de ville. 1829. 8vo.,
pp., verso of title-page 'personnages' 'acteurs', with a footnote :
'Toutes les phrases guillemettés ont étés retranchées à la seconde
représentation; on trouvera au bas de chaque page celles qui leur on
été substituées.', (3)-107. Théatre français moderne ou Choix de
pièces de Théatre nouvelles représentés avec succes sur le théatres
de Paris. Série 1. Livraison II. "Henri III et sa cour", Drame
historique en cinq actes et en prose par Alexandre Dumas. Dessau
1829, chez G. Ackermann, libraire, 24mo., pp. viii (preface, signed
'J. Louis'), 144.

"Henri III et sa cour"; Drame historique en cinq actes et en prose,
par Alexandre Dumas. Représenté sur le théatre français, par les
comédiens du roi, le 11 février 1829. Troisième édition. (Vignette)
Paris. Vezard, rue des Marais-Saint-Germain, NO17; Le Normant, rue
Seine, NO 8. 1833. 8vo., half-title (imprimerie Le Normant, rue de
Seine, no. 8, on verso), title, verso blank, pp. (vii)-ix "Un mot"
signed 'Alexandre Dumas', another half-title with 'personnages' on
verso, (13)-108. Brown wrappers repeating title-page and same vignette as the first and second editions.

"Henri III et sa cour", drame historique en cinq actes et en prose, par M. Alexandre Dumas; Représenté sur le Théatre Français, par les comédiens ordinaires du Roi, le 11 février 1829. Pale green wrappers : La France dramatique au dix-neuvième siècle. Théâtre Français. "Henri III" drame historique en cinq actes. (Vignette) 8e et 9e livraisons. Paris : J.N. Barba, Pollet, Bezou, on souscrit également ment dans les bureaux de la France pittoresque, 1834, 8vo., pp. (51)-84 in double columns, followed by 2 pages of the publishers' prospectus. Impr. normale de J. Didot.

Théatre de Alex. Dumas. "Henri III". (Vignette) Bruxelles. E. Laurent, 1834, 32mo., pp. (5)-76 "Comment je devins auteur dramatique" signed : Alex. Dumas 20 décembre 1833; half-title "Henri III et sa cour", verso 'personnages', (79)-209. Buff wrappers repeating title-page.

"Henri III et sa cour", drame historique en cinq actes et en prose, par M. Alexandre Dumas. Paris, J.N. Barba, 1835, large 8vo., pp. (51)-83 in double columns. (Added title-page: La France dramatique au dix-neuvième siècle. Théâtre Francais.) Impr. normale de Jules Didot l'ainé.

"Henri III et sa cour". Drame. Par Alexandre Dumas. (Vignette) Bruxelles, Meline, Cans et compagnie, 1838, 16mo., pp. (5)-61 "Comment je devins auteur dramatique", verso blank, "Henri III et sa cour", verso 'Personnages', (65)-216. Yellow wrappers.

Ibid   Same publishers, year, format and pagination, but on the yellow wrappers : Bibliothèque des châteaux et des campagnes. 9e Série. Bruxelles, Livourne, Meline, Cans et compagnie; Leipzig, J.P. Meline.

Oeuvres de Alex. Dumas. Tome second. (Vignette) Bruxelles, Meline, Cans et compagnie, 1838, large 8vo. "Henri III et sa cour". 'Personnages' on verso of title-page, pp. (25)-62 in double columns.

Répertoire du Théâtre français à Berlin. No. 206. "Henri III et sa cour", drame historique en cinq actes et en prose, par Alexandre Dumas. Berlin, chez Ad. Mt. Schlesinger, Libraire et Editeur de Musique, 1839, 8vo., pp. 63. Imprimé chez I.W. Krause.

"Henri III et sa cour"; drame en cinq actes et en prose. Par Alexandre Dumas. Paris, Tresse et Stock, n.d. (1840), large 8vo., pp. (51)-84 in double columns.

Théatre de Alex. Dumas. "Henri III et sa cour". (Vignette) Bruxelles, Mme. Laurent, 1841, 32mo., pp. 128. Yellow wrappers.

"Henri III et sa cour". Drame en cinq actes et en prose. Par Alexandre Dumas. Bruxelles, Société belge de librairie. Hauman et cie., 1842, 18 mo., pp. (1)-54 "Comment je devins auteur dramatique", 55-125, "Henri III et sa cour".

La France dramatique au dix-neuvieme siècle, Choix de Pièces Modernes. Théâtre-Français. "Henri III et sa cour", drame historique en cinq actes. 8-9. Paris, C. Tresse, éditeur, acquéreur des fonds de J.-N. Barba et V. Bezou, seul propriétaire de la France dramatique, ... , 1845, 8vo., pp. 52-83 in double columns.

"Henri III et sa cour", drame historique en cinq actes et en prose. Par Alexandre Dumas. Représenté sur le Théâtre Français, par les comédiens ordinaires du Roi le 11 février 1829. Paris, Tresse, 1856, large 8vo., pp. 52-83 in double columns. La France dramatique au dix-neuvième siècle. Choix de pièces modernes.

"Henri III et sa cour" drame en cinq actes, en prose Théâtre-Francais. - 11 février 1829. Dédicace "A mon ami, le baron Taylor ..."; pp. (115)-118 'un mot', 118 'Distribution', 119-198. Théatre complet de Alex. Dumas Tome 1ᵉʳ. Paris Calmann Levy éditeur ancienne maison Michel Lévy frères, 1874. 12 mo. "Théatre complet" in 25 volumes.

There were five parodies of "Henri III et sa cour" :

"La cour du Roi Petard", vaudeville, par MM. Alexandre et Henri. This was by Dumas himself in collaboration with MM. Cavé, Langlé et de Leuven. It was first performed at the Vaudeville Theatre, 28th February, 1829.

"Cricri et ses mitrons" Petite Parodie en vers et en cinq Tableaux, d'une grande pièce en cinq actes et en prose, par MM. Carmouche, Jouslin de la Salle et Dupeuty. Représentée pour la première fois, à Paris, sur le Théatre des Variétés, le 7 mars 1829. Paris, Quoy, Libraire-Editeur, 1829, 8vo., pp. 39.

"Le Brutal, Episode de Henri III", en deux tableaux, par MM. Armand Dartois, Masson et Bartélemy, représenté pour la première fois à Paris, sur le théatre de la Gaité, le 27 mars 1829. Apparently this parody ran for 61 performances.

"Le duc de Frise, ou le mouchoir criminel". The author/s are not known and the parody was probably written anonymously. It was performed at the théâtre du Luxembourg, 3rd April, 1829.

"La cour du roi Pétaud" Opéra bouffe en trois actes par Adolphe Jaime et Philippe Gille Musique de Léo Delibes (Paris, Théâtre des Variétés, 24 avril 1869). Paris, Michel Lévy frères, Editeur, 1869, 12 mo., pp. iv, 101.

Additionally, there was a comic opera based on the play : Biblio-thèque-Leduc-P.L. (i.e. Paul et Lucien) Hillemacher. "Saint-Mégrin", opéra-comique en 4 actes et 5 tableaux, d'après "Henri III", d'Alex-andre Dumas. Poème d'Ernest Dubreuil et Eugène Adenis. Partition chant et piano. Paris, Alphonse Leduc, n.d. (1886), 4to., pp. 283, (Représenté pour la première fois ... à Bruxelles, le 2 mars 1886.)

"LES DERNIERS ADIEUX"   1830

        A poem of five verses each of 6 lines.

Original edition.
In the "Revue des deux mondes", avril, 1830.

In the "Almanach des dames", in the same year.

"L'EMBARQUEMENT"   1830

        This poem consists of fifteen verses each of 6 lines. In the original manuscript draft it was entitled "A bord de la 'Pauline'", and the published version was lengthened.

Original edition.
In the "Revue des deux mondes", towards the end of 1830.

"Le Sélam", Morceaux choisis, inédits, de littérature contemporaine. Orné de dix vignettes anglaises. 1834. Paris. F. Astoin, éditeur, A. Levavasseur ... , 12mo., pp. 'Introduction "Le Sélam" ' (v)-ix signed 'T.G.', verso blank, 'Liste des vignettes' (unnumbered), verso blank, 'Liste des vignettes' (in full and comprising 10) (unnumbered), verso blank, (1)-4 "L'Embarquement", signed 'Alex. Dumas', frontispiece engraving. Imprimerie, de A. Pinard.

"Le Talisman", par Messieurs A. Dumas, ..., ...; Ornée de six vignettes anglaises. Deuxième année. Paris, Félix Astoin, éditeur. 1835. 12mo., pp. 'Liste des Vignettes' (unnumbered), verso blank, (1)-4 "L'Embarquement", signed 'Alex. Dumas'; frontispiece engraving. Everat, imprimeur.

The poem is included in Glinel's "Alexandre Dumas et son oeuvre", pp. 327-329.

"LA LETTRE"   1830

A poem of six verses each of 4 lines. It is the fifteenth piece in the "Préludes poétiques", pp. 135-138.

Original edition.
In "Le Livre: Revue littéraire du monde", Paris, A. Quantin, octobre 1886, pp. 293-294.

"REVERIE"   1830

The poem comprises eleven verses each of 4 lines. It is the fourteenth piece in the "Préludes poétiques", pp. 129-134.

Original edition.
In "Le Livre: Revue littéraire du monde", Paris, A. Quantin, octobre 1886, pp. 292-293.

"LES AMES"   1830

This poem consists of twelve verses each of 4 lines.

Original edition.
In "Les annales romantiques", Paris, Louis Janet, 1832.

It is the twelfth piece in the "Préludes poétiques", pp. 115-120.

The poem is included in Glinel's "Alexandre Dumas et son oeuvre", pp. 308-309.

"A MADAME MELANIE WALDOR"   c 1830

A short poem of only three verses, each of 4 lines. Dumas used the first three verses in his "Le mari de la veuve", scene iii, the second verse differing from the original.

14

Original edition in its original form.
In "Alexandre Dumas 1802-1870 Sa Vie intime. Ses oeuvres", by L.-
Henry Lecomte, Paris, J. Tallandier, n.d. (1902), 8vo., pp. 238-239.

"PRELUDES POETIQUES"   1830 and earlier
    The volume comprises a collection of verse entirely in Dumas'
handwriting, written out for and presented by him to Mélanie Waldor.
It consists of 150 pages, large 8vo., handsomely bound in violet
morocco and gilt edged.   The spine has the lettering "Préludes Poétiques" - Alex. Dumas, and the cover "Mme. Waldor" lettered in gold.
This bound manuscript was left to the Institut de France by vicomte
de Spoelberch de Louvenjoul.
    Following two blank pages the third carries the title : "Pré-
ludes Poétiques", par Alex. Dumas, followed by an epigraph. On the
final leaf Dumas has written the twelve lines which appear at the
beginning of his "Comment je devins auteur dramatique", these in turn
being part of his "A toi".
    The volume contains sixteen poems; in some cases titles have
been changed, and Glinel in his "Alexandre Dumas et son oeuvre" and
other works has noted a number of variants in the published versions
from the original manuscript.

    1. "Foy"   pp.   5-22

    2. "L'Enfant malade"   22-32

    3. "Le sylphe"   33-36

    4. "Canaris"   37-46

    5. "Le mancenillier"   47-52

    6. "L'Aigle blessé"   53-58

    7. "Souvenirs"   59-66

    8. "Le poète"   67-74

    9. "Leipsick"   75-88

   10. "La nereide"   89-96

   11. "Le Signe de croix"   97-114

   12. "Les âmes"   115-120

   13. "Le pâtre"   121-128

   14. "Rêverie"   129-134

   15. "La lettre"   135-138

   16. "Les génies"   139-146

"CHRISTINE, ou STOCKHOLM, FONTAINEBLEAU ET ROME"   1830
    Some three years before this trilogie finally appeared Dumas had
conceived the idea of a drama from a bas-relief on exhibition at the
Salon de Paris. The various holograph manuscripts of the play indicate how often it was reshaped; indeed, one particular revised version in the handwriting of both Dumas and Mélanie Waldor takes account

of two separate censors' reports, the first asking that Le Père Lebel should not be dressed as a clergyman and the other approving a new epilogue - but the main changes in this particular version are the introduction of Paula, the mistress of Monaldeschi, and the inclusion of that portion entitled "Rome".

The work was originally entitled simply "Christine à Fountaine-bleau" and consisted of five acts comprising 1,950 alexandrines. Modified, it was entitled in the original edition "Stockholm, Fon-tainebleau et Rome", to be altered again later to "Christine, ou Stockholm, Fontainebleau et Rome", the final version consisting of 2,583 alexandrines and a post-scriptum.

It should be mentioned here that editions published in France after the 1834 'collected edition' published by Charpentier do not contain the note by Dumas explaining the alternative matter included there, and which the Belgian editions added between Act 5 and the Epilogue.

Original edition.
"Stockholm, Fontainebleau et Rome", Trilogie dramatique sur la vie de Christine, cinq actes en vers, avec prologue et épilogue, par Alex. Dumas. Représenté a Paris, sur le théatre royal de l'Odéon, le 30 mars 1830. (Throughout ... Paris, Barba, Palais-Royal, grande cour, Derrière le Théatre Français. 1830. 8vo., pp. half-title "Stockholm, Fontainebleau et Rome", verso 'on trouve chez le même libraire. HENRI III, drame en cinq actes du même auteur. HERNANI, ou l'honneur Castillan, drame en cinq actes et en vers, par M.V. Hugo.', title, 'A Son Altesse Royale Monseigneur Le duc d'Orleans. Hommage De Respect et de Reconnaissance, Alexandre DUMAS. Paris, 30 mars 1830, 11 heures du soir' (unnumbered), verso 'personnages', unnumbered page 'Prologue. Descartes.', verso blank, (3)-14, 'acte I. Paula', verso blank, "Christine". (17)-187, verso blank, (189)-191 'post scriptum' signed 'Alex. Dumas'. 2 pages of advertisements. This first edition has a lithograph by Charlet after Raffet, of Christine and Paula in Act V, scene vi, facing the title-page. Buff wrappers repeating the title-page. Imprimerie de Lachevardiere, rue du Colombier, N⁰ 30.

Ibid   Seconde édition. Paris, Barba, Palais-Royal, grande cour, Derrière le Théâtre Français. 1830. 8vo., half-title "Stockholm, Fontainebleau et Rome" with on verso same announcement as in the first edition, 2 unnumbered pages publisher's advertisements, same pagination as the first edition. This second edition does not contain the lithograph. Buff wrappers, with on verso of the front wrapper publisher's advertisements. Imprimerie de Lachevardiere, rue du Colombier, N⁰ 30.

Répertoire dramatique de la scène française. "Stockholm, Fontaine-bleau et Rome". Trilogie dramatique sur le vie de Christine, cinq actes en vers avec prologue et épilogue, par Alex. Dumas. Représ-enté pour la première fois à Paris, sur le Théatre Royal de l'Odéon, le 30 mars 1830. (Throughout ... A Bruxelles, au bureau du réper-toire, chez Ode et Wodon, 1830, 24mo., pp. 157, blank, (159)-161 postscriptum signed : 'Alex. Dumas'. Brown wrappers - "Stockholm, Fontainebleau et Rome, trilogie dramatique.

Théatre français moderne. Série II. Livraison 1. "Stockholm,

Fontainebleau et Rome", Trilogie dramatique sur la vie de Christine, cinq actes en vers, avec prologue et épilogue, par Alexandre Dumas. Publié par J. Louis. Dessau, chez C.G. Ackermann, 1830, 18mo., pp. 174.

"Stockholm, Fontainebleau et Rome", trilogie dramatique sur la vie de Christine, cinq actes en vers, avec prologue et épilogue, par Alexandre Dumas. Berlin, Charles Heymann, n.d. (c 1830), 18mo., pp. 174.

Théatre de Alex. Dumas. "Christine". (Vignette) Bruxelles. E. Laurent, 1834, 32mo., pp. half-title "Christine. Stockholm, Fontainebleau et Rome", verso 'personnages', (7)-163. Buff wrappers repeating title-phage, but dated 1835.

"Christine". Drame. Par Alexandre Dumas. (Vignette) Bruxelles, Meline, Cans et compagnie, 1838, 16mo., pp. 177. Yellow wrappers.

Oeuvres de Alex. Dumas. Tome second. (Vignette) Bruxelles, Meline, Cans et compagnie, 1838, large 8vo. "Christine. Stockholm, Fontainebleau et Rome", pp. 'Personnages' (unnumbered), frontispiece, (103)-106 Prologue, (107)-145 in double columns.

Répertoire du Théâtre français á Berlin. No. 236. "Stockholm, Fontainebleau et Rome", trilogie dramatique sur la vie de Christine, 5 actes en vers, avec prologue et épilogue, par Alexandre Dumas. Berlin, Ad. Mt. Schlesinger, Libraire et Editeur de Musique, 1841, 8vo., pp. 84. Imprimé chez I.W. Krause.

"Christine, ou Stockholm et Fontainebleau", drame en cinq actes, en vers, par M. Alexandre Dumas. Représenté sur le Théâtre Royal de l'Odéon, le 30 mars 1830, et repris au Théâtre-Français en 1841. Conforme à la représentation. Caption title. Paris, Imprimerie de Boulé et Cie., n.d., (1841), 8vo., pp. (1)-34 in double columns.

'Nouvelle édition publiée à l'occasion de la reprise de la pièce au Théatre Français en 1841'; in 'La France dramatique au XIXe siecle.'

"Christine. (Stockholm, Fontainebleau et Rome.)" S.1., n.d. (c 185), 8vo., verso of half-title 'Personnages'; Prologue. 'Descartes', again verso 'Personnages'; Prologue (5)-16; 1. 'Paula', again 'personnages', (19)-213.

"Christine ou Stockholm, Fontainebleau et Rome" trilogie dramatique en cinq actes, en vers avec prologue et épilogue Odéon. - 30 mars 1830. ("Throughout! ... 'A son altesse royale monseigneur le duc d'Orléans Hommage de respect et de reconnaissance. Alex. Dumas! Paris, 30 mars 1830, onze heures du soir'. 'Distribution' on title-page, pp. (199)-304, 'post-scriptum' 304-306. Théatre complet de Alex. Dumas Tome 1er. Paris Calmann Lévy, éditeur ancienne maison Michel Lévy frères, 1874. 12mo. "Théatre complet" in 25 volumes.

There was one parody of the play :
"Tristine, ou Chaillot, Surêne et Charenton" Trilogie sans préambule et sans suite en trente actes d'une scène, et en vers alexandrines, par MM. Carmouche, de Courcey et Dupeuty. Musique arrangée par M. André. Représentée, pour la première fois, sur le Théatre de l'ambigu-Comique, le 26 avril 1830. Paris, chez R. Riga, Editeur, A. Boulland, à la Librairie Centrale, 1830, 8vo., pp. 35.

(In "Choix de poésies françaises. Poètes modernes", Stuttgart,

Edouard Hallberger, n.d. (c 1856), 12mo., appeared "Regrets de Christine du Suède pour le pays natal". (Alexandre Dumas. "Christine".)

"RAPPORT AU GENERAL LAYFAYETTE, ..., REDIGE PAR   1830
ALEXANDRE DUMAS"

This is the official report of Dumas' journey to Soissons for
gun-powder required by the insurgents in Paris.

It first appeared in the issue of "Le Moniteur" for the 9th août
1830. (No. 221.)

Original edition in book-form.
"Rapport au Général La Fayette sur l'enlèvement des poudres de Sois-
sons", rédigé par Alex. Dumas et signé par Bard, Hutin, Lenoir,
Morand et Gilles. Paris, Impr. de Sétier, n.d. (1830), 8vo., pp. 7.

(A much more lively account of the trip to Soissons may, of course,
be read in Dumas' "Memoirs".)

"NAPOLEON BONAPARTE, ou TRENTE ANS DE   1831
L'HISTOIRE DE FRANCE"   (Drama)

Even as soon as 1831 Napoleon was becoming a legendary figure in
France and there was a demand for plays dealing with him. The theatre
manager Harel urged Dumas to write a play with a Napoleonic theme,
despite the fact that six such plays had already been performed.
Dumas was reluctant, but Harel finally got his way, it is said, by
having Dumas immured to all intents and purposes in the actress
Mademoiselle George's rooms until he had completed the writing of it.

Here can be seen the further blossoming of the man as a dramatist
and notwithstanding that Dumas has written, quite unjustifiably, that
this prose drama was a matter of scissors and paste it is well written
and was most successful; Frédérick Lamaître was magnificent in the
rôle of Napoleon. Originally the play amounted to about 9,000 lines,
but it was much reduced in the final version. There are seventy-six
rôles, not all of which had speaking parts.

Napoleon's mother attended the first performance.

Original edition.
"Napoléon Bonaparte", ou trente ans de l'histoire de France". Drame
en six actes, par Alex. Dumas. Représenté pour la première fois,
sur le théatre royal de l'Odéon, le 10 janvier 1831. 'D'ici à dix
ans, toute l'Europe sera républicaine ou cosaque.' Napoléon. (Mémor.
de Ste-Hélène.) Paris. Chez Tournachon-Molin, libraire, rue de pont-
de-Lodi, N° 5. 1831. 8vo., half-title "Napoléon Bonaparte", verso
'imprimerie de Amb. Firmin Didot, rue Jacob, N° 24.', title, unnumbered page "A la Nation Française. Alex. Dumas.", verso blank, pp. (i)-
xii 'préface' signed 'Alex. Dumas', (xiii)-xvi 'personnages', (1)-219
"Napoléon Bonaparte, ou trente ans de l'histoire de France." Drame
en six actes, en 19 tableaux. Buff wrappers; front cover repeating
title-page and rear cover with vignette of Napoleon's head.

"Napoléon Bonaparte; ou 30 ans de l'histoire de France"; drame en
cinq (sic) actes, par Alex. Dumas. (Odéon, Paris, 1831.) The quota-

18

tion in the original edition repeated. (Vignette) Bruxelles, J.P.
Meline, 1831, 24mo., pp. (5)-8 'Personnages', (9)-184.

Ibid   Bruxelles, F. Cannongette, 1831, same format and
pagination.

"Napoléon Bonaparte, ou trente ans de l'histoire de France", Drame
en six acts, par Alexandre Dumas. Publié par J. Louis. Dessau, chez
C.G. Ackermann, libraire. 1831. 18mo., 4 unnumbered pages 'Préface'
signed 'Dessau. J. Louis', 2 unnumbered pages 'Personnages', (7)-244.
"Théatre français moderne. II Série. Livraison 7, 8." Livraison 7
ends on page 112 - Fin du troisième acte - and pp. 115-244 comprise
livraison 8. Grey wrappers dated 1832, being the actual year of
issue.

"Napoléon Bonaparte", drame en six actes et en vingt-trois tableaux,
par M. Alexandre Dumas, représenté pour la première fois, sur le
théatre Royal de l'Odéon, le 10 janvier 1831. Paris, Marchant, 1835,
8vo., pp. 55 in double columns. Caption title. Le magasin théatral.
Vol. VI.

Napoléon Bonaparte", drame en six actes et en vingt-trois tableaux,
Par M. Alexandre Dumas, représenté pour la première fois, sur le
theatre royal de l'Odéon, le ... . Paris, Marchant; Bruxelles, Aug.
Jouhaut, 1835, 8vo., pp. 55 in double columns. Supplement au Magasin
Théatral, choix de pièces jouées sur les théatres de Paris; Imprimerie
Dondey-Dupré. Caption title.

Ibid   Paris, n.d. (c 1835), same format and pagination.
Imprimerie normale de Jules Didot l'aîné.

Théatre de Alex. Dumas. "Napoléon Bonaparte". Bruxelles, E. Laurent,
1835, 32mo., pp. 230. Buff wrappers.

"Napoléon Bonaparte", drame en six actes et en vingt-trois tableaux,
Par M. Alexandre Dumas, représenté pour la première fois, sur le
théatre Royal de l'Odéon, le ... . Caption title. Yellow wrappers :
Quatrième année. Magasin théatral, choix de pièces nouvelles jouées
sur tous les théatres de Paris. Theatre de l'Odéon. "Napoleon",
Drame en cinq (sic) actes. (Vignette) Paris, Marchant; A Bruxelles,
Chez MM. Francois et Delavau, 1837, 8vo., pp. 55 in double columns.

Oeuvres de Alex. Dumas. Tome seconde. (Vignette) Bruxelles, Meline,
Cans et compagnie, 1838, large 8vo. "Napoléon Bonaparte". 'Personnages' on verso of title, pp. (337)-442 in double columns.

"Napoléon Bonaparte, ou Trente ans de l'histoire de France", par
Alexandre Dumas. Drame en 6 actes. Berlin, chez Ad. Mt. Schlesinger,
editeur de musique et libraire, 1839, 8vo., pp. 111. No. 203 of the
'Répertoire du théâtre français à Berlin.

Théatre de Alex. Dumas. "Napoléon Bonaparte". Bruxelles, Meline,
Cans et Compagnie, 1842, 32mo., pp. 230. Buff wrappers.

"Napoléon Bonaparte". Drame en six actes et en prose, par Alexandre
Dumas. Bruxelles, Société belge de librairie Hauman et cie., 1842,
16mo., pp. 217. Brown wrappers.

Napoléon Bonaparte", drame en six actes et en vingt-trois tableaux,
Par M. Alexandre Dumas, représenté pour la première fois, sur le
théatre Royal de l'Odéon, le ... . Caption title. Yellow wrappers :
Magasin théatral, choix de pièces nouvelles, jouées sur tous les

théatres de Paris. Théatre Royal de l'Odéon. "Napoléon". Drame en six actes. Paris, Marchant; Bruxelles, Tarride, 1845, 8vo., pp. 55 in double columns.

"Napoléon Bonaparte" ou trente ans de l'histoire de France" drame en six actes, en vingt-trois tableaux. Odéon. - 10 janvier 1831. 'D'ici à cinquante ans, toute l'Europe sera républicaine ou cosaque.' Napoléon (Mémorial de Sainte-Hélène). 'Préface' signed 'Alex. Dumas' pp. (1)-9, 'distribution' pp. 10-11, 11-157. Théatre complet de Alex. Dumas Tome II Paris, Calmann Lévy, éditeur ancienne maison Michel Lévy frères, 1874. 12mo. "Théatre complet" in 25 volumes.

"ANTONY"   1831

Dumas' infatuation with Mélanie Waldor, his liaison with her and his subsequent jealousy, form the basic subject of this play - particularly in its first drafting. The second and modified form was the one to be staged. The play ran for one hundred and thirty successive performances, probably an unprecedented thing in those days, and for a number of years it remained one of the most popular plays on the Paris stage.

The nine verses, each of 4 lines, which appear at the start of all editions of the play were written in 1829, and besides being printed in Dumas' "Mémoires" were published by Glinel in his "Alexandre Dumas et son oeuvre", pp. 293-294.

Original edition.
"Antony", drame en cinq actes, en prose, par Alexandre Dumas. Représenté pour la première fois sur le théatre de la Porte-Saint-Martin, le mardi 3 mai 1831. ("Ils ont dit que Childe Harold, c'est moi ... Que m'importe!" - Byron.) Paris, Auguste Auffray, éditeur, rue des Beaux-Arts, N° 6, 1831, 8vo., pp. 5 blanks, 106, 1 unnumbered 'postscriptum', with vignette facing title-page by Tony Johannot transferred to wood by Tellier and engraved by Thompson, of Antony and Adèle after the episode of the ball in Act 4, scene viii. Some copies included portraits of Dumas and Madame Dorval, others lacked them. Paper wrappers. Impr. Aug. Auffray.

"Antony", drame en cinq actes, en prose, par M. Alexandre Dumas, représenté pour la première fois, sur le théâtre de la Porte-Saint-Martin, le mardi 3 mai 1831. Paris, Dondey-Dupré, 1831, 8vo., pp. 26 in double columns. Caption title. Le Magasin théatral.

"Antony", drame en cinq actes en prose, par Alexandre Dumas. Représenté pour la première fois, sur le théatre de la Porte-Saint-Martin, le mardi 3 mai 1831. (Quotation from Byron). (Vignette) Bruxelles, chez Jouhard, 12mo., pp. 56.

"Antony". Drame en cinq actes, en prose. Par Alexandre Dumas. Porte-Saint-Martin - 3 mai 1831. (Quotation from Byron). S.l., Impr. F. Aureau, n.d. (1831), 12mo., pp. 67.

"Antony", drame en cinq actes, en prose, par Alexandre Dumas. Représenté pour la première fois sur le théatre de la Porte-Saint-Martin, le mardi 3 mai 1841. (Quotation from Byron). 2e édition. Paris, Auguste Auffray, éditeur, ... , 1832, 8vo., pp. viii, 101, with the same vignette as the first edition. Paper wrappers.

20

"Antony", drame en cinq actes et en prose, par Alexandre Dumas.
(Paris, représenté sur le théâtre de la Porte-Saint-Martin, 1831.)
(Quotation from Byron). (Vignette) Bruxelles, F. Canongette, 1832,
18mo., pp. 80. Blue wrappers. (There is in existence a copy of the
Canongette edition bound in dark brown paper covers - "Antony", drame
en 5 actes et en prose. 20e livraison. Deuxième série. (Vignette)
Bruxelles J.P. Meline, 1831, same format and pagination.

"Antony", drame en cinq actes et en prose, par Alexandre Dumas.
(Paris, représenté sur le théâtre de la porte-Saint-Martin, 1831.)
(Vignette) Bruxelles, Jules Boquet et Cie., 1832, 18mo., pp. 80.
Blue wrappers : "Antony", drame en 5 actes et en prose. 20e liv-
raison. Deuxième série. (Vignette) Bruxelles, Jules Boquet et Cie.,
1831.

"Antony", Paris, imprimé Terzuolo, n.d. (c 1833), 8vo. Preceded by
"Comment je devins auteur dramatique", dated '20 décembre 1833'. The
Bibliothèque Nationale copy has no title-page.

Théatre de Alex. Dumas. "Antony". Bruxelles, E. Laurent, 1834, 32mo.,
pp. 115. Vignette on title-page.

Théatre de Alex. Dumas. "Antony". Bruxelles, E. Laurent, 1834,24mo.,
pp. 108. Buff wrappers.

"Antony", drame en cinq actes. Par M. Alexandre Dumas, ... Paris,
Marchant; Bruxelles, Aug. Jouhaud, 1835, 8vo., pp. 26 in double columns. Caption title. Supplement au Magasin Théatral, choix de pièces
jouées sur les théatres de Paris. Pink wrappers.

Ibid   Paris, Marchant; Bruxelles, A la librairie Belge-
Francaise, n.d. (1835), 8vo., pp. 26 in double columns. Caption title.
Magasin théatral, choix de pièces nouvelles jouées tous les théatres
de Paris. Théatre de la Porte-Saint-Martin. "Antony", drame en
cinq actes. (Vignette) Names of publishers repeated. Blue wrappers.

Ibid   Paris, Marchant; Bruxelles, Tarride, n.d. (1835),
8vo., pp. 26 in double columns. Caption title. Magasin théatral.
Yellow wrappers.

Ibid   Paris, Marchant; Bruxelles, Auguste Jouhaud, 1836,
8vo., pp. 26 in double columns. Caption title. Troisième année.
Magasin théatral choix de pièces jouées sur tous les théatres de
Paris. (Vignette) Names of publishers repeated. Green wrappers.

"Antony", drame en cinq actes, par M. Alexandre Dumas. Paris, J.N.
Barba, 1836, 8vo., pp. 26 in double columns. Caption title. La
France dramatique au dix neuvième siècle. Le Magasin théatral.
Impr. Dondey-Dupré. Buff wrappers.

"Antony". Drame. Par Alexandre Dumas. (Vignette) Bruxelles,
Meline, Cans et compagnie, 1838, 12mo., pp. 134. Bibliothèque des
châteaux et des campagnes. 3e série.

Oeuvres de Alex. Dumas. Tome second. (Vignette) Bruxelles, Meline,
Cans et compagnie, 1838, large 8vo. "Antony". Pp. Dumas' verses
(unnumbered), half-title with epigraph, 'Personnages' on verso, (69)-
99 in double columns.

Théatre de Alex. Dumas. "Antony". (Vignette) Bruxelles, Mme. Laurent, 1840, 24mo., pp. 108. Buff wrappers.

"Antony", drame en cinq actes, en prose, par Alexandre Dumas. Brux-elles, Société belge de librairie, 1842, 16mo., pp. 125.

"Antony" drame en cinq actes et en prose, par Alexandre Dumas. Bruxelles et Livourne, Meline, Cans et compagnie; Leipzig, J.P. Meline, 1853, 16mo., pp. 125, Yellow wrappers.

"Antony". Drame en cinq actes par M. Alexandre Dumas. Représenté pour la première fois sur le théâtre de la Porte-Saint-Martin, le mardi 3 mai 1831. Paris, N. Tresse 1854, 8vo., pp. 26 in double columns. La France dramatique au dix-neuvième siècle, choix de pièces modernes. Impr. Dubuisson et Cie.

"Antony", drame en cinq actes, Par M. Alexandre Dumas, représenté pour la première fois, sur le théatre de la Porte-Saint-Martin, le mardi 3 mai 1831. Caption title. La France dramatique au dix-neuvième siècle choix de pièces modernes. Paris, Tresse, Successeur de J.-N. Barba, 1872, 8vo., pp. 26 in double columns, the last 2 pages being unnumbered. Yellow wrappers.

"Antony" drame en cinq actes, en prose Porte-Saint-Martin. - 3 mai 1831. (Quotation from Byron) Pp. (159)-160 "A ***", 161 'distribu-tion', 161-226, 226 "Post-scriptum". Théatre complet de Alex. Dumas Tome II Paris Calmann Lévy, éditeur ancienne maison Michel Lévy frères, 1874. 12mo. "Théatre complet" in 25 volumes.

"Antony"; drame en cinq actes, par Alexandre Dumas. Paris, Calmann-Lévy, 1892, 4to., pp. 24 in double columns. Caption title. Paper covers.

There was one parody of the play :
"Batardi, ou le désagrément de n'avoir ni mère ni père" Existence d'Homme en cinq portions de M. (Henri) Dupin (et Ach. Dartois). Rep-reséntée pour la première fois, à Paris, sur le Théâtre des Variétes, le 30 mai 1831. Paris, J.-N. Barba, Libraire, 1831, 8vo., pp. 38.

Ibid.   (Paris, sur le théatre des Variétés, le 30 mai 1831.) (Vignette) Bruxelles, J.P. Meline, 1832, 24 mo., pp. 44 Nouveau répertoire dramatique.

"CHARLES VII CHEZ SES GRANDS VASSAUX"   1831

The germ idea of this tragedy was obtained from "La Chronique du Roi Charles VII" by Maître Alain Chartier, who has been described as 'un homme fort honorable'. Dumas has said that it was a work of assimilation and not an original drama, and one which had cost him more labour than "Antony". At any rate, it is one of his finest plays and his one real tragedy. The time of its action is, of course, when France was at its lowest ebb in its history immediately previous to the appearance on the European scene of Joan of Arc. The tragedy comprises 1,817 alexandrines.

Original edition.
"Charles VII chez ses grands vasseaux", tragédie en cinq actes, par Alexandre Dumas. Représentée pour la première fois, sur le Théâtre Royal de l'Odèon, le 20 octobre 1831. ("Cur non? ... ". Paris, Publications de Charles Lemesle. Se vend chez Veuve Charles-Bechet, Werdet, Lecointe et Pougin, Riga, Barba, 1831, 8vo., pp. 120. Paper wrappers. Impr. David.

"Charles VII chez ses grands vassaux" Tragédie en Cinq Actes par Alex. Dumas; représentée pour la première fois, sur le théatre Royal de l'Odéon, le 20 octobre 1831. Deuxième édition, augmentée d'une preface. ("Cur non? ... " Paris, Publication de Charles Lemesle. 1831, 8vo., pp. (1)-7 'Préface', (9)-124. Buff wrappers, repeating title-page.

"Charles VII chez ses grands vassaux". Tragédie en cinq actes, Par M. Alexandre Dumas; représentée pour la première fois, sur le théatre de la Porte-Saint-Martin (sic) le ... . Caption title : Yellow wrappers - Magasin théatral, choix de pièces jouées sur tous les théatres de Paris. Théatre-Français (sic). "Charles VII". Tragédie en cinq actes. (Vignette) Paris, Marchant; Bruxelles, Tarride, n.d. (1831), 8vo., pp. 28 in double columns.

"Charles VII chez ses grands vassaux", par Alexandre Dumas. Bruxelles, J.-A. Lelong, 1833, 18mo., pp. 108.

Théatre de Alex. Dumas. "Charles VII". (Vignette) Bruxelles. E. Laurent, 1835, 32mo., half-title "Charles VII chez ses grands vassaux". Pp. (3)-10 unsigned introduction by Dumas, (13)-130. Buff wrappers repeating title-page.

"Charles VII chez ses grands vassaux", tragédie en cinq actes, Par M. Alexandre Dumas; représentée pour la première fois, sur le théatre de la Porte-Saint-Martin (sic), le ... . Paris, Marchant; Bruxelles, Aug. Jouhaut, 1835, 8vo., pp. 28 in double columns. Caption title. Supplement au Magasin Theatral, choix de pièces jouées sur tous les théatres de Paris.

Reprinted, same format and pagination, 1836 and 1837.

"Charles VII chez ses grands vassaux". Tragédie en cinq actes, par M. Alexandre Dumas; représentée, pour la première fois, sur le théatre de porte-Saint-Martin (sic) le ... . Paris, Imprimerie de Dubuisson et Ce., n.d. (c 1835), 8vo., pp. 28 in double columns. (A former owner of the copy in Bibliothèque Historique de la Ville de Paris has struck out the words 'la porte-Saint-Martin' and replaced them with the equal solecism 'le theatre d'Orléans'.)

"Charles VII chez ses grands vassaux", tragédie en cinq actes, Par M. Alexandre Dumas; représentée pour la première fois, sur le théatre de la Porte-Saint-Martin (sic), le ... . Caption title. Imprimerie de Ve Dondey-Dupré, n.d. (1835), 8vo., pp. 28 in double columns.

"Charles VII chez ses grands vassaux". Drame. Par Alexandre Dumas. (Vignette) Bruxelles, Meline, Cans et compagnie, 1838, 18mo., pp. 136.

Oeuvres de Alex. Dumas. Tome second. (Vignette) Bruxelles, Meline, Cans et compagnie, 1838, large 8vo. "Charles VII chez ses grands vassaux", pp. (149)-150 'préface', half-title with 'personnages' on verso, (153)-184 in double columns.

"Charles VII chez ses grands vassaux", tragédie en cinq actes, par Alexandre Dumas. Bruxelles, Société belge de librairie, 1842, 16mo., pp. 126. Buff wrappers.

"Charles VII chez ses grands vassaux" tragédie en cinq actes Odéon. - 20 octobre 1831. ("Cur non? ... " 'Préface'signed Alex. Dumas pp. (227)-230, p. 231 'Distribution', 231-314, Théatre complet de Alex. Dumas Tome II Paris, Calmann Lévy, éditeur ancienne maison Michel

Lévy frères, 1874. 12mo. "Théatre complet" in 25 volumes.

"RICHARD DARLINGTON"   1831

This drama was written in collaboration with MM. Beudin et
Goubaux, but its actual construction is clearly almost entirely by
Dumas. It is recorded that so much did his collaborators realise
the enormous importance of Dumas' share that again and again on the
first night which was an amazing success, they begged him to have his
name alone acclaimed. Dumas refused, but he retained the right to
include the work in the collected edition of his plays.

Dumas has openly admitted in his "Mémoires" that the prologue was
based on the beginning of Sir Walter Scott's "The Surgeon's Daughter",
but the play itself has not the remotest connection with the rest of
Scott's story - it presents a character consumed by political ambition.
Jenny's murder in Act 3 is one of Dumas' most masterly stage effects,
and at the first performance Madame Noblet, who played the part, was
herself terrified, as was the audience.

Original edition.
"Richard Darlington", drame en trois actes et en prose, précédé de
"La Maison du Docteur", prologue, par MM. Dinaux, représenté,
pour la première fois, a Paris, sur le théatre de la porte-Saint-
Martin, le 10 décembre 1831. (Vignette) Paris. J.N. Barba, libraire,
palais-royal grand cour, derrière le théatre-francais. 1832. 8vo.
Unnumbered page "La maison du docteur", prologue, with a quotation
from Terence in Latin and in French translation, verso 'personnages'
'acteurs' (unnumbered), pp. (1)-20 (last page misnumbered 18) "La
Maison du Docteur", prologue, unnumbered page "Richard Darlington",
drame en trois actes, verso 'personnages' 'acteurs' (unnumbered),
(23)-132. Yellow paper wrappers. Imprimerie de E. Duverger, rue de
Verneuil, n. 4.

(There is a 'rogue' copy held by the Bibliothèque de la Société des
Auteurs et Compositeurs Dramatiques : "Richard Darlington", drame
en trois actes et en prose, précédé de "La maison du docteur", prologue, par M. Alexandre Dumas, représenté pour la premiere fois, a
Paris, sur le théâtre de la Porte-Saint-Martin, le 10 décembre 1831.
Paris. J.N. Barba, libraire, 1832. The same format and pagination as
the preceding.)

Musée théatral Galerie Pittoresque. "Richard Darlington". Huit
dessins de Victor Adam, gravés par Branche, a l'eau-forte sur acier,
accompagnées D'une Analyse de la Pièce. 1ʳᵉ livraison. Paris,
Bartélemy, Editeur; Louis Janet, libraire; Madame Armand Christophe;
1832, pet. in-12 oblong (14.8 x 11.9 cms.), pp. (1)-4 'Prospectus', 2
unnumbered pages, title-page with list of 'Personnages' on verso, 4
unnumbered pages 'Introduction', 1 unnumbered page "La maison du
docteur", 9 unnumbered pages "Richard Darlington". Brown paper covers
: Musée théatral galerie pittoresque Des Pièces modernes le plus
en Vogue Première Livraison "RICHARD D'ARLINGTON" (sic) huit
dessins de Victor Adam Graves par Branche. 1832. On back cover :
Le MUSEE THEATRAL est mis en Vente; de Paris, chez BARTHELEMY,
EDITEUR, rue du pot-de-fer-S.-Sulpice 14; Louis Janet, libraire, rue
Saint-Jacques, 59; Mᵐᵉ Armand Christophe, Boulevard Bonne-Nouvelle,

2. Dans la Province, Chez tous les Libraires, Marchands d'Estampes et de Musique. Paris, imprimerie de Ducessois, Quai des Augustins, 55. "Richard Darlington". Drame. Par Alexandre Dumas. Bruxelles, Meline, Cans et Cie., 1833, 12mo., pp. 239.

"Richard Darlington", drame en trois actes et en prose, précédé de "La maison du docteur", prologue, par MM. Dinaux; Représenté pour la première fois, a Paris, sur le theatre de la Porte-Saint-Martin, le 10 décembre 1831. Caption title. Buff wrappers : La France dramatique au dix-neuvieme siècle. Porte ST. Martin. "Richard Darlington", drame en trois actes et en prose. 41e et 42e livraisons. Paris : J.N. Barba, Pollet, Bezou, on souscrit également dans les bureaux de la France pittoresque, 1834, 8vo., pp. "La maison du docteur" (111)-118, "Richard Darlington" (119)-161 in double columns.

Théatre de Alex. Dumas. "Richard Darlington". (Vignette) Bruxelles. E. Laurent, 1834, 32mo., pp. half-title "Richard Darlington", verso 'personnages', (7)-194. Buff wrappers repeating title-page.

"Richard Darlington", drame en trois actes et en prose, précédé de "La maison du docteur", prologue, par MM. Dinaux. Paris, J.N. Barba, 1835, 8vo., pp. (111)-161 in double columns. La France dramatique au dix-neuvième siècle. Porte-Saint-Martin. Imprimerie normale de Jules Didot l'aîné.

"Richard Darlington". Drame. Par Alexandre Dumas. (Vignette) Bruxelles, Meline, Cans et compagnie, 1838, 12mo., pp. 'Personnages' and epigraph (2 leaves unnumbered with 'personnages' for the Prologue on verso), Prologue (9)-40, "Richard Darlington" Acte premier (unnumbered with 'personnages' for the first act on verso), (43)-239. Yellow wrappers.

Ibid   Same publishers, format and pagination. On front
cover : Bibliothèque des châteaux et des campagnes. 7e Série.

Oeuvres de Alex. Dumas. Tome second. (Vignette) Bruxelles, Meline, Cans et compagnie, 1838, large 8vo. "Richard Darlington", pp. 'personnages' on verso of title, prologue (265)-275, (276)-323 in double columns.

"Richard Darlington", drame en trois actes et en prose, précédé de 'La maison du docteur", prologue, par MM. Dinaux; Représenté pour la première fois, à Paris, sur le théatre de la Porte-Saint-Martin, le 10 décembre 1831. Paris, Imprimerie normale de Jules Didot l'ainé, n.d. (1843), 8vo., pp. (111)-161 in double columns. La France dramatique du XIXe siècle. Volume 12.

"Richard Darlington", par A. Dumas et Dinaux. Paris, chez N. Tresse, 1859, 8vo., pp. (111)-161. Caption title.

Ibid   Paris, Imp. de Walder, 1866, same format and pagination as the preceding. Caption title.

"Richard Darlington" drame en trois actes, en huit tableaux précédé d'un prologue en société avec MM. Goubaux et Beudin Porte-Saint-Martin. - 10 décembre 1831. 'Distribution' on title-page. Prologue "La maison du docteur", pp. 2-22, "Richard Darlington", pp. 23-134. Théatre complet de Alex. Dumas Tome III Paris, Calmann Lévy, éditeur ancienne maison Michel Lévy frères, 1874. 12mo. "Théatre complet" in 25 volumes.

There was one parody of the play which, to my knowledge, was never published. "Piffard Droldeton", en trois actes, précédé de "La mansarde de la sage-femme", prologue, par MM. Dumersan, Brazier er Saint-Hilaire. Apparently it was performed at the Theatre de l'Odéon on the 31st December, 1831.

(I should add here that Charles Beaumont-Wicks in his "Parisian Stage 1800-1850", University of Alabama Press, 1950, mentions a parody with a slightly different title and by different authors which was also performed at the Odéon on the 31st December, 1831 : "Piffard Drôle-de-ton" imitation grivoise en 3 actes et en prose, par MM. Dumersan, L. Lhérie et A.V. de St. Hilaire.)

"LA VENDEE APRES LE 29 JUILLET"   1831

La Vendée was staunchly Royalist, and after the Revolution of 1830 Dumas toured there for the purpose of estimating the possibilities of organising a National Guard in the region. On his return he wrote a report for Louis-Philippe and La Fayette in which, besides deprecating the possibility of any sudden changes there, he made some suggestions which he thought would be helpful towards its successful pacification.

Original edition.
"La Vendée après le 29 juillet". Signed : Alex. Dumas. Paris, Revue des deux mondes", Volume 1. Série i. 1831, pp. (114)-133.

"Le château d'Eppstein", par Alexandre Dumas. Paris, L. de Potter, 1844, 3 vols. Volume 3 is completed by "Fra Bartolomeo", "Le curé Chambard", "La Vendée après le 29 juillet", pp. 233-288, and "Un miracle au XVe siècle".

Dumas quoted a large portion of it in his "Mémoires".

"A TOI"   1832

This poem comprises five verses of unequal length totalling 70 lines, and rhyming in couplets. The 12 lines making up the last strophe but one were the epigraph to Charpentier's 1834 edition of Dumas'plays, and they were also written on the back fly-leaf of the "Préludes poètiques".

Original edition.
"A toi", signed : Alex. Dumas, 15 septembre 1831, pp. 167-170, in "Nouveau Keepsake Français. Souvenir le littérature contemporain", Paris, Louis Janet, libraire, n.d. (1831), 24mo.; illustrated with steel engravings.

In "La France Littéraire", 1832, Volume IV, pp. 203-205.

In "Souvenirs poétiques de l'école romantique 1825 a 1840", par M. Edouard Fournier, Paris, Laplace, Sanchez et Cie., 1880, pp. 119-121.

In "Le Livre", octobre 1886, pp. 296-297.

26

"LA GRANDE CHARTREUSE"   1832
    Twenty-nine verses, each of 4 lines.

Original edition.
"La Grande Chartreuse", signed : Alexandre Dumas, pp. 130-136 in
"Annales Romantiques Receuil de morceaux choisis De Littérature
Contemporaine", Paris, Louis Janet, 1835, 24mo.; illustrated with
steel engravings.

In "Le Petit Journal", 8 novembre 1864, with Dumas' comments and
dedicated to Dom Mortes, Superior of the Grand Chartreuse, Grenoble;
here Dumas says that the poem was written in 1832.

In Glinel's "Alexandre Dumas et son oeuvre", pp. 334-337. Glinel
points out eighteen variants in the two preceding printings.

"TERESA"   1832
    Dumas was never particularly enthusiastic about this play. It
was written from a draft made by Anicet Bourgeois, and yet some critics have praised it as being one of the best of Dumas' earlier dramas.

Original edition.
"Teresa", drame En Cinq Actes et en Prose, par Alex. Dumas. Représenté, pour la première fois, sur le théatre Royal de l'Opera-
Comique, le 6 février 1832. Publication de Charles Lemesle. Paris.
Barba, éditeur. v^e Charles-Bechet, libraire, Lecointe et Pougin,
libraires, 1832, 8vo., unnumbered page following title : "A mes
jeunes compatriots et amis. C'est à Villers-Côterets (sic), au
milieu de nos fêtes, de nos soirées et de nos chasses, que ce drame
a été composé et écrit. Je vous le dédie : Frères, recevez-le
comme un frère, car Villers-Côterets (sic) est aussi son pays natal.
6 février 1832 - 11 heures du soir. Amitié Alex. Dumas.", pp. (5)-164.
Brown wrappers repeating title-page.

"Teresa", drame en cinq actes et en prose, par Alex. Dumas. Genève,
Ch. Gruaz, imprimeur-éditeur; A. Cherbuliez, libraire, au haut de la
cité. En Suisse, chez les principaux libraires. 1833. 8vo., pp. 126.

Théatre de Alex. Dumas. "Teresa". (Vignette) Bruxelles, E. Laurent,
1834, 32mo., pp. 165. Buff wrappers repeating title-page.

"Teresa", drame en cinq actes, Par M. Alexandre Dumas, représenté
pour la première fois, sur le théatre Royal de l'Opéra-Comique, le
... . Caption title. Yellow wrappers : Supplément au magasin
théatral, choix de pièces jouées sur les théatres de Paris. Tome
deuxième. Théâtre de la Porte-Saint-Martin (sic). "Théresa". (sic),
Drame en cinq actes, par M. Alexandre Dumas. (Vignette) Paris, Marchant; Bruxelles, Aug. Jouhaud, 1835, 8vo., pp. 36 in double columns.

"Teresa", drame en cinq actes, Par M. Alexandre Dumas, représenté
pour la première fois, sur le theatre royal de l'Opéra-Comique, le
6 février 1832. Caption title. Buff wrappers - Quatrième année.
Magasin théatral, choix de pièces nouvelles, jouées sur les théatres
de Paris. Théatre de la Porte-Saint-Martin (sic). "Théresa" (sic),
Drame en cinq actes. (Vignette) Paris, Marchant, 1837, 8vo., pp. 36
in double columns.

"Teresa", drame en cinq actes, par M. Alexandre Dumas, représenté pour la première fois sur le Théâtre Royal de l'Opéra-Comique, le 6 février 1832. Paris, Marchant; Bruxelles, Librairie belge-francaise, 1838, 8vo., pp. 36 in double columns. Caption title Le Magasin théâtral. Tome VI.

"Teresa". Drame. Par Alexandre Dumas. (Vignette) Bruxelles, Meline, Cans et compagnie, 1838, 16mo., pp. 205. Yellow wrappers.

Oeuvres de Alex. Dumas. Tome second. (Vignette) Bruxelles, Meline, Cans et compagnie, 1838, large 8vo. "Teresa", pp. 'Personnages' on verso of title, (213)-261 in double columns.

"Teresa", drame en cinq actes, par Alexandre Dumas. Bruxelles, Société belge de librairie, 1842, 16mo., pp. 165. Buff wrappers.

"Teresa" drame en cinq actes, en prose Salle Ventadour (sic). - 6 février 1832. "A mes jeunes compatriotes et amis ... " and 'distribution' below caption title, pp. 136-240. Théatre complet de Alex. Dumas Tome III Paris Calmann Lévy, éditeur ancienne maison Michel Lévy frères, 1874. 12mo. "Théatre complet" in 25 volumes.

There was one parody of the play :
"Thérèse ou ange et diable", comédie-vaudeville en deux actes par MM. Bayard et Arthur de Beauplan, représentée pour la première fois, a Paris, sur le théatre du Gymnase, le 29 octobre 1852. Paris, Michel Lévy frères, n.d. (1853), 4to., pp. 23 in double columns. Caption title with woodcut. Théatre contemporain illustré.

"LE MARI DE LA VEUVE"   1832

This was the first of Dumas' comedies. Assistance in its preliminary rough draft was given by Eugène Durieu and Anicet Bourgeois, but the play in its final form was solely by Dumas. It has been stated that it was written, rehearsed, and the first performance given, in one week. This first performance was a benefit one for Mademoiselle Dupont. The play became a great favourite, and up to 1872 it had been played more than one hundred and eighty times at the Théâtre-Francais alone.

Original edition.
"Le mari de la veuve", comédie en un acte et en prose. Par M. ***. Représentée pour la première fois sur le Théatre Français, le 4 avril 1832. Paris, Auguste Auffray, 1832, 8vo., 'personnages' and 'acteurs' on verso of title, pp. (5)-60; 'Variantes pour les scènes iii et iv', pp. (61)-63. Buff wrappers repeating title-page; on back wrapper "Ouvrages Dramatiques de M. Alex. Dumas."

"Le mari de la veuve", comédie en un acte et en prose, par M. Alexandre Dumas. Paris, Dondey-Dupré, 1832, 8vo., pp. 18 in double columns. Caption title. Le Magasin théatral.

"Le mari de la veuve", comédie en un acte et en prose, par MM. Alexandre Dumas et ***, représentée pour la première fois, à Paris, sur le Théatre-français, le 4 avril 1832. Paris, Imprimerie de Ve Dondey-Dupré, n.d. (1835), 8vo., pp. 18 in double columns. Caption title. Le Magasin théatral.

"Le mari de la veuve", comédie en un acte et en prose, Par M. Alexandre Dumas, ... Paris, Marchant; Bruxelles, Aug. Jouhaud, 1835, ivo., pp. 20 in double columns. Caption title. Supplement au Magasin Théatral, choix de pièces jouées sur les théatres de Paris.

Théatre de Alex. Dumas. "Le mari de la veuve". (Vignette) Bruxelles. E. Laurent, 1836, 32mo., verso of half-title 'personnages', pp. (7)-84. Buff wrappers repeating title-page.

"Le mari de la veuve", comédie en un acte et en prose, par M. Alexandre Dumas, représentée pour la première fois, à Paris, sur le Théâtre-Français, le 4 avril 1832. Paris, Marchant, 1836, 8vo., pp. 20 in double columns. Caption title. Le Magasin théatral.

Oeuvres de alex. Dumas. Tome second. (Vignette) Bruxelles, Meline, Cans et compagnie, 1838, large 8vo. "Le mari de la veuve", pp. (187)-209 in double columns.

"Le mari de la veuve", comédie en un acte et en prose, Par MM. Alexandre Dumas et ***, représentée pour la première fois, a Paris, sur le Théatre-Français, le 4 avril 1832. Paris, Marchant; Bruxelles, A la libraire belge-française,1838, 8vo., pp. 18 in double columns. Caption title. Le magasin théatral. Green wrappers, the back cover announcing the publication of a new translation of Shakespeare's works "précédée d'une introduction sur le génie de Shakspeare (sic), par Alexandre Dumas."

"Le mari de la veuve", comédie en un acte et en prose, par Alexandre Dumas. Bruxelles, Société belge de librairie, 1842, 16mo., pp. 80. Buff wrappers.

Repértoire du Théâtre français à Berlin. No. 330. Deuxième Série. (No. 80.) "Le mari de la Veuve". Comédie en un acte, et en prose, par MM. Alexandre Dumas et ***. Berlin, Ad. Mt. Schlesinger, Libraire et Editeur de Musique, 1847, 8vo., pp. 36. Imprimé chez I.W. Krause.

"Le mari de la veuve", comédie en un acte et en prose, par M. Alexandre Dumas, représentée pour la première fois, à Paris, sur le Théâtre-Français, le 4 avril 1832. Paris, La Librairie théâtrale, 1851, 8vo., pp. 18 in double columns. Caption title.

"Le mari de la veuve", comédie en un acte et en prose, Par M. ***. Représentée pour la première fois sur le Théatre Français, le 4 avril 1852 (sic). Nouvelle édition, conforme à la représentation. Paris, a Ta librairie théatrale, 1853, 8vo., pp. 72.

"Le mari de la veuve", comedie en un acte et un prose, par Alexandre Dumas. Bruxelles, Livourne, Meline, Cans et compagnie; Leipzig, J.P. Meline, 1853, 12mo., pp. 80. Yellow wrappers.

"Le mari de la veuve", comédie en un acte et en prose, par M. Alexandre Dumas, représentée pour la première fois, à Paris, sur le Théâtre-Français, le 4 avril 1832. Paris, Barbré, 1860, 8vo., pp. 18 in double columns. Caption title.

"Le mari de la veuve", comédie en un acte et en prose, Par MM. Alexandre Dumas et ***, représentée pour la première fois, a Paris, sur le Théatre-Français, le 4 avril 1832. Caption title. Yellow wrappers : Magasin théatral pièces nouvelles jouées sur tous les théatres de Paris. (Vignette) Paris, Barbré, 1868, 8vo., pp. 18 in double columns.

"Le mari de la veuve" comédie en un acte, en prose en société avec
MM. Anicet Bourgeois et Durieu Théâtre- Français. - 4 avril 1832.
'Distribution' page (241), pp. (241)-296. Théâtre complet de Alex.
Dumas Tome III Paris, Calmann Lévy, éditeur ancienne maison Michel
Lévy frères, 1874, 12mo. "Théatre complet" in 25 volumes.

"LA TOUR DE NESLE"   1832

Very probably the germ idea for this play originates as far back
as Villon, where he related the incident of Buridan being thrown from
the Tour de Nesle in a sack. Around this particular incident Frédéric
Gaillardet fashioned a play which was quite unsuitable for the stage.
Jules Janin was asked by Harel, the manager of the Porte-Saint-Martin,
to work on it and re-adapt it. The manuscript was in due course returned as an impossible one to redraft. Harel then persuaded Dumas,
considerably against his will, to accept the task.

Dumas proceeded to write a whole tableau to precede what had
already been written, probably used part of Gaillardet's second tableau, and then completed the drama in his own fashion. Janin may at
an early stage have conceivably made some small contribution. Madame
la comtesse Dash has stated (and she handled both Gaillardet's MSS
and Dumas') that there is no question but that the play as finally
staged was Dumas'. He, however, had insisted that the first playbills
should read : "par MM. F. Gaillardet et ***", which were later
changed by Harel to read : "par MM. *** et F. Gaillardet", but nevertheless there was continuous acrimony, lawsuits, and ultimately a duel
between the two men. In 1887 the heirs of Gaillardet, and he had
earlier acknowledged the real value of the work Dumas had put into the
play, brought a suit to prevent its title appearing on the statue
erected to Dumas in the Place Malesherbes in Paris. The suit failed.

The play's success was enormous. For years it was repeatedly
revived, and just as frequently interdicted by the censorship.
During some thirty odd years after its first performance there were
over eight hundred performances of this extraordinarily powerful
drame.

Original edition.
"La tour de Nesle", Drame en cinq actes et en neuf tableaux, par
MM. Gaillardet et ***, représenté, pour la première fois, a Paris,
sur le théatre de la Porte-Saint-Martin, le 29 mai 1832. Paris, J.N.
Barba, Libraire, Palais-Royal, grande cour, Derrière le Theatre-
Français. 1832. 8vo., 'Personnages' 'Acteurs' verso of title, 4
unnumbered pages of introduction, (1)-98, and 2 pages of publisher's
advertisements. Greyish yellow paper wrappers.
(One copy of this edition was printed on parchment for Jules Janin.)

"La tour de Nesle", drame en cinq actes et neuf tableaux, par MM.
Alexandre Dumas et F. Gaillardet. Représenté, pour la première fois,
a Paris, sur le théatre de la Porte-Saint-Martin, le 29 mai 1832.
Genève, Ch. Gruaz, imprimeur-éditeur, Rue du Puits-Saint-Pierre. Ab.
Roullier, libraire, rue de Bourg. 1832. 8vo., pp. verso of title-
page 'personnages' 'acteurs', 4 unnumbered pages comprising intro-
ductory history material (unsigned), (7)-115. De l'Imprimerie Ch.
Gruaz, rue du Puits-Saint-Pierre.

"La tour de Nesle", Drame en cinq actes et en neuf tableaux, per MM. Gaillardet et ***, représenté, pour la première fois, a Paris, sur le théatre de la Porte-Saint-Martin, le 29 mai 1832. Nouvelle édition. (Vignette) Paris, J.N. Barba, 1833, same format and pagination as the original edition. Beige wrappers with a vignette differing from that on the title-page. Imprimeur, Marlin, Versailles.

"La tour de Nesle", drame en cinq actes et en neuf tableaux, Par MM. Gaillardet et ***. Représenté, pour la première fois, à Paris, sur le théâtre de la Porte-Saint-Martin, le 29 mai 1832. A Bruxelles, J.-A. Lelong, n.d. (1833), 32 mo., pp. (i)-iii "Préface", (1)-134.

"La tour de Nesle", drame en cinq actes et en neuf tableaux, par MM. Gaillardet et ***, Représenté pour la première fois, à Paris, sur le théatre de la Porte-Saint-Martin. Paris, J.N. Barba, Delloye, Bezou, 1835, 8vo., pp. (205)-242 in double columns, followed by 2 pages of publishers' advertisements. Brown paper wrappers : La France dramatique au dix-neuvième siècle. Porte-St. Martin. "La tour de Nesle", drame en cinq actes et en neuf tableaux, par MM. Frédéric Gaillardet et ***.

"La tour de Nesle", drame en cinq actes et en neuf tableaux, par MM. Gaillardet et ***. Paris, J.N. Barba, 1835, 8vo., pp. (205)-242 in double columns. La France dramatique au dix-neuvième siècle. Porte Saint-Martin. Impr. normale de Jules Didot l'ainé.

"La tour de Nesle". Drame. Par Alexandre Dumas. (Vignette) Bruxelles, Meline, Cans et compagnie, 1838, 16mo., pp. 180. Yellow wrappers.

Ibid   Same publishers, format and pagination. Bibliothèque des châteaux et des campagnes, in the same year.

Oeuvres de Alex. Dumas. Tome second. (Vignette) Bruxelles, Meline, Cans et compagnie, 1838, large 8vo. "La tour de Nesle". 'Personnages' on verso of title, pp. (327)-370 in double columns.

"La tour de Nesle", drame en cinq actes et en neuf tableaux, par MM. Frédéric Gaillardet et Alexandre Dumas; Représenté pour la première fois, à Paris, sur le théatre de la Porte-Saint-Martin, le 29 mai 1832. (Paris, J.N. Barba, 1839), 8vo., pp. (205)-242 in double columns. Caption title. Imprimerie normale de Jules Didot l'ainé.

Théatre de Alex. Dumas. "La tour de Nesle". (Vignette) Bruxelles, Mme. Laurent, 1840, 32 mo., pp. 142. Buff wrappers.

"La tour de Nesle" drame en cinq actes et en prose par Alexandre Dumas. Bruxelles, Société belge de librairie Hauman et cie., 1842, 16 mo., pp. 143. Brown wrappers. (The advertisements on the back wrapper include the announcement of a work by Dumas to be entitled "Godefroid de Harcourt", 2 volumes in-18.)

"La tour de Nesle", drame en cinq actes et en neuf tableaux, par MM. Gaillardet et *** ... (Paris, Barba, Pollet et Bezou, n.d. 184), 8vo., pp. (205)-242 in double columns.

"La tour de Nesle", drame en cinq actes et en neuf tableaux par MM. Frédéric Gaillardet et Alexandre Dumas, Représenté pour la première fois, à Paris, sur le théâtre de la Porte-Saint-Martin, le 29 mai 1832. Caption title. Pink wrappers : "La tour de Nesle" drame en cinq actes par F. Gaillardet et A.Dumas. Paris, Tresse et Stock, n.d.

(c 1860), 8vo., pp. 38 (last page unnumbered) in double columns.

Ibid   Caption title.   Blue wrappers : La France dramatique au dix-neuvième siècle   Choix de Pièces Modernes.   Porte-Saint-
Martin.   "La tour de Nesle" drame en cinq actes et neuf tableaux.
Paris, N. Tresse, Successeur de J.-N. Barba, 1861, 8vo., pp. 38 in
double columns.

"La tour de Nesle", drame en cinq actes et en neuf tableaux,   par MM.
Frédéric Gaillardet et Alexandre Dumas; Représenté pour la première
fois, à Paris, sur le théâtre de la Porte-Saint-Martin, le 29 mai 1832.
Caption title.   Paris, Imprimerie normale de Jules Didot l'aîné, n.d.
(1866)ₐ 8vo., pp. (205)-242 in double columns.   La France dramatique
au XIXᵉ siècle.

"La tour de Nesle" drame en cinq actes, en neuf tableaux en société
avec M. Fréderic Gaillardet Porte-Saint-Martin. - 29 mai 1832.
'Distribution' on title-page, pp. 2-98.   Théatre complet de Alex.
Dumas Tome IV Paris Calmann Lévy, éditeur ancienne maison Michel
Lévy frières, 1874.   12mo.   "Théatre complet" in 25 volumes.

There were three parodies of the play :
"La tour de Nesle à pont-à-Mousson" parodie-vaudeville en trois acte-
et six tableaux par MM Theodore Cogniard et Clairville représentée
pour la première fois, à Paris, sur le théâtre des Varietes, le 30
mai 1861.   Paris, Michel Lévy frères, n.d. (1861), 4to., pp. 11 in
double columns.   Caption title with woodcut at head.   Théâtre contemporain illustré 636ᵉ livraison.

Ibid   Représentée pour la première fois, à Paris, sur
le théâtre des Variétés le 30 mai 1861. Paris, Calmann-Lévy, n.d.
(188), large 8vo., pp. 38 in double columns and 2 pages of publisher's
advertisement.   Caption title.

"La Tour de Nesle pour de bon" par L. Beauvallet et M. Leprévost.
Parodie en trois actes représentée sur le Théâtre Dejazet.

"La Tour de Nesle pour rire" par E. Blum et A. Flan. Parodie-revue-
ballet en trois actes representée sur le Théâtre des Délassements-
Comiques.

I have never been able to trace a printing of the last two parodies.

"LE FILS DE L'EMIGRE, ou LE PEUPLE"   1832

     In his article'Le théatre inconnu d'Alexandre Dumas père' pub-
lished in the "Revue Biblio Iconographique" Charles Glinel stated
that this drama consisted of four acts and eight tableaux. Earlier
in his work "Alexandre Dumas et son oeuvre" he had written that it
consisted of five acts, in prose, always being preceded by a prologue
"L'armurier de Brientz". In the latter work Gline wrote : 'L'idée
du "Fils de l'Emigré" était de lui (Anicet Bourgeois); l'exécution   -
dans les premiers actes surtout   - fut entièrement de Dumas.'

     Despite the fact that it was a well-constructed and powerful
play it was a failure, probably because of the brutality of the plot;
the final act aroused the hostility of the audience. The play's
failure hurt Dumas' feelings considerably, and he did no more playwriting under his own name until "Angèle" more than a year later.

The play was never published in full, but a summary of the prologue and the first three acts, and the full fourth act, may be read
in L.Henry Lecomte's "Alexandre Dumas 1802-1870 Sa Vie intime. Ses
Oeuvres", Paris, Tallandier, (1902). "Le fils de l'emigré, ou le
peuple" drame en quatre actes et huit tableaux, en prose, precédé de
"L'armurier de Brientz", prologue en prose, par M. Anicet Bourgeois
(et Alexandre Dumas). Représenté sur le théatre de la Porte-Saint-
Martin, le 28 aoôt 1832.

(A copy of the original manuscript, made by an amanuensis in the 19th.
century, of "Le fils d'un emigré" is held by the Bibliothèque de
l'Arsenal, Paris; it consists of 70 leaves. Rondel Ms, 484.)

"PERRINET LECLERC, ou PARIS EN 1418"   1832

This prose drama has an interesting history. The authors,
Anicet Bourgeois and Lockroy, drew its plot from Dumas' "Scènes historiques" which had appeared in the 'Revue des deux mondes' and which
were later incorporated in his "Isabel de Bavière". In 1832 Dumas
was in Switzerland and could, therefore, have taken no part in the
play's writing; his permission to use his material was never asked
for and, indeed, no credit was given to him.

In his "Mémoires" Dumas wrote that 'the "Scènes historiques"
caused no particular stir but the play was a great success', and
added that 'the authors were very careful not to mention my name'.

I am referring to it in this Bibliography if only because after
the publication of "Isabel de Bavière" Dumas was unjustly accused by
some who were ignorant of the periodical publication of his historical
studies of having taken his material from the drama.

Original edition.
"Perrinet Leclerc, ou Paris en 1418" Drame historique en cinq actes
par MM. Anicet Bourgeois et Lockroy. Musique de M. A Piccini.
Représenté pour la première fois, à Paris, sur le théatre de la Porte-
Saint-Martin, le 3 novembre 1832. Paris; J.-N. Barba, Delloye, Bezou
On souscrit également dans les bureaux de la France Pittoresque, 1832,
8vo., pp. 110, and plate.
Reprinted in 1833 and 1836, same publishers, format and pagination.

Ibid   (1857), Imprimerie de Dubuisson, large 8vo., pp.
363-401.

Ibid   (1866) and (1875), imprimerie de Walder, same format and pagination as the (1857) edition.

"L'ANGE DE POESIE"   1833

This poem comprises five verses, each of 8 lines. The original
date of its writing was 18th December, 1833, in an album then be-
longing to Madame Mennessier-Nodier.

Original edition.
In "Leben sie Wohl", edited by MM. Taxile Delord and Adolphe Carle,
Marseille, Feissart l'ainé et Demonchy, 19, rue Canebière, 1835,
12mo.

In "La Perce-Neige", which comprised pieces of contemporary poetry
collected by Madame Mennessier-Nodier. Paris, Heideloff et Campé, 16
rue Vivienne, 1836, 18mo.

The poem was set to music by Ch. Glantade. Paris, Madame Cristriez,
N°1, Faubourg Poissonnière, n.d. (c 18), with a vignette on the
title-page by A. Deveria lithographed by Guillet.

The first verse only is quoted in "Charles Nodier et la groupe romantique" d'après des documents inédits (par) Michel Salomon, Paris, ...
Perrin et Cie., 1908, 8vo., pp. 163-164.

"LES ENFANTS DE LA MADONE"   1833

This was the first of Dumas' brigand stories; it was later renamed "Cherubino et Celestini" to appear as the first story in his
"Souvenirs d'Antony".

Original edition.
"Les enfants de la Madone", Par M. Alexandre Dumas. Included in
"Les Cent-et-une nouvelles des cent-et-un, ornées des cent-et-un
vignettes" Dessinées et gravées par cent-et-un artistes. Tome Second.
(Vignette) A Paris, Chez Ladvocat, libraire de S.A.R. Le duc d'Or-
léans, 1833, 8vo., pp. (3)-32.

"UNE JOUTE"   1833

A little known story and something of a mystery.

Original edition.
"Une joute". Alexandre Dumas. Included in "Le livre des conteurs".
Tome III. Paris, Allardin, 1833, 8vo., pp. (353)-368 in double
columns.

Reprinted, Paris, chez Lequien fils, 1834, same format and pagination
as the preceding.

"Une joute au Moyen Age". In "Revue pittoresque musée littéraire"
illustré par les premiers artistes. Deuxième Série. Tome II. Paris,
37, Rue Neuve-Saint-Augustin, 1844, 4to., pp. (337)-340 in double
columns, signed 'Alexandre Dumas'; engraving on first page, 1
illustration.

"ANGELE"   1833

In 1832 there was written, and produced at the Théâtre de la
Porte-Saint-Martin, a prose drama entitled "Le fils de l'émigré"
signed by Anicet Bourgeois. It can be assumed that Dumas had a
major part in the writing of it. It was a disastrous failure on the
stage and, to my knowledge, was never published.

However, with the production of "Angèle" Dumas' reputation was
re-established, certainly with admirers of his plays. Dumas has
described it as 'a drama of manners', and this is quite true.

Original edition .
"Angèle" drame en cinq actes, par Alexandre Dumas. Paris, Charpen-

tier, 1834, 8vo., half-title following title, 'Personnages' on verso
of half-title, pp. (3)-254, and 1 unnumbered page with the following
inscription : "Aux acteurs qui ont joué dans 'Angèle'. Mes amis,
Nous avons eu un succès de famille; prenons et partageons. A vous,
Alex. Dumas. Paris, 8 janvier 1834." Etched frontispiece by Celestin
Nanteuil. Yellow paper wrappers with "Représenté pour la première
fois à la Porte-Saint;Martin, le 28 décembre 1833".
(Some copies included at the back an 8 page prospectus by Charles
Nodier of Dumas' works, and 4 pages of Charpentier's catalogue. There
also exist, according to Quérard in his "Supercheries littéraires",
Volume 1, column 1065, some copies bearing the name of Anicet Bour-
geois as author instead of Dumas, but I have never seen one.)

"Angèle". Drame en cinq actes, per Alexandre Dumas. (Vignette)
Bruxelles, J.P. Meline, 1834, 18mo., pp. 167.

"Angèle", drame en cinq actes, par Alexandre Dumas. Bruxelles,
J.-A. Lelong, 1834, 18mo., pp. 144. Nouveau répertoire dramatique de
la scène française : 11ème année. 2ème série, 4ème livraison.

Théatre de Alex. Dumas. "Angèle". Bruxelles, E. Laurent, 1834, 32mo.,
pp. 165. Buff wrappers.

"Angèle", Drame, par Alexandre Dumas. Représenté, pour la première
fois, sur le théatre de la Porte-Saint-Martin, le 28 décembre 1833.
(Vignette) Bruxelles. E. Laurent, 1834, 32mo., pp. 165, verso blank,
unnumbered page "Aux acteurs qui ont joué dans 'Angèle' ... ... "
signed 'A. Dumas'. Paris, 8 janvier 1834". Buff wrappers repeating
title-page.

"Angèle", Drame en cinq actes, par Alexandre Dumas. (Vignette)
Berlin, chez Ad. Mt. Schlesinger, Libraire et Editeur de Musique,
1834, 8vo., pp. (3)-108. 'Personnages' on verso of title. Répertoire
du Théâtre français à Berlin. No. 124. Imprimé chez L.W. Krause.

"Angèle", drame en cinq actes, Par M. Alexandre Dumas, représenté
pour la première fois, sur le théatre de la Porte-Saint-Martin, le 28
décembre 1833. Paris, Marchant; Bruxelles, Aug. Jouhaud, 1835, 8vo.,
pp. 36 in double columns. Caption title. Supplement au Magasin
théatral, choix de pièces jouées sur les théatres de Paris.

Ibid   Caption title. Pink paper wrappers - Troisième
année. Magasin théatral, choix de pièces nouvelles, jouées sur tous
les théatres de Paris. (Vignette) Paris, Marchant; Bruxelles, Auguste
Jouhaud, 1836, 8vo., pp. 36 in double columns.

Ibid   Caption title. Yellow paper wrappers - Magasin
théatral, choix de pièces nouvelles, jouées sur tous les théatres de
Paris. Théatre de la Porte-Saint-Martin. "Angèle", Drame en cinq
actes. (Vignette) Paris, Marchant; Bruxelles, Tarride, n.d. (1836),
8vo., pp. 36 in double columns.

"Angèle", drame en cinq actes, par M. Alexandre Dumas, représenté
pour la première fois, sur le théâtre de la Porte-Saint-Martin, le 28
décembre 1833. Paris, Marchant; Bruxelles, Librairie belge-française,
1837, 8vo., pp. 36 in double columns. Caption title. Le Magasin
théatral, Tome VI.

"Angèle". Drame. Par Alexandre Dumas. (Vignette) Bruxelles, Meline,
Cans et compagnie, 1838, 16mo., pp. 198. Yellow wrappers.

Ibid   In the Bibliothèque des châteaux et des campagnes,
same publishers, year, format and pagination.

Oeuvres de Alex. Dumas.   Tome second.   (Vignette) Bruxelles, Meline,
Cans et compagnie, 1838, large 8vo.   "Angèle", pp. 'Personnages' on
verso of title, (445)-493 in double columns.

"Angèle" Drame en cinq actes et en prose, par Alexandre Dumas.
Bruxelles. Meline, Cans et Cie., 1853, 18mo. pp. 159.

Ibid   Bruxelles, Livourne, Meline, Cans et compagnie;
Leipzig, J.P. Meline, 1853, same format and pagination as the preceding.

"Angèle" drame en cinq actes, par M. Alexandre Dumas, représenté
pour la première fois, sur le théatre de la Porte-Saint-Martin, le 28
décembre 1833. Paris, N. Tresse, successeur de J.-N. Barba, 1861,
8vo., pp. 36 in double columns. Caption title. Yellow wrappers.

"Angèle" drame en cinq actes, en prose Porte-Saint-Martin. - 28
decémbre 1833. "Aux acteurs qui ont joué dans 'Angèle' ... ... " and
'Distribution' on title-page, pp. (100)-204. Théatre complet de Alex.
Dumas Tome IV Paris Calmann Lévy, éditeur ancienne maison Michel
Lévy frères, 1874. 12 mo. "Théatre complet" in 25 volumes.

Reference should be made here to :
"Angèle", drame en cinq actes, narré et commenté par Madame Gibou à
ses commères Mesdames Pochet, la Lyonnaise, etc. En prose, "par
l'auteur de 'Marie Tudor' racontée par Madam Pochet à ses voisines".
Paris, Marchant, Laisné, 1834, 8vo., pp. 56.

"Angèle", drame, vengé des critiques et des détracteurs. Paris,
Setier, 1834, 8vo., pp. 8.

"GAULE ET FRANCE"   1833

     This is Dumas' first piece of serious historical writing, and
covers the history of France from the earliest times to the death of
Charles IV and the succession of Philippe de Valois in 1328.

     Some editions published in France, and all those published in
Belgium, include the famous epilogue in which Dumas prophesied the re-
establishment of a Republic with : 'un président élu pour cinq ans,
sortant du peuple, d'une fortune particulière modeste, et pourvu d'une
liste civile restreinte', a prophecy which was fulfilled in 1848 for
a short time, and again later.

Original edition.
"Gaule et France", par Alex. Dumas. ('Sans haine, sans crainte'.
Paris. U. Canel, rue de Bac, 104. A. Guyot, place du Louvre, 18.
M D CCC XXXIII. 8vo., pp. half-title with on verso : imprimerie de
Aug. Auffray, rue des filles-S.-Thomas, 5, place de la Bourse, title,
verso blank, (1)-14 'Prologue', (15)-156 'Gaule. Race conquérante.
Monarchie Franco-Romaine', (157)-337 'France. Race Nationale. Mon-
archie Française', verso blank, (339)-375 'Epilogue'. Grey paper
wrappers repeating title-page. On back wrapper : 'sous presse
pour faire suite a ce volume : Chroniques de France, par Alex. Dumas.
Première livraison. 2 vol. in 8e.; prix : 15 fr.'
This first edition was published, August, 1833.

"Gaule et France", par Alex. Dumas. ('Sans haine, sans crainte'. (Vignette) Bruxelles, Ant. Peeters, libraire; Leipzig, Allgemeine Niederlandische Buchhandlung, 1833, 16mo., pp. (5)-21 'Prologue', (23)-171 'Gaule, Race conquérante. Monarchie Franco-Romaine', (175)-361 'France. Race nationale. Monarchie Française', (365)-400 'Epilogue'. Buff wrappers.

Ibid   Bruxelles, J.P. Meline, 1833, 16mo., same pagination as the preceding.

"Gaule et France", par Alexandre Dumas. ('Sans haine, sans crainte'. Deuxième Edition. Paris, Victor Magen, éditeur ... . 1835, 8vo., pp. 375 of which the epilogue comprises pp. 341-375. Typographie de A. Pinard.

Oeuvres de Alex. Dumas. Tome premier. (Vignette) Bruxelles, Meline, Cans et compagnie, 1838, large 8vo. "Gaule et France", pp. (557)-658 in double columns, and includes the epilogue.

"Gaule et France", avec Une introduction aux Scènes historiques, par Alex. Dumas. (Vignette) Paris. Librairie de Charles Gosselin, éditeur de la bibliothèque d'élite, 9, rue Saint-Germain-des Prés. MDCCCXLII. 16mo., pp. half-title with on verso : imprimé par Béthune et Plon, a Paris, title, verso blank, (1)-10 'Introduction', (11)-24 'Prologue', (25)-152 'Gaule. Race conquérante. Monarchie Franco-Romaine' (page 132 misnumbered 123), (153)-321 'France. Race Nationale. Monarchie Française', verso blank, (323)-347 'Epilogue', and 8 pages of publisher's advertisements. On cover : Bibliothèque d'Elite. (The introduction referred to in this edition has been taken from the 2 volume, 1839, edition of Dumas' "La comtesse de Salisbury", where it also served as an introduction. It refers to Dumas' ideas regarding the writing of historical romances.)

Oeuvres de Alex. Dumas. Tome deuxième. (Vignette) Bruxelles, Societe belge de librairie Hauman et Ce. 1843, large 8vo. "Gaule et France", pp. (351)-461 in double columns including the epilogue.

'Le Siècle'. Oeuvres complètes d'Alexandre Dumas Douxième série. "Gaule et France". Paris, au bureau du Siècle, ... (1857), 4to., pp. (361)-422 in double columns.

"Gaule et France" par Alexander Dumas. Paris, Michel Lévy frères, 1863, 4to., pp. 72 in double columns, and including the epilogue. Caption title with woodcut. Yellow wrappers with woodcut. Musée littéraire contemporain.

"LA VENDEE ET MADAME"   1833

     Although this account of the arrest of the duchesse de Berry, daughter of Francis I of Naples, at Nantes was first published under the name of General Dermoncourt it was well-known then, as it is to-day, that the first edition was written by Dumas. Dermoncourt had related to Dumas details of the Duchess' expedition to La Vendée and of her subsequent arrest by Dermoncourt who was then military governor of Nantes. Dermoncourt had no literary pretensions and asked Dumas to do the actual writing of the book. Later, greatly dissatisfied with the way the government of Louis-Philippe handled the aftermath of the arrest his political views changed, and the second edition was 'revised, corrected and augmented', and for these changes Dermoncourt was solely responsible.

Original edition. (Dumas)
"La Vendée et madame", par le Gal Dermoncourt. Paris, Adolphe Guyot, 18 place du Louvre. Urbain Canel, 104, rue de Bac. Londres, Bailli- ère, 219, Regent Street. 1833. 8vo., pp. half-title with on verso the printer's name Auffray, front-piece 'Château de la Penissière', title, verso blank, pp. (i)-iv 'Avis. Paris 15 septembre 1833', (1)- 323, verso blank, (325)-362 'Pièces justificatives', unnumbered page 'Erratum', verso blank.
Reprinted, same publishers, year, format and pagination.

"La Vendée et madame', par le général Dermoncourt. (Vignette) Bruxelles, J.P. Meline, libraire-éditeur. 1833. 12mo., pp. half- title, verso A. Wahlen, imp.-lib. de la cour, title, (v)-vi 'Avis. Paris. 15 septembre 1833'. (7)-256,(257)-288 'Pièces justificatives'. Buff wrappers repeating title-page.
(This, the first and only Belgian edition, appeared almost immediately after the first French edition.)

Second edition. (Dermoncourt)
"La Vendée et madame", par le général Dermoncourt. Deuxième édition véritable, revue, corrigée et augmentée du double, sur des notes authentiques communiqués a l'auteur depuis la première. (Verso quotation from Ch. Nodier.) Paris. L.F. Hivert, libraire-éditeur, quai des Augustins, N° 55. 1834. 8vo., pp. half-title with on verso : imprimerie de Béthune, Belin et Plon, rue de Vaugirard, N° 36, frontispiece 'Combat de la Pénissière', title, verso blank, (5)-17 'Avertissement sur cette édition', verso blank, (19)-453, (454)-460 'Pièce justificative'. In addition to the frontispiece there is one other lithograph - 'Général, je me rends à vous, et me remets à votre loyauté ...' - facing page 369.
Each of the ten sections into which the work is divided bears a motto consisting of one or more phrases to be found later in the body of that section. The verso quotation from Nodier on the title-page is part of the second verse of his "La Napoléone". Most of the 'pièces justificatives' of the original edition are here transferred to the main text.

"COMMENT JE DEVINS AUTEUR DRAMATIQUE"   1833
    The title is self-explanatory. The article's usual appearance is as introductory matter to editions of "Henri III et sa cour" pub- lished in Belgium.
    Originally it appeared, signed 'Par Alexandre Dumas' in the 'Revue des deux mondes', 1er décembre, 1833, pp. 603-618.

Original edition in introductory form.
Théatre de Alex. Dumas. "Henri III". (Vignette) Bruxelles. E. Laur- ent, 1834, 32mo., pp. half-title 'Théatre de Dumas', verso Bruxelles. - imprimerie de E. Laurent, title, (5)-76 "Comment de devins auteur dramatique" signed : Alex. Dumas. 20 décembre 1833, half-title "Henri III et sa cour", verso 'personnages', (79)-209. Buff wrappers : Théatre Alex. Dumas. "Henri III" (Vignette) Bruxelles. E. Laurent, imprimeur-éditeur, place de Louvain, N° 547. 1834.

"Henri III et sa cour". Drame en cinq actes et en prose par Alexandre Dumas. Bruxelles, Société belge de librairie. Hauman et cie., 1842, 18mo., pp. (1)-54 "Comment je devins auteur dramatique", (55)-125 "Henri III et sa cour".

"Antony", Paris, imprimé Terzuolo, n.d. (c 1833), 8vo., pp. i-xlvii "Comment je devins auteur dramatique" signed : Alex. Dumas. 20 décembre 1833, and followed by the text of the play.

"Comment je devins auteur dramatique" signed : Alex. Dumas 20 décembre 1833. Pp. (1)-34. Théatre complet de Alex. Dumas Tome I Paris Calmann Lévy, éditeur ancienne maison Michel Lévy frères, 1874. 12mo. "Théatre complet" in 25 volumes.

"IMPRESSIONS DE VOYAGE" (EN SUISSE)   1833

In his "Mémoires" Dumas tells how, intending to go to Switzerland, he sought out Gosselin the publisher and offered to write a two volume work describing his travels in that country. Gosselin could not be persuaded to take any interest, but Dumas nevertheless set out with the intent of holidaying there. Needless to say he wrote.

In 1833 the following articles by him were published in the 'Revue des deux mondes' :

15 février	-	"Une pêche de nuit".
15 mars	-	"Un beefsteak d'ours".
		"Le col de Balme".
		"Jacques Balmat".
1 mai	-	"Le mont Saint-Bernard".
1 juillet	-	"Les eaux d'Aix".
15 juillet	-	"Le tour du lac".
1 novembre	-	"La mer de glace".

And in the issue of that journal for 1 avril, 1836, appeared "Voyages de Gabriel Payot". All these articles formed part of the final work : "Impressions de voyage." (En Suisse).

The work was, in fact, completed over the years and amounted finally to five volumes. As will be read below the original edition to be published in France came from three quite separate publishers. I can find no published reference to the reason for this; it could be surmised that Dumas had differences of opinion on questions of paymen- with both Guyot and Charpentier, and eventually decided that the last three volumes should be offered to Dumont. There may well exist correspondence between Dumas and Dumont in which an agreement was reached that if Dumont published these final volumes then future works by Dumas would also be published by him; as was the case, indeed, for a number of subsequent works.

Original edition.
"Impressions de voyage" par Alexandre Dumas. (Paris, Adolphe Guyot, Charpentier, and Dumont.) 8vo., 5 volumes.

Volume 1 - Paris, Au bureau de la revue des deux mondes; Librairie d'Adolphe Guyot, MDCCCXXXIV, 8vo., pp. half-title, 388 and unnumbered page table of contents; water-colour frontispiece by Célestin Nanteuil. The half-title is in place of a title-page. Impr. de H. Fournier.

Volume 2 - Paris, Charpentier, MDCCCXXXIV, 8vo., pp. half-title, 368 and unnumbered page table of contents; with the same frontispiece as for Volume 1 but less well produced. Again the half-title is in place of a title-page. Impr. de Corbeil.

Volume 3-5 - Paris, Dumont, 1837, 8vo., pp. 372, 340 and 404.

(I think that it may usefully be added here that the only complete 'run' of these five volumes appears to be held in the New York Public Library.)

Volumes 1 and 2 were immediately pirated in Belgium and Germany. The first such edition to appear was :

"Impressions de voyage" par Alexandre Dumas. Bruxelles, A. Peeters, libraire; Leipzig, Allegemeine Niederlandische Buchhandlung, 1834, 24mo., 2 volumes, pp. 292 and 295, each with an additional unnumbered page table of contents; the title-page of volume 2 has additionally above the colophon 'Deuxième série'. The contents are : Volume 1 - 'Exposition. Montereau. Jeans-sans-peur. Napoléon. Lyon. Le tour de lac. Une pêche de nuit. Les salines de Bex. Le beefsteak d'ours. Le col de Balme. Jacques Balmat, dit Mont-Blanc. La mer de glace. Marie Coutet. Retour à Martigny. Le Saint-Bernard.' Volume 2 - 'Les eaux d'Aix. Adventicum. Charles-le-Téméraire. Fribourg. Les ours de Berne. Le lac de Thun. La vallée de Lauterbrunnen. Passage de la Vengenalp. Le Faulhorn. Rosenlauwi.'

"Impressions de voyage", par Alexandre Dumas. (Vignette) Bruxelles, J.P. Meline, 1834, 16mo., 2 vols., pp. 292 and 295, each with an unnumbered page table of contents; the first volume ends with the chapter 'Le Saint-Bernard', and the second with 'Rosenlauwi.' Imprimerie de Vanderborght fils.

"Impressions de voyage", par Alexandre Dumas. La Haye, G. Vervloet, éditeur, 1834, same format and pagination as the preceding edition.

A second edition of the Guyot and Charpentier first two volumes was published in 1835, same format and pagination.

"Impressions de voyage", par Alexandre Dumas, troisième édition, revue, corrigée et augmentée de plusieurs impressions nouvelles. Paris, Charpentier, libraire-éditeur, rue de Seine, N°31, 1835, 8vo., 2 vols., pp. 476 and 352, each with an additional unnumbered page table of contents; Vol. 2 is completed with 'Notes', pp. (347)-352, the first such note comprising for the most part a letter to Dumas from baron Dermoncourt, and the second Dumas' comments on Interlaken.

"Fragments tirés des 'Impressions de voyage' "par Alexandre Dumas". A l'usage des enfants. Londres, P. Rolandi, 1835, 12mo., pp. 166.

"Impressions de voyage", par Alexandre Dumas. (Vignette) Bruxelles, J.P. Meline, 1835, 16mo., pp. 293 and 293, each with an additional unnumbered page table of contents. (As with the 1834 edition the first volume ends with 'Le Saint-Bernard', and the second with 'Rosenlauwi'.) Volume 1 has a steel engraving frontispiece facing the title-page.

An accompanying volume was issued :

"Nouvelles impressions de voyage", par Alexandre Dumas. (Same vignette as the 2 preceding volumes) Bruxelles, Meline, Cans et comp-

agnie, 1837, 16mo., pp. 319 with an additional unnumbered page table
of contents.
As will be seen this volume has a different pagination from the other
1837 edition noted and, moreover, the contents differ - the volume
starts with the chapter 'Pauline' and ends with 'Prosper Lehmann',
and omits five chapters which were included in the 1838, large 8vo.,
edition. There is no indication at the end of this third volume as
to whether there should be a fourth and final volume. Imp. de Ode et
Wodon.

"Impressions de voyage", par Alexandre Dumas. Paris, (Charpentier
et Dumont.) The Charpentier, troisième édition, is referred to above.
The volumes of the two publishers ran in series, Charpentier being
followed by : "Impressions de voyage", par Alexandre Dumas. Deuxième édition. Paris, Dumont, 1837, 8vo., 3 vols., pp. 370, 338 and
404; the first two volumes each have an additional unnumbered page
table of contents, the table of contents in the final volume being
included in the pagination.

"Nouvelles impressions de voyage". Par Alex. Dumas. Paris. Publications du Figaro, rue coq-héron, 8 ... . Pour Paris et les Départements. 1837. 8vo., pp. (5)-410 and table of contents (1)-2. L.
Herhan, imprimeur.
(This work comprises what were eventually chapters XXXIV-XLVIII of
the Calmann-Lévy edition of the 'complete works'.)

"Nouvelles impressions de voyage", par Alexandre Dumas. (Vignette)
Bruxelles, Meline, Cans et compagnie, 1837, 16mo., 3 vols., pp. 319,
157 and 280, each with an additional unnumbered page table of contents.
Pale yellow wrappers repeating the title-pages.
This is the complete edition of the "Impressions de voyage", but the
arrangement of the chapters is altered.

Ibid   (Vignette) Bruxelles et Leipzig, C. Hochhausen
et Fournes, 1837, 3 vols., same format and pagination as the preceding.

"Nouvelles impressions de voyage", Par M. Alex. Dumas. (Monogram)
Leipzig, Avenarius et Friedlein, 1837. 18mo., pp. 354; there is no
table of contents.
(It would appear that the edition traced is incomplete.)

"Impressions de voyage", par Alexandre Dumas. Troisième édition.
Paris, Dumont, 1838, 8vo., 3 vols.

"Impressions de voyage". Par Alexandre Dumas. (Vignette) Bruxelles,
Meline, Cans et compagnie, 1838, 16mo., 4 vols., pp. 261, 265, 317 and
344, each with an additional unnumbered page table of contents. Green
wrappers repeating the title-pages.

Oeuvres de Alex. Dumas. Tome premier. (Vignette) Bruxelles, Meline,
Cans et compagnie, 1838, large 8vo. "Impressions de voyage", pp.
(165)-484 in double columns.

"Impressions de voyage", par Alexandre Dumas. Quatrième édition.
Paris, Dumont, 1839, 8vo., 3 vols.

"Impressions de voyage" par Alex. Dumas. Nouvelle édition revue et
corrigée. (Monogram) Paris. Librairie de Charles Gosselin, 9, rue
Saint-Germain-des-prés. MDCCCXL. 12mo., 2 vols., pp. (1)-4 'Exposition', (5)-423, verso blank, 1 unnumbered page table of contents; (1)-
466, 2 unnumbered pages table of contents. The end of the 'exposition'

reads : '... mon médecin m'ordonna ce qu'un médecin ordonne lorsqu'il
ne sait plus qu'ordonner : Un voyage en Suisse. En conséquence le 21
juillet 1832, je partis de Paris.'
Reprinted, 1842, same format and pagination.

"Impressions de voyage" par Alexandre Dumas. Bruxelles. Société
belge de librairie; Hauman et Ce., 1841, 16mo., 4 vols., pp. 270, 266
(ending with the chapter 'Rosenlauwi'), 345 and 341, each with an
additional unnumbered page table of contents. Volume 4 ends at page
335, blank, (337)-341 'Notes' as in the Charpentier, 1835, edition.

"Comment Saint-Eloi fut guéri de la vanité". Alexandre Dumas. In
'Le livre des feuilletons Receuil de nouvelles, contes, épisodes,
extraits de la presse contemporaine'. Nancy, Imprimerie Hinzelin,
1843, 8vo., pp. (95) in double columns. Deuxième volume.
(This is a reprint of Chapter 65, "En Suisse".)

Echo des feuilletons Choix de nouvelles, épisodes, anecdotes,
extraits de la Presse contemporaine. Paris, 1844, large 8vo., "Le
Pont du Diable", pp. 143-144 in double columns, extrait - 'Revue des
deux mondes'.
(This is a reprint of the relevant chapter in "En Suisse".)

"Guillaume Tell". Volume 9 of the Alexandre Cadot, 1847-1848, edition
of "Le batard de Mauléon" is completed by "Guillaume Tell", pp. (101)-
317, blank, 319 table of contents. The individual chapter heads are
: 'Werner Stauffbacher. Conrad de Baumgarten. Guillaume Tell.
Guessler. L'Empereur Albert'.

"Impressions de voyage. Suisse", par Alexandre Dumas. Paris, Michel
Lévy frères, 1851, 12mo., 3 vols., pp. 309, and 3 additional pages of
which 1 is table of contents and the others advertisements, 299, and
additional page table of contents, 284, and 4 additional pages of
which 1 is table of contents and 2 are pages of advertisements.
This was the first separate edition reprinted in France from the 1834-
1837 edition.
Reprinted many times both by Michel Lévy frères and Calmann-Lévy.

"Impressions de voyage" par Alexandre Dumas. Edition nouvelle revue
par l'auteur. Illustrée par Coppin, Lancelot, J.-A. Beaucé, Staal,
etc. Publiée par Dufour et Mulat. "Suisse". (Engraving) Paris,
chez Marescq et Cie., libraires, 1853, 4to., in 2 parts. Part 1, pp.
162 in double columns, with 17 plates; Part 2, pp. 96 in double columns with 14 plates, and followed by "Histoire d'un mort" pp. 1-12,
and "Une âme à naître" pp. 13-16, both in double columns; unnumbered
pages table of contents and 'placement des gravures'. A peculiarity
of the work is that the left hand column of the table of contents
refers to the second part of the volume (i.e. pp. 96), while the right
refers to the first part (i.e. pp. 162). There are numerous small
illustrations throughout the text.

"Impressions de voyage" par Alexandre Dumas Edition nouvelle revue
par l'auteur Illustrée par Coppin, Lancelot, J.-A. Beaucé, Staal,
etc. Publiée par Dufour et Mulat in 3 parts, the first 2 dated 1853
and the third dated 1854, 4to., pp. Part 1, 'Exposition' 1-2, (3)-162;
Part 2, 154; Part 3, 153, all in double columns, and each with an
additional unnumbered page table of contents and 'placement des gravures'; frontispieces, and vignettes on title-pages.

42

Le Siecle. Oeuvres complètes d'Alexandre Dumas. Huitième série.
"Impressions de voyage "Suisse... ... ". Paris, au bureau du Siècle
... 1855. 4to., pp. 210 and 'Notes' (211)-212, all in double columns;
table of contents at foot of page 212.

"Le touriste nouveau guide de l'étranger a Genève et dans des en-
virons suivi de 'Tour de lac' D'après Murray, Joanne, Baedecker,
Ebel, etc." avec un Notice historique et descriptive d'Alexandre
Dumas accompagné de deux cartes et d'une vue de Genève. prix : 1
franc. Genève chez Bécherat, libraire-éditeur place du lac, 171.
Paper covers repeating title-page but with, at foot, Genève chez
Mlle. Bécherat, ... 1856. 8vo., pp. 108, of which "Notice historique
et description de Genève" par Alexandre Dumas, occupies pp. (7)-11.

"Impressions de voyage" par Alexandre Dumas Edition nouvelle revue
par l'auteur. Illustrée par Coppin, Lancelot, J.-A. Beaucé, Staal,
etc. Publiée par Dufour et Mulat. "Suisse". (Woodcut) Paris,
L'écrivain et Toubon, 1860, 4to., same pagination as the Dufour et
Mulat edition, 1853-1854.

"Impressions de voyage. Suisse" par Alexandre Dumas. Paris, Imprimerie de J. Voisvenel, n.d. (c 1861), 4to., pp. 212. Caption title
with illustration at head of title. Running title : oeuvres complètes d'Alexandre Dumas. VIII.

"Guillaume Mona". In "Le chien de Brisquet" and other stories, edited
for school use by L.C. Syms. New York, American Book company, n.d.
(c 1896), 8vo. "Guillaume Mona" occupies pp. 15-24, and is a modified
version of "Le bifteck d'ours".

Alexandre Dumas. "Impressions de voyage". Edition nouvelle revue par
l'auteur; illustrée par Coppin, Lancelot, J.-A. Beaucé, Staal, etc.;
publiée par Dufour et Mulat. "Suisse". Paris, Calmann-Lévy, 1896,
4to., 3 parts, pp. 162, 154 and 153 in double columns, with table of
contents, bound in 1 volume.

"ZAWISKA-LE-NOIR"   1834

     This poem, which consists of thirteen verses each of 6 lines, is
a French version by Dumas of a song of 1420 that had been developed
from a Polish legend. It carries the epigraph : 'A moi, Auvergne,
voilà les ennemis! - Le chevalier d'Assas.'

Original edition.
In "La vieille Pologne" ... ", par M. Niemcewicz. Paris, 1834, 4to.

In "La vieille Pologne". Album historique et poétique composé de
chants et légendes, imités du Polonais, ou composés par le plus
célèbres poëtes français par Ch. Forster. Paris, Londres, Dresden,
1836, 4to. 36 lithographiques romantiques hors-texte par Léon Noël
d'après Vlad; Oleszcynski, Charlet, Norblin, J. David, Sarnecki,
Deveria, Princess Sulkowska, Rigo, Forster, Lafosse.

Ibid   Paris, Bossange, Didot, 1836, 4to. Dumas' poem
was accompanied by a steel engraving by Sarrien, lithographed by
Villain.

There was a third edition of the book - Paris et Leipsic, Brockhaus
et Avenarius, 18 , 4to.

"LA VENITIENNE"   1834

Dumas had a considerable share in the writing of this play which
was announced, and published, as by Anicet Bourgeois. Bourgeois admitted this collaboration in the dedication to Dumas in the original
edition.

Original edition .
"La Vénitienne" Drame en cinq actes et huit tableaux par Anicet
Bourgeois Représenté pour la première fois, à Paris, sur le Théatre
de la Porte-Saint-Martin, le 7 mars 1834. Paris, J.-N. Barba, 1834,
8vo., pp. 229, with an engraved frontispiece and dedication.

"La Vénitienne", drame en cinq actes, par MM. Anicet-Bourgeois et
Alexandre Dumas. A Bruxelles, Aug. Jouhaud, 1834, 32mo., pp. (3)-94;
a woodcut of M. Bocage in the rôle of 'Le Bravo' faces the title-
page.

"La Vénitienne", drame en cinq actes et en huit tableaux, Par M.
Anicet Bourgeois; représenté pour la première fois sur le théatre de
la Porte-Saint-Martin, le 18 (sic) mars 1834. Deuxième édition,
(Vignette) A Paris, chez Marchant, éditeur, Boulevart (sic) St.
Martin, 12. 1834. 8vo., pp. title-page with 'Personnages' 'Acteurs'
on verso, (3)-32 in double columns. Le magasin théatral. Impr. de
J.-R. Mevrel, passage du Caire, 54.

"La Vénitienne", drame en cinq actes et en huit tableaux, Par M.
Anicet Bourgeois; représenté pour la première fois, sur le théatre
de la Porte-Saint-Martin, le 7 mars 1834. Paris, Barbré, s.d. (1834),
folio, pp. 16 in double columns. Caption title with woodcut at head
of title.

Ibid   Paris, Librairie théâtrale, s.d. (185), same
format and pagination as the preceding. Caption title with woodcut
at the head of title. Magasin théatral illustré.

"La Vénitienne", drame en cinq actes et huit tableaux Par M. Anicet
Bourgeois. Lyon, imprimerie de J.-M. Boursy, s.d., 8vo., pp. 8.
Analyse de pièce.

"CATHERINE HOWARD"   1834

This play was written solely by Dumas. He refers to it in his
"Mémoires" as "Edith aux longs cheveux", and it seems that he must
have been working on it somewhere between the end of 1829 and the
early months of 1830 at about the time that Harel was pressing him
to write the play with a Napoleonic theme. The writing of the play,
then to be simply entitled "Edith", was dropped and could only have
been resumed some considerable number of months later. Again in his
"Mémoires" Dumas tells how the play was ultimately submitted to the
Théâtre Français and rejected. Mademoiselle Mars then comes into
the picture by pointing out to Dumas the play's incompleteness as it
stood. Dumas rewrote it under the title as we now know it.

Original edition.
"Catherine Howard", drame en cinq actes et en huit tableaux, par
Alexandre Dumas. Représenté pour la première fois à la Porte-Saint-
Martin, le 2 avril 1834. Paris, Charpentier, 1834, 8vo., pp. iv, 208;

44

water-colour frontispiece by Célestin Nanteuil. Yellow wrappers.
(Another frontispiece drawn by the same artist was suppressed and
never published.)
The first performance was on the 2nd April according to Asselineau,
and on 2nd June according to Talvart at Place.

"Catherine Howard", drame en cinq actes et en huit tableaux, par
Alexandre Dumas. (Vignette) Bruxelles, J.P. Meline, 1834, 16mo.,
pp. (v)-ix, 194. Blue wrappers.

"Catherine Howard", drame en cinq actes et en huit tableaux; par
Alexandre Dumas. A Bruxelles, J.-A. Lelong, 1834, 24mo., pp. 149.
Buff wrappers - Nouveau répertoire dramatique de la scène francaise.
IIe année - IVe série - 1re liv. "Catherine Howard".

Théatre de Alex. Dumas. Tome III. (Vignette) Bruxelles. E. Laurent,
1834, 32mo., pp. half-title "Catherine Howard"., title, pp. (5)-11
Introduction signed : Alexandre Dumas 15 juin 1834, 2 unnumbered
pages 'personnages', (17)-178. Buff wrappers - Théatre de Alex.
Dumas. "Catherine Howard". (Vignette) Bruxelles, E. Laurent, 1838
(sic).

"Catherine Howard", drame en cinq actes et en huit tableaux, par M.
Alexandre Dumas, représenté pour la première fois, à Paris, sur le
théatre de la Porte Saint-Martin, le 2 juin 1834. Paris, n.d. (1834),
8vo., pp. 42 in double columns. Caption title. Imprimerie normale
de Jules Didot l'ainé.

Théâtre francais ou Choix de pièces de Théâtre nouvelles. Série III.
Livraison 6. "Catherine Howard", Drame en cinq actes et en huit
tableaux. Par Alexandre Dumas. Publié par J. Louis. Dessau, Imprimerie de la cour, 1834, 24mo., pp. 182.

"Catherine Howard", drame en cinq actes et en huit tableaux, Par M.
Alexandre Dumas, ... Paris, Marchant, 1835, 8vo., pp. 42 in double
columns. Le Magasin théatral.

Ibid   Paris, Marchant; Bruxelles, Aug. Jouhaud, 1835,
same format and pagination as the preceding. Caption title. Supplement au Magasin Théatral, choix de pièces jouées sur le théatres de
Paris.

"Catherine Howard", drame en cinq actes et en huit tableaux, par M.
Alexandre Dumas, représenté pour la première fois, à Paris, sur le
théatre de la Porte-Saint-Martin, le 2 juin 1834. (Paris). Imprimerie
de Dondey-Dupré, n.d. (1836), 8vo., pp. 42 in double columns. Caption
title.

Ibid   Paris, J.N. Barba, 1836, same format and pagination as the preceding. Caption title. Paper covers - La France
dramatique au dix-neuvième siècle ... . Le Magasin théatral.

Oeuvres de Alex. Dumas. Tome second. (Vignette) Bruxelles, Meline,
Cans et compagnie, 1838, large 8vo. "Catherine Howard", pp. (497)-498
'Avertissement' signed : Alexandre Dumas 15 juin 1834, half-title,
'Personnages' on verso, (501)-549 in double columns.

Théâtre francais moderne ou Choix de pièces de Théâtre nouvelles.
Série III. Livraison 6. "Catherine Howard", Drame en cinq actes et
en huit tableaux. Par Alexandre Dumas. Publié par J. Louis. Dessau,
Imprimerie de la cour, 1839, same format and pagination as the Dessau,

1834, edition. Blue wrappers.

Répertoire du Théâtre francais à Berlin. No. 231. "Catherine Howard",
drame en cinq actes et en huit tableaux, par Alexandre Dumas. Berlin,
Chez Ad. Mt. Schlesinger, Libraire et Editeur de Musique, 1841, 8vo.,
pp. (3)-78; 'Personnages' on verso of title-page. Imprimé chez L.W.
Krause.

"Catherine Howard" drame en cinq actes, en huit tableaux Porte-Saint-
Martin. - 2 juin 1834. 'Avertissement' pp. (205)-207, signed :
Alex. Dumas 15 juin 1834; 'Distribution' on verso, pp. 208-312.
Théatre complet de Alex. Dumas Tome IV Paris Calmann Lévy, éditeur
ancienne maison Michel Lévy frères, 1874. 12mo. "Théatre complet"
in 25 volumes.

"Catherine Howard", drame en cinq actes et en huit tableaux, par M.
Alexandre Dumas, représenté pour la première fois, à Paris, sur le
théâtre de la Porte-Saint-Martin, le 2 juin 1834. Paris, Calmann-
Lévy, 1892, 8vo., pp. 60 double columns. Yellow wrappers.

Footnote - Reference should be made to "Catherine Howard", drame en
cinq actes et en huit tableaux, par M. Alexandre Dumas, and "Catherin-
Howard", 'd'après Voltaire et d'autres historiens', Paris, Impr. de
Sétier, 1834, 12mo., pp. 12, held in the Bibliothèque Nationale,
Paris.

"LA TOUR DE BABEL"   1834

     This one act review was, seemingly, the work of no less than
thirty-six collaborators of whom Dumas was one. The censorship
intervened before its first performance and cut it about severely;
even so it was stopped by the censorship after its tenth performance.

Original (and only) edition.
"La tour de Babel", revue épisodique en un acte, Par MM. *********
********** représentée pour la première fois à Paris, sur le théatre
des Variétés, le 24 juin 1834. Prix : 3 sous. (Vignette) Paris,
au magasin théatral, Marchant, Boulevart (sic) Saint Martin, N° 12.
1834. 8vo., pp. 'Personnages' 'Acteurs' on verso of title, (3)-16 in
double columns. Imp. de J.-R. Mevrel, passage du Caire, 54.

"LA MEDITERRANEE ET SES COTES"   1834

     Dumas, in 1834, thought of touring the Mediterranean with the
artist Jadin, and he drew up and signed a prospectus to attract subscribers for the travel book that would be the result; Jadin was to
contribute twenty-five illustrations. An itinerary was made for him
by MM. Amédée Jaubert, Alex. Delaborde and Alphonse de Lamartine.
(This may be read in the 'Revue Biblio-Iconographique', III Série,
1902, pp. 183-185). In 1858 Dumas issued another prospectus for a
similar projected tour, and this in turn may be read in the issue of
his journal "Le Monte Cristo" for the 22nd April, 1858. In so far as
the 1834 prospectus was concerned it was published as follows -

Original (and only) edition.
"La Méditerranée et ses côtes", signed on page 3 : Alex. Dumas, 10

octobre 1834. (Paris) Imprimerie de Dondey-Dupré, n.d. (1834), 8vo., pp. 4.

"ISABEL DE BAVIERE"   1835

   This work is more a chronicle than a romance, and it should be pointed out that of its twenty-eight chapters eleven appeared as : "Chroniques de France : Scènes historiques" in the 'Revue des deux mondes' in 1831-1832; these eleven chapters are numbered in the full work - XVI-XXIII and XXV-XXVII, both inclusive. Dumas' main sources were Monstrelet, Froissart, and Prosper Brugière de Barante's "Histoire des ducs de Bourgogne". Later Dumas was to draw on "Isabel de Bavière" for his play "La tour Saint-Jacques-la-Boucherie"; while in 1832, as I have mentioned, Anicet Bourgeois and Lockroy had based their drama "Perrinet Leclerc, ou Paris en 1418" on the 'Revue des deux mondes' material.

   With regard to the 'Revue des deux mondes' articles the first, dated 15th December, 1831, quickly sold out and a reprinting was made to which Dumas wrote a three page preface, without any separate title; the pagination of the printings was 609-646 and 659-690 respectively. For the proper bibliographical history of the entire work it is necessary to set out the articles as they appeared in the 'Revue des deux mondes' - the confusion in the numbering of the series is probably due to the fact that after the first five sections had appeared Dumas had gone to Switzerland. Presumably on his return after an absence of three months he saw No. III, forgot that Nos. IV and V had appeared in the same issue of the journal, and numbered the first of his new series IV. Here, then, are the articles :

15 décembre, 1831.   I. "Le chevalier de Bourdon, 1417."
                       II. "Laissez passer la justice du roi."
15 janvier, 1832.   III. "Perrinet le Clerc."
                       IV. Epigraph "C'est infernal, dit
                            Charlotte."
                        V. Epigraph "Tous criaient 'Notre Dame
                            de la Paix! Vive le roi! Vive
                            Bourgoyne! Que ceux qui veulent la
                            paix s'arment et nous suivent!"
1 novembre, 1832.   IV. "La terrace de Bastille."
1 décembre, 1832.   V. "Maître Capeluch."
                       VI. "Le Sire de Giac." (This is the
                            first part of the short historical
                            story published under the title of
                            "La main droite du Sire de Giac -
                            1425-1426", q.v.).
15 décembre, 1832.   VI. "La traite." (This is the second
                            part of "Le main droite du Sire de
                            Giac - 1425-1426, and being regarded
                            as a continuation of the preceeding
                            issue has been given the same num-
                            ber by the publishers.)
                     VIII. "Le pont de Montereau."
                       IX. "La course."

Original edition.
"Chroniques de France. Isabel de Bavière (Règne de Charles VI). Par
Alexandre Dumas. Paris, librairie de Dumont, 1835, 8vo., 2 vols., pp.
(i)-iv 'Preface', (7)-406 and (1)-419. There are no tables of con-
tents; illustrated at head of Chapter 1, volume 1, with a vignette by
Paul Huet, and repeated on the beige wrappers. Impr. de Bourgogne et
Martinet.

"Isabel de Bavière, Règne de Charles VI". Par Alexandre Dumas.
(Vignette) Bruxelles, Ad. Wahlen, Impr.-Libr. de la cour, 1835, 18mo.,
2 vols., pp. 270 and 276. There are no tables of contents. Brown
wrappers repeating title-pages. Nouvelle bibliothèque economique.

"Chroniques de France. Isabel de Bavière. (Règne de Charles VI)".
Par Alexandre Dumas. Bruxelles, J.P. Meline, 1835, 16mo., 2 vols.,
pp. (v) - with vignette at head - viii, (9)-319 and (5)-319. There
are no tables of contents.

"Chroniques de France. Isabel de Bavière. (règne de Charles VI)"
par Alexandre Dumas. Bruxelles et Leipzig, Allgemeine Niederlandische
Buchhandlung, 1835, same format and pagination as the preceding edition.

"Chroniques de France. Isabel de Bavière (Règne de Charles VI)". Par
Alexandre Dumas. Paris, Librairie de Dumont, 1836. Deuxième édition.
8vo., 2 vols., pp. 338 and 345, each with a differing vignette at the
head of the first chapter of each volume. Impr. A. La Boyer et Cie.,
Lagny.

Ibid   Bruxelles, Meline, Cans et compagnie, 1838, 18mo.,
2 vols., pp. (v)-viii, (9)-300 and (5)-305.

Oeuvres de Alex. Dumas. Tome premier. (Vignette) Bruxelles, Meline,
Cans et compagnie, 1838, large 8vo. "Isabel de Bavière". Pp. (3)-4,
(5)-161 in double columns.

"Isabel de Bavière" par Alexandre Dumas. Nouvelle Edition revue et
corrigée. Paris, Pascal jeune, libraire-éditeur, ... 1846, 8vo.,
3 vols., pp. 343, 340 and 376. There are no tables of contents.
Imprimerie de E. Dépée, à Sceaux (Seine).

"Isabel de Bavière" par Alexandre Dumas Paris Michel Lévy frères,
libraires-éditeurs des Oeuvres complétes d'Alexandre Dumas, de la
bibliothèque dramatique et du théatre de Victor Hugo, ... 1848, 12mo.,
2 vols., pp. 286 and 2 pages of publishers' advertisements, and 303.
There are no tables of contents. "Isabel de Bavière" ends on page 213
of vol. 2, verso blank, and is followed by "Praxède" pp. (215)-257,
verso blank, and "Pierre-le-cruel" pp. (259)-303. Green wrappers.
Paris - Imp. Lacrampe fils et Comp.

Le Siècle. "Isabel de Bavière" par Alexandre Dumas. Paris, au
bureau du Siècle, 16, rue de Croissand, ancien hotel Colbert, 1850,
4to., pp. (147)-248 in double columns.

Ibid   Paris, Impr. de Walder, n.d. (1861), same format
and pagination as the preceding. Romans illustrés.

"SOUVENIRS D'ANTONY"   1835
    This work comprises a collection of his short stories, the com-

bined title being chosen purely and simply because of the advertising value from the "Antony" of his famous play of that name.

Original edition.
"Souvenirs d'Antony", par Alexandre Dumas. Paris, Librairie de Dumont, 1835, 8vo., pp. 360. The contents are : "Cherubino et Celestini", pp. 3-42; "Antonio", pp. 43-76; "Maria, suite d'Antonio", pp. 79-117; "Le cocher de Cabriolet", pp. 121-170; "Blanche de Beaulieu", pp. 173-263; "Un bal masqué", pp. 267-284; "Jacques 1er et Jacques II", pp. 287-360, with an additional unnumbered page table of contents. Yellow paper wrappers.

Reprinted, 1836, same publisher, format and pagination.

"Souvenirs d'Antony". Par Alexandre Dumas. (Vignette) Bruxelles, J.P. Meline, 1835, 18mo., pp. 305, verso unnumbered page table of contents. Contents : "Cherubino et Celestini", pp. (5)-96; "Le cocher de cabriolet", pp. (97)-137; "Blanche de Beaulieu", pp. (139)-220; "Un bal masqué", pp. (221)-238; "Jacques I et Jacques II", pp. (239)-305.

"Souvenirs d'Antony", par Alexandre Dumas. Bruxelles, Ad. Wahlen, 1835, 18mo., pp. 281 and unnumbered page table of contents. Contents : "Cherubino et Celestini", pp. 5-36; "Antonio", pp. 37-61; "Maria. Suite d'Antonio", pp. 63-92; "Le cocher de cabriolet", pp. 93-131; "Blanche de Beaulieu", pp. 133-205; "Un bal masqué", pp. 207-222; "Jacques 1er et Jacques II", pp. 223-281.

"Souvenirs d'Antony". Par Alexandre Dumas. (Vignette) Bruxelles et Leipzig, Allgemeine Niederlandische, 1835, 18mo., pp. 305, and unnumbered page table of contents; same contents and pagination as the J.P. Meline, 1835, edition. Green wrappers.

"Souvenirs d'Antony". Par Alexandre Dumas. (Vignette) Bruxelles, Meline, Cans et compagnie, 1838, 16mo., pp. 267 and unnumbered page table of contents. Contents : "Cherubino et Celestini", pp. (7)-33; "Antonio", pp. (34)-56; "Maria suite d'Antonio", pp. (59)-84; "Le cocher de cabriolet", pp. (87)-120; "Blanche de Beaulieu", pp. (123)-192; "Un bal masqué", pp. (195)-208; "Jacques I et Jacques II", pp. (211)-267. Green wrappers.

Oeuvres de Alex. Dumas. Tome premier. (Vignette) Bruxelles, Meline, Cans et compagnie, 1838, large 8vo. "Souvenirs d'Antony". Pp. (487)-553 in double columns. Contents : "Cherubino et Celestini", pp. (487)-494; "Antonio", pp. 494-500; "Maria, suite d'Antonio", pp. 500-507; "Le cocher de cabriolet", pp. 507-516; "Blanche de Beaulieu", pp. 517-535; "Un bal masqué", pp. 535-538; "Jacques I et Jacques II", pp. 539-553.

Oeuvres de Alex. Dumas. Tome deuxième. (Vignette) Bruxelles, Société belge de librairie Hauman et Ce. 1843. Large 8vo. "Souvenirs d' Antony". Pp. (203)-260 in double columns. Contents : "Cherubino et Celestini", pp. (203)-211; "Antonio", pp. 211-218; "Maria". (suite d'Antonio), pp. 218-226; "Le cocher de cabriolet", pp. 226-236; "Blanche de Beaulieu", pp. 236-255; "Un bal masqué", pp. 256-260.

Here it is necessary to interpose that later printings of this work omitted one or two of the stories referred to above, and added others. Detailed pagination, with the rare exception, is not being given as it is not really vital to the bibliography.

"Souvenirs d'Antony", par Alexandre Dumas. Paris, Michel Lévy frères, 1848, 12mo., pp. 315 and unnumbered page table of contents. Contents : "Cherubino et Celestini. Le cocher de cabriolet. Blanche de Beaulieu. Un bal masqué. Jacques I et Jacques II. Bernard. Don Martin de Freytas".

Ibid   Nouvelle édition. Paris, Michel Lévy frères, 1862, 12mo., pp. 323 and unnumbered page table of contents. Oeuvres complètes d'Alexandre Dumas. Reprinted, 1868.

Ibid   Nouvelle édition. Paris, Michel Lévy frères, 1874, 12mo., pp. 319 and unnumbered page table of contents. Contents : "Cherubino et Celestini. Le cocher de cabriolet. Blanche de Beaulieu. Un bal masqué. Bernard. Don Martin de Freytas. Le curé de Chambard". Frequently reprinted by Calmann-Lévy, same format, pagination and contents.

Alexandre Dumas Oeuvres illustrées Edition illustrée par J.-A. Beaucé, Staal, et Rieux. Paris, Calmann-Lévy, 1890, 4to., (but on title-page 'dessins par J.-A. Beaucé, G. Staal, Andrieux, Coppin, etc.), buff wrappers with woodcut. Contents : "Blanche de Beaulieu. Un bal masqué. Le cocher de cabriolet. Bernard. Cherubino et Celestini. La main droite du sire de Giac. Histoire d'un mort. Une ame a naître. Don Martinn de Freytas", comprising pp. (1)-146 in double columns.

Another edition of the 'Oeuvres illustrées d'Alexandre Dumas' was published : Paris, Calmann-Lévy, 1891-1897, 4to., in separate volumes and printed in double columns, 'dessins par J.-A. Beaucé, Staal, C. Nanteuil, Ed. Coppin'. These were : "Un bal masqué", pp. 6; "Bernard, histoire pour les chasseurs", pp. 16; "Blanche de Beaulieu", pp. 24; "Le cocher de cabriolet", pp. 16; "Cherubino et Celestini", pp. 28; "Don Martinn de Freytas", pp. 24; "Jacques I et Jacques II", pp. 24.

Separate publications of individual titles :
"Antonio" and "Maria, suite d'Antonio" were published in 'Le journal des enfants', 183 .

"Un bal masqué", drame. Signed : Alex. Dumas, pp. (165)-182, in 'Album de la mode. Chronique du monde fashionable ou chois de Morceaux de Littérature contemporaines'. ... . Paris, Louis Janet, libraire, 1833, 8vo., pp. (v)-vi, Préface de l'Editeur, table des matières (unnumbered), (1)-376; there are no illustrations. "Un bal masqué" occupies pp. (165)-182. Imprimerie et fonderie de Rigoux et Cie, rue des Francs-Bourgeois-S.-Michel, No° 8.

"Un bal masqué" was included in 'Le journal des enfants', (183) as well as in 'Scènes du beau monde' and in volume 2 of 'Le conteur', the last two mentioned being published in 1833.

"Un bal masqué" par Alexandre Dumas, pp. 1-27, in 'Veillées d'hiver (le conteur)', par MM. Alexendre Dumas, Charles Nodier, ... , Paris, Charpentier, 1834, 8vo.; there are no illustrations and Dumas' contribution was in Volume 2.

"Un bal masqué"; "Un cocher de cabriolet", par Alexandre Dumas. Paris, Marescq, 1852, large 8vo., pp. 16, illustrated.

Ibid   Paris, Imp. de Gaittet, n.d. (1861), same format and pagination, illustrated.

Ibid   Paris, S. Raçon et Cie., n.d. (1861) same format
and pagination, illustrated.

"Un bal masqué" par Alexandre Dumas Dessins par Andrieux Paris Calmann Lévy, Editeur ancienne maison Michel Lévy frères, 1887, 4to.,
pp. 6 in double columns. Alexandre Dumas oeuvres illustrées.

"Bernard, histoire pour les chasseurs", par Alexandre Dumas. Bruxelles, Société typographique belge, Ad. Wahlen et compagnie, 1843,
16mo., pp. (113)-147, and unnumbered page table of contents.

"Un mari" par Madam la comtesse Dash. "Bernard histoire pour les
chasseurs" par Alexandre Dumas. Bruxelles, Société belge de librairie Hauman et Ce., 1843, 12mo., pp. 8 (unnumbered), 165. "Bernard
... ... " occupies pp. 123-165. Bibliothèque des châteaux et des
campagnes. 9e série.

"Un mari" par madame la comtesse Dash. "Bernard Histoire pour les
chasseurs", Par A. Dumas. A Bruxelles, Imprimerie du politique,
1843, 18mo., pp. (1)-165. "Bernard ... ...", Par Alexandre Dumas.
Pp. (123)-165.

"Bernard. Histoire pour les chasseurs". Signed : Alex. Dumas. In
'Le courier des lectures ou choix de feuilletons, nouvelles, contes,
anecdotes, épisodes, faites curieux, bons mots, etc.' Directeurs :
Fellens frères (Vignette) Paris. 1843. Large 8vo., pp. 274-285 in
double columns.

"Bernard, histoire pour les chasseurs" par Alexandre Dumas. In 'Echo
des feuilletons Choix de nouvelles, épisodes, anecdotes, extraits
de la Presse contemporaine'. Paris, 1844, large 8vo., pp. (279)-288
in double columns.

"Bernard. Histoire pour les chasseurs". Signed : Alexandre Dumas.
In 'Revue pittoresque musée littéraire' illustré par les premiers
artistes. Deuxième Série. Tome II. Paris, 37, Rue Neuve-Saint-
Augustin, 1844, 4to. Pp. (325)-335 in double columns; engraving on
first page, illustrated.

"Bernard" appeared serially in 'La Presse' in 1844.

"Cécile" par Alexandre Dumas. Paris, Dumont, éditeur ... 1844, 8vo.,
2 vols.; the pagination of volume 2 is (5)-324, "Cécile" ending on
page 254 and followed by "Bernard. Histoire pour les chasseurs", pp.
(255)-324; there is no table of contents. Yellow wrappers.

Le Siècle. Oeuvres complètes d'Alexandre Dumas. Troisième série.
"Bernard Histoire pour les chasseurs". Paris, au bureau du Siècle,
1848, 4to., pp. (373)-379 in double columns.

"Nouvelles", par Alexandre Dumas. Paris, au bureau du Siècle, 1850,
4to., pp. 343-390. "Bernard ... ..." was one of the stories included.

"Bernard, histoire pour les chasseurs", par Alexandre Dumas. Première
édition séparée (France). Paris, Marescq, 1852, large 8vo., pp. 16 in
double columns; illustrated.

Ibid   Paris, Impr. de Gaittet, n.d. (1861), same format
and pagination; illustrated.

Ibid   Paris, S. Raçon et Cie., n.d. (1861), same format

and pagination; illustrated.

"Bernard histoire pour les chasseurs" par Alexandre Dumas Dessins par Ed. Coppin, etc. Paris, Calmann Lévy, Editeur ancienne maison Michel Lévy frères, 1887, 4to., pp. (1)-16 in double columns. Alexandre Dumas oeuvres illustrées.

"La dame de Monsoreau" par Alexandre Dumas. Paris, Pétion, libraire-éditeur, 1846, 8vo., 8 vols.; volume 8 consists of pp. 299, verso blank, and unnumbered page table of contents. "La dame de Monsoreau" ends on page 93, verso blank, and is followed by "Le cocher de cabriolet" pp. (95)-155, verso blank, and "Blanche de Beaulieu" pp. (157)-299. Green wrappers. Corbeil - imprimerie de Crété.

"Blanche de Beaulieu" par Alexandre Dumas. Paris, Schneider, n.d. (c 1850), large 8vo., pp. 24 in double columns, 4 plates. Reprinted, same publishers, format and pagination, n.d. (c 1861).

"Blanche de Beaulieu" par Alexandre Dumas. Publié par Dufour et Mulat. Edition illustrée par J.-A. Beaucé et G. Staal. Paris, Marescq et Cie., 1852, 4to., pp. 24 in double columns.

"Ingénue", ("Blanche de Beaulieu"). Par Alex. Dumas. Edition autorisée pour la Belgique et l'étranger, interdite pour la France. Bruxelles, A. Lebègue, 1854-1855, 32mo., 5 vols.; "Ingénue" ends on page 112 of volume 5 (1855), which is completed by "Blanche de Beaulieu", pp. 113-189, and curiously all the pages are headed "Ingénue".

Ibid Bruxelles et Leipzig, Kiessling, Schnée et Cie.; Bâle, J. G. Neukirch, 1854-1855, 32mo., 5 vols. This edition conforms in every way with that published by Lebègue.

"Blanche de Beaulieu" par Alexandre Dumas Dessins par J.-A. Beaucé, G. Staal, Andrieux, Coppin, etc. (Vignette) Paris Calmann Lévy, Editeur ancienne maison Michel Lévy frères, 1887, 4to., pp. 24 in double columns. Alexandre Dumas oeuvres illustrées.

Alexandre Dumas illustré. Par Andrieux. "Cherubino et Celestini". (Engraving) Paris, 1852, chez Marescq et Cie., libraires, 4to., pp. 28 in double columns. Reprinted, 1853, same publishers, format and pagination.

"Cherubino et Celestini", par Alexandre Dumas. Paris, Imp. de Gaittet, n.d. (1861), 4to., pp. 28 in double columns; illustrated.

Ibid Paris, S. Raçon et Cie., n.d. (1861), same format and pagination; illustrated.

"Cherubino et Celestini" par Alexandre Dumas Dessins par Andrieux. Paris Calmann Lévy, Editeurs ancienne maison Michel Lévy frères, 1887, 4to., pp. (1)-28 in double columns. Alexandre Dumas oeuvres illustrées.

"Le cocher de cabriolet" in : 'Paris, ou le livre des cent-et-un'. Tome second. (Vignette) A Paris, chez Ladvocat, librairie de S.A.R. le duc d'Orléans. M DCCC XXXI. 8vo., pp. (1)-422, and unnumbered page table of contents. "Le cocher de cabriolet", signed : Alex. Dumas, pp. (251)-288. Typographie de Firmin Didot frères.

"Le cocher de cabriolet" in : 'Paris, ou le livre des cent-et-un'. Tome second. Stuttgart, chez Charles Hoffmann, libraire. 1831. 12mo., pp. (250)-280, signed : Alex. Dumas. "Nouveautés de la littérature française", 1831-1833, 10 volumes.

"La dame de Monsoreau" par Alexandre Dumas. Paris, Pétion, libraire-éditeur, 1846, 8vo., 8 vols.; volume 8 consists of pp. 299, verso blank, and unnumbered page table of contents. "La dame de Monsoreau" ends on page 93, verso blank, and is followed by "Le cocher de cabriolet" pp. (95)-155, verso blank, and "Blanche de Beaulieu" pp. (157)-299. Green wrappers. Corbeil - imprimerie de Crété.

"Un bal masqué"; "Un cocher de cabriolet", par Alexandre Dumas. Paris Marescq, 1852, large 8vo., pp. 16, illustrated.

Ibid   Paris, Imp. de Gaittet, n.d. (1861), same format
and pagination, illustrated.

Ibid   Paris, S. Raçon et Cie., n.d. (1861), same format
and pagination, illustrated.

"Le cocher de cabriolet" (par Alexandre Dumas) Dessins par Andrieux Paris Calmann Levy, Editeur ancienne maison Michel Lévy frères, 1887, 4to., pp. (7)-16 in double columns. Alexandre Dumas oeuvres illustrées

"Le curé de Chambard". Par M. Alexandre Dumas. In : 'La bibliothèque des feuilletons receuil de romans, nouvelles et feuilletons'., janvier 1844, 8vo., pp. 75-93.

"Le château d'Eppstein", par Alexandre Dumas. Paris, L. de Potter, 1844, 8vo., 3 volumes. Volume 3 is completed, among other short works by Dumas, by "Le curé de Chambard", pp. 113-232.

"Le curé Chambard", par M. Alexandre Dumas. Paris, Boulé Editeur, rue Coq-Héron, 5. 1849, 8vo., pp. 75-93.

"Le curé de Chambard". Par M. Alexandre Dumas. In : 'L'Echo des feuilletons receuil de nouvelles, légendes, anecdotes, épisodes, ...'. Paris, chez les éditeurs, 1856, large 8vo., pp. 560-574 in double columns.

"Jacques 1er et Jacques II" in : 'Le journal des enfants'. Deuxième année. Undated (c 183), 8vo., signed : A. Dumas, pp. 361-365 in double columns.

"Pauline de Meulien" "Aventures de Lyderic" "Jacques 1er et Jacques II" par Alexandre Dumas. Publiés par Dufour et Mulat. Dessins par J.-A. Beaucé, Staal, C. Nanteuil, Ed. Coppin. (Woodcut) Paris, chez Marescq et Cie. 1852. 3 parties en 1 volume, 4to., pp. 80, 48 and 24 respectively in double columns.
Reprinted, 1855 and 1856.

Oeuvres diverses. "Jacques 1er et Jacques II. Fragments historiques" par Alexandre Dumas. Illustrations par Cel. Nanteuil. Paris, Imp. Simon Raçon et Cie., n.d. (1854), 4to., pp. 2-24 in double columns; 2 plates and 11 other illustrations.

"Jacques 1er et Jacques II, fragments historiques" par Alexandre Dumas. Paris, Impr. de Gaittet, n.d. (1861), 4to., pp. 24 in double columns; illustrated.

Ibid   Paris, S. Raçon et Cie., n.d. (1861), same format
and pagination as the preceding, 2 illustrations.

"Jacques 1er et Jacques II fragments historiques" par Alexandre Dumas Dessins par Nanteuil. Paris Calmann Lévy, Editeur ancienne maison Michel Lévy frères, 1885, 4to., pp. (1)-24 in double columns. Alexandre Dumas oeuvres illustrées.

53

"Pauline de Meulien" "Aventures de Lyderic" "Jacques 1er et Jacques
II (fragments historiques)" par Alexandre Dumas Dessins par J.-A.
Beaucé, Staal, C. Nanteuil, Ed. Coppin. (Woodcut) Paris, Calmann-
Lévy, n.d. (1890), 4to.; "Jacques 1er ... ... ", pp. (1)-24 in double
columns. Buff wrappers : Alexandre Dumas Oeuvres illustrées.

"LE CHATEAU DE LA ROCHE-POT"   1835
    This is a very brief anecdote concerning a trickster's sharp
practice.

Original edition.
"Le château de la Roche-Pot". Signed : Alex. Dumas. In : 'Hommage
aux dames', Paris, Louis Janet, n.d. (1835), 18mo.

Ibid   In : 'Le courrier des lectures ou choix de
feuilletons, nouvelles, contes, anecdotes, épisodes, faites curieux,
bons mots, etc'. Directeurs : Fellens frères (Vignette) Paris.
1843. Large 8vo., pp. 151-152 in double columns.

"CROMWELL ET CHARLES 1er"   1835
    Charles Glinel in his article 'Théâtre inconnu d'Alexandre Dumas'
published in the issue of the 'Revue biblio-iconographique', 1898, 3^e
série, pp. 512-513, stated that he owned the manuscript of this play
written in Dumas' hand and consisting of ninety-two pages. On the
final page is written : 'Fini le 3 mars à 5.h. ½ du soir. Al.
Dumas.' Glinel added that a comparison between the manuscript and
the printed version showed a number of variants.

Original edition.
"Cromwell et Charles 1er.", drame en cinq actes, précédé de "Un
dernier hour de la popularité", prologue en un acte, par M. Corde-
llier Delanoue, représenté pour la première fois, a Paris, sur le
théâtre de la Porte-Saint-Martin, le 21 mai 1835. Caption title
followed by 'personnages' 'acteurs', large 8vo., pp. (1)-35 in
double columns. Yellow wrappers repeating caption title. Paris, Marchant, 1835. Librairie Théatrale. Imprimerie Dondey-Dupré.

Ibid   Paris, Marchant, 1835, same format and pagination
as the preceding. Magasin théatral.

"LA DIVINE COMEDIE"   1836
    This poem consists of 144 lines rhyming in couplets, and is a
translation of the first canto of Dante's "Inferno".

Original edition.
In the 'Revue des deux mondes', 1 mars 1836, where it appeared in
articles by Dumas entitled "Guelfes et Gibelins", the first half bearing that title and the second "Dante et la Divine Comédie".

    The whole was later combined in one to form part of "Les hommes
de fer".

54

"LE CID"   1836
    Six verses each of 8 lines.

Original edition.
In : 'L'Ariel', 5 mars 1836.
In : 'Le chansonnier des graces', Paris, Mme. Louis, libraire, 1838, pp. 249-251.
In : 'L'Illustration', 8 octobre 1847.
And finally, in : 'Le Pays', 23 juin 1864, under the title of "La romance du Cid".

"LE CONSEIL DU MAUVAIS ANGE, ou LA COQUETTE"   1836
    Five verses each of 6 lines.

Original edition.
In Dumas' "Don Juan de Marana", Acte II, tableau ii, scène iv; then in : "Ne m'oubliez pas Keepsake", Paris, Louis Janet, n.d. (1837), 18mo., pp. 107-108, with an additional verse of 6 lines.

"ARRANGEMENT A L'AIMABLE, ou L'ECHANGE"   1836
    Three verses each of 4 lines. As "L'Echange" it was set to music by Henri Reber, Paris, Richault.

Original printing.
In : "Souvenirs poétiques de l'école romantique 1825-1840" ... par M. Edouard Fournier Paris Laplace, Sanchez et Cie, libraires-éditeurs, 1880, 12mo., page 118, with an introductory note by Fournier.

"LE MARQUIS DE BRUNOY"   1836
    This vaudeville, with music written by M. Masset, was announced as being by MM. Théaulon and Jaime (Ernest Rousseau), but Dumas is believed to have contributed to its writing. Lecomte adds the name of Armand Dartois as another contributor.

Original edition.
"Le marquis de Brunoy", pièce en cinq actes, par MM. Théaulon et Jaime; musique nouvelle de M. Masset. Représentée pour la première fois, à Paris, sur le théâtre des Variétés, le 14 mars 1836. Caption title. Yellow paper covers - La France dramatique au dix-neuvième siècle. Variétés. "Le marquis de Brunoy", pièce en cinq actes. (nos.) 177-178. Paris : J.N. Barba ... ; Delloye, ... ; Bezou, ... ; on souscrit également dans les bureaux de la France pittoresque, ... 1836. Large 8vo., pp. 152 in double columns. Imprimerie et fonderie de Jules Didot l'aîne.

"Le marquis de Brunoy", pièce en cinq actes, par MM. Théaulon et Jaime; musique nouvelle de M. Masset. Représentée pour la première fois A Paris, sur le Théâtre des Variétés, le 14 mars 1836. (Vig-

nette) Paris, Marchant, éditeur, Boulevart (sic) Saint-Martin, 12.
1836. 24mo., pp. (3)-79, verso of title-page 'personnages' 'acteurs'.
Buff wrappers - Répertoire général de pièces nouvelles, a 25 centimes,
par abonnement. "Le marquis de Brunoy". prix séparément 50 centimes.
(Vignette, differing from that on title-page) Bruxelles, Auguste
Jouhaud, imprimeur-éditeur Passage de la Comédie. Imprimerie :
Auguste Jouhaud, imprimeur, éditeur. 3 passage de la Comédie Brux-
elles. On the back wrapper the advertisement : publication de mars
- "Jean-Jean Don Juan", parodie. No further trace of this exists.

"DON JUAN DE MARANA, ou LA CHUTE D'UN ANGE"   1836

This play, based on the more well-known legends surrounding Don
Juan, is wholly by Dumas. There are two versions, the first in which
Don Juan dies unrepentant in the last act, and another which is substituted in the Michel Lévy frères edition of the "Théâtre complet"
published subsequent to 1861 where he repents at the very end.

Original edition.
"Don Juan de Marana ou la chute d'un ange", mystère en cinq actes,
par Alexandre Dumas. Musique de M. Piccini; décors de MM. Cicéri,
Nolau, Devoir et Pourchet. Paris, Marchant, éditeur du magasin théatral, 1836, 8vo., pp. half-title, title, 4, 5-303. Yellow paper
wrappers - Représenté pour la première fois à la Porte-Saint-Martin,
le 30 avril 1836.
(The copy held by the Bibliothèque de l'Arsenal has a frontispiece by
Celestin Nanteuil.)

"Don Juan de Marana, ou la chute d'un ange", mystère en cinq actes,
par Alexandre Dumas; musique de M. Piccini, décors de MM. Cicéri,
Nolau, Devoir et Pourchet. (Vignette) Bruxelles, Aug. Jouhaud,
1832, 32mo., pp. 146.

Ibid   Bruxelles, J.-A. Lelong, 1836, 24mo., pp. (5)-160.
Verso of title : 'Personnages' 'Acteurs'.

"Don Juan de Marana, ou la chute d'un ange", mystère en cinq actes,
par Alex. Dumas. (Vignette) Bruxelles. E. Laurent, 1836, 32mo., pp.
half-title "Don Juan de Maranna", verso blank, 2 unnumbered pages
'personnages', (9)-165. Buff wrappers - Théâtre de Alex. Dumas.
"Don Juan de Marana", Bruxelles, E. Laurent, 1836.

"Don Juan de Marana, ou la chute d'un ange", mystère en cinq actes
et sept tableaux, Par M. Alexandre Dumas, musique de M. Piccini,
décors de MM. Cicéri, Nolau, Devoir et Pourchet, représenté pour la
première fois, a Paris, sur le théâtre de la Porte-Saint-Martin, le
30 avril 1836. Paris, Marchant, 1836, 8vo., pp. 36 in double columns.
Caption title. Le Magasin théatral. Imprimerie de Ve Dondey-Dupré.

Répertoire du Théâtre français. No. 161. "Don Juan de Marana, ou le
chute d'un ange", mystère en cinq actes, par Alexandre Dumas. Berlin, Chez Ad. Mt. Schlesinger, Libraire et Editeur de Musique, 1836,
8vo., pp. 36 in double columns. Imprimé chez L.W. Krause.

"Don Juan de Marana ou la chute d'un ange", mystère en cinq actes
et sept tableaux, Par M. Alexandre Dumas, musique de M. Piccini;
décors de MM. Cicéri, Nolau, Devoir et Pourchet; représenté pour la
première fois, a Paris, sur le théâtre de la Porte-Saint-Martin, le

30 avril 1836. (Vignette) Bruxelles, Neirinckx et Laruel, 1836, 24mo., pp. (3)-112. Plum paper wrappers - Bibliothèque dramatique de la scène française, ou collection choisie de nouvelles pièces de théâtre. Deuxième année. IIe série - 24e livraison.

"Don Juan de Marana ou la chute d'un ange", mystère en cinq actes et sept tableaux, par M. Alexandre Dumas, musique de M. Piccini; décors de MM. Cicéri, Nolau, Devoir et Pourchat; représenté pour la première, à Paris, sur le Théâtre de la Porte-Saint-Martin, le 30 avril 1836. (Vignette) Bruxelles, Neirinckx et Laruel, 1836, 24mo., pp. (3)-112. Brown wrappers - "Don Juan de Marana. Mystère en cinq actes et sept tableaux", par M. Alexandre Dumas, musique de M. Piccini. Bruxelles, Société belge de librairie ... Hauman, Cattoir et cie., 1837.
(On the back cover in 'Collection de pièces de théatre' are advertised "Charles VII" and "Kean".)

"Don Juan de Marana, ou la chute d'un ange". Mystère en cinq actes. Par Alexandre Dumas. (Vignette) Bruxelles, Meline, Cans et compagnie, 1838, 16mo., pp. 201. Yellow wrappers.

Oeuvres de Alex. Dumas. Tome second. (Vignette) Bruxelles, Meline, Cans et compagnie, 1838, large 8vo. "Don Juan de Marana", pp. 'Personnages' on verso of title, (553)-604 in double columns.

"Don Juan de Marana". Drame en cinq actes et sept tableaux, par Alexandre Dumas. Bruxelles, Livourne, Meline, Cans et compagnie; Leipzig, J.P. Meline, 1853, 16mo., pp. 173. Yellow wrappers.

"Don Juan de Marana ou la chute d'un ange" mystère en cinq actes, en neuf tableaux Porte-Saint-Martin. - 30 avril 1836. "Distribution" on title-page, pp. (2)-100. Théâtre complet de Alex. Dumas Tome V Paris Calmann Lévy, éditeur ancienne maison Michel Lévy frères, 1874. 12mo. "Théâtre complet" in 25 volumes.

There was one parody of the play :
"Don Juan de Marana, ou la chute d'un ange ... ". Raconté par Robert Macaire et Bertrand; drame en dix tableaux. Paris, Bezou, 1836, 8vo., pp. 36.

"KEAN"   1836
(Sometimes entitled : KEAN, ou DESORDRE ET GENIE".)

In a letter to Charles Glinel Dumas fils has stated that one, Théaulon, had collaborated in the first drafting of this comedy, but such assistance as may have been given cannot have been of great consequence.

Apparently Dumas wrote a new fifth act for the play for subsequent performances at the Odéon, but to my knowledge that comedy as so revised has never been published.

"Kean" was first performed at the Théâtre des Variétés on the 31st August, 1836. It was highly regarded by both French critics and the public; the title-rôle was one of Frédérick Lemaître's great successes.

Original edition.
"Kean", comédie en cinq actes, par Alexandre Dumas. Paris, J.-B.

Barba, libraire, palais royal, galerie de Chartres, 2 et 3, derrière le Théâtre-Français. 1836. 8vo., pp. half-title, title, unnumbered page 'A Mme la Duchesse d'Abrantès, hommage de haute estime et de respecteux amitié. Alex. Dumas', another half-title with 'Personnages' on verso, (3)-263. Yellow wrappers repeating title-page. Imprimerie de Ve Dondey-Dupré.

"Kean, ou désordre et génie", comédie en cinq actes, mêlée des chants, par M. Alexandre Dumas, représentée pour la première fois, à Paris, sur le théatre des Variétés, le 31 aout 1836. (Paris) Imprimerie de Ve Dondey-Dupré, n.d. (1836), 8vo., pp. 38 in double columns. Caption title.

Ibid   Paris, Marchant, 1836, same format and pagination as the preceding. Le Magasin théatral.

"Kean, ou désordre et génie", comédie en cinq actes, mêlée des chants, Par M. Alexandre Dumas; représentée pour la première fois, sur le théatre des Variétés, le 31 aout 1836. (Vignette) Bruxelles, Neirinckx et Laruel, 1836, 24mo., pp. 100. Pink wrappers - "Kean", comédie en cinq actes, mêlée des chants. Par M. Alexandre Dumas. Bruxelles, Société belge de librairie ... Hauman, Cattoir et Ce., 1837.

Théatre de Alex. Dumas. "Kean", par Alexandre Dumas. Bruxelles, E. Laurent, 1836, 32mo., pp. 154. Buff wrappers.

"Kean". Comédie en cinq actes, par Alexandre Dumas. Publié par J. Louis. Dessau, Imprimerie de la Cour. 1836. 18mo., 'Personnages' on verso of title-page, pp. 175.

"Kean, ou désordre et génie", comédie en cinq actes, mêlée de chants, par M. Alexandre Dumas. Représentée pour la première fois, à Paris, au Théatre des Variétés, le 31 août 1836. Anvers, H. Ratinckx, 1836, 16mo., pp. 125.

"Kean, ou désordre et génie". Drame. Par Alexandre Dumas. (Vignette) Bruxelles, Meline, Cans et compagnie, 1838, 16mo., pp. 189. Yellow wrappers.

Oeuvres de Alex. Dumas. Tome second. (Vignette) Bruxelles, Meline, Cans et compagnie, 1838, large 8vo. "Kean, ou désordre et génie", 'Personnages' on verso of title-page, pp. (607)-655 in double columns.

"Kean", comédie en cinq actes par Alexandre Dumas. Berlin, au Bureau du Théâtre français, chez Charles Heyman, n.d., (c 1840), 24mo., pp. 190, ix.

Théatre de Alex. Dumas. "Kean". Bruxelles, Meline, Cans et compagnie, 1842, 32mo., pp. 153. Buff wrappers.

"Kean" drame en cinq actes et en prose par Alexandre Dumas. Bruxelles, Société belge de librairie Hauman et cie., 1842, 24mo., pp. 163. Yellow wrappers.

"Kean", comédie en cinq actes, par Alexandre Dumas. Publié par J. Louis. Nouvelle Edition. Avec des notes explicatives. Leipzig. C.P. Melzer, imprimeur libraire, 1843, 24mo., pp. 180. "Kean" ends on page 174 and the 'notes' occupy pp. 175-180. Théâtre moderne ou Choix de pièces de Théâtre nouvelles. Série IV Livraison 6. Blue wrappers.

Répertoire du Théâtre français à Berlin. No. 316. "Kean", comédie
en 5 actes, par Alexandre Dumas. Berlin, chez Ad. Mt. Schlesinger,
Libraire et Editeur de Musique, 1846, 8vo., pp. 76. Imprimé chez I.W.
Krause.

Théatre Français publié par G. Schutz. Septième série. XII livraison.
"Kean, ou désordre et génie", comédie en cinq actes. Par Alex.
Dumas. Bielefeld. Velhagen & Klasing, 1846, 24mo., pp. 112.
Several reprints were issued, the fifth being in 1872.

"Kean, ou désordre et génie", Comédie en cinq actes et en prose,
par Alexandre Dumas. Bruxelles, Livourne, Meline, Cans et Cie.; J.P.
Meline, 1853, 12mo., pp. 163.

"Kean, ou désordre et génie", comédie en cinq actes, mêlée de chants,
Par M. Alexandre Dumas, représentée pour la première fois, a Paris,
sur le théâtre des Variétés, le 31 août 1836. Caption title. Violet
wrappers - Kean, ou désordre et génie" comédie en cinq actes mêlée
de chants Par M. Alexandre Dumas. Paris, N. Tresse, successeur de
J.-N. Barba, 1868, 8vo., pp. 38 in double columns.

La France dramatique au dix-neuvième siècle choix de pièces modernes.
"Kean, ou désordre et génie", comédie en cinq actes mêlée de chant
par M. Alexandre Dumas. Paris, N. Tresse, successeur de J.-N. Barba,
1872, same format and pagination as the preceding. Yellow wrappers.

"Kean ou désordre et génie" comédie en cinq actes, en six tableaux
Variétés. - 31 août 1836. "Distribution" on title-page, pp. 102-212.
Théatre complet de Alex. Dumas Tome V Paris Calmann Lévy, éditeur
ancienne maison Michel Lévy frères, 1874. 12mo. "Théatre complet" in
25 volumes.

"Kean ou désordre et génie". Comédie en cinq actes par Alex. Dumas.
Avec notes ... par G. van Muyden ... . Berlin, Friedberg et Mode,
1878, 18mo., pp. 132. Théâtre français. No. 60.
Several reprints were issued, the fifth being in 1896.

"Kean ou désordre et génie" comédie en cinq actes par Alexandre
Dumas. Paris, Tresse, 1876, 8vo., pp. 38 in double columns.

Alexandre Dumas. "Kean" comédie en cinq actes. Paris, Calmann-
Lévy, 1892, 4to., pp. 38 in double columns. Caption title. "Kean,
ou désordre et génie", comédie en cinq actes, mêlée de chants, Par
M. Alexandre Dumas, représentée ...; left-hand pages have the running
title 'Le magasin théâtral' and the right-hand pages the running title
'Kean'.

There was one parody of the play :
"Kinne ou que de génie en désordre" Variété en 99 couplets.

    'Aussi, sans r'tard, Kean je veux te connaître
    Et bon Dartois, je vous jur' qu'a gogo,
    Pour prononcer son nom comme il doit l'être
    Pendant huit jours je vais jouer au loto.'

4 sous. A Paris, chez l'éditeur, rue du Bac, 126. Et dans tous les
dépots de publications a bon marché. 1836. Caption title. "Kinne,
ou que de génie en désordre". Variété en 99 couplets. Large 8vo.,
pp. (1)-9 in double columns. Imprimerie de Baudoin, rue Mignon, 2.

  1836

    In or just previous to 1836 Dumas was approached for a contribution
to a work entitled "La Plutarque Français". It is not known whether
the subject of Napoleon was suggested or whether, as seems more likely,
Dumas suggested it, particularly since in his reading for the play
"Napoléon Bonaparte, ou Trente Ans de l'Histoire de France", which he
had written in 1831, he would have been helped in the planning of the
later biographical work.

    As it first appeared in "Le Plutarque Français" the work consisted
of six articles, and not four as Quérard in his "Supercheries littéraires devoilées" and, later, Glinel in "Alexandre Dumas et son oeuvre"
have wrongly stated. These articles were : 'Napoléon Bonaparte',
'Bonaparte Général', 'Bonaparte Premier Consul', 'Napoléon Empereur',
'Napoléon à l'Ile d'Elbe: les cent jours', and 'Napoléon à Saint-
Hélène'. The work's first appearance in this form was in :

"Le Plutarque Français", édité par Monsieur Mennechet. Paris, Imprimerie Crapelet, 1836, large 8vo., 8 vols.; the six sections occupied
96 pages and were accompanied by 4 full-length portraits. This was
reprinted in 1844-1847 :

"Le Plutarque Français, Vie des Hommes et des Femmes illustres de la
France, depuis le Ve siècle jusqu'à nos jours, avec les portraits
en pied gravés sur acier. 2e édition, publiée sous la direction de
T. Hadot. Paris, 4to., 6 vols; 185 beaux portraits hors-texte, gravés
sur acier et tirés sur chine monté avec pour chacun une notice biographique par les plus grands noms de l'époque. Mennechet, éditeur.

    When reprinted by Delloye to the original six articles were added
: 'Gouvernement de Napoléon' and 'Testament de Napoléon'.

Original edition (as a separate work).
"Napoléon", par Alexandre Dumas, Avec douze Portraits en pied.
Graves sur acier par les meilleurs artistes, d'après les peintures et
les dessins de Horace Vernet, Tony Johannot, Isabey, Jules Boïlly, etc.
(Decorative cross). Paris. Au Plutarque Français, 17, rue Duphet.
Delloye, éditeur, 13, place de la Bourse. 1840. Large 8vo., half-
title, title, pp. (1)-410, unnumbered page 'Table', verso blank; 12
steel engravings. Full calf, gilt decorated spine - "Al. Dumas"
"Napoléon". Imprimé par Bethune et Plon, 36, rue de Vaugirard. (Quérard refers to an edition published by Delloye, 1839, pp. 256, and
mentions the 12 steel engravings; this edition is not known to the
Bibliothèque Nationale, nor have I discovered any other reference to
it and its existence is dubious.)

"Histoire de Napoléon" par Alexandre Dumas. Bruxelles, Société belge
de librairie. Hauman et ce, 1840, 16mo., pp. 319 and unnumbered page
table of contents. The edition consists of 8 unnumbered chapters, the
text ending on page 296 and being followed by pp. (297)-319 'Testament
de Napoléon'. Brown wrappers.

"Napoléon", Par Alexandre Dumas. (Vignette) Bruxelles, Meline, Cans
et compagnie, 1840, 18mo., pp. 355 and unnumbered page table of contents. This edition comprises the 8 articles in the original French
volume edition. Yellow wrappers.

Oeuvres de Alex. Dumas. Tome quatrième. (Vignette) Bruxelles,
Meline, Cans et compagnie, 1840, large 8vo. "Napoléon", pp. frontis-

piece, (317)-411 in double columns. The same text as in the preceding edition.

"Napoléon". Par Alexandre Dumas. Berlin : Liebmann & Cie., 1841, 18mo., pp. (8)-305 and unnumbered page table of contents. Facing the title-page is : Collection des meilleurs ouvrages français modernes. No. 1. "Napoleon". Par Alexandre Dumas. Berlin : Liebmann & Cie., 1841. This edition follows the Delloye text.

"Histoire de Napoléon" par Alexandre Dumas. Mit Erl grammat. Bemerkungen und einem Wörterbuche. Hrsg. von E. Hoche. Leipsic : Fleischer, 1841, 8vo., pp. iv, 243.

Ibid   Stockholm, Zacharias Haeggstrom, 1845, 8vo., pp. 207, (1), and dictionary, pp. 1-35. Pink wrappers.

Ibid   Enrichi d'un vocabulaire et de notes grammaticales par E.I. Hauschild. Leipsic, Renger, libraire-éditeur, 1846, 8vo., pp. 2 preliminary leaves, 170; frontispiece portrait of Napoleon.

"L'Ile d'Elbe et les cent jours". Alexandre Dumas. In : Le livre des feuilletons, receuil de nouvelles, contes, épisodes, anecdotes, ... Extraits de la presse contemporaine. Paris, n.d. (November 1851), 8vo., unnumbered pages but totalling 24. Volume V, 11e livraison. This is a reprint of 'Napoléon à l'Ile d'Elbe et les cent jours' in the original 1840 edition.

"Napoléon", par Alexandre Dumas ... With conversational exercises, explanatory notes, and references to the 'New French Method" ... by Louis Fasquelle ... . New York, Ivison & Phinney, 1855, 8vo., pp. vi, (7)-273. At head of title : Translation, composition, conversation. Reprinted several times, same format and pagination.

"Histoire de Napoléon" par Alexandre Dumas. Mit Erl grammat. Bemerkungen und einem Wörterbuche ... Dr. Ed. Hoche ... . Leipzig, Verlag von Ernst Fleicher, 1856, 12mo., pp. iv, (2), 220, and 49 pages of vocabulary.

Ibid   Enrichie de notes historiques et géographiques. Munster. Imprimerie et Librairie de Theissing, 1860, 18mo., pp. vi, 314. Bibliotek gediegener und interessanter franzosischer werke. 30. Reprinted : Deuxième édition, soigneusement corrigée, 1865, 1869 and 1870, same format and pagination.

"Napoléon", par Alexandre Dumas. Paris, Michel Lévy frères, 1862, 12mo., pp. 309, blank, table of contents, verso blank. This edition, and succeeding editions by the same publishers and by Calmann-Lévy, contain the 6 sections as listed above in the "Plutarque Français" issue of 1836, but with "Napoleon a l'Ile d'Elbe : les cent jours" divided into separate parts, thus making 7 sections; included is the section "Testament de Napoléon" but not "Gouvernement de Napoléon". Reprinted several times, same format and pagination.

"Napoléon", par Alexandre Dumas. For the use of colleges and schools. With conversational exercises, explanatory notes, and references to the 'New French Method' ... by Louis Fasquelle ... . New York, Ivison, Phinney, Blakeman & Co.; Chicago, S.C. Griggs & Co., 1866, 8vo., pp. vi, (7)-273). At head of title : Translation, composition, conversation.
Reprinted by the same firms, 1869, 1875 and 1882, same format and pagination, and similar head of title.

"Napoléon" par Alexandre Dumas. Nouvelle édition. Paris, Calmann-Lévy, 1881, 12mo., 2 preliminary leaves, pp. 309, (2). Oeuvres complètes d'Alexandre Dumas. Collection Michel Lévy. Reprinted several times.

"Napoléon" par Alexandre Dumas. Munchen, Lindauer, 1893, 8vo., pp. iv, 134, and 3 maps.

"DEUTZ; ou IMPOSTURE, INGRATITUDE ET TRAHISON"   1836

Barbier, in his "Dictionnaire des ouvrages anonymes", Volume 1, column 917, quoting M. de Manne (conservateur-adjoint of the Bibliothèque Royale) states that this work was by Dumas. However, it is apparent from the 'Avis Essentiel' that the references to "La Vendée et madame" are those to be found in the second edition of that work published in 1834 with which Dumas had nothing to do, and which was written by General Dermoncourt. R.S.Garnett, in his translation of Dumas' "Le dernier roi des français, 1771 à 1851", has stated that the book was signed 'M. Davy', a nom-de-plume sometimes used by Dumas. But this is not so. It is, however, curious that Dumas was familiar with Deutz's activities, as can be seen in his references to him in "Le dernier roi ..." and in his "Mémoires".

Original edition.
"Deutz; ou Imposture, Ingratitude et Trahison". Par l'auteur de "La Vendée et Madame". Paris, Dentu, 1836, 8vo., pp. xi, 132.

Collection Hetzel. "Les louves de Machecoul" par Alex. Dumas. Edition autorisée pour la Belgique et l'étranger, interdite pour la. France. Bruxelles, Meline, Cans et compagnie, 1858, 24mo., 8 vols.; the pagination of the last volume is 194 of which pp. (174)-194 are occupied by 'Note' on Hyacinthe-Simon Deutz (Extrait de "Mémoires" d'Alex. Dumas.)

Collection Hetzel.   Ibid   Leipzig, Alphonse Dürr, 1858, same number of volumes, format and pagination.

"Les louves de Machecoul" par Alexandre Dumas. Paris Alexandre Cadot, éditeur, 1859, 8vo., 10 vols.; "Les louves de Machecoul" ends on page 86 of volume 10 and is followed by, inter alia, 'Note' on Hyacinthe-Simon Deutz, pp. (99)-136. Yellow wrappers. Fontainebleau - Imp. de E. Jacquin.

"GUELFES ET GIBELINS"   1836

Originally this historical article appeared in the issue of the 'Revue des deux mondes' for 1 mars 1836 as follows:

Tome 5. Pp. (513)-527, with no individual chapter heading; 527-533, 'Dante Alighieri'; 534-539, 'La Divina Commedia'; 539-544, 'Chant premier'. All in single columns, and signed : Alex. Dumas.

Subsequent editions.
"Les hommes de fer", par Alexandre Dumas. Paris, Michel Lévy frères, 1867, 12mo., pp. 305 and 2 unnumbered pages table of contents. "Guelfes et Gibelins" occupies pp. 243-305, the work divided into 2 parts without sub-titles.

Ibid   Nouvelle édition. Paris, Calmann-Lévy, 1888,
same format and pagination as the preceding. Oeuvres complètes d'Alexandre Dumas. Collection Michel Lévy.

"VOYAGES DE GABRIEL PAYOT"   1836

    This was Dumas' last contribution to the 'Revue des deux mondes',
and consists of his epilogue to "Impressions de voyage. En Suisse".
"Voyages de Gabriel Payot", par Alex. Dumas. Paris, Revue des deux
mondes, 1 avril 1836, pp. (46)-66.

"LA MAIN DROITE DU SIRE DE GIAC"   1837

    This brief historical study is, in fact, the completion of the
adventures of the Sire de Giac of which the earlier portion can be
found in "Isabel de Bavière" : Chapters XXIII, XXV, XXVI and XXVII.
It first appeared in the issue of the 'Revue des deux mondes', 1 and
15 décembre 1832.

Original edition (in volume form).
"La main droite du Sire de Giac" : in 'Dodecaton ou le livre des
douze'. Tome second. Paris. Victor Magen, éditeur 1837. 8vo.,
pp. (1)-409, verso blank, unnumbered page table of contents. Pp.
(157)-223, half-title "La main droite du sire de Giac", verso blank,
"Scènes historiques. La main droite du sire du Giac. 1425-1426",
signed : Alex. Dumas. Imprimerie et fonderie de A. Finard.

"Le capitaine Paul". Par Alexandre Dumas. Paris, Dumont, 1838, 8vo.,
2 volumes; "La main droite ... ... " occupies pp. 221-323 of volume
II.

"Contes et nouvelles". Par Alexandre Dumas. (Vignette) Bruxelles,
Meline, Cans et compagnie, 1838, 16mo., pp. 259. "La main droite du
Sire de Giac. Scènes historiques. 1425-1426" occupies pp. (5)-54.
Yellow wrappers.

Oeuvres de Alex. Dumas. Tome premier. (Vignette) Bruxelles, Meline,
Cans et compagnie, 1838, large 8vo. "Contes et nouvelles". "La main
droite du sire de Giac. Scenes historiques. - 1425-1426", pp. (661)-
673 in double columns.

Alexandre Dumas. "L'abbaye de Peyssac" (the fourth part of "La guerre
des femmes") Paris, L. de Potter, 1846, 8vo., 2 volumes, pp. 324 and
363; the second volume is completed by, inter alia, "La main droite
du sire de Giac. 1425-1426", pp. (249)-363. Yellow wrappers. Fontainebleau - Impr. de E. Jacquin.

"Le capitaine Paul" par Alexandre Dumas Paris Michel Lévy frères,
libraires-éditeurs de la bibliothèque dramatique Rue Vivienne, 1.
1846. 12mo., pp. (1)-6 'Préface' (Unsigned), (7)-238. "La main
droite du sire de Giac", pp. (241)-284. Half-title : oeuvres complètes d'Alexandre Dumas. Paris. - Typ. Lacrampe et Comp., rue
Damiette, 2.

Le Siècle. Oeuvres complètes d'Alexandre Dumas Troisième série. "La
main droite du sire de Giac". Paris, du bureau du Siècle, 1848, 4to.,
pp. (364)-372 in double columns.

"Nouvelles", par Alexandre Dumas. Paris, au bureau du Siècle, 1850, 4to., pp. 343-390. "La main droite ... ..." was one of the stories included.

"Le capitaine Paul", par Alexandre Dumas. Paris, Michel Lévy frères, 1850, 12mo., pp. 285. "La main droite ... ..." occupies pp. (239)-285.

"La main droite du sire de Giac", par Alexandre Dumas. Paris, Marescq et Cie., 1852, 4to., pp. 16 in double columns; illustrated.

"Nouvelles", par Alexandre Dumas. Paris, Impr. de Morris, n.d. (1854), 4to., pp. 343-372. "La main droite ... ..." is included; illustrated.

"La main droite du sire de Giac", par Alexandre Dumas. Paris, Impr. de S. Raçon et Cie., n.d. (1855), 4to., pp. 16 in double columns; 2 illustrations.
Reprinted, n.d. (1861), same format and pagination; 2 illustrations.

Ibid   Paris, Impr. de Gaittet, n.d. (1861), same format, pagination and illustrations as the preceding.

"Les hommes de fer", par Alexandre Dumas. Paris, Michel Lévy frères, 1867, 12mo., pp. 305 and 2 unnumbered pages table of contents. "Le sire de Giac; la main droite du sire de Giac", pp. 181-241.
Reprinted, 1888, same format and pagination.

"La main droite du sire de Giac" par Alexandre Dumas Dessins par Andrieux. Paris Calmann Lévy, Editeur ancienne maison Michel Lévy frères, 1887, 4to., pp. (1)-16 in double columns. Alexandre Dumas oeuvres illustrées.

Alexandre Dumas oeuvres illustrées Edition illustrée par J.-A. Beaucé, Staal, Andrieux. "La main droite du sire de Giac" par Alexandre Dumas. Paris, Calmann-Lévy, 1890, 4to., pp. (1)-16 in double columns.

"TEMPLE ET HOSPICE DU MONT-CARMEL. ... ..."   1837

After its publication in the issue of 'La Presse", 31 mai 1837, this article was later printed as a pamphlet. It was written by Dumas, jointly with Adolphe Dumas, for the Paris Committee of the Church and Alms-house.

Original edition.
"Temple et hospice du Mont-Carmel. Frère Jean-Baptiste, architecte du Carmel". Paris, Impr. d'Adrien le Clerc, 1837, 8vo., pp. 8, and signed 'Alexandre Dumas' on the final page.
Reprinted, same format and pagination, 1841, and later, undated.

"Temple et hospice du Mont-Carmel en Palestine", par MM. Alexandre Dumas et Adolphe Dumas, au nom du Comité de Paris; Paris, Impr. de Fain et Thunot, n.d. (1844), 8vo., 2 preliminary leaves, 16.

"PIQUILLO"   1837

There is no doubt that this is the joint work of Dumas and Gérard de Nerval. In his 'Préface en forme de causerie ou causerie en forme de préface' to "Les armes et le duel" by A. Grisier, Dumas gives an

amusing account of the origin of this comic opera - Monpou, the composer of the music, had worried him continually for the libretto, but
at that particular time Dumas was in arrears with his guard duty and
had various ways of entering and leaving his rooms without being
caught. Monpou finally gave him away to the National Guard on condition that Dumas should be provided with a private room to serve his
term of imprisonment. Hence, according to Dumas, "Piquillo".

Original edition.
"Piquillo", opéra-comique en trois actes, par M. Alexandre Dumas,
musique de M.H. Monpou, représenté pour la première fois, a Paris,
sur le théatre royal de l'Opéra-Comique, le 31 octobre 1837. Paris.
Marchant, Editeur, Boulevart (sic) Saint-Martin, 12. 1837. 8vo.,
pp. 'personnages' 'acteurs' verso of title-page, (5)-82. Buff
wrappers repeating title-page. Imprimerie de Ve Dondey-Dupré, rue
Saint-Louis, N° 46, au Marais.

"Piquillo", opéra-comique en trois actes, par M. Alexandre Dumas.
Musique de M.H. Monpou. Représenté pour la première fois, à Paris,
sur le Théatre Royal de l'Opéra-Comique, le 31 octobre 1837. Paris,
Ve Dondey-Dupré, n.d. (1837), 8vo., pp. 23 in double columns. Caption
title.

"Piquillo", opéra-comique en trois actes, Par M. Alexandre Dumas,
musique de M.H. Monpou, représenté pour la première fois, a Paris, sur
le théatre royal de l'Opéra-Comique, le 31 octobre 1837. Caption
title. Woodcut at head of title, Acte III, scène vi. Blue wrappers
: Magasin théatral. Choix de pièces nouvelles, jouées sur tous les
théatres de Paris. Théatre royal de l'Opéra-Comique. "Piquillo",
Opéra-comique en trois actes. (Vignette) Paris, Marchant; A Bruxelles, A la librairie belge-française, 1837, 8vo., pp. 23 in double
columns.

"Piquillo", opéra-comique, en trois actes, par M. Alexandre Dumas;
musique de M. Monpou. Représenté, pour la première fois, a Paris,
sur le théatre royal de l'Opéra-Comique, le 31 octobre 1837. (Vignette) Bruxelles : J.-A. Lelong; Gambier, 1837, 18mo., pp. 85. Buff
wrappers : Nouveau répertoire de la scène française, ou bibliothèque
dramatique.

"Piquillo". Opéra Comique en trois Actes. Paroles de M^r· Alex. Dumas.
Mis en musique. Dédie a son Ami Chollet par Hipp. Monpou. Représenté
pour la 1er fois sur le théatre R^{al} de l'opéra-comique le 30 (sic)
octobre 1837. Paris, J. Meissonier, n.d. (1837), 4to., pp. 343; list
of 'Personnages' and 'Catalogue des morceaux' on unnumbered page
following the title. In this edition the words accompany the musical
score.

"Piquillo", opéra-comique en trois actes, par M. Alexandre Dumas,
musique de M.H. Monpou, représenté pour la première fois, à Paris,
sur le théatre royal de l'Opéra-comique, le 31 octobre 1837. Paris,
Marchant, 1838, 8vo., pp. 23 in double columns. Caption title.

"Piquillo" opéra-comique en trois actes musique d'Hippolyte Monpou
Opéra-Comique. - 31 octobre 1837. "Distribution" on title-page,
pp. (213)-282. Théatre complet de Alex. Dumas Tome V Paris Calmann
Levy, éditeur ancienne maison Michel Lévy frères, 1874. 12mo.
"Théatre complet" in 25 volumes.

"CALIGULA" 1838

This fine play (and the prologue has been particularly praised) is solely by Dumas and was dedicated to someone unknown at its first performance - the 'unknown' is generally supposed to have been Dumas' friend the duc d'Orléans, eldest son of Louis-Philippe. The elaborately decorated holograph manuscript of the play was given to him. In his preface Dumas explains how the idea of the play came to him.

Original edition.
"Caligula", tragédie en cinq actes et en vers, avec un prologue, par M. Alexandre Dumas. Représentée pour la première fois, a Paris, sur le Théatre-Français, le 26 décembre 1837. Paris, Marchant, Editeur du Magasin Théatral, 1838, 8vo., pp. xiii, 170. Paper wrappers. Imprimerie de Ve Dondey-Dupré.

"Caligula", tragédie en cinq actes et en vers, précédée d'un prologue, Par M. Alexandre Dumas, représentée pour la première fois, a Paris, sur le Théatre-Français, le 26 décembre 1837. (Paris) Imprimerie de Ve Dondey-Dupré, n.d. (1838). Caption title. Woodcut at head of title, Acte IV, scene ii. 8vo., pp. 39 in double columns.

"Caligula". Tragédie en cinq actes et en vers, avec un prologue. Par Alexandre Dumas. (Vignette) Bruxelles, Meline, Cans et compagnie, 1838, 18mo., unnumbered page 'Note' by Dumas, pp. (vii)-xv Dumas' introduction, half-title with 'Personnages' on verso, (17)-182. Yellow wrappers.

Théatre de Alex. Dumas. "Caligula". (Vignette) Bruxelles. E. Laurent, 1838, 32mo., pp. half-title "Caligula", tragédie. 26 décembre 1837; pp. 155. Buff wrappers repeating title-page.

"Caligula". Tragédie en cinq actes et en vers, avec un prologue. Par Alexandre Dumas. (Vignette) Bruxelles, Meline, Cans et compagnie, 1838, 16mo., unnumbered page 'Note' by Dumas, pp. (vii)-xv Dumas' introduction, 182. Buff wrappers. Bibliothèque des châteaux et des campagnes. 5e Série. Bruxelles, Livourne, Meline, Cans et compagnie; Leipzig, J.P. Meline.

Oeuvres de Alex. Dumas. Tome second. (Vignette) Bruxelles, Meline, Cans et compagnie, 1838, large 8vo. "Caligula". Pp. (659)-661 'Préface' signed : A. Dumas; half-title with 'Personnages' on verso, (665)-674 prologue, (675)-707 in double columns.

"Caligula", Tragédie en 5 actes et en vers, précédée d'un prologue. Bruxelles, J.-A. Lelong, 1838, 24mo., pp. 121.

"Caligula", tragédie en cinq actes et en vers, précédée d'un prologue, par Alexandre Dumas. Représentée pour la première fois a Paris, sur le Théatre français, le 26 décembre 1837. (Vignette) Bruxelles, Th. Lejeune, même maison a La Haye, 1838, 18mo., pp. 132. Grey wrappers repeating the title-page, but omitting vignette.

Théatre français moderne ou Choix de pièces de Théatre nouvelles représentés avec succès sur les théatres de Paris. Série IV. Livraison 11. "Caligula". Tragédie en cinq actes et en vers. Précédée d'un prologue. Par M. Alexandre Dumas, publié par J. Louis. Dessau, Imprimerie de la cour, 1838, 8vo., pp. 164.

"Caligula", tragédie en cinq actes et en vers, précédée d'un prologue, par M. Alexandre Dumas; représentée, pour la premiere fois, a Paris,

66

sur le Théatre-Français, le 26 décembre 1837. (Vignette) Bruxelles
: J.-A. Lelong ... ; Gambier, 1838, 24mo., pp. (5)-121. Yellow
wrappers : Nouveau repertoire de la scène française, ou Bibliothèque dramatique. "Caligula", tragédie en cinq actes. Bruxelles,
J.-A. Lelong, 1838.

"Caligula", tragédie en cinq actes et en vers, précédée d'un prologue, Par M. Alexandre Dumas, représentée pour la première fois,
a Paris, sur le Théatre-Français, le 26 décembre 1837. Caption title.
Woodcut at head of title, Acte IV, scène ii. Green wrappers : Magasin théatral, choix de pièces nouvelles, jouées sur tous les théatres
de Paris. Théatre-Français. "Caligula", Tragédie en cinq actes.
(Vignette) Paris, Marchant; Bruxelles, A la librairie Belge-Française,
1838, 8vo., pp. 39 in double columns.

Ibid   But on wrappers : Paris, Marchant; Bruxelles,
Tarride, n.d. (c 1839), same format and pagination.

"Caligula". "Lorenzino". Par Alex. Dumas. Bruxelles, Meline, Cans
et Cie., 1855, 24mo., pp. 174 and 132 respectively.

"Caligula" tragédie en cinq actes, en vers précédée d'un prologue
Théâtre-Français. - 26 decembre 1837. 'Note' signed : Alex.
Dumas. 30 décembre 1837 on title-page, pp. (1)-7 'Préface' and page
7 'Distribution', 8-35 Prologue, 35-122. Théatre complet de Alex.
Dumas Tome VI Paris Calmann Lévy, éditeur ancienne maison Michel
Lévy frères, 1874. 12mo. "Théatre complet" in 25 volumes.

Théâtre nationale de l'Odéon. Direction de M. Porel. "Caligula"
Drame d'Alexandre Dumas. Musique de scène de Gabriel Fauré. Op. 52
... . Partition d'orchestre ... . Paris, J. Hamelle, n.d. (1888),
folio, pp. 1 preliminary leaf, 75. Full score. First produced at
Paris, 8 novembre 1888.

There was one parody of the play :
"Caligula" Pot-pourri par Romain Duclacour (J.-L. - Jules Lantin)
Citoyen Gaulois de Pontoise Paris Imprimerie de Stahl, 33 quai
Napoléon, 1838, 12mo., pp. 36.

"SUR LA MORT DE MADAME DUMAS"   1838

A poem of 12 lines rhyming alternately.

Dumas was terribly fond of his mother. She died on the 1st
August, 1838, and Amaury Duval drew her picture on her death-bed and
under it Dumas wrote this poem.

It may be found on page 355 of Glinel's "Alexandre Dumas et son
oeuvre", as well as on page 314 of Blaze de Bury's "Alexandre Dumas
Sa Vie Son Temps Son Oeuvre" (Paris, Calmann-Lévy, 1885) and on page
45 of L.-Henry Lecomte's "Alexandre Dumas 1802-1870 Sa Vie intime
Ses Oeuvres" (Paris, J. Tallandier, n.d. (1902).)

"LA SALLE D'ARMES. (PAULINE. PASCAL BRUNO. MURAT)"   1838

As can be seen this work consists of three quite separate stories,
and it is best to deal with each under its own individual title. Dumas
has said that he obtained the general material for them in the fencing-
school of the famous Grisier. But nevertheless "Pauline" has been

further developed from incidents described in his "Impressions de voyage. En Suisse". The title of this story was chosen to fulfil a promise made to a young bride whom he had met during his travels in La Vendée just as she was leaving for Guadeloupe with her husband.

Original edition.
"La salle d'armes. Pauline", par Alexandre Dumas. Paris, Dumont, 1838, 8vo., pp. 375 and unnumbered page table of contents. Volume 2, published in the same year by Dumont, pp. 350 and unnumbered page table of contents, comprised "Murat" and "Pascal Bruno".

Dumont published a second edition of Volume 1 in 1840, 8vo., pp. 376 including table of contents.

"Pauline", par Alexandre Dumas. (Vignette) Bruxelles, J. Jamar, 1838, 24mo., pp. 204, the last page being wrongly numbered 104.

"Pauline". Par Alexandre Dumas. (Vignette) Bruxelles, Meline, Cans et compagnie, 1838, 16mo., pp. (5)-309 and (311)-312 table of contents. "Pauline" occupies pp. (5)-234, and is followed by "Murat" only. Pale pink wrappers.

"Pauline", par Alexandre Dumas. Bruxelles, Meline, Cans et cie., 1839, 18mo., pp. 294 and unnumbered page table of contents. Blue wrappers.

Oeuvres de Alex. Dumas. Tome troisième. (Vignette) Bruxelles, Meline, Cans et compagnie, 1839, large 8vo. "Pauline". Pp., frontispiece, (7)-66 in double columns.

"Pauline" et "Pascal Bruno" ("Murat"). Par Alexandre Dumas. Paris, Michel Lévy frères, 1848, 12mo., pp. 319 and unnumbered page table of contents. "Pauline" occupies pp. (1)-157.

Le Siècle. "La salle d'armes. Pauline - Murat - Pascal Bruno" par Alexandre Dumas. Paris. Au bureau du Siècle, 1850, 4to. "Pauline" occupies pp. (253)-290 in double columns.

"Pauline" et "Pascal Bruno", par Alexandre Dumas. Bruxelles, Librairie du Panthéon, 1851, 18mo., 2 volumes, pp. 175 and 163. "Pauline" fills the whole of Volume 1 and ends on page 35 of volume 2. La Nouveauté littéraire. Yellow wrappers.

"Pauline de Meulien". "Aventures de Lyderic". "Jacques 1er et Jacques II". Par Alexandre Dumas. Publiés par Dufour et Mulat. Dessins par J.-A. Beaucé, Staal, C. Nanteuil, Ed. Coppin. (Engraving) Paris, 1853, chez Marescq et Cie. 3 parties en 1 volume, 4to., "Pauline" pp. 80 in double columns. Reprinted, 1855 and 1856, same format and pagination.

"Pauline de Meulien" par Alexandre Dumas. Paris, Impr. de S. Raçon et Cie., n.d. (1860), 4to., pp. 80 in double columns; 6 illustrations.

Ibid   Paris, Impr. de Gaittet, n.d. (1861), same format, pagination and illustrations as the preceding.

"La salle d'armes Pauline et Pascal Bruno". Par Alexandre Dumas. Paris, Impr. de J. Voisvenel, n.d. (c 1862), 4to., pp. 80 in double columns; 6 illustrations.

"Pauline de Meulien" par Alexandre Dumas Dessins par J.-A. Beaucé, Staal, C. Nanteuil, Ed. Coppin. (Vignette) Paris Calmann Lévy,

Editeur ancienne maison Michel Lévy frères, 1885, 4to., pp. (1)-80
in double columns. Alexandre Dumas Oeuvres illustrées.

"Pauline de Maulien" "Aventures de Lyderic" "Jacques 1er et Jacques
II" par Alexandre Dumas Dessins par J.A. Beaucé, Staal, C. Nanteuil,
Ed. Coppin. (Engraving) Paris, Calmann-Lévy, n.d. (1890), 4to.,
"Pauline de Meulien" pp. (1)-80 in double columns. Buff wrappers.
Alexandre Dumas oeuvres illustrées.

"LA SALLE D'ARMES. (PAULINE. PASCAL BRUNO. MURAT)" 1838

"Pascal Bruno" is one of Dumas' brigand stories and it achieved
considerable popularity not only in France but also in English translation. The main incidents in the story were adapted for the stage
for production in Britain and the United States and the plot differs
considerably from the French original.

Original edition.
"La salle d'armes. Pauline", par Alexandre Dumas. Paris, Dumont,
1838, 8vo., 2 volumes. Volume 1 is occupied solely by "Pauline";
Volume 2, pp. 350 and unnumbered page table of contents includes
"Pascal Bruno", pp. 123-350.
Dumont published a second edition in 1840, volume 2 then consisting
of pp. 304; "Pascal Bruno", pp.

"Contes et nouvelles". Par Alexandre Dumas. (Vignette) Bruxelles,
Meline, Cans et compagnie, 1838, 18mo., pp. 259 and unnumbered page
table of contents. "Pascal Bruno. Roman historique", pp. (55)-199.
Yellow wrappers repeating title-page.

Oeuvres de Alex. Dumas. Tome premier. (Vignette) Bruxelles, Meline,
Cans et compagnie, 1838, large 8vo. "Pascal Bruno. Roman historique".
pp. 674-710 in double columns.

"Pauline" et "Pascal Bruno' ("Murat"). Par Alexandre Dumas. Paris,
Michel Lévy frères, 1848, 12mo., pp. 310 and unnumbered page table of
contents. "Pascal Bruno" occupies pp. 211-310.

Le Siècle. "La salle d'armes. Pauline - Murat - Pascal Bruno"
par Alexandre Dumas. Paris. Au bureau du Siècle, 1850, 4to. "Pascal
Bruno" occupies pp. (307)-330 in double columns.

"Pauline" et "Pascal Bruno", par Alexandre Dumas. Bruxelles,
Librairie du Panthéon, 1851, 18mo., 2 volumes, pp. 175 and 163.
"Pascal Bruno" occupies pp. (37)-163 of Volume 2. La Nouveauté
littéraire. Yellow wrappers.

"Pascal Bruno" par Alexandre Dumas. Paris, Imprimerie Schneider,
n.d. (c 1851), large 8vo., pp. 56; illustrated.

"Les mille et un fantômes". "Pascal Bruno". Par Alexandre Dumas.
Publiés par Dufour et Mulat. Edition illustrée par Andrieux et Ed.
Coppin. (Vignette) Paris, 1852, chez Marescq et Cie.; "Pascal Bruno"
occupies pp. 56 in double columns.
Reprinted, 1854, same format, pagination and illustrations.

"La salle d'armes. "Pascal Bruno", par Alexandre Dumas. Paris,
Impr. de Walder, n.d. (1854), 4to., pp. 305-330 in double columns;
illustrated.

Ibid   Paris, Impr. de Morris, n.d. (1855), same format,
pagination and illustrations as the preceding.

"Pascal Bruno" par Alexandre Dumas. Paris, Impr. de S. Raçon et Cie.,
n.d. (1860), pp. 56 in double columns; 4 illustrations.

Ibid   Paris, Impr. de Gaittet, n.d. (1861), same format,
pagination and illustrations as the preceding.

"Les mille et un fantômes". "Pascal Bruno", par Alexandre Dumas.
Edition illustrée par Andrieux et Ed. Coppin. Paris, Impr. de Gaittet,
n.d. (1861), 4to., pp. 56 in double columns.

"La salle d'armes. Pauline et Pascal Bruno". Par Alexandre Dumas.
Paris, Impr. de Voisvenel, n.d. (c 1862), 4to., pp. 56 in double
columns.

Alexandre Dumas. "Pascal Bruno". ("Murat"). Paris, Michel Lévy
frères, 1864, 4to., pp. 56 in double columns.

"Pascal Bruno" par Alexandre Dumas Paris, Calmann-Lévy, 1889, 4to.,
pp. 56 in double columns. Caption title. Illustrated.

"Pascal Bruno" par Alexandre Dumas Edition illustrée par Andrieux
et Ed. Coppin. Paris, Calmann-Lévy, n.d. (1891), 4to., pp. 56 in
double columns. Alexandre Dumas Oeuvres illustrées.

"LA SALLE D'ARMES. (PAULINE. PASCAL BRUNO. MURAT)"   1838

    This account of the capture and execution of the King of Naples
was, with the exceptions mentioned below, used as one of the articles
comprising "Les crimes célèbres".

Original edition.
"La salle d'armes. Pauline", par Alexandre Dumas. Paris, Dumont,
1838, 8vo., 2 volumes. Volume 1 is occupied solely by "Pauline";
Volume 2, pp. 350 and unnumbered page table of contents includes
"Murat" pp. 11-113.
Dumont published a second edition in 1840, volume 2 then consisting
of pp. 304; "Murat", pp.

"La capitaine Paul" suivi de "Murat" par Alexandre Dumas. (Vignette)
Bruxelles, J. Jamar, 1838, 18mo., 2 volumes, pp. 139 and 143. "Le
capitaine Paul" ends on page 78 of volume 2, "Murat" occupying pp.
(79)-143 with no separate title.

"Le capitaine Paul", par Alexandre Dumas. (Vignette) Bruxelles,
Société encyclographique, A. Mertens et comp., 1838, same format and
pagination as the preceding edition.

"Pauline" et "Pascal Bruno" ("Murat"). Par Alexandre Dumas. Paris,
Michel Lévy frères, 1848, 12mo., pp. 310 and unnumbered page table of
contents. "Murat" occupies pp. (159)-209.

Le Siècle. "La salle d'armes. Pauline - Murat - Pascal Bruno"
par Alexandre Dumas. Paris. Au bureau du Siècle, 1850, 4to. "Murat"
occupies pp. (293)-304 in double columns.

Alexandre Dumas. "Pascal Bruno". ("Murat"). Paris, Michel Lévy
frères, 1864, 4to., pp. 24 in double columns.

"Murat" par Alexandre Dumas Edition illustrée par les principaux artistes Paris Calmann Lévy, Editeur ancienne maison Michel Lévy frères, 1887, 4to., pp. 24 in double columns. Alexandre Dumas oeuvres illustrées.

Alexandre Dumas "Le capitaine Paul" "Murat" "Le Kent" "Pierre le cruel" "Don Bernardo de Zuniga" édition illustrée par les principaux artistes Paris, Calmann Lévy, éditeur ancienne maison Michel Lévy frères, 1887, 4to., pp. 24 in double columns.

Ibid (Vignette) Paris, Calmann-Lévy, n.d. (1890), 4to., same pagination as the preceding. Alexandre Dumas oeuvres illustrées.

"LE BOURGEOIS DE GAND, ou LE SECRETAIRE DU DUC D'ALBE" 1838

This drame was signed by Hippolyte Romand, but L.-Henry Lecomte in his "Alexandre Dumas 1802-1970 Sa Vie intime. Ses oeuvres" (Paris, J. Tallandier, 1902) states explicitly that Dumas assisted in its writing.

Original (and only) edition.
"Le bourgeois de Gand, ou le secrétaire du duc d'Albe" Drame en cinq actes et en prose par M. Hippolyte Romand Représenté pour la première fois, à Paris, sur le théatre royal de l'Odéon, par les comédiens ordinaires du Roi, le 21 mai 1838. Paris, Imprimerie de J. Didot l'aîné, n.d. (1838), 4to., pp. 543-584 in double columns.

"QUINZE JOURS AU SINAI" 1838

Dumas never travelled in the Holy Land or Egypt. Two of his friends, Baron Taylor and Dauzats the artist, did as members of a scientific party in 1830. They gave him a detailed account of what they had seen and done; one reason for the journey being to finalise arrangements for the transfer to France of the obelisk at Luxor which was to finally stand in the Place de la Concorde in Paris.

There can be no question of Dumas filching someone else's work, or resorting to inferior journalism, when he decided to do the writing. This is a unique piece of descriptive work and so filled with the genuine atmosphere of the Middle East that, some time later, Ibraham Pacha sent him a message of congratulations saying that 'of all men who had visited Egypt, he had best described it as it is'. A number of people, however, refused to believe that he had not been a member of the party. The final part of the book is devoted to a description of the expedition of Louis IX of France to Egypt in 1249.

The work is also unique in that its first printing in French was made outside Europe; this points to it having been published earlier in serial form in a French journal.

Original edition.
"Le Sinaï. (Impressions de voyage.)" Par A. Dauzats et Alexandre Dumas. (Vignette) New-York, Foreign and Classical bookstore, 94 Broadway, 1838, (the uncut pages vary in size between 24.3 x 23.4 and 15.7 x 14.5 cms.), pp. (1-5), 6-458, (459)-(461), 462 and 2 unnumbered pages; paper covers.

"Nouvelles impressions de voyage. Quinze jours au Sinaï", par MM.

Alex. Dumas et A. Dauzats. Paris, Dumont, Libraire-éditeur, palais royal, 88, au Salon Littéraire. 1839. 8vo., 2 volumes. Volume 1 : half-title, title with an engraved frontispiece 'Mont Sinaï', pp. 356; Volume 2 : half-title, title with an engraved frontispiece 'Rocher de Moise', pp. 404, each volume with 2 additional unnumbered pages table of contents. The frontispieces were by Dauzats.
A second edition was published in the same year by Dumont, same format and pagination, but with vignettes facing the title-pages.
Also in the same year from Dumont came an edition, same format and pagination 'imprimée sur grand papier vélin' with the frontispieces of the first Dumond edition.

"Quinze jours au Sinaï". Par Alexandre Dumas. (Vignette) Bruxelles, Meline, Cans et compagnie, 1839, 12mo., 2 volumes, pp. 238 and 290, each with an additional unnumbered page table of contents. Some copies have blue wrappers, others yellow.

Oeuvres de Alex. Dumas. Tome troisième. (Vignette) Bruxelles, Meline, Cans et compagnie, 1839, large 8vo. "Quinze jours au Sinaï", frontispiece, pp. (159)-282 in double columns.

"Quinze jours au Sinaï", par MM. Alex. Dumas et A. Dauzats. Paris, Librairie de Charles Gosselin, 1841, 12mo., pp. iv, 401.
Reprinted, 1842, same format and pagination.

"Mort de Kleber". Alexandre Dumas. In : Le livre des feuilletons Receuil de nouvelles, contes, épisodes, extraits de la presse contemporaine. Nancy, Imprimerie Hinzelin, 1843, deuxième volume, 8vo., pp. 104-106 in double columns.
This is an extract from the chapter entitled : 'Soleyman-el-Haleby'.

"Quinze jours au Sinaï". Par Alexandre Dumas. Paris, Recoules, 1846, 8vo., 2 volumes.

"Quinze jours au Sinaï", par Alexandre Dumas. Paris, Boulé, 1846, large 8vo., pp. 189 and unnumbered page table of contents. In : Les mille et un romans. Volume XVII.

Alexandre Dumas. "Quinze jours au Sinaï". Paris, Desessart, éditeur ... . M DCCC XLVI. 8vo., 2 volumes, pp. (1)-335, verso blank, unnumbered page table of contents; (1)-367, verso blank, unnumbered page table of contents.

Ibid (Deuxième édition) Paris, Desessart, same year, format and pagination as the preceding.

"Quinze jours au Sinaï" par Alexandre Dumas. Paris. Boulé, Editeur, rue Coq-Héron, 5. 1849, 8vo., pp. (1)-189, verso blank, unnumbered page table of contents.

"Voyage en Orient. Quinze jours au Sinaï". Par Alexandre Dumas. ('... La main d'un enfant peut t'ouvrir au hasard Sans qu'un mot corrupter étonne son regard.') Stuttgart, n.d. (1851), 12mo., pp. 158. Additional title-page : Bibliothèque française du Choix de livres interessants destinés à la jeunesse allemande des deux sexes ... , receuillis par Charles Zoller ... . Série 1, Tome X.
The book consists of extracts from the work; a second edition, same format and pagination, was published in 1856.

"Quinze jours au Sinaï" par Alexandre Dumas. Publié par Dufour et Mulat. Illustrés par J.-A. Beaucé, Ed. Coppin, Lancelot, etc. (Vignette) Paris, Marescq et cie., 1853, 4to., pp. (1)-170 in double columns, and two additional unnumbered pages table of contents and

72

'placement des gravures'.
The wrappers are dated 1854.
Reprinted, 1854, same format, pagination and illustrations.

"Impressions de voyage. Quinze jours au Sinaï", par Alexandre Dumas.
Paris, Impr. de Walder, n.d. (1854), 4to., pp. 80 in double columns.
Caption title. Woodcut at head of title.
Le Siècle. Oeuvres complètes d'Alexandre Dumas. Dixième série.
"Impressions de voyage. Quinze jours au Sinaï". Paris, au bureau du
Siècle, n.d. (1855), 4to., pp. (1)-80 in double columns, and including
table of contents.

"Quinze jours au Sinaï" : this edition in the Stad Antwerpen Biblio-
teken lacks the title-page. It has a frontispiece engraving 'Le mont
Sinaï' with beneath it 'A. Dumas'; it is in 8vo., pp. 159-282 in
double columns, and was certainly published around the middle of the
19th century.

"Impressions de voyage. Quinze jours au Sinaï", par Alexandre Dumas.
Paris, Michel Lévy frères, 1855, 12mo., pp. 299, verso unnumbered
page table of contents.

"Quinze jours au Sinaï" par Alexandre Dumas. Publié par Dufour et
Mulat. Illustrés par J.-A. Beaucé, Ed. Coppin, Lancelot, etc. (Vignette) (Paris) Lécrivain et Toubon, 1860, 4to., pp. 170 in double
columns.

"Impressions de voyage. Quinze jours au Sinaï", par Alexandre Dumas
et A. Dauzats. Nouvelle édition. Paris, Michel Lévy frères, 1961,
12mo., pp. 299, verso unnumbered page table of contents.
Frequently reprinted, same format and pagination, by Michel Lévy
frères and Calmann-Lévy.

Ibid   Paris, Calmann-Lévy, 1881, 4to., pp. 80 including
table of contents in double columns. Caption title. Woodcut at head
of title, repeated on pale pink wrappers. Musée littéraire contemporain.
Reprinted, 1888, same format and pagination.

Prosateurs français. 72. Lieferung. "Quinze jours au Sinaï". par
A. Dumas père et A. Dauzats. Auszug. Mit Ammerkungen zum Schulebrauch
herausgegeben von Dr. Adolf Meyer ... . Bielefeld und Leipzig, Velhagen & Klasing, 1889, 8vo., pp. (1)-8 'Introduction', (9)-133 French
text, and additional unnumbered page table of contents.

As a footnote to the above :
Feuilleton du journal l'Ordre. "La mer rouge, journal de deux voyageurs, pour faire suite a 'Quinze jours au Sinaï'," par Alexandre
Dumas et Dauzatz. Signed : Arnaud et Vayssièrs. Paris, impr. de
Firmin-Didot frères, n.d. (1849), oblong folio (20 x 44 cms.), pp. 24
in treble columns. The first 6 pages consist of a letter from Dumas
to 'Monsieur le gérant de l'Ordre', and page 7 of a letter from the
authors to Dumas, dated 15 mars 1849.

"LE CAPITAINE PAUL"   (Romance)
"PAUL JONES" ("PAUL LE CORSAIRE")   (Drama)   1838

    The history of these two works is interwoven. In 1830 Dumas was
visiting Mélanie Waldor in La Vendée and in the course of his travels
stayed at Lorient which had been used on several occasions by Captain

Paul Jones as a convenient harbour. Dumas claims, with probably an author's licence, that a servant's son of the Auray family had narrated to him the incidents on which the romance is based. The subject continued germinating in his mind until 1836; in that year Dumas was travelling in Italy and, in October, on board his 'speronare' off the coast of Sicily the play "Paul Jones" was written. On his return to Paris it was submitted to the producer Harel, but it was not accepted.

Temporarily financially embarrassed Dumas 'pledged' the play to Porcher, the ever accommodating theatre-ticket seller and friend-in-need to so many writers. Early in 1838 the management of the journal "Le Siècle" approached Dumas for a serial for that paper. They were in a hurry and were willing to allow him only two months for the writing. Dumas thought of his rejected drama and from it drew "Le capitaine Paul". This was an unusual thing for him to do, a parallel being in 1842 with the drawing of the romance "Une nuit à Florence" from the not very successful drama "Lorenzino".

Dumas was travelling with Gérard de Nerval in the Rhine valley between August and November, 1838, when he heard from a friend in Paris that the play he had handed over to Porchet was being rehearsed at the very third-rate Théâtre du Panthéon by the then manager Théodore Nezel, Porchet's son-in-law and in financial difficulties. To convince a somewhat sceptical public that the play was indeed by Dumas the holograph manuscript was exhibited in the theatre vestibule. What had happened was that Dumas had quite forgotten his 'pledge' and Porcher, although with considerable misgivings, had handed the play over to Nezel to help put him on his feet again. The play was, in fact, successful and Dumas on his return bore Porcher no malice, although its production at such a theatre could have been detrimental to his reputation.

The vicissitudes of the play and the romance have been told by Dumas in the issues of his journal "Le Mousquetaire" for 28 and 29 février, and 1 and 2 mars, 1856, and also as a preface to the edition of the romance published by Charlieu in that year, being reprinted in later French editions. It may be added here that Dumas was a great admirer of the works of Fenimore Cooper whose influence, with that of Sir Walter Scott, he felt in his early career. (Dumas regarded "Le capitaine Paul" as a sequel to "The Pilot", but American readers may find this rather difficult to understand.) Dauzats, the painter, is generally considered to have helped Dumas with the nautical technicalities.

"LE CAPITAINE PAUL" : The romance ran in the columns of "Le Siècle" from 30 mai to 23 Juin, 1838.

Original edition.
"Le capitaine Paul" suivi de "Murat" par Alexandre Dumas. (Vignette) Bruxelles, J. Jamar, 1838, 18mo., 2 volumes, pp. 139 and 143. "Le capitaine Paul" ends on page 78 of Volume 2; "Murat" occupying pp. 79-143 with no separate title.

"Le capitaine Paul", par Alexandre Dumas. (Vignette) Bruxelles, Société encyclographique, A. Merten et comp., 1838, same format and pagination as the preceding edition.

"Le capitaine Paul". Par Alexandre Dumas. Paris, Dumont, 1838, 8vo.,
2 volumes, pp. 316 and 323. "Le capitaine Paul" ends on page 220 of
Volume 2 and is followed by "La main droite du sire de Giac". Yellow
wrappers.
A copy of this first edition published in France was sent by Dumas to
Dauzats 'en hommage', and inscribed 'Dauzats invenit. A. Dumas sc'.

"Le capitaine Paul". Par Alexandre Dumas. (Vignette) Bruxelles,
Meline, Cans et compagnie, 1838, 18mo., pp. (v)-x, (11)-269. Green
wrappers repeating title-page. (This edition does not include "Murat".)

Ibid   (Vignette) Bruxelles et Leipzig, C. Hochhausen
et Fournes, 1838, same format and pagination as the preceding edition.

Oeuvres de Alex. Dumas. Tome troisième. (Vignette) Bruxelles,
Meline, Cans et compagnie, 1838, large 8vo. "Le capitaine Paul", pp.
(91)-92 préface, (93)-156 in double columns.

"Le capitaine Paul" par Alexandre Dumas Paris Michel Lévy frères,
libraires-éditeurs de la bibliothèque dramatique Rue Vivienne, 1.
1846. 12mo., pp. (1)-6 préface (unsigned), (7)-238. "La main droite
du sire de Giac", pp. (241)-284. Half-title : oeuvres complètes
d'Alexandre Dumas. Paris. - Typ. Lacrampe et Comp., rue Damiette, 2.
The preface to this first Lévy edition is shorter than that published
in 1850 and subsequent editions.
Reprinted, 1847, same format and pagination.

Ibid   Paris, Michel Lévy frères, 1850, 12mo., pp. 1
preliminary leaf, 285. "Le main droite ... ... " occupies pp. (239)-
285. Bibliothèque contemporaine.

"Le capitaine Paul", par Alexandre Dumas. Bruxelles, Librairie du
Panthéon, 1851, 24mo., 2 volumes, pp. 162 and 157. La Nouveauté
littéraire.

"Le capitaine Paul", par Alexandre Dumas. Paris, Librairie Théâtrale,
1856, 12mo., pp. 313, including the preface.

Ibid   Paris, Charlieu, 1856, 12mo., pp. 313 including
the preface.
(The Librairie Théâtrale was published by Charlieu.)

"Le capitaine Paul", Par Alexandre Dumas. Paris, Michel Lévy frères,
1858, 12mo., pp. xlviii, 223. Oeuvres complètes d'Alexandre Dumas.
Reprinted, 1862, 1869 and by Calmann-Lévy, 1889, 1895, same format
and pagination.

Journal du dimanche. "Le capitaine Paul". No. 297, 2 septembre 1860,
through to No. 308, 11 octobre 1860, in treble columns. 'Alexandre
Dumas'; 4to., woodcut at head of each issue.

"Le capitaine Paul". Par Alexandre Dumas. Paris, Michel Lévy frères,
n.d. (c 1865), 4to., pp. 43 in double columns. Illustrated paper
covers.

Alexandre Dumas "Le capitaine Paul" "Murat" "Le Kent" "Pierre le
cruel" "Don Bernardo de Zuniga" édition illustrée par les principaux
artistes (Vignette) Paris Calmann Lévy, éditeur ancienne maison
Michel Lévy frères, 1887, 4to., pp. (1)-52 in double columns. Brown
paper covers with different vignette : Illustrés par J.-A. Beaucé
et les principaux artistes. Alexandre Dumas oeuvres illustrées.
Reprinted, n.d. (1890), 1897, same format and pagination.

"PAUL JONES" ("PAUL LE CORSAIRE")

There is a difference of opinion as to when the drama was first performed. The Marchant and Imprimerie de Walder editions state that it was first staged on the 8th October, 1838, but the Calmann-Lévy complete editions of Dumas' plays gives the 12th October of that year; for what it is worth the former date is also given by Quérard. It was re-staged on the 16th October, 1841, at the Théâtre de la Porte-Saint-Martin under the altered title of "Paul le Corsaire" where it ran for forty performances.

De Mirecourt, and later Quérard, gives Nezel some hand in the writing of the play, but this, in the circumstances of the actual original writing as outlined in my introduction to the romance and the drama, is manifestly impossible. No other collaborator has ever been suggested.

Original edition.
"Paul Jones", drame en cinq actes, par Alexandre Dumas, représenté pour la première fois, à Paris, le 8 octobre 1838. Paris, Marchant, (1838), 4to., pp. 32 in double columns. Caption title. Engraving at head of title, Acte V, scène v. Le Magasin théatral; Imprimerie de Vᵉ Dondey-Dupré.

"Paul Jones", drame en cinq actes, Par Alexandre Dumas, représenté pour la première fois, a Paris, le 8 octobre 1838. Caption title. Woodcut at head of title. Yellow wrappers : Magasin théatral, choix de pièces nouvelles, jouées sur tous les théatres de Paris. Théatre du Panthéon, "Paul Jones", Drame en cinq actes. (Vignette) Paris, Marchant; Bruxelles, A la librairie Belge-Française, 1838, 8vo., pp. 32 in double columns.

Ibid   With on yellow wrappers : Théâtre de la Porte-Saint-Martin, "Paul Jones", Drame en cinq actes. (Vignette) Paris, Marchant; Bruxelles, Tarride, n.d. (c 1840). Same format and pagination as the preceding edition.

"Paul Jones" ("Paul le Corsaire"). Drame en cinq actes par Alexandre Dumas, représenté pour la première fois, à Paris, le 8 octobre 1838. Paris, Impr. de Walder, n.d. (1866). Caption title. Same format and pagination as the preceding editions.

"Paul Jones" drame en cinq actes, en prose Panthéon. - 12 octobre 1838. "Distribution" on title-page, pp. (123)-206. Théatre complet de Alex. Dumas Tome VI Paris Calmann Lévy, éditeur, ancienne maison Michel Lévy frères, 1874. 12mo. "Théatre complet" in 25 volumes.

Between the publication of the romance and the staging of the play, two other plays were staged both of which it is stated by Quérard were based on the former. To my knowledge neither was ever printed.

"Le capitaine Paul", drame en cinq actes, en prose, par Dautrevaux. This was performed at the Théâtre Dorsay, 30 août 1838.

"Le capitaine Paul", drame en trois actes, en prose, par MM. Durand de Valley (Em. Gautrot) et Léon Angot. This was performed at the Théâtre du Luxembourg, 6 octobre 1838.

"ACTE"   1838
    Dumas' researches for the writing of "Caligula" led him to study

the career of Nero. The character of the freedwomen Acté, Nero's mistress, gave him the idea he wanted for the writing of an historical romance. The period is from A.D. 57 to 68. Hippolyte Parigot has written : 'Scott could never have written the first two hundred pages. Renan who related the martyrdom of Blandina would not have been ashamed of them. Tacitus, Suetonius and St. Paul are authorities for his facts. Dumas did not advance a single step without a document to support him .....'

Unfortunately when he was nearing the end of writing the work his much-loved mother, whom he had brought to Paris from Villers-Cotterets, died on the 1st August, 1838. It would seem that its conclusion was wanted urgently by the journal in which it was appearing as a serial, and that, greatly bereaved by his mother's death, Dumas quickly brought the work to a conclusion by extensively using material from Chateaubriand's "Martyrs". The book bears the dedication : 'A la memoire de ma mère, morte pendant que j'achevais cet ouvrage, Alex. Dumas'.

Sienkiewics has said that it was this romance which gave him the idea for his "Quo vadis?"

Original edition.
"Acté". Par Alexandre Dumas. Bruxelles, Société typographique belge Adolphe Wahlen et Cie., 1838, 18mo., 2 volumes, pp. 266 and 251. (This is a typical 'pré-façon' belge.)

"Acté" ("Monseigneur Gaston Phoebus, chronique dans laquelle est racontée l'histoire du démon familier du sire de Corasse".) par Alexandre Dumas. Paris, Libraire de Dumont, palais-royal, 88, au salon littéraire. 1839. 8vo., 2 volumes, pp. half-title, title, unnumbered page bearing Dumas' dedication, verso blank, (1)-342 (the last page being wrongly numbered 242), and (1)-123; pp. (125)-302 are occupied by "Monseigneur Gaston Phoebus, ...". Yellow wrappers. Corbeil. Imprimerie de Crété.

"Acté", par Alexandre Dumas. (Vignette) Bruxelles, J. Jamar, 1839, 18mo., 2 volumes, pp. 179 and 171. "Acté" ends on page 85 of Volume 2; pp. (87)-171 comprise "Monseigneur Gaston Phoebus, ...", Par Alexandre Dumas.

"Acté". Par Alexandre Dumas. (Vignette) Bruxelles, Meline, Cans et compagnie, 1839, 18mo., 2 volumes, pp. 278 and 260.

Oeuvres de Alex. Dumas. Tome troisième. (Vignette) Bruxelles, Meline Cans et compagnie, 1839, large 8vo. "Acté". Pp. frontispiece, (285)-361 in double columns.

Echo des feuilletons Choix de nouvelles, épisodes, anecdotes, extraits de la Presse contemporaine. Paris, 1844, large 8vo. "Une fête a Rome", pp. 26-30 in double columns. This is a reprint of an extract from "Acté".

"Acté" par Alexandre Dumas. Montmirail - Imp. de Brodart, n.d. (1847), 8vo., 2 volumes, pp. (1)-342 and (1)-302. "Acté" ends on page 123 of Volume 2, verso blank, and is followed by "Monseigneur Gaston Phoebus, ...", pp. (125)-302.

Le Siècle. Oeuvres complètes de M. Alexandre Dumas. "Acté". Paris, 1852, 4to., pp. 50 in double columns. Impr. de Lange Lévy.

"Acté", par Alexandre Dumas. Paris, Michel Lévy frères, 1854, 12mo., pp. 266.
Frequently reprinted by Michel Lévy frères and Calmann-Lévy.

Ibid   Paris, Michel Lévy frères, 1854, 4to., pp. 50 in double columns; illustrated. Caption title.

Ibid   Paris, Impr. de J. Voisvenel, n.d. (1855), same format and pagination as the preceding edition; illustrated. Caption title.

Ibid   Couloummiers, Typ. de A. Moussin et Charles Unsinger, n.d. (1867), 12mo., pp. (1)-252.

Ibid   Paris, Calmann-Lévy, n.d. (1890), 4to., pp. 50 in double columns; illustrated. Caption title.

"MARGUERITE DE BRANKSOME (LAI DU DERNIER MENESTREL)"   1839

This poem consists of 80 lines, rhyming in couplets, and in verses of irregular length. It is an adaptation rather than a translation of stanzas XI to XVIII of the first canto of Sir Walter Scott's "Lay of the last minstrel".

Dumas has given to Margaret those powers of sorcery that Scott attributed to her mother, the daughter of the clerk of Béthune.

Original edition.
"Beautés de Walter Scott", magnifiques portraits des héroines de Walter Scott accompagnés chacun d'un portrait littéraire, par MM. Alexandre Dumas, ..., ... Paris. chez l'Editeur, A la librairie, Boulevard Saint-Martin, 13. Garnier freres, Editeur, Rue Richelieu, 10. N.d. (c 1839), large 8vo. Dumas' contribution pp. (29)-32, with a lithographic portrait of Marguerite de Branksome facing the first unnumbered page. Violet boards decorated in gold on the front and back covers and spine. Paris. - Typ. de Mme Ve Dondey-Dupré, rue Saint-Louis, 46, au Marais.

"Calerie des femmes de Walter Scott", quarante portraits gravés sur acier, accompagnés chacun d'un portrait littéraire. Paris, Marchant, éditeur, boulevart (sic) Saint-Martin, 12. 1842. Slightly smaller format than the preceding, with the same pagination and lithograph. Black boards with gilt decorated spine. On verso of half-title : imprimerie de Mme Ve Dondey-Dupré, rue Saint-Louis, 46, au marais.

"JACQUES ORTIS"   1839

This work is a translation of Ugo Foscolo's "Les dernières lettres de Jacopo Ortis".

Original edition.
"Jacques Ortis", par Alexandre Dumas. Paris, Dumont, 1839, 8vo., pp. (i)-xvi 'Préface de Piers-Angelo-Fiorentino' : Paris, 2 janvier 1839, 312. Yellow wrappers.

"Jacques Ortis" par Alexandre Dumas. (Vignette) Bruxelles. Meline, Cans et compagnie, 1839, 18mo., pp. (i)-xvii preface signed and dated as in the original edition, (19)-298.

Ibid   (Same vignette) Bruxelles et Leipzig, Meline,
Cans et compagnie, 1839, same format and pagination as the preceding
edition. Pale green wrappers.

Oeuvres de Alex. Dumas. Tome troisième. (Vignette) Bruxelles,
Meline, Cans et compagnie, 1839, large 8vo. "Jacques Ortis". Pp.
signed and dated preface (501)-504, (505)-566 in double columns.

"Jacques Ortis", par M. Alex. Dumas, précédé d'un essai sur le vie
et les écrits D'Ugo Foscolo, par Eugène de Montlaur, et suivi d'une
traduction inédite de ses oeuvres par M.L. Delatre. (Monogram) Paris
Librairie de Charles Gosselin, éditeur de la bibliothèque d'élite, 9,
rue Saint-Germain-des-Prés. MDCCCXLII. 12mo., pp. (i)-x preface
signed and dated as in the original edition, (xi)-lii 'Essai sur la
vie et les écrits d'Ugo Foscolo' signed : Eug. de Montlaur, (1)-220
"Jacques Ortis", (221)-(281) 'oeuvres choisies d'Ugo Foscolo', verso
blank, unnumbered page table of contents. Verso of half-title publisher's advertisements for "Quinze jours au Sinaï" and "Gaule et
France"; Paris. - Imprimerie de Béthune et Plon. Brown paper
wrappers repeating title-page and headed 'Bibliothèque d'Elite'.

"Jacques Ortis", par Alexandre Dumas. Paris, Desessard, 1846, 8vo.,
pp. 325.

"Jacques Ortis", par Alexandre Dumas précédé d'un essai sur la vie
et les écrits d'Ugo Foscolo par Eugène de Montlaur et suivi d'une
traduction inédite de ses oeuvres choisies par M.L. Delatre. Paris,
Michel Lévy frères, 1847, 12mo., pp. 281 and unnumbered page table of
contents.
Occasionally reprinted.

"Jacques Ortis". "Les fous du docteur Miraglia". Par Alexandre Dumas.
Avec notice sur U. Foscolo par E. de Montlaur (pp. (1)-14) et traduc-
tion inédite de ses oeuvres choisies par M.L. Delatre. Paris, Michel
Lévy frères, 1867, 12mo., pp. 306 and unnumbered page table of contents
"Jacques Ortis", pp. (15)-260; "Les fous du docteur Miraglia", pp.
(261)-306.
Reprinted 1885 and 1897, same format and pagination, by Calmann-Lévy.

"LA COMTESSE DE SALISBURY" ("EDOUARD III")   1839

     One of the "Chroniques de France" series, this work covers
approximately the years 1338 to 1377 of the Hundred Years' War. Dumas'
most excellent 'Introduction' to the book, giving his ideas as to the
writing of historical romances, was republished in the 1842 edition of
his "Gaule et France". Dumas claims to have introduced the 'feuilleton' romances with this work, and said that had the instalments
appeared daily instead of only on Sundays it must have been a greater
success. It did, in fact, appear serially in "La Presse" during 1838.

     The original edition is the cause of some mystery. Talvart et
Place state. : "Chroniques de France. La comtesse de Salisbury",
par Alexandre Dumas. Paris, Dumont (et Alexandre Cadot), 1839-1848,
8vo., 5 volumes, pp. 333, 340, 315, 320 and 317, without giving the
years of the individual volumes. Quérard says : 'Tomes I et II,
1839, 2 vols. in-8⁰, ... II doit avoir deux autres volumes'. The
publisher Dumont was still advertising the work as of two volumes as
late as 1842, and despite this Parran says : 'Paris, Dumont, 1839-

1840, 6 volumes'. Glinel follows Parran. The Bibliothèque Nationale has volumes 1 and 2 of the Dumont, 1839, edition, and then next refers to : '2e édition, Paris, Alexandre Cadot, 1848, 6 volumes'. Several of the Belgian pirated editions publish the work with "La comtesse de Salisbury" ending abruptly at Chapter XI, and then continuing under the title of "Edouard III".

I consider that in all probability the first half of the work to be published in volume form constituted solely the 'feuilleton' issue, and that it was only after some years thay the remainder was published.

Original edition.
"Chroniques de France. La comtesse de Salisbury", par Alexandre Dumas. Paris. Dumont, libraire-éditeur, palais-royal, 88, au salon littéraire. 1839. 8vo., 2 volumes.

Volume 1 : 16 pages of publisher's announcements including books in print and those to be published by Dumont, half-title with verso again listing Dumas' works published or to be published, title, verso blank, pp. (1)-21 'Introduction', 22-333.

Volume 2 : half title with verso once more listing Dumas' works published or to be published, title, verso blank, (3)-340. Yellow wrappers repeating title-pages. Paris. - imprimerie de Ve Dondey-Dupré, Rue Saint-Louis, N° 46, au Marais.

(It may be remarked here that among the publisher's announcements described above is mentioned "Godefroi de Marcour" par A. Dumas, and which is announced on the verso of the half-title as "Godefroy de Harcourt", and announced again on the back wrapper of volume 2 as 'sous presse' - "Godefroy de Marcourt". Curiously, on the back wrapper of the Bruxelles, Société belge de librairie Hauman et Cie., edition of Dumas' "Les demoiselles de Saint-Cyr", 1844 on the title-page, 1843 on the wrappers, is given among 'Ouvrages du même auteur - "Godefroid de Harcourt", 2 vols.)

"La comtesse de Salisbury", par Alexandre Dumas. (Vignette) Bruxelles, Société belge de librairie, etc., Hauman et compe., 1839, 24mo., 2 volumes, pp. xi, 177 and 193; the chapters run continuously : I-XXI.

"Chroniques de France. La comtesse de Salisbury". Par Alexandre Dumas. 4 volumes : Vols. 1 and 2, Bruxelles, Meline, Cans et compagnie, 1839, and Vols. 3 and 4, Bruxelles, Livourne, Meline, Cans et Cie.; Leipzig, J.P. Meline, 1849, 18mo., pp. xix, 266, (1)-283, 228 and 228.

"La comtesse de Salisbury" par Alexandre Dumas. (Monogram) Bruxelles, Alphonse Lebègue, imprimeur-éditeur, Rue Jardin d'Idalie, 1. Près la rue Notre-Dame-aux-Neiges 60. 1848. 2 volumes, 18mo., pp. (5)-136 and (5)-152. Muséum littéraire. Buff wrappers.

"Edouard III" Suite de "La comtesse de Salisbury" par Alexandre Dumas. Bruxelles, Livourne, Meline, Cans et Cie.; Leipzig, J.P. Meline, 1849, 18mo., 2 volumes, pp. 236 and 228.

"Chroniques de France. La comtesse de Salisbury". Par Alexandre Dumas. Bruxelles et Leipzig, Meline, Cans et compagnie, 1839, 18mo., 2 volumes, pp. xix, 266 and (1)-283. Yellow wrappers.

"Edouard III" Suite de "La comtesse de Salisbury" par Alexandre

Dumas. Bruxelles, Livourne, Meline, Cans et Cie., 1849, 18mo., 2 volumes, pp. 236 and 228. Yellow wrappers.

"Chroniques de France. La comtesse de Salisbury". Par Alexandre Dumas. 18mo., 4 volumes : Volumes 1 and 2, Bruxelles et Leipzig, Meline, Cans et compagnie, 1839, pp. 266 and 228; Volumes 3 and 4, Bruxelles, Livourne, Meline, Cans et Cie.; Leipzig, J.P. Meline, 1849, pp. 236 and 283. The variant pagination should be noted.

"La comtesse de Salisbury" par Alexandre Dumas. Deuxième édition. Paris, Alexandre Cadot, éditeur, 1848, 8vo., 6 volumes, pp. (1)-30, 'Introduction', (31)-312, 327, 352, 315 verso blank and 4 pages of publisher's advertisements, 320, and 317 verso blank and 1 page of publisher's advertisements. Yellow wrappers. Impr. de E. Dépée, à Sceaux.

"La comtesse de Salisbury" par Alexandre Dumas. (Vignette) Bruxelles et Leipzig, Ch. Muquardt, 1848, 18mo., 2 volumes, pp. 136 and 152.

"Edouard III". Suite de "La comtesse de Salisbury". Par Alexandre Dumas. (Vignette) Bruxelles et Leipzig, Ch. Muquardt, 1848, 18mo., 2 volumes, pp. 139 and 135.

"Edouard III", par Alexandre Dumas. Bruxelles, Alp. Lebègue; Et chez tous les libraires correspondants du Muséum Littéraire, 1848, 18mo., 2 volumes, pp. 139 and 135.

"Edouard III" Suite de "La comtesse de Salisbury" par Alexandre Dumas. Bruxelles, Livourne, Meline, Cans et Cie.; Leipzig, J.P. Meline, 1849, 18mo., 2 volumes, pp. 236 and 228.

Ibid   La Haye, chez les héritiers Doorman, 1849, same format and pagination as the preceding edition.

"La comtesse de Salisbury", par Alexandre Dumas. Paris, Michel Lévy frères, 1856, 12mo., 2 volumes, pp. 290 and 277. Reprinted, Michel Lévy frères, 1861, and Calmann-Lévy, 1878, 1879, 1886 and 1890, same format and pagination.

Ibid   Paris, Walder, n.d. (1860), 4to., pp. 273-406 in double columns. Caption title. Romans illustrés.

Ibid   Paris, Calmann-Lévy, n.d. (c 1890), 4to. Caption title. Woodcut at head of title. Alexandre Dumas oeuvres illustrées.

"MONSEIGNEUR GASTON PHOEBUS ... ..."   1839

     This is one of Dumas' series of "Chronique-romans" and the period is that of the Hundred Years' War in the lull between 1385 and 1391.

     It first appeared as a serial in "Le Siècle".

Original edition.
"Acte" ("Monseigneur Gaston Phoebus, chronique dans laquelle est racontée l'histoire du démon familier du sire de Corasse".) par Alexandre Dumas. Paris, Libraire de Dumont, palais-royal, 88, au salon littéraire. 1839. 8vo., 2 volumes, of which "Monseigneur Gaston Phoebus ... ... " occupies pp. (125)-302 of Volume 2. Yellow wrappers. Corbeil. Imprimerie de Crété.

"Acté", par Alexandre Dumas. (Vignette) Bruxelles, J. Jamar, 1839,

18mo., 2 volumes. "Monseigneur Gaston Phoebus, ...", Par Alexandre Dumas occupies pp. (87)-171 of Volume 2.

Oeuvres de Alex. Dumas. Tome troisième. (Vignette) Bruxelles, Meline, Cans et compagnie, 1839, large 8vo. "Monseigneur Gaston Phoebus, ...", frontispiece, pp. (363)-388 in double columns.

"Acté" par Alexandre Dumas. Montmirail - Imp. de Brodart, n.d. (1847), 8vo., 2 volumes. "Acté" ends on page 123, verso blank, of Volume 2 and is followed by"Monseigneur Gaston Phoebus ... ...", pp. (125)-302.

"Salvator", - suite et fin des "Mohicans de Paris", par Alexandre Dumas. Paris, Michel Lévy frères, 1862-1863, 12mo., 5 volumes. "Salvator" ends on page 196 of volume 5 (1863) and is followed bu "Monseigneur Gaston Phoebus, ...", pp. (197)-255. Reprinted many times by both Michel Lévy frères and Calmann-Lévy in the same format and pagination.

"BATHILDE"   1839
        This play, which is signed by Auguste Maquet alone, was first intended to be entitled "Un soir de carnaval". Maquet could not get it accepted and approached Gérard de Nerval for him to make emendations; de Nerval in turn went to Lockroy who, after some hesitation, refused to help. Dumas was at the time working on "L'Alchimiste", but he was induced by de Nerval to assist in rewriting it. In fact, according to a letter from de Nerval to Maquet, Dumas rewrote the whole play and it was arranged that he should be introduced to Maquet. The play served as the début of Ida Ferrier who, on the 5th February, 1840, married Dumas.

Original edition.
"Bathilde", drame en trois actes, par M. Auguste Maquet. Magasin théatral, choix de pièces nouvelles, jouées sur tous les théatres de Paris. Théatre de la Renaissance. Paris, Marchant; Bruxelles, à la librairie Belge-Française, n.d. (1839), 8vo., pp. 26 in double columns. Caption title. Blue wrappers.
(The Royal Library in The Hague gives the date of publication as 1839, the year the play was 'représenté, pour la première fois, a Paris, sur le théatre de la Renaissance (Salle Ventadour), le 14 janvier 1839', and states categorically that the authors were Auguste Maquet, A. Dumas and Cordellier-Delanoue.)

"Bathilde", drame en trois actes, Par M. Auguste Maquet, représenté, pour la première fois, a Paris, sur le théatre de la Renaissance (Salle Ventadour), le 14 janvier 1839. Paris, Marchant, 1843, 8vo., pp. 26 in double columns. Caption title. Steel engraving at head of title, Acte III, scène v. Magasin Théatral. Choix de pièces nouvelles jouées sur tous les théatres de Paris. Bibliothèque de Ville et de Campagne.

"MADEMOISELLE DE BELLE-ISLE"   1839
        This is the most famous of Dumas'comedies; it was not written in collaboration despite Quérard in his "Supercheries littéraires devoilées" suggesting an anonymous writer, and de Mirecourt in his various

pamphlets naming Comte Walewski.

The play has a curious history. One, Lhérie, had written a vaudeville which no theatre manager would accept, and he offered Dumas the general outline of the plot. Dumas agreed to pay him 300 francs against the receipts of the first night's performance of his, Dumas', play whenever it should be written and staged. Lhérie accepted, but after five years grew tired of waiting and offered Dumas' 'note' to Charlieu the publisher for its face value. Charlieu accepted and spoke of the matter to Dumas who promptly changed the 300 to 3,000 francs.

During that long wait of five years Dumas had at last found the opening to the play that he wanted, the incident of the sequin. He mentioned the play to the Comédie Française and a reading was suggested then and there - but the comedy was not yet on paper. However, he stood before the theatre committee and related the whole of it, taking several hours. It was accepted with acclamation. It was written almost immediately, and Dumas used the bundle of quills given to him by the duc d'Orléans on the day following that prince's marriage in May, 1837.

The play was an enormous success, with Mademoiselle Mars in the title-rôle.

Original edition.
"Mademoiselle de Belle-Isle", drame en cinq actes, en prose, par Alexandre Dumas, représenté, pour la première fois, sur le Théatre-Français, le 2 avril 1839. Paris, Dumont, 1839, 8vo., pp. 202 and 2 pages 'Post-face note sur les artistes', signed by Dumas; the play was dedicated 'A Mademoiselle Mars - Hommage d'admiration profonde et de sincère reconnaissance'. Yellow wrappers.
(Quérard, Parran, and Glinel all give a wrong pagination of 208.)

"Mademoiselle de Belle-Isle". Drame par Alexandre Dumas. Représenté pour la première fois, sur le Théatre Français, le 2 avril 1839. (Vignette) Bruxelles, Meline, Cans et compagnie, 1839, 16mo., pp. dedicatory page to Mademoiselle Mars (unnumbered), second half-title with 'Personnages' on verso, (9)-168, and post-scriptum signed : Alex. Dumas, (169)-171. Yellow wrappers.

Ibid   (Vignette) Bruxelles et Leipzig, Meline, Cans et compagnie, 1839, same format and pagination as the preceding edition.

Ibid   (Vignette) Bruxelles, Meline, Cans et compagnie, 1839, 24mo., pp. 'Préface' (1)-9, 10-171, (1).

"Mademoiselle de Belle-Isle", drame en cinq actes en prose. Par Alexandre Dumas. Bruxelles, J.-A. Lelong, 1839, 18mo., pp. 123.

"Mademoiselle de Belle-Isle". Drame par Alexandre Dumas. Publié par J. Louis. Leipsic. En commission chez Charles Drobisch, Libraire, 1839, 24mo., pp. 154. Blue wrappers : Théâtre français moderne ou Choix de pièces de Théâtre nouvelles. Série V Livraison 4.

Oeuvres de Alex. Dumas. Tome troisième. (Vignette) Bruxelles, Meline, Cans et compagnie, 1839, large 8vo. "Mademoiselle de Belle-Isle", pp. 'Personnages' on verso of title, (569)-610, Dumas' post-scriptum (unnumbered), in double columns.

"Mademoiselle de Belle-Isle". Bruxelles, Mme. Laurent, 1839, 32mo., pp. 138 and 2 pages Dumas' post-scriptum. Buff wrappers : Théatre de Alex. Dumas.

"Mademoiselle de Belle-Isle", drame en cinq actes en prose, par Alexandre Dumas, représenté pour la première fois, a Paris, sur le Théatre-français, le 2 avril 1839. Caption title. Woodcut at head of title, Acte V, scène iii. Paris, Marchant, 1839, 8vo., pp. 38 in double columns. Le Magasin théatral. Volume XXIV.

Ibid   Yellow wrappers. Magasin théatral, choix de pièces nouvelles, jouées sur tous les théatres de Paris. (Vignette) Paris, Marchant; Bruxelles, A la librairie belge-française, 1839, same format and pagination as the preceding edition.

Répertoire du Théâtre français a Berlin. No. 204. "Mademoiselle de Belle-Isle". Drame en cinq actes, en prose par Alexandre Dumas ... . Berlin, chez Ad. Mt. Schlesinger, Libraire et Editeur de Musique, 1839, 8vo., pp. 69.

"Mademoiselle de Belle-Isle" comédie en cinq actes et en prose, par Alexandre Dumas. Bruxelles, Société belge de librairie Hauman et Ce., 1842, 16mo., pp. (i)-iv 'Préface', 143.

Oeuvres de Alex. Dumas Tome deuxième. (Vignette) Bruxelles, Société belge de librairie Hauman et Cᵉ. 1843. Large 8vo. "Mademoiselle de Belle-Isle" comédie en cinq actes, pp. verso of title-page 'personnages' (unnumbered), (119)-159, followed by 'poste-face' signed : Alexandre Dumas, all in double columns.

"Mademoiselle de Belle-Isle", drame en cinq actes, en prose, par Alexandre Dumas, représénte pour la première fois, a Paris, sur le Théatre-Français, le 2 avril 1839. Caption title. Woodcut at head of title, Acte V, scène iii. Paris, Marchant, 1843, 8vo., pp. 38 in double columns. Magasin théatral. Choix de pièces nouvelles jouées sur tous les théatres de Paris. Bibliothèque de Ville et de Campagne.

Ibid   Paris, Imprimerie de Mᵐᵉ Vᵉ Dondey-Dupré, n.d. (c 184), same format and pagination as the preceding edition.

Théatre français publié par G. Schutz. Sixième série. 1 livraison. "Mademoiselle de Belle-Isle". Par Alexandre Dumas. Bielefeld, Velhagen & Klasing, 1845, 24mo., pp. 109. Reprinted, 1846, same format and pagination.

"Mlle. de Belle-Isle" drame en cinq actes par Alex. Dumas. Paris, Michel Lévy frères, 1851, 12mo., pp. 150. (In this edition the dedication is omitted and a different list of the performers is given.)

"Mademoiselle de Belle-Isle", Comédie en cinq actes et en prose, par Alexandre Dumas. Bruxelles, Livourne, Meline, Cans et compagnie; Leipzig, J.P. Meline, 1853, 18mo., pp. 143. Yellow wrappers.

Théatre français publié par G. Schutz. Sixième série. 1 livraison. "Mademoiselle de Bellf-Isle", drame en cinq actes, en prose, par Alexandre Dumas. Bielefeld, Velhagen & Klasing, 1854, 16mo., pp. 99, (1).

Ibid   Deuxième édition. 1865, same format and pagination as the preceding.

"Mademoiselle de Belle-Isle", drame en cinq actes, en prose, par

Alexandre Dumas, représenté pour la première fois, a Paris, sur le théatre français, le 2 avril 1839. 'Personnages' 'Acteurs' on title-page. Caption title. Woodcut at head of title, Acte V, scène iii. 8vo., pp. (1)-38 in double columns. Yellow wrappers : "Mademoiselle de Belle-Isle" drame en cinq actes, en prose par M. Alexandre Dumas représenté pour la 1er fois, a Paris, sur le theatre-français le 2 avril 1839. Paris N. Tresse, Editeur Successeur de J.-N. Barba palais-royal, galerie de Chartres, Nos 10 et 1 (sic) derrière le Théatre-Français. 1871. Paris. Typ. Alder, rue Bonaparte, 44.

Mademoiselle de Belle-Isle" drame en cinq actes, en prose Théâtre-Français. - 12 (sic) avril 1839. "Dédicace" and "Distribution" on title-page, pp. (2)-96; pp. (96)-98 "Post-scriptum". Théatre complet de Alex. Dumas Tome VII Paris Calmann Lévy, éditeur, ancienne maison Michel Lévy frères, 1874. 12mo. "Théatre complet" in 25 volumes.

"Mademoiselle de Belle-Isle". (There is no title-page to this edition held by the Wesleyan Library, Connecticut.) Half-title, no name of printer on verso, 8vo., (c 18), pp. 1 preliminary leaf, (375)-616, (1), in double columns; plate.

"Mademoiselle de Belle-Isle". Drame en cinq actes par Alexandre Dumas. Avec notes ... ... par A.W. Kastan. Berlin, Friedberg & Mode, n.d. (c 189), 24mo., pp. 93; notes, etc., pp. 94-101. Théatre Français. No. 77.
There were two subsequent reprints, same format and pagination, the third of which was published in 1900.

"L'ALCHIMISTE"   1839

      This play was mainly written in 1838 when Dumas was travelling along the Rhine with Gérard de Nerval and Ida Ferrier; it may well be that de Nerval gave some slight assistance in its construction. It consists of 1.857 alexandrines and a lyric of 36 lines.

      The plot apparently originated in Grazzini's novella "The story of Fazio" from which Milman took his drama entitled, simply, "Fazio". It is obvious that Dumas knew both of these works for he used the material which each included. However, he altered the plot for the better, introduced the important new character Lelio and changed the original tragic ending to a comparatively happy one. Lemaître has stated that Dumas offered Anténor Joly, the manager of the Renaissance Theatre, the choice of this play or "Mademoiselle de Belle-Isle". He chose "L'Alchimiste", which he must later have greatly regretted doing

      The play was dedicated "A Madam I.F.", signed : Alexandre Dumas in a poem of three verses each of 5 lines.*

Original edition.
"L'Alchimiste" drame en cinq actes, en vers, par Alexandre Dumas, représenté pour la première fois, sur le théatre de la Renaissance, le mercredi 10 avril 1839. Paris, Dumont, 1839, 8vo., unnumbered page dedicatory verses, pp. 176. Yellow wrappers.
(The Houghton Library, Harvard University, holds a copy of this edition on rose-coloured paper; it is obviously a presentation copy but the recipient's name has become indecipherable.)

"L'Alchimiste". Drame par Alexandre Dumas. Représenté pour la première fois, sur le théatre de la Renaissance, le mercredi 10 avril 1839.
(Vignette) Bruxelles. Meline, Cans et compagnie, 1839, 16mo., pp.
(v)-vi 'A Madame I.F.', (7)-133. Yellow wrappers repeating title-
page.

Ibid   (Vignette) Bruxelles et Leipzig, Meline, Cans et
compagnie, 1839, same format and pagination as the preceding edition.

"L'Alchimiste", drame en cinq actes, en vers. Par Alexandre Dumas.
Bruxelles, J.-P. Meline, 1839, 24mo., pp. 133.

Oeuvres de Alex. Dumas. Tome troisième. (Vignette) Bruxelles, Meline,
Cans et compagnie, 1839, large 8vo. "L'Alchimiste", unnumbered page
dedicatory verses, 'Personnages' on verso, pp. (617)-647 in double
columns.

Théatre de Alex. Dumas. "L'Alchimiste". (Vignette) Bruxelles, Mme.
Laurent, 1839, 32mo., pp. 116, including the dedicatory verses. Buff
wrappers repeating the title-page.

"L'Alchimiste", drame en cinq actes, en vers, par Alexandre Dumas,
représenté, pour la première fois, à Paris, sur le théatre de la Renaissance, le 10 avril 1839. Paris, Marchant, 1839, 8vo., pp. 31 in
double columns. Caption title. Woodcut at head of title, Acte V,
scène vi. Le Magasin théatral.

Ibid   Same caption title and woodcut. Yellow wrappers
: Magasin théatral, choix de pièces nouvelles, jouées sur tous les
théatres de Paris. Théatre de la Renaissance. "L'Alchimiste", Drame
en cinq actes. (Vignette) Paris, Marchant; Bruxelles, A la librairie
Belge-Française, 1839, same format and pagination as the preceding.

Ibid   Same caption title and woodcut. Paris, Marchant,
1843, 8vo., pp. 31 in double columns. Magasin théatral. Choix de
pièces nouvelles jouées sur tous les théatres de Paris. Bibliothèque
de Ville et de Campagne.

Oeuvres de Alex. Dumas Tome deuxième. (Vignette) Bruxelles, Société
belge de librairie Hauman et Ce. 1843. Large 8vo. "L'Alchimiste".
Unnumbered page 'A madam J. (sic) F ***' signed : Alexandre Dumas,
verso 'personnages', pp. (167)-199, all in double columns.

"L'Alchimiste". Drame. Par Alexandre Dumas, Bruxelles, Livourne,
Meline, Cans et compagnie; Leipzig, J.P. Meline, 1853, 16mo., pp. 118.
Yellow wrappers.

"L'Alchimiste" drame en cinq actes, en vers Renaissance. - 10
avril 1839. 'A madame Ida Ferrier' signed : Alex. Dumas on title-
page, page 208 "Distribution", pp. 208-288. Théatre complet de Alex.
Dumas Tome VI Paris Calmann Lévy, éditeur, ancienne maison Michel
Lévy frères, 1874. 12mo. "Théatre complet" in 25 volumes.

----

* These dedicatory verses were reprinted, but with a variation in the
final line. This originally read :
" 'Faites vite pour moi ce drame' - Le voila!", and was changed
to read :
" 'Faites vite pour moi quelques vers! - Les voila!" Moreover, the
title of the poem was changed, as were the dedications.

Its first appearance was
"Obéissance" in 'La Sylphide', 1841, with the dedication to Madame E.
de H. (La comtesse de Hanska, née Eveline Rzewuske.)

"Obéissance" in 'Le Keepsake Français' published by "La Chronique",
1842, with the dedication to Madame D. de H. In both instances the
poem is signed : Alex. Dumas.

The poem may be found in Glinel's "Alexandre Dumas et son oeuvre", pp.
364-365.

"LEO BURCKART"   1839

     This play was signed by Gérard de Nerval but Dumas is generally
acknowledged to have had a hand in its writing during their travels
along the Rhine in 1838. The play has a German setting, and Gautier
in his "L'Art dramatique en France depuis vingt-cinq ans", published
in 1858, praised it.

Original edition.
"Léo Burckart", drame en cinq actes, par Monsieur Gérard, accompagné
de mémoires et documents inédits sur les sociétés secrètes d'Allemagne.
Paris, Barba, Desessart, Brockhaus et Havenarius, 1839, 8vo., pp. 340.
(Dumas had nothing to do with the writing of the accompanying memoirs
and documents.)

"Léo Burckhart" Drame en cinq actes par Alexandre Dumas et Gérard
de Nerval Bruxelles. Société belge de librairie. Hauman et Cie.,
1840, 18mo.
(Following the title-page is : "Léo Burckhart accompagné de Mémoires
et Documents inédits sur les Sociétes secrètes d'Allemagne" par M.
Gérard.)

Footnote : "Lorely souvenirs d'Allemagne" par Gérard de Nerval.
'A Jules Janin'. 'Sensations d'un voyageur enthousiaste'. 'Souvenirs
de Thuringe'. 'Scènes de la vie allemande. Léo Burckhart'. - 'Rhin
et Flandre'. Paris D. Giraud et J. Dagneau, libraires-éditeurs 7,
rue Vivienne, au premier, 7 Maison du Coq d'or. 1852. 16mo.
'Scènes de la vie allemande. Léo Burckhart', pp. 103-270.

"LE CAPITAINE PAMPHILE"   1839

     Dumas wrote the first few chapters of this children's book in
1834 when they first appeared as "Jacques 1er et Jacques II" in the
second volume published that year of "Le journal des enfants", the
story being continued in the third and sixth volumes and completed in
the seventh volume. In 1835 the same chapters now entitled "Jacques
1er et Jacques II : fragments historiques" were reprinted in Dumas'
"Souvenirs d'Antony". Dumas, in due course, completed the work with
the adventures of the piratical Captain Pamphile which, according to
both Quérard and Parran, both wrongly, was first published in 1840.
For general reading in France the work as first issued was entirely
superseded by the issue of the edition illustrated by Bertall.

     It is interesting to note that the original stories of 1834 are
written in exactly the same style as Dumas' famous "Histoire de mes
bêtes" which was published some twenty-five years later.

Original edition.
"La capitaine Pamphile", par Alexandre Dumas. Paris, Dumont, 1839,
8vo., 2 volumes, pp. 307 and 296. The second volume includes the
letter to Dumas from Alphonse Karr.

"Le capitaine Pamphile", par Alexandre Dumas. Bruxelles, J. Jamar,
1839, 24mo., 2 volumes, pp. 4 preliminary leaves, ii, (3)-182, and
4 preliminary leaves, 141, (1). "Le capitaine Pamphile" ends on page
7 of Volume 2, the remainder of the volume being filled by "Don Martinn de Freytas".

"Le capitaine Pamphile". Par Alexandre Dumas. (Vignette) Bruxelles,
Meline, Cans et compagnie, 1839, 16mo., pp. (v)-vi 'Note des éditeurs',
(7)-290, (291)-292 'Note des éditeurs', (293)-306 'Pièces justificatives' which include the letter from Alphonse Karr. Green wrappers
repeating the title-page, but with a different vignette.

"Le capitaine Pamphile" par Alexandre Dumas. (Vignette) Bruxelles
et Leipzig, Meline, Cans et compagnie, 1839, 18mo., pp. vi, (7)-360.

"Le capitaine Pamphile", par Alexandre Dumas. Bruxelles, Société
typographique belge, 1839, same format and pagination as the Bruxelles,
J. Jamar, edition referred to above.

Oeuvres de Alex. Dumas. Tome quatrième. (Vignette) Bruxelles, Meline, Cans et compagnie, 1840, large 8vo. "Le capitaine Pamphile",
pp. 'Note des éditeurs' (unnumbered), frontispiece, (37)-131, (132)-
135 'Pièces justificatives' which include Alphonse Karr's letter, in
double columns.

"Le capitaine Pamphile" par Alexandre Dumas. Bruxelles, Société
belge de librairie, Hauman et cie., 1840, 16mo., 2 volumes, pp. 265,
blank, 3 pages table of contents, and 244, 3 pages table of contents.
Brown wrappers.

Ibid   Bruxelles, Société belge de librairie Hauman et
ce., 1840, same format and pagination as the preceding edition.
Bibliothèque des châteaux et des campagnes. 6ᵉ série.

Oeuvres de Alex. Dumas. Tome deuxième. (Vignette) Bruxelles, Société
belge de librairie Hauman et Cᵉ. 1843. Large 8vo. "Le capitaine
Pamphile", pp. (263)-345, 345-348 'Pièces justificatives' which include
the letter from Alphonse Karr.

"Le capitaine Pamphile", par Alexandre Dumas. Nouvelle édition.
Paris, Michel Lévy frères, 1862, 12mo., pp. ii, (3)-297, blank, (299)-
300 table of contents. "Le capitaine Pamphile" ends on page 273, the
rest of the volume being filled by "Le fléau de Naples" by Dumas.
Frequently reprinted, same format and pagination, by Michel Lévy
frères and Calmann-Lévy.

"Nouvelles pittoresques". Par Souvestre, Al. Dumas, J. Arago, ...
... . Edition stéréotype. Munster, Imprimerie et librairie de
Theissing, n.d. (c 1862), 18mo., pp. xi, 262. "Partie et revanche
ou Péripéties du capitaine Pamphile" par Al. Dumas occupies pp. (64)-
94.

"Le capitaine Pamphile" par Alexandre Dumas édition illustrée de
103 vignettes dont 26 hors texte par Bertall Paris Calmann Lévy,
éditeur ancienne maison Michel Lévy frères rue Auber, 3, et boulevard des Italiens, 15 a la librairie nouvelle Droits de traduction

et de reproduction réservés N.d. (1878), large 8vo., pp. half-title with engraved frontispiece of Pamphile on verso, title, full-page illustration 'J'aperçus un Anglais qui retournait une tortue en tous sens', (1)-349, verso blank, (350)-364 'Pièces justificatives', including letter from Alphonse Karr, (365)-366 table of contents. Scarlet boards illustrated in black and gold; gilt-lettered spine; grey end-papers. Corbeil - Typ. et stér. de CRETE. This is the first illustrated edition. There were published in the same year issues on special paper limited to 25 copies at 20 francs, and 10 at 30 francs.

"MAITRE ADAM LE CALABRAIS"   1839

In writing of Maître Adam, the humble Calabrian painter of frescoes, Dumas drew a picture of a man after his own heart.

The period of the story lies between 1798 and 1835. Perhaps the only criticism that can be made of this tale of artists, bandits, priests and executioners is that Maître Adam's adventure with the robbers is so reminiscent of Grimm's "Travelling Musicians" as to possibly suggest that he borrowed it from the German; but when it is realised that different versions of the same story are found in different countries it may well be that Chapter IX 'Souls in purgatory' was a version current in Calabria and there was, therefore, no anachronism in relating it.

The work first ran as a serial in "Le Siècle", and it is worth noting that what became the first chapter in the Dumont edition appeared as the final one in the Meline, Cans pirated edition.

Original edition.
"Maître Adam le Calabrais", par Alexandre Dumas. Paris, Auguste Ozanne, 1839, 18mo., pp. 150. Pink wrappers.

"Maître Adam le Calabrais". Par Alexandre Dumas. (Vignette) Bruxelles, Meline, Cans et compagnie, 1839, 24mo., pp. (7), 8-237 and additional unnumbered page table of contents.

Ibid   (Vignette) Bruxelles et Leipzig, Meline, Cans et compagnie, 1839, same format and pagination as the preceding edition. Buff wrappers.

"Maître Adam le Calabrais", par Alexandre Dumas. Bruxelles, J. Jamar, 1839, 18mo., pp. 150. Buff wrappers. Muséum littéraire.

"Maître Adam le Calabrais" par Alexandre Dumas. (Vignette) Bruxelles Société belge de librairie, Hauman et Compie., 1839, 18mo., pp. 270. Pink wrappers.

"Maître Adam le Calabrais", par Alexandre Dumas. Paris, Dumont, 1840, 8vo., pp. 347 and additional unnumbered page table of contents. Yellow wrappers.

Oeuvres de Alex. Dumas. Tome quatrième. (Vignette) Bruxelles, Meline, Cans et compagnie, 1840, large 8vo. "Maître Adam le Calabrais", pp. frontispiece, (7)-51 in double columns.

"Maître Adam le Calabrais". Par Alexandre Dumas. In : 'Le livre des feuilletons Receuil de nouvelles, contes, épisodes, extraits de la presse contemporaine'. Nancy, Imprimerie Hinzelin, n.d. (1846), 8vo., pp. (37)-85 in double columns.

"Maître Adam le Calabrais", par Alexandre Dumas. New-York : Courrier des Etats-Unis, 1853, 8vo., pp. 45 in double columns.

"Maitre Adam le Calabrais", (no title-page), yellow wrappers : Paris, Dufour, Mulat et Boulanger, éditeurs ... 1857, large 8vo., pp. (1)-56 in double columns; woodcut at head of first page and 2 full-page woodcut illustrations. It is followed by "Les étoiles commis voyageurs", pp. (57)-64 in double columns. Alexandre Dumas illustré.

"Maître Adam, le Calabrais". "Les étoiles commis-voyageurs". Publié par Dufour, Mulat et Boulanger. Par Alexandre Dumas. Paris : Bureau de l'Echo des feuilletons, 1857, 4to., pp. (1)-64 in double columns; 2 plates. "Maître Adam, le Calabrais" occupies pp. (1)-56. Alexandre Dumas illustré.

"La colombe". "Maître Adam le Calabrais". Par Alexandre Dumas. Paris, Michel Lévy frères, 1863, 12mo., pp. 304 and unnumbered page table of contents. "Maître Adam ... " occupies pp. (137)-304. Reprinted, 'nouvelle édition', 1871, same format and pagination. Oeuvres complètes d'Alexandre Dumas.

Romans historiques, aventures, anecdotes, mystères par Alexandre Dumas. "Maître Adam le Calabrais". Paris, Boulanger et Legrand ... , 1864, large 8vo., pp. (1)-56 in double columns; illustrated. Lagny, Imprimerie de A. Varigault.

"VIE ET AVENTURES DE JOHN DAVYS"   1839

     This tale of travel and adventure has some resemblance to Captain Marryat's style of writing. John Davys and Dumas were on friendly terms, and in 1857 Davys translated Laurence Sterne's "A Sentimental Journey" for publication in the journal "Le Monte-Cristo" journal hebdomadaire de romans, d'histoire, de voyages et de poésie publié et rédigé par Alexandre Dumas, seul.

     The work must, presumably, have been first published as a serial since the pirated Belgian editions appeared before the first edition in volume form was published in France.

Original edition.
"Vie et aventures de John Davys". Par Alex. Dumas. Bruxelles, Société typographique belge, Adolph Wahlen et Cie., 1839, 18mo., ... volumes. The pagination of volume 1 is (1)-342, and is the only existing one in the Library of Bratislava University; it is not known whether a further volume was published. Green wrappers.

"Vie et aventures de John Davys". Par Alexandre Dumas. (Vignette) Bruxelles, Meline, Cans et compagnie, 1840, 18mo., 2 volumes, pp. 273 and 375; "Journal de Fatinitza" occupies pp. 351-375 of Volume 2. There are no tables of contents.

Ibid   (Vignette) Bruxelles et Leipzig, Meline, Cans et compagnie, 1840, same format and pagination as the preceding edition. (It is known that these two Meline, Cans editions were published three months before the Paris, Dumont, edition.)

"Vie et aventures de John Davys" par Alexandre Dumas. Bruxelles, Société belge de librairie Hauman et Ce., 1840, 18mo., 2 volumes, pp. 231 and 386; Volume 1 comprises Chapters I-XIV and Volume 2

Chapters XV-XXXIII, "Journal de Fatinitza" begins on page 361 (part
of Chapter XXXIII) and ends on page 386. There are no tables of contents.

"Aventures de John Davys", par Alexandre Dumas. Paris, Librairie
de Dumont, 1840, 8vo., 4 volumes, pp. 322, 321, 336 and 300. There
are no tables of contents, and there are 8 pages of publishers' advertisements at the end of Volume 4.

Oeuvres de Alex. Dumas. Tome quatrième. (Vignette) Bruxelles,
Meline, Cans et compagnie, 1840, large 8vo. "Vie et aventures de John
Davys", pp. frontispiece, (139)-313 in double columns.

Alexandre Dumas illustré. "Les aventures de John Davys". Illustré
de 9 gravures et divisé en 16 livraisons à 25 cent. Complet : 4 frs.
(Woodcut) Paris, Bureaux de l'écho des feuilletons, 1857, 4to., pp.
254, paged continuously. Caption title for each separate livraison.

"Aventures de John Davys", par Alexandre Dumas. Paris, Michel Lévy
frères, 1861, 12mo., 2 volumes, pp. 322 and 314. There are no tables
of contents.
Quite frequently reprinted by both Michel Lévy fréres and Calmann-Lévy.

Romans historiques, aventures, anecdotes, mystères par Alexandre Dumas.
"Les aventures de John Davys". Paris, Boulanger et Legrand ... , 1864,
large 8vo., pp. (1)-256; illustrated. There is no table of contents.
Lagny, Imprimerie de A. Varigault.

"CRIMES CELEBRES"   1839-1840

In this long collection of articles of historical criminal signi-
ficance, where in a number of cases the principal character or characters was or were victims and not criminals, Dumas had the assistance
of several friends for the final collection of eight volumes. The
work is a bibliographer's nightmare, as may be seen from what follows.

It may well be that the research for some of the articles helped
Dumas with some of his later writings. For example, "Urbain Grandier"
for the play of that name, "L'homme au masque de fer" for "Le vicomte
de Bragelonne", and, conceivably, "Ali Pacha" for "Le comte de Monte-
Cristo".

Original collected edition.
"Crimes célèbres" par Alexandre Dumas (Volumes 1 - part, 6), et par
MM. Alex. Dumas, Arnould, Fournier, Fiorentino et Mallefille (Volumes
part, 6-8). Paris, Administration de librairie, rue Louis-le-Grand,
18; 1839-1840, large 8vo.
Pagination : Volume 1, 1839; "Les Cenci, 1598" (3)-52, 'Notes' (53)-
              57; "La marquise de Brinvilliers. 1676" (61)-174,
              'Notes' (175)-180; "Karl Ludwig Sand. 1819" (183)-268,
              'Notes' (269)-(271); "Marie Stuart. 1587" (275)-318;
              unnumbered page table of contents.
              Volume 2, 1839; "Marie Stuart" (3)-241, 'Notes' (243)-
              249; "La marquise de Ganges. 1667" (253)-314; unnum-
              bered page table of contents.
              Volume 3, 1839; "La marquise de Ganges" (3)-18, 'Notes'
              (19)-22; "Murat. 1815" (25)-84, 'Notes' (85)-87; "Les
              Borgia. 1492-1507" (91)-316; unnumbered page table of
              contents.

Volume 4, 1839; "Les Borgia. 1492-1507" (Seconde
partie) (3)-86, 'Notes' (87)-(89); "Urbain Grandier.
1634" (93)-228, 'Notes' (229)-232; "Vaninka. 1800-1801"
(235)-321, 'Notes' (323)-(325); unnumbered page table
of contents.
Volume 5, 1839; "Massacres du Midi. 1551-1815", Première partie, (3)-321; unnumbered page table of contents.
Volume 6, 1840; "Massacres du Midi. 1551-1815" (3)-32,
'Notes' (33)-43; "La comtesse de Saint-Géran" (47)-117;
"Jeanne de Naples. 1343-1382" (121)-275, 'Notes' (277)-
(279); "Nisida. 1825" (283)-306; unnumbered page table
of contents.
Volume 7, 1840; "Nisida. 1825" (Second partie) (3)-41
signed : Pier Angelo Fiorentino, 'Notes' (43)-(45);
"Derues" (49)-224 signed : A. Arnould, 'Notes' (225)-
231; "Martin Guerre" (235)-303 signed : N. Fournier;
"Ali Pacha" (307)-334; unnumbered page table of contents.
Volume 8, 1840; "Ali Pacha" (Seconde partie) (3)-146
signed : Mallefille; "La Constantin. 1660" (149)-241
signed : A. Arnould; "L'homme au masque de fer" (245)-
309 signed : A. Arnould, 'Notes' (311)-318; unnumbered
page table of contents.

The first six volumes each contain 4 illustrations drawn by L. Boulanger and engraved by N. Desmadryl; volume 7 has 4 illustrations drawn
by Bourdet and Vernier and engraved by A. Billy, Lafon and J. Lesueur;
volume 8 has 4 illustrations drawn by Bourdet and Vernier.

Ibid   All the volumes are dated 1840, and each has an
additional unnumbered page table of contents; frontispieces to Volumes
1 and 4, and all volumes illustrated with steel engravings.
Pagination : Volume 1; "Les Cenci. 1598" (3)-52, 'Notes' (53)-57;
"La marquise de Brinvilliers. 1676" (61)-174, 'Notes'
(175)-180; "Karl Ludwig Sand. 1819" (183)-268, 'Notes'
(269)-(271); "Marie Stuart. 1587" (275)-318.
Volume 2; "Marie Stuart" (3)-241, 'Notes' (243)-249;
"La marquise de Ganges. 1667" (253)-314.
Volume 3; "La marquise de Ganges. 1658" (sic), 'Notes'
(19)-22; "Murat". 1815" (25)-84, 'Notes' (85)-(87);
"Les Borgia" (91)-316.
Volume 4; "Les Borgia. 1492-1507" (Seconde partie)
(3)-86, 'Notes' (87)-(89); "Urbain Grandier. 1634"
(93)-228, 'Notes' (229)-232; "Vaninka. 1800-1801"
(235)-321, 'Notes' (323)-(325).
Volume 5; "Massacres du Midi. 1551-1815" (Première
partie) (3)-321.
Volume 6; "Massacres du Midi. 1815" (sic) (Seconde
partie) (3)-32, 'Notes' (33)-43; "La comtesse de Saint-
Géran" (47)-117; "Jeanne de Naples. 1343-1382" (121)-
275, 'Notes' (277)-(279); "Nisida. 1825" (283)-306.
Volumes 7 and 8, "Crimes célèbres par MM. Alex. Dumas,
Arnould, Fournier, Fiorentino et Mallefille.
Volume 7; "Nisida. 1825" (Seconde partie) (3)-41
signed : Pier-Angelo Fiorentino, 'Notes' (43)-45;
"Derues" (49)-224 signed : A. Arnould, 'Notes' (225)-
231; "Martin Guerre" (235)-303 signed : N. Fournier;

"Ali-Pacha" (307)-334.
Volume 8; "Ali-Pacha" (Seconde partie) (3)-146 signed
: Mallefille; "La Constantin. 1660" (149)-241 signed
: A. Arnould; "L'homme au masque de fer" (245)-309
signed : A. Arnould, 'Notes' (311)-318. Imprimerie
de Ve Dondey Dupré.

The 'Administration de librairie' edition was reprinted over the years 1841-1842, 1842-1843, 1846, 1850, 1851 and 1853; a number of libraries have obvious broken sets with the year of publication of each individual volume falling within the range of the above dates.
It may usefully be added here that there was published in 1842, 8vo., 6 volumes : "Nouvelles causes célèbres, faisant suite aux 'Crimes célèbres' d'Alexandre Dumas par l'avocat Moquard; Dumas had nothing to do with the writing of this work.

"Crimes célèbres" par Alexandre Dumas (Volumes 1-5); par MM. Alex. Dumas, Arnould, Fournier, Fiorentino et Mallefille (Volume 6); par MM. Arnould, Fournier, Fiorentino et Mallefille (Volumes 7 and 8). Bruxelles, Société belge de librairie. Hauman et Ce., 1841, 16mo., 8 volumes.
Pagination and contents : Volume 1, 1-344 and unnumbered page table of contents. "Les Cenci. La marquise de Brinvilliers. Karl Ludwig Sand. Marie Stuart". Volume 2, 1-351, with no table of contents. "Marie Stuart. La marquise de Ganges". Volume 3, 1-347 and unnumbered page table of contents. "La marquise de Ganges. Murat. Les Borgia". Volume 4, 1-353, blank, and unnumbered page table of contents. "Les Borgia. Urbain Grandier. Vaninka". Volume 5, (1)-374, with no table of contents. "Massacres du Midi". Volume 6, 1-318 and unnumbered page table of contents. "Massacres du Midi. La comtesse de Saint-Géran. Jeanne de Naples. Nisida". Volume 7, 1-358 and unnumbered page table of contents. "Nisida. Derues. Martin Guerre. Ali-Pacha". Volume 8, 1-349, blank, and unnumbered page table of contents. "Ali-Pacha. La Constantin. L'homme au masque de fer".

"Crimes célèbres" par Alexandre Dumas. Bruxelles et Leipzig, Meline, Cans et compagnie, 1841, 18mo., 4 volumes.
Pagination and contents : Volume 1, 1-339, "Les Borgia". Volume 2, 1-83 "La comtesse de Saint-Géran"; 85-259 "Jeanne de Naples"; 261-328 "Nisida". Volume 3, 1-130 "La marquise de Brinvilliers"; 131-188 "Les Cenci"; 189-275 "La marquise de Ganges". Volume 4, 1-150 "Urbain Grandier"; 151-245 "Karl-Ludwig Sand"; 247-340 "Vaninka".

Oeuvres de Alex. Dumas Tome deuxième. (Vignette) Bruxelles, Société belge de librairie Hauman et Ce. 1843. Large 8vo. "Crimes célèbres". Pp. (1)-22 "Nisida. (1825)"; (23)-81 "Derues" signed : A. Arnould; (83)-105 "Martin Guerre" signed : N. Fournier; (107)-116 and (465)-512 "Ali-pacha" signed : Mallefille; (513)-543 "La Constantin (1660)" signed : A. Arnould; (545)-568 "L'homme au masque de fer" signed : A. Arnould. All in double columns.

"Pauline". Par Alexandre Dumas. Bruxelles, Meline, Cans et compagnie, 1838, 16mo., pp. (5)-309, (311)-312 table of contents. "Pauline" ends on page 234, and is followed by "Murat", pp. (235)-309. Pale pink wrappers.

Oeuvres de Alex. Dumas. Tome troisième. (Vignette) Bruxelles, Meline, Cans et compagnie, 1839, large 8vo. "Murat" pp. (69)-88 in double columns.

"Jean Cavalier", par Alexandre Dumas. Bruxelles, A. Jamar, 1841, 18mo., pp. 232. This work comprises the first two-thirds of "Massacres du Midi".

"Karl Sand". "Les Cenci" par Alexandre Dumas. Bruxelles, A. Jamar, 1841, 18mo., pp. 144. "Karl Ludwig Sand. 1819", pp. 1-87, verso blank, "Les Cenci", verso blank, "Les Cenci. 1598", pp. (91)-144.

"Urbain Grandier". Par Alexandre Dumas. Bruxelles, A. Jamar, 1841, 18mo., pp. 138.

"Vaninka". "Urbain Grandier". Par Alexandre Dumas. Bruxelles, A. Jamar, 1841, 18mo., pp. 221. "Vaninka", pp. 1-83; "Urbain Grandier", pp. 87-221.

"Vaninka". "Urbain Grandier" par Alexandre Dumas. Bruxelles, A. Jamar, 1841, 24mo., pp. 224. "Vaninka", pp. (1)-83, blank, "Urbain Grandier", pp. (85)-224.

"Nisida". Par Alexandre Dumas. Bruxelles, A. Jamar, 1842, 18mo., pp. 62.

"Le Spéronare", par Alexandre Dumas. Bruxelles, A. Jamar, 1842, 4mo., 3 volumes, pp. 199, 157 and 160. "Nisida", par Alexandre Dumas, occupies pp. (101)-160 of Volume 3.

"Jean Cavalier" par Alexandre Dumas. Bruxelles, A. Jamar, 1843, large 8vo., pp. 62 in double columns.

"Les crimes célèbres" par Alexandre Dumas. Edition illustrée de vignettes sur bois. (Vignette) Paris, Librairie Charlieu frères et Huillery, Huillery successeur, n.d. (c 1850), large 8vo., pp. 304 in double columns.

"Les crimes célèbres" par Alexandre Dumas. Paris, Librairie théâtrale, n.d. (1851), 4to., pp. 304 in double columns. Contents and pagination : "La marquise de Brinvilliers. 1676", 1-20; "La comtesse de Saint-Géran", 20-31; "Karl Ludwig Sand. 1819", 31-45; "Murat", 45-54; "Les Cenci. 1598"; (End of the first part or instalment) "Marie Stuart. 1587", 65-112; (End of the second part) "Les Borgia. 1492-1507", 113-162; "La marquise de Ganges. 1667", 163-176; (End of the third part) "Massacres du Midi. 1551-1815", 177-234; "Urbain Grandier. 1634", 234-256; (End of the fourth part) "Jeanne de Naples. 1343-1382", 257-282; "Vaninka. 1800-1801", 282-296. (End of the fifth part). At the foot of page 296 : 'Fin des crimes célèbres, par Alexandre Dumas'. Then follows another instalment : "Nisida. 1825", par Pier Angelo Fiorentino, pp. 297-304. Caption titles. Illustrated with woodcuts by L. Deghouy and Bara, after drawings by A. Belin.

"Les frères Corses; Othon l'archer; "Murat". Par Alexandre Dumas. Publiés par Dufour et Mulat; illustrés par J.-A. Beaucé, Ed. Coppin et Gerard Séguin. Paris, chez Marescq, 1853, 4to., (one title-page for all three works), "Murat", pp. 23 in double columns.

"Les crimes célèbres. Les Borgia" par Alexandre Dumas. Paris, Passard, 1854, 8vo., 3 volumes, pp. 318, 329 and 16 pages of publisher's advertisements, and (151); followed by "Les Cenci", pp. (153)-293. There are no tables of contents. Yellow wrappers.

"Les crimes célèbres. Jeanne de Naples" par Alexandre Dumas. Suivi de "La Constantin" par A. Arnould. Paris, Passard, 1854, 8vo., 2 vol-

94

umes, pp. 318 and 62; followed by "La Constantin", pp. (63)-309 and
2 pages of publisher's advertisements. There are no tables of contents. Yellow wrappers.

"Murat" par Alexandre Dumas. Paris, Impr. de Walder, n.d. (1854),
large 8vo., pp. 293-304 in double columns. Caption title.

Alexandre Dumas. "Massacres du Midi. Urbain Grandier" Paris, Librairie théatrale éditeur de la société des gens de lettres, 1856,
12mo.; "Massacres du Midi", pp. 257, and "Urbain Grandier", pp. (259)-
357, and unnumbered page table of contents.

Alexandre Dumas. "Les Borgia - La marquise de Ganges - Les Cenci".
Paris, Librairie théatrale, 1856, 12mo., pp. 317, and unnumbered page
table of contents.

Alexandre Dumas. "Marie Stuart - Karl Ludwig Sand - "Murat".
Paris, Librairie théatrale, 1856, 12mo., pp. 310, and unnumbered
page table of contents.

Alexandre Dumas. "La marquise de Brinvilliers - La comtesse de
Saint-Géran - Jeanne de Naples - Vaninka". Paris, Librairie
théatrale, 1856, 12mo., pp. 315, and unnumbered page table of contents.

Alexandre Dumas. "Massacres du Midi - Urbain Grandier". Paris,
Librairie théatrale, 1856, 12mo., pp. 357, and unnumbered page table
of contents.

"Murat" par Alexandre Dumas. Paris, S. Raçon et Cie., n.d. (c 1860),
4to., pp. 24 in double columns; 2 plates. Caption title. Alexandre
Dumas. Oeuvres.

"Murat", par Alexandre Dumas. Paris, Impr. de Gaittet, n.d., (1861),
4to., pp. 24 in double columns. Caption title.

"Murat" par Alexandre Dumas. Paris, Impr. de J. Voisvenel, n.d.
(1862), 4to., pp. 293-304 in double columns. Caption title.

"I Borboni di Napoli" par Alessandro Dumas. ... Napoli, 1862-1863,
8vo., 10 volumes. Volumes 7-10 are concerned with "Murat".

"Les crimes célèbres" par Alexandre Dumas. Nouvelle édition. Paris,
Librairie internationale A. Lacroix, Verboeckoven et Cie., Même
Maison à Bruxelles, à Leipzig et à Livourne, 1865, 12mo., 4 volumes.
Volume 1 : "Les Borgia La marquise de Ganges"; Volume 2 : "Marie
Stuart Karl Ludwig Sand Murat"; Volume 3 : "Les massacres du Midi
Urbain Grandier"; Volume 4 : "La marquise de Brinvilliere La com-
tesse de Saint-Géran Jeanne de Naples Vaninka".

Alexandre Dumas. "Marie Stuart Karl Ludwig Sand Murat". Nouvelle
édition. Paris, Librairie internationale A. Lacroix, Verboeckhoven
et Cie., Même Maison à Bruxelles, à Leipzig et à Livourne, 1865,
12mo., pp. 319 and unnumbered page table of contents.

Alexandre Dumas. "La marquise de Brinvilliers. La comtesse de Saint-
Géran. Jeanne de Naples. Vaninka". Nouvelle édition. Paris, Librairie internationale A. Lacroix, Verboeckhoven et Cie., Même Maison
à Bruxelles, à Leipzig et à Livourne, 1865, 12mo., pp. 313 and unnumbered page table of contents. Pagination : "La marquise de Brinvilliers", (1)-86; "La comtesse de Géran", 87-137; "Jeanne de Naples.
1343-1382", 139-249; "Vaninka", 251-313.

Alexandre Dumas. "Massacres du Midi. Urbain Grandier". Nouvelle édition. Paris, Librairie internationale A. Lacroix, Verboeckhoven et Cie., Même Maison à Bruxelles, à Leipzig et à Livourne, 1865, 12mo., pp. 359 and unnumbered page table of contents.

"Les crimes célèbres" Par Alexandre Dumas "Marie Stuart" : 'L'Omnibus' No. 1275 of 18 mars 1868 to No. 1294 of 23 mai 1868, 4to., in three columns; illustrated.

"Les crimes célèbres" Par Alexandre Dumas "Les Cenci" : 'L'Omnibus' No. 1295 of 27 mai 1868 to No. 1300 of 13 juin 1868, 4to., in three columns; illustrated.

"Les crimes célèbres" Par Alexandre Dumas "La comtesse de Saint-Géran" : 'L'Omnibus' No. 1301 of 17 juin 1868 to No. 1306 of 4 juillet 1868, 4to., in three columns; illustrated.

"Les crimes célèbres", par Alexandre Dumas. Paris, Impr. de E. Blot, n.d. (1871), 4to., pp. 304 in double columns; illustrated.

Ibid.   Paris, Impr. de C. Blot, n.d. (c 187), same format and pagination as the preceding.

"Les crimes célèbres La marquise de Brinvilliers La comtesse de Saint-Géran Jeanne de Naples". Par Alexandre Dumas. Paris, E. Flammarion, n.d. (c 1890), 8vo., pp. 249 and unnumbered page table of contents. Auteurs célèbres. No. 152.

"Les crimes célèbres Les massacres du Midi Urbain Grandier". Par Alexandre Dumas. Paris, E. Flammarion, n.d. (c 1890). 8vo., pp. 247 and unnumbered page table of contents. Auteurs célèbres. No. 192.

"Les crimes célèbres Les Borgia La marquise de Ganges Les Cenci". Par Alexandre Dumas. Paris, E. Flammarion, n.d. (c 1890), 8vo., pp. 316 and unnumbered page table of contents. Auteurs célèbres. No. 221.

"Les crimes célèbres Marie Stuart Karl-Ludwig-Sand Murat". Par Alexandre Dumas. Paris, E. Flammarion, n.d. (c 1890), 8vo., pp. 315 and unnumbered page table of contents. Auteurs célèbres. No. 231.

Alexandre Dumas. "Les Borgia La marquise de Ganges Les Cenci". Nouvelle edition. Paris, Librairie Marpon et Flammarion, n.d. (c 1893), 8vo., pp. 316 and unnumbered page table of contents. "Les Borgia", pp. (1)-219; "La marquise de Ganges", pp. (221)-278; "Les Cenci", pp. (279)-316. Auteurs célèbres. No. 221.

"Les crimes célèbres. La marquise de Brinvilliers. La comtesse de Saint-Géran. Jeanne de Naples. Vaninka". Par Alexandre Dumas. Paris, Librairie Marpon et Flammarion, E. Flammarion, succ., n.d. (1893), 8vo., pp. 313 and unnumbered page table of contents. "La marquise de Brinvilliers", pp. (1)-86; "La comtesse de Saint-Géran", pp. (87)-137; "Jeanne de Naples". 1343-1382, pp. 139-249; "Vaninka", pp. 251-313.

"PRAXEDE"   1839-1841
"PIERRE-le-CRUEL"
"DON MARTIN DE FREYTAS" (With the alternative spelling of
                          "Don Martinn ... .)

        These are three chronicle stories dealing with individual Spaniards and which were subsequently published in the first

French edition under the title of the first-named. Previous to volume publication "Pierre-le-cruel" had appeared in "Le Siècle" in 1839 and later in "Nouveau musée français", 1841, Nos. 47-50; "Don Martin de Freytas" was also printed in "Le Siècle" in 1839 and, again later, in the "Revue des feuilletons", mai, 1845.

"Praxède" and "Pierre-le-cruel" are included in the standard Calmann-Lévy edition printed along with "Jehanne la Pucelle", while "Don Martin de Freytas" is included with the other stories in "Souvenirs d'Antony".

Original edition.
"La capitaine Pamphile", par Alexandre Dumas. Bruxelles, Société typographique belge, 1839, 24mo., 2 volumes, pp. 182 and 141. "Don Martinn de Freytas", par Alexandre Dumas, occupies pp. (91)-141 of Volume 2.

Ibid   Bruxelles, J. Jamar, 1839, same format and pagination as the preceding edition.

Oeuvres de Alex. Dumas. Tome quatrième. (Vignette) Bruxelles, Meline, Cans et compagnie, 1840, large 8vo. "Praxède". Suivi de "Don Martinn de Freytas" et de "Pierre le cruel". Separate pagination : (652)-665; blank; "Don Martinn de Freytas", 667-683; blank; "Pierre le cruel", (685)-699, all in double columns.

"Praxède", suivi de "Don Martinn de Freytas" et de "Pierre-le-cruel" par Alexandre Dumas. Paris, Dumont, éditeur, palais-royal, 88, au salon littéraire. 1841. 8vo., half-title "Praxède", verso 'ouvrages de M. Alexandre Dumas', another half-title "Praxède", pp. (3)-92; half-title "Don Martinn de Freytas", verso blank, (95)-203); verso blank, half-title "Pierre-le-cruel", verso blank, (207)-307. There is no table of contents. Yellow wrappers. Sceaux. - Impr. de E. Dépée.

"Praxède", suivi de "Pierre le Cruel". Par Alexandre Dumas. Bruxelles, A. Jamar, 1841, 24mo.; "Praxède", pp. (1)-46; "Pierre le Cruel", pp. (47)-97; followed by "Impressions de voyages. Le Midi de la France", pp. (99)-163. There is no table of contents.

"Praxède" suivi de "Don Martinn de Freytas" et de "Pierre le cruel". Par Alexandre Dumas. Bruxelles, Société belge de librairie, Hauman et Ce., 1841, 18mo.; "Praxède", pp. (1)-74; "Don Martinn de Freytas", pp. (75)-162; "Pierre le cruel", pp. (163)-247. There is no table of contents.

"Praxède", Suivi de "Don Martinn de Freytas" et de "Pierre le cruel". Par Alexandre Dumas. (Vignette) Bruxelles, Meline, Cans et compagnie, 1841, 18mo.; "Praxède", pp. (5)-67; "Don Martinn de Freytas", pp. (69)-144; "Pierre le cruel", pp. (145)-214; unnumbered page table of contents.

"Légende de Pierre-le-cruel", par M. Alexandre Dumas. In : 'Revue des feuilletons journal littéraire illustré composé de romans, voyages, légendes, anecdotes, contes nouvelles historiques, etc.', par J. Arago, H. de Balzac, A. Dumas, ... Première année. Paris, au bureaux (sic) du journal, 1841, 8vo., pp. (5)-25. Reprinted from "Le Siècle".

"Don Martinn de Freytas", par Alexandre Dumas. The copy in the Stad Antwerpen Bibliotheken is bound in with several other works by various

authors, and there is no title-page or indication of publisher or
printer. 8vo., pp. (71)-84 in double columns, and preceded by "Le
capitaine Pamphile", par Alexandre Dumas, same format, pp. (1)-71 in
double columns. Possible date of publication : circa 1841.

"Don Martinn de Freytas", par M. Alexandre Dumas. In : 'Revue des
feuilletons journal littéraire illustré composé de romans, voyages,
légendes, anecdotes, contes nouvelles, historiques, etc.', par J.
Arago, H. de Balzac, A. Dumas, ... Cinquième année. Paris, au
boureaux (sic) du journal, 1845, 8vo., pp. (198)-222.

Le Siècle. Oeuvres complètes d'Alexandre Dumas. Troisième série.
"Don Martinn de freytas". Paris, au bureau du Siècle, 1848, 4to.,
pp. (380)-390 in double columns.

"Isabel de Bavière" par Alexandre Dumas Paris Michel Lévy frères,
libraires-éditeurs ... 1848. 12mo., 2 volumes; the pagination of
Volume 2 is 303 with "Isabel de Bavière" ending on page 213, verso
blank, followed by "Praxède", pp. (215)-257, blank, "Pierre-le-cruel",
pp. (259)-303. There is no table of contents. Green wrappers.
Paris - Imp. Lacrampe fils et Comp.

"Nouvelles", par Alexandre Dumas. Paris, au bureau du Siècle, 1850,
4to., in double columns. "Don Martinn de Freytas" was one of the
stories included in this collection.

"Praxède". "Pierre le Cruel". "Cécile". Par Alexandre Dumas. Paris,
au bureau du Siècle, 1850, 4to., in double columns. The total pagination of the three works is (249)-322.

"Légende de Pierre-le-cruel". Alexandre Dumas. In : 'L'Echo des
feuilletons'. Paris, Dufour et Mulat, 1849, 8vo., pp. 446-462 in
double columns.
Reprinted, 1857, same format and pagination.

"Praxède". "Pierre le cruel". Par Alexandre Dumas. Paris, Impr.
de Ve Dondey-Dupré, n.d. (c 1850), 4to., pp. (249)-268 in double
columns. Caption titles.

"Don Martin de Freytas" par Alexandre Dumas. Paris, S. Raçon et Cie.,
n.d. (c 1850), 4to., pp. 24 in double columns; 2 plates.

"Praxède", suivi de "Pierre le cruel" par Alexandre Dumas. Bruxelles, Librairie du Panthéon, 1851, 18mo., pp. 146.

"Don Martinn de Freytas", par Alexandre Dumas. Paris, Marescq, 1852,
4to., pp. 24 in double columns; illustrated.

Alexandre Dumas. "Une vie artiste (Mélingue)". "Chronique de Charle-
magne". "Praxède". "Pierre le cruel". Edition illustrée par J.-A.
Beaucé et Ed. Coppin. Paris, Marescq, 1857, 4to.; "Praxède" and
"Pierre le cruel" each have a pagination of 24 in double columns.

"Légende de Pierre-le-cruel". Alexandre Dumas. In : 'L'Echo des
feuilletons'. Paris, chez les éditeurs, 1862, 8vo., pp. 446-462 in
double columns. Tome septième.

"Jehanne la Pucelle", with "Praxède" and "Pierre le Cruel". Par Alexandre Dumas. Paris, Impr. de Walder, n.d. (c 1862), 4to., pp. (249)-
268 in double columns for the two latter works. Caption titles.

"Don Martinn de Freytas" par Alexandre Dumas Dessins par Andrieux.
Paris Calmann Lévy, éditeur ancienne maison Michel Lévy frères, 1887,

4to., pp. (1)-24 in double columns. Alexandre Dumas oeuvres illustrees.

Alexandre Dumas "Le capitaine Paul" "Murat" "Le Kent" "Pierre le cruel" "Don Bernardo de Zuniga" Edition illustrée par les principaux artistes. (Vignette) Paris, Calmann-Lévy, 1887, 4to.; "Pierre le cruel", pp. (1)-16 in double columns. Brown paper wrappers with 'Illustrées par J.-A. Beaucé et les principaux artistes'. Alexandre Dumas oeuvres illustrées. Reprinted, 1862 and 1872, same format and pagination.

"Praxède" par Alexandre Dumas édition illustrée par J.-A. Beaucé et Ed. Coppin Paris, Calmann-Lévy éditeur ancienne maison Michel Lévy frères, 1889, 4to., pp. (1)-16 in double columns.

"Don Martinn de Freytas" par Alexandre Dumas. Edition illustrée par J.-A. Beaucé, Staal, Andrieux. Paris, Calmann-Lévy, n.d. (1890), 4to., pp. (1)-24 in double columns. Buff paper wrappers. Alexandre Dumas oeuvres illustrées.

Alexandre Dumas. "Praxède". "Pierre le Cruel". "Don Martinn de Freytas". Edition illustrée par les principaux artistes. Paris, Calmann-Lévy, 1897, 4to., pp. 24, 16 and 24 in double columns. Alexandre Dumas oeuvres illustrées.

"OTHON L'ARCHER"   1840

     "Othon l'archer" belongs to that category of stories which have been drawn from the reservoir of German mediaeval legend, and which Dumas has chosen to place in the fourteenth century.

     It was published serially in "Le Siècle" during 1838 and, curiously, did not seem to have attracted the attention of any Belgian publisher.

Original edition.
"Othon l'archer", par Alexandre Dumas. Paris, Librairie de Dumont, 1840, 8vo., pp. 324. There is no table of contents. Yellow wrappers.

"Othon L'archer. Chronique des bords du Rhin". Signed : Alex. Dumas. In : 'Le courrier des lectures ou choix de feuilletons, nouvelles, contes, anecdotes, épisodes, faites curieux, bons mots, etc.' Directeurs : Fellens frères (Vignette) Paris. 1843. Large 8vo., pp. 481-516 in double columns.

"Les frères Corses", par Alexandre Dumas. Paris, Michel Lévy frères, 1851, 12mo., pp. 294 and unnumbered page table of contents. "Othon l'archer" occupies pp. (159)-294.
Frequently reprinted by both Michel Lévy frères and Calmann-Lévy.

"Les frères Corses"; "Othon l'archer"; "Murat". Par Alexandre Dumas. Publiés par Dufour et Mulat. Illustrés par J.-A. Beaucé, Ed. Coppin et Gerard Séguin. Paris, chez Marescq, 1853, 4to., (one title-page for the three works); "Othon l'archer", pp. 64 in double columns.

"Othon l'archer" par Alexandre Dumas. Paris, Imp. de Raçon et Cie., n.d. (c 186), 4to., pp. 64 in double columns.

"Les frères Corses". "Othon l'archer", par Alexandre Dumas. Edition illustrée par J.-A. Beaucé, Ed. Coppin, Gerard Séguin. Paris, Calmann-

Lévy, n.d. (1884), 4to., pp. 64 in double columns. Oeuvres illustrées
d'Alexandre Dumas.
Reprinted, 1891, same format and pagination.

It has been stated that Thackeray's "A legend of the Rhine" is a bur-
lesque of this romance; if that is so it is not a very good one.

"MEMOIRES D'UN MAITRE D'ARMES"   1840

     As was the case with "La salle d'armes. Pauline" this story has
been stated by Dumas to have been related to him by the fencing-master
Grisier. Grisier had earlier spent a number of years in St. Petersbourg and had, indeed, become involved in the Pestel conspiracy of
1824-1826 to overthrow Czar Nicholas I. This was one of Dumas'
successful descriptions of a land which he was not to visit until
eighteen years later, when he had the pleasure of being warmly wel-
comed by the hitherto unknown hero and heroine of the story. The work
was in fact interdicted in Russia.

     It first appeared serially during 1849 in the 'Revue de Paris'.

Original edition.
"Mémoires d'un maître d'armes ou dix-huit mois a St-Petersbourg". Par
Alexandre Dumas. Bruxelles, Meline, Cans et compagnie, 1840, 16mo.,
2 volumes, pp. (5)-276 and (5)-233. Green wrappers.

"Mémoires d'un maître d'armes", par Alexandre Dumas. Bruxelles, A.
Jamar, 1840, 16mo., 2 volumes, pp. 200 and 235. Green wrappers.
Muséum littéraire.

"Mémoires d'un maître d'armes". Par Alexandre Dumas. Bruxelles,
Société belge de librairie (Volume 1), Société belge de librairie.
Hauman et Ce. (Volumes 2 and 3), 1840, 18mo., pp. 276, 235 and 197.
"Mémoires d'un maître d'armes" end on page 138 of Volume 3, and is
followed by "Une mort, un succés, une chute" by Dumas which subsequently appeared as part of the chapter 'Bellini' in his "Le capitaine Aréna". There are no tables of contents.

Ibid   Bruxelles, Société belge de librairie, Hauman et
Cie., 1840, same format and pagination as the preceding edition.

Oeuvres de Alex. Dumas. Tome quatrième. (Vignette) Bruxelles,
Meline, Cans et compagnie, 1840, large 8vo. "Mémoires d'un maître
d'armes", frontispiece, pp. (513)-647 in double columns.

"Le maître d'armes", par Alexandre Dumas. Paris, Dumont, 1840-1841,
8vo., 3 volumes, pp. (Volumes 1 and 2, 1840) 320 and 322, (Volume 3,
1841) 336. Yellow wrappers.
The Biblioteca Nazionale 'Vittoria Emanuele III', in Naples, possesses
a copy, same publishers, format and pagination, with the third volume
dated 1844.

"L'assassinat de Paul 1er., empereur de Russie". In : 'Le courrier
des lectures ou choix de feuilletons, nouvelles, contes, anecdotes,
épisodes, faites curieux, bons mots, etc.' Directeurs: Fellens
frères (Vignette) Paris. 1843. Large 8vo., pp. 323-334 in double
columns. 'Ce récit dramatique et intéressant est extrait d'un ouvrage
de M. Alex. Dumas, publié à la libraire de Dumas sous le titre de :
"Mémoires d'un maître d'armes".'

Echo de feuilletons Choix de nouvelles, épisodes, anecdotes, extraits de la Presse contemporaine. Paris, 1844, large 8vo., "Mort de Paul premier", pp. 139-145 in double columns. 'Les derniers volumes des "Mémoires d'un Maître d'armes" par Alexandre Dumas, nous fournissent le chapitre suivant dans lequel l'auteur raconte à sa manière un des événements les plus remarquables de l'histoire de Russie. Cet épisode si dramatique ne saurait manquer d'intéresser vivement nos lecteurs'.

Le Siècle. Oeuvres complètes d'Alexandre Dumas Troisième série. "Le maître d'armes". Paris, au bureau du Siècle, 1848, 4to., pp. (113)-196 in double columns.

"Le maître d'armes", par Alexandre Dumas. Paris, Michel Lévy frères, 1848, 12mo., pp. 312 and unnumbered page table of contents. Frequently reprinted, same format and pagination, by Michel Lévy frères and Calmann-Lévy.

"Le maître d'armes". Par Alexandre Dumas. Episodes. Edited, with English notes, by H. Lallemand and E. Joel. London, David Nutt, 1891, 8vo., pp. vi, 231.

"JARVIS L'HONNETE HOMME"   1840

As can be seen this was originally a play in two acts; at some later date after its performance at the Gymnase it was restaged at the Porte-Saint-Martin being retitled "Le marchand de Londres", and the two acts were divided to make three. Although it was announced as being by Charles Lafont it was in fact written by Dumas.

Original edition.
"Jarvis l'Honnête homme", drame en deux actes, par M. Charles Lafont, représenté pour la première fois, sur le théatre Gymnase-Dramatique, le 3 juin 1840. A Paris, Chez Ch. Tresse, successeur de J.-N. Barba, 1840, 8vo., pp. 63. Librairie théatrale de E. Michaud, ... Maison de l'Ambigue.

"Jarvis l'honnête homme", drame en deux actes, par M. Charles Lafont (et A. Dumas). Paris, Henriot, n.d. (1840), large 8vo., pp. 24 in double columns. Caption title. Impr. de Mme. de Lacombe.

"Jarvis l'honnête homme", drame en deux actes, par M. Charles Lafont. Représenté pour la première fois, à Paris, sur le théâtre du Gymnase-Dramatique, le 3 juin 1840. Pink wrappers : Répertoire dramatique des auteurs contemporains. N. 100. Paris, Beck, éditeur, Tresse, successeur de J.N. Barba, 1842, large 8vo., pp. 24 in double columns.

"LES STUARTS"   1840

This work is a chronicle history of the House of Stuart, covering more particularly the period of approximately 1437-1587.

Original edition.
"Les Stuarts" par Alexandre Dumas. Paris. Dumont, libraire-éditeur, Palais-Royal, 88, salon littéraire; Baudry, rue Coquillière, 34. 1840. 8vo., 2 volumes, pp. (1)-303 and (1)-304. There are no tables of contents. Yellow wrappers. Imprimerie de Vᵉ Dondey-Dupré.

"Les Stuarts", par Alexandre Dumas. Bruxelles, A. Jamar, 1840, 18mo.,

2 volumes, pp. 163 and 152. Green wrappers. Muséum littéraire.

"Les Stuarts" par Alexandre Dumas. Bruxelles, Société belge de librairie, Hauman et cie., 1840, 16mo., 2 volumes, pp. 228 and 224.

Ibid   Bruxelles, Meline, Cans et compagnie, 1840, 16mo., 2 volumes, pp. 266 and 263.

"Les Stuarts", par Alexandre Dumas. Bruxelles, Meline, Cans et cie.; Leipzig, J.P. Meline, 1840, same format and pagination as the preceding edition.

Oeuvres de Alex. Dumas. Tome quatrième. (Vignette) Bruxelles, Meline, Cans et compagnie, 1840, large 8vo. "Les Stuarts", pp. (415)-510 in double columns.

"Jacques IV et Jacques V". In : 'Babel' publication de la Société des Gens de Lettres. Tome troisième. Paris, librairie Jules Renouard et Cie., ... 1840, 8vo., pp. (1)-452 and unnumbered page table of contents. "Jacques IV et Jacques V, rois d'Ecosse, Fragment de l'histoire des Stuarts", signed : Alexandre Dumas. Frontispiece facing title-page, pp. (83)-145. Imprimé chez Paul Renouard.

"Un épisode de la vie de Marie Stuart" - Extrait d'un ouvrage de M. Alexandre Dumas, intitulé "Les Stuarts" et publié par M. Dumont. In : 'Le courrier des lectures ou choix de feuilletons, nouvelles, contes, anecdotes, épisodes, faites curieux, bons mots, etc.' Directeurs : Fellens frères (Vignette) Paris. 1843, large 8vo., pp. 184-186 in double columns.

"Les Stuarts", par Alexandre Dumas. Paris, Michel Lévy frères, 1863, 12mo., pp. 307. There is no table of contents.
Reprinted, but not frequently, by both Michel Lévy frères and Calmann-Lévy.

"UN MARIAGE SOUS LOUIS XV"   1841

     Without any doubt this is Dumas' finest full-length comedy (it should be remembered that he regarded "Mademoiselle de Belle-Isle" as a drama) and was written in Italy. There can be no question of any collaborator. In 1861 the actor Regnier abridged it by omitting the first scene from Act IV, combined the third and fourth acts, and made sundry alterations. Therefore, to read the play in its original form one must go to the early French and Belgian editions, and not to the text as later published by Michel Lévy frères and Calmann-Lévy. The whole play takes place with no change of scenery.

Original edition.
"Un mariage sous Louis XV", comédie en cinq actes, par Alexandre Dumas. Représentée pour la première fois, sur le Théatre-Français, le 1er juin 1841. Paris, Marchant; Tresse, 1841, 8vo., pp. 140. Blue wrappers repeating the title-page and with the dedication : 'A la ville de Florence Souvenir de sa bonne hospitalité. Alex. Dumas'.

"Un mariage sous Louis XV". Comédie en cinq actes par Alexandre Dumas. Représentée, pour la première fois, sur le Théatre-Français, le 1er juin 1841. (Vignette) Bruxelles, Meline, Cans et compagnie, 1841, 16mo., pp. 223. Yellow wrappers.

Ibid   (Vignette) Bruxelles et Leipzig, Meline, Cans et compagnie, 1841, same format and pagination as the preceding edition. Yellow wrappers.

"Un mariage sous Louis XV" comédie en cinq actes par Alex. Dumas. Bruxelles, Société belge de librairie, 1841, 16mo., pp. 226.

"Un mariage sous Louis XV", comédie en cinq actes, par Alexandre Dumas, représentée pour la première fois, par les comédiens ordinaires du roi, sur le Théâtre-français, le 1er juin 1841. Paris, Marchant, 1841, 8vo., pp. 47 in double columns. Caption title. Woodcut at head of title, Acte IV, scène ii.
Reprinted, 1843, same format and pagination.

Ibid   Caption title. Woodcut at head of title, Acte IV, scène ii. Yellow wrappers. Magasin théatral. Choix de pièces nouvelles, jouées sur tous les théatres de Paris. Théatre-Français. "Un mariage sous Louis XV", Comédie en cinq actes. (Vignette) Paris, Marchant; Bruxelles, Tarride, n.d. (1841), same format and pagination as the preceding edition.

Théatre de Alex. Dumas. "Un mariage sous Louis XV". (Vignette) Bruxelles, Meline, Cans et compagnie, 1842, 32mo., pp. 174. Buff wrappers.

Oeuvres de Alex. Dumas. Tome cinquième. (Vignette) Bruxelles, Meline, Cans et compagnie, 1842, large 8vo. "Un mariage sous Louis XV", frontispiece, pp. 'personnages' on verso of title-page, (193)-247 in double columns.

"Un mariage sous Louis XV", comédie en cinq actes, par Alexandre Dumas, représentée pour la première fois, par les comédiens ordinaires du roi, sur le Théâtre-Français, le 1er juin 1841. Paris, Marchant, 1843, 8vo., pp. 47 in double columns. Caption title. Woodcut at head of title, Acte IV, scène ii. Magasin théatral. Choix de pièces nouvelles, jouées sur tour les théatres de Paris. Bibliothèque de la Ville et de la Campagne. Imprimerie de Ve Dondey-Dupré.

Alexandre Dumas. "Un mariage sous Louis XV". Comédie en cinq actes. Bruxelles, J.-A. Lelong, 1847, 24mo., pp. 148. Répertoire de la scène française. IXe année, 27.

"Un mariage sous Louis XV", comédie en cinq actes, en prose, par Alexandre Dumas ... . Paris, Impr. de E. Blot, n.d. (c 1860), 8vo., pp. 47 in double columns. Caption title. Woodcut at head of title, Acte IV, scène ii.

"Un mariage sous Louix XV" comédie en quatre actes, en prose Théâtre-Français. - 1er juis 1841. 'A la ville de Florence Souvenir de sa bonne hospitalité. Alex. Dumas'. Paris, Michel Lévy frères, 1864, 12mo., pp. 100-196.

Ibid   Théatre complet de Alex. Dumas Tome VII Paris Calmann Lévy, éditeur ancienne maison Michel Lévy frères, 1874. 12mo. "Théatre complet" in 25 volumes.

Alexandre Dumas. "Un mariage sous Louis XV" comédie en quatre actes. Paris, Calmann-Lévy, n.d. (1894), 12mo., pp. (including two half-titles, the second repeating the title-page but with dedication and 'distribution'), 100-196. Orange covers.

Ibid   With the first half-title : "Un mariage sous Louis XV" comédie. Représentée pour la première fois, à Paris, sur

le théâtre de la Comédie-Française (sic), le 1er juin 1841. Conforme
à la représentation (1894). Same format as the preceding edition,
but with pp. 132.

"JEANNIC LE BRETON, ou LE GERANT RESPONSABLE"   1841

It is well-known that Dumas collaborated with Bourgeois in the
writing of this play, but he refused to allow his name to be connected
with it.

At about this time Dumas was preoccupied with the possibility of
his election to the Académie Française, and Lecomte in his "Alexandre
Dumas 1802-1870 Sa vie intime Ses oeuvres" mentions him saying to
Lemaître : 'Le silence interprète désigné "Jeannic le Breton", le
silence le plus absolu est ma condition. Dans ce moment-ci une chute
ou une oeuvre peu littéraire me rejetterait à cent lieues de l'Académie
...'. It was the intention that Lemaître should play the leading rôle
but, in the event, Bocage took the part of Jeannic Mauclerc (appelé
Jeannic-le-Chouan).

Original edition.
"Jeannic-le-Breton, ou le gérant responsable", drame en cinq actes
et en prose, par M. Eugène Bourgeois, Représenté pour la première
fois, à Paris, sur le théâtre de la Porte-Saint-Martin, le samedi 27
novembre 1841. Caption title, followed by 'Distribution', large 8vo.,
pp. (1)-40 in double columns. Blue wrappers. Répertoire dramatique
des auteurs contemporaines : No. 177. Théâtre de la Porte-Saint-
Martin. "Jeannic-le-breton". Drame en cinq actes et en prose. Paris,
Beck, éditeur, ... Tresse, successeur de J.N. Barba, Palais-Royal.
1842. Impr. de Mme. Delacom.

"Jeannic-le-Breton ou le gérant responsable", drame en cinq actes,
par MM. E. Bourgeois et *** (A. Dumas), Représenté pour la première
fois, à Paris, sur le théâtre de la Porte-Saint-Martin, le samedi 27
novembre 1841. (Vignette) Bruxelles, J.-A. Lelong, Imprim.-libr.-
éditeur, rue des Pierres 46; Gambier, au Théâtre; Ve Neirinckx, Grand'
Place, et chez les principaux Libraires du Royaume. 1842. 24mo., pp.
'personnages' 'acteurs' on verso of title-page, (5)-128. Répertoire
de la scène française. 10e année, 6.
The Bibliothèque de l'Arsenal holds a copy, same format and pagination,
in pink wrappers with Lelong only named as the publisher.

"NOUVELLES IMPRESSIONS DE VOYAGE : LE MIDI DE LA FRANCE"   1841

Dumas left Paris in the middle of October, 1834, with the painter,
Godefroy Jadin, and the bulldog, 'Milord', for Marseilles. The journey
was subsequently continued into Italy, and the travels there were duly
described in "Une année à Florence", "Le Speronare", "Le capitaine
Aréna" and "Le Corricolo". The present work was rounded off, seemingly
almost as an afterthought, by "La chasse au chastre".

Original edition.
"Nouvelles impressions de voyage (Midi de la France)" par Alexandre
Dumas. Paris, Dumont, 1841, 3 volumes, pp. 340, 326 and 357. There
are no tables of contents. Yellow wrappers.

Ibid   Paris, Ozanne, 1840, 18mo., 3 volumes.

Ibid   Bruxelles, Société belge de librairie. Hauman et
ce., 1841, 18mo., 2 volumes, pp. 302 and 303. Yellow wrappers.

"Nouvelles impressions de voyage (Midi de la France)". Par Alexandre
Dumas. Bruxelles, A. Jamar, 1841, 24mo., 3 volumes, pp. 194, 192 and
215. On the verso of the half-title of Volume 1 appears : 'Les for-
malités voulues par la loi pour assurer la propriété de cet ouvrage
ont été remplies'.

"Praxède", suivi de "Pierre le Cruel". Par Alexandre Dumas. Bruxelles, A. Jamar, 1841, 24mo.; the volume is completed by "Impressions
de voyage. Le Midi de la France", pp. (99)-163.

"Nouvelles impressions de voyage. (Midi de la France)", par Alexandre
Dumas. Bruxelles, Meline, Cans et compagnie, 1841, 16mo., 2 volumes,
pp. 364 and 330, each with an additional page table of contents, that
in volume 2 being unnumbered.

"Nouvelles impressions de voyage (Midi de la France)" par Alexandre
Dumas. Bruxelles et Leipzig, Meline, Cans et compagnie, 1841, 2 volumes, same format and pagination as the preceding edition.

Oeuvres de Alex. Dumas. Tome cinquième. (Vignette) Bruxelles,
Meline, Cans et compagnie, 1842, large 8vo. "Nouvelles impressions
de voyage. (Midi de la France)", frontispiece, pp. (3)-190 in double
columns.

"Impressions de voyage" par Alexandre Dumas "Midi de la France".
Paris, Michel Lévy frères, 1851, 12mo., 2 volumes, pp. 290 and additional unnumbered page table of contents, and 323, verso unnumbered
page table of contents. "Midi de la France" ends on page 214 of
Volume 2 and is followed by "La chasse au chastre", pp. 214-323.
Frequently reprinted, same format and pagination, by Michel Lévy
frères and Calmann-Lévy.

"Nouvelles impressions de voyage (Midi de la France)" par Alexandre
Dumas. Paris, Vᵉ Dondey-Dupré, n.d. (c 1853), 4to., pp. 213-328 in
double columns. Caption title. Romans illustrés.

Le Siècle. Oeuvres complètes d'Alexandre Dumas. Huitième série.
"Impressions de voyage Suisse. - Midi de la France. - Une année a
Florence". Paris, au bureau du Siècle ... . 1855, 4to., pp. (213)-
328 in double columns.

"Contes et nouvelles". Par Alexandre Dumas. (Vignette) Bruxelles,
Meline, Cans et compagnie, 1858, 18mo., pp. 259, unnumbered page table
of contents. The chapter "Une visite à Nimes" is included, pp. (243)-
253, and is followed by 'A M. Alexandre Dumas. Les arènes de Nimes'
par J. Reboul, pp. (255)-259. Yellow wrappers.

Alexandre Dumas "Voyage en Bourbonnais une visite à Achille Allier"
(Vignette) Moulins, Imprimerie de C. Desrosiers. 1884. Large 8vo.,
pagination : (1)-2 introduction signed : 'A.R.', and 3-39; 1
illustration and 2 vignettes. Blue paper wrappers repeating the title-
page.
This is an extract from 'La Revue Bourbonnais' of février, mars, avril,
1884, and is a reprint of pp. 64-98 of Volume 1 of "Impressions de
voyage Midi de la France", Paris, Michel Lévy frères, 1851.

"Impressions de voyage. Le midi de la France" par Alexandre Dumas.
Paris, Calmann-Lévy, n.d. (189), 4to., pp. 168 in double columns.
There is no table of contents.

"Le midi de la France" ends on page 138, and is followed by Chapter XXXII "La chasse au chastre", pp. 138-168. Caption title. Woodcut at head of title. Blue wrappers repeating the title-page. Musée littéraire contemporain.

"LA CHASSE AU CHASTRE"   1841

The plot of this short story which, in part, turns to an adventure with brigands, was first told to Dumas by Joseph Méry. For some time Dumas did nothing with it and Méry decided to write it himself. Almost simultaneously Dumas' version appeared at the end of his travel book "Le Midi de la France" and he was accused of plagiarism. Méry immediately wrote explaining how the position had arisen. The first part of each version has some similarity, but the adventure with the brigands is absent from Méry's story.

The story was not published as a separate work in France, and when printed to fill up the last of the two volumes of "Le Midi de la France" published by Michel Lévy frères the type used was smaller, almost as if to indicate that its inclusion was an afterthought. As will be seen the story was also used to complete the Alexandre Cadot edition of "Le chevalier de Maison-Rouge".

Original edition in separate volume form.
"Le chasse au chastre" par Alexandre Dumas. Bruxelles, Société belge de librairie. Hauman et Ce., 1841, 18mo., pp. (3)-244. Imp. de Hauman et Ce.

"Le chevalier de Maison-Rouge" par Alexandre Dumas. Paris, Alexandre Cadot, 1845-1846, 8vo., 6 volumes; the pagination of Volume 6 (1846) is 332 and unnumbered page table of contents, "Le chevalier de Maison-Rouge" ending on page 58 and being followed by "La chasse (au chastre)", pp. (59)-332. Yellow wrappers. Sceaux - imp. de E. Dépée.

"UNE ANNEE A FLORENCE"   1841

This part of the "Nouvelles impressions de voyage" is, in fact, a continuation of Dumas' "Le Midi de la France" and the period covered is 1835.

Original edition.
"Une année à Florence" par Alexandre Dumas. Paris, Dumont, 1841, 8vo., 2 volumes, pp. 340 and 343. Yellow wrappers.

"Souvenirs de voyage (Italie)". Par Alexandre Dumas. Bruxelles, Société belge de librairie, Hauman et Ce., 1841, 16mo., pp. 279. Green wrappers.
This work, published as a separate third volume but simultaneously, with "Nouvelles impressions de voyage (Midi de la France)" is a continuation of the latter. It ends with Chapter XII 'Les fêtes de la Saint-Jean à Florence', and these twelve chapters are included as the first twelve in the work with the title "Souvenirs de voyage en Italie" to which reference should be made under "Le capitaine Aréna" from which selected chapters were included.

"La Siècle. "Impressions de voyage. Une année à Florence", par Alexandre Dumas. Paris, au bureau du Siècle, 1851, 4to., pp. 329-502 in double columns. Romans illustrés.

"Impressions de voyage" par Alexandre Dumas "Une année à Florence".
Paris, Michel Lévy frères, 1851, 12mo., pp. 278 and unnumbered page
table of contents.
Reprinted, same format and pagination, by both Michel Lévy frères and
Calmann-Lévy.

Le Siecle. Oeuvres complètes d'Alexandre Dumas Huitième série.
"Impressions de Voyage Suisse. - Midi de la France. - Une année à
Florence". Paris, au bureau du Siècle. ... . 1855, 4to., pp. (329)-
401 (wrongly numbered 501), 502 (sic) table of contents, in double
columns.

"Impressions de voyage. Une année à Florence" par Alexandre Dumas.
Paris Calmann-Lévy, n.d. (1899), 4to. Caption title. Woodcut at
head of title. Musée littéraire contemporain.

"SOUVENIRS DE VOYAGE EN ITALIE"   1841-1843
"LE CAPITAINE ARENA"

     The first of the above titles comprises part of "Une année à
Florence" and since, as will be seen, some chapters were incorporated
in "Le capitaine Aréna" it is considered best to deal with the two
works together. It will be noted that a further and quite separate
edition of "Souvenirs de voyage (Italie)" was published in 1841 by
the Société belge de librairie. Hauman et Ce., in Bruxelles.

Original edition.
"Souvenirs de voyage (Italie)" Par Alexandre Dumas. Bruxelles.
Société belge de librairie. Hauman et Ce., 1841, 16mo., pp. (1)-279.
This edition comprises the last thirteen chapters of "Une année à
Florence".
"Souvenirs de voyage en Italie". Par Alexandre Dumas. Bruxelles,
Meline, Cans et compagnie, 1841-1842, 18mo., 5 volumes; Volume 1 (1841),
pp. 270, Volumes 2-5 (1842), pp. 261, 214, 241 and 273 (the wrappers
of Volumes 2 and 3 are dated 1841). Brown wrappers. Volume 5 con-
tains chapters later included in "Le capitaine Aréna".

Ibid   Bruxelles, Meline, Cans et Cie.; Leipzig, J.P.
Meline. Same years of publication, format and pagination, as the
preceding edition.

Ibid   La Haye. Chez les héritiers Doorman, with the
same years of publication, format and pagination, as the preceding
two editions. Buff wrappers, those for Volumes 2 and 3 being dated
1841.
In none of the three above editions is there any table of contents.

"Le capitaine Aréna". Par Alex. Dumas. (Vignette) Béthune, éditeur.
Paris, Dolin, Librairie - commissionaire, 1842, 8vo., 2 volumes, pp.
309 and 2 unnumbered pages table of contents, and 314 and 1 unnumbered
page table of contents. Yellow wrappers.

Oeuvres de Alex. Dumas. Tome cinquième. (Vignette) Bruxelles, Mel-
ine, Cans et compagnie, 1842, large 8vo. "Souvenirs de voyage en
Italie", frontispiece, pp. (251)-448 in double columns, ending with
Chapter XXV 'Le souterrain'.

Oeuvres de Alex. Dumas. Tome sixième. (Vignette) Bruxelles, Meline, Cans et compagnie, 1843, large 8vo. "Souvenirs de voyage en Italie" (suite), pp. (385)-522 in double columns, beginning with Chapter XXVI 'Un requin' and ending with Chapter XLVI 'Arrivée à Naples'. This edition includes chapters from "Le capitaine Aréna"; the chapter 'Le Pizzo' is entitled 'Murat'.

Oeuvres de Alex. Dumas. "Souvenirs de voyage en Italie". Bruxelles, Société belge de librairie, Hauman et Cie., 1843, large 8vo. This is Volume 5 of the series, pp. 475-521 in double columns. This, again, included portions of "Le capitaine Aréna" among which three chapters are entitled 'Excursions aux Iles Eoliennes' and five 'Voyage en calabre'. (Part of the chapter entitled 'Bellini' was published in the last volume of "Mémoires d'un maître d'armes". Par Alexandre Dumas. Bruxelles, Société belge de librairie, Hauman et Cie., 1840, 18mo., 3 volumes, under the title of 'Une mort'.)

"Le capitaine Aréna", par Alexandre Dumas ... . Paris, Boule, 1847, large 8vo., pp. 184 in double columns. There is no table of contents. Caption title. Les mille et un romans, nouvelles et feuilletons. No. XX.

Oeuvres d'Alexandre Dumas. "Impressions de voyage. Le capitaine Aréna". Paris, au bureau de Siècle, 1853, 4to., pp. 209-285 in double columns. Série IX.

"Impressions de voyage" par Alexandre Dumas "Le capitaine Aréna". Paris, Michel Lévy frères, 1855, 12mo., pp. 290 and unnumbered page table of contents.
Frequently reprinted, same format and pagination, by both Michel Lévy frères and Calmann-Lévy.

Le Siècle. Oeuvres complètes d'Alexandre Dumas. Neuvième série. "Impressions de voyage. Le capitaine Aréna". Paris, au bureau du Siècle, 1855, 4to., pp. 209-285 in double columns and including table of contents.

"Impressions de voyage. Le capitaine Aréna" par Alexandre Dumas. Paris, Michel Lévy frères, n.d. (187), 4to., pp. 77 in double columns and unnumbered page table of contents. Caption title. Woodcut at head of title. Brown wrappers repeating caption title and woodcut.

"EXCURSIONS SUR LES BORDS DU RHIN"   1841

     In company with Gérard de Nerval Dumas made this journey between August and November, 1838, and from it there sprang another series of "Impressions de voyage". It is probable that de Nerval gave Dumas some assistance in the writing.

Original edition.
"Excursions sur les bords du Rhin" par Alexandre Dumas. Paris, Dumont, 1841, 8vo., 3 volumes, pp. 328 (and 16 pages of publisher's advertisements), 326 and 334. Yellow wrappers. (The advertisements bound into Volume 1 include the announcement of 'Publications sous presse' by Dumas of : L'anneau mystérieux" and "La chambre rouge"; while Volume 3, on the page facing the title-page, announces 'sous presse' "Le bonhomme Buva" (sic).)

"Excursions en Belgique", par Alexandre Dumas. Bruxelles, A. Jamar,

1841, 18mo., pp. 196, with a frontispiece and illustrations. (This work comprises the smaller first part of "Excursions sur les bords du Rhin", beginning with the chapter 'Bruxelles' and ending with the chapter 'Le banquet de Warfusée'.)

"Excursions sur les bords du Rhin", par Alexandre Dumas. Bruxelles, Société belge de librairie, Hauman et cie., 1842, 16mo., 3 volumes, pp. 251, 261 and 260. There are no tables of contents.

"Excursions sur les bords du Rhin" par Alexandre Dumas. Bruxelles, Meline, Cans et compagnie, 1842, 16mo., 3 volumes, pp. 247, 254 and 260. There are no tables of contents.

"Excursions sur les bords du Rhin", par Alexandre Dumas. Bruxelles, Livourne, Meline, Cans et cie.; Leipzig, J.P. Meline, 1842, same format and pagination as the preceding edition.

Ibid   La Haye, chez les héritiers Doorman, 1842, same format and paginations as the two preceding editions.

Oeuvres de Alex. Dumas. Tome cinquième. (Vignette) Bruxelles, Meline, Cans et compagnie, 1842, large 8vo. "Excursions sur les bords du Rhin", frontispiece, pp. (451)-567 in double columns.
Oeuvres de Alex. Dumas. Tome sixième. (Vignette) Bruxelles, Meline, Cans et compagnie, 1843, large 8vo. "Excursions sur les bords du Rhin" (suite), pp. (247)-305 in double columns.

"Impressions de voyage" par Alexandre Dumas "Les bords du Rhin". Paris, Michel Lévy frères, 1854, 12mo., 2 volumes, pp. 285 and 280, each with an unnumbered page table of contents.
Frequently reprinted, same format and pagination, by both Michel Lévy frères and Calmann-Lévy.

"Impressions de voyage. Excursions sur les bords du Rhin", par Alexandre Dumas. Paris, Impr. de Morris, n.d. (1854), 4to., pp. 81-192 in double columns; illustrated. Caption title.

"Le Siècle. Oeuvres complètes d'Alexandre Dumas. Dixième série. "Impressions de voyage. Excursions sur les bords du Rhin". Paris, au bureau du Siècle, n.d. (c 1855), 4to., pp. (81)-192 in double columns, and including table of contents.

"Impressions de voyage. Excursions sur les bords du Rhin" par Alexandre Dumas. Paris, Michel Lévy frères, n.d. (c 1855), 4to., pp. (81)-192 in double columns. Caption title. Woodcut at head of title. Pink wrappers repeating caption title and woodcut. Musée littéraire du siècle.

Ibid   Paris, Calmann-Lévy, n.d. (c 187), 4to., pp. (81)-191 in double columns, and page 192 table of contents. Caption title. Oeuvres complètes d'Alexandre Dumas.

Ibid   Paris, Calmann-Lévy, n.d. (189), 4to., pp. 141 in double columns. Caption title. Woodcut at head of title. Yellow wrappers repeating caption title and woodcut.

"GALERIE DE FLORENCE"   1841 and 1844

This magnificently produced work is, as will be seen, inter-related with Dumas' other works on the major Italian and Flemish artists dealt with later in this Bibliography. Apart from my own set

in six volumes only one other set has been traced and that is held in
The Royal Library in The Hague. I can only presume that other copies
have been broken up for the separate sale of the quite superb engravings. All volumes are uniform in 'elephant folio' (55½ x 39 cms.),
and the work was printed and engraved on heavy hand-made paper.

Original edition.
"Galerie de Florence" gravée sur cuivre, et publiée par une société
d'amateurs, sous la direction de L. Bartolini, J. Bezzuoli et S. Jesi
avec un texte en français par Alexandre Dumas Tome premier. (Monogram) Florence a la société de publication rue Saint-Egide, numéro
6638, palais Magnani MDCCCXLI. (On the spine : Dumas Galerie de
Florence portraits et peintures.)
There is no French text to this volume which comprises 110 engravings.

Ibid   Again 'Tome premier' with the same title-page and
year of publication as the preceding volume, but with on the spine :
Dumas Galerie de Florence tableaux d'histoire.
This volume comprises 81 engravings, with introductory matter by Dumas
to an individual plate or set of plates.

"Galerie de Florence" gravée sur cuivre, et publiée par une société
d'amateurs, sous la direction de Bartolini, Bezzuoli et Jesi avec un
texte en français par Alexandre Dumas, dediée a Sa Majesté Nicolas
premier empereur et autocrate de toute les Russies. Tome premier.
(Russian imperial coat-of-arms) Florence chez la société éditrice,
MDCCCXLIV.
Pagination : 4 unnumbered pages of handwritten copperplate script
serving as an introduction to : "Les Médicis, branche ainée, (1)-
69, verso blank, "Les Médicis, branche cadette", (71)-129, verso
blank, "Maison de Lorraine François second et ses descendants", (131)-
135, verso blank, "La peinture chez les anciens", (5)-94, leaf with
title : "Histoire des peintres faisant suite a l'histoire de la
peinture.", verso blank, "Histoire des peintres faisant suite a
l'histoire de la peinture Massacio de S-Giovanni. Ne en 1401, mort
en 1442 (97)-100, "Le Perugin" (100)-107, "Léonard de Vinci" 107-125,
"Michel-Ange Buonarroti" (125)-169, "Raphaël Sanzio d'Urbin" 169-196,
"Titien Vecello" 196-242, "Giorgione" 242-254. (On the spine :
Dumas Galerie de Florence Tome I.)

"Histoire de la peinture depuis les égyptiens jusqu'à nos jours" par
Alexandre Dumas, Dediée à Sa Majesté Nicolas premier empereur et
autocrate de toutes les Russies. Tome premier. (Russian imperial
coat-of-arms.) Florence chez la société éditrice MDCCCXLIV. This
volume comprises 6 engravings with introductory matter by Dumas to an
individual plate or set of plates. (On the spine : Dumas Galerie
de Florence tableaux de histoire II.)

Ibid   Tome deuxième, with the same title-page, publishers
and year of publication as the preceding volume. "Histoire des peintres, faisant suite à l'histoire de la peinture". "Jean Bellin" (5)-
13, "Andre del Sarto" 13-48, "Fra Bartolomeo" 48-58, "Jules Romain"
58-68, "Le Primaticcio" 68-80, "Luc Kranac" (sic) but all pages are
headed "Luc Cranach" 80-84, "Quentin Metsys" 85-91, "Baccio Bandinelli" 91-108, "Jean Holbein" 109-121, "Jean-Antoine Razzi" dit le
Sodoma et le Mataccio 121-129, "Bernardino Pinturicchio" 130-135,
"Baldasarre Peruzzi" 136-146, "André de Mantegna" 146-151, "Albert
Durer" 151-162, "Pierre Paul Rubens" 162-208, "Antoine Allegri" dit

le Corrège 209-215, "Giorgio Vasari" 215-231, verso blank, "Les
peintres espagnols" revue retrospective les écoles de Tolède, de
Valence, de Séville et de Madrid. - pp. 2 (unnumbered), "École de
Tolède Feran Gonzales, el Greco, Luis Tristan, Morales blas de,
Prado Fray Juan Bantista Mayno, Orrente, oeuvres principales de ces
maîtres", pp. (235)-240. There are no illustrations to this volume.
(On the spine : Dumas Galerie de Florence Tome II.)

The sixth, and final, volume has no title-page. It comprises 29
engravings with introductory matter by Dumas to an individual engraving
or set of engravings. The volume is completed by "Ecole de Tolède",
pp. 241-246, "Ecole de Valence" 246-255, and stops abruptly with pp.
255-256 "Ecole de Seville", the last sentence being incomplete. It
is my belief that Dumas had no connexion with the writing of "Les
peintres espagnols .....", and this belief is borne out by the following work held in the Bibliothèque Nationale : "Galerie de Florence"
gravée sur cuivre et publié par une société d'amateurs sous la direction d'un comité artistique, avec un texte français par Alexandre
Dumas, continué par Hector de Garriod, ... Florence, A. Paris, 1859,
folio, 95° livraison.
N.B. - The catalogue card of the Bibliothèque Nationale has a note
saying : 'Il n'y a rien de Dumas dans cette volume.' All the above
volumes, with the exception of the sixth which has no half-title, bear
on the verso of the half-title : Imprimerie de Vincent Batelli et
Comp. It may be taken that the sixth volume was also printed by this
Company, for the engravers and the paper used are exactly the same as
in the other five volumes.

"ARMEE FRANÇAISE"   1841-1845
     Dumas' friend, the duc d'Orléans, suggested to him that he should
write a series of regimental histories. In fact only three volumes
were ever published, and these at irregular intervals. It is generally
assumed that Adrien Pascal helped considerably in their writing. These
histories were never included in any of the collected editions of
Dumas' works.

Original (and only) editions.
"Armée française. Histoire du 23e régiment d'infanterie de ligne"
... (Par Alexandre Dumas). Publiée par ordre de S.A.R. Mgr. le duc
d'Orléans, prince royal. Paris, Impr. de Vve Dondey-Dupré, rue Saint-
Louis, 46. 1841. 32mo., pp. 597.

"Armée française. Histoire du 2e régiment d'infanterie de légère"...
(Par Alexandre Dumas). Publiée par ordre de S.A.R. feu Mgr. le duc
d'Orléans. Paris, Imprimé par Béthune et Plon, 1843. 32mo., pp. 504.

"Armée française. Histoire du 24e régiment d'infanterie de ligne" ...
(Par Alexandre Dumas). Publiée par ordre de S.A.R. feu Mgr. le duc
d'Orléans. Paris, Imprimé par Plon frères, 1845. 32mo., pp. 616.

"PAGE D'ALBUM. A MADAME LA COMTESSE DE REVIESKI"   1842
     This poem consists of five verses each of 6 lines. Glinel has
noted variations in the different texts, and has drawn attention to
the resemblance of these verses to some written by Dumas, fils, under
the title : "Vers mis sur un album".

111

Original edition.
In : 'La Chronique', Paris, Béthune et Plon, 1842, pp. 202-203.
In : 'Paris-Londres Keepsake Français', Paris, H.-L. Delloye et Garnier frères, 1842.
In the issue of 'Le Mousquetaire' for 15 mars, 1854.
The verses were also printed in facsimile in 'L'Autograph', 1864, page 61.

"LORENZINO"   1842

Whether Dumas had any collaborator in the writing of this not very successful play, and Glinel has written that there were only seven performances, is very much open to doubt. Parigot in his "Le drame d'Alexandre Dumas" (Paris, Calmann Lévy, 1899) refers to Dumas' "Fiesque de Lavagna", drame en cinq actes et en vers, which Dumas drew from Schiller and wrote in 1827 which was neither staged nor published, and suggests that it was the inspiration for "Lorenzino".

The action is centred around the assassination in Florence in 1537 of Alexander de Medici by his cousin Lorenzino, and from the play Dumas drew his romance "Une nuit à Florence".

Original edition.
"Lorenzino", drame en cinq actes et en prose, par Alexandre Dumas, représenté pour la première fois, a Paris, sur le Théatre- Français, le 24 février 1842. Caption title. Woodcut at head of title, Acte IV, scene v. Paris, Marchant, n.d. (1842), large 8vo., pp. 35 in double columns.

Ibid   Yellow wrappers : Magasin théatral. Choix de pièces nouvelles. Jouées sur tous les théatres de Paris. Théatre Français. "Lorenzino", Drame en cinq actes. (Vignette) Paris, Marchant; Bruxelles, Tarride, n.d. (1842), same format and pagination as the preceding edition.

"Lorenzino", drame en cinq actes et en prose, par M. Alexandre Dumas, représenté pour la première fois, a Paris, sur le théatre Français, le 24 février 1842. (Vignette) Bruxelles, J.-A. Lelong, Imprim.-libr.-éditeur, rue des pierres, 46; Gambier, au Théâtre; Vᵉ Neirinckx, Grand'Place et chez les principaux Libraires du Royaume, 1842, 18mo., pp. (5)-112.

"Lorenzino". Drame en cinq actes et en prose par Alexandre Dumas. Bruxelles, Société belge de librairie. Hauman et cie., 1842, 16mo., pp. 132. Brown wrappers.

Répertoire du Théâtre français à Berlin. Deuxième série. No. 14. "Lorenzino", drame en cinq actes et en prose, par Alexandre Dumas. Répertoire No. 264. Berlin, 1842, Ad. Mt. Schlesinger, Libraire et Editeur de Musique, 8vo., pp. (2), 63. Imprimé chez I.W. Krause.

"Lorenzino", drame en cinq actes et en prose, par Alexandre Dumas, représenté pour la première fois, à Paris, sur le Théâtre-Français, le 24 février 1842. Paris, Marchant, 1844, large 8vo., pp. 35 in double columns. Caption title. Woodcut at head of title, Acte IV, scène v.

Ibid   Paris, Imprimerie de Mme Ve Dondey-Dupré, n.d.
(c 1845), same format and pagination as the preceding edition. Caption title. Woodcut at head of title, Acte IV, scène V. Le magasin
théatral.

"Caligula". "Lorenzino". Par Alex. Dumas. Bruxelles, Meline, Cans
et Cie., 1855, 24mo., pp. 174 and 132.

"Lorenzino" drame en cinq actes, en prose Théâtre-Français. - 24
février. "Distribution" on title-page, pp. (197)-280. Théatre complet de Alex. Dumas. Tome VII Paris Calmann Levy, éditeur, ancienne maison Michel Lévy frères, 1874. 12mo. "Théatre complet" in
25 volumes.

"LE SPERONARE"   1842

        This is another work by Dumas devoted to his travels in Italy.
It was first published as a serial in 'La Presse'.

Original edition.
"Le Spéronare", par Alexandre Dumas. Bruxelles, A. Jamar, 1842,
24mo., 3 volumes, pp. 199, 157 and 160. "Le Spéronare" ends on page
98 of Volume 3, the volume being completed by "Nisida", par Alexandre Dumas, pp. (101)-160.

Ibid   Bruxelles, Ch. Hen, éditeur-libraire, 1842, 18mo.,
2 volumes, pp. 199 (followed by "Le dimanche" par Victor Joly, 4 pages),
and 157.

"Le Spéronare". par Alexandre Dumas. Bruxelles, Société belge de
librairie. Hauman et Ce., 1842, 24mo., 4 volumes, pp. 270, 218, 241
and 305. Yellow wrappers.

"Le Spéronare", par Alexandre Dumas. Paris, Dumont, 1842, 8vo., 4
volumes, pp. 329, 337, 348 and 306. Yellow wrappers.

Oeuvres de Alex. Dumas. Tome sixième. (Vignette) Bruxelles. Société belge de librairie Hauman et Ce. 1843, large 8vo. "Le Speronare" (Deuxième série.), pp. (381)-531 in double columns.

"La chapelle gothique". Alexandre Dumas. In : Le livre des feuilletons Receuil de nouvelles, contes, épisodes, extraits de la presse
contemporaine. Nancy, Imprimerie Hinzelin, 1843, 8vo., pp. (177)-216
in double columns.
This is a reprint of the chapter bearing the same title in "Le Spéronare".

Echo des feuilletons Choix de nouvelles, épisodes, anecdotes, extraits
de la Press contemporaine. Paris, 1844, large 8vo., "Les Bénédictines
de Saint-Nicolas-le vieux", pp. (42)-48 in double columns.
This is a reprint of Chapter 8 of "Le Spéronare".

"Les Bénédictines de Saint-Nicolas-le Vieux", signed : Alexandre
Dumas, pp. 84-96, in : Album littéraire ou nouveaux choix de lectures, Copenhague chez MM. Hoest et Reitzel, libraires de l'université, 1853, 8vo., pp. (iii)-vi 'preface', (1)-304 and 2 unnumbered
pages table of contents.
Again, a reprint of Chapter 8.

"Impressions de voyage. Le Spéronare", par Alexandre Dumas. Paris,

Impr. de Walder, n.d. (1854), 4to., pp. 75-208 in double columns. Caption title; illustrated.

Le Siecle. Oeuvres complètes d'Alexandre Dumas. Neuvième série. "Impressions de voyage. Le Speronare". Paris, au bureau du Siècle, 1855, 4to., pp. 75-207 in double columns and unnumbered page table of contents. Caption title.

"Impressions de voyage. Le Spéronare", par Alexandre Dumas. Paris, Impr. de J. Voisvenel, n.d. (c 1855), 4to., pp. 75-208 in double columns. Caption title; illustrated.

Ibid   Paris, Michel Lévy frères, 1855, 12mo., 2 volumes, pp. 319, verso table of contents, and 297 with additional unnumbered page table of contents. Frequently reprinted, same format and pagination, by Michel Lévy frères and Calmann-Lévy.

"Les Bénédictines de Saint-Nicolas-le-Vieux", signed : Alexandre Dumas, pp. 122-136, in : Album littéraire ou nouveaux choix de lectures. Deuxième édition refondue et augmentée Copenhague chez MM. Hoest et Reitzel libraires de l'université 1859. 8vo., pp. 348 including table of contents.

"Les Bénédictines de Saint-Nicolas-le-Vieux" signed : Alexandre Dumas, pp. 143-159, in : Album littéraire ou nouveaux choix de lectures, offert aux amateurs de la langue française suivies de notes littéraires et explicatives par L.-S. Borring Professeur de la langue française Troisième édition refondue et augmentée Copenhague a la librairie de J.-H. Schuhothe 1866. 8vo., pp. viii, 442 including table of contents. This particular edition also includes "Le chant des Girondins", par A. Maquet (sic), pp. part of 385-386.

"Impressions de voyage. Le Spéronare" par Alexandre Dumas. Paris, Calmann-Lévy, 1894, 4to., pp. 157 in double columns. Caption title. Woodcut at head of title, repeated on brown wrappers. Musée littéraire contemporain.

"JEHANNE LA PUCELLE. 1429-1431"   1842

        This is purely and simply a colourful chronicle relating to Joan of Arc. In a later work, "Les étoiles du monde", Dumas wrote about her again using material from the 1842 publication.

Original editioh.
"Jehanne la Pucelle. 1429-1431". Par Alex. Dumas. ('Il y a trois voix crieront éternellement vengeance contre l'Angleterre: c'est celle de Jeanne d'Arc sur son bûcher; celle de Marie Stuart sur son échefaud; et celle de Napoléon sur son rocher'. (Monogram) Béthune, éditeur. Paris. Magen et Comon, libraires, quai des Augustins. M DCCC XLII. 8vo., unnumbered page following title-page 'A la Mémoire de S.A.R. la PRINCESSE MARIE. Hommage de respect à la Fille de France; Hommage d'admiration à l'Artiste européenne. Alex. Dumas', pp. (iii)-vii, verso blank, (1)-327. On verso of half-title : Paris, imprimé par Béthune et Plon, Rue de Vaugirard, 36.

"Jehanne la Pucelle 1429-1431" par Alex. Dumas. (Quotation) Bruxelles, Société belge de librairie Hauman et Ce., 1842, 18mo., pp. 301.

"Jehanne la Pucelle 1429-1431". Par Alexandre Dumas. Bruxelles, Meline, Cans et compagnie, 1842, 16mo., pp. preliminary leaf, (3)-275. Brown wrappers repeating title-page.

Ibid   Bruxelles et Leipzig, Meline, Cans et compagnie, 1842, same format and pagination as the preceding edition.

Oeuvres de Alex. Dumas. Tome sixième. (Vignette) Bruxelles, Meline, Cans et compagnie, 1843, large 8vo. "Jehanne la Pucelle", pp. (171)-244 in double columns.

Oeuvres de Alex. Dumas. Tome sixième. $_e$(Vignette) Bruxelles. Société belge de librairie Hauman et Ce. 1843, large 8vo. "Jehanne la Pucelle", unnumbered page 'A la mémoire de S.A.R. la princesse Marie. Hommage de respect à la fille de France; Hommage d'admiration à l'artiste européenne. Alex. Dumas', pp. (241)-312 in double columns.

"Jeanne d'Arc", par M. Alexandre Dumas; suivi d'un appendice contenant une analyse raisonnée des documents anciens et des nouveaux documents inédits sur la pucelle d'Orléans, par J.-A. Buchon; avec une introduction par M. Charles Nodier de l'Académie Française. (Vignette) Paris. Librairie de Charles Gosselin, éditeur de la bibliothèque d'élite, ... MDCCCXLIII, 8vo., pp. (i)-xv 'Introduction' signed : Ch. Nodier, verso blank, (1)-173 "Jehanne-la-pucelle. 1429-1431", verso blank, (175)-453 'Appendice contenant une analyse ... ...', par J.-A. Buchon. Yellow wrappers repeating title-page with the addition : 'Bibliothèque d'Elite' at the head. Paris, imprimé par Béthune et Plon.

"Jehanne la Pucelle" (with "Praxède" and "Pierre le Cruel"). Par Alexandre Dumas. Paris, Impr. de Walder. n.d. (1855), 4to. "Jehanne la Pucelle" occupies pp. 267-308 in double columns.

"Jehanne la Pucelle", par Alexandre Dumas. Paris, Michel Lévy frères, 1862, 12mo., pp. 295, verso table of contents. "Jehanne la Pucelle" occupies pp. (1)-206, being followed by "Praxède" and "Pierre le Cruel".
Reprinted, same format and pagination, by both Michel Lévy frères and Calmann-Lévy.

"Jehanne la Pucelle" par Alexandre Dumas. Paris, Calmann-Lévy, 1883, 4to., pp. 56 in double columns including table of contents. Caption title. Woodcut at head of title, repeated on brown wrappers. Musée littéraire contemporain.

"AVENTURES DE LYDERIC"   1842

     This is a chronicle story, half-legendary and half-fictitious, of Lyderic, first Count of Flanders, in the seventh century.

Original edition.
"Aventures de Lyderic" (with "Chronique du roi Pépin" and "Chronique de Charlemagne") Par Alexandre Dumas. Paris, Dumont, 1842, 8vo., pp. 359. "Aventures de Lyderic" occupies pp. (1)-159. Yellow wrappers.

"Aventures de Lyderic" par Alexandre Dumas. Bruxelles, Meline, Cans et compagnie, 1842, 18mo., pp. 280; the work occupies pp. (1)-124, and is followed by "Chronique du roi Pépin" and "Chronique de Charlemagne".

Ibid   Bruxelles et Leipzig, Meline, Cans et compagnie,
1842, same format and pagination as the preceding edition. Pink
wrappers.

"Lyderic" par Alexandre Dumas. Bruxelles. Société belge de librairie
Hauman et Ce., 1842, 24mo., pp. 122, followed by "Charlemagne" (with
no title-page), pp. 123-215.

"Lyderic" par Alexandre Dumas. Bruxelles, Société belge de librairie
Hauman et Ce., 1842, 18mo., pp. 231. Bibliothèque des châteaux et des
campagnes. 4e série.

Oeuvres de Alex. Dumas. Tome sixième. (Vignette) Bruxelles, Meline,
Cans et compagnie, 1843, large 8vo. "Aventures de Lyderic", pp. (309)-
338 in double columns.

Oeuvres de Alex. Dumas. Tome sixième. (Vignette) Bruxelles. Société
belge de librairie Hauman et Ce. 1843. Large 8vo. "Lyderic", pp.
(315)-347 in double columns.

"Pauline de Meulien". "Aventures de Lyderic". "Jacques 1er et Jacques
II" par Alexandre Dumas. Publié par Dufour et Mulat. Dessins de
J.-A. Beaucé, Staal, C. Nanteuil, Ed. Coppin. (Woodcut) Paris, 1853,
chez Marescq et Cie. 3 parties en 1 volume, 4to., pp. 80, 48 and 24
respectively in double columns.
Reprinted, same format and pagination, 1855 and 1856.

Le Siècle. "Les aventures de Lyderic". "Gabriel Lambert". Par Alexandre Dumas. Paris, Bureau du Siècle, 1855, 4to. "Les aventures de
Lyderic", pp. (309)-328 in double columns. Caption title.

"Les aventures de Lyderic". "Gabriel Lambert". Par Alexandre Dumas.
Paris, Impre. de Walder, n.d. (1855), same format and pagination as
the preceding edition. Caption title.

Ibid   Paris, Impr. de J. Voisvenel, n.d. (1855), same
format and pagination as the preceding edition. Caption title.

Collection Hetzel. "L'horoscope" par Alex. Dumas. Edition autorisée
pour la Belgique et l'étranger, interdite pour la France. Bruxelles,
Meline, Cans et Cie., 1858, 24mo., 3 volumes, the pagination of the
last volume being 233 and unnumbered page table of contents. "L'horoscope" ends on page 101, verso blank, "Aventures de Lyderic", verso
blank, "Aventures de Lyderic, comte de Flandre", pp. (105)-233. On
verso of half-title of each volume : 'Déposé aux terms de la loi'.
Green wrappers.

Ibid   Bruxelles, Office de Publicité; Leipzig, Alphonse
Dürr, libraire-éditeur, 1858, same format and pagination as the preceding edition. Bruxelles. Impr. Guyot.

Ibid   Leipzig, Alphonse Dürr, libraire, éditeur, 1858,
same format and pagination as the preceding edition. Bruxelles. Imp.
de E. Guyot.

"Aventures de Lyderic", par Alexandre Dumas. Paris, Impr. de Gaittet,
n.d. (1861), large 8vo., pp. 48 in double columns. Caption title;
illustrated.

Ibid   Paris, Impr. de S. Raçon, n.d. (1861), same format
and pagination as the preceding edition. Caption title; 4 illustrations.

"La bouillie de la comtesse Berthe", par Alexandre Dumas. Paris, Michel Lévy frères, 1862, 12mo., pp. 240, (241)-242 table of contents. "Aventures de Lyderic comte de Flandre", pp. (95)-240. Frequently reprinted, same format and pagination, by Michel Lévy frères and Calmann-Lévy.

"Aventures de Lyderic" par Alexandre Dumas Dessins par J.-A. Beaucé. Paris, Calmann-Lévy, Editeur ancienne maison Michel Lévy frères, 1885, 4to., pp. (1)-48 in double columns. Alexandre Dumas oeuvres illustrées.

"Pauline de Meulien" "Aventures de Lyderic" "Jacques 1er et Jacques II" par Alexandre Dumas. Dessins par J.-A. Beaucé, Staal, C. Nanteuil, Ed. Coppin. (Vignette) Paris, Calmann-Lévy, n.d. (1890), 4to. "Aventures de Lyderic", pp. 48 in double columns. Caption title. Woodcut at head of title. Buff wrappers. Alexandre Dumas oeuvres illustrées.
Reprinted, same format and pagination, 1891.

"Aventures de Lyderic, comte de Flandre". By Alexandre Dumas. Edited with notes by A.K. Cook. London, Rivington, 1890, 16mo., pp. viii, 155. Episodes from modern French authors.

"CHRONIQUE DU ROI PEPIN"   1842

This, another chronicle story, belongs to the period 740 to 768 A.D. and calls for no particular notice.

It was first published as a feuilleton in 'Le Siècle' in 1841.

Original edition.
"Aventures de Lyderic" (with "Chronique du roi Pépin" and "Chronique de Charlemagne") Par Alexandre Dumas. Paris, Dumont, 1842, 8vo., pp. 359. "Chronique du roi Pépin" occupies pp. (161)-224. Yellow wrappers.

"Aventures de Lyderic" par Alexandre Dumas. Bruxelles, Meline, Cans et compagnie, 1842, 18mo., pp. 280. "Aventures de Lyderic" ends on page 124, and is followed by "Chronique du roi Pépin", pp. 125-176, and by "Chronique du Charlemagne".

Ibid   Bruxelles et Leipzig, Meline, Cans et compagnie, 1842, same format and pagination as the preceding edition. Pink wrappers.

"Le chevalier d'Harmental" par Alexandre Dumas. Bruxelles, Société belge de librairie, Hauman et ce., 1842, 18mo., 3 volumes. "Le chevalier d'Harmental" ends on page 191 of Volume 3 and is followed by "Chronique du roi Pépin", pp. (195)-242.

Oeuvres de Alex. Dumas. Tome sixième. (Vignette) Bruxelles, Meline, Cans et compagnie, 1843, large 8vo. "Chronique du roi Pépin", pp. (341)-353 in double columns.

Oeuvres de Alex. Dumas Tome sixième. (Vignette) Bruxelles. Société belge de librairie Hauman et Ce. 1843, large 8vo. "Chronique du roi Pépin", pp. (223)-236 in double columns.

"Histoire d'une colombe" par Alexandre Dumas. Paris, Alexandre Cadot, éditeur, 1851, 8vo., 2 volumes, pp. 303 and 319. There are no tables of contents. "Histoire d'une colombe" ends on page 57 of Volume 2, verso blank, "Chateaubriand", pp. (59)-235, verso blank, "Le roi Pépin", pp. (237)-319. Yellow wrappers. Sceaux, impr. de E. Dépée.

"Histoire nautique. Episodes de la mer" par Alexandre Dumas. Bruxelles, Alphonse Lebègue, 1852, 18mo., pp. 158. Contents and pagination : "Bontekoe 1619", pp. (5)-116; "Le roi Pépin", pp. (117)-158.

Ibid   Bruxelles et Leipzig, Kiessling et compagnie; Vienne, à la librairie de J.F. Gress, 1852, same format and pagination as the preceding edition.

"Les hommes de fer" par Alexandre Dumas. Paris, Michel Lévy frères, 1867, 12mo., pp. 305, and unnumbered page table of contents. "Pépin" occupies pp. (1)-58.
Reprinted, same format and pagination, by both Michel Lévy fréres and Calmann-Lévy.

"CHRONIQUE DE CHARLEMAGNE"   1842

To all intents and purposes this further chronicle story is a continuation of "Chronique du roi Pépin" covering the years 768 to 814 A.D.

Original edition.
"Aventures de Lyderic" (with "Chronique du roi Pépin" and "Chronique de Charlemagne") Par Alexandre Dumas. Paris, Dumont, 1842, 8vo., pp. 359. "Chronique de Charlemagne" occupies pp. (225)-359. Yellow wrappers.

"Aventures de Lyderic" par Alexandre Dumas. Bruxelles, Meline, Cans et compagnie, 1842, 18mo., pp. 280. "Chronique de Charlemagne" is the third work in the volume and occupies pp. 177-280.

Ibid   Bruxelles et Leipzig, Meline, Cans et compagnie, 1842, same format and pagination as the preceding edition.

"Lyderic" par Alexandre Dumas. Bruxelles. Société belge de librairie Hauman et Ce., 1842, 24mo., pp. 122; it is followed by "Charlemagne" (with no title-page), pp. 123-215.

Oeuvres de Alex. Dumas. Tome sixième. (Vignette) Bruxelles, Meline, Cans et compagnie, 1843, large 8vo. "Chronique de Charlemagne", pp. (357)-382 in double columns.

Oeuvres de Alex. Dumas Tome sixième. (Vignette) Bruxelles. Société belge de librairie Hauman et Ce. 1843, large 8vo. "Chronique de Charlemagne", pp. (351)-377 in double columns.

"Le trou d l'enfer" (with "Chronique de Charlemagne") Par Alexandre Dumas. Paris, Alexandre Cadot, 1851, 8vo., 4 volumes. "Chronique de Charlemagne" occupies pp. 165-354 of Volume 4. Yellow wrappers.

Alexandre Dumas illustré par J.-A. Beaucé. "Chronique de Charlemagne". Publié par Dufour et Mulat. (Vignette) Marescq et Cie., éditeurs. Paris, 1856, 4to., pp. 32 in double columns.

Alexandre Dumas. "Une vie artiste (Mélingue)". "Chronique de Charlemagne". "Praxède". "Pierre le Cruel". Edition illustrée par J.-A. Beaucé et Ed. Coppin. Paris, Marescq, 1857, same format and pagination as the preceding edition.

118

"Chronique de Charlemagne", par Alexandre Dumas. Paris, Impr. de
Gaittet, n.d. (1861), 4to., pp. 32 in double columns; illustrated.
"Les hommes de fer" par Alexandre Dumas. Paris, Michel Lévy frères,
1867, 12mo., pp. 305, and unnumbered page table of contents. "Charle-
magne" occupies pp. (59)-180.
Reprinted, same format and pagination, by both Michel Lévy frères and
Calmann-Lévy.
"Chronique de Charlemagne" par Alexandre Dumas édition illustrée
par J.-A. Beaucé et Ed. Coppin Paris Calmann-Lévy éditeur ancienne
maison Michel Lévy frères, 1889, 4to., pp. (1)-32 in double columns.
Alexandre Dumas. "Chronique de Charlemagne." Edition illustrée par
J.-A. Beaucé et Ed. Coppin. Paris, Calmann-Lévy, 1897, same format
and pagination as the preceding edition. Alexandre Dumas oeuvres
illustrées.

"LE CHEVALIER D'HARMENTAL"   1842

     This romance deals with the Cellamare conspiracy of 1718, and
is the first with which Auguste Maquet had any connexion. Maquet had
written a short story from an incident in the "Mémoires de Jean Buvat".
This story was rejected wherever it was submitted, and Dumas hearing
of it offered to take it with him to Florence and there make a play out
of it. Instead he wrote a romance which Buloz, most unwisely, declined
for publication in the "Revue de Paris". It was accepted by "Le
Siècle", the first feuilleton appearing in the issue for 18 juin,
1841.

     It should be mentioned here that "Une fille du Régent" is more
of a companion story than the sequel that it has been claimed to be.

Original edition.
"Le chevalier d'Harmental" par Alexandre Dumas. Bruxelles, Société
belge de librairie, Hauman et ce., 1842, 18mo., 3 volumes, pp. 396,
233 and 242. The work ends on page 191 of Volume 3 and is followed
by "Chronique du roi Pépin", pp. (195)-242.

"Le chevalier d'Harmental", par Alexandre Dumas. Bruxelles, Ch. Hen,
Editeur-libraire, 1842, 18mo., 3 volumes, pp. 223, 4; 216, 4; 202, 4.
The four pages at the end of each volume are entitled : "Le dimanche.
Chronique des Salons, des Arts, de la Littérature et de la Politique"
and have nothing to do with Dumas.

"Le chevalier d'Harmental". Par Alexandre Dumas. (Vignette) Bruxelles, Meline, Cans et compagnie, 1842, 18mo., 3 volumes, pp. 265, 259
and 250.

Ibid   Bruxelles et Leipzig, Meline, Cans et compagnie,
1842, 3 volumes, same format and pagination as the preceding edition.

"Le chevalier d'Harmental", par Alexandre Dumas. Paris, Dumont,
1842, 8vo., 4 volumes, pp. 326, 305, 340 and 337. Yellow wrappers.

Oeuvres de Alex. Dumas. Tome cinquième. (Vignette) Bruxelles,
Meline, Cans et compagnie, 1842, large 8vo. "Le chevalier d'Harmental"
pp. (571)-617 in double columns. Oeuvres de Alex. Dumas. Tome sixième. (Vignette) Bruxelles, Meline, Cans et compagnie, 1843, large

8vo. "Le chevalier d'Harmental" (suite), frontispiece, pp. (7)-168 in double columns.

Oeuvres de Alex. Dumas Tome sixiéme. (Vignette) Bruxelles. Société belge de librairie Hauman et Ce. 1843, large 8vo. "Le chevalier d'Harmental", frontispiece, pp. (3)-220 in double columns.

"Le chevalier d'Harmental" par Alexandre Dumas. Paris, Michel Lévy frères, 1846, 12mo., 2 volumes, pp. 309 and 326 with 'post-scriptum' pp. 327-330, each with an additional unnumbered page table of contents.

"Le Chevalier d'Harmental", Par M. Alexandre Dumas. Reprinted from "Le Siècle" in 'L'Echo des feuilletons', Paris, 1849, 8vo., pp. (149)-341 in double columns. Caption title.

"Le chevalier d'Harmental" par Alexandre Dumas. Publié par Dufour et Mulat. Edition illustrée par J.-A. Beaucé. (Vignette) Paris, Marescq et Cie., 1854, 4to.; Partie I et Partie II, pp. 146 with 19 illustrations, and 148 with 18 illustrations, each with an additional unnumbered page table of contents and, on verso, 'placement des gravures', all in double columns.

Ibid   Paris, Marescq et Cie, éditeurs chez Malmenayde et de Riberolles, libraires, 1854, same format and pagination as the preceding edition. Buff wrappers with vignette illustrations.

Alexandre Dumas. "Le chevalier d'Harmental". Paris, Michel Lévy frères, 1854, 4to., pp. (89)-221 in double columns and including table of contents. Caption title. Woodcut at head of title. Pink wrappers repeating woodcut.

"Le chevalier d'Harmental" par Alexandre Dumas. Edition illustrée par J.-A. Beaucé. Paris, Lécrivain et Toubon, 1860, 4to., pp. (1)-146 in double columns and unnumbered page table of contents, verso 'Placement des gravures'; frontispiece.

"Le chevalier d'Harmental" par Alexandre Dumas. Nouvelle édition. Paris, Michel Lévy frères, 1860, 12mo., 2 volumes, pp. 295 and 320, including 'post-scriptum', 1 additional unnumbered page table of contents to Volume 1 and 2 pages to Volume 2.
Frequently reprinted, same format and pagination, by both Michel Lévy frères and Calmann-Lévy.

Journal du dimanche. "Le chevalier d'Harmenthal". No. 387, 14 juillet 1861, through to No. 413, 13 octobre 1861, in treble columns, signed : Alexandre Dumas. 4to., woodcut at head of each issue.

"Le chevalier d'Harmental" par Alexandre Dumas Edition illustrée par J.-A. Beaucé. Paris, Calmann-Lévy, 1897, 4to., 2 volumes. Première partie, pp. (1)-146 and Deuxième partie, pp. (1)-148, each in double columns and with an additional unnumbered page table of contents. First volume with yellow, and second volume with green, wrappers. Oeuvres illustrées.

"LE SEDUCTEUR ET LE MARI"   1842

        Although this play was announced as having been written by Charles Lafont it is well-known that Dumas helped considerably in the writing of it.

Original (and only) edition.
"Le séducteur et le mari", drame en trois actes, par M. Ch. Lafont,
représenté, pour la première fois, a Paris, le 5 novembre 1842. Caption title. Woodcut at head of title, Acte III, scène vi. Yellow
wrappers : Magasin théatral. Choix de pièces nouvelles, jouées
sur tous les théatres de Paris. Théatre des Délassemens Comiques.
"Le séducteur et le mari", Drame en trois actes. (Vignette) Paris,
Marchant; Bruxelles, Tarride, n.d. (1842), 8vo., pp. 27 in double
columns. (The Bibliothèque de l'Arsenal copy has 'et Alexandre Dumas'
in ink on the title-page after 'Lafont'.)

"HALIFAX"   1843

        The period of this play is the reign of Charles II of England,
and it has been stated that Adolphe d'Ennery helped in the writing.
At any rate the prologue was an afterthought, for Dumas at the end of
the final rehearsal told the actors and actresses that the play needed
some sort of an introduction - he would write it at once if they could
learn it before the opening performance. He did, and they did. Dumas
had himself announced on the first night under the pseudonym of Davy.

        It may be noted that the Calmann-Lévy collected editions of his
plays both state that the first performance was 30th November, 1842.

Original edition.
"Halifax", comédie mêlée de chant, en trois actes, avec un prologue,
par Alexandre Dumas, représentée, pour la première fois, a Paris, sur
le Théatre des Variétés, le 2 décembre 1842. Caption title. Woodcut
at head of title, Prologue, scène v. Yellow wrappers : Magasin
théatral. Choix de pièces nouvelles, jouées sur tous les théatres de
Paris. Théatre des Variétés. "Halifax", Comédie en trois actes et
un prologue. (Vignette) Paris, Marchant, n.d. (1843), 8vo., pp. 36
in double columns.

Ibid   Paris, Marchant; Bruxelles, Tarride, n.d. (1843),
same format and pagination as the preceding edition.

Théatre de Alex. Dumas. "Halifax". (Vignette) Bruxelles, Meline,
Cans et compagnie, 1843, 32mo., pp. 130. Buff wrappers.

"Halifax", comédie mêlée de chant, en trois actes, par Alexandre
Dumas. Représentée, pour la première fois sur le théatre des Variétés,
le 2 décembre 1842. A Bruxelles, J.-A. Lelong, Imprim.-Libr.-Editeur,
1843, 12mo., pp. 114. Yellow wrappers : Repértoire de la scène
française. IIme année. No. 1.

Théatre français en prose publié par G. Schutz. Quatrième série. X
livraison. "Halifax". Comédie mêlée de chant, en 3 actes, avec un
prologue, par Alexandre Dumas. Bielefeld, Velhagen & Klasing, 1843,
24mo., pp. 110.
Ibid   Deuxième édition. 1861. Same format and pagination as the preceding edition.
Ibid   Troisième édition. 1876. 18mo., pp. 96.

"Halifax", comédie mêlée de chant, en trois actes, avec un prologue,
par Alexandre Dumas, représentée, pour la première fois, à Paris, sur
le théatre des Variétés, le 2 décembre 1842. Paris, Impr. de Mme V^e
Dondey-Dupré, n.d. (c 1845), 8vo., pp. 36 in double columns. Caption
title. Woodcut at head of title, Prologue, scène v.

"Halifax" comédie en trois actes et en prologue Variétés. - 30 novembre 1842. "Distribution" on title-page, pp. (1)-92. Théatre complet de Alex. Dumas. Tome VIII Paris Calmann Lévy, éditeur ancienne maison Michel Lévy frères, 1874. 12mo. "Théatre complet" in 25 volumes.

"Halifax". Comédie mêlée de chant, en trois actes, avec un prologue. Par Alexandre Dumas. Avec notes et vocabulaire par A.W. Kastan ... . Berlin, Friedberg et Mode, 1880, 8vo., pp. 92. 'Notes et vocabulaire', pp. 93-98. Théâtre français. No. 98.

"A I ..." (Ida Ferrier)   1843

This poem which, according to the late André Fossé d'Arcosse, was written for Ida Ferrier who became Dumas' wife consists of six verses each of 4 lines.

Original edition.
In : No. 38 of 'Le Foyer', 8 janvier 1843.
In : 'Le Livre', 10 avril 1887, page 107.
In : 'L'Intermédiaire des chercheurs et curieux', 20 mars 1898, under the title "Pièce de vers écrit par Alexandre Dumas père dans l'album de la comtesse d'A ... ."
In : 'Le centenaire d'Alexandre Dumas : 1802-1902', Soissons, 'L'Argus Soissonnais', 1902.

(The first two verses, in Dumas' holograph and signed, were printed in 'Revue des autographes' published by Eugène Charavay, issue No. 84, janvier 1886.)

"LE CORRICOLO"   1843

This is the final work covering Dumas' travels in Italy and Sicily. It was published as a feuilleton in "Le Siècle" between 24th June, 1842, and 17th January, 1843.

Original edition.
"Le Corricolo", par Alexandre Dumas. Bruxelles, Alp. Lebègue et Sacré fils, 1842-1843, 18mo., 3 volumes, pp. Volume 1 (1842), 192, and Volumes 3 and 4 (1843), 192 and 192. Green wrappers.

Ibid   Bruxelles et Leipzig, C. Muquardt, 1842-1843, same format and pagination as the preceding edition.

"Le Corricolo" par Alexandre Dumas. Bruxelles, Hauman et Cie., 1843, 16mo., 4 volumes, pp. 263, 241, 253 and 239, each with an additional unnumbered page table of contents.

"Le Corricolo", par Alexandre Dumas. Bruxelles, J. Jamar, 1843, 18mo., 3 volumes, each of 192 pages.

"Le Corricolo" par Alexandre Dumas. (Vignette) Bruxelles, Meline, Cans et Cie., 1843, 16mo., 3 volumes, pp. (v)-ix 'Préface', (11)-270, 248 and 203, each with an additional unnumbered page table of contents.

"Le Corricolo". Par Alexandre Dumas. (Vignette) Bruxelles et Leipzig, Meline, Cans et compagnie, 1843, same format and pagination as the preceding edition.

Oeuvres de Alex. Dumas. Tome sixième. (Vignette) Bruxelles, Meline, Cans et compagnie, 1843, large 8vo. "Le Corricolo", pp. (525)-715 in double columns.

"Le Corricolo", par Alexandre Dumas. Paris, Dolin, 1843, 8vo., 4 volumes, pp. 342, 327, 334 and 324. Yellow wrappers.

"Comment fut composé 'L'Othello' de Rossini". Alexandre Dumas. In : 'Le livre des feuilletons Receuil de nouvelles, contes, épisodes, extraits de la presse contemporaine'. Nancy, Imprimerie Hinzelin, 1843, 8vo., pp. 35-38 in double columns. Premier volume. (This is a reprint of Chapter V, Volume 1, of "Le Corricolo".)

"Le Corricolo" par Alexandre Dumas. Bruxelles, Société belge de librairie Hauman et ce., 1843-1844, 16mo., 4 volumes, pp. Volumes 1-2 (1843), 263 and 241, and Volumes 3-4 (1844), 253 and 239, each with an additional unnumbered page table of contents.

"Salvator-Rosa". Alexandre Dumas. In : 'Echo des feuilletons Choix de nouvelles, épisodes, anecdotes, extraits de la Presse contemporaine'. Paris, 1845, large 8vo., pp. (22)-32 in double columns.
Ibid   Paris, 1849, same format and pagination as the preceding edition.
(This is Chapter 44, Volume 2, of the Levy édition of "Le Corricolo", entitled there 'Les héritiers d'un grand homme'.)

"Le Corricolo" par Alexandre Dumas Paris, Chez Boulé, 1846, large 8vo., pp. 380, (381)-382 table of contents. Les mille et un romans, Nouvelles et Feuilletons. No. XVI.

"Impressions de voyage. Le Corricolo" par Alexandre Dumas. Paris, Michel Lévy frères, 1851, 12mo., 2 volumes, pp. 315, verso table of contents, and 310, and unnumbered page table of contents.
Frequently reprinted, same format and pagination, by both Michel Lévy frères and Calmann-Lévy.

Ibid   Paris, Michel Lévy frères, n.d. (1853), 4to., pp. 159 in double columns. Caption title, illustrated.

Le Siècle. Oeuvres complètes d'Alexandre Dumas. Neuvième série. "Impressions de voyage. Le Corricolo". Paris, au bureau du Siècle, 1855, 4to., pp. (1)-158 in double columns, and unnumbered page table of contents. Caption title.

"Impressions de voyage. Le Corricolo" par Alexandre Dumas. Paris, Calmann-Lévy, 1888, 4to., pp. 166 in double columns and unnumbered page table of contents. Caption title. Woodcut at head of title. Brown wrappers with the same woodcut. Musée littéraire contemporain.

"LA VILLA PALMIERI"   1843

    This work is purely and simply a collection of articles describing places and occurrences connected with Florence. Its title comes from the name of the house Dumas occupied while he was living in Florence. Included in the work is the account of the arrival of the news of the death of his friend the duc d'Orléans, which was later rewritten and enlarged for the work "Les morts vont vite".

Original edition.
"La villa Palmieri", par Alexandre Dumas. Paris. Dolin, librairie-

commissionaire, 1843, 8vo., 2 volumes, pp. (i)-lxvi 'Préface. Un alchimiste au dix-neuvième siècle', (1)-278, and (1)-337, each with an
additional unnumbered page table of contents; verso of half-titles
'extrait du Catalogue de Dolin, Libraire' which includes three titles
by Dumas. Yellow wrappers. Paris, Imprimé par Béthune et Plon.
(The preface is a biography of vicomte Henri de Ruolz, composer and
chemist.)

"L'ange de la réconciliation". Alexandre Dumas. In : 'Le livre des
feuilletons Receuil de nouvelles, contes, épisodes, extraits de la
presse contemporaine'. Nancy, Imprimerie Hinzelin, 1843, 8vo., pp.
129-133 in double columns. Premier volume.

Ibid   In : 'L'Echo des feuilletons'. Paris, Dufour
et Mulat, 1843, 8vo., pp. 277-281 in double columns.
Reprinted, 1850 and 1863, same format and pagination.

Ibid   In : 'La Chronicle. L'Echo des feuilletons',
Paris, 1857, 8vo., same format and pagination as the preceding.
(The above are reprints of the Chapter entitled 'Hippolyte et Dianora',
Volume 2.)

"La villa Palmieri", par Alexandre Dumas. Paris, Boulé, 1847, 8vo.,
pp. (1)-20 'Préface : Un Alchimiste au dix-neuvième siècle', (21)-
197, and unnumbered page table of contents. Caption title. Les mille
et un romans, Nouvelles et Feuilletons. No. XXII.

"Impressions de voyage. La villa Palmieri" par Alexandre Dumas.
Paris, Michel Lévy frères, 1855, 12mo., pp. 278 and unnumbered page
table of contents.
Several times reprinted, same format and pagination, by both Michel
Lévy frères and Calmann-Lévy.

Le Siècle. Oeuvres complètes d'Alexandre Dumas. Neuvième série.
"Impressions de voyage La villa Palmieri". Paris, au bureau du
Siècle, 1855, 4to., pp. (1)-73 in double columns, and unnumbered page
table of contents.

"La villa Palmieri" par Alexandre Dumas. Paris, Michel Lévy frères,
n.d. (1855), same format and pagination as the preceding edition.
Caption title; illustrated.

"Impressions de voyage. La villa Palmieri", par Alexandre Dumas.
Paris, Impr. de J. Voisvenel, n.d. (1855), same format and pagination
as the two preceding editions. Caption title; illustrated.

"UN ALCHIMISTE AU DIX-NEUVIEME SIECLE"   1843

      As mentioned in the note to the original edition of "La villa
Palmieri" this is a brief biography of vicomte Henri de Ruolz, musical
composer and chemist.

Original edition (in separate form).
"Un alchimiste au dix-neuvième siècle" par Alexandre Dumas. Paris,
Imprimerie de Paul Dupont, 1843, 8vo., pp. 23. The printed cover takes
the place of the title-page.

Then, as a preface to "La villa Palmieri", Paris, Dolin, 1843, edition,
q.v.

"Une fille du Régent" Par Alexandre Dumas. Bruxelles, Société belge de librairie, Hauman et cie., 1844, 24mo., 5 volumes, the pagination of Volume 5 being 152 and pp. (99)-152 being filled by "Un alchimiste au XIXe siècle".

Ibid   Bruxelles, Société belge du librairie, Hauman et ce., 1844, 16mo., 3 volumes, the pagination of Volume 3 being 248 and pp. (193)-248 being filled by "Un alchimiste au XIXe siècle".

Then, as a preface to "La villa Palmieri", Paris, Boulé, 1847, edition, q.v.

"LE MARIAGE AU TAMBOUR"   1843

        Quérard has written that on the first night of this comedy's performance the author's name was announced as M. de Villers; this was considered by one reviewer to conceal the name of Alexandre Dumas of Villers-Cotterets. Dumas has always been associated with its writing.

Original edition.
"Le mariage au tambour", comédie en trois actes, mêlée de chant, par MM. de Leuven et Brunswick, Représentée pour la première fois, à Paris, sur le théâtre des Variétés, le 9 mars 1843. Caption title. Yellow wrappers : Répertoire dramatique des auteurs contemporains. N. 240. Théâtre des Variétés. "Le mariage au tambour", comédie en trois actes, mêlée de chant. (Vignette) Paris, au bureau ... Tresse, successeur de J.N. Barba, 1843, 8vo., pp. 31 in double columns. (The copy in the Bibliothèque de l'Arsenal has 'et Alex. Dumas' in ink after Brunswick's (Lhérie) name.

"Le mariage au tambour", comédie en trois actes, mêlée de chant, par MM. A. Dumas, de Leuven et Brunswick, Représentée, pour la première fois, à Paris, sur le théâtre des Variétés, le 9 mars 1843. (Vignette) A Bruxelles, J.-A. Lelong, 1843, 18mo$_{me}$ pp. 96. Yellow wrappers : Répertoire de la scène française. IIme année. No. 15.

"Le mariage au tambour", opéra-comique en 3 actes et 6 tableaux, d'après Alexandre Dumas, de Leuven et Brunswick, par Paul Burani, musique de M. Léon Vasseur ... . (Paris, Châtelet, 4 avril 1885.) Paris, Enoch frères et Costallat, 1885, 16mo., pp. 103.

"ALBINE" "LE CHATEAU D'EPPSTEIN"   1843

        This is one of Dumas' least successful romances and, because of its dual title by Belgian and French publishers, has been the cause of some confusion. It would appear to have been drawn from a story by August Lafontaine, a German despite his name, and is Dumas' first attempt at dealing with the supernatural in his romances.

Original edition (as "Albine").
"Albine", par Alexandre Dumas. Bruxelles, Alph. Lebègue et Sacré fils, 1843, 18mo., 2 volumes, pp. 151 and 152.

Ibid   (Vignette) Bruxelles et Leipzig, C. Muquardt, 1843, same format and pagination as the preceding edition. Yellow wrappers.

"Albine" par Alexandre Dumas. (Vignette) Bruxelles. Meline, Cans et compagnie librairie, imprimerie et fonderie. 1843, 16mo., 2 volumes, pp. (1)-50 'Introduction', (51)-226 (comprising Chapters I-VIII), and (1)-252 (comprising Chapters IX-XXII).

Ibid   Bruxelles et Leipzig, Meline, Cans et compagnie, 1843, same format and pagination as the preceding edition.

Original edition (as "Le château d'Eppstein").
"Le château d'Eppstein", par Alexandre Dumas. Paris, L. de Potter, 1844, 8vo., 3 volumes, pp. 324, 354 and 322. "Le château d'Eppstein" ends on page 70 of Volume 3, and is followed by "Fra Bartolomeo", pp. 71-112; "Le curé Chambard", pp. 113-232; "La Vendée après le 29 juillet", pp. 233-288; and "Un miracle au XVe siècle", pp. 289-322. Yellow wrappers.

Collection Hetzel. "Le château d'Eppstein" par Alexandre Dumas. Edition autorisée pour la Belgique et l'étranger, interdite pour la France. Leipzic, Alph. Dürr, 1852, 24mo., 2 volumes, pp. 195 and 180. Green wrappers.

Collection Hetzel. "Le château d'Eppstein", par Alexandre Dumas. Edition autorisèe pour la Belgique et l'ètranger, interdite pour la France. Bruxelles, Meline, Cans et cie., 1859, same format and pagination as the preceding edition.

"Le château d'Eppstein" par Alexandre Dumas. Paris, Michel Lévy frères, 1860, 12mo., 2 volumes, pp. 261 and 243.
Reprinted, same format and pagination, by both Michel Lévy frères and Calmann-Lévy.

Ibid   Paris, Michel Lévy frères, 1860, 4to., pp. 85 in double columns. Caption title; illustrated.

"FILLES LORETTES ET COURTISANES"   1843

    In his brief introduction to this work Dumas wrote that he under-took it because no one else dared.

Original edition.
"Filles lorettes et courtisanes" signed : Alex. Dumas. In : "La grande ville nouveau tableau de Paris comique, critique et philosophique" par H. de Balzac, Alex. Dumas, Frédéric Soulié, ...
... . Illustrations de Gavarni, Victor Adam, Daumier, d'Aubigny, H. Emy, Traviès et Henri Monnier. 2 Paris au bureau central des publications nouvelles, rue des Prêtres Saint-Germain-l'Auxerrois, 11. 1843. Large 8vo., 2 volumes. Volume 2 : "Filles", pp. (317)-344; "Lorettes", pp. (345)-367; "Courtisanes", pp. (369)-396; each sub-title with a facing steel engraving, vignettes. Pp. (417)-418 table of contents. Paris, imprimerie de Maulde et Renou, rue Bailleul, 9 et 11.

"Filles lorettes et courtisanes" par Alexandre Dumas. Paris Dolin, libraire-commissionaire, quai des Augustins, 47. 1843 8vo., pp. (1)-4 'Avant-propos', (5)-91 "Filles", verso blank, (93)-160 "Lorettes", (161)-245 "Courtisanes", verso blank. The volume is completed by "Mme de Saint-Colombe" par Marc Fournier. There is no table of contents. Verso of half-title 'Extrait du Catalogue de Dolin, Libraire' which includes four of Dumas' works. Green wrappers. Imp. de Maulde et Renou, rue Bailleul, 9 et 11.

"Nouveau tableau de Paris". Comique, Critique et Philosophique par MM. Balzac, A. Dumas, Soulié, Gozlan, ... Illustrations de Gavarni, Victor Adam, Daumier, d'Aubigny, ... Paris, Marescq, libraire-éditeur, 1845, 4to. "Filles, lorettes et courtisanes" occupies pp. 315-396 in double columns. The volume has 26 illustrations.

Alexandre Dumas. "Filles, lorettes et courtisanes". Vienne, Rhombus, n.d. (c 1860), 8vo., pp. 101.

Later editions of this work had additional material entitled "Les serpents", an article written by Dumas of the same genre as the earlier work.

"Filles, lorettes et courtisanes - les serpents" par Alexandre Dumas. Paris, Michel Lévy frères, 1874, 12mo., pp. 282 and additional unnumbered page table of contents. "Les serpents", pp. (139)-282. Fairly frequently reprinted, same format and pagination, by both Michel Lévy frères and Calmann-Lévy.

"Filles lorettes et courtisanes" par Alexandre Dumas. Paris, Michel Lévy frères, 1875, 4to., pp. 35 in double columns, followed by "Les serpents", pp. 35-71 also in double columns. Caption title. Woodcut at head of title. Pale mauve wrappers repeating woodcut. Musée littéraire contemporain.

"GEORGES"   1843

    Mauritius, in the years 1810 to 1824, is the setting for this romance and it is the only occasion on which Dumas ever touched upon the colour problem. The capital of the island at that time was named Port Napoléon and the story opens with the description of a battle fought offshore from that port. Dumas' account of the battle was for long considered to be false in that it differed from the official version published in 'Le Moniteur'; it has, however, since been proved that his description was the correct one, the official version having been distorted for political reasons.

    At the time of writing the book one of Dumas' friends was Félicien Malleville, who had been brought up in Mauritius, and it can be assumed that it was from him that Dumas obtained the local 'colour' given in his story.

Original edition (to be published in France).
"Georges", par Alexandre Dumas. Paris, Dumont, 1843, 8vo., 3 volumes, pp. 330, 323 and 322. Yellow wrappers.

It is very probable that the Dumont edition was preceded by the following four Belgian editions, and very possibly too by a London reprint. The particular spelling of the book's title in the Belgian and London editions should be noted.

"George" par Alexandre Dumas. (Vignette) Bruxelles, Meline, Cans et compagnie, 1843, 16mo., 2 volumes, pp. 305 and 262. There are no tables of contents. Blue wrappers.

Ibid   Bruxelles, Société Typographique belge, Ad. Wahlen et Compagnie, 1843, 18mo., 3 volumes, pp. 167, 174 and 183, each with an additional unnumbered page table of contents. Yellow wrappers imprinted 'Distribution de l'émancipation'.

Ibid   (Vignette) Bruxelles, Société typographique belge, 1843, 12mo., 3 columes, pp. 203, 213 and 226, each with an additional unnumbered page table of contents.

"George", par Alexandre Dumas. A Bruxelles, Imprimerie Politique, (half-title : Bibliothèque du journal le politique), 1843, 18mo., 3 volumes, pp. 181, 195 and 200, each with an additional unnumbered page table of contents.

Ibid   London, Courrier de l'Europe's Office, 1843, same format and pagination as the preceding edition.

Oeuvres de Alex. Dumas. Tome septième. (Vignette) Bruxelles, Meline, Cans et compagnie, 1845, large 8vo. "George".

"Georges" par Alexandre Dumas. Paris, Michel Lévy frères, 1848, 12mo. This edition includes "Amaury".

"Georges" par Alexandre Dumas. Paris, L. Grimaux et Cie., n.d. (c 185), 4to., pp. 90 in double columns. Caption title; illustrated. Romans illustrés.

"Georges" par Alexandre Dumas. Nouvelle édition. Paris, Michel Lévy frères, 1860, 12mo., pp. 309, verso blank, (311)-312 table of contents.
Frequently reprinted, same format and pagination, by both Michel Lévy frères and Calmann-Lévy.

Footnote : A play was taken from the romance. "Georges le mulâtre", drame en cinq actes, huit tableaux, d'après le roman "Georges" d'Alexandre Dumas, par Charles Garand. Représenté pour la première fois, à Paris, sur le Théâtre du Château d'Eau, le samedi 26 janvier 1878. Paris, Calmann-Lévy, n.d. (1878), 4to., pp. 23 in double columns. Caption title.

"ASCANIO"   1843

     The period of this work is from 1539 to 1545 and centres around Benvenuto Cellini and the court of Francis I. It is partly based on the great craftsman's memoirs. Probably correctly, Paul Meurice has been credited with some participation towards the writing, but this would have been limited to sketching out the main theme of the story. To Dumas' great annoyance Meurice drew from it a five act drama entitled "Benvenuto Cellini" which was produced at the Porte-Saint-Martin in 1852.

     The work first appeared serially in "Le Siècle" from 31st July to 4th October, 1843.

Original edition.
"Ascanio", par Alexandre Dumas. (Vignette) Bruxelles, Alph. Lebégue et Sacré fils, 1843, 18mo., 3 volumes, pp. 192, 191 and 192. Green wrappers. Galérie littéraire, 7me. série.

Ibid   Bruxelles et Leipzig, C. Muquardt, 1843, same format and pagination as the preceding edition. Blue wrappers.

La Semaine Littéraire du Courrier des Etats-Unis. "Ascanio", par

128

Alexandre Dumas. New-York, Bureaux de la Semaine Littéraire, 1843,
4to., pp. 1 preliminary leaf, 90 in double columns. La Semaine Littéraire, 2ᵉ serie no. 31-42, "Ascanio" no. 1-11.

"Ascanio", par Alexandre Dumas. Bruxelles et Leipzig, Meline, Cans
et cie., 1843-1844, 24mo., 3 volumes, pp. Volume 1 (1843), 286, and
Volumes 2 and 3 (1844), 258 and 264.

Ibid   Bruxelles, Société belge de librairie, Hauman
et Cie., 1844, 16mo., 3 volumes, pp. 325, 263 and 316.

Ibid   Paris, Pétion, MDCCXLIV, 8vo., 5 volumes, pp. 329,
334, 325, 294 and 282, with 1 additional unnumbered page table of
contents for Volumes 1-4 and 2 additional unnumbered pages for
Volume 5.

Ibid   Paris, Michel Lévy frères, 185 , 2 volumes, pp. 299
and 342, each with an additional unnumbered page table of contents.
Frequently reprinted, same format and pagination, by both Michel Lévy
frères and Calmann-Lévy.

Ibid   Paris, Michel Lévy frères, n.d. (186), 4to.,
pp. 227-360 in double columns. Caption title. Musée littéraire du
siècle.

Ibid   Lagny, Typ. de A. Varigault, n.d. (186), 4to.,
pp. 161 in double columns; illustrated. Caption title.

"Ascanio" par Alexandre Dumas. Paris, Calmann-Lévy, n.d. (189),
4to., pp. 161 in double columns and unnumbered page table of contents.
Caption title. Woodcut at head of title. Blue wrappers with similar
woodcut. Musée littéraire contemporain.

"LES DEMOISELLES DE SAINT-CYR"   1843
     The action of this play takes place in France and Spain centring
around Madame de Maintenon's school for young ladies of respectable
families and the flight of the young couples forced into marriage and,
as a consequence, estranged to Spain. Altogether it was performed
more than 220 times at the Théatre-Français up to the early 1890s.

     In 1855 it was performed, by special request at Saint-Cloud, be-
fore Queen Victoria and the Prince Consort. The original had been
abridged by the actor Regnier, who did not do as much damage this
time as he did to "Un mariage sous Louis XV". Regnier compressed the
fifteen scenes of Act V into six and added them to Act IV; this version
is the one published in the collected editions of Dumas' "Theatre",
neither of which contains the letter from Dumas to Jules Janin, but
instead a note of appreciation to the cast as a post-scriptum dated
'28 juillet 1843' and signed : Alex. Dumas.

Original edition.
"Les demoiselles de Saint-Cyr", comédie en cinq actes, par M. Alexandre Dumas, représentée pour la première fois, a Paris, sur le
Théatre-Français, le 25 juillet 1843. Caption title. Woodcut at head
of title, Acte 1ᵉʳ, scène xii. Yellow (some copies buff) wrappers :
2ᵐᵉ. série du magasin théatral pièces nouvelles, jouées sur tous les
théatres de Paris. Théatre Français. "Les demoiselles de Saint-Cyr".
Comédie en cinq actes. (Vignette) Paris, chez Marchant, et tous les

marchands de nouveautés, n.d. (1843), 8vo., pp. 1 (lettre de Dumas à son éditeur), 38, and viii (lettre à J. Janin, 'le 23 juillet 1843'), in double columns. Dedicated 'A mon excellente ami madame la comtesse Dash'.

Feuilleton de la presse : 27 juillet 1843. "Les demoiselles de Saint-Cyr", comédie en cinq actes. Printed in 3 columns occupying 14 half-pages; each act has 'Alexandre Dumas' printed at the end.

"Les demoiselles de Saint-Cyr", comédie en cinq actes, par M. Alexandre Dumas. Bruxelles, J.-A. Lelong, chez Gambier, librairepapetier, au Magasin de pièces de Théâtre, 1843, 16mo., pp. 128, with Dumas' letter to the publisher facing the title-page.

Théâtre de Alex. Dumas. "Les demoiselles de Saint-Cyr". Bruxelles, Meline, Cans et Compagnie, 1843, 32mo., pp. 169. Green wrappers.

Théâtre français. IV série. 12e livraison. "Les demoiselles de Saint-Cyr" par Alexandre Dumas. A l'usage des écoles. Revue et annotée par Chr. Rauch ... . Bielefeld, Velhagen & Klasing, 1843, 18mo., pp. 137.
Frequently reprinted; the fourth edition, 1862, and subsequent editions all being in the same format but with a pagination of 156.

"Les Demoiselles de Saint-Cyr", comédie en cinq actes par Alexandre Dumas. Bruxelles, Société belge de librairie Hauman et Cie., 1844 on the title-page, the buff wrapper giving the year 1843, 18mo., pp. 208.
(On the back wrapper under 'Ouvrages de même auteur' is "Godefroid de Harcourt", 2 vols.)

Répertoire du Théâtre français à Berlin. Deuxième série. No. 37 (287). "Les demoiselles de Saint-Cyr", comédie en cinq actes et en prose, par A. Dumas. Berlin, 1844, Ad. Mt. Schlesinger, Libraire et Editeur de Musique. 8vo., pp. (1)-79. Imprimé chez I.W. Krause.

Théâtre français. VII Série. Livraison I (No. 37). "Les demoiselles de Saint-Cyr", Comédie en cinq actes et en prose, par A. Dumas. Berlin, chez Ad. Mt. Schlesinger. Petersbourg chez Graeff, Stockholm chez Bonniers, n.d. (1844), 24mo., pp. (3)-138, verso of title 'Personnages'; 2 pages of advertisements which include "Lorencino", par Dumas.

"Les demoiselles de Saint-Cyr", comédie en cinq actes, par Alexandre Dumas. Paris, Librairie théâtrale, 1854, 8vo., pp. 38 in double columns. Caption title.

"Les demoiselles de Saint-Cyr", comédie en cinq actes, par M. Alexandre Dumas, représentée pour la première fois, à Paris, sur le Théâtre-Français, le 25 juillet 1843. Paris, Impr. de Mme Ve Dondey-Dupré, n.d. (1854), 8vo., pp. 38 in double columns. Caption title.

"Les demoiselles de Saint-Cyr" comédie en quatre actes, en prose Théâtre-Français. - 25 juillet 1843. "Dédicace" and "Distribution" on title-page, pp. (93)-197. Théâtre complet de Alex. Dumas. Tome VIII Paris Calmann Lévy, éditeur ancienne maison Michel Lévy frères, 1874. 12mo. "Théâtre complet" in 25 volumes.

"Les Demoiselles de Saint-Cyr". Comédie en cinq actes. Par Alexandre Dumas. Pourvue de notes ... par Charles Ansorg. Berlin, Friedberg et Mode, 1877, 8vo., pp. 123, 7. Théâtre français. Collection Friedberg et Mode. No. 17.
Frequently reprinted, same format and pagination.

Le théâtre français du XIXe siècle. No. 8. "Les demoiselles de Saint-Cyr". Par Alexandre Dumas. With explanatory notes by Francis Tarver
.... London : Dulau and Co.; Hachette and Co., 1877, 16mo., pp. iv, 1-116, and 117-124, notes.

"Les demoiselles de Saint-Cyr", comédie par Alexandre Dumas; with introduction and notes by Victor Oger. London, Macmillan and co., 1886, 8vo., pp. 1 preliminary leaf, (1), vi-viii, (1), 152. Macmillan's series of Foreign School Classics, etc.

It is proper that reference should be made here to : "Le critique Jules Janin et le dramaturge Alexandre Dumas, à propos des 'Demoiselles de Saint-Cyr', comédie en cinq actes". Extraits du 'Journal des débats' et de 'La Presse' - Paris, chez tous les libraires, 1843, 12mo., pp. 44.
A second edition was published in the same year - Paris, rue des Prêtres-Saint-Germain-l'Auxerrois, 11; same format and pagination.

"LOUISE BERNARD"   1843
        The first draft of this play, which was written with the assistance of de Leuven and Léon Lhérie, was entitled "François". The period is the reign of Louis XV.

Original edition.
"Louise Bernard", drame en cinq actes, par M. Alex. Dumas, représenté pour la première fois, a Paris, sur le théatre de la Porte-Saint-Martin, le 18 novembre 1843. Paris, Marchant, n.d. (1843), 8vo., pp. 34 in double columns. Caption title. Woodcut at head of title, Acte IV, scène vii.

"Louis Bernard, drame en cinq actes; Par M. Alex. Dumas, représenté pour la première fois, a Paris, sur le théatre de la Porte-Saint-Martin, le 18 novembre 1843. Caption title. Woodcut at head of title, Acte IV, scène vii. Yellow wrappers : Magasin théatral. Choix de pièces nouvelles, jouées sur tous les théatres de Paris. Théatre de la Porte-Saint-Martin. "Louise Bernard". Drame en cinq actes. (Vignette) Paris, Marchant; Bruxelles, Tarride, n.d. (1843), 8vo., pp. 34 in double columns.

"Louise Bernard", drame en cinq actes, par M. Alexandre Dumas, Représentée pour la première fois, à Paris, sur le théâtre de la Porte-Saint-Martin, le 18 novembre 1843. (Vignette) Bruxelles, J.-A. Lelong, 1844, 18mo. pp. 112. Blue wrappers : Repértoire de la scène française, 12me année. No. 1.

"Louise Bernard"; drame en cinq actes. Par M. Alex. Dumas, représenté pour la première fois, à Paris, sur le Théatre de la Porte-Saint-Martin, le 18 novembre 1843. Paris, Impr. de Dondey-Dupré, n.d. (c 1845), 8vo., pp. 34 in double columns. Caption title. Woodcut at head of title, Acte IV, scène vii.

"Louise Bernard" drame en cinq actes, en prose Porte-Saint-Martin. - 18 novembre 1843. "Distribution" on title-page, pp. (199)-294. Théatre complet de Alex. Dumas. Tome VIII. Paris Calmann Levy, éditeur ancienne maison Michel Lévy frères, 1874. 12mo. "Théatre complet" in 25 volumes.

"FIESOLE" 1843

Early in 1842 Dumas was staying at the Villa Palmieri in Florence.
The book "La villa Palmieri", although sometimes indicated as the
volume following "Une année à Florence", was really a later production
and is, in reality, a kind of guide book to Florence, or to such
parts of it as appealed to Dumas; it is freely interspersed with
stories, more particularly those of an historical nature.

The interesting thing about "Fiesole" is that it is not a reprint
of a chapter, or even part of one, of "La villa Palmieri". Seemingly
it was written specially for the December "Keepsake" published by 'La
Chronique' and is, therefore, a separate bibliographical item in its
own right.

Original (and only) edition.
"Keepsake de 'La Chronique'". (Vignette) Paris, au bureau de la
Chronique, rue Neuve-S.-Augustin, 37. décembre 12mo., pp. (7)-159,
4 pages of facsimile MS and autographs, unnumbered page table of contents, frontispiece and vignettes. "Fiesole", signed : Alexandre
Dumas occupies pp. (7)-28. Grey board decorated covers repeating
title-page and with the date '1843'. Blois, Felix Jahyer, imprimeur.

"AMAURY" 1843

Dumas has stated that this pathetic story was based upon the case
of a boyhood companion, Félix Deviolaine, who went through all the
stages of pulmonary consumption but eventually, and miraculously,
recovered. The work first appeared as a feuilleton in 'La Presse'.
A Monsieur de Noailles, whose daughter was 'poitrinaire' like the
heroine of the romance, and who was intensely interested in the successive instalments, asked Dumas to suspend publication; this was done
and the instalments were resumed only after her death. It has also
been said, and this may be apocryphal, that Dumas improvised in manuscript a happy ending to the story for the girl's benefit.

Original edition.
Courrier des Etats-Unis. Semaine littéraire. "Amaury" par Alexandre
Dumas. New-York, F. Gaillardet, 1843, large 8vo., pp. 289-388 in
double columns. Série 3, no. 1.

"Amaury", par Alex. Dumas. Paris, Hippolyte Souverain, 1844, 8vo.,
4 volumes, pp. 313, 329, 323 and 301 (but according to Talvart et
Place the pagination of the last volume is wrong, pp. 295 and 296
having been skipped over); only Volumes 1 and 2 have an additional
unnumbered page table of contents.

"Amaury", par Alexandre Dumas. Bruxelles, Alph. Lebègue et Sacré
fils, 1844, 16mo., 2 volumes, pp. (5)-12 'Préface', (13)-158, and
(5)-202.

Ibid   Bruxelles et Leipzig, C. Muquardt, 1844, same
format and pagination as the preceding edition.

Ibid   Bruxelles, Meline, Cans et Cie., 1844, same format
and pagination as the two preceding editions.

"Amaury" par Alexandre Dumas. Bruxelles, Société belge de librairie
Hauman et Ce., 1844, 18mo., 2 volumes, pp. 243 and 250.

132

Ibid   (Vignette) Bruxelles, Meline, Cans et compagnie,
1844, 18mo., 2 volumes, pp. 254 and 260.

Ibid   (Vignette) Bruxelles et Leipzig, Meline, Cans et
compagnie, 1844, same format and pagination as the preceding edition.

"Amaury" par Alexandre Dumas. Paris, Michel Lévy frères, 1848, 12mo.,
pp. (1)-6 'Préface', 7-283.
Frequently reprinted same format and pagination, by both Michel Lévy
frères and Calmann-Lévy.

"Amaury", par Alexandre Dumas. Paris, Michel Lévy frères, n.d.
(18), 4to., pp. 177-252 in double columns. Caption title. Woodcut
at head of title. Musée littéraire du siècle.

"SYLVANDIRE"   1843

This is the second work in which Dumas and Maquet collaborated.
Probably Maquet found the source of the story in "Les mémoires de
madame la marquise de Fresne", by Gatien de Courtilz. The period is
that of the last years of Louis XIV and the ascendancy of Madame de
Maintenon, approximately 1708-1716.

It is very possible that the work was first issued in serial
form in 1843.

Original edition.
"Sylvandire", par Alexandre Dumas. (Vignette) Bruxelles, Alph.
Lebègue et Sacré fils, 1843, 18mo., 2 volumes, pp. 215 and 211, with
4 pages of publishers' advertisements at the end of Volume 2.

"Sylvandire" par Alexandre Dumas. Bruxelles, Société belge de librairie Hauman et Ce., 1843, 18mo., 2 volumes, pp. 284 and 322.

"Sylvandire", par Alexandre Dumas. Bruxelles, Société belge de librairie, Hauman et cie., 1843, same format and pagination as the preceding edition. Bibliothèque des châteaux et des campagnes. 9e série.

Ibid   (Vignette) Bruxelles, Meline, Cans et Cie., 1843,
16mo., 2 volumes, pp. 216 and 212.

"Sylvandire" par Alexandre Dumas. (Vignette) Bruxelles et Leipzig,
Meline, Cans et compagnie, 1843, 12mo., 2 volumes, pp. 277 and 280.

"Sylvandire", par Alexandre Dumas. Bruxelles, A. Jamar, 1843, 18mo.,
2 volumes, pp. 270 and 280. Blue wrappers.

"Sylvandire" par Alexandre Dumas. (Vignettes on title-pages and on
the last page of Volume 2) Bruxelles, A. Jamar, 1843, 16mo., 2 volumes, pp. 215 and 211.

"Sylvandire", par Alexandre Dumas. Bruxelles, Langlet et Prodhomme,
1843, same format and pagination as the preceding edition.

"Sylvandire", par Alexandre Dumas. Paris, Dumont, 1844, 8vo., 3 volumes, pp. 318, 310 and 324. Yellow wrappers.

Ibid   Bruxelles, a la librairie générale de Prodhomme,
1845, 18mo., 3 parties, pp. 126, 132 and 130.

"Sylvandire" par Alexandre Dumas. Paris, Michel Lévy frères, 1848,
12mo., pp. 334.

Ibid   Paris, Michel Lévy frères, n.d. (c 185), 4to.,
pp. 324-412 in double columns. Caption title. Woodcut at head of
title.

Ibid   Nouvelle édition. Paris, Michel Lévy frères,
1861, 12mo., pp. (1)-315, verso blank, (317)-319 table of contents.
Frequently reprinted, same format and pagination, by both Michel Lévy
frères and Calmann-Lévy.

Ibid   Paris, Calmann-Lévy, n.d. (c 189), 4to. Musée
littéraire contemporain.

"GABRIEL LAMBERT"   1843
    The story of a forger and a coward - there could hardly be a
less attractive subject, and it could not be expected that an agreeable
story should result. It is as a study of human nature at its lowest
that it is remarkable. Dumas set himself to develop the character of
a vulgar swindler and its only literary rival is, conceivably, Stubbs
in Thackeray's "The Fatal Boots".

    It was published serially in 'La Chronique' between 15th March
and 1st May, 1844.

Original edition.
"Gabriel Lambert" in : 'Revue pittoresque musée littéraire' illustré par les premiers artistes. Première Série. Tome 1. Paris, 37,
Rue Neuve-Saint-Augustin, 1843, 4to., pp. (241)-298 in double columns,
signed : Alexandre Dumas. Engraving on first page; illustrated.

"Gabriel Lambert" par Alexandre Dumas. (Vignette) Bruxelles, Meline, Cans et compagnie, 1844, 16mo., pp. 271. Green wrappers.

Ibid   (Vignette) Bruxelles et Leipzig, Meline, Cans et
compagnie, 1844, same format and pagination as the preceding edition.
Blue wrappers.

Ibid   Bruxelles, Sociéte´belge de librairie, Hauman et
cie., 1844, 18mo., pp. 238.

Ibid   (Vignette) Bruxelles, Alph. Lebègue et Sacré fils,
1844, 18mo., pp. 166.

"Gabriel Lambert". Par Alexandre Dumas. (Vignette) Bruxelles et
Leipzig, Ch. Muquardt, 1844, same format and pagination as the preceding edition.

"Gabriel Lambert", par Alexandre Dumas. Paris, Hippolyte Souverain,
1844, 8vo., 2 volumes, pp. 295 and 303, each with an additional unnumbered page table of contents. Bibliothèque des romans nouveaux. Nos.
69-70.
(There are two errors of pagination. In Volume 1 the first chapter
starts with the page number 17, and the final page of Volume 2 has the
wrong number of 383.

Le Siècle. "Les aventures de Lyderic". "Gabriel Lambert" par Alexandre Dumas. Paris, aux bureaux du Siècle, 1855, 4to., "Gabriel Lambert", pp. (329)-364 in double columns.

"Gabriel Lambert" par Alexandre Dumas. Paris, Impr. de Walder, n.d.
(1855), 4to., pp. 329-364 in double columns, illustrated. Caption
title.

134

Ibid   Paris, Impr. de J. Voisvenel, n.d. (1855), same
format and pagination as the preceding edition. Illustrated. Caption
title.

"Gabriel Lambert" par Alexandre Dumas. Paris, Michel Lévy frères,
1856, 12mo., pp. 275, table of contents on verso. "Gabriel Lambert"
occupies pp. (1)-175, the rest of the volume comprising "La pêche aux
filets", "Invraisemblance" and "Une Ame à maître".
Reprinted, same format and pagination, by both Michel Lévy frères and
Calmann-Lévy.

Ibid   Paris, Michel Lévy frères, n.d. (1864), 4to.
Musée littéraire contemporain.

"L'HORLOGER"   circa 1843
     Whether this work is by Dumas is something that would be difficult
to prove for the very good reason that no French, Belgian, or other,
edition is known and neither has any serial issue ever been traced.
There were, however, several English translations of the work attribut-
ing it to Dumas published both in Britain and the United States of
America, the earliest being that 'entered according to Act of Congress,
1844' under the imprint of Williams Bros., New-York, and with the title
of "The Devil's Wedding-ring; or, The Adventures of a Watchmaker".

     The plot of the story, quite a reasonable one but bearing no
comparison on merit with any of Dumas' earlier or later romances, is
placed towards the end of the 18th century and is almost certainly
taken from some German source which Dumas may have come across in the
course of his travels along the Rhine. There are at times glimpses of
his own particular style of writing at about the period suggested for
the work's publication, but these are few and far between.

     Taken all in all, and assuming that the work can be attributed
to him, the facts would point to a serial issue in some little known
journal; it may not necessarily have been published under the title
quoted above.

"L'ECOLE DES PRINCES"   1844
     Glinel, quoting Quérard, has written that Dumas had a share in
the writing of this comedy. Lecomte agrees, as does Noel Parfait.

Original (and only) edition.
"L'école des princes", comédie en cinq actes et en vers, par M.
Louis Lefèvre, Représentée sur le second Théatre Francais, le 29
novembre 1843. Caption title. Brown wrappers : "L'ecole des
princes", comédie en cinq actes et en vers, par M. Louis Lefèvre.
Second Théâtre Francais. Paris, C. Tresse, libraire acquéreur du
fonds du Barba et Vezou. 1844, 8vo., pp. 32 in double columns.
(The copy held by the Bibliothèque de l'Arsenal has 'et Alex. Dumas'
in ink after 'Lefèvre' on the wrapper.)

"LE LAIRD DE DUMBIKY"   1844
     Dumas has written in his "Mémoires" that this comedy was one of
the only two which had been failures on their first nights. This is

difficult to understand for it is very amusing. Théophile Gautier has suggested that the choice of title was an unhappy one, and this may well be true since it may have given theatre-goers the wrong impression of what they could expect. The action takes place in London and Windsor about the year 1660, with Charles II and Nell Gwynn as prominent characters. It is generally agreed that de Leuven and Léon Lhérie gave some help in the writing.

Original edition.
"Le laird de Dumbiky", comédie en cinq actes, en prose, par M. Alexandre Dumas, représentée, pour la première fois, à Paris, sur le théatre royal de l'Odéon, le 30 décembre 1843. Caption title. Woodcut at head of title, Acte II, scène xii. Yellow wrappers : Magasin théatral. Choix de pièces nouvelles, jouées sur tous les théatres de Paris. Théatre royal de l'Odéon. "Le laird de Dumbiky". Comédie en cinq actes. (Vignette) Paris, Marchant; Bruxelles, Tarride, n.d. (1844), 8vo., pp. 42 in double columns. Reprinted, same format and pagination, n.d. (1847).

Ibid   Paris, Impr. de Mme. Ve Dondey-Dupré, n.d. (c 1845), same format and pagination as the preceding edition.

"Le laird de Dumbiky" comédie en cinq actes, en prose Odéon. - 30 décembre 1843. "Distribution" on title-page, pp. (1)-136. Théatre complet de Alex. Dumas. Tome IX. Paris Calmann Lévy, éditeur ancienne maison de Michel Lévy frères, 1874. 12mo. "Théatre complet" in 25 volumes.

"CECILE"   "LA ROBE DE NOCE"   1844

"Cécile" or as it was first announced "La robe de noce", is the herald of Dumas' golden year. He was ambitious to succeed in every style of fiction, and although this work is in no sense characteristic of him it deserves its place, along with "Amaury", as an unaffected and pathetic story in a 'genre' seldom attempted by him.

Original edition.
"Cecile" par Alexandre Dumas. Paris, Dumont, éditeur ... 1844, 8vo., 2 volumes, pp. (5)-47 'Introduction', (49)-330, and (5)-324. There are no tables of contents. "Cécile" ends on page 254 of Volume 2 and is followed by "Bernard. Histoire pour les chasseurs", pp. (255)-324. Yellow wrappers.

"La robe de noce", par Alexandre Dumas. (Vignette) Bruxelles, Meline, Cans et compagnie, 1844, 16mo., pp. 332. Yellow wrappers repeating title-page, but with a different vignette.

Ibid   (Vignette) Bruxelles et Leipzig, Meline, Cans et compagnie, 1844, same format and pagination as the preceding edition. Blue wrappers.

"La Robe de noce". Par Alexandre Dumas. Edition autorisée pour la Belgique et l'étranger, interdite pour la France. Bruxelles, Leipzig, C. Muquardt, 1844, 18mo., pp. 250.

Oeuvres de Alex. Dumas. Tome septième. (Vignette) Bruxelles, Meline, Cans et compagnie, 1845, large 8vo.

"La robe de noce" par Alexandre Dumas. (Same vignette as the Meline,

Cans et compagnie, 1844, edition) Bruxelles. Meline, Cans et compagnie. Librairie, imprimerie et fonderie. 1846. 12mo., pp. (1)-306.

Ibid   Leipzig, Ernst Schaeffer, 1846, 24mo., pp. 223.
Buff wrappers.

"Cécile". par Alexandre Dumas. Paris, Michel Lévy frères, 1848, 12mo., pp. 281 and additional unnumbered leaf table of contents. Frequently reprinted, same format and pagination, by both Michel Lévy frères and Calmann-Lévy.

"La robe de noce" par Alexandre Dumas. Avec le portrait de Msr. Dumas. Leipsic. Librairie de Ferd. Rubach. (Guillaume Baensch) 1849 (the year is added in ink on the title-page), 32mo., pp. 223; the portrait is by 'Wrankmore sculps'.

"Cécile". Par Alexandre Dumas. Paris, Michel Lévy frères, n.d. (c 1850), 4to., pp. 269-322 in double columns.

"La robe de noce", par Alexandre Dumas. Bruxelles, Librairie du Panthéon, 1850, 24mo., 2 volumes.

Le Siècle. "Praxède". "Pierre le Cruel". "Cécile". Par Alexandre Dumas. Paris, au bureau du Siècle, 1850, 4to., pp. 269-322 in double columns.

"La robe de noce" par Alexandre Dumas. Avec le portrait de Msr. Dumas. Leipsic. 1851. Librairie de Guillaume Baensch, 1851, 32mo., pp. (5)-223; engraved portrait of Dumas ('Wrankmore sculps') with facsimile signature facing the title-page.

"La robe de noce" par Alexandre Dumas. Nouvelle édition. Leipzig, Charles Wilfferodt, libraire-éditeur, 1877, 24mo., pp. 239 and additional unnumbered page table of contents.

"FERNANDE"   1844

     If this book had been dated '1854' instead of '1844' one could easily have attributed it to Dumas, fils. The fact remains that no critic, friendly or hostile, has allowed it to be the unaided work of Dumas, père, and usually St. Hippolyte Auger is attributed to having been the collaborator. It first appeared serially in 1844 in 'La Revue de Paris'.

Original edition.
"Fernande" par Alexandre Dumas. Bruxelles, Société belge de librairie Hauman et ce., 1844, 24mo., 3 volumes, pp. 175, 125 (with extra page 'errata'), and 230.
(The 'errata' reads as follows : 'Une erreur de pagination s'est glissée dans ce volume: de la page 21 à 84 les folios se trouvent en double, ce qui, cependant, n'interdit en rien l'ordre des matières'.)

Ibid   Bruxelles, Société belge de librairie, Hauman et Ce., 1844, 18mo., 2 volumes, pp. 275 and 314.

"Fernande", par Alexandre Dumas. (Vignette) Bruxelles, Livourne, Meline, Cans et cie.; Leipzig, J.-P. Meline, 1844, 16mo., 2 volumes, pp. 290 and 292.

Ibid   (Vignette) Bruxelles, Alph. Lebègue et Sacré fils, 1844, 18mo., 2 volumes, pp. 194 and 217. Galérie littéraire, 94 et 98; 9e série, 5 et 9.

Ibid   (Vignette) Bruxelles et Leipzig, C. Muquardt,
1844, same format and pagination as the preceding edition.

Ibid   Paris, Dumont, éditeur ... 1844, 8vo., 3 volumes,
pp. 320, 336 and 320. There are no tables of contents. Yellow
wrappers.

Ibid   Paris, Michel Lévy frères, 1848, 12mo., pp. 312.
There is no table of contents.
Reprinted, same format and pagination, by both Michel Lévy frères and
Calmann-Lévy.

"Fernande". Par Alexandre Dumas. Bruxelles et Leipzig, Meline, Cans
et compagnie, 1852, 16mo., 2 volumes, pp. 290 and 292.

"Fernande" par Alexandre Dumas. Paris, Michel Lévy frères, n.d.
(186), 4to. Caption title. Musée littéraire contempain.

"UNE FAMILLE CORSE" "LES FRERES CORSES"   1844

        Dumas relates this story in the first person, an unusual thing
for him to do. In many ways it is a minor masterpiece, the plot like
that of the "Menaechmi" and "The Comedy of Errors", and so many other
dramas and stories of all countries, revolving on the remarkable like-
ness of two brothers. The period is around 1841. It is curious that
Dumas never dramatised the work, and that as will be seen was left to
other hands.

        I do not think it is generally known that the romance is, to a
certain extent, founded on fact. In real life the brothers were Louis
and Charles Blanc. Charles was a French Academician, distinguished
art critic and historian. He died in 1882. Louis was known as 'the
tribune of the people', or some such similar title. On their mother's
side they were Corsican and related to that Signor Pozzo del Borgo
who, it has been stated, never forgave Napoleon for on one occaaion
taking all the gravy of a leg of mutton. In 1830 Charles went to
visit a friend, a doctor, who lived some 450 miles from Paris. One
evening after dinner he was walking with friends in the garden when
he jumped in agony crying that he had been hit, and said that he was
sure that something had happened to his brother Louis. The next day
a letter arrived announcing that Louis had been knocked down on the
street by a blow on his forehead. Charles Blanc later told this story
to Dumas. It was adapted by him to form the base of his novel.

Original edition.
"Une famille corse" suivie de "Histoire d'un mort racontée par lui-
même" par Alexandre Dumas. Bruxelles, Meline, Cans et compagnie,
1844, 16mo., pp. 242, of which "Une famille corse" occupies pp. (3)-
202. Yellow wrappers.

"Une famille corse" par Alexandre Dumas. Bruxelles, Société belge de
librairie, Hauman et Ce., 1844, 18mo., pp. 184.

"Une famille corse" par Alexandre Dumas. "Jules Chaumelle" Par Marie
Aycard. "Un legs" nouvelle par Mme. Louise Collet. Bruxelles, Société belge de librairie, Hauman et ce., 1844, 24mo., 2 volumes, pp.
143 and 147.
Even although the title-pages of the two volumes are similar, Dumas'
work occupies only the whole of Volume 1, Volume 2 comprising the
other two titles.

138

"Une famille corse", suivie de "Histoire d'un mort racontée par lui-
même. Par Alexandre Dumas. Bruxelles, Ch. Muquhardt, 1844, 24mo.,
pp. (5)-155, of which "Une famille corse" occupies pp. (5)-128.

Ibid   Bruxelles et Leipzig, C. Muquardt, 1844, same
format and pagination as the preceding edition.

Semaine littéraire du courrier des Etats-Unis. Receuil choisi de
romans, feuilletons, ouvrages historiques et dramatiques, en prose et
en vers, des auteurs modernes les plus renommés. Sixième série. New-
York, F. Gaillardet, Bureau du Courier des Etats-Unis, 1844. "Une
famille corse", par Alexandre Dumas. 8vo., pp. (3)-40 in double
columns.

"Une famille corse" suivie de "Histoire d'un mort racontée par lui-
même". Par Alexandre Dumas. Bruxelles, Alph. Lebègue et Sacré fils,
1845, 24mo., pp. (5)-155, of which "Une famille corse" occupies pp.
(5)-128.

Le Nord revue de la littérature française 1re série. 1845 Large
8vo., the total series comprising 26 numbers each of 16 pages printed
in double columns. "Une famille corse" par A. Dumas was published
in Nos. 1-9 inclusive, pp. 10-14, 10-14, 8-12, 10-13, 11-14, 7-12,
1-11, 1-12 and 1-8. On the final page of each number is : 'Le journal parait toutes les semaines. Lund. Copenhague. Christiana. Chez
Schubothe, commis. en chef. Rédacteur : Thisted, cand. Bern. Rée,
libraire-éditeur. Imprimeur : E.C. Löser à Copenhague'. (On page
16 of No. 26 is printed : 'Aux souscripteurs. Il est de notre devoir
de prévenir nos honorés lecteurs que ce journal cessera dès aujourd'
hui de paraître'.)

"Les frères corses" par Alexandre Dumas. Hippolyte Souverain, éditeur, rue des beaux-arts, 5, a l'entresol, a Paris, 1845, 8vo., 2 volumes, pp. the title-page is followed by a quotation from Prosper
Mérimée's "Colomba" and : 'Mon cher Mérimée, Permettez-moi de vous
emprunter cette épigraphe et de vous offrir ce livre. A vous de coeur,
Alexandre Dumas' (unnumbered), (11)-302, and (7)-312. "Les frères
corses" ends on page 178 of Volume 2, and is followed by "Mes infortunes de garde national", pp. (179)-312. There are no tables of contents. Green wrappers : Bibliothèque de romans nouveaux, par les
meilleurs écrivains, formera 100 volumes in-8. Tome - 89 et 90. The
wrappers are ornamented with an engraving by Cherrier in a frame designed by E. Bourguignon.

"Les frères corses" par Alexandre Dumas. Paris, Michel Lévy frères,
1851, 12mo., pp. 294, verso table of contents. The work occupies pp.
(3)-155, and is followed by "Othon l'archer".
Frequently reprinted, same format and pagination, by both Michel Lévy
frères and Calmann-Lévy.

"Les frères Corses". Par Alexandre Dumas. Publié par Dufour et Mulat.
Illustré par J..A. Beaucé, Ed. Coppin, Gerard Séguin. Paris, Marescq
et Cie., 1852, 4to., pp. 64 in double columns; illustrated.

Alexandre Dumas. "Les frères corses". Paris Michal Lévy frères, 1853,
4to., pp. 331-358 in double columns; illustrated. Caption title.

"Les frères Corses"; "Othon l'archer"; "Murat". Par Alexandre Dumas.
Publiés par Dufour et Mulat. Illustrés par J.-A. Beaucé, Ed. Coppin,
Gerard Séguin. Paris, chez Marescq, 1853, 4to., (one title-page for
all three works), "Les frères Corses", pp. 64 in double columns.

"Les frères corses" par Alexandre Dumas. Paris, S. Raçon et Cie., n.d. (c 185), 4to., pp. 64 in double columns; 4 illustrations.

Ibid   Poissy, Impr. de A. Bouret, 4to., n.d. (c 186), same format, pagination and illustrations as the preceding edition.

Ibid   Paris, Calmann-Lévy, n.d. (c 187), 4to., pp. (331)-358 in double columns. Caption title. Oeuvres complètes d'Alexandre Dumas.

"Les frères Corses". "Othon l'archer", par Alexandre Dumas. Edition illustrée par J.-A. Beaucé, Ed. Coppin, Gerard Séguin. Paris, Calmann-Lévy, n.d. (1884), 4to., pp. each of 64 in double columns. Oeuvres illustrés d'Alexandre Dumas.
Reprinted, 1891, same format and pagination.

"HISTOIRE D'UN MORT ... "   (or "INVRAISEMBLANCE")
"HISTOIRE D'UNE AME"   (or "UNE AME A NAITRE").
"UN MESSAGE"   1844
"FRA BARTOLOMEO"

Originally these four brief works were invariably used to fill up any remaining space at the end of a major work. The four do not call for any particular comment except, perhaps, that "Un message" describes how Dumas sent readers of his "Les trois mousquetaires" to the Bibliothèque Royale, as it then was, to ask for a copy of "Les mémoires du comte de la Fère" knowing full well that these existed only in his own imagination. It is proper that "Fra Bartolomeo" should be dealt with fully under "L'histoire des peintres" ... series later in this Bibliography.

Original edition.
"Une famille corse" suivie de "Histoire d'un mort racontée par lui-meme" par Alexandre Dumas. Bruxelles, Meline, Cans et compagnie, 1844, 16mo., pp. 242, of which "Histoire d'un mort ..." occupies pp. (203)-242.

"Une famille corse", suivie de "Histoire d'un mort racontée lui-même". Par Alexandre Dumas. Bruxelles, C. Muquardt, 1844, 24mo., pp. 155, of which "Histoire d'un mort ..." occupies pp. (131)-155.

Ibid   Bruxelles et Leipzig, C. Muquardt, 1844, same format and pagination as the preceding edition.

"Les trois mousquetaires". par Alexandre Dumas. Paris, Baudry, ... M DCCC XLIV. 8vo., 8 volumes, the work ending on page 131 of Volume 8 and being followed by "Un Message", pp. (136)-145; "Histoire d'un Mort", pp. 150-233; "Histoire d'Une Ame", pp. 238-271; and "Fra Bartolomeo", pp. 276-329.
The Baudry edition was reprinted in 1845.

"Une famille corse" suivie de "Histoire d'un mort racontée par lui-même". Par Alexandre Dumas. Bruxelles, Alph. Lebègue et Sacré fils, 1845, 24mo., pp. 155, of which "Histoire d'un mort ..." occupies pp. (131)-155.

Alexandre Dumas. "L'abbaye de Peyssac" (the fourth part of "La guerre des femmes") Paris, L. de Potter, 1846, 8vo., 2 volumes, pp. 324 and 363; the second volume, following "La pêche aux filets" is

140

filled with, inter alia, "Invraisemblance" pp. (127)-214, and "Une âme à naître" pp. (215)-247, verso blank. Yellow wrappers. Fontaine-bleau - Impr. de. E. Jacquin.

Le Siècle. Oeuvres complètes d'Alexandre Dumas. Troisième série. "Invraisemblance". Paris, au bureau du Siècle, 1848, 4to., pp. (355)-361 in double columns.

Le Siècle. Oeuvres complètes d'Alexandre Dumas. Troisième série. "Une âme à naître". Paris, au bureau du Siècle, 1848, 4to., pp. 361-363 in double columns.

"Nouvelles". Par Alexandre Dumas. Paris, au bureau du Siècle, 1850, 4to., pp. 343-390. "Invraisemblance" and "Une âme à naître" are two of the six stories included in this collection.

"Histoire d'un mort racontée par lui-même" ("Invraisemblance") and "Une âme à naître" par Alexandre Dumas. Publiée par Dufour et Mulat. Paris, chez Marescq et Cie., 1852, 4to., pp. (1)-12 and 13-16 respectively, both in double columns.
Reprinted, same format and pagination, both 'Alexandre Dumas illustré'. The illustrations were by Ed Coppin.

"Nouvelles", par Alexandre Dumas. Paris, Impr. de Morris, n.d. (1854), 4to., pp. 343-372. "Invraisemblance" and "Une âme à naître" were two of the four stories included in this collection.

Ibid   Paris, Impr. de S. Raçon, n.d. (1855) same format and pagination as the preceding edition.
Reprinted, same format and pagination, (c 1861).

"Gabriel Lambert", par Alexandre Dumas. Paris Michel Lévy frères, 1860, 12mo., pp. 275, verso table of contents. Both "Invraisemblance" and "Une âme à naître" were used to fill this volume occupying pp. (235)-264 and (265)-275 respectively.
Reprinted, same format and pagination, by both Michel Lévy frères and Calmann-Lévy.

"Invraisemblance", par Alexandre Dumas. Paris, Michel Lévy frères, 1864, 4to., pp. (16)-23 in double columns. Included with "La pêche aux filets". Musée littéraire contemporain.

"Une âme à naître", par Alexandre Dumas. Paris, Michel Lévy frères, 1864, 4to., pp. (24)-26 in double columna. Included with "La pêche aux filets". Musée littéraire contemporain.

"Histoire d'un mort racontée par lui-même - Invraisemblance" par Alexandre Dumas Dessins par Ed. Coppin. Paris, Calmann Lévy, Editeur ancienne maison Michel Lévy frères, 1887, 4to., pp. (1)-12 in double columns. Alexandre Dumas oeuvres illustrées.

"Une âme à naître" (par Alexandre Dumas) Paris, Calmann Lévy, Editeur ancienne maison Michel Lévy frères, 1887, 4to. ppl (13)-16 in double columns. Alexandre Dumas oeuvres illustrées.

"Histoire d'un mort racontée par lui-même - Invraisemblance" par Alexandre Dumas. "Une âme à naître". Edition illustrée par J.-A. Beaucé, Staal, Andrieux. Paris, Calmann-Lévy, n.d. (1890), 4to., pp. (1)-12 and (13)-16 respectively in double columns. Buff wrappers. Alexandre Dumas oeuvres illustrées.
Reprinted, same format and pagination, 1897.

"UNE FILLE DU REGENT"   (Romance)   1844

This work has for long been commonly regarded as being a sequel
to "Le chevalier d'Harmental". It is neither more nor less than a
companion story. It again deals with the Cellamare Conspiracy of the
early 18th century.

The success of "Le chevalier d'Harmental" gave Dumas the idea of
writing a play covering the same period; this was, in fact, written
in 1843, and perhaps earlier, for the first draft (which was later
greatly modified) was accepted by the reading committee of the Théâtre-
Français in December, 1843. Thus the romance is one of the very few
which Dumas drew from a play. It should be noted here that Maquet
has admitted to have had nothing to do with the writing of the play,
but he did help with the romance the first publication of which was
as a serial in 'Le Commerce'.

Original edition.
"Une fille du régent" par Alexandre Dumas. Bruxelles, Meline, Cans
et compagnie, 1844, 18mo., 3 volumes, pp. 287, 272 and 215.

Ibid   Bruxelles et Leipzig, Meline, Cans et compagnie,
1844, 3 volumes, same format and pagination as the preceding edition.

Ibid   Bruxelles, Société belge de librairie, Hauman
et ce., 1844, 24mo., 5 volumes, pp. 150, 159, 162, 134 and 152. The
work ends on page 96 of Volume 5 and is followed by "Un alchimiste
au XIXe siècle", pp. (99)-152.

Ibid   Bruxelles, Société belge de librairie, Hauman
et ce., 1844, 16mo., 3 volumes, pp. 256, 246 and 248. The work ends
on page 192 of Volume 3 and is followed by "Un alchimiste au XIXe
siècle", pp. (193)-248.

Ibid   Bruxelles, Alph. Lebègue et Sacré fils, 1844,
24mo., 3 volumes, pp. 170, 177 and 150.

"Une fille du régent". Par Alexandre Dumas. Bruxelles, Ch. Muquardt,
same format and pagination as the preceding edition.

"Une fille du régent" par Alexandre Dumas. Bruxelles et Leipzig,
C. Muquardt, 1844, same format and pagination as the preceding editions.
Yellow wrappers.

Semaine littéraire du Courrier des Etats-Unis. Receuil choisi de
romans, feuilletons, ouvrages historiques et dramatiques, en prose et
en vers, des auteurs modernes les plus renommés. Sixième série. New-
York, F. Gaillardet, Bureau du Courrier des Etats-Unis, 1844. "Une
fille du régent", par Alexandre Dumas. 8vo., pp. (41)-185 in double
columns.

"Une fille du régent" par Alexandre Dumas. Paris, Alexandre Cadot,
1845, 8vo., 4 volumes, pp. 304, 319, 319 and 335. Yellow wrappers.

"Une fille du régent" par Alexandre Dumas Paris Michel Lévy frères,
libraires-éditeurs des Oeuvres complètes d'Alexandre Dumas, de la
bibliothèque dramatique et du théatre de Victor Hugo Rue Vivienne,
1. 1848 12mo., pp. (1)-358, (359)-360 table of contents. Paris. -
Imp. Lacrampe fils et Comp., rue Damiette, 2.

"Une fille du régent" par Alexandre Dumas publié par Dufour et Mulat
édition illustrée par J.-A. Beaucé, etc. (Vignette) Paris, Marescq

et Cie, éditeurs, librairie centrale des publications illustrées, 1857, 4to., pp. (1)-190 and unnumbered page table of contents, all in double columns. Pale green wrappers with vignette.

"Une fille du régent" par Alexandre Dumas. Publié par Dufour et Mulat. Edition illustrée par J.-A. Beaucé, ... (Vignette) Paris, Lécrivain et Toubon, 1860, same format and pagination as the preceding edition with 23 illustrations of which 3 are 'hors-texte'.

Ibid   Nouvelle édition. Paris, Michel Lévy frères, 1860, 12mo., pp. (1)-353, verso blank, (355)-356 table of contents. Frequently reprinted, same format and pagination, by both Michel Lévy frères and Calmann-Lévy.

Ibid   Paris, Calmann-Lévy, n.d. (c 187), 4to., pp. (1)-96 in double columns. Caption title. Woodcut at head of title.

Ibid   Edition illustrée par J.-A. Beaucé, etc. Paris, Calmann-Lévy, 1890, same format and pagination as the preceding edition. Caption title. Woodcut at head of title. Alexandre Dumas oeuvres illustrées.

"LES TROIS MOUSQUETAIRES"   1844

It should be remembered with regard to this, the greatest of Dumas' romances, that there are three differing texts in the original French. For his historical study "Louis XIV et son siècle" Dumas had read "Les mémoires de Monsieur d'Artagnan" by Gatien de Courtilz and was impressed by two things : first, the curious names of the three musketeers, Athos, Portos (as first spelt) and Aramis, and secondly, by the intrigues centred around Milady. He suggested to Maquet that the memoirs provided a suitable background for a romance. It is known that Maquet wrote the early chapters with no settled plan in his brain and with no idea of a plot, for, except for Milady's appearance in the opening pages, there was no vestige of a plot until Bonacieux approached d'Artagnan with the request for help in the recovery of his abducted wife. Dumas changed all that and the great romance gradually took shape.

Its first appearance was a serial in 'Le Siècle' from 14th March to 14th July, 1844. Belgian publishers gathered from 'Le Siècle' daily the material of the story, and when it was completed simply bound and entitled the sectors and placed the volumes on the market. With the romance's completion there was keen competition for the right of publication in book form in France. The successful tender was made by Baudry. Dumas wrote to Baudry asking that proofs should be sent to him as there were errors which, in the common interests of author and publisher, required correction. The proofs were duly sent, but Dumas instinctively improvised and expanded.

Thus, when examination is made of the pirated Belgian editions and of Baudry's text, since perpetuated in the Michel Lévy frères and Calmann-Lévy issues, not only are small corrections found but also well over two hundred major alterations many of which extended into paragraphs. Dumas never modified his main plot but, strangely, in spite of certain improvements, the original text on the whole reads better.

Nor does the matter end here. In 1846 Fellens et Dufour published the first illustrated edition of the romance. This followed neither of

the above-mentioned texts accurately. Use was made in turn of which-
ever appealed most to the 'éditeurs'. Not only did they take a passage from the serial (and Belgian) printing, sometimes from Baudry,
but they even had the temerity to combine sentences from both to
yield a paragraph, or phrases from both to yield a sentence. The
production of such combinations would have been too dreary a task for
Dumas, but I am inclined to think that he probably gave his consent.
There is the further, but comparatively minor, complication that the
texts of the Fellens et Dufour edition and that of the subsequent
Marescq et Cie. illustrated edition, while almost identical yet the
paragraphs in the latter are often broken into much smaller fragments.

At the conclusion of the Baudry edition can be read : 'Fin
d'Athos, Porthos et Aramis'. This is interesting because the title
of the work was thus announced before publication, and evidently was
so written on the original manuscript. It can thus only have been
the editor who, disliking it, changed the title to that which we know
so well.

Original edition.
"Les trois mousquetaires" par Alexandre Dumas. Bruxelles, Alph. Lebegue et Sacre fils, 1844, 18mo., 5 volumes, pp. (1)-8 'préface', (9)-
181, 172, 171, 163 and 223. Muséum littéraire. Green wrappers.

"Les trois mousquetaires" par Alexandre Dumas. Bruxelles, Société
belge de librairie Hauman et ce., 1844, 18mo., 5 volumes, pp. 250,
239, 262, 254 and 263.

"Les Trois mousquetaires". Par Alexandre Dumas. Bruxelles, Ch.
Muquardt, 1844, 18mo., 5 volumes, pp. (1)-8 'préface', (9)-181, 172,
171, 163 and 223.

"Les trois mousquetaires" par Alexandre Dumas. Bruxelles, Alph.
Legègue et Sacré fils, 1844, 24mo., 5 volumes, pp. 276, 303, 268, 262
and 293. Galerie littéraire, nos. 102, 103, 106, 113 and 114. 10^e
série; 3, 4 and 7, and 4 and 5 in 11e serie.

"Les trois mousquetaires" par Alexandre Dumas. Bruxelles, Meline,
Cans et compagnie, 1844, 18mo., 5 volumes, pp. 276, 303, 268, 262 and
293.

Ibid   Bruxelles et Leipzig, Meline, Cans et compagnie,
1844, same format and pagination as the preceding edition.

Oeuvres de Alex. Dumas. Tome huitième. (Vignette) Bruxelles, Société
belge de librairie Hauman et ce., 1844, large 8vo. "Les trois mousquetaires", pp. (287)-599 in double columns.

"Les trois mousquetaires". par Alexandre Dumas. Paris. Baudry,
libraire-éditeur, 34, rue coquillière; et rue de la chaussée, 22.
M DCCC XLIV. 8vo., 8 volumes. Yellow wrappers. Impr. Béthune et
Plon.

Volume 1 : half-title, title, verso blank, pp. 1-349 (page 349 is
            misnumbered 449), verso blank, table of contents.
       2 : half-title, title, verso blank, pp. 1-329, verso blank,
            table of contents.
       3 : half-title, title, verso blank, pp. 1-386, table of
            contents.
       4 : half-title, title, verso blank, pp. 1-363, table of
            contents.

Volume 5 : half-title, title, verso blank, pp. 1-310, table of
       contents.
    6 : half-title, title, verso blank, pp. 1-287, table of
       contents.
    7 : half-title, title, verso blank, pp. 1-297, verso blank,
       table of contents.
    8 : half-title, title, verso blank, pp. 1-329, verso blank,
       table of contents.

"Les trois mousquetaires" ends in Volume 8 on page 131 with 'Fin
D'Athos, Porthos et Aramis', verso blank. This is followed by :
"Un Message", pp. (136)-145, verso blank; "Histoire d'Un mort" (147-
148 blank -149) 150-233; 234 blank; "Histoire d'Une Ame" (235-236
blank 237) 238-271; 272 blank; "Fra Bartolomeo" (273, 274 blank,
275), 276-329.
The Baudry edition was reprinted in 1845.

"Les trois mousquetaires" par Alexandre Dumas. (Vignette) Bruxelles,
Meline, Cans et compagnie, 1845, 16mo., 4 volumes, pp. 287, 280, 287
and 285.

"Les trois mousquetaires" par M. Alexandre Dumas. Paris, MM. J.-B.
Fellens et L.-P. Dufour, editeurs, rue Saint-Thomas-du-Louvre, 30.
1846. Large 8vo., pp. (i)-iii 'préface', verso blank, (5)-515, verso
blank, 517-518 'epilogue' with 'fin des trois mousquetaires', (519)-
521 table of contents, verso blank, unnumbered page 'Classement des
Gravures'. Frontispiece portrait of Dumas and 32 plates; head and
tale pieces. The portrait of Dumas is engraved by Hébert after Beaucé;
the plates are engraved by A. Gusman, G. Lecestre, Jahyer, A. Vien,
Pisau, Trichon, Faxardo, A. Pollet, Laisné and Vivet after V. Beaucé,
Bourgue, Ed. Frère, Marckl and Wattier. Imprimerie de Bureau, rue
coquillière, 22. Various board bindings with gilt decorated spine.
This first illustrated edition was also published in instalments in
pink wrappers.

"Les trois mousquetaires". Par Alexandre Dumas. Deuxième édition.
Bruxelles, Alph. Lebègue et Sacré fils, 1846, 18mo., 5 volumes, pp.
152, 143, 143, 135 and 194. Yellow wrappers.

Semaine Littéraire du Courrier des Etats-Unis. XIII série; Vol. 4,
1846. "Les Trois mousquetaires", par Alexandre Dumas. 1846. New-
York: F. Gaillardet 1846. At head of page (3) : "Les trois mous-
quetaires", par Alexandre Dumas. 8vo., pp. (3)-268 in double columns.
(The work is preceded in the bound volume by "Clarissa Harlowe" de
Samuel Richardson (traduit) par Jules Janin.)

"Les trois mousquetaires", par Alexandre Dumas. Paris, Michel Lévy
frères, 1846-1847, 12mo., 2 volumes; pp. : Volume 1 (1846), 336, and
Volume 2 (1847), 326, each with 2 additional unnumbered pages table of
contents.

Le Siècle. "Les mousquetaires", trilogie (sic) par Alexandre Dumas.
Première partie : "Les trois mousquetaires". Seconde partie :
"Vingt ans après" ... Paris, au bureau du Siècle, 1847, large 8vo.,
pp. 351 in double columns; illustrated.

Oeuvres de Alex. Dumas. Tome neuvième. (Vignette) Bruxelles, Société
belge de librairie Hauman et ce., 1847, large 8vo. "Les trois mousquetaires".

"Les trois mousquetaires" Par Alexandre Dumas. (Troisième édition.)

Bruxelles, Alph. Lebègue, 1848, 18mo., 5 volumes, pp. 152, 143, 143, 135 and 194.

"Les trois mousquetaires", par M. Alexandre Dumas. Paris, Dufour et Mulat, 1849, large 8vo., pp. (i)-iii, (5)-521, (2), with the same portrait and engravings as the Fellens et Dufour edition of 1846. Reprinted, same format, pagination and illustrations, 1850. Reprinted, 1851, same format but pp. 518 and additional pages table of contents and 'classement des gravures', frontispiece portrait of Dumas by Beaucé.

"Les trois mousquetaires". Par M. Alexandre Dumas. Paris, Dufour, Mulat et Boulanger, 1849, large 8vo., pp. (i)-iii, (5)-521, (2), with the same portrait and engravings as the Fellens et Dufour edition of 1846. Reprinted, same format, pagination and illustrations, 1856.

"Les trois mousquetaires". Par Alexandre Dumas. Bruxelles, Alphonse Lebègue, 1849-1850, 18mo., 5 volumes, pagination : Volume 1 (dated 1850 in error), 148; Volumes 2 and 3 (1849), 139 and 140; Volume 4 (1850), 132; Volume 5 (dated 1849 in error), 188. Green wrappers, printed 'Quatrième édition', the wrappers being dated : Volume 1, 1850, and Volumes 2-5, 1849.

"Les trois mousquetaires" suivi de "Vingt ans après" et du "Vicomte de Bragelonne", par Alex. Dumas. Bruxelles, Meline, Cans et compagnie, 1851, 4to. Pagination of "Les trois mousquetaires", (3)-4 'préface', (5)-294 in double columns, the whole being followed by 3 pages of tables of contents.

"Les trois mousquetaires" Par Alexandre Dumas. Bruxelles, Alphonse Lebègue, 1852, 18mo., 5 volumes, pp. 148, 139, 140, 132 and 188.

"Les trois mousquetaires" par Alexandre Dumas illustrés par J.-A. Beaucé, F. Philippoteaux, etc. publiés par Dufour et Mulat Paris chez Marescq et Cie, libraires ... 1852, 4to., published in 2 parts. Pagination : Première partie, (1)-2 'préface', (3)-166; deuxième partie, (1)-157; both in double columns and with an additional unnumbered page table of contents and 'placement des gravures'. Vignette on the title-page of each part. No portrait of Dumas was published with this edition but it has the 32 illustrations, initial letters and tail-pieces of the Fellens et Dufour, 1846, edition. Reprinted, same format, pagination and illustrations, 1853.

"Les trois mousquetaires" par Alexandre Dumas. Paris, Michel Lévy frères, n.d. (1852), 4to., pp. 156 in double columns. Caption title. Woodcut at head of title. Musée littéraire du siècle. Reprinted, same format and pagination in the same series, 1863.

"Les trois mousquetaires". Par Alexandre Dumas. Bruxelles, Alphonse Lebègue, 1853, 18mo., 5 volumes, pp. 144, 132, 148, 143 and 132.

"Les trois mousquetaires" par Alexandre Dumas. Paris, Impr. de Mme. Ve Dondey Dupré, n.d. (1855), 8vo., 2 volumes, pp. 351 and 488, with head-piece to each chapter.

"Les trois mousquetaires", par Alexandre Dumas. Paris, Michel Lévy frères, 1858, 12mo., 2 volumes, pp. 350 and 340, each with 2 additional unnumbered pages table of contents; Volume 1 has pp. 4 'préface' included in the pagination. Oeuvres complètes d'Alexandre Dumas. Over the intervening years between 1858 and 1900 this work was re-

146

printed, both by Michel Lévy frères and Calmann-Lévy, a very great
many times in the same format as the preceding edition but with varying paginations - sometimes Dumas' preface was included and sometimes
not, and also in some reprintings the tables of contents were not
included.

"Les Trois mousquetaires" par Alexandre Dumas. Illustrés par J.-A.
Beaucé, F. Philippoteaux, etc. Paris, Lécrivain et Toubon, n.d.
(c 1860), same format, pagination and illustrations as the Marescq
et Cie., 1852, edition.

Alexandre Dumas "Les trois mousquetaires" "Vingt ans après" Paris
Jules Rouff et Cie., éditeurs ... (Propriété Calmann-Lévy), n.d.
(1887-1891). Second illustrated title-page. 4to. "Les trois mousquetaires", pp. (1)-629. Deuxième partie "Vingt ans après", pp.
(630)-1164, continued into Volume 2, pp. 1165-1435; "Le vicomte de
Bragelonne" occupies pp. (1436)-2328, each volume had 4 unnumbered
pages tables of contents; illustrated.
Reprinted, same format, pagination and illustrations, n.d. (1893-1895).

"Les trois mousquetaires" par Alexandre Dumas dessins par J.-A.
Beaucé, F. Philippoteaux, etc. (Vignette) Paris, Calmann-Lévy, n.d.
(1893), 4to., 2 volumes, pp. 166 and 158 in double columns. Caption
title. Woodcut at head of title. Alexandre Dumas oeuvres illustrées.

Alexandre Dumas "Les trois mousquetaires" avec une lettre d'Alexandre
Dumas fils compositions de Maurice Leloir gravures sur bois de J.
Huyot (Woodcut vignette) Paris Calmann Lévy, éditeur ancienne
maison Michel Lévy frères 3, rue Auber, 3 1894 2 volumes, 4to.,
pagination : Volume 1, full-page woodcut following title-page, (vii)-
xvi 'lettre d'Alexandre Dumas fils', (xvii)-xx 'preface dans laquelle
il est établi que, malgré leurs noms en os et en is, les héros de
l'histoire que nous allons avoir l'honneur de raconter a nos lecteurs
n'ont rien de mythologique', (1)-471, verso blank, (473)-474, 'table
des chapitres du tome premier', (475)-479, 'table des gravures du
tome premier'; Volume 2, (1)-462, (463)-464, 'table des chapitres du
tome second', (465)-469, verso blank, unnumbered page : 'achevé
d'imprimer pour Calmann Lévy, éditeur par Chamerot et Renouard Le
25 novembre 1893'.
On verso of half-title of Volume 1 : Edition de grand luxe il a été
tiré de cette édition 1 Un exemplaire unique sur papier des Manufactures impériales du Japon, accompagné des dessins originaux de M.
Maurice Leloir et des fumés des deux cents cinquante bois gravés. 2
Cent cinquante exemplaires numérotés sur papier de Chine, dont cent
avec les tirages à part de chaque gravure.
Twelve copies of each of the illustrator's two original water-colours
were printed for sale by Librairie Michaud de Reims.

"Les trois mousquetaires", par Alexandre Dumas; abridged with notes
by J.H.T. Goodwin. London, Macmillan and company, 1895, 8vo., pp.
xii, 260. Macmillan's foreign school classics.

"Les trois mousquetaires" par Alexandre Dumas. Paris, Calmann-Lévy,
1895, 4to., pp. 188 in double columns, including table of contents.
Caption title. Woodcut at head of title. Red wrappers with the same
woodcut. Musée littéraire contemporain.

"SIMPLE LETTRES SUR L'ART DRAMATIQUE"   1844

These five letters were the result of the quarrel between Dumas

and François Buloz and the Comédie-Française, of which Buloz was at
the time commissaire royal. The letters were addressed to the Rédacteur of 'La Démocratique pacifique', and were published first in
that journal towards the end of 1844. They were never published in
volume form in France.

Original edition.
"Simple letteres sur l'art dramatique" par Alexandre Dumas. Bruxelles,
Hauman et Cie., 1844, 18mo., pp. 132.

Ibid_e   Bruxelles. Société belge de librairie Hauman
et Ce. 1845. Same format and pagination as the preceding edition.
On verso of half-title : imp. de Hauman et Ce. - Deltombe, Gérant
....

"Simples lettres sur l'art dramatique" A M.D.L. rédacteur de la
'Démocratie pacifique'. Pp. (193)-246. Théatre complet de Alex.
Dumas Tome XXV Paris Calmann Lévy, éditeur ancienne maison Michel
Lévy frères, 1874. 12mo. "Théatre complet" in 25 volumes.

"TROIS MAITRES"   1844

     As will be seen the three 'maîtres' concerned are Michel-Ange,
Titien and Raphaël and the volume was published as a separate entity,
for no very apparent reason, in the collected edition of Dumas'
works by Michel Lévy frères and Calmann-Lévy and, later, in the early
19th century by Le Vasseur in 'Alexandre Dumas illustré'.

     "Titien Vecelli" first appeared in issues of 'La Chronique' be-
tween 1st December, 1843, and 15th January, 1844, that is before its
publication in Dumas' "Galerie de Florence".

Original edition (in volume form).
"Trois maîtres" par Alexandre Dumas. Paris Michel Lévy frères,
1861, 12mo., pp. "Michel-Ange" (1)-100; "Titien" (101)-203, verso
blank; "Raphaël" (205)-263, verso table of contents.
Reprinted several times, same format and pagination, by both Michel
Lévy frères and Calmann-Lévy.

Ibid   Paris, Michel Lévy frères, n.d. (c 187), 4to.
Musée littéraire contemporain.

"HISTOIRE D'UN CASSE-NOISETTE"   1844

     Always a great favourite with French children, and now similarly
in the English speaking world because of its most recent translation
and the fact that Tchaikovsky's 'Nutcracker Suite' was based to a
large extent on Dumas' story, it is an adaptation of Hoffmann's "The
Nutcracker and the Mouse-king". Ernst Theodor Amadeus Hoffmann was
born in Konigsberg, Germany, in 1776 and died in 1822, and he is probably mostly remembered by his "Contes Fantastiques".

     In his adaptation Dumas, as is the usual case when he handled
someone else's material, has greatly improved upon the original; in
addition he wrote a brief introduction. The story originally appeared
in "le Nouveau Magasin des Enfants' in 1844 in 40 parts, each consisting of 16 pages.

148

Original edition .
"Histoire d'un casse-noisette" par Alexandre Dumas. Illustré par
Bertall. (Vignette) Paris, publié par J. Hetzel, 1845, 8vo., 2 volumes, pagination : Volume 1, (7)-14 'préface', (15)-131 and unnumbered page table of contents; Volume 2, (with a different vignette) (5)-
122 and unnumbered page table of contents. Frontispiece to Volume 1
and 136 woodcut illustrations; no frontispiece to Volume 2 and 99
woodcut illustrations. Illustrated wrappers.

'Le nouveau magasin des enfants' par Alexandre Dumas et Alphonse
Karr. 300 vignettes par Bertall et Laurentz (sic). (Vignette) Paris,
Edition Hetzel, Librairie de L. Hachette et Cie., 1860, large 8vo.,
pagination : "Histoire d'un casse-noisette" (Première partie), (1)-8
'préface', (9)-126; Seconde partie "suite de l'histoire de la nois-
ette krakatuk et de la princesse Pirlipate", (127)-244. Alexandre
Dumas. Pages (245)-334 are occupied by "Les fées de la mer", by
Alphonse Karr, and an additional unnumbered page table of contents.
Frontispiece to Part 1 and 131 vignettes, 154 vignettes to Part 2, all
by Bertall. The illustrations to Karr's work are by Lorentz.
Reprinted in the same year, same format, pagination and illustrations.

'Le nouveau magasin des enfants' par Alexandre Dumas - Paul de
Musset et Edouard Ourliac. 315 vignettes par Bertall - Gerard
Séguin - Eugène Lacoste. (Vignette) Paris Edition Hetzel Librairie de L. Hachette et Cie., 1860, 8vo., pp. (1)-118 "Histoire d'un
casse-noisette" Alexandre Dumas.

"Histoire d'un casse-noisette". Par Alexandre Dumas. Paris, Michel
Lévy frères, 1860, 12mo., pp. 283 and unnumbered page table of contents. Pagination : (1)-9 'préface', (11)-91 "Histoire d'un casse-
noisette", (91)-233 "Histoire de la noisette krakatuk et de la princesse Pirlipate". The rest of the volume is completed by Dumas'
"L'égoïste", pp. (235)-263, and "Nicolas le philosophe", pp. (265)-283.
Frequently reprinted, same format but with varying paginations, by
both Michel Lévy frères and Calmann-Lévy.

'Le nouveau magasin' contes du premier age "Histoire
d'un casse-noisette" par Alexandre Dumas. "Les fées de la mer" par
Alphonse Karr. Vignettes par Bertall et Lorentz. (Vignette) Bibliothèque d'éducation et de récréation Paris, J. Hetzel et Cie., n.d.
(c 186), same format, pagination and illustrations as the Paris,
Edition Hetzel, Librairie de L. Hachette et Cie., 1860, edition.

"Histoire d'un casse-noisette" par Alexandre Dumas. Illustré par
Bertall. (Vignette) Paris, J. Hetzel, n.d. (1889), same format,
pagination and illustrations as the Paris, Edition Hetzel, Librairie
de L. Hachette et Cie., 1860, edition, but not including Karr's work.

"Histoire d'un casse-noisette" par Alexandre Dumas. Paris, Michel
Lévy frères, n.d. (c 189), 4to. Musée littéraire contemporain.

"LA BOUILLIE DE LA COMTESSE BERTHE"   1844

     As with "Histoire d'un casse-noisette" this is a story taken from
a German source, and although this source has never been stated it
could, conceivably, have been E.T.A. Hoffmann. And, again, it has
always been very popular with French and British children. Like
"Histoire d'un casse-noisette" it first appeared in 'Le nouveau magasin
des enfants' in 1844 in 20 parts.

Original edition.
"La bouillie de la comtesse Berthe" par Alexandre Dumas. Illustré par
Bertall. (Vignette) Paris, publié par J. Hetzel, 1845, 12mo., pp.
125 and 3 unnumbered pages comprising table of contents and publisher's
announcements. The illustrations consist of a frontispiece and 144
woodcuts of which 7 are vignettes. Illustrated binding with on the
front cover: 'Le nouveau magasin des enfants'.

"La bouillie de la comtesse Berthe", par Alexandre Dumas. Illustré
par Bertall. Bruxelles, J. Hetzel et Meline, Cans et cie., 1854,
12mo., pp. 126 and unnumbered page table of contents. Coloured frontispiece.

"La bouillie de la comtesse Berthe" par Alexandre Dumas. Illustré par
Bertall. Deuxieme édition. (Vignette) Paris, E. Blanchard, ancienne
librairie Hetzel, 1854, 12mo., pp. 128 and unnumbered page table of
contents. Additional title-page consists of full-page woodcut. There
are 150 illustrations. Cream wrappers with 'Le nouveau magasin des
enfants'.

"La bouillie de la comtesse Berthe", par Alexandre Dumas. Paris,
Michel Lévy freres, 1862, 12mo., pp. (1)-4 'préface', (5)-93 "La
bouillie de la comtesse Berthe", (95)-240 "Aventures de Lyderic comte
de Flandre", (241)-242 table of contents.
Frequently reprinted, same format and pagination, by both Michel Lévy
frères and Calmann-Lévy.

"La bouillie de la comtesse Berthe" par Alexandre Dumas Illustré par
Bertall. (Vignette) Petite bibliothèque blanche éducation et récréation J. Hetzel et Cie., ... Paris, n.d. (c 1860), 12mo., pp. (5)-8
'préface', (9)-126 and unnumbered page table of contents. Frontispiece
and numerous vignettes. Buff wrappers, illustrated.

"La bouillie de la comtesse Berthe" par Alexandre Dumas. Paris,
Michel Lévy frères, n.d. (c 189), 4to. Musée littéraire contemporain.

"LES MEDICIS"   1844

     This historical account of the Médicis and their great influence
on the arts in Florence really serves as a link between "Galerie de
Florence" and Dumas' "Histoire des peintres, faisant suite à l'histoire
de la peinture".

Original edition.
This appeared in the "Galerie de Florence" and reference should be
made to the bibliography of that work.

"Les Médicis". ("La peinture chez les ancienne". Histoire des
peintres, faisant suite à l'histoire de la peinture".) Par Alexandre
Dumas. Paris, Recoules, 1844, 8vo., 2 volumes, pp. 343 and 345 each
with an additional unnumbered page table of contents. Yellow wrappers.
Reprinted, same format and pagination, 1845.

"Les Médicis" par Alexandre Dumas. Bruxelles, Alph. Lebègue et Sacré
fils, 1845, 24mo., pp. 155; Branche ainée, pp. (5)-85, blank, Branche
cadette, pp. (87)-155, the final page misnumbered 165.

Ibid   Bruxelles, Meline, Cans et compagnie, 1845, 18mo.,
pp. 278; Branche ainée, pp. (1)-150, Branche cadette, pp. (151)-278.

150

Ibid   La Haye, chez les héritiers Doorman, 1845, same
format and pagination as the preceding edition. Pink wrappers.

Ibid   Bruxelles et Leipzig, Meline, Cans et compagnie,
1845, same format and pagination as the two preceding editions.

Omnibus littéraire. "Les Médicis" par Alexandre Dumas. Bruxelles,
Meline, Cans et compagnie, 1845, 24mo., pp. 182; Branche ainée, pp.
(1)-98, Branche cadette, pp. 99-182. Yellow wrappers.

"Les Médicis". Par Alexandre Dumas. Bruxelles, Ch. Muquardt, 1845,
24mo., pp. 155; Branche ainée, pp. (5)-85, blank, Branche cadette,
pp. (87)-155, the final page misnumbered 165.

"Les Médicis" par Alexandre Dumas. Bruxelles et Leipzig, C. Muquardt,
1845, same format and misnumbered pagination as the preceding
edition; vignette on title-page.

"Les mariages du père Olifus". "Les Médicis". Par Alexandre Dumas.
Edition illustrée par J.-A. Beaucé, Ed. Coppin, etc. Paris, Marescq
et Cie., 1856, large 8vo.; "Les Médicis", pp. 36 in double columns;
Branche ainée, pp. (1)-20, Branche cadette, pp. 20-36.

"Les Médicis" par Alexandre Dumas. Paris, Michel Lévy frères, 1860,
12mo., pp. 269 and additional unnumbered page table of contents;
Branche ainée, pp. (1)-146, Branche cadette, pp. (147)-269.
Several times reprinted, same format and pagination, by both Michel
Lévy frères and Calmann-Lévy.

Ibid   Paris, Michel Lévy frères, 1861, 4to., pp. 36
including table of contents in double columns. Caption title. Woodcut at head of title. Green wrappers repeating woodcut. Musée
littéraire contemporain.

Ibid   Paris, Calmann-Lévy, 1887, 4to., pp. 64. Caption
title; illustrated.

Alexandre Dumas. "Les Médicis". Edition illustrée par J.-A. Beaucé,
Ed. Coppin, etc. Paris, Calmann-Lévy, n.d. (1897), 4to., pp. 36 in
double columns.

"HISTOIRE DES PEINTRES faisant suite à
L'HISTOIRE DE LA PEINTURE"
"LA PEINTURE CHEZ LES ANCIENS"   1844
"ITALIENS ET FLAMANDS"

     These works comprise a series of articles on some of the great
Italian and Flemish artists and sculptors. The list of such artists
is a formidable one as will be seen from the details incorporated
in various editions. "Michel-Ange", "Titien Vecelli" and "Raphaël
Sanzio d'Urbin" were incorporated into a work entitled "Trois maîtres";
"Titien Vecelli" was published in : 'Revue pittoresque musée littéraire' illustré par les premiers artistes. Première Série. Tome 1.
Paris, Rue Neuve-Saint-Augustin, 1843, 4to., pp. (5)-32 in double
columns, signed : Alexandre Dumas, with an engraved portrait of
the artist and 2 engraved illustrations; "Jules Romain" was not included in 'Le Mousquetaire' reprint; and as will be seen from the
bibliography of "Italiens et Flamands" in the Lévy collected edition
of Dumas' works there are a number of artists not represented or published in other editions. It should be added here that the introductory chapter to the collected Lévy comprises in its entirety "La peinture chez les anciens".

For simplicity's sake, following on the 1844 Florence edition of "Galerie de Florence", it is best to treat the individual articles as separate issues or helping to fill up the final volume of some other work by Dumas, and to continue from there to the main titles as given above.

Original edition.
"Le château d'Eppstein", par Alexandre Dumas. Paris, L. de Potter, 1844, 8vo., 3 volumes, the pagination of the final volume being 322. "Le château d'Eppstein" ends on page 70 of Volume 3 and is followed, inter alia, by "Fra Bartolomeo", pp. 71-112, and "Un miracle au XVe siècle" (which is, in fact) "Quentin Metzys", pp. 289-322. Yellow wrappers.

"Les trois mousquetaires". par Alexandre Dumas. Paris, Baudry, libraire-éditeur, ... , M DCCC XLIV. 8vo., 8 volumes, the pagination of the final volume being 329, verso blank, table of contents. "Les trois mousquetaires" ends on page 131 of Volume 8 and is followed, inter alia, by "Fra Bartolomeo", pp. (273, 274 blank, 275) 276-329. Yellow wrappers.
The Baudry edition was reprinted in 1845.

"Michel-Ange" par Alexandre Dumas. (Vignette) Bruxelles, Alph. Lebègue et Sacré fils, 1844, 18mo., pp. 167. "Michel-Ange" occupies pp. (5)-84, and is followed by "Titien Vecelli", pp. (85)-167.

"Michel-Ange". Par Alexandre Dumas. Bruxelles, Ch. Muquardt, 1844, same format and pagination as the preceding édition.

"Michel-Ange" par Alexandre Dumas. (Vignette) Bruxelles et Leipzig, C. Muquardt, 1844, same format and pagination as the preceding editions. Light green wrappers.

Vies des peintres italiens. "Michel-Ange" suivi de "Titien Vecelli". Par Alex. Dumas. Bruxelles, Meline, Cans et compagnie, 1844, 16mo., pp. 278. "Michel-Ange" occupies pp. (5)-139, verso blank, "Titien Vecelli", pp. (141)-278. Light green wrappers repeating title-page.

Ibid   Bruxelles et Leipzig, Meline, Cans et compagnie, 1844, same format and pagination as the preceding edition and with the same light green wrappers.

"La reine Margot" par Alexandre Dumas. Bruxelles, Société belge de librairie, Hauman et ce., 1845, 24mo., 5 volumes, the pagination of the final volume being 290. "La reine Margot" ends on page 186 of Volume 5 and is followed by "Rubens", pp. (187)-290. Buff wrappers.

Ibid   Bruxelles, Société belge de librairie Hauman et Ce., 1845, 18mo., 8 volumes, the pagination of the final volume being 144. "La reine Margot" ends on page 40 of Volume 8 and is followed by "Rubens", pp. (41)-144. Light blue wrappers on which is : 'Bibliothèque littéraire'.

"Michel-Ange" et "Raphaël Sanzio", par Alex. Dumas. Paris, Recoules, 1845, 8vo., 2 volumes, pp. 345 and 306 each with an additional unnumbered page table of contents.
Reprinted, same format and pagination, 1846.

"Michel-Ange", par M. Alexandre Dumas. In : Revue des feuilletons journal littéraire illustré composé de romans, voyages, légendes, anecdotes, contes nouvelles, historiques, etc., par J. Arago, H. de

Balzac, A. Dumas, ... Cinquième année. Paris, au boureaux (sic) du journal, 1845, 8vo., pp. (243)-282.

"Le Primatice et François 1er" signed : Alexandre Dumas. In : Revue pittoresque musée littéraire illustré par les premiers artistes Troisième Série. Tome III. Paris, Aubert, éditeur, 29, Place de la Bourse, 1845, 4to., pp. (179)-186 in double columns; vignette headpiece, 2 illustrations.

"La peinture chez les anciens suivie de l'histoire des peintres" par Alexandre Dumas. Bruxelles, Meline, Cans et compagnie, 1845, 16mo., 2 volumes, pp. 252 and 284. Pagination : Volume 1, "La peinture chez les anciens", (3)-185. "Histoire des peintres faisant suite à l'histoire de la peinture" : "Masaccio de San Giovanni" (189)-200, "Jean Bellin" (201)-228. "Le Perugin" (229)-252. Volume 2, "Léonard de Vinci" (1)-60, "Pinturiccio" (61)-80, "Fra Bartolomeo" (81)-113, "Albert Durer" (115)-151, "Luca Cranach" (153)-168, "Quentin Metzys" (169)-189, "André de Mantegna" (191)-207, "Baldassare Peruzzi" (209)-242, "Giorgione" (243)-284. There are no tables of contents. Green wrappers differing only from the title-page in that 'Par Alex. Dumas' replaces 'par Alexandre Dumas'.

Ibid   La Haye, chez les héritiers Doorman, 1845, 2 volumes, same format and pagination as the preceding edition. Buff wrappers.

Ibid   Bruxelles et Leipzig, Meline, Cans et compagnie, 1845, 2 volumes, same format and pagination as the two preceding editions. Blue wrappers.

"Vingt ans après", suite des "Trois mousquetaires" Par Alexandre Dumas. Paris, Baudry, ... , 1845, 8vo., 10 volumes, the pagination of the final volume being 302 with an additional page table of contents. "Vingt ans après" ends on page 201 of Volume 10, the remainder of the volume being filled up by "Giorgione".

"Les peintres célèbres. Cimabué. - Giotto". Alexandre Dumas. In : $_e$Musée des familles lectures du soir. Janvier 1846 - 2e série. - 13e volume. - No. 4. Au bureau de la direction, rue Gaillon, 4, a Paris. 4to., pp. 112-116 in double columns; 1 illustration.

"Vingt ans après", par Alexandre Dumas. Deuxième édition. Paris, Michel Lévy frères, éditeurs; Pétion, éditeur. 1846, 8vo., 8 volumes; "Vingt ans après" ends on page 213 of Volume 8, verso blank, and is followed by "Giorgione", pp. (215)-294.

Alexandre Dumas. "La peinture chez les anciens". "Léonard de Vinci, Masaccio de San-Giovanni, Le Pérugin, Jean Bellin, Luca Cranach, Albert Durer, Fra Bartolomeo, André de Mantegna, Pinturiccio, Baldassare Peruzzi, Giorgione, Quentin Metzys". // "Les deux étudiants de Bologne". "Dom Bernardo de Zuniga". // Publiée par Dufour et Mulat. Edition illustrée par J.-A. Beaucé, etc. (Vignette) (Paris) Marescq et Cie., n.d. (1856), large 8vo., pp. 40, and then 5 separate sections each of 16 pages; 25 illustrations and 6 illustrations 'hors-texte'.

"Receuil de biographies de peintres célèbres". Par Alexandre Dumas. Paris, Impr. de Gaittet, n.d. (1861), 4to., each of 16 pages and illustrated :

    1. "Albert Dürer et Fra Bartolomeo".
    2. "Giorgione et Quentin Metzis".

3. "Léonard de Vinci et Masaccio de S. Giovanni".
4. "Le Perugin, Jean Bellin et Luca Cranach".

"Italiens et Flamands" par Alexandre Dumas Paris Michel Lévy frères, 1862, 12mo., 2 volumes, pp. 305 and 300 each with an additional page table of contents. Pagination - Volume 1 : 'Introduction' (1)-145, verso blank, "Masaccio de San-Giovanni" (147)-154. "Jean Bellin" (155)-173, "Le Perugin" (175)-191, "Léonard de Vinci" (193)-232, "Pinturiccio" (233)-246, "Fra Bartolomeo" (247)- 268, "Albert Durer" (269)-293, "Luca Cranach" (295)-305. Volume 2 : "Quentin Metzys" (1)-14, "André de Mantegna" (15)-25, "Baldasarre Perruzi" (27)-49, "Giorgione" (51)-78, "Jean-Antoine Razzi, dit il Sodoma et il Mataccio" (79)-98, "Baccio Bandinelli" (99)-137, "André del Sarto" (139)-215, "Guerard Berck-Heyden" (217)-223, "Jules Romain" (225)-246, "Jacques de Pontormo" (247)-250, "Jean-Antoine Sogliani" (251)-256, "Corneille Bega" (257)-258, "François Miéris" (259)-261, "Alexandre Botticelli" (263)-269, "Ange Gaddi" (271)-276, "Jean Holbein" (277)-300. Reprinted, same format and pagination, by both Michel Lévy frères and Calmann-Levy.

Nouvelle bibliothèque française à l'usage de la jeunesse. Collection ouvrages choisies redigée et munie de notes explicatives par Louis Paban. Quatrieme livraison. Contenant VIII. "Michel Ange" par Alexandre Dumas. IX. Alphonse de Lamartine. "Scenes de sa vie racontées par lui-même". Stockholm, Aux dépens de P. Ad. Huldberg, Au Bazar de Norrbro, n.d. (1862), 8vo., 'Avertissement' (unnumbered), pp. (1)-75, "Michel Ange", notes on "Michel Ange" pp. 133-138.

"La peinture chez les anciens", par Alexandre Dumas. Paris : Impr. S. Raçon et Cie., n.d. (c 186), 4to., pp. 40 in double columns; illustrated.

"Albert Dürer et Fra Bartolomeo", par Alexandre Dumas. Paris : S. Raçon et Cie, n.d. (c 186), 4to., pp. 16 in double columns; illustrated.

"Giorgione et Quentin Metzis", par Alexandre Dumas. Paris : S. Raçon et Cie., n.d. (c 18), 4to., pp. 16 in double columns; illustrated.

"Leonard de Vinci et Massacio de S. Giovanni", par Alexandre Dumas. Paris : S. Raçon et Cie., n.d. (c 186), 4to., pp. 16 in double columns; 1 illustration.

"Les Médicis", par Alexandre Dumas. Paris : S. Raçon et Cie., n.d. (c 186), 4to., pp. 64 in double columns, 8 illustrations. (This edition of this work has been included here for the sake of continuity of the Raçon series.)

"Le Perugin, Jean Bellin et Luca Cranach", par Alexandre Dumas. Paris : S. Raçon et Cie., n.d. (c 186), 4to., pp. 16 in double columns; 1 illustration.

"Italiens et Flamands" par Alexandre Dumas. Paris Michel Lévy frères, n.d. (c 186), 4to. Musée littéraire contemporain.

"LE COMTE DE MONTE-C(H)RISTO"   1844-1845

In 1842 Dumas visited Elba with Prince Napoléon, the son of Jerome, and on their return journey they sailed around the island of

Monte-Cristo. Dumas told his companion that, some day, he would use
either it or its name in a romance to commemorate their journey.
Somewhere about that time Dumas was approached by Béthune et Plon
to write a work to be entitled "Impressions de voyage dans Paris",
but they later asked that instead the work should be a romance in
the style of Eugène Sue.

Dumas has written that he found the germ of the plot for this
famous work in "Le diamant et la vengeance" in Peuchet's "La police
dévoilée", although later this brief documental narrative came to be
called "François Picaud". His original intention was that the story
should start in Rome with the adventures of de Morcerf and Franz
d'Epinay, and he had, indeed, written several chapters before mention-
ing anything about the work to Maquet. The latter, however, insisted
that the story should start at Marseilles. Dumas finally agreed, and
divided the romance into three parts : Marseilles, Rome, Paris.
The period is 1815-1838. Dumas did at one time have the idea of
writing a sequel, but this never eventuated.

With some interruption the work appeared serially in 'Le journal
des débats' from 28th August, 1844, to 15th January, 1846, under the
title of "Le comte de Monte-Christo". This title was perpetuated
through most of the Belgian pirated editions, the first to be published
in volume form in France, and, with certain exceptions, right up to
the Lécrivain et Toubon illustrated edition of 1860. The first illustrated edition, au bureau de l'Echo des Feuilletons, 1846, printed the
title with the spelling as it is now known.

The years of the first publication of the work in volume form
in France in its now very rare first edition, and the names of the
original Paris publishers, have been the subject of controversy.
Talvart et Place state that the publisher was Pétion, librairie-
éditeur des oeuvres complètes d'Eugène Sue, 11, rue du Jardinet, the
printers being Cosson, Béthune et Plon, and Plon frères, and the
years of publication being 1845-1846. However, Glinel, Quérard, and
Parran, all state 1844-1845 - which is proved by the fact that a set
of the volumes (eighteen in all) bearing these dates was sold at the
Hotel Drouot in 1921, possibly from Parran's library. The curious
thing is that Talvart et Place state categorically that Volumes 1 to
14 are dated 1845, and Volumes 15 to 18, 1846. The Bibliothèque
Nationale possesses only the first twelve volumes, which are dated
1845 and were published by Pétion. In his introduction to the 'Class-
iques Garnier' edition of the work published in 1962 Professor Bornecque, on page lxi, gives the original edition as follows : Paris,
Pétion, Libraire-Editeur des Oeuvres complètes d'Eugène Sue, 11, rue
du Jardinet ou : Baudry, 34, rue Coquillière et rue de la Chausée
d'Antin, 22. (Impr. Cosson; Impr. Béthune et Plon, et Impr. Plon
frères). 1845-1846. 18 vol. in-8; but he goes on to add that the
'Journal de la Librairie' "annonce les Tomes I-II à la date du novembre
1844, n'annonce pas les Tomes III-IV, puis mentionne les Tomes V-VI le
19 juillet 1845, les Tomes VII-VIII le 30 août, les Tomes IX-X le 25
octobre, les Tomes XI-XII le 20 décembre. Je n'ai trouvé aucune mention des derniers."

I am of the first belief that the evidence provided by the Hotel
Drouot sale is conclusive that the first edition to be published in
volume form in France is dated 1844-1845, the first two volumes being
dated 1844 and the remaining 16, 1845.

In different editions, both Belgian and French, there are very minor variations in the text of the work; as an instance, the date of the arrival of the 'Pharaon' in Marseilles is given in some texts as 24th February and in others the 28th of that month. The first illustrated edition published 'Au bureau de l'Echo des Feuilletons' has been stated to have been 'revised, corrected and with an epilogue', but my copy contains no such statement and it certainly does not differ very much textually from the Belgian and early French editions in my library - there is the alteration that the last chapter's final portion has been detached to be entitled 'Conclusion'.

Based on what has been written above, therefore, the original edition was :

"Le comte de Monte-Christo" par Alexandre Dumas. Paris, (publishers as set out above), 1844-1845, 8vo., 18 volumes, pagination : Volumes 1 and 2 (1844), 321 and 334, each with an additional unnumbered page table of contents; Volumes 3-18 (1845), 312 including table of contents, 325, 338, each with an additional unnumbered page table of contents, 324 including table of contents, 310, 329, 320, 312, 312, 309, 309, all with an additional unnumbered page table of contents, 318 including table of contents, 310, 367, 309 and 307, all with an additional unnumbered page table of contents. Yellow wrappers.

"Le comte de Monte-Christo". Par Alexandre Dumas. Bruxelles, Alph. Lebègue et Sacré fils, 1845, 24mo., 15 volumes, pp. 160, 167, 160, 160, 166, 163, 164, 159, 166, 162, 165, 142, 151, 157 and 187.

Omnibus littéraire. "Le comte de Monte-Christo" par Alexandre Dumas. Bruxelles, Meline, Cans et compagnie, 1845, 18mo., 12 volumes, pp. 163, 157, 151, 156, 152, 160, 154, 149, 162, 154, 155 and 140.

"Le comte de Monte-Christo". par Alexandre Dumas. Paris. Pétion, libraire-éditeur des oeuvres complètes d'Eugène Sue, 11, rue du Jardinet. 1845. 8vo., 18 volumes, pagination : 321, 334, each with an additional unnumbered page table of contents, 311 verso table of contents and unnumbered, 325, 338, 323, 310, 329, all with an additional unnumbered page table of contents, 320 with no table of contents, (5)-313, (5)-312, 309, 309, all with an additional unnumbered page table of contents, 315 with table of contents numbered (317)-318, 310, 287, 309 and 305, all with an additional unnumbered page table of contents. All title-pages are identical with the exception that in Volumes 1-6 inclusive there is a full-stop after "Christo", while in Volumes 7-18 the full-stop is lacking. Volumes 1-4 were printed by Béthune et Plon, Volumes 5 and 6 by Plon frères, and Volumes 7-18 by A. Henry. Yellow wrappers.

Supplément au journal Le Siècle. Oeuvres complètes d'Alexandre Dumas. "La comte de Monte-Christo". The publication dates were : 28th September, 1845, to 1st February, 1846. 4to., pp. (1)-403 in double columns, followed by "François Picaud histoire contemporaine", pp. (404)-408. Frontispiece portrait of Dumas and 28 steel engravings. (The date of the arrival of the 'Pharaon' at Marseilles is given in this instance as 24th February.)

Omnibus littéraire. "Le comte de Monte-Christo" par Alexandre Dumas. Bruxelles, Meline, Cans et compagnie, 1845-1846, 18mo., same number of volumes and pagination as the Meline, Cans edition of 1845.

"Le comte de Monte-Christo" par Alexandre Dumas. Bruxelles Société

156

belge de librairie, 1845-1846, 18mo., same number of volumes and pagination as the preceding edition.

Ibid   Rio-de-Janeiro, Désiré Dujardin, libraire, 1845-1846, 18mo., same number of volumes and pagination as the preceding two editions.

Ibid   Bruxelles, Livourne, Meline, Cans et cie.; Leipzig, J.-P. Meline, 1845-1846, 16mo., 8 volumes, pagination : Volumes 1-6 (1845), 280, 269, 308, 281, 292 and 292; Volumes 7-8 (1846), 282 and 375.

"Le comte de Monte-Christo", par Alexandre Dumas. Bruxelles, Société belge de librairie, Hauman et Ce., 1845-1846, 16mo., same number of volumes and pagination as the preceding edition.

Ibid   La Haye, chez les héritiers Doorman, 1845-1846, 16mo., same number of volumes and pagination as the two preceding editions.

"Le comte de Monte-Christo" Par Alexandre Dumas. Bruxelles et Leipzig, C. Muquardt, 1845-1846, 24mo., 15 volumes, pagination : Volumes 1-14 (1845), 160, 167, 160, 160, 166, 163, 164, 159, 166, 162, 165, 142, 151 and 157; Volume 15 (1846), 259 'Fin du quinzieme volume' and Chapter X, followed by (161)-187, Chapter XI, 'Le 5 octobre'.

Ibid   Bruxelles, Alph. Lebègue et Sacré fils, 1846, 18mo., 10 volumes, pp. 162, 172, 161, 175, 156, 168, 172, 143, 162 and 175.

"Le comte de Monte-Christo" par Alexandre Dumas. Bruxelles, Société typographique belge, Ad. Wahlen et compagnie, 1846, 18mo., 13 volumes, pp. 182, 178, 178, 167, 175, 173, 166, 173, 154, 158, 161, 157 and 159. Pink wrappers with the imprint 'Distribution de l'émancipation'.

Ibid   Bruxelles, Société typographique, Ad. Wahlen et compagnie, 1846, 16mo., 9 volumes, pp. 300, 296, 263, 309, 277, 287, 317, 322 and 279.

Semaine littéraire du Courrier des Etats-Unis. "Le comte de Monte-Christo", par Alexandre Dumas. New-York, F. Gaillardet, éditeur, Bureau du Courrier des Etats-Unis ... . 1846, large 8vo., 2 volumes, pp. (3)-547 continuously in double columns. The final chapter is numbered 'LVI' : 'Le pardon', and shows that the edition was an abbreviated one. There is added, pp. (549)-556 "Histoire de François Picaud". The work is divided into four parts and consists of : Part 1, 30 chapters; Part 2, 9 chapters; Part 3, 21 chapters, Part 4, 57 chapters. On the verso of the title-page of Volume 1 is : "Conditions d'Abonnement ... Le roman de MONTE-CHRISTO forme un supplément à la SEMAINE LITTERAIRE. Cet ouvrage, qui a été publié à Paris en 12 volumes in-octavo, se vend $3, et $2 seulement pour les abonnés du Courrier des Etats-Unis et de la Semaine Littéraire."

"Le comte de Monte-Christo" par Alexandre Dumas. (Vignette) Bruxelles, Meline, Cans et compagnie, 1846, large 8vo., pp. 618 in double columns.

"Le comte de Monte-Cristo" par M. Alexandre Dumas Paris au bureau de l'écho des feuilletons rue Saint-Thomas-du-Louvre, 30. 1846. Large 8vo., 2 volumes, pp. (1)-476, (477)-478 table of contents, (489) 'avis au relieur pour le placement des gravures du Monte-Cristo illustré', and (1)-499, verso (unnumbered) table of contents. Frontispiece

portrait of Dumas to Volume 1 engraved by Le Couterier after Eugène
Giraud and 14 plates engraved on steel by Ch. Colin, Goulu, Rose,
Pardinel, Carey, Lichard, Audibran, Caren, A. Portier, A. Gabriel,
after Gavarni and Tony Johannot; Volume 2 has 15 plates by Gabriel,
Rebel, Carey, Pardinel, Riffaut, Lochard, Masson, Audibran, A. Portier,
after Gavarni and Tony Johannot. Typographie Lacrampe et Cie rue
Damiette, 2.
This is the first illustrated edition of the work which initially
appeared in 60 parts at 40 centimes each, and 24 francs for the com-
plete work, in the same year.

Ibid   1846. Large 8vo. 2 volumes, pp. (1)-478 including
2 pages table of contents, and with 15 plates, and (1)-500 including
1 page table of contents, also with 15 plates. This edition includes
as an addendum to Volume 2 "François Picaud, Histoire contemporaine".
(Professor Bornecque refers to a single volume 4to. edition published
by L'écho des feuilletons' in 1846 which includes "François Picaud
... ", but this edition is unknown to me.)

Ibid   1846-1849, 2 volumes, same format, pagination and
illustrations as the original 1846 edition with the wrappers bearing
the date '1850'.
Reprinted, same format, pagination and illustrations, 1850.

"Le comte de Monte-Cristo" par Alexandre Dumas. Bruxelles, Livourne,
Meline, Cans et compagnie; Leipzig, J.P. Meline, 1846, 8vo., 4 volumes,
pp. 375, 378, 378 and 327. There are no tables of contents. Green,
some copies buff, wrappers.

Oeuvres complètes de M. Alexandre Dumas. "Le comte de Monte-Cristo"
par Alexandre Dumas. Publié par 'Le Siècle'. 1846, 4to., pp. 'Table
des chapitres' (unnumbered); Supplément du journal 'Le Siècle' du 28
septembre 1845. "Le comte de Monte-Christo", pp. (1)-403 in double
columns. The supplement was published in weekly instalments from 28
septembre 1845 to 1er février, 1846, and thereafter the supplements
were not dated but ran as a continuation from the last-mentioned date.

"Le comte de Monte-Cristo" par Alexandre Dumas Paris Michel Lévy
frères, libraires-éditeurs, 1846, 12mo., 6 volumes, pagination : 299,
verso unnumbered page table of contents, 328, and unnumbered page table
of contents, 319, verso unnumbered page table of contents, 308, and
unnumbered page table of contents, 286, and unnumbered page table of
contents, 278, and unnumbered page table of contents.
Reprinted, same format and pagination, 1847.

"Le comte de Monte-Cristo". Par Alexandre Dumas. Bruxelles, Wouters
frères, Imprimeurs-libraires, 1847, 18mo., 10 volumes, pp. 189, 188,
194, 182, 164, 168, 161, 149, 150 and 139.

"Le comte de Monte-Cristo" Par Alexandre Dumas. Bruxelles, C.-G.
Vogler, 1847, 18mo., 10 volumes, pp. 189 (1), 188, 194 (2), 182, 164,
168 (2), 161 (1), 149 (1), 150 and 139 (3).

Ibid   Bruxelles et Leipzig, C. Muquardt, 1847, 18mo.,
10 volumes, pp. 189, 188, 194, 182, 164, 168, 161, 149, 150 and 139.

"Le comte de Monte-Cristo" par Alexandre Dumas Paris Michel Lévy
frères, 1850, same format and pagination as the Michel Lévy frères,
1846 and 1847 editions.
This work was many times reprinted in the same format but with

varying pagination over the years between 1850 and 1900 by both Michel Lévy frères and Calmann-Lévy.

"Le comte de Monte-Christo" par Alex. Dumas. (Vignette) Bruxelles, Livourne, Meline, Cans et compagnie; Leipzig, J.P. Meline, 1851, large 8vo., pp. (426)-1030 in double columns, and 2 unnumbered pages table of contents also in double columns.

"Le comte de Monte-Christo" par M. Alexandre Dumas. Paris, Dufour, Mulat et Boulanger, éditeurs, 4to., 2 volumes; Volume 1, 1855, and Volume 2, 1851; pagination : Volume 1, (1)-476, (477)-478 table of contents, and unnumbered page 'avis au relieur pour le placement des gravures'; Volume 2, (1)-499, verso unnumbered page table of contents. Frontispiece portrait of Dumas to Volume 1. Buff wrappers : "Le comte de Monte-Christo" par M. Alexandre Dumas. (Vignette) Paris, au bureau de l'Echo des feuilletons, and dated 1856.

"Le comte de Monte-Christo" par Alexandre Dumas publié par Dufour et Mulat illustré par G. Staal et J.-A. Beaucé. (Vignette) Paris - 1852-1853 chez Marescq et Cie., libraires, 4to., in six parts, the text being in two columns. Pagination : Première partie, (1)-158; Deuxième partie, (1)-162, both published in 1852; Troisième partie, (1)-258; Quatrième partie, (1)-157; Cinquième partie, (1)-150; Sixième partie, (1)-138 and (139)-149 "François Picaud Histoire contemporaine". Each part has an additional unnumbered page table of contents, with on verso 'placement des gravures', and each part has a frontispiece and the following number of plates : 19, 19, 19, 18, 17 and 18 respectively.
Reprinted, same format, pagination and illustrations, 1853-1854.

"Le comte de Monte-Cristo" par M. Alexandre Dumas. Paris, Legrand, Troussel et Pomey, n.d. (c 1857), large 8vo., 2 volumes, pp. 478 and 500, each volume with a frontispiece and 14 illustrations; Volume 1 includes a notice to the binder as to the location of the illustrations, and Volume 2 has an index to the illustrations.

"Le comte de Monte-Cristo" was published as a serial in Dumas' journal 'Le Monte-Cristo' as follows : 'Un mot à propos du comte de Monte-Cristo', pp. 342-354 of issue no. 22 for 17th September, 1857 (1re année), the first instalment also appearing in that issue and continuing to be published weekly, with only five lapses, throughout the remainder of the first, all of the second, and part of the third years of the journal's publication up to and including issue no. 10 for 23rd June, 1859. It was followed in this last issue, and in the subsequent one, by "François Picaud Histoire contemporaine" from the 'Archives de la police'. The journal was published in double columns.

"Le comte de Monte-Cristo" par M. Alexandre Dumas. Paris, Dufour, Mulat et Boulanger, large 8vo., 2 volumes, pagination : Volume 1 (1860), 476, 2 unnumbered pages table of contents and 1 page 'Avis au relieur pour le placement des gravures du Monte-Cristo illustré', frontispiece portrait of Dumas by Beaucé, 15 engravings, initial ornaments for each of the 55 chapters and a number of ornamental tail-pieces; Volume 2 (1859), 499, 2 unnumbered pages table of contents and 'classement des gravures' (there are no instructions to the binders), 10 engravings, initial ornaments for each of the 64 chapters and a number of ornamental tail-pieces.

"Le comte de Monte-Christo" par Alexandre Dumas illustré par G.

Staal, J.A. Beaucé, etc. (Vignette) Paris, Lécrivain et Toubon,
n.d. (c 186), 4to., in six parts, same pagination and illustrations
as the Paris, Marescq et Cie., edition of 1852-1853 referred to above.

"Le comte de Monte-Cristo" par Alexandre Dumas. Tome premier. (Vignette) Paris Ch. Crouzet, libraire-éditeur, n.d. (c 1865), large 8vo.,
pp. (1)-476, (477)-478 table of contents. Tome deuxième. Paris,
Legrand et Crouzet, libraires-éditeurs, n.d. (c 1865), large 8vo.,
pp. (1)-499, verso unnumbered page table of contents; both volumes
illustrated. Paris - Société d'Imprimerie Paul Dupont.

"Le comte de Monte-Cristo", par M. Alexandre Dumas. Paris, Legrand
et Crouzet, n.d. (1865), n.d. (1865), large 8vo., 2 volumes, same
pagination and illustrations as the Paris, 'L'Echo des feuilletons'
edition of 1846.

Musée littéraire contemporain. Alexandre Dumas. "Le comte de Monte-
Cristo". Paris, Michel Lévy frères, n.d. (c 186), 4to., pp. 403
in double columns, and unnumbered page table of contents. Caption
title. Woodcut at head of title repeated on wrappers.

"Le comte de Monte-Cristo", par Alexandre Dumas. Paris, Jules Rouff
et Cie., n.d. (1887), 4to., pp. 1389 and 3 unnumbered pages table of
contents. Illustrations by Riou, Gavarni, Tony Johannot, etc.
This edition appeared in 174 parts, each with a woodcut frontispiece.
Reprinted, same format, pagination and illustrations, 1893 and 1894.

Alexandre Dumas. "Le comte de Monte-Cristo". Illustré par G. Staal,
J.-A. Beaucé. Paris, Calmann-Lévy, 1896-1897, 4to., in six parts.
Volumes 1-2 (1896), Volumes 3-4 (1897), Volume 5 (1892) (sic), and
volume 6 was undated. This edition comprised the same pagination,
with the same illustrations, as the Paris, Marescq et Cie., 1852-1853,
edition.

"Le comte de Monte-Cristo", par Alexandre Dumas. Paris, Calmann-
Lévy, 1896-1897, 12mo., 6 volumes; Volumes 1-2 (1896), pp. 299, 328;
Volumes 3-4 (1897), 322, 308; Volumes 5-6 (1896), 286, 278; each with
an additional unnumbered page table of contents.

"LOUIS XIV ET SON SIECLE"   1844-1845

     This is the first of a long series of historical studies extending
to the reign of Louis-Philippe. These studies may,indeed, be extended
back considerably earlier if "Les grands hommes en robe de chambre" are
taken into account.

Original edition.
"Louis XIV et son siècle", Par M. Alexandre Dumas. Paris, chez MM.
J.-B. Fellens et L.-P. Dufour, 1844-1845, royal 8vo., 2 volumes. Pagination : Volume 1 (1844), (1)-482, (483)-488 'appendice', (489)-492
table of contents, unnumbered page 'avis au relieur pour le placement
des gravures', frontispiece and 29 plates; Volume 2 (1845), (1)-500,
(501)-508 'appendice', (509)-512 table of contents, unnumbered page
'avis au relieur pour le placements des gravures', frontispiece and
29 plates. Blue wrappers : Illustré par les premiers Artistes de
Paris. Imprimerie de BUREAU, rue Coquillière, 22. Tiré sur presses
mécaniques par ARISTIDE.
The engravings in Volume 1 are by Lesestre, Brugnot, Hébert, Pisan,
Piaud, Trichon and Bernard, after Rouargue, Marckl, Guérin and Wattier;

in Volume 2 by Hébert, Pisan, Lesestre, Trichon, Bernard, Brevière, Piaud, A. Vien, Duhardin, etc., after Marckl, Wattier, Valentin and The. Guérin. There are numerous vignettes.
The work was originally issued in 63 parts at 60 centimes each, and 30 francs for the complete set of parts.
Reprinted, same format, pagination and illustrations, 1850.

Omnibus littéraire. "Louis XIV et son siècle" par Alexandre Dumas. Bruxelles, Société belge de librairie; Hauman et Cie., 1844-1846, 18mo., 9 volumes. Pagination : Volumes 1-3 (1844), 156, 154, 153; Volumes 4-6 (1845), 155, 147, 145; Volumes 7-9 (1846), 165, 107, 95. The text of the work ends on page 68 of Volume 9, pp. 69-95 consisting of the 'Appendix'.

Ibid   Bruxelles, Société belge de librairie; Hauman et Cᵉ, 1844-1846, same format and pagination as the preceding edition.

Ibid   Bruxelles, Meline, Cans et compagnie, 1844 and 1846; Volumes 1-5, 1844, and 6-9, 1846, same format and pagination as the preceding edition.

Ibid   Bruxelles, Meline, Cans et compagnie, 1846, same format and pagination as the preceding editions.

"Louis XIV et son siècle" par Alexandre Dumas. (Vignette) Bruxelles et Leipzig, Meline, Cans et compagnie, 1844-1846, 16mo., 5 volumes. Pagination : Volume 1 (1844), 282, Volumes 2-4 (1845), 295, 308, 315; Volume 5 (1846), 393. The appendix occupies pp. (367)-393 of Volume 5.

"Louis XIV et son siècle", par Alexandre Dumas. La Haye, chez les héritiers Doorman, 1844-1846, same format and pagination as the preceding edition.

Louis XIV et son siècle", par M. Alexandre Dumas. Nouvelle édition. Paris, Passard, 1845, 8vo., 9 volumes, pp. (i)-viii, 304, 327, 358, 392, 326, 320, 364, 297 and 308.

Collection des meilleurs auteurs modernes français, italiens et espagnols. Alexandre Dumas. "Louis XIV et son siècle". Grimma, imprimerie du bureau d'édition, 1845-1846, 16mo., 4 volumes. Pagination : Volumes 1-3 (1845), 306, 308-604 (volumes 2 and 3 being paged continuously); Volume 4 (1846), 282.

Oeuvres de Alex. Dumas. Tome dixième. (Vignette) Bruxelles, Livourne, Meline, Cans et compagnie; Leipzig, J.P. Meline, 1846, large 8vo. "Louis XIV et son siècle", pp. (1)-413 in double columns.

"Louis XIV et son siècle". Par Alexandre Dumas. Paris, Publié par MM. Dufour et Mulat, 1850, 4to., 2 volumes, pp. 492 and 512, with 29 and 30 plates respectively. The engravings were by MM. Marckl. Wattier, J.-A. Beaucé, Valentin, etc.
Reprinted, same format, pagination and illustrations, 1851, 1852, 1853.

"Louis XIV et son siècle" par Alexandre Dumas. Bruxelles, Livourne, Meline, Cans et cie.; Leipzig, J.P. Meline, 1850-1851, 16mo., 5 volumes. Pagination : Volumes 1-2 (1850), 239, 226; Volumes 3-5 (1851), 215, 267, 242. Blue wrappers.

"Louis XIV et son siècle" par Alexandre Dumas illustré par MM. Marckl, Wattier, J.-A. Beaucé, Valentin, etc., etc. Publié par MM. Dufour et Mulat. (Vignette) Paris chez Marescq et Cie., 1851, 4to., pp. (1)-2 'Préface' signed : Alexandre Dumas, (3)-402, and 402-408

'Appendice', (409)-412 table of contents and 'placement des gravures imprimées a part'; frontispiece and 15 illustrations.
Reprinted, same format, pagination and illustrations, 1853, 1856, 1867.

"Louis XIV et son siècle" par M. Alexandre Dumas. Paris, Dufour, Mulat et Boulanger, 1856, large 8vo., 2 volumes; pagination : Volume 1, (i)-ii 'Préface' signed : Alexandre Dumas, (1)-482, (483)-499 'Appendice', frontispiece and 25 illustrations, vignettes; Volume 2, (1)-500, (501)-508 'Appendice', (509)-512 table of contents, frontis-piece and 23 illustrations, vignettes.
Reprinted, same format, pagination and illustrations, Volume 1, 1857, and Volume 2, 1859.

Ibid   Paris, Lécrivain et Toubon, 1861, large 8vo., same pagination and illustrations as the Marescq et Cie., 1851, edition.

"Louis XIV et son siècle", par Alexandre Dumas. Paris, Dufour, Boulanger et Legrand, Volume 1, 1862, Volume 2, 1861 (sic), large 8vo., pp. 482, (483)-488 'Appendice', and 4 unnumbered pages table of con-tents, and pp. 500, (501)-508 'Appendice', and 4 unnumbered pages table of contents.

Ibid   Paris, Legrand, Poumey et Crouzet, n.d. (c 1862), large 8vo., 2 volumes. Illustrated with frontispieces and a total of 56 plates.

"Louis XIV et son siècle" par Alexandre Dumas. Paris, Michel Lévy frères, 1866, 12mo., 4 volumes, pp. 316, 305, 308 and 283, each in-clusive of table of contents; pp. (269)-277 of Volume 4 comprise 'Notes'.
Several times reprinted, same format and pagination, by both Michel Lévy frères and Calmann-Lévy.

Ibid   Paris, Michel Lévy frères, n.d. (c 187), 4to., 4 volumes. Caption title. Woodcut at head of title.

"MES INFORTUNES DE GARDE NATIONAL"   1845

     This is a piece of purely personal reminiscence.

Original (and only) edition.
"Les frères corses" par Alexandre Dumas. Hippolyte Souverain, éditeur, rue des beaux-arts, 5, a l'entresol, a Paris, 1845, 8vo., 2 volumes. The pagination of Volume 2 is (7)-312, "Les frères corses" ending on page 178 and being followed by "Mes infortunes de garde national", pp. (179)-312. Green wrappers : Bibliothèque de romans nouveaux, par les meilleurs écrivains, formera 100 volumes in-8. Tome 90. The wrappers are ornamented with an engraving by Cherrier in a frame designed by E. Bourguignon.

"LA REINE MARGOT"   (Romance)   1845

     On the 3rd December, 1844, 'La Presse', which was owned by Emile de Girardin, published the first chapter of Balzac's "Les Paysans". Three days later the following announcement was made : '... In the course of the month and immediately after the first part of "Les Paysans" 'La Presse' will publish "La Reine Margot" by M. Alexandre Dumas'. Balzac's work far from being read with interest had brought threats of stopping subscriptions to the journal, and Girardin, fearful of the dreaded 31st December on which day subscriptions for the following year fell due, had had to promise a romance by the author of "Monte-Cristo". The first instalment of "La reine Margot" duly appeared on Christmas Day, to the infinite joy of the bored readers of "Les Paysans". Subscriptions were renewed and Girardin was saved.

Dumas was fortunate again in that he had found in memoirs of the sixteenth century the names of two men whose tragic history strangely, attracted him. The names of the two men - La Mole and Coconnas. Before the concluding chapters were reached the work, by common consent, was considered one of the best of his historical romances; it was seen to be better constructed and, by and large, better written than the immortal "Les trois mousquetaires". The period is 1572-1575, a terrible one, taking within it the Massacre of Saint-Bartholomew's Eve, the rivers of blood, the poisonings, and the torture-chambers.

Original edition.
"La reine Margot" par Alexandre Dumas. Bruxelles, Société belge de librairie, Hauman et ce., 1845, 24mo., 5 volumes, pp. 277, 256, 240, 228 and 290. "La reine Margot" ends on page 186 of Volume 5, and is followed by "Rubens", pp. (187)-290. Buff wrappers.

Ibid   Bruxelles, Société belge de librairie Hauman et Ce., 1845, 18mo., 8 volumes, pp. 187, 181, 168, 176, 156, 154, 135 and 144. "La reine Margot" ends on page 40 of Volume 8, and is followed by "Rubens", pp. (41)-144. Light blue wrappers on which is : Bibliothèque littéraire.

Ibid   Bruxelles, Meline, Cans et compagnie, 1845, 24mo., 4 volumes, pp. 277, 286, 285 and 351.

Ibid   Bruxelles et Leipzig, Meline, Cans et compagnie, 1845, 4 volumes, same format and pagination as the preceding edition.

Ibid   Bruxelles, Alph. Lebègue et Sacré fils, 1845, 18mo., 5 volumes, pp. 173, 164, 172, 176 and 166.

"La reine Margot", par Alexandre Dumas. Bruxelles, Leipzig, Librairie de Ch. Muquardt, 1845, 18mo., 5 volumes, same pagination as the preceding edition.

Ibid   Paris, Garnier frères, 1845, 8vo., 6 volumes, pp. 322, 319, 318, 365, 351 and 349, each with an additional unnumbered page table of contents. Yellow wrappers. Impr. Béthune et Plon et Impr. Plon frères.

Publication du journal 'Le Siècle'. Oeuvres complètes de M. Alexandre Dumas. "La reine Margot". Paris, Bureaux du Siècle, 1845-1846, 4to., pp. 1-168 in double columns. There is no table of contents. Caption title. The first date to appear of an instalment is on page 25 '12 octobre 1845', and the last on page 161 '8 février 1846'.

Oeuvres de Alex. Dumas. Tome dixième. (Vignette) Bruxelles, Livourne, Meline, Cans et compagnie; Leipzig, J.P. Meline, 1846, large 8vo. "La reine Margot", pp. 1-250 in double columns.

"La reine Margot" par Alexandre Dumas. Paris, Michel Lévy frères, 1847, 12mo., 2 volumes, pp. 364 and 342, each with an additional un-

numbered page table of contents.
Reprinted 1851, and 'nouvelle édition' 1860.
Frequently reprinted in the same format but with varying paginations
by both Michel Lévy frères and Calmann-Lévy.

"La reine Margot" par Alexandre Dumas publiée par Dufour et Mulat.
Edition illustrée par E. Lampsonius et Lancelot. (Vignette) Paris,
chez Marescq et Cie., 1853, 4to., in two parts. Pagination : Première partie, (1)-(180), Seconde partie, (1)-(188), in double columns,
with 73 and 69 illustrations respectively.

"La reine Margot" par Alexandre Dumas Edition illustrée par E. Lampsonius et Lancelot Paris Lécrivain et Toubon, ... 1860, 4to.,
in two parts. Pagination : Première partie, (1)-178, Seconde partie,
(1)-186, in double columns, each with an additional unnumbered page
table of contents. Woodcuts on title pages, 57 illustrations. Alexandre Dumas. Oeuvres illustrées.

"La reine Margot" par Alexandre Dumas Paris, Calmann-Lévy, n.d.
(c 187), 4to., pp. (1)-148 in double columns including table of contents. Caption title. Woodcut at head of title.

Ibid   Edition illustrée par E. Lampsonius et Lancelot.
Paris, Calmann-Lévy, 1885, 4to., 2 volumes, same format and pagination
as the Lécrivain et Toubon, 1860. Caption title. Alexandre Dumas
oeuvres illustrées.
Reprinted, same format and pagination, 1889, 1894, 1896.

"La reine Margot", par Alexandre Dumas. Paris, J. Rouff, n.d. (c
189), large 8vo., 3 volumes; "La reine Margot"; "La dame de Monsoreau"; "Les quarante-cinq". Illustrated.

"LE GARDE FORESTIER"   1845

        This comedy was signed by de Leuven and Brunswick (Lhérie) only,
but Dumas is considered to have had a hand in its writing. It must
on no account be confused with Dumas' own play "Les gardes forestiers"
which was produced in 1858.

Original edition.
"Le garde forestier", comédie en deux actes et deux époques, mêlée
de couplets, par MM. de Leuven et Brunswick, Représentée pour la
première fois, à Paris, sur le théâtre des Variètès, le 15 mars 1845.
Paris, Beck, 1845, 8vo., pp. 28 in double columns. Caption title.

"Le garde forestier" comédie en deux actes et deux époques mêlée de
couplets par MM. de Leuven et Brunswick. Représentée pour la premiere
fois, à Paris, sur le théâtre de Variétés le 15 mars 1845. Paris,
C. Tresse, éditeur, 1845, same format and pagination as the preceding
edition. Caption title. Impr. de Boulé. La France dramatique au
dix-neuvième siècle.

"UNE CONTE DE FEES"   1845

        The collaboration of Dumas is known to have been sought in the
writing of this comedy, even although it bore the signatures only of
de Leuven and Brunswick (Lhérie).

Original edition.
"Une conte de fées", comédie en trois actes mêlée de chant, par MM. de Leuven et Brunswick, Représentée, pour la première fois, à Paris, sur le théâtre des Variétés, le 29 avril 1845. (Paris, Beck, 1845), 8vo., pp. 32 in double columns. Paris, Imprimerie de Boulé et Ce.

"Une conte de fées" comédie en trois actes mêlée de chant, par MM. de Leuven et Brunswick. Représentée, pour la première fois, à Paris, sur le théâtre des Variétés, le 29 avril 1845. Paris, C. Tresse, 1845, same format and pagination as the preceding edition. Impr. de Boulé. La France dramatique au dix-neuvième siècle.

"SYLVANDIRE"   (Drama)   1845

        Drawn from Dumas' romance of the same name he is properly credited with having helped de Leuven and Vanderbuch in the writing of this play. The period of the romance was the last years of Louis XIV and the ascendancy of Madame de Maintenon, but the action of the play is brought forward to the reign of Louis XV.

Original edition.
"Sylvandire", roman d'Alexandre Dumas, mis en quatre chapitres, par MM. de Leuven et Vanderbuch, représentée, à Paris, sur le théâtre du Palais-Royal, le 7 juin 1845. Paris, (Marchant) Magasin théatral, n.d. (1845), 8vo., pp. 32 in double columns. Caption title. Woodcut at head of title, Chapître IV scène iii. Yellow wrappers. Imp. de Mme Vve Dondey-Dupré.

Ibid   Yellow wrappers : Magasin théatral. Choix de pièces nouvelles, jouées sur tous les théatres de Paris. Théâtre du Palais-Royal. "Sylvandire", Roman en quatre chapitres. (Vignette) Paris, Marchant; Bruxelles, Tarride, n.d. (1845), same format and pagination as the preceding edition.

"VINGT ANS APRES"   1845

        Following on the tremendous success of "Les trois mousquetaires" 'Le Siècle' asked Dumas for another romance to be published serially. He offered to write a sequel to that work, an offer which was declined by one of the editors. Dumas approached his friend Louis Desnoyers, the then general manager of that journal, and to him he unfolded the proposed plot. A contract was signed on the spot.

        Whether "Vingt ans après" does or does not share the usual fate of sequels, which so often lack the vigour of the original, is an open question. But what could be more impressive than the opening chapter with Mazarin sitting in solitary and gloomy reverie in Richelieu's chair in Richelieu's room, while he can hear outside the noise of the sullen and discontented Parisian crowds. The book is notable for having absolutely no love interest; the only women who play even insignificant parts are Anne of Austria, and the wife and daughter of Charles 1st. There is certainly a glimpse of Louise de la Vallière, but that only as a preparation for meeting her in another work, her companion being Athos' son, Raoul de Bragelonne.

        The romance was a great success in 'Le Siècle', and it seems unlikely that Dumas either corrected or revised the 1845 serial publication, as it is known he did with "Les trois mousquetaires" before its issue in volume form. There is, however, one interesting point which must be made - in certain of the Belgian pirated editions there is included a chapter entitled 'Le bonhomme Broussel' which is not to be found in either the Baudry first edition to be published in France or in the subsequent Michel Lévy frères and Calmann-Lévy editions, although it is included in the illustrated editions of both Fellens et Dufour, and Marescq.

The period is that of the Fronde in the years 1648-1649.

Original edition.
"Vingt ans après" (Suite des Trois Mousquetaires) par Alexandre Dumas. Bruxelles, Société belge de librairie Hauman et Ce., 1845, 16mo., 7 volumes, pp. 198, 229, 240 ('Le bonhomme Broussel', Ch. VIII, pp. (89)-102), 226, 235, 274 and 287. "Vingt ans après" ends on page 191 of Volume 7; "La plus romanesque aventure de ma vie", par le Bibliophile Jacob, filling pp. (195)-287.

"Vingt ans après" (Suite des Trois Mousquetaires). Par Alexandre Dumas. Bruxelles, Société belge de librairie Hauman et ce., 1845, 18mo., 10 volumes, pp. 178, 173, 178 ('Le bonhomme Broussel' pp. (165)-178 and 177-178 bound between pp. 160 and 161), 166, 167, 166, 171, 167, 166 and 167. This edition does not include the above-mentioned work by Le Bibliophile Jacob.

"Vingt ans après" (Suite des Trois Mousquetaires) par Alexandre Dumas. (Vignette) Bruxelles, Meline, Cans et compagnie, 1845, 18mo., 6 volumes, pp. 283, 295, 295 ('Le bonhomme Broussel', Ch. I, pp. (1)-16), 257, 312 and 379.

Ibid (Vignette) Bruxelles et Leipzig, Meline, Cans et compagnie, 1845, 18mo., 6 volumes, pp. 286, 296, 297, 257, 314 and 380.

"Vingt ans après" (Suite des Trois Mousquetaires) par Alexandre Dumas. Bruxelles, Alphonse Lebègue et Sacré fils, 1845, 18mo., 8 volumes, pp. 141, 145 (and 8 pages of advertisements), 139 ('Le bonhomme Broussel', Ch. VII, pp. 88-98) (and 4 pages of advertisements), 146 (and 8 pages of advertisements), 159, 149, 153 and 140. Muséum littéraire, comprising parts of the 14th, 15th, 16th and 17th series of the 'Galerie littéraire'. Green wrappers.

"Vingt ans après" par Alexandre Dumas. Bruxelles et Leipzig, C. Muquardt, 1845, 18mo., 8 volumes, pp. 129, 135, 128 ('Le bonhomme Broussel', Ch. VII, pp. 81-90), 134, 146, 139, 143 and 128.

Semaine littéraire du Courrier des Etats-Unis. Receuil choisi de romans, feuilletons, ouvrages historiques et dramatiques, en prose et en vers, des auteurs modernes les plus renommés. VIII série - Vol. II. New-York, F. Gaillardet. Bureau du Courrier des Etats-Unis. 1845. "Vingt ans après, ou les trois mousquetaires sous Mazarin", par Alexandre Dumas. 8vo., pp. (3)-348 in double columns, and unnumbered page table of contents divided into : 'Prologue' and 'Première-Neuvième partie'.

(It should be added here that "Vingt ans après", suite des trois mousquetaires, par Alexandre Dumas, was published in : Nouvelle Orléans, Imprimerie de l'Abeille, 1845; the only copy that I have been able to trace was in the Howard-Tilton Memorial Library of Tulane University, U.S.A., but unfortunately that Library's copy has disappeared.)

"Vingt ans après", suite des Trois Mousquetaires Par Alexandre Dumas. Paris, Baudry, 34 rue Coquillière, 1845, 8vo., 10 volumes. Pagination : 332 including table of contents, 334, 334 both with an additional unnumbered page table of contents, 320 including table of contents, 324, 315, 312, 312, 296 and 302 all with an additional unnumbered page table of contents. "Vingt ans après" ends on page 221 of Volume 10, the remainder being occupied by "Giorgione" later included in "Italiens et Flamands" ("Histoire des peintres".) Yellow wrappers. Impr. Plon frères.

"Vingt ans après", suite Des "Trois mousquetaires", par M. Alexandre Dumas. (Monogram) Paris, MM. J.-B. Fellens et L.-P. Dufour, éditeurs, rue Saint-Thomas-du-Louvre, 30. 1846. Large 8vo., pp. (1)-591, verso blank, (593)-595 table of contents. 'Le bonhomme Broussel', Ch. XXIX, pp. 189-193. This, the first illustrated edition, has an engraved frontispiece and 36 plates by Marckl, Th. Guérin, Coppin, Wattier, Beaucé, Georges Fischer, etc., engraved by Thévenon, Hébert, Pisan, Fagnion, Lesestre, Carbonneau, Polet, A. Vien, Pierdon, Linton et Baudeville, Stypulkowski, Adèle Lajsné and Trichon. Pink wrappers. Imprimerie de BUREAU, rue Coquillière, 22. Tiré sur presses mécaniques par ARISTIDE.
This edition was initially published in 30 parts.

"Vingt ans après", par Alexandre Dumas. Deuxième édition. Paris, Michel Lévy frères, éditeurs; Pétion, éditeur. 1846. 8vo., 8 volumes, pp. 236, 316, each with an unnumbered page table of contents, 313, 321, 317, each with verso blank and unnumbered page table of contents, 310, and unnumbered page table of contents, 295, verso unnumbered page table of contents, 294, and unnumbered page table of contents. "Vingt ans après" ends on page 213 of volume 8, verso blank, and is followed by "Giorgione", pp. (215)-294. Sceaux - Imprimerie de E. Dépée.

"Vingt ans après". Suite des "Trois mousquetaires". Par Alexandre Dumas. Paris, Imprimerie de Bureau, 1846, large 8vo., pp. 596, and 37 illustrations.

Le Siècle. "Les Mousquetaires", trilogie (sic) par Alexandre Dumas. Première partie : "Les trois mousquetaires". Seconde partie : "Vingt ans après". ... Paris, au bureau du Siècle, 1847, 4to., pp. 351; illustrations.

"Vingt ans après" (Suite des "Trois mousquetaires") par Alexandre Dumas. (Vignette) Bruxelles, Livourne, Meline, Cans et compagnie; Leipzig, J.P. Meline, 1847, 16mo., 4 volumes, pp. 350, 326, 332 and 321.

Oeuvres de Alex. Dumas. Tome neuvième. (Vignette) Bruxelles, Meline, Cans et compagnie, 1847, large 8vo. "Vingt ans après".

"Vingt ans après", par Alexandre Dumas. Paris, Michel Lévy frères, (1846), 12mo., 3 volumes, pp. 280, 284 and 276. (The Bibliothèque Nationale copy carries the year '1849' on the wrappers of each volume and on the title-page of Volume 3.)

The preceding edition may be a 'rogue' copy, for in the years 1846-1847 Michel Lévy frères published a three volume edition as follows : 12mo., pagination : Volume 1 (1846), 278, Volumes 2 and 3 (1847), 281 and 276, each with an additional unnumbered page table of contents. Frequently reprinted in the same format, but with varying paginations, by both Michel Lévy frères and Calmann-Lévy.

"Vingt ans après" suite des "Trois mousquetaires" par M. Alexandre
Dumas. Paris, MM. Dufour et Mulat, éditeurs, 1849, 4to., pp. 595
including 3 pages table of contents; illustrated with 37 plates by
Marckl, Wattier, Beaucé, Coppin, etc.
Reprinted, same format and pagination, and with the same number of
illustrations, 1850, 1851.

"Vingt ans après" par Alexandre Dumas. Bruxelles, Alph. Lebègue,
1849-1850, 18mo., 8 volumes; pagination : Volume 1 (1849), 115;
Volumes 2-5 (1850), 120, 115, 121 and 131; Volumes 6-8 (wrongly dated
1849) 1850, 124, 128 and 115. Green wrappers stating that this is the
'Troisième édition'; the wrapper of Volume 4 is dated 1849 and the
wrappers of Volumes 5-8 are dated 1850.

"Les trois mousquetaires" suivi de "Vingt ans après" et du "Vicomte
de Bragelonne", par Alex. Dumas. Bruxelles, Livourne, Meline, Cans
et compagnie, 1851, 4to. "Les trois mousquetaires" ends on page 294;
"Vingt ans après" and "Le vicomte de Bragelonne" are paged continuously
(297)-675 in double columns, with 3 unnumbered pages table of contents.

"Les mousquetaires" "Vingt ans après" par Alexandre Dumas illustrés
par J.-A. Beaucé, F. Philippoteaux, etc. Publiés par Dufour et Mulat
Paris chez Marescq et Cie., libraires, 1852, in three parts, each
with a different vignette on the title-pages. 4to. Pagination :
Première partie (1)-169, Deuxième partie (1)-157, Troisième partie
(1)-137, all in double columns and with at the end of each part an
unnumbered page table of contents and on verso 'Placement des gravures'.

Bibliothèque contemporaine, 1ère Série. Alexandre Dumas. Oeuvres
complètes. "Vingt ans après". Suite de "Trois mousquetaires".
Paris, Michel Lévy frères, 1852, 12mo., 3 volumes, pp. 280, 284 and
276 all including table of contents.

Alexandre Dumas "Vingt ans après" suite des "Trois mousquetaires"
Paris, Michel Lévy frères, libraires-éditeurs ... . Bureaux du journal Le Siècle, ... 1853. 4to. pp. 351 in double columns and
unnumbered page table of contents. Caption title. Woodcut at head
of title. Pink wrappers with vignette. Musée littéraire du siècle.

"Vingt ans après", suite des "Trois mousquetaires" par Alexandre
Dumas. Paris, Legrand, Pomey et Crouzet, n.d. (1857), large 8vo.,
pp. (4). 595, (1) including table of contents; frontispiece and 37
illustrations.

"Les mousquetaires" "Vingt ans après" par Alexandre Dumas. Paris,
Lécrivain et Toubon, n.d. (1860), large 8vo., with the same pagination
and illustrations as the Marescq et Cie., 1852, edition.

"Vingt ans après", suite des "Trois mousquetaires" par Alexandre
Dumas. Paris, Legrand et Crouzet, n.d. (1872), large 8vo., same pagination and illustrations as the Legrand, Pomey et Crouzet edition of
(1857).

Ibid   Paris, Polo, n.d. (1875), large 8vo., pp. 556,
frontispiece portrait of Dumas, and illustrations.

"Vingt ans après" par Alexandre Dumas. Edition illustrée par J.-A.
Beaucé. Paris Calmann Lévy, 1885. (Additional title-page : "Vingt
ans après". Suite des "Trois mousquetaires" par Alexandre Dumas.)
(Vignette) 4to., pp. 554 and 2 unnumbered pages table of contents;
frontispiece portrait of Dumas and approximately 70 illustrations.

Alexandre Dumas "Les trois mousquetaires" "Vingt ans après" Paris
Jules Rouff et Cie., éditeurs ... . (Propriété Calmann-Lévy), n.d.
(1887-1891). Second illustrated title-page. 4to. "Les trois mousquetaires", pp. (1)-629. Deuxième partie "Vingt ans après", pp.
(630)-1164 continued into volume 2 pp. 1165-1435; "Le vicomte de
Bragelonne" occupies pp. (1436)-2328, each volume with 4 unnumbered
pages table of contents; illustrated.
Reprinted, n.d. (1893-1895), same format, pagination and illustrations.

"Vingt ans après" (suite des "Trois mousquetaires") par Alexandre
Dumas. Paris, Calmann-Lévy, 1891, 4to., pp. 239 in double columns.
Caption title. Woodcut at head of title. Brown wrappers. Musée
littéraire contemporain.

"L'évasion du duc de Beaufort", par Alexandre Dumas. Edited with
notes by D.B. Kitchin, M.A., ... Boston, D.C. Heath & Co., 1892,
8vo., pp. (3)-95.
Several times reprinted in a revised edition after 1900.

"Les mousquetaires". "Vingt ans après", par Alexandre Dumas; illustrés par J.-A. Beaucé, F. Philippoteaux, etc. Paris, Calmann-Lévy,
1893, 4to., same pagination and illustrations as the Marescq et Cie.,
1852, edition.

"LA PECHE AUX FILETS"   1845
    Dumas knew Naples thoroughly and this work's opening paragraph
would seem to relate to his Italian travels in the late 1830s. The
story is brief, more romance than history, and could well have been
founded on some old legend.   The period is 1414, at Naples, in the
days of Ladislas of Hungary and Joanna II of Naples.

Original edition.
"La pêche aux filets", par M. Alexandre Dumas. In : Revue des
feuilletons journal littéraire illustré composé de romans, voyages,
légendes, anecdotes, contes nouvelles, historiques, etc., par J.
Arago, H. de Balzac, A. Dumas, ... Cinquième année. Paris, au
boureaux (sic) du journal, 1845, 8vo., pp. (70)-96.
(The work has been stated to have appeared in 'Le Monde' at about the
same time.)

Alexandre Dumas. "L'abbaye de Peyssac" (the fourth part of "La
guerre des femmes") Paris, L. de Potter, 1846, 8vo., 2 volumes, pp.
324 and 363. "L'abbaye de Peyssac" ends on page 276 of Volume 1, and
is followed by "La pêche aux filets", pp. (277)-324 and is continued
on into Volume 2 to page 126. Yellow wrappers. Fontainebleau -
Impr. de E. Jacquin.

Le Siècle. Oeuvres complètes d'Alexandre Dumas Troisième série. "La
pêche aux filets". Paris, au bureau du Siècle, 1848, 4to., pp. (343)-
354 in double columns.

Semaine littéraire du Courrier des Etats-Unis. "La pêche aux filets",
par Alexandre Dumas. New-York, F. Gaillardet, (P. Arpin), 1849, 8vo.,
pp. (246)-262 in double columns.

"Nouvelles". Par Alexandre Dumas. Paris, au bureau du Siècle,
1850, 4to., pp. 343-390. "La pêche aux filets" was one of the six
stories included in this collection.

"Nouvelles", par Alexandre Dumas. Paris, Impr. de Morris, n.d.
(1854), 4to., pp. 343-372. "La pêche aux filets" was one of the four
stories included in this collection.

Ibid   Paris, Impr. de S. Raçon, n.d. (1855), same format
and pagination as the preceding edition.

"Gabriel Lambert" par Alexandre Dumas. Paris, Michel Lévy frères,
1856, 12mo., pp. 275 and table of contents on verso; "La pêche aux
filets" was used to fill the volume, pp. (177)-234.
Reprinted, same format and pagination, by both Michel Lévy frères and
Calmann-Lévy.

"La pêche aux filets" par Alexandre Dumas. Paris, Michel Lévy frères,
1864, 4to., pp. 15 in double columns. Caption title. Woodcut at head
of title, repeated on yellow wrappers. Musée littéraire contemporain.

"PORTHOS A LA RECHERCHE D'UN EQUIPEMENT"   1845

Since this comedy was based on a well-known incident in "Les
trois mousquetaires" it is not, I think, out of place to refer to it
in a Bibliography of Dumas. As a matter of slight interest, perhaps,
its first performance was as a 'benefit' for 'General Tom Thumb'.

Original edition.
"Porthos à la recherche d'un equipement", comédie-vaudeville en un
acte, par MM. Anicet, Dumanoir et Ed. Brisebarre, Représentée pour
la première fois, à Paris, sur le théâtre Vaudeville, le 23 juin 1845.
Caption title. Pink wrappers repeating caption title. Paris, Beck,
Editeur, ... Tresse, successeur de J.-N. Barba, 1845, 8vo., pp. 18
in double columns.

It was reissued : Paris, Michel Lévy frères, 1848, 12mo.

"LES MOUSQUETAIRES"   (Drama)   1845

The title of this play is quite misleading, for Dumas and Maquet
drew it from "Vingt ans après"; it was at a later date that "La jeunesse des mousquetaires" was drawn from "Les trois mousquetaires".

The curtain was raised at 6.30 and not finally lowered until
after one o'clock the next morning. The play was a great success and
on the first night the duc de Montpensier summoned Dumas to his box
to congratulate him and to ask why it was performed at such an inferior
theatre. Dumas' reply was that he had no theatre of his own and was
thus forced to have his plays produced wherever he was able; de Montpensier arranged for a license to be granted to his friend and the outcome was the Théâtre-Historique where, in due course, "La jeunesse
des mousquetaires" was produced.

Original edition.
"Les mousquetaires" drame en cinq actes et douze tableaux, precédé
de "L'auberge de Béthune", prologue, par MM. Alexandre Dumas et
Auguste Maquet, représenté, pour la première fois, a Paris, sur le
théâtre de l'Ambigu-Comique, le 27 octobre 1845. ('Distribution de
la pièce'.) Paris. Marchant, éditeur du magasin théatral, boulevard
Saint-Martin, 12. 1845. 8vo., pp. 59 in double columns. Imprimerie
de Dondey-Dupré.

"Les mousquetaires", drame en cinq actes et douze tableaux, precédé de "L'auberge de Béthune", prologue, par MM. Alexandre Dumas et Auguste Maquet, représenté, pour la première fois, a Paris, sur le théatre de l'Ambigu-Comique, le 27 octobre 1845. Paris, Marchant, éditeur du magasin théatral, ... , 1846, 8vo., pp. 58 in double columns followed by 3 pages of unsigned 'post factum'. Green wrappers. Edition illustrée de cinq belles vignettes sur bois dessinées par Alex. Lacauchie et gravées sur bois par H. Faxardo. Sujet des vignettes : 1, 'La confession du Bourreau de Béthune'; 2, "L'évasion des Mousquetaires'; 3, 'Les adieux de Charles 1er '; 4, 'La maison de Cromwell'; 5, 'La mort de Mordaunt'.

Ibid   S.1., s.a., same format and pagination as the above, including the 'post factum'. Caption title. Woodcut at head of title, but only 4 illustrations. Imprimerie Dondey-Dupré.

Ibid   Paris, Imprimerie Walder, n.d. (c 1846), same format and pagination as the preceding edition. Caption title. Woodcut at head of title, Prologue, scène viii.

Ibid   Paris, Imprimerie de C.-H. Lambert, n.d. (c 1847), same format and pagination as the preceding editions, and same woodcut at head of title.

Ibid   Paris, imprimerie française et espagnole de Du Buisson et Cie., 1856, same format and pagination as the preceding editions, and same woodcut at head of title.

"Les mousquetaires", drame en cinq actes et douze tableaux, précédé de "L'auberge de Béthune", prologue, par MM. Alexandre Dumas et Auguste Maquet. Paris, N. Tresse, 1864, same format and pagination as the preceding editions, and same woodcut at head of title.

"Les mousquetaires" drame en cinq actes, en treize tableaux dont un prologue en société avec M. Auguste Maquet Ambigu-Comique. - 27 octobre 1845. "Distribution" on title-page, pp. 202-383. Théatre complet de Alex. Dumas. Tome XIV Paris Calmann Lévy, éditeur ancienne maison Michel Lévy frères, 1874. 12mo. "Théatre complet" in 25 volumes.

Here I should interpolate that Maquet also included the play in his collected "Theatre" :
"Les mousquetaires" drame en cinq actes, en treize tableaux dont un prologue en société avec Alexandre Dumas Ambigu-Comique. - 27 octobre 1845. "Distribution" on title-page, pp. 202-383. Théatre complet de Auguste Maquet Tome I Paris Calmann Lévy, éditeur rue Auber 3, et boulevard des Italiens, 15 a la librairie nouvelle 1893 12mo. "Théatre" in 4 volumes.

Two analyses were published of the play :
"Analyse des 'Mousquetaires', drame en cinq actes et onze (sic) tableaux, précédé de 'L'auberge de Béthune', prologue, par MM. A. Dumas et A. Maquet ... '. Nantes, impr. de V. Mangin, février 1846, 8vo., pp. 13.

"Les trois mousquetaires" (sic), drame en cinq actes et onze (sic) tableaux, précédé d'un prologue, par MM. Alexandre Dumas et A. Maquet. 'Analyse'. Metz, impr. de J. Mayer, n.d. (1861), 8vo., pp. 4.

There were the following parodies of the work :
"Marie Michon", comédie-vaudeville en deux actes, Tirée de la seconde

partie des "Mousquetaires", d'Alexandre Dumas, par MM. E. Vanderburch et A. de Leuven, representée pour la première fois, à Paris, sur le théâtre du Palais-Royal, le 11 mars 1846. Paris, Impr. de Boulé, n.d. (1846), 8vo., pp. 26 in double columns.

"Les trois gendarmes" Parodie en un acte et en vers des "Mousquetaires" de MM. A. Dumas et A. Maquet par MM. Gabriel Richard et Charles Monselet Représentée pour la première fois sur le Théâtre des Variétés, à Bordeaux, le 18 avril 1846. Bordeaux Chez les principaux libraires. N.d. (1846), large 8vo., pp. 11 in double columns. Impr. de F. Causserouge.

"Fanfan le bâtonniste à la représentation des 'Mousquetaires'" Parodie pot-pourri en 30 couplets Prix : 15 cent. Paris Chez Pierre Vinçard, éditeur, rue Montmartre, N° 1. Dépôt : chez M. Eyssautier, passage Bourg-l'Abbé, 30, et chez les Marchands de Pittoresques. 1846. 8vo.

"Encore des mousquetaires" "Vaudeville en un acte par MM. Varin et Paul Vermond Représenté pour la première fois, à Paris, sur le théâtre de Vaudeville, le 26 octobre 1851, 12mo., verso of the title-page "Personnages" (unnumbered) pp. (3)-44. Yellow wrappers : Théatre de Vaudeville. Bibliothèque théatrale Auteurs contemporains. "Encore des mousquetaires" vaudeville en 1 acte Par MM. Varin et Paul Vermond. Paris D. Giraud et J. Dagneau, libraires-éditeurs ... Maison du Coq d'or.
(The Bibliothèque de l'Arsenal copy has 'et Jaime' written in ink after 'Vermond' on the title-page.)

Bibliothèque musicale illustrée "Les Mousquetaires au couvent" opéracomique en trois actes Musique de Louis Varney Partition complète - piano et chant. Paris, Montgredien et Cie éditeurs. Publié avec l'autorisation de Choudens, Editeur. Représenté pour la première fois au Théâtre des Bouffes-Parisiens le 16 mars 1880. N.d. (1880), large 8vo.; pp. (I)-XII "Ouverture", 3-304. Woodcut following the title-page, and illustrated with woodcuts.

"Les petits mousquetaires" opéra comique en trois actes, cinq tableaux, paroles de Paul Ferrier et Jules Prével, musique de Louis Varney. Paris, Calmann-Lévy, 1885, 12mo., on verso of title-page "Personnages", pp. (3)-175. Blue wrappers : Représenté pour la première fois, à Paris, sur le Théâtre des Folies Dramatiques, le 5 mars 1885.

Ibid Paris, Calmann Lévy ancienne maison Michel Lévy frères, 1886, same format and pagination as the preceding edition.

"Les mousquetaires de la reine" opéra-comique en trois actes par M. de Saint-Georges musique de F. Halévy Paris, Calmann-Lévy, 1889, 12mo., on verso of title-page "Personnages", pp. (1)-78. Brown wrappers. Nouvelle édition.

"LA GUERRE DES FEMMES" (Romance) 1845-1846

When Dumas was researching for his "Louis XIV et son siècle" he came across "Les mémoires de M. L ***, Conseiller d'Etat" which he found to have been written by Pierre Lenet, a member of a family closely associated with the House of Condé. Lenet's memoirs contained a narrative of the Civil War which became known as the 'New Fronde' or,

from the number of women who were moving spirits in it, as 'la guerre
des femmes'. The period is, of course, 1650. Nearly all of Dumas'
best qualities are to be found in the work and probably none of his
romances are so crowded with inspired subsidiary characters, nor contain more vivid scenes - whether tragic or comic.

The work ran serially in 'La Patrie' in 1844, but as will be seen
when first published in volume form in France it was divided into four
parts. At the time of the publication of "L'abbaye de Peyssac" the
publisher had in stock a number of surplus copies of Mélanie Waldor's
novel "Charles Mandel", and Dumas made it a condition that with the
purchase of this fourth part a copy must also be bought of "Charles
Mandel".

The romance was published in Bruxelles before the final serial
part was available in Paris and the pirated editions, therefore, lack
the two chapters of 'Epilogue'. It should be added here that in the
Belgian issues the chapters are numbered consecutively throughout,
and thus follow the serial issue.

Original edition.
"La guerre des femmes", par Alexandre Dumas. Bruxelles, Alph. Lebègue
et Sacre fils, 1845, 18mo., 4 volumes, pp. 180, 170, 185 and 170.
Green wrappers. Museum littéraire.

"La guerre des femmes" par Alexandre Dumas. Bruxelles, Société belge
de librairie Hauman et Ce., 1845, 24mo., 4 volumes, pp. 223, 249,
255 and 233.

Ibid   Bruxelles, Meline, Cans et compagnie, 1845, 4 volumes, pp. 239, 256, 257 and 286.

"La guerre des femmes", par Alexandre Dumas. La Haye, chez les héritiers Doorman, 1845, same format and pagination as the preceding
edition.

"La guerre des femmes" par Alexandre Dumas. Bruxelles et Leipzig,
C. Muquardt, 1845, 18mo., 4 volumes, pp. 180, 170, 185 and 170.

As has been said this work was first published in France in four parts.
These are :
Alexandre Dumas. "Nanon de Lartiques" Paris, L. de Potter, libraire-
éditeur, Rue Saint-Jacques, 38. 1845. 8vo., 2 volumes, pp. 324 and
331.
Alexandre Dumas. "Madame de Condé" Paris, L. de Potter, libraire-
éditeur, Rue Saint-Jacques, 38. 1845. 8vo., 2 volumes, pp. 315 and
307.
Alexandre Dumas. "La vicomtesse de Cambes" Paris, L. de Potter,
libraire-éditeur, Rue Saint-Jacques, 38. 1845. 8vo., 2 volumes, pp.
334 and 324.
Alexandre Dumas. "L'abbeye de Peyssac" Paris, L. de Potter, libraire-
éditeur, Rue Saint-Jacques, 38. 1846. 8vo., 2 volumes, pp. 324 and
363.
"L'abbaye de Peyssac" ends on page 197 of Volume 1, being followed by
the two chapters of epilogue entitled 'L'abbesse de Sainte-Radigonde'
and 'Le frère et la soeur' occupying pp. 199-276. The remaining
pages of this volume are filled by "La pêche aux filets", pp. (277)-
324 and continued in the second volume to page 126; the rest of this
latter volume comprises "Invraisemblance", pp. (127)-214, "Une âme à

naître, pp. (215)-247, verso blank, "La main droite du Sire de Giac.
1425-1426", pp. (249)-363. Yellow wrappers. Fontainebleau - Impr.
de E. Jacquin.

Oeuvres de Alex. Dumas. (Vignette) Bruxelles, Meline, Cans et compagnie, 1846, large 8vo. 2 volumes. "La guerre des femmes", pp. 422
and 248, with two additional numbered pages table of contents.
This particular Belgian edition includes the two chapters of epilogue
referred to above.

Le Siècle. Oeuvres complètes d'Alexandre Dumas Troisième série. "La
guerre des femmes". Paris, au bureau du Siècle, 1848, 4to., pp. (197)-
342 in double columns.

"La guerre des femmes" par Alexandre Dumas. Paris, Michel Lévy Frères,
1848, 12mo., 2 volumes, pp. 336 and 299, each with an unnumbered page
table of contents; the two chapters comprising the epilogue occupy pp.
(279)-299.
Several times reprinted, same format and pagination, by both Michel
Lévy frères and Calmann-Lévy.

"La guerre des femmes" par Alexandre Dumas. Paris, au bureau du
Siècle, 1852, 4to., pp. (197)-342 in double columns. Caption title.

Ibid   Paris, Ve Dondey-Dupré, n.d. (c 1855), same format
and pagination as the preceding edition. Romans illustrés.

Ibid   Paris, Michel Lévy frères, n.d. (c 187), 4to.,
2 volumes. Musée littéraire contemporain.

"LE CHEVALIER DE MAISON-ROUGE"   (Romance)   1845-1846

     This work, which was originally announced before publication as
"Geneviève, ou un épisode de 1793", was later changed to "Le chevalier
de Rougeville, ou an épisode de 1793", to be finally altered to its
present title, opens at the time of Marie-Antoinette's imprisonment
in the Temple, deals with the conspiracy of the carnation and ends,
historically, with the Queen's execution. The period is from March to
October, 1793.

     It is very possible that Dumas, taking the name of 'Maison-Rouge',
intended that this work should take its place at the end of the long
series of romances known as "Mémoires d'un médecin". He was unsuccess-
ful, for Taverney de Maison-Rouge cannot be regarded as anything like
the same person as the Maison-Rouge of the carnation conspiracy, and
in any event Taverney disappears at the end of "Le collier de la reine",
and does not reappear in either of its two sequels. Yet "Le chevalier
de Maison-Rouge" is often described as a sequel to "La comtesse de
Charny". It is not, except in the historical sense that the one
follows upon the other.

     The romance ran serially in 'La Democratique Pacifique', a journal
with no very great circulation, and previous to its publication in volume form a short extract was printed from it as :
"Episode de 1793", extrait du roman "Le chevalier de Maison-Rouge,
par Alex. Dumas. Paris, Desloges, 1845, 16mo., pp. 34.

Original edition.
"Le chevalier de Maison-Rouge (Episode de 1793)" par Alexandre Dumas.

Bruxelles, Société belge de librairie Hauman et Ce., 1845-1846, 16mo., 3 volumes. Pagination : Volumes 1 and 2 (1845), 250 and 252; Volume 3 (1846), 295.

Ibid   Bruxelles, Société belge de librairie, Hauman et Ce., 1845-1846, 18mo., 5 volumes. Pagination : Volume 1-3 (1845), 169, 172 and 164; Volumes 4 and 5 (1846), 159 and 159.

"Le chevalier de Maison-Rouge. Episode de 1793" par Alexandre Dumas. Bruxelles, Meline, Cans et compagnie, 1845-1846, 16mo., 4 volumes. Pa-gination : Volumes 1-3 (1845), 260, 205 and 209; Volume 4 (1846), 185.

"Le chevalier de Maison-Rouge" par Alexandre Dumas. Bruxelles et Leipzig, Meline, Cans et compagnie, 1845-1846, same format and pagination as the preceding edition.

Omnibus littéraire. "Le chevalier de Maison-Rouge" par Alexandre Dumas. Bruxelles, Meline, Cans et compagnie, 1845-1846, 18mo., 5 volumes. Pagination : Volumes 1-3 (1845), 156, 141 and 126; Volumes 4 and 5 (1846), 124 and 115.

Le chevalier de Maison-Rouge (Episode de 1793)" par Alexandre Dumas. Bruxelles, Meline, Cans et cie.; Leipzig, J.P. Meline, 1845-1846, 16mo., 3 volumes. Pagination : Volumes 1 and 2 (1845), 250 and 252; Volume 3 (1846), 295.

"Le chevalier de Maison-Rouge" par Alexandre Dumas. Paris, Alexandre Cadot, 1845-1846, 8vo., 6 volumes. Pagination : Volume 1 (1845), 305, verso blank, unnumbered page table of contents; Volume 2 (1845), 315, verso table of contents; Volumes 3-6 (1846), 293, verso blank, unnumbered page table of contents, 311, verso table of contents, 302 and unnumbered page table of contents, 332 and unnumbered page table of contents. "Le chevalier de Maison-Rouge" ends on page 58 of Volume 6 and is followed by "La chasse (au chastre)", pp. (59)-332. Yellow wrappers. Fontainebleau, Impr. E. Jacquin, et Sceaux, Impr. de E. Dépée.

Semaine littéraire du Courrier des Etats-Unis. Receuil choisi de romans, feuilletons, ouvrages historiques et dramatiques, en prose et en vers des auteurs modernes les plus renommés. XIII série; Vol. 3. 1846. New-York, F. Gaillardet 1846. At the top of page (3) : "Le chevalier de Maison-Rouge", par Alexandre Dumas. 8vo., pp. (3)-160 in double columns.

"Le chevalier de Maison-Rouge" par Alexandre Dumas. Paris, Michel Lévy frères, 1848, 12mo., pp. 412.

Le Siècle. Oeuvres complètes d'Alexandre Dumas. Troisième série. "Le chevalier de Maison-Rouge". Paris, au bureau du Siècle, 1848, 4to., pp. (1)-112 in double columns.

"Le chevalier de Maison-Rouge" par Alexandre Dumas. Paris, Michel Lévy frères, 1850, 12mo., pp. 406, including table of contents pp. (405)-406.

"Le chevalier de Maison-Rouge" par Alexandre Dumas publié par Dufour et Mulat édition illustrée par E. Lampsonius (Woodcut) Paris 1852 chez Marescq et Cie., ... Large 8vo., pp. (1)-225 in double columns, verso blank, unnumbered page table of contents with, on verso, 'placement des gravures tirées a part'; numerous illustrations including 11 full-page plates.

"Le chevalier de Maison-Rouge. Episode de 1793". Par M. Alexandre Dumas. Paris, L'Echo des feuilletons, 1856, large 8vo., pp. (425)-574 in double columns.

Journal du dimanche. "Le chevalier de Maison-Rouge". No. 271, 3 juin 1860, through to No. 296, 30 août, 1860, in treble columns. Signed : Alexandre Dumas. 4to., woodcut at head of each issue.

"Le chevalier de Maison-Rouge" par Alexandre Dumas. Paris, Michel Lévy frères, 1863, 4to., pp. 134 in double columns. Caption title. Woodcut at head of title. Musée littéraire contemporain.

Ibid   Paris, Michel Lévy frères, 1863, 12mo., 2 volumes, pp. 311 and 295, each with an additional unnumbered page table of contents on verso of last page.
Frequently reprinted, same format but with occasional variations in pagination, by both Michel Lévy frères and Calmann-Lévy.

Ibid   Paris, Calmann-Lévy, n.d. (c 187), 4to., pp. 112 in double columns. Caption title. Oeuvres completes d'Alexandre Dumas.

Ibid   Edition illustrée par E. Lampsonius. Paris, Calmann-Lévy, éditeur, 1885, 4to., pp. (1)-225 in double columns, and unnumbered page table of contents. Caption title. Woodcut at head of title. Alexandre Dumas oeuvres illustrées.
Reprinted, same format and pagination, 1896.

Alexandre Dumas "Le chevalier de Maison-Rouge" Illustrations de Julien le Blant gravées sur bois par Léveillé (Vignette) Paris librairie de l'édition nationale Emile Testard, éditeur 18, rue de Condé, 18 1894. 4to., 2 volumes, pp. (1)-290 and (291)-292 table of contents; (1)-283, verso blank, (285)-286 table of contents. 74 and 82 illustrations respectively, with different vignettes on the title-pages which are printed in black and red. Vellum wrappers reproducing title-pages, and illustrated spines and back wrappers. On verso of half-title : Tirage de grand luxe a cent exemplaires numérotés a la presse savoir : Nos. 1 à 75. - 75 exemplaires sur papier des manufactures Impériales du Japon. Nos. 76 à 110. - 35 exemplaires sur papier de Chine extra-fort. Le tirage sur papier de Chine à 35 exemplaires (nos. 76 à 110) a été entièrement souscrit par M.A. Ferroud. (Librairie des Amateurs.) 'Edition autorisée par MM. Calmann-Lévy.' On the leaf following the table of contents of each volume : achevé d'imprimer par Charles Hérissey d'Evreux (monogram) pour le compte de M. Emile Testard éditeur a Paris.

In the same year, and published separately :
Alexandre Dumas "Le chevalier de Maison-Rouge" compositions de Julien le Blant gravées a l'eau-forte par Géry-Bichard Préface par G. Larroumet Paris librairie de l'édition nationale Emile Testard, éditeur 18, rue de Condé, 18 1894. 4to., pp. (i)-xiv 'préface', unnumbered page 'liste des gravures' and the relative positions of the 10 illustrations, 5 to each of the above two volumes; verso : imprimé par Chamerot et Renouard 19, Rue des Saints-Pères, 19 Paris. In loose cover with : collection artistique Emile Testard "Le chevalier de Maison-Rouge" eaux-fortes with on verso : justification du tirage il a été un tirage en grand papier ainsi composé : 75 exemplaires sur papier du Japon (quatre états) 1 à 75 35 exemplaires sur papier du Chine (quatre états) 76 à 110. Brown cloth cover repeating the title-page.

"LA DAME DE MONSOREAU"   (Romance)   1845-1846

This work is not, as has been stated, a sequel to "La reine Margot". The two works follow each other closely only in so far as the
time of action is concerned and, naturally enough, the same historical
characters appear.

One of Dumas' very finest romances, in it there is met for the
first time Chicot, the king's jester. In his own different way Chicot
is a possible rival to d'Artagnan in his courage and ability to pene-
trate to the heart of an intrigue, and he has the added attraction of
a quick wit and biting sense of humour. For his foil there is the
Rabelaisian Dom Gorenflot. The period of the romance falls between
February, 1578, and August, 1579, with its accompaniment of bloodshed -
the death of Bussy d'Amboise, and the duel between Quelus and his
friends with the Angevins.

Maquet helped in the work's composition and he, some twenty years
after Dumas' death, produced an opera from it with the same title as
the romance. "Le dame de Monsoreau" was first published as a serial
in 'Le Constitutionnel' between August, 1845, and February, 1846.

Original edition.
"La dame de Monsoreau". Par Alexandre Dumas. Bruxelles, Alph. Lebègue
et Sacré fils, 1845-1846, 24mo., 7 volumes. Pagination : Volumes
1-6 (1845), 174, 154, 158, 157, 159 and 155; Volume 7 (1846), 200.

Ibid   Same format and pagination, but volumes 1-5 are
dated 1845 and volumes 6 and 7, 1846. Blue wrappers.

"La dame de Monsoreau" par Alexandre Dumas. Bruxelles, Meline, Cans
et compagnie, 1845-1846, 16mo., 6 volumes. Pagination : Volumes
1-2 (1845), 285 and 321; Volumes 3-6 (1846), 325, 280, 229 and 190.

"La dame de Monsoreau", par Alexandre Dumas. Bruxelles, Meline, Cans
et cie.; Leipzig, J.P. Meline, 1845-1846, 16mo., 6 volumes. Pagination
: Volume 1 (1845), 285; Volumes 2-6 (1846), 321, 325, 280, 229 and
190.

Ibid   La Haye, chez les héritiers Doorman, 1845-1846,
same format, pagination and split years as the preceding edition.

"La dame de Monsoreau" Par Alexandre Dumas. Bruxelles et Leipzig,
C. Muquardt, 1845-1846, 24mo., 7 volumes. Pagination : Volumes 1-5
(1845), 174, 154, 158, 157 and 159; Volumes 6-7 (1846), 155 and 200.
Vignettes on title-pages. Blue wrappers.

"La dame de Monsoreau" par Alexandre Dumas. Leipzig, Brockhaus &
Avenarius, 1845-1846, 16mo., 6 volumes. Pagination : Volumes 1-4
(1845), 147, 157, 185 and 176; Volumes 5 and 6 (1846), 191 and 147.
Typographie de F.A. Brockhaus.

"La dame de Monsoreau" par Alexandre Dumas. Paris, Pétion, libraire-
éditeur, 1846, 8vo., 8 volumes. Pagination : 329, verso blank,
(331)-332 table of contents; 346, (347)-348 table of contents; 316
(misnumbered, should be 318), (319)-320 table of contents; 318 and
unnumbered page table of contents; 333, verso blank, (335)-336 table
of contents; 326, (327)-328 table of contents; 314, (315) table of
contents; 299, verso blank, and unnumbered page table of contents.
"La dame de Monsoreau" ends on page 93 of volume 8, verso blank,
followed by "Le cocher de cabriolet", pp. (95)-155, verso blank,

"Blanche de Beaulieu", pp. (157)-299. Green wrappers. Corbeil - imprimerie de Crété.

Semaine Littéraire du Courrier des Etats-Unis. Receuil Choisi de romans, feuilletons, ouvrages historiques et dramatiques, en prose et en vers des auteurs modernes les plus renommés. XI série; Vol. 1, 1846. New-York, F. Gaillardet 1846. At the top of page (3) : Semaine littéraire Du Courrier des Etats-Unis. "La dame de Monsoreau", par Alexandre Dumas. 8vo., pp. (3)-325 in double columns, followed by a work by Soulié.

"Le dame de Monsoreau" par Alexandre Dumas. Paris, Michel Lévy frères, 1846-1847, 12mo., 3 volumes.

Publication du journal 'Le Siècle'. Oeuvres complètes de M. Alexandre Dumas. "La dame de Monsoreau". Paris, Bureaux du Siècle, 1847, 4to., pp. (1)-230 in double columns, and 2 unnumbered pages table of contents. Blue wrappers. The first number is dated '22 février' and the last '23 août', being completed with the twenty-ninth issue. (These serial issues were given as a bonus to subscribers to the journal.)

"La dame de Monsoreau". Par M. Alexandre Dumas. In : L'Echo des feuilletons receuil de nouvelles, légendes, anecdotes, épisodes, ... Paris, chez les éditeurs, 1848, large 8vo., pp. (301)-480 in double columns; illustrated.

"La dame de Monsoreau" par Alexandre Dumas. Paris, Michel Lévy frères, 1849, 12mo., 3 volumes, pp. 303, 316 and 279 each with an additional 2 unnumbered pages table of contents. Frequently reprinted, same format but sometimes with varying paginations, by both Michel Lévy frères and Calmann-Lévy.

"La dame de Monsoreau" par Alexandre Dumas. Depot de vente à la librairie illustrée, 16, rue de Croissant, Ancien Hotel Colbert. Propriété de MM. Michel Lévy frères, n.d. (185). large 8vo., pp. (1)-558 in double columns, (559)-560 table of contents. Illustrated by Beaucé.

"La dame de Monsoreau". Par M. Alexandre Dumas. In : L'Echo des feuilletons. Paris, Dufour, Mulat et Boulanger, 1857, large 8vo., pp. (301)-480 in double columns; illustrated.

"La dame de Monsoreau" par Alexandre Dumas Publiée par Dufour et Mulat Edition illustrée par J.-A. Beaucé, etc. (Woodcut vignette) Paris, Marescq et Cie., 1857, large 8vo., 3 parts each of 158 pages in double columns and each with an additional unnumbered page table of contents, verso 'placement des gravures'; frontispiece to each part and 24 illustrations in all, with numerous vignettes.

"La dame de Monsoreau". Par M. Alexandre Dumas. In : L'Echo des feuilletons receuil de nouvelles, légendes, anecdotes, épisodes, ... Paris, chez les éditeurs, 1862, large 8vo., pp. (301)-480 in double columns; illustrated.

"La dame de Monsoreau" par Alexandre Dumas. Edition illustrée par J.-A. Beaucé. (Vignette) Paris, Lécrivain et Toubon, n.d. (186), large 8vo., in 3 parts with the same pagination as the Marescq et Cie., 1857, edition.

Ibid   (Paris), à la librairie illustrée, n.d. (1875), large 8vo., pp. (1)-558 in double columns, (559)-560 table of contents. Illustrated by Beaucé.

"La reine Margot", par Alexandre Dumas. Paris, J. Rouff, n.d. (189), large 8vo., 3 volumes. "La reine Margot"; "La dame de Monsoreau"; "Les quarante-cinq"; illustrated.

Alexandre Dumas. "La dame de Monsoreau". Edition illustrée par J.-A. Beaucé. Paris, Calmann-Lévy, 1897, 4to. Alexandre Dumas oeuvres illustrées.

"UNE FILLE DU REGENT"   (Drama)   1846

This play, unlike the romance of the same name, was solely Dumas' work. It was first entitled "Une conspiration sous le régent" and as such was accepted by the Comédie Française in December, 1843. Dumas, however, withdrew it and although keeping to the main plot there were changes. It was renamed "Hélène de Saverny". There was still no prologue, but there were five acts of which the fourth took place in the Bastille - this was removed from the text in the fresh rewriting and a prologue introduced to the play as it is now known. Unlike the romance the play has a happy ending.

It should be added that on 23rd September, 1850, there was produced at the Théâtre Historique a drama in five acts entitled "Le capitaine Lajonquière" which was a slight modification of "Une fille du régent"; this was never published.

Original edition.
"Une fille du régent", comédie en cinq actes et en prose, par Alexandre Dumas, représentée pour la première fois, à Paris, sur le Théâtre-français, le 1ᵉʳ avril 1846. Paris, Marchant, 1846, large 8vo., pp. 35 in double columns. Caption title. Woodcut at head of title, Acte V, scène ix. Le Magasin théatral.

"Une fille du régent", comédie en cinq actes et en prose, dont un prologue, par M. Alexandre Dumas. Représentée pour la première fois, à Paris, sur le Théâtre Français, le 1 avril 1846. Bruxelles, J.-A. Lelong, 1846, 12mo., pp. 116. Répertoire de la scène française, 14ᵐᵉ année.

"Une fille du régent", comédie en cinq actes et en prose, par Alexandre Dumas, représentée pour la première fois, à Paris, sur le Théâtre Français, le 1ᵉʳ avril 1846. (Paris), Imprimerie de Madame veuve Dondey-Dupré, n.d. (1846), large 8vo., pp. 35 in double columns. Caption title. Woodcut at head of title, Acte V, scène ix. (The Bibliothèque de l'Arsenal copy has written in ink under 'représentée pour la première fois ...' "au Th. Historique sous le titre de : Le Capitaine Lajonquière", which is patently wrong.)

"Une fille du régent" comédie en quatre actes et un prologue Théâtre-Français. 1ᵉʳ avril 1846. "Distribution" on title-page, pp. 138-248. Théatre complet de Alex. Dumas Tome IX Paris Calmann Lévy, éditeur ancienne maison Michel Lévy frères, 1874. 12mo. "Théatre complet" in 25 volumes.

"ECHEC ET MAT"   1846

This comedy, which was first performed at the Odéon on 23rd May, 1846, was signed : 'MM. Octave Feuillet, Paul Bocage et ***'.

Reference should be made here to Philibert Audebrand's "Alexandre
Dumas a la maison d'or souvenirs de la vie littéraire", (Paris,
Calmann Lévy, ..., 1888), page 225 : 'On n'a pas "Echec et mat", un
épisode de l'histoire d'Espagne, un mélange d'aventures galantes et
de duels, avec les beaux costumes et les grands panaches de l'ancien
régime. Non seulement le drame était très intéressant, mais encore
il marchait avec une étonnante rondeur. A la vérité, pour le mettre
tout à fait au point, Alexandre Dumas père y avait mis la main.'

It is now included in Volume 5 of Feuillet's "Théâtre complet",
Paris, Calmann-Lévy, 1892-1893.

Original edition.
"Echec et mat" drame en cinq actes, en prose, par MM. Octave Feuillet
et Paul Bocage. Paris Jérome, libraire-éditeur, rue Saint-Jacques,
326. 1846. Large 8vo., pp. (3)-63 in single columns; verso of title-
page 'Personnages' 'Acteurs'. Buff wrappers. Paris - Imprimerie de
Cossé : J. Dumaine et N. Delamotte.

"Echec et mat", drame en cinq actes, en prose, par MM. Oct. Feuillet
et P. Bocage. Représenté, pour la première fois, à Paris, sur le
Théâtre Royal de l'Odéon, le 23 mai 1846. (Vignette) Bruxelles.
J.-A. Lelong, imprim.-lib.-éditeur, rue des Pierres, N° 46, le soir
au théâtre royal. 1846. 18mo., pp. 92; verso of title-page 'personnages' 'acteurs'. Pale blue wrappers : répertoire de la scène
française. 14ᵐᵉ année. No. 42. "Echec et mat", drame en cinq
actes. Bruxelles. J.-A. Lelong, imprim. lib. édit. Rue des Pierres,
46. Le soir au théâtre royal. 1846. Bruxelles : Imprimerie J.A.
Lelong.

"Echec et mat" drame en cinq actes, en prose par MM. Octave Feuillet
et Paul Bocage représenté pour la première fois, a Paris, sur le
théâtre royal de l'Odéon, le 23 mai 1846. Paris, Michel Lévy frères,
n.d. (c 186), 4to., pp. 21 in double columns. Caption title. Woodcut at head of title. Théâtre contemporain illustré.

"A ANA, A PETRA, A CARMEN" ("LA DANSE")   1846
This poem consists of six verses, each of 4 lines. In the issue
of 'La Presse', 25 novembre, 1846, there appeared : 'Les journeaux
espagnols nous apportent des vers improvisée à Seville par M. Alexandre
Dumas. C'est à la sortie d'un bal que l'auteur de "La reine Margot"
a envoyé les stances suivantes à 'L'Indépendant' de Seville; No. du
12 novembre 1846.'

From the above original publication the poem was reprinted in
'Le journal du dimanche', 29 novembre, 1846, and later under the
title "La danse" in 'Revue de Paris et de Saint-Petersbourg', 15
janvier, 1888.

"JEANNE D'ARC AU BUCHER".   1846
Set to music by Franz Liszt in the same year as it was written
this poem comprises three verses, each of 8 lines. The verses and
the music were published : Paris, Meissonnier.

In (1876) there was published :
"Jeanne d'Arc au bûcher". Scène dramatique. Paroles d'Alex. Dumas

composées pour mezzo-soprano, avec accompagnement d'Orchestra ou piano par F. Liszt. Mayence, chez les fils de B. Schott; Londres, Schott & Cie.; Bruxelles, Schott frères. Folio, pp. 1 preliminary leaf, 36. "Jeanne d'Arc au bûcher", par A. Dumas père. - "Hymne de l'enfant à son réveil", par Lamartine. Paris, impr. de Chaix, n.d. (1886), 8vo., pp. 4.

"LE BATARD DE MAULEON"   1846-1847

This was one of the half-dozen works left unfinished when Dumas and his son, accompanied by Maquet, left on their travels through Spain and to North Africa in October, 1846. Dumas was completely run-down through overwork, and the advice that he should rest coincided with an invitation to the wedding of the duc de Montpensier in Madrid on the 10th of that month.

It is not one of the most satisfactory of his works; the ending is weak and this part of the romance has usually been attributed to Maquet. The period dealt with is between May, 1358, and March, 1369, in the earlier part of the Hundred Years' War, commencing historically with the murder by Pedro of Castile of his half-brother Don Fadrique and ending with Pedro's own death at the hands of his other half-brother Henry of Trastamara. Dumas based Fadrique's dog on his own animal, Mouton. He was writing the early chapters of his romance when he saw Mouton rooting up dahlias in the garden of the house he had rented, the Villa Médicis, in Saint-Germain. He gave the dog a kick and it turned on him and went for his throat. Dumas put up his right hand, which was severely mauled, and it was some days before he could again hold a pen.

Parran has written that the work was declined by 'La Presse', but stated, along with Glinel, that it was published serially in 'Le Commerce' during 1846-1847. Dumas, however, in his preface to Grisier's "Les armes et le duel" says in 'L'Espagnol'. It could, conceivably, have appeared in both these journals.

Original edition.
"Le batard de Mauléon". Par Alexandre Dumas. Bruxelles, Alph. Lebègu et Sacré fils, 1846-1847, 18mo., 4 volumes. Pagination : Volumes 1 and 2 (1846), 172 and 150; Volumes 3 and 4 (1847), 165 and 200.

"Le batard de Mauléon" par Alexandre Dumas. (Vignette) Bruxelles, Meline, Cans et compagnie, 1846-1847, 16mo., 4 volumes. Pagination : Volumes 1 and 2 (1846), 279 and 252; Volume 3 and 4 (1847), 250 and 388.
The title-pages of volumes 3 and 4 bear the additional publisher's name ; Leipzig, J.P. Meline.

"Le batard de Mauléon" Par Alexandre Dumas. (Vignette) Bruxelles et Leipzig, C. Muquardt, 1846-1847, 18mo., 4 volumes. Pagination : Volume 1 (1847 - sic), 172, Volumes 2 and 3 (1846), 150 and 165, Volume 4 (1847), 200.

"Le bâtard de Mauléon" par Alexandre Dumas. Paris, Alexandre Cadot, 1846-1847, 8vo., 9 volumes. Pagination : 299 and 2 unnumbered pages table of contents, 304, 304, 304, 320 and 267 each with an unnumbered page table of contents, 304, 307 and 317 with an unnumbered page table of contents. "Le bâtard de Mauléon" ends on page 98 of Volume 9; half-title "Guillaume Tell", pp. (101)-317. Yellow wrappers. "Guillaume Tell" is a reprint of the chapter bearing that title in "Impressions de voyage : en Suisse". At least one copy known to me does not include "Guillaume Tell".

"Le Batard de Mauléon". Alexandre Dumas. Bruxelles, A. Christiaens, n.d. (1847), large 8vo., pp. 311 in double columns, blank, (313)-314 table of contents. Green wrappers.

"Le bâtard de Mauléon" par Alexandre Dumas. Paris, Alexandre Cadot, 1847-1848, 8vo., 9 volumes. Pagination : Volume 1, 299, blank, (301)-303 table of contents, and dated 1848 (sic); Volumes 2-6 (1847), 301, blank, 303-304 table of contents; 302, 303-304 table of contents; 302, 303-304 table of contents; 317 blank, 319-320 table of contents; 267, blank, 269 table of contents, 3 blanks; Volumes 7-9 (1848), 303, 304 table of contents; 307, 308 table of contents; 317, blank, (319) table of contents for "Le bâtard de Mauléon" and Guillaume Tell". As with the Alexandre Cadot, 1846-1847, edition "Le bâtard de Mauléon" ends on page 98 of Volume 9; Half-title "Guillaume Tell", pp. (101)-317.

"Le bâtard de Mauléon", par Alexandre Dumas. Paris, S. Raçon et Cie., n.d. (c 1850), large 8vo., pp. 215-385 in double columns.

"Le bâtard de Mauléon" par Alexandre Dumas. Paris Michel Lévy frères, 1851, 12mo., 3 volumes.
Reprinted a number of times, same format but with varying paginations, by both Michel Lévy frères and Calmann-Lévy.

"Le bâtard de Mauléon" par Alexandre Dumas. Paris, Michel Lévy frères, c 186 , 4to. Musée littéraire contemporain.

"LES DEUX DIANES"   (Romance)   1846-1847

This work has been the subject of quite considerable controversy. It may be accepted (pace : Aksel J. Nielsen in his "Bibliographie d'Alexandre Dumas", Copenhague, 1964, page 66) that Paul Meurice was principally responsible for the writing of it - that is apparent from its style. But it is curious that the band of adventurers, nine in all, appeared in "Le page du duc de Savoie" which Dumas wrote unaided in Bruxelles in the 1850s; three of these had appeared earlier in his "Ascanio", and six of them made their appearance in "Les deux Diane". Dumas also introduced two of them in his play "La tour Saint-Jacques-la-Boucherie" produced in 1856. The only feasible suggestion can be that Dumas talked with Meurice about the plot, outlined the characters of the adventurers, and Meurice wrote a preliminary draft. At this time Dumas was writing six serials simultaneously and conceivably Meurice, tired of waiting for further action from Dumas, wrote the romance in its present form himself.

The story is readable, but it is not Dumas. The two Dianas are Diane de Castro, the illegitimate daughter of Henri II, and Diane de Poitiers. The period is that of Henri II's last years, the siege of Saint-Quentin, the taking of Calais, and the brief reign of François II. It opens in 1557 and closes with the death of the boy-king in December, 1560, and the departure of Mary, Queen of Scots, to her own country in 1561. It should be regarded as a companion romance to "Ascanio" and "Le page du duc de Savoie".

The work did not appear in serial form before its original publication by Cadot. Meurice drew a play from it in 1865. (See pages
365-366).

Original edition.
"Les deux Diane", par Alexandre Dumas. Paris, Alexandre Cadot, 1846-
1847, 8vo., 10 volumes. Pagination : 310 and 304 both including
table of contents, 299, 333 and 304 with additional unnumbered page
table of contents, 308 including table of contents, 332 and 315 with
additional unnumbered page table of contents, 324 including table
of contents, and 357 with additional unnumbered page table of contents.

"Les deux Diane" par Alexandre Dumas. Bruxelles, Alphonse Legègue et
Sacré fils, 1846-1847, 24mo., 9 volumes. Pagination : Volumes 1-3
(1846), 121, 118 and 115; Volumes 4-9 (1847), 122, 146, 158, 155, 123
and 130. Volume 9 bears the sole imprint : 'Alph. Lebègue'.

"Les deux Diane", par Alexandre Dumas. Bruxelles, Meline, Cans et
Cie., 1846-1847, 16mo., 10 volumes. Pagination : Volumes 1 and 2
(1846), 233 and 231; Volumes 3-10 (1847), 225, 237, 224, 218, 238,
220, 226 and 255.

"Les deux Diane" par Alexandre Dumas. Bruxelles, Meline, Cans et
compagnie; Leipzig, J.P. Meline, 1846-1847; same years of publication
for each volume, format and pagination as the preceding edition.

Ibid   (Vignette) Bruxelles et Leipzig, C. Muquardt,
1846-1847, 24mo., 9 volumes. Pagination : Volumes 1 and 2 (1846),
121 and 118; Volumes 3-9 (1847), 115, 122, 146, 158, 155, 123 and 130.

"Les deux Diane" par Alexandre Dumas. Bruxelles, Alph. Lebègue et
Sacré fils, 1847, 24mo., 9 volumes, pp. 121, 118, 115, 122, 146, 158,
155 (and 8 pages of publishers' advertisements), 123 and 130. Volume
3 bears the date 1846, and Volume 6, 1848. (sic).

Ibid   Bruxelles, Alp. Lebègue or Alphonse Lebègue,
1849-1851, 24mo., 9 volumes. Pagination : Volume 1 (1849), 113;
Volume 2 (1851 - sic), 108; (both with the imprint of Alp. Lebègue);
Volume 3 (1849), 107; Volume 4 (1850), 115; Volumes 5 and 6 (1851),
140 and 147; Volumes 7-9 (1850 - sic), 146, 116 and 120; (all with
the imprint of Alphonse Lebègue). The edition is uniform in every
respect save the oddities of years of publication and these can, I
think, only be explained as printers' errors.

"Les deux Diane" par Alexandre Dumas. Paris, Michel Lévy frères,
1853, 12mo., 3 volumes, pp. 294, (295)-296 table of contents, 291,
verso table of contents, 268, (269)-270 table of contents.
Often reprinted, same format and pagination, by both Michel Lévy frères
and Calmann-Lévy.

Ibid   Paris, Impr. de J. Voisvenel, n.d. (c 186), 4to.,
pp. (51)-272 in double columns. Oeuvres complètes d'Alexandre Dumas.

Ibid   Paris, Michel Lévy frères, 187 , 4to. Musée
littéraire contemporain.

"MEMOIRES D'UN MEDECIN : JOSEPH BALSAMO"   1846-1849

     According to Quérard, Emile de Girardin, the founder and owner
of the journal 'La Presse', began publishing in 1841 two stories which

were to be the beginning of a series taken from the original Italian
manuscript of "Les mémoires du comte Cagliostro". Their publication
aroused strong protests from readers for they were expecting something quite different. A rival journal, 'Le National", stated that
these articles were purely and simply the material of two stories published some thirty years earlier, the only difference being that the
names of characters had been altered. The outcome was a lawsuit.
While all this was going on the subscribers to 'La Presse' were becoming more and more outraged. Cagliostro was still very much a matter
of popular interest - his memoirs had been promised and his memoirs
were what readers wanted. The result was that Girardin finally
approached Dumas to write a romance centring around Cagliostro.

Dumas refused. It was 1844 by now and he was totally preoccupied
with not only "Les trois mousquetaires" and "Le comte de Monte-Cristo",
but also with "La reine Margot" for which he had signed a serial contract with Girardin. Finally, Dujarrier, the editor of 'La Presse',
persuaded him but Dumas insisted that he be given time. It was not
until the end of May, 1846, that eight of the promised nineteen volumes having been started, 'La Presse' began to publish "Mémoires d'un
médecin : première partie, Joseph Balsamo". But even Dumas' powers
of endurance could not stand up to the strain of writing simultaneously
the number of works on which he was then engaged and, as is known, he
dropped everything in October, 1846, for three months' rest, travelling
in Spain and North Africa. It was not until September, 1847, that
serial resumption was made, and from then on apparently the work continued to be published with any serious interruptions.

Joseph Balsamo is normally considered to have been Cagliostro's
real name. The period covered is from Marie-Antoinette's arrival in
France in May, 1770, to Louis XV's death in May, 1774. It was to be
followed by "Le collier de la reine", "Ange Pitou", and "La comtesse
de Charny". Once again Maquet was the collaborator, using possibly
as one of his sources the spurious "Mémoires de madame du Barry".

Original edition.
Semaine littéraire du Courrier des Etats-Unis. "Les mémoires d'un
médecin", par Alexandre Dumas. New-York, F. Gaillardet, éditeur,
Bureau du Courrier des Etats-Unis ... . 1846. Large 8vo., printed
in double columns as follows : (3)-364, 265-462; page numbers 265-
364 having been repeated (i.e. totalling 100 pages), and the last page
number should therefore read 562.

Ibid   1847, same format and pagination as the preceding.
(The above consists of that amount of the work Dumas had completed
before his departure for Spain.)

"Mémoires d'un médecin" Par Alexandre Dumas, ... Bruxelles, Alph.
Lebègue et Sacré fils, 1846-1848, 18mo., 10 volumes. Pagination :
Volumes 1-5 (1846), 188, 194, 192, 134 and 146; Volume 6 (1847), 146;
Volumes 7-10 (1848), 160, 148, 144 and 148.

"Mémoires d'un médecin. Joseph Balsamo", par Alexandre Dumas. Bruxelles, Meline, Cans et comp., 1846-1848, 16mo., 11 volumes. Pagination
: Volumes 1-5 (1846), 234, 259, 236, 240 and 234; Volume 6 (1847),
239; Volumes 7-11 (1848), 249, 265, 259, 261 and 264. Yellow wrappers.

"Mémoires d'un médecin", par Alexandre Dumas. La Haye, chez les héritiers Doorman, 1846-1848, 16mo., 11 volumes; same years of publication
and pagination as the preceding edition.

184

"Mémoires d'un médecin" par Alexandre Dumas. Bruxelles, Livourne, Meline, Cans et compagnie; Leipzig, J.P. Meline, 1846-1848, 16mo., 11 volumes; same years of publication and pagination as the preceding editions. Yellow wrappers.

Ibid Bruxelles, Livourne, Meline, Cans et compagnie; Leipzig, J.P. Meline, 1846-1848, 18mo., 16 volumes. Pagination : Volumes 1-7 (1846), 171, 176, 160, 182, 174, 138 and 152; Volumes 8-11 (1847), 150, 153, 154 and 160; Volumes 12-16 (1848), 171, 159, 169, 157 and 227.

"Mémoires d'un médecin. Joseph Balsamo", par Alexandre Dumas. Bruxelles, N.-J. Slingemeyer jeune and Librairie de Tarride, 1846-1848, 24mo., 16 volumes. Pagination : Volumes 1-8 (N.-J. Slingemeyer jeune) - 1-7 (1846), 172, 146, 155, 175, 141, 148 and 120; Volume 8 (1847), 134; Volumes 9-16 (Librairie de Tarride) - 9-13 (1847), 129, 146, 146, 132 and 137; Volumes 14-16 (1848), 136, 136 and 116. I would note here I have found another copy, same format and pagination but with the difference that Volumes 1-7 were published by N.-J. Slingemeyer jeune and Volumes 8-16 by Librairie de Tarride : 'première partie' Volumes 1-4; 'deuxiéme partie' Volumes 5-7; 'troisiéme partie' Volumes 8-16.

"Mémoires d'un médecin" Par Alexandre Dumas. Auteur de "Monte-Christo", des "Trois mousquetaires", etc. Bruxelles et Leipzig, C. Muquardt, 1846-1848, 18mo., 10 volumes. Pagination : Volumes 1-5 (1846), 188, 194, 192, 134 and 146; Volume 6 (1847), 146; Volumes 7-10 (1848), 160, 148, 144 and 148.

"Mémoires d'un médecin" par Alexandre Dumas. Berlin, Librairie B. Behr, 12 et 13 Oberwallstrasse, 1846-1848, 8vo., 7 volumes. Pagination : Volumes 1-3 (1846), (3)-37 'introduction', 220 and unnumbered page table of contents, 256 and no table of contents, 297 and unnumbered page table of contents; Volumes 4-5 (1847), 219 and 227 both with an additional unnumbered page table of contents; Volumes 6-7 (1848), 251 and 169 both with an additional unnumbered page table of contents. The work ends on page 160 'Fin de Joseph Balsamo' and is followed by an epilogue pp. 161-169. Each volume has a half-title with : "Mémoires d'un médecin" par Alexandre Dumas. Première - troisième partie de "Joseph Balsamo". Imprimé chez Jules Sittenweld, à Berlin. On the verso of the half-title of Volume 7 appears : 'La première partie des "Mémoires d'un médecin" comprenant le temps écoulé depuis le mariage de Marie-Antoinette, jusqu'à l'année 1774 est terminée'. 'La seconde partie, que M. Alexandre Dumas nous a promis de ne pas faire longtemps attendre à nos lectures, comprendra les six années de 1789 à 1794, c'est à dire depuis le prise de la Bastille jusqu'à la fin de la Terreur.' 'Puis viendront tour à tour le Directoire, l'Empire, la Restauration; tous les événements contemporains repasseront ainsi devant les yeux, tu public, dont la curiosité a été si vivement excitée par la lecture de la première partie des "Mémoires d'un médecin".'

"Mémoires d'un médecin" par Alexandre Dumas. "Joseph Balsamo ... Lettres sur le magnétisme". Paris, Fellens et Dufour (et Alexandre Cadot), 1846-1848, 8vo., 19 volumes. Pagination : Volume 1 (Première partie - Joseph Balsamo), 317, 341, 345, 321, 301 and 325, each with an additional unnumbered page table of contents; Volume 7 (Joseph Balsamo, deuxième partie. Andrée de Taverney), 326, 327, 333, 310,

310 and 333, each with an additional unnumbered page table of contents; Volume 13 (Joseph Balsamo, troisième partie. Andrée de Taverney), 329, 302, 302, 315, 318, 300, each with an additional unnumbered page tabl- of contents, and 312.
"Mémoires d'un médecin" par Alexandre Dumas. Leipzig, Brockhaus & Avenarius, F.A. Brockhaus, 1846-1851, 12mo., 22 volumes. Pagination : Volumes 1-15 (Brockhaus & Avenarius - Typ. de F.A. Brockhaus); Volumes 1-5 (1846), 166, 160, 169, 146 and 169; Volumes 6-9 (1847), 144, 155, 144 and 138; Volumes 10-11 (1848), 156 and 157; Volumes 12- 15 (1849), 147, 160, 156 and 142; Volumes 16-22 (F.A. Brockhaus - Impr. de F.A. Brockhaus à Leipzig), Volumes 16-17 (1850), 150 and 179; Volumes 18-22 (1851), 166, 164, 156, 160 and 83. There are no tables of contents.
That this is a rogue edition can be seen from the following : Vol- umes 1-3 : Première partie Joseph Balsamo, with on page 169 'Fin de la première partie de Joseph Balsamo'; Volumes 4-5 : Deuxième partie Joseph Balsamo, with on page 169 'Fin de la deuxième partie de Joseph Balsamo'; Volumes 6-11 : Troisième partie Joseph Balsamo, with on page 157 'Fin de la première (sic) partie; Volume 12 : Quatrième partie Les Prédictions, pp. 1-47 'prologue', pp. 48 through to Volume 17 "Le collier de la reine" with on page 179 of Volume 17 'Fin du tome dix-septième et du collier de la reine'; Volumes 18-22 : Cinquième partie "Ange Pitou", with on page 83 'Fin du tome vingt-deuxième, d'Ange Pitou et des Mémoires d'un Médecin.' Misprints - Volume 6, numbers on pp. 48 and 72 are omitted; Volume 7, page 36 is misnumbered 63 and page 56 is misnumbered 65; Volume 8, page 113 is misnumbered 311 and page 120 is misnumbered 20; Volume 9, page 135 is misnumbered 351 and page 60 is misnumbered 06.
I have traced one other copy of this edition. It is exactly as des- cribed above but with the variation that Volumes 1-16 were published by Brockhaus & Avenarius, and Volumes 17-22 by F.A. Brockhaus.

Semaine littéraire du Courrier des Etats-Unis. Receuil Choisi de romans, feuilletons, ouvrages historiques et dramatiques, en prose et en vers des auteurs modernes les plus renommés. Volume 3. 1848. New-York, F. Gaillardet 1848. At the top of Page (3) : "Les mémoires d'un médecin. Joseph Balsamo". Large 8vo., pp. (3)-462 in double columns with the same pagination errors noted in the 'Semaine littér- aire ... ', 1846 and 1847 editions.

"Mémoires d'un médecin" par Alexandre Dumas. "Joseph Balsamo". Paris, Michel Lévy frères, 1850, 12mo., 5 volumes.
Frequently reprinted in the same format but with occasional varying paginations by both Michel Lévy frères and Calmann-Lévy.

"Mémoires d'un médecin Joseph Balsamo" par Alexandre Dumas Paris Dufour, Mulat et Boulanger, éditeurs (se reservant le droit de repro- duction et de traduction à l'étranger.) 21 quai Malaquais 1856, large 8vo., 2 volumes, pp. (1)-518, (519)-520 table of contents, and (1)- 503, verso blank, (505)-507 table of contents, verso blank, 2 unnumber- ed pages 'classement des gravures'; frontispiece to each volume and each with 32 full-page illustrations.
Reprinted, same format, pagination and illustrations, 1857, 1861.

Ibid   Paris, Dufour et Mulat, chez Marescq et Cie., 1859, same format, pagination and illustrations as the preceding edition. Reprinted, 1863.

Ibid   Paris, Dufour Boulanger et Legrand, 1862, same format, pagination and illustrations as the preceding editions.

Ibid   Paris, Imprimerie Pillet fils, n.d. (c 186),
4to., pp. 407 in double columns, and unnumbered page table of contents.
Caption title. Woodcut at head of title; illustrated.

Alexandre Dumas. "Mémoires d'un médecin : Joseph Balsamo". (Clichy,
Impr. de M. Loignon et cie.), n.d. (188), 4to., same pagination as
the preceding edition. Caption title. Woodcut at head of title;
illustrated.

"Mémoires d'un médecin - Joseph Balsamo" par Alexandre Dumas. Paris,
Michel Lévy frères, 188 , 4to., same pagination as the preceding
editions. Caption title. Woodcut at head of title. Musée littéraire
contemporain.

"LA REINE MARGOT"   (Drama)   1847

    At long last Dumas had a theatre of his own, the Théâtre Histor-
ique, and the first play to be presented there was taken from the
romance of the same name. Maquet collaborated. On the whole the
romance is followed closely, but there is a difference in the conclusion in the dramatised version. The stamina of audiences in the mid-
nineteenth century must have been amazing for the performance lasted
nine hours. But in any event the play was a tremendous success.

Original edition.
"La reine Margot", drame en 5 actes et en 13 tableaux, par MM.
Alexandre Dumas et Auguste Maquet, représenté pour la première fois,
a Paris, pour l'ouverture du Théâtre Historique, le 20 février 1847.
Paris, Michel Lévy frères, 1847, 12mo., pp. (1)-152. Paper covers.
Bibliothèque Dramatique. Théâtre moderne. 2ᵉ série.

"La reine Margot", drame en cinq actes et treize tableaux, par MM.
Alex. Dumas et A. Maquet. Représenté, pour la première fois, à Paris,
sur le théâtre Historique, le 20 février 1847. Bruxelles, J.-A. Lelong,
1847, 12mo., pp. 154.

"La reine Margot"; drame en cinq actes et treize tableaux, par Alexandre Dumas et Auguste Maquet ... la musique de M. Varney. Paris :
Vᵉ Dondey-Dupré, n.d. (1847), 12mo., pp. 152. Caption title. (The
music is not included.)

"La reine Margot" drame en cinq actes et treize tableaux, par MM.
Alexandre Dumas et Auguste Maquet, représenté pour la première fois,
a Paris, pour l'ouverture du Théatre-Historique. (Paris), Typographie
de Lacrampe fils et Comp., n.d. (1847), 12mo., pp. (1)-152. Caption
title with "distribution de la pièce" and "Les décorations sont de
MM. Desplechin, Diéterie et Séchan; les costumes de MM. Bonhomme, L.
Lasalle et Bailue; la musique de M. Varney."

Bibliothèque dramatique. Théâtre moderne. "La reine Margot" drame
en 5 actes et 13 tableaux par MM. Alexandre Dumas et Auguste Maquet.
Paris, Michel Lévy frères, 1850, 12mo., pp. (1)-157, including title-
page.

"La reine Margot" drame en cinq actes et treize tableaux par MM.
Alex. Dumas et A. Maquet représenté pour la première fois, á Paris,
sur le Théâtre-Historique, le 20 février 1847. Paris, Michel Lévy
frères, n.d. (1853), 8vo., pp. 42 in double columns. Caption title.
Engraving at the head of title. Théâtre contemporain illustré. No. 14.
Reprinted, same format and pagination, n.d. (1868).

Ibid   Paris, Calmann-Lévy, n.d. (c 187), 4to., pp. 44
in double columns.   Caption title.   Engraving at head of title.

"La reine Margot"   drame en cinq actes, en treize tableax   en société
avec M. Auguste Maquet Théâtre-Historique. - 20 février 1847.   "Distribution" on title-page, pp. 2-188.   Théâtre complet de Alex. Dumas
Tome X   Paris   Calmann Lévy, éditeur   ancienne maison Michel Lévy
frères, 1874.   12mo.   "Théâtre complet" in 25 volumes.

"La reine Margot"   drame en cinq actes, en treize tablezux   en société
avec Alexandre Dumas   Théâtre-Historique. - 20 février 1847.   "Distribution" on title-page, pp. 2-188.   Théatre de Auguste Maquet   Tome IV
Paris   Calmann-Lévy, éditeurs 3, rue Auber, 3 (n.d.), 1893   12mo.
"Théatre" in 4 volumes.

"La Reine Margot",   drame en 5 actes et 13 tableaux,   par MM. Alexandre Dumas et A. Maquet.   Toulouse, Impr. de Troyes, n.d. (1865),
8vo., pp. 4.
This comprises the distribution of the parts and an analysis of the
play.

There were three parodies of the play :
"La reine argot"   parodie   de "La reine Margot"   en trois actes, sept
tableaux et en vers   par MM. Lubize, A. Guénée et Marc-Leprevost,
représentée pour la première fois a Paris sur le théatre des Folies-
Dramatiques, le 23 mars 1847.   Caption title.   'Distribution' on title-
page.   12mo., pp. (1)-60, and 4 pages of publishers' announcement of
'oeuvres completes d'Alexandre Dumas' format de la bibliothèque
Charpentier. Yellow wrappers : Bibliothèque dramatique Théâtre
moderne. - 2e Série.   "La reine argot"   parodie de "La reine Margot"
en 3 actes, 7 tableaux, et en vers.   60 centimes.   Michel Lévy frères,
libraires-éditeurs des oeuvres d'Alexandre Dumas, ... , et du théâtre
de Victor Hugo   rue Vivienne, 1.   Paris, - 1847.   Paris. - Typ. La-
champe et Ce., 2, rue Damiette.

"Fouyou" au Théâtre Historique   Représentation de la "Reine Margot"
Pot Pourri en 14 tableaux   Prix : 15 centimes.   Paris, L.Vieillot,
édit. des Chansons de MM. L. Festeau et A. Jacquenart.   32, Rue Notre-
Dame-de-Nazareth.   1847, 12mo.

"Apothéose de M. A. Dumas à la suite de la première représentation
de 'La reine Margot'"   Air : Saint-Esprit, descends, descends jusqu'
en bas. (Béranger).   Parodie en 6 couplets imprimée par Lacour et
Cie., 1847, 8vo., pp. 4.

"INTRIGUE ET AMOUR"   1847

     Dumas has stated that this play was a translation from Schiller
but, as with "Fiesque de Lavagna" (also after Schiller but never
published), it is clear that he was no translator in the strict sense
of the word. He modified and reconstructed, although closely following
the main plot. The play was very successful. Maquet had no share in
its composition, but he did have a share in the rights from it in
payment of debts due to him.

Original edition.
"Intrigue et amour" drame en cinq actes et neuf tableaux, Traduit de
Schiller. Par Alexandre Dumas, représenté pur la première fois, a
Paris, sur le Théâtre Historique, le 11 juin 1847. Paris, Michel Lévy
frères, 1847, 12mo., pp. (2)-99. Blue wrappers : Bibliothèque dramatique Théâtre moderne. - 2e Série. Poissy, imprimerie française
et étrangère de G. Oliver.

"Intrigue et amour", drame en cinq actes et neuf tableaux, (traduit
de Schiller) par Alexandre Dumas. Représenté, pour la première fois,
à Paris, sur le Théâtre-Historique, le 11 juin 1847. Bruxelles, J.-
A. Lelong, 1847, 16mo., pp. 127.

"Intrigue et amour" drame en cinq actes et neuf tableaux. Traduit
de Schiller par M. Alexandre Dumas. Représenté pour la première
fois, à Paris, sur le théâtre historique, le 11 juin 1847. Paris,
Michel Lévy frères, n.d. (1853), 4to., pp. 27 in double columns. Caption title. Woodcut at head of title. Théâtre contemporain illustré,
No. 61.

"Intrigue et amour", drame en 5 actes et 9 tableaux, traduit de
Schiller, par Alexandre Dumas ... . Poissy, Impr. de G. Olivier,
n.d. (c 1864), 12mo., pp. (2)-99.

"Intrigue et amour" drame en cinq actes, en neuf tableaux traduit
de Schiller. Théâtre-Historique. - 11 juin 1847. "Distribution" on
title-page, pp. (189)-306. Théâtre complet de Alex. Dumas Tome X
Paris Calmann Lévy, éditeur ancienne maison Michel Lévy frères,
1874. 12mo. "Théâtre complet" in 25 volumes.

"LE CHEVALIER DE MAISON-ROUGE"   (Drama)   1847

     The claim has been made that this enormously popular play, which
was written in collaboration with Maquet, had some influence towards
the outbreak of the 1848 Revolution which sent Louis-Philippe into
exile.

     As so often happens with Dumas the drama was in some ways an
improvement on the romance; in point of fact the play ends on a happy
note with the escape of Maurice and Genevieve, in happy and direct
contrast with the tragic ending to the romance. The effect of the
introduction of the song "Mourir pour la Patrie", and in addition the
famous verses sung by the Girondins, was remarkable. The play lasted
a marathon eight hours, and after its withdrawal from the Théâtre-
Historique was later staged at the Porte-Saint-Martin where, for some
unaccountable reason, Dumas' second verse sung by the Girondins was
omitted and replaced by two other verses allegedly written by Maquet.

Original edition.
"Le chevalier de Maison-Rouge, épisode du temps des Girardins", drame
en cinq actes et douze tableaux, par MM. Alexandre Dumas et Auguste
Maquet. Représenté, pour la première fois, a Paris, sur le Théâtre
Historique, le 3 aout 1847. Paris, Michel Lévy frères, 1847, 12mo.,
pp. (2)-139. Caption title, which includes "Distribution". Blue
wrappers : Bibliothèque dramatique Théâtre moderne "Le chevalier
de Maison-Rouge épisode du temps des Girondins" Drame en 5 actes et
12 tableaux par MM. Alexandre Dumas et Auguste Maquet. Imprimerie
Dondey-Dupré.

Le chevalier de Maison-Rouge, épisode du temps des Girondins", drame
en cinq actes et douze tableaux, par MM. Alex. Dumas et Aug. Maquet.
Représenté, pour la première fois, à Paris, sur le Théâtre-Historique,
le 3 Août 1847. (Vignette) Bruxelles, J.-A. Lelong, imprim.-lib.-
éditeur, 1847, 16mo., pp. 130.

Le chevalier de Maison-Rouge" drame en cinq actes et douze tableaux
par MM. Alex. Dumas et A. Maquet représenté pour la première fois,
à Paris, sur le Théatre-historique, le 3 août 1847. Paris, Michel
Lévy frères, n.d. (1847), 4to., pp. 40 in double columns. Caption
title. Woodcut at head of title. Théâtre contemporain illustré.

Théatre Français publié par G. Schutz. Neuvième série. I. livraison.
"Le chevalier de Maison-Rouge. Episode du temps des Girondins". Par
MM. Alex. Dumas et Aug. Maquet. Bielefeld, Velhagen & Klasing, 1847,
24mo., pp. 155.
Reprinted, same format and pagination, 1858, 1862, 1876.

"Le Chevalier de Maison-Rouge, épisode du temps des Girardins". Drame
en cinq actes et douze tableaux, représenté, pour la première fois,
à Paris, sur le Théatre Historique, le 3 août 1847. Par Alexandre
Dumas et Auguste Maquet. Paris, Michel Lévy frères, n.d. (1849),
12mo., pp. (2)-139. Bibliothèque dramatique. Théâtre moderne.

"Le chevalier de Maison-Rouge" drame en cinq actes et douze tableaux
par MM. Alex. Dumas et A. Maquet représenté pour la première fois à
Paris sur le Théatre-Historique, le 3 août 1847. Paris, Michel Lévy
frères, n.d. (1853), 4to., pp. 40 in double columns. Caption title.
Woodcut at head of title. Théatre contemporain illustré. No. 9.

"Le chevalier de Maison-Rouge ou les Girondins". Drame en cinq actes
et douze tableaux, en prose, par Alexandre Dumas et A. Maquet. Paris,
Michel Lévy frères, 1868, 4to., pp. 22-61, in double columns. Chefs-
d'oeuvre du Théâtre moderne. Vol. 2.

"Le chevalier de Maison-Rouge" drame en cinq actes en douze tableaux
par Alexandre Dumas et Auguste Maquet. Représenté, pour la première
fois, a Paris, sur le Théatre-Historique, le 3 aout 1847 et repris
au Théatre de la Porte-Saint-Martin, le 11 novembre 1869. (Paris)
Calmann-Lévy, n.d. (1870), 4to., pp. 40 in double columns. Caption
title. Woodcut at head of title.

"Le chevalier de Maison-Rouge" drame en cinq actes, en douze tableaux
en société avec M. Auguste Maquet Théâtre-Historique. - 3 août 1847.
"Distribution" on title-page, pp. 2-166. Théatre complete de Alex.
Dumas Tome XI Paris Calmann Lévy, éditeur ancienne maison Michel
Lévy frères, 1874. 12mo. "Théatre complet" in 25 volumes.

"Le Chevalier de Maison-Rouge", drame en 4 actes, 10 tableaux, par
Alexandre Dumas et Auguste Maquet. Nouvelle édition, conforme à la
représentation. (Repris sur le théâtre de la Porte-Saint-Martin, à
Paris, le 28 décembre 1888.) Paris, Calmann-Lévy, 1889, 8vo., pp. 146.

"LES GIRONDINS" "MOURIR POUR LA PATRIE"   1847

        It is apposite that full reference should be made here to these
two verses each of 6 lines, the two last forming a common refrain to
both verses. They were sung by the condemned Girondins in prison in
the play "Le chevalier de Maison-Rouge". They do not appear in the

romance of that name. The first verse is in Act V, scene i, and the second in the same act, scene v. In so far as the first four lines of each verse are concerned the music was by Alphonse Varney, but that for the refrain was from Rouget de l'Isle, the lines of the refrain being taken from a poem entitled "Roland" written by de l'Isle.

Dumas is said to have remarked to Varney, the leader of the orchestra at the performance of the drama, that 'our next Revolution will march to this song'. His percipience proved to be correct for the song was, indeed, heard sung throughout Paris in February, 1848. I have no knowledge of the separate publication of the words and music in France, but these must undoubtedly have been so published. The song achieved a degree of fame outside France and : "Mourir pour la Patrie". Musique d'Alphonse Varney, was published : London, 'Illustrated London News', 11th March, 1848, together with an English rendering of Dumas' verses. In the same issue the journal published a drawing of 'Alexandre Dumas borne in triumph by the people', and another drawing by Valentin entitled 'Singing the "Choeur des Girondins" in the galerie d'Orléans, at the Palais Royal'.

"Les Girondins : Mourir pour la Patrie". Revolutionary song of '48. As sung at Paris during the struggle, February 22, 23 and 24. Written by Alexander Dumas. Music composed by Alphonse Varney. New York : Atwill, copyright 1848, folio, pp. 4.

'Album litteraire ou nouveau choix de lectures, offert aux amateurs de la langue française suivies de notes littéraires et explicatives' par L.-S. Borring Professeur de langue française Troisième édition refondue et augmentée Copenhague a la librairie de J.-H. Schubothe 1866. 8vo., pp. viii, 442 including table of contents. "Le chant des Girondins", par A. Maquet (sic), pp. 385-386, the first two verses being on page 385 and the last on page 386. The work also includes "Les Bénédictines de Saint-Nicolas-le-vieux", being a chapter from Dumas' "Le Speronare".

With the restaging of the play in 1869 in a different political climate Dumas' second verse was replaced by two others allegedly written by Maquet. This three-verse piece, with music by Varney but without using de l'Isle's music for the refrain, was published under the title : "Choeur des Girondins : Mourir pour la Patrie, Chant National", Chanté au Théâtre de la Porte-Saint-Martin dans "Le chevalier de Maison-Rouge", drame en 5 actes par MM. Alexandre Dumas et Auguste Maquet, Paris, M. Labbé, year, format and pagination unknown. It was dedicated to Lamartine, but the important thing is that it bore the words 'Paroles de M.A. Maquet'. There then followed :

"Le chant des Girondins", hymne nationale, paroles d'Alex. Dumas et Maquet; this was published together with "Le chant du départ", paroles de M.-J. Chénier. Saint-Quentin, Langlet, n.d. (1870), 12mo., pp. 4.

"LES QUARANTE-CINQ"   1847

A true sequel to "La dame de Monsoreau" this great romance continues the Guise and League intrigues against Henri III, Chicot's adventures in combatting these intrigues, the capture of Cahors, and Diane de Méridor's vengeance on the duc d'Anjou for the murder of

Bussy d'Amboise. The period of the story is from October, 1582, to June, 1584. Several times Dumas promised a further sequel but this never eventuated.

Maquet was again the collaborator and it has been suggested that he finished the work alone. This is untenable, for the manuscript was on display at the centenary celebrations of Dumas' birth at Villers-Cotterets, the first portion in the hand of Dumas, père, and the remainder in that of his son with a signed declaration by the latter that his father had dictated it to him because he was confined to his bed through illness.

The work appeared serially in 'Le Constitutionnel' between 13th May and 20th October, 1847.

Original edition.
"Les quarante-cinq" par Alexandre Dumas. 'Etiam omnes' Bruxelles, Alph. Lebègue et Sacré fils, 1847, 18mo., 6 volumes, pp. 172, 175, 143, 144, 144 and 129. It should be noted that Volumes 4-6 bear only the imprint : Alph. Lebègue.

Ibid   Bruxelles, Librairie de Ch. Muquardt, 1847, 24mo., 6 volumes, pp. 203, 201, 277, 282, 268 and 268.

"Les quarante-cinq" par Alexandre Dumas. Bruxelles, Livourne, Meline, Cans et compagnie; Leipzig, J.P. Meline, 1847, 18mo., 6 volumes, pp. 277, 282, 268, 268, 262 and 225. "Les quarante-cinq" ends on page 108 of Volume 6 and is followed by "Une amazone", pp. 109-192, and "Une séance de magnétisme chez M. Alexandre Dumas", pp. 193-225.

Ibid   La Haye, chez les héritiers Doorman, 1847, same format and pagination as the preceding edition.

Semaine Littéraire du Courrier des Etats-Unis. Receuil Choisi de romans, feuilletons, ouvrages historiques et dramatiques, en prose et en vers des auteurs modernes les plus renommés. XVII série : Vol. 3, nos. 1-10. 1847. New-York : F. Gaillardet 1847. At the top of the page 3 : "Les Quarante-cinq", par Alexandre Dumas. 8vo., pp. (3)-304 in double columns.

"Les quarante-cinq" par Alexandre Dumas. Bruxelles, Alph. Lebègue et Sacré fils, 1847-1848, 18mo., 6 volumes. Pagination : Volumes 1-5 (1847), 203, 201, 277, 282 and 268; Volume 6 (1848), 268.

"Les quarante-cinq", par Alexandre Dumas. Bruxelles, Livourne, Meline, Cans et compagnie; Leipzig, J.P. Meline, 1847-1848, 16mo., 6 volumes. Pagination : Volumes 1-5 (1847), 203, 201, 205, 190 and 197; Volume 6 (1848), 158.
This edition is complete in itself and does not, as with the Meline, Cans ... edition of 1847, include other works by Dumas.

"Les quarante-cinq" par Alexandre Dumas. Bruxelles et Leipzig, C. Muquardt, 1847-1848, 6 volumes, same format and pagination as the preceding edition.

"Les quarante-cinq" par Alexandre Dumas. Paris, Alexandre Cadot, 1847-1848, 8vo., 10 volumes. Pagination : Volumes 1-8 (1847), 331, 308, 327, 343, 307, 327, 324 and 311; Volumes 9-10 (1848), 317 and 311, each with an additional unnumbered page table of contents. 'Le billet de spectacle' occupies pp. 163-311 of Volume 10, with continuous pagination, and is described in the table of contents as Chapter VII, although on page 163 no chapter number is given. Yellow wrappers.

Le Siècle. Oeuvres complètes d'Alexandre Dumas. "Les quarante-cinq". Paris, au bureau du Siècle, 1849, 4to., pp. 214 in double columns.

"Les quarante-cinq". Par M. Alexandre Dumas. In : 'L'Echo des feuilletons receuil de nouvelles, légendes, anecdotes, épisodes, ... '. Paris, chez les éditeurs, 1849, large 8vo., pp. (265)-409 in double columns; illustrated.

"Les quarante-cinq" par Alexandre Dumas. Paris, Michel Lévy frères, 1850, 12mo., 3 volumes, pp. 318, (319)-320 table of contents; 314, (315)-316 table of contents; 266, (267)-268 table of contents. Frequently reprinted, same format but sometimes with varying pagination by both Michel Lévy frères and Calmann-Lévy.

"Les quarante-cinq" par Alexandre Dumas. Illustrés par J.-A. Beaucé et Coppin. Publiés par Dufour et Mulat. (Vignette) Paris, Marescq et Cie., 1857, large 8vo., in 3 parts; pp. 154, 155 and 152, each with an additional unnumbered page table of contents and list of illustrations, all in double columns. Each part has 8 plates and 24 woodcuts.

"Les quarante-cinq". Par M. Alexandre Dumas. Paris, Dufour, Mulat et Boulanger, 1857, large 8vo., pp. (265)-409 in double columns; illustrated.

"Les quarante-cinq" par Alexandre Dumas. Paris, Lécrivain et Toubon, n.d. (1861), large 8vo.

"Les quarante-cinq". Par M. Alexandre Dumas. In : 'L'Echo des feuilletons, receuil de nouvelles, légendes, anecdotes, épisodes, ... '. Neuvième année. Paris, chez les éditeurs, 1863, large 8vo., pp. (265)-409 in double columns; illustrated.

"Les quarante-cinq" par Alexandre Dumas Paris, Calmann-Lévy, n.d. (c 187), 4to., pp. (1)-229 in double columns, unnumbered page table of contents. Caption title. Woodcut at head of title.

"La reine Margot", par Alexandre Dumas. Paris, J. Rouff, n.d. (189), large 8vo., 3 volumes. "La reine Margot"; "La dame de Monsoreau"; "Les quarante-cinq". Illustrated.

Alexandre Dumas. "Les quarante-cinq". Illustrés par J.-A. Beaucé et Coppin. Paris, Calmann-Lévy, n.d. (1897), 4to., pp. 152 in double columns. Caption title. Woodcut at head of title. Alexandre Dumas oeuvres illustrés.

"NOTICE NECROLOGIQUE SUR MELCHIOR FREDERIC SOULIE ..."   1847

     Soulié was one of Dumas' friends and on his death, when he was only 47, Dumas and several others wrote appreciative articles about him. These were collected and published with, as will be seen, a complete list of Soulié's works.

Original (and only) edition.
"Notice nécrologique sur Melchior Frédéric Soulié, poète et littérateur, décoré de juillet, mort a Bièvre, près Paris, le 23 septembre 1847"; par MM. Victor Hugo, Alexandre Dumas, Jules Janin, Paul Lacroix (le bibliophile Jacob), Antony Béraud, Charles de Matharel et Charles Monselet, Et terminée par la liste complète des Oeuvres de Frédéric Soulié. (Vignette) Extrait du nécrologe universel du XIXe

siècle. E. Saint-Maurice Cabany, Directeur et Rédacteur en chef. Au bureau de rédaction et a l'administration, Rue Cassette, 8, faubourg St. Germain, et chez tous les libraires. Paris, 1847. Large 8vo., pp. (5)-79. Brown wrappers repeating the title-page and with Soulié's 'romans' listed on the back cover. Dumas' contribution occupies pp. 69-77, and Soulié's complete works are listed on pp. 78-79. Paris. Imprimé par Plon frères, rue de Vaugirard, 36.

"HERMINIE"   "UNE AMAZONE"   1847

     Under the title of "Une amazone" this work first appeared serially in 'Le Siècle' from 29th September to 3rd October, 1845, to be sub-sequently entitled alternatively "Herminie" or "Herminie l'amazone" when it was published in volume form. Dumas has claimed that, apart from the alteration of names, it is based on fact. The work was republished in his journal 'Le Monte-Cristo' between 3rd and 17th June, 1862, but here he states that the incidents occurred in the 1850s, which indicates alterations in the story as it originally appeared in 'Le Siècle'.

Original edition.
"Les quarante-cinq" par Alexandre Dumas. Bruxelles, Livourne, Meline, Cans et compagnie; Leipzig, J.P. Meline, 1847, 18mo., 6 volumes, the final volume pp. 225. "Les quarante-cinq" ends on page 108 and is followed by "Une amazone", pp. 109-192, and "Une séance de magnétisme chez M. Alexandre Dumas", pp. 193-225.

Ibid   La Haye, chez les héritiers Doorman, 1847, same format and pagination as the preceding edition.

'Le foyer de l'opéra - moeurs fashionables' - par Alexandre Dumas etc. Volume 9. Paris, Hippolyte Souverain, 1848, 8vo., "L'Amazone", pp. 252. Brown wrappers with on cover : 'Le foyer de l'opéra' 9 Alex. Dumas. "Une amazone". (The full work comprised 12 volumes, published 1840-1848.)

Collection Hetzel. "Herminie" & "Marianna" par Alexandre Dumas. Edition autorisée pour la Belgique et l'étranger, interdite pour la France. Bruxelles, Meline, Cans et compagnie, 1859, 24mo., pp. 174, unnumbered page table of contents, and 16 pages of publishers' adver-tisements. "Herminie", pp. (1)-96, and "Marianna", pp. 97-174. Typ. J. Nys.

Ibid   La Haye, chez les héritiers Doorman, 1859, same format and pagination as the preceding edition.

Ibid   Leipzig, Alph. Dürr, 1859, same format and pagina-tion as the preceding editions.

"Une aventure d'amour" (with "Herminie") par Alexandre Dumas. Paris, Michel Lévy frères, 1862, 12mo., pp. 274 and unnumbered page table of contents. "Herminie" occupies pp. (191)-274.
This is the first edition of the work to appear under this title in France.
Often reprinted, same format and pagination by both Michel Lévy frères and Calmann-Lévy.

"Herminie - L'Amazone" par Alexandre Dumas Paris Calmann-Lévy,

1888, 8vo., pp. (1)-111, and additional unnumbered page table of contents. Illustrated with a frontispiece and 14 vignettes by Robaudi engraved by Deville. This was a limited edition of which 25 copies were printed on 'papier Japon', and 225 copies on 'vélin du Marais', all numbered. Bound in buff stiff paper wrappers.

"LE VICOMTE DE BRAGELONNE, OU DIX ANS PLUS TARD" 1847- ...

This long romance completes the trilogy which started with "Les trois mousquetaires". The work opens with Louis XIV's visit to Blois in July, 1659 (for his own purposes Dumas brought the year forward to 1660), and ends with d'Artagnan's death at Maestricht on 25th June, 1673. The story does not open particularly well and its action only really starts with the seventeenth chapter; from then we have amongst a great deal else Monk kidnapped, Mazarin's death, the adventure of Belle-Isle, Aramis made General of the Jesuits, the love intrigues of the Court and of La Vallière, Fouquet's fall from power, Porthos' death, and the man in the iron mask - in all a feast of epic variety. Dumas at one time meditated writing a further sequel and, indeed, in 1854 he went so far as to announce its title as "Le maréchal de Ferrant", but no chapter of the work ever appeared, if, for that matter, anything was ever written.

As with its two predecessors in the trilogy the work was published serially in 'Le Siècle', between 20th October, 1847, with some lapses, to 12th January, 1850.

It should be noted that d'Artagnan's final words differ in the Dufour et Mulat, - Marescq et Cie., illustrated editions from those in the serial issue, and therefore in the Belgian pirated editions, and the Michel Lévy frères edition which was the first to be published in France. Maquet again collaborated.

Original edition.
Semaine Littéraire du courrier des Etats-Unis. Receuil Choisi de romans, feuilletons, ouvrages historiques et dramatiques, en prose et en vers, des auteurs modernes les plus renommés. XVIII série - Volume 4. New-York, F. Gaillardet, Bureau du Courrier des Etats-Unis, 1847 (sic). "Le vicomte de Bragelonne", (Suite des "Trois Mousquetaires" et de "Vingt ans après".) Par Alexandre Dumas. Large 8vo., pp. (3)-289, Fin de la sixième partie; (291)-839, Septième partie, to the end of the published work, all in double columns. Followed by "Mocquet", pp. (841)-849 in double columns, and dated 'Villers-Cotterets, 19 décembre 1849'.
It is obvious from the dates of the feuilleton issue that this is an incomplete work, with the important proviso that copies of some at least of Dumas' manuscript sheets may have reached New York.

"Le vicomte de Bragelonne", par Alexandre Dumas. Bruxelles, Librairie de la rue de la fourche, 1847-1848, 24mo., 8 volumes. Pagination : Volume 1 (1847), 146; Volumes 2-8 (1848), 155, 135, 136, 151, 141, 134 and 126.
(I have never heard of this publisher in connexion with any other of Dumas' pirated editions, and it could possibly be that he went out of business before the edition could be completed.)

"Le Vicomte de Bragelonne" par Alexandre Dumas. Bruxelles, Librairie de Tarride, 1847-1850, 24mo., 25 volumes. Pagination : Volume 1 (1847), 146; Volumes 2-10 (1848), 155, 135, 136, 151, 141, 134, 126, 125 and 128; Volumes 11-24 (1849), 138, 125, 125, 128, 126, 130, 129, 144, 143, 151, 139, 142, 132 and 148; Volumes 25 (1850), 161.

"Le vicomte de Bragelonne" par Alexandre Dumas. Bruxelles, 1848-1850, 18mo., 18 volumes, of which Volumes 1-6 were published in 1848, 7-17 in 1849, and 18 in 1850. Publisher's imprint and pagination : Volumes 1-3 (Alph. Lebègue), 139, 118 and 123; Volume 4 (Alp. Lebègue), 136; Volumes 5-7 (Alphonse Lebègue), 147, 128 and 144; Volume 8 (Alp. Lebègue), 167; Volumes 9-13 (Alph. Lebègue), 148, 148, 147, 148 and 138; Volume 14 (Alphonse Lebègue), 148; Volume 15 (Alp. Lebègue), 145; Volumes 16-17 (Alphonse Lebègue), 136 and 127; Volume 18 (Alp. Lebègue), 182 - the past page stating : 'Fin du vicomte de Bragelonne, trois- ième et dernière partie des Trois Mousquetaires'.

"Le vicomte de Bragelonne" (Suite de "Vingt ans après") par Alexandre Dumas. Bruxelles et Leipzig, C. Muquardt, 1848-1850, 18mo., 16 vol- umes. Pagination : Volumes 1-4 (1848), 185, 179, 177 and 179; Vol- umes 5-11 (1849), 171, 159, 176, 172, 179, 177 and 172; Volumes 12-16 (1850), 177, 176, 156, 168 and 164.

"Le vicomte de Bragelonne" (Suite de "Vingt ans après") par Alex- andre Dumas. Bruxelles, Livourne, Meline, Cans et compagnie; Leipzig, J.P. Meline, 1848-1850, 16mo., 13 volumes. Pagination : Volumes 1-4 (1848), 283, 285, 263 and 276; Volumes 5-10 (1849), 283, 277, 284, 279, 278 and 257; Volumes 11-13 (1850), 251, 281 and 329. Volumes 1-8 : Imprimerie de la société typographique belge Ad. Wahlen et compagnie; Volumes 9-13 : Imprimerie de G. Stapleaux.

Ibid   La Haye, les heritiérs Doorman, 1848-1850, same individual years of publication, format and pagination as the preceding edition.

Ibid   Bruxelles, Livourne, Meline, Cans et compagnie; Leipzig, J.P. Meline, 1848-1850, 18mo., 16 volumes. Pagination : Volumes 1-4 (1848), 185, 179, 177 and 179; Volumes 5-11 (1849), 171, 159, 176, 172, 179, 177 and 172; Volumes 12-16 (1850), 177, 176, 156, 168 and 164. Volumes 1-5 are in green wrappers and Volumes 6-16 in blue.

"Le vicomte de Bragelonne" (Suite de "Vingt ans après") Par Alex- andre Dumas. Bruxelles, Livourne, Meline, Cans et compagnie; Leipzig, J.P. Meline, 1848-1850, 18mo., 16 volumes. This particular edition is a reprint of the preceding with the differ- ence that Volumes 1-5 were published in 1848, Volumes 6-11 in 1849, and Volumes 12-16 in 1850 with the same pagination except that Volume 16 is misnumbered 161. All the volumes were in blue wrappers.

"Le vicomte de Bragelonne, ou dix ans plus tard", suite de "Trois mousquetaires" et de "Vingt ans après". Par Alexandre Dumas. Paris, Michel Lévy frères, 1848-1850, 8vo., 26 volumes. Pagination : 322, 326, 326, 308 (all with an additional unnumbered page table of con- tents), 324 (including table of contents), 318, 317 (both with an additional unnumbered page table of contents), 312 (including table of contents), 306 (and additional unnumbered page table of contents), 320 (including table of contents), 317, 301, 318 (all with an addition- al unnumbered page table of contents), 312 (including table of con- tents), 305 (an additional unnumbered page table of contents), 328

(including table of contents), 305, 317 (both with an additional unnumbered page table of contents), 308 (including table of contents),
299 (with an additional unnumbered page table of contents), 308 (including table of contents), 305, 300, 277, 292 and 292 (all with an
additional unnumbered page table of contents.) "Le vicomte de Bragelonne" ends on page 178 of Volume 26 and is followed by "Histoire
contemporaine" pp. (179)-292. Yellow wrappers. Impr. de E. Dépée,
a Sceaux.
The individual years of publication of the 26 volumes cannot be given
because the Bibliothèque Nationale copy is lacking Volumes 11 and 12,
and the pagination is taken from Talvart et Place who do not supply
this break-down.

"Histoire contemporaine" is a reissue of Dumas' "Révélations sur
l'arrestation d'Emile Thomas".

Oeuvres de Alex. Dumas. Tome dixième. (Vignette) Bruxelles, Meline,
Cans et compagnie, 1850, large 8vo. "Le vicomte de Bragelonne".

"Le vicomte de Bragelonne : ou, dix ans plus tard", complément des
"Trois mousquetaires" et de "Vingt ans après", par Alexandre Dumas.
Nouvelle édition. Paris, Michel Lévy frères, 1851, 12mo., 6 volumes,
pp. 351, 344, 352, 356, 348 and 330, each with additional unnumbered
pages table of contents.
Frequently reprinted, sometimes in 3 volumes, in the same format and
with varying paginations by both Michel Lévy frères and Calmann-Lévy.

"Le vicomte de Bragelonne", par Alexandre Dumas. Bruxelles, Librairie
du Panthéon, 1851, 18mo., 25 volumes, pp. 146, 135, 135, 136, 131, 141,
134, 126, 125, 128, 140, 125, 125, 128, 126, 130, 129, 144, 143, 151,
139, 142, 132, 148 and 160.

"Les trois mousquetaires" suivi de "Vingt ans après" et du "Vicomte
de Bragelonne", par Alex. Dumas. Bruxelles, Livourne, Meline, Cans
et compagnie, 1851, 4to., of which "Vicomte de Bragelonne" together
with "Vingt ans après" occupies pp. (297)-675 in double columns, with
2 additional unnumbered pages table of contents.

"Le vicomte de Bragelonne", par Alexandre Dumas. Paris, Dufour et
Mulat, 1851, 4to., 2 volumes. Pagination : Volume 1, 548 (the last
page misnumbered 545) with 33 illustrations by Philippoteaux and Piaud
engraved by Léchard, Piaud, Pouget and Trichon; Volume 2, 556 and
'Placement des gravures', with 25 illustrations by the same artists
and engravers. The frontispiece of each volume is on steel and the
others are woodcuts. This is the first illustrated edition, having
been published originally in 70 parts in pink wrappers.

Ibid   Paris, Dufour, Mulat et Boulanger, 1851, same format and pagination as the preceding edition and with the same illustrations.
Reprinted, same format, pagination and illustrations, 1853.

"Le vicomte de Bragelonne" par Alexandre Dumas publié par Dufour et
Mulat édition illustrée par J.-A. Beaucé, Philippoteaux, etc. (Vignette) Paris chez Marescq et Cie, libraires, ... 1852, 4to., pp.
(1)-479 in double columns, unnumbered table of contents on verso of
last page; numerous illustrations throughout the text.
Reprinted, same format, pagination and illustrations, 1853.

"Le vicomte de Bragelonne", complément des "Trois mousquetaires" et de "Vingt ans après" par Alexandre Dumas. Paris, Michel Lévy frères, n.d. (1852), 4to., pp. 549 in double columns, and additional unnumbered page table of contents. Caption title. Woodcut at head of title. Musée littéraire du siècle.

Le siècle. "Les Mousquetaires" trilogie par Alexandre Dumas. Troisième partie. "Le vicomte de Bragelonne". Paris, au bureau du Siècle, 1854, 4to., pp. 486 in double columns, and 2 unnumbered pages table of contents.

Alexandre Dumas. "Le vicomte de Bragelonne". Complément des "Trois mousquetaires" et de "Vingt ans après". Seule édition complète publiée dans ce format. Paris, Michel Lévy frères, 1854, pp. 486 in double columns, and 2 unnumbered pages table of contents.

"Le vicomte de Bragelonne", par Alexandre Dumas. Paris, Lécrivain et Toubon, n.d. (1861), 4to., pp. 480 in double columns; illustrated.

"D'Artagnan le mousquetaire, sa vie aventureuse, ses duels ... " par Alexandre Dumas. Paris, S. Raçon et Cie., n.d. (1860), 4to., pp. 80 in double columns. Caption title. (According to the New York Public Library this appears to be a series of extracts from "Le vicomte de Bragelonne".)

"Le vicomte de Bragelonne", par Alexandre Dumas. Paris, Legrand et Crouzet, n.d. (1872), 4to., pp. 480 in double columns; illustrated.

Ibid   Paris, Librairie illustrée, n.d. (1876), large 8vo., pp. 811; illustrated and with a frontispiece portrait of Dumas.

"Le vicomte de Bragelonne", complément des "Trois mousquetaires" et de "Vingt ans après" par Alexandre Dumas. Paris, Calmann-Lévy, 1874, 4to., 2 volumes. Pagination : 289 and 261 in double columns, each with an additional unnumbered page table of contents. Caption titles. Woodcuts at head of titles. Buff wrappers repeating woodcuts.
Often reprinted, same format and pagination, up to and including 1895.

Alexandre Dumas "Les trois mousquetaires" "Vingt ans après" Paris Jules Rouff et Cie., éditeurs ... . (Propriété Calmann-Lévy), n.d. (1887-1891). Second title-page, illustrated. 4to., 2 volumes. "Les trois mousquetaires", pp. (1)-629. Deuxième partie "Vingt ans après", pp. (630)-1164 continued into Volume 2 pp. (1165)-1435; "Le vicomte de Bragelonne", pp. (1436)-2328; each volume with 4 unnumbered pages table of contents; illustrated.
Reprinted, same format, pagination and illustrations, n.d. (1893-1895).

Alexandre Dumas. "Le vicomte de Bragelonne". Illustré par G. Staal, J.-A. Beaucé, etc. Paris, Calmann-Lévy, 1897, 4to., pp. 479 in double columns, table of contents on verso of final page.

Pitt Press Series. "La fortune de d'Artagnan" an episode from "Le vicomte de Bragelonne" by Alexandre Dumas. With introduction ... edited by Arthur R. Ropes, M.A. ... . Stereotyped edition. Cambridge: at the University Press, 1898, 12mo., pp. (vii)-viii 'Contents', (ix)-xvi 'Introduction', (1)-182 "La fortune de d'Artagnan", (183)-344 'Notes, etc.'.

"Le vicomte de Bragelonne", par Alexandre Dumas; illustré par G. Staal, J.-A. Beaucé, etc. ... Paris, Calmann-Lévy, n.d. (c 1899), 4to., 3 volumes.

"DE PARIS A CADIX"   1847 -

By 1846 Dumas was at the height of his fame, but worn out through overwork. Fortuitously in October of that year he was invited to attend the duc de Montpensier's wedding to the Spanish Infanta in Madrid on the 10th of the month. On 3rd October he travelled south with his son, Louis Boulanger the painter, and Auguste Maquet. Two months were spent in Spain and the literary outcome of his travels was this work written in the form of letters to an unknown woman; Glinel has suggested that she was Suzanne Brohan. The work first appeared serially in 'La Presse'.

Original edition.
"Impressions de voyage. De Paris à Cadix" par Alexandre Dumas. Paris.
Ancienne maison Delloye, Garnier frères, 1847-1848, 8vo., 5 volumes.
Pagination : Volumes 1-4 (1847), 346, 303, 300 and 300; Volume 5 (1848), 261. Yellow wrappers.

"Un combat de taureaux", pp. 414-424. Signed : Alexandre Dumas.
In : 'L'Echo des feuilletons Choix de nouvelles, épisodes, anec-dotes, extraits de la Presse contemporaine'. Paris, 1847, large 8vo.
('Extrait des lettres sur "L'Espagne et l'Afrique", i.e. "Impressions de voyage. De Paris à Cadix".')
Reprinted, same format and pagination : Dufour, Mulat et Boulanger, 1857, and in : 'L'Echo des feuilletons ...', 1862.

"De Paris à Cadix", par Alexandre Dumas. Bruxelles, Meline, Cans et compagnie, 1847 and 1849, 18mo., 4 volumes. Pagination : Volumes 1 and 2 (1847), 251 and 220; Volumes 3 and 4, (1849), 288 and 276.
Pale green wrappers.

Ibid   La Haye, chez les heritiers Doorman, 1847 and 1849, same format and pagination as the preceding edition.

"De Paris a Cadix" par Alexandre Dumas. Bruxelles, Livourne, Meline, Cans et compagnie; Leipzig, J.P. Meline, 1847 and 1849, same format and pagination as the preceding editions. Pale blue wrappers.

"L'Espagne, le Maroc et L'Algérie" par Alexandre Dumas. (Vignette) Bruxelles, Alph. Lebègue, 1848-1849, 18mo., 4 volumes. Pagination : Volumes 1 and 2 (1848), 148 and 111; Volumes 3 and 4 (1849), 156 and 148. Green wrappers. Muséum littéraire.

Ibid   (No vignette) Bruxelles, Alphonse Lebègue, 1848-1849, same format and paginations the preceding edition.
(Despite the misleading title these are printings of "De Paris à Cadix".)

"Impressions de voyage. De Paris a Càdix", par Alexandre Dumas.
Paris, Michel Lévy frères, 1854, 12mo., 2 volumes, pp. 306 and 305.
Frequently reprinted, same format and pagination, by both Michel Lévy frères and Calmann-Lévy.

Le Siècle. Oeuvres complètes d'Alexandre Dumas. Dixième série. "Im-pressions de voyage. De Paris à Cadix". Paris, au bureau du Siècle, n.d. (c 1855), 4to., pp. (193)-319 in double columns.

"Impressions de voyage. De Paris à Cadix, par Alexandre Dumas.
Paris, Michel Lévy frères, n.d. (c 186), same format and pagination as the preceding edition. Caption title. Woodcut at head of title.
Musée littéraire du siècle.

"HAMLET, PRINCE DE DANEMARK"   1848

Based on Shakespeare's play this work by Dumas and Paul Meurice
is included in the collected editions of both men. Liberties have
been taken with Shakespeare's text, most notably in the ending. For
twenty years it remained the standard text for stage presentation in
France. Gautier in his "Art dramatique en France ... " states that
before its first performance at the Théâtre Historique it had been
played at the theatre in Saint-Germain-en-Laye. The play was revived
in 1886 at the Théâtre Français, and in that year and the four following it was performed more than one hundred times.

Original edition.
"Hamlet, prince de Danemark". (Shakspeare's (sic) "Hamlet Prince of
Denmark".) drame en cinq actes et huit parties, en vers, par MM.
Alexandre Dumas et Paul Meurice, représenté pour la première fois,
a Paris, sur le Théâtre-historique, le 15 décembre 1847. Paris,
Michel Lévy frères, 1848, 12mo., caption title followed by 'distribu-
tion de la pièce', pp. 106 and 2 unnumbered pages advertising 'oeuvres
complètes d'Alexandre Dumas, format de la bibliothèque Charpentier'
Yellow wrappers : bibliothèque dramatique Théâtre moderne. - 2^e
série. Imprimerie Dondey-Dupré.

Shakspeare (sic). "Hamlet, prince de Danemark", étude en 5 actes,
en vers, sur le drame de Shakspeare, par MM. Alexandre Dumas et Paul
Meurice. Paris, Théâtre Historique, le 15 décembre 1847. Edition
accompagnée d'une notice historique sur W. Shakspeare, (sic) et la
traduction textuelle, en prose, de l'oeuvre originale, par M. Benjamin Laroche ... . Paris, bureaux du Siècle, n.d. (1850), 4to.,
pp. (177)-259.
There were three reprintings in (1863), (1866), and (1867).

"Hamlet, prince de Danemark", drame en vers en 5 actes et 8 parties,
par MM. Alex. Dumas et Paul Meurice, représenté pour la première
fois, a Paris, sur le Théâtre historique, le 15 décembre 1847. Paris,
Michel Lévy frères, 1853, folio, pp. (1)-31 in double columns. Caption title. Woodcut at head of title. Théâtre contemporain illustré.
No. 18.
There were at least three reprintings in (1863), (1866) and (1868).

"Hamlet prince de Danemark" (Shakspeare's (sic) "Hamlet, prince
of Denmark") drame en cinq actes (huit parties), en vers par Alexandre Dumas en société avec M. Paul Meurice. Théâtre-Historique. -
15 décembre 1847. Paris, Michel Lévy frères, 1865, 12mo., pp. 154.

Ibid   "Distribution" on title-page, pp. 168-268.
Théâtre complete de Alex. Dumas Tome XI Paris Calmann Lévy, éditeur
ancienne maison Michel Lévy frères, 1874. 12mo. "Théâtre complet"
in 25 volumes.

Alexandre Dumas - Paul Meurice "Hamlet prince de Danemark" (Shakespeare's "Hamlet, prince of Denmark") drame en cinq actes, en vers.
Paris Calmann Lévy, éditeur 1886, 12mo.; pagination : unnumbered
page following title-page 'personnages' 'acteurs' (Théâtre Historique
1847. Comédie-Française 1886). verso blank, (1)-154. Half-title :
"Hamlet prince de Danemark" drame Représenté pour la première fois
à Paris, sur le Théâtre-Historique, le 15 décembre 1847 Repris à la
Comédie-Française le 28 septembre 1886. Bourloton - Imprimeries
réunies, B, rue Mignon, 2.

Of this edition there was a limited issue of 1 copy on 'papier
hollande' and 15 on 'papier japonnais'.

Ibid   Paris, Calmann Lévy, éditeur 1896, 8vo.; pagination
: unnumbered page following title-page 'personages' 'acteurs'
(Théâtre-Historique 1847. Comédie-Française, 1886, 1896), verso blank,
(7)-151. Half-title : "Hamlet prince de Danemark drame Représenté
pour la première fois à Paris, sur le Théatre-Historique, le 15 décembre 1847. Repris à la Comédie-Française le 28 septembre 1886. Verso
of half-title : oeuvres de Paul Meurice .... Printed on 'papier
japonnaise'. Stiff yellow wrappers : Théatre de Paul Meurice "Hamlet prince de Danemark". Lib-Imp. réunies, 7, rue Saint-Benoit,
Paris.

There was an opera drawn from the play :

"Hamlet" opéra on cinq actes paroles de MM. Michel Carré et Jules
Barbier d'après Shakespeare c'est-à-dire, d'après la version française d'Alexandre Dumas. Musique d'Ambroise Thomas. Première pré-
sentation à Paris sur l'Opéra, 9 février 1868. Paris, Michel Lévy
frères. 1868. 12mo., pp. 60.

"Etude sur Hamlet et sur W. Shakspeare" (sic), par Alexandre Dumas.
Paris, Michel Lévy frères, 1867, 4to., pp. 16.
This is a reprint of the article "Hamlet" which was published in 'Le
Monte-Cristo' on 21st, 28th May, and 4th June, 1857.

"LE VELOCE, OU TANGER, ALGER ET TUNIS"   1848 -
        This work is really a continuation of "De Paris à Cadix". The
background to it is that in 1846 the Minister of Public Instruction
was M. le comte de Salvandy; he was most anxious that his fellow
countrymen should be better informed about North Africa, and Algeria
in particular. He accordingly arranged for Dumas, before he left for
Madrid, to continue his journey from Cadiz and to write a narrative
of his travels. To assist him he arranged for the corvette "Le
Véloce" to await him at that port. This rather high-handed action
led to a heated debate in the Chamber of Deputies. The actual journey
lasted from near the end of November, 1846, to the beginning of January, 1847. The work was never published as a serial.

Original edition.
"Le Véloce, ou Tanger, Alger et Tunis" par Alexandre Dumas. Ouvrage
entièrement inédit. Paris, Alexandre Cadot, Bertonnet, 1848-1851,
8vo., 4 volumes. Pagination : Volume 1, (Vignette on title-page of
'Le Véloce') pp. 362 and unnumbered page table of contents; frontispiece by L. Boulanger engraved on steel by Ch. Geoffroy, 3 plates
hors-texte and woodcuts by Giraud engraved by Montigneul; Volume 2,
(No vignette) but dedicatory page to S.A.R. monseigneur le duc de
Montpensier, pp. 329 and unnumbered page table of contents; no plates,
but vignettes; Volume 3, (No vignette), pp. 308 and unnumbered page
table of contents; 1 plate engraved on steel and 1 woodcut, vignettes;
Volume 4, (No vignette), pp. 342 and unnumbered page table of contents; 1 plate hors-texte by Giraud engraved on steel by Geoffroy

and 1 woodcut, vignettes. Illustrated wrappers. Typ. Schneider, et Sceaux, impr. E. Dépée.

Ibid   Ouvrage entièrement inédit. Paris, Alexandre Cadot, éditeur Bertonnet, éditeur, 1848-1851, same format and pagination as the preceding but limited to a very few copies on fine light blue paper.

"Le véloce ou Tanger, Alger at Tunis" par Alexandre Dumas. Bruxelles, Meline, Cans et compagnie, 1849-1851, 18mo., 4 volumes. Pagination : Volume 1 (1849), (xiv) 'Préface' of 14 lines signed : Alexandre Dumas, (5)-295; Volume 2 (1849), i dedication 'A son altesse royale Monseigneur le duc de Montpensier' of 7 lines signed : Alexandre Dumas, 24 février 1849, (iii) 'Sidi-Ibrahim', (5)-284; Volume 3 (1851), (i) 'Le tombeau de Saint-Louis', (3)-267; Volume 4 (1851), (i) 'Le général Dedeau', (3)-304.

Ibid   La Haye, chez les héritiers Doorman, 1849-1851, same format and pagination as the preceding edition.

Ibid   Bruxelles, Livourne, Meline, Cans et compagnie; Leipzig, J.P. Meline, 1848-1851, same format and pagination as the preceding editions.

"Le Véloce ou Tanger, Alger et Tunis". Par Alexandre Dumas. (Vignette) Bruxelles, Alp. Lebegue, 1849-1851, 18mo., 4 volumes. Pagination : Volumes 1 and 2 (1849), (1)-(5), 6-141 and (1)-(5), 6-136; Volumes 3 and 4 (1851), (1)-(5), 6-128 and (1)-(5), 6-149, Green wrappers. Muséum littéraire.

Ibid   (Including the Lebègue vignette) Bruxelles, Librairie de Ch. Muquardt, même maison a Leipzig et a Gand, 1849-1851, same format and pagination as the preceding edition.

Le Siècle. Oeuvres complètes d'Alexandre Dumas. Dixième série. "Impressions de voyage. Le Véloce, ou Tanger, Alger et Tunis". Paris, au bureau du Siècle, n.d. (c 1855), 4to., pp. (321)-445 in double columns and unnumbered page table of contents.

"Impressions de voyage. Le Véloce" par Alexandre Dumas. Paris, Michel Lévy frères, 1861, 12mo., 2 volumes, pp. 303 and 294, each with an additional unnumbered page table of contents.
Frequently reprinted, same format and pagination, by both Michel Lévy frères and Calmann-Lévy.

Ibid   Paris, Michel Lévy frères, n.d. (c 186), 4to. Musée littéraire contemporain.

"MONTE-CRISTO" : "LE COMTE DE MORCERF" : "VILLEFORT" 1848 & 1851

For continuity's sake the two later plays, "Le comte de Morcerf" and "Villefort", are included here. As will be seen "Monte-Cristo" itself required two evenings for its performance, and it was originally intended that this particular play should be the opening attraction for the Théâtre Historique. Dumas, however, changed his mind and substituted "La reine Margot". All three plays were written in collaboration with Maquet. Some details in the romance were altered to meet the needs of a stage production.

Original editions.
N. Tresse, éditeur. "Monte-Cristo" drame en cinq actes et onze tableaux, de MM. Alexandre Dumas et Auguste Maquet, musique de MM. Warney (sic), Stoepel et Mangeant; Décors de MM. Cambon, Thiery, Sechan, Dieterle, Desplechin et Lechavellier. Costumes dessinés par MM. Gavarni, Louis Lassalle et Giraud. Machines de M. Adolphe Pierart. Costumes exécutés par M. Ferdinand et Mlle. Philis. Représenté pour la première fois, a Paris, sur le Théatre-Historique, le 3 février 1848. Première soirée. Caption title. Yellow wrappers : Magasin théatral pièces anciennes et modernes jouées sur les théatres de Paris. (Vignette) Paris, Barbré, n.d. (1848), 8vo., pp. 48 in double columns.

Ibid   Paris, N. Tresse, 1878, same format and pagination as the preceding edition. La France dramatique au XIXe siècle. Imprimerie de Boulé.

N. Tresse, éditeur. "Monte-Cristo" drame en cinq actes et six tableaux. ... . Représenté pour la première fois, a Paris, sur le Théatre-Historique, le 4 février 1848. Deuxième soirée. Caption title. Blue wrappers : Magasin théatral pièces anciennes et modernes jouées sur les théatres de Paris. (Vignette) Paris, N. Tresse, 1848, 8vo., pp. (49)-87 in double columns.

Ibid   Paris, N. Tresse, 1878, same format and pagination as the preceding edition. La France dramatique au XIXe siècle. Imprimerie de Boulé.

"Le comte de Morcerf" drame en cinq actes et dix tableaux, de MM. Alexandre Dumas et Auguste Maquet. Représenté pour la première fois, à Paris, sur le théatre de l'Ambigu-Comique, le 1er· avril 1851. 3e partie de "Monte-Cristo". Paris, imprimerie de Dubuisson et Ce., n.d. (1851), 8vo., pp. (89)-138 in double columns. Caption title.

"Villefort" drame en cinq actes et dix tableaux, de MM. Alexandre Dumas et Auguste Maquet. Représenté pour la première fois, à Paris, sur le théatre de l'Ambigu-Comique, le 8 mai 1851. 4e partie de "Monte-Cristo". Paris, imprimerie de Dubuisson, n.d. (1851), 8vo., pp. (139)-197 in double columns. Caption title.

"Monte-Cristo" drame en 5 actes et 11 tableaux, de MM. Alex. Dumas et Aug. Maquet, musique de MM. Varney, Stoepel et Mangeant. Représenté pour la première fois, à Paris, sur le Théatre-Historique, le 3 février 1848. Première soirée. Bruxelles, J.-A. Lelong, 1848, 18mo., pp. 139. Blue wrappers. Répertoire de la scène française. 16me année. No. 10.

"Monte-Cristo" drame en 5 actes et 6 tableaux, de MM. Alex. Dumas et Aug. Maquet, musique de M. Varney, ..., ... Représenté pour la première fois, à Paris, sur le Théatre-Comique, le 4 février 1848. Bruxelles, J.-A. Lelong, 1848, 18mo., pp. (143)-244. Blue wrappers. Répertoire de la scène française. 16me année. No. 11.

"Le comte de Morcerf" drame en cinq actes et dix tableaux, par Alex. Dumas et A. Maquet. Représenté pour la première fois, à Paris, sur le théatre de l'Ambigue-Comique, le 1er avril 1851. Troisième partie de "Monte-Cristo". Bruxelles, J.-A. Lelong, 1851, 18mo., pp. 150.

"Villefort" drame en cinq actes et dix tableaux, par MM. A. Dumas et A. Maquet. Représenté pour la première fois, à Paris, sur le théatre de l'Ambigu-Comique, le 8 mai 1851. Quatrième partie de "Monte-Cristo" Bruxelles, J.-A. Lelong, 1851, 18mo., pp. 176,

"Monte-Cristo" (première partie) drame en cinq actes, en onze tableaux en société avec M. Auguste Maquet Théâtre-Historique. - 3 février 1848. "Distribution" on title-page, pp. 2-132. Théatre complet de Alex. Dumas Tome XII Paris Calmann Lévy, éditeur ancienne maison Michel Lévy frères, 1874. 12mo. "Théatre complet" in 25 volumes.

"Monte-Cristo" (deuxième partie) drame en cinq actes, en six tableaux en société avec M. Auguste Maquet Théâtre-Historique. - 4 février 1848. "Distribution" on title-page, pp. 134-234. Théatre complet de Alex. Dumas Tome XII Paris Calmann Lévy, éditeur ancienne maison Michel Lévy frères, 1874. 12mo. "Théatre complet" in 25 volumes.

"Le comte de Morcerf" (troisième partie de "Monte-Cristo") drame en cinq actes, en dix tableaux en société avec M. Auguste Maquet Ambigu-Comique. - ler. avril 1851. "Distribution" on title-page, pp. 2-122. Théatre complet de Alex. Dumas Tome XIII Paris Calmann Lévy, éditeur ancienne maison Michel Lévy frères, 1874. 12mo. "Théatre complet" in 25 volumes.

"Villefort" (quatrième partie de "Monte-Cristo") drame en cinq actes, en dix tableaux en société avec M. Auguste Maquet Ambigu-Comique. - 8 mai 1851. "Distribution" on title-page, pp. 124-267. Théatre complet de Alex. Dumas Tome XIII Paris Calmann Lévy, éditeur ancienne maison Michel Lévy frères, 1874. 12mo. "Théatre complet" in 25 volumes.

Alexandre Dumas et Auguste Maquet. "Monte-Cristo", drame en cinq actes, quinze tableaux. Paris, Calmann-Lévy, 1894, 12mo., pp. 195. Described as the 'Version nouvelle et définitive comprenant les quatre soirées'. First performed at the Théâtre de la Porte-Saint-Martin, le 15 mars 1894.

"Monte-Cristo" (première partie) drame en cinq actes, et onze tableaux en société avec Alexandre Dumas Théâtre-Historique. - 3 février 1848. "Distribution" on title-page, pp. 2-132. Théatre complet de Auguste Maquet Tome II Paris Calmann Lévy, éditeur rue Auber, 3, et boulevard des Italiens, 15 a la librairie nouvelle 1897 12mo. "Théatre" in 4 volumes.

"Monte-Cristo" (deuxième partie) drame en cinq actes, en six tableaux en société avec M. Auguste Maquet (sic) Théâtre-Historique. - 4 février 1848. "Distribution" on title-page, pp. 134-234. Théatre complet de Auguste Maquet Tome II Paris Calmann Lévy, éditeur rue Auber, 3, et boulevard des Italiens, 15 a la librairie nouvelle 1897 12mo. "Théatre" in 4 volumes.

There was one parody, and it has the peculiar distinction of having been written nearly a year previous to the first performance of "Monte-Cristo"; it was based on the romance.
"Le comte de Monte-Fiasco, ou la Répétition générals d'un drame en trente actes et cent tableaux", par MM. Deforges et Clairville. Paris, Delacombe, 1847, 8vo.

During 1848 Dumas was heavily engaged in political affairs, and his "Révélations sur l'arrestation d'Emile Thomas" bears at least one witness to this. Miscellaneous material was written for political periodicals, and he wrote electoral addresses. But he did not succeed in being elected to the Chamber of Deputies.

The following is a very brief list of such material, all of which
can be found in L.-Henry Lecomte's "Alexandre Dumas 1802-1870 Sa
Vie intime Ses Oeuvres" (Paris, J. Tallandier, Editeur, n.d. (1902).);
the relevant pagination is given in each instance.

"A la garde nationale". The National Guard in question was that of
Saint-Germain-en-Laye, and is dated from there 'le 27 février 1848'.
(Lecomte, pp. 189-190).

"Aux travailleurs". This electoral address, dated 'mars 1848', sets
out details of the amount of work he has accomplished and the amounts
that have been earned as a result by printers, bookbinders, actors,
musicians, etc. (Lecomte, pp. 191-192; and also Claretie's article
'Alexandre Dumas, homme politique' in 'La nouvelle revue', 1881,
No. VIII, pp. 405-407.)

"Aux pasteurs d'âmes parisiens". Dumas' appeal to the curés of Paris
because of his loyalty to the Christian faith and the Church. (Lecomte, pp. 192-193.)

"A messieurs les électeurs de la Gironde". An open letter in which
he states that he had intended offering himself as a candidate for
the Gironde, but having learned that Thiers and Girardin were to
stand he would withdraw in their favour. It is dated '28 mai'.
(Lecomte, pp. 193-194.)

"A ses concitoyens de Seine-et-Oise, Alexandre Dumas, candidat à la
représentation nationale". Paris, Impr. E. Brière, 1848, 8vo., pp.
13. The text may also be read in H. Hostein's "Historiettes et
souvenirs d'un homme de théâtre" (Paris, E. Dentu, 1878, pp. 281-
311.)

"Aux électeurs de l'Yonne". Dumas made two appeals to the Yonne elec-
tors, the first on the 29th June, 1848, and the second some four
months later. (Lecomte, pp. 194-195, and 195-197.)

"A M. Emile Barrault à propos de sa lettre à M. Lamartine". Signed
: Alex. Dumas. Paris, au bureau de 'Le France nouvelle'. Impr. de
E. Briere, n.d. (1848), folio, pp. 2 in treble columns. This provoked
a reply :

"Réponse à M. Alexandre Dumas, à propos de sa lettre à M.E. Barrault,
sur M. Lamartine". Signed : Louvet. Seemingly Barrault had attacked
Dumas' friend Lamartine and in defending him he had, in turn, attacked
the 'Saint-Simoniens' to whom Barrault was at least sympathetically
inclined.

"LA FRANCE NOUVELLE ... ... "   1848

    Early in 1848 Dumas wrote a letter to the chief editor of the
journal 'La Liberté' protesting against the law of exile. The letter
was not accepted for publication, but was later published by 'L'Assem-
blée Nationale' and again, by Dumas himself, in the issue for the 1st
November, 1849, of his own journal 'Le Mois'. On the face of it, and
this may be purely conjectural, this particular letter may have lead
Dumas to become ultimately rédacteur-en-chef of "La France nouvelle
... ... ", the contents of which were almost solely political, although
occasionally some foreign news was published. The journal's life was
brief; 30 numbers in all were published, more or less regularly, in

issues each of 4 pages printed in four columns. The pages measured
43 x 30 centimetres. In it Dumas published "Révélations sur l'arrestation d'Emile Thomas" as well as starting the reissue in feuilleton
form of "Les trois mousquetaires".

The dates of publication of 'La Presse du Dimanche Réunie.' "La
France Nouvelle journal politique et littéraire" during the period of
its existance in 1848 were as follows :

Numéro 1 Samedi, 20 mai.
2 Dimanche, 21 mai.
3 Mardi, 23 mai.
4 Mercredi, 24 mai.
5 Jeudi, 25 mai.
6 Vendredi, 26 mai.
7 Samedi, 27 mai.
8 Dimanche, 28 mai.
9 Lundi et Mardi, 29
   et 30 mai.
10 Mercredi, 31 mai.
11 Jeudi, 1 juin.
The issue for the 1st June is the
first to state under the journal's
title : 'M. Alexandre Dumas,
rédacteur-en-chef'.
12 Samedi, 3 juin.
13 Dimanche, 4 juin.

14 Mardi, 6 juin.
15 Mercredi, 7 juin.
16 Jeudi, 8 juin.
17 Vendredi, 9 juin.
18 Samedi, 10 juin.
19 Dimanche, 11 juin.
20 Mardi, 13 juin.
21 Mercredi, 14 juin.
22 Jeudi, 15 juin.
23 Vendredi, 16 juin.
24 Samedi, 17 juin.
25 Dimanche, 18 juin.
26 Mardi, 20 juin.
27 Mercredi, 21 juin.
28 Jeudi, 22 juin.
29 Vendredi, 23 juin.
30 Samedi, 30 juin.

"LE MOIS"   1848-1850

This journal was the most important of Dumas' purely political
ventures. It can properly be compared only with his "L'Indipendente.
L'Indépendant" which appeared between 1860 and 1864 when he was closely
connected with Garibaldi. The sub-title of "Le Mois" stated that it
was a 'Revue historique et politique De tous les événements qui se
produisent en France et à l'étranger depuis Février 1848', although
sub-titles varied slightly in some instances. The arrangement of the
journal is largely that of a diary, and it was entirely written by
Dumas. By the end of 1848 the paper had 20,000 subscribers, and this
despite the fact that it contained no 'causeries' or feuilletons
except for the two final numbers for 1850, each of which started with
9 and 6 pages respectively of the first two chapters of his "Montevideo, ou une nouvelle Troie".

Publication ceased abruptly with no indication in the final
number for 1st February, 1850, that that would be the last issue.
There are two possible reasons for the sudden termination - the tur-
moil of events following February, 1848, was dying out and politics
could be of less interest to the Parisian public, but possibly more
important was that Dumas' Théâtre-Historique (like many other theatres
in Paris) was having serious financial trouble. It may well be that
Dumas found it financially impossible to continue publishing his paper.

The format was large 8vo., 32 pages to each number, and printed
in two columns. As will be seen it was published irregularly, and in
several of the later issues Dumas apologised to his subscribers for
its erratic appearance from the press. Subscription was 75 centimes
per single number, or 4 francs per annum.

No.	1 Mars	1848	No.	14 1 Février	1849
	2 Avril	1848		15 1 Mars	1849
	3 16 Mai	1848		16 1 Avril	1849
	4 31 Mai	1848		17 1 Mai	1849
	5 16 Juin	1848		18 1 Juin	1849
	6 30 Juin	1848		19 1 Juillet	1849
	7 16 Juillet	1848		20 1 Août	1849
	8 31 Juillet	1848		21 1 Septembre	1849
	9 31 Août	1848		22 1 Octobre	1849
	10 15 Septembre	1848		23 1 Novembre	1849
	11 15 Octobre	1848		24 1 Décembre	1849
	12 30 Novembre	1848		25 1 Janvier	1850
	13 1 Janvier	1849		26 1 Février	1850

The issue for December, 1849, contained 'Table of contents' for the 23 preceding numbers.

At the end of each of the first two years an annual volume was issued consisting of the 12 numbers bound in a buff wrapper, the last page of which printed a notice to subscribers of future plans, together with the announcement of a new portrait of the editor which was, in fact, bound in with the annual number for 1849.

"REVELATIONS SUR L'ARRESTATION D'EMILE THOMAS"   1848

This pamphlet throws an interesting light on the political and social disorder in 1848. When the 'national workshops' were established as the result of the Revolution in that year Emile Thomas proposed a central bureau to regulate the many applications for work and bread. For no very explicit reason he was arrested, but later set free without any compensation or apology. Dumas, with his sense of right and justice, took up Thomas' case and wrote this pamphlet, complete with 'pièces justificatives'.

Original edition.
"Révélations sur l'arrestation d'Emile Thomas" par Alexandre Dumas suivi de pièces justificatives. (Quotation from Emile de Girardin.) Paris Michel Lévy frères, libraires-éditeurs des oeuvres d'Emile de Girardin, Rue Vivienne, 1. 1848. 12mo., pp. (3)-41; 'pièces justificatives' (42 - not numbered)-54. Brown wrappers. "Révélations sur l'arrestation d'Emile Thomas" par Alexandre Dumas Prix : 50 centimes. Paris Michel Lévy frères, libraires-éditeurs des oeuvres complètes d'Alexandre Dumas de la Bibliothèque dramatique et du Théâtre de Victor Hugo rue Vivienne, 1. Août 1848 Poissy. - Imprimerie de G. OLIVIER.

Under the title of "Histoire contemporaine" it was reissued to complete Volume 26 of the Michel Lévy frères, 1848-1850, edition of "Le vicomte de Bragelonne", there occupying pp. (179)-292.

"MARCEAU, OU LES ENFANTS DE LA REPUBLIQUE"   1848

Written by Anicet Bourgeois and Michel Masson the central idea of this prose drama was drawn from Dumas' "Blanche de Beaulieu, ou la rose rouge". Obviously a good deal of extraneous matter was added to Dumas' short story. Gautier in his "L'art dramatique en France" wrote : 'Voilà une pièce qui reflète encore les préoccupations du moment. Pourtant, elle n'a, au point de vue de l'art, rien de révolutionnaire; elle est jetée dans le vieux moule des mélodrames du boulevard, et n'avait pas besoin, pour être possible, de la chute d'une monarchie. ... La forme 'biographique' que ce drame affecte n'a jamais cependant exclu la touche du génie'.

It should be added that Dumas had nothing to do with the writing of the play but it should, nevertheless, because of its source be mentioned in this Bibliography.

Original (and only) edition.
"Marceau, ou les enfants de la République" Drame en cinq actes et dix tableaux par MM. Anicet Bourgeois et Michel Masson. Représenté, pour la première fois, à Paris, sur le Théâtre de la Gaité, le 22 juin 1848. Paris, Calmann Lévy, Editeur Ancienne maison Michel Lévy frères, n.d. (1863), 4to., pp. 24 in double columns. Caption title. Woodcut at head of title. Théâtre contemporain illustré.

"CATILINA"   1848
This play deals with the violent times in Rome between the civil wars in the declining years of the Republic. Although it was announced as being written by Dumas and Maquet, Blaze de Bury in his "Alexandre Dumas Sa vie, son temps, son oeuvre" (Paris, Calmann Lévy, 1885) wrote : 'Maintenant si quelqu'un m'interroge sur le collaborateur de la circonstance, je répondrai qu'il s'appelait Théodore Burette. C'était un aimable garcon, érudit et viveur, bon latiniste sans cuistrerie, ...'

Original edition.
"Catilina" drame en cinq actes et sept tableaux, par MM. Alexandre Dumas et Auguste Maquet, représenté, pour la première fois, a Paris, sur le Théatre Historique, le 14 octobre 1848. Caption title followed by 'distribution de la pièce' and the note : 'La musique est de M. Warney (sic). - s'adresser pour la mise en scène, à M. Caron, régisseur général du Théâtre Historique.' Green wrappers : Bibliothèque dramatique Théatre moderne. "Catilina" Drame en 5 actes et 7 tableaux, par MM. Alexandre Dumas et Auguste Maquet. Paris, Michel Lévy frères, 1848, 12mo., pp. 'avant-propos' unsigned and unnumbered on verso of caption title, 'prologue' pp. (3)-20 (page 4 unnumbered), 20-151. Imprimerie de Mme Ve Dondey-Dupré.

"Catilina" drame en cinq actes et sept tableaux, par MM. Alexandre Dumas et Auguste Maquet, représenté, pour la première fois, a Paris, sur le théatre historique, le 14 octobre 1848. La musique est de M. Warney (sic). - S'adresser pour la mise en scène, à M. Caron, régisseur général du Théâtre Historique. Paris, Imprimerie de Mme. Ve Dondey-Dupré, n.d. (c 1849), 8vo., pp. unsigned 'Avant-propos' on verso of title-page (unnumbered), (3)-151. Caption title.

"Catilina" drame en cinq actes et sept tableaux par MM. Alexandre Dumas et Auguste Maquet. Représenté pour la première fois, à Paris, sur le Théatre-historique, le 14 octobre 1848. Paris, Michel Lévy frères, n.d. (1854), 8vo., pp. 43 in double columns. Caption title. Woodcut at head of title. Théâtre contemporain illustré. No. 111. Reprinted, same format and pagination, n.d. (1861).

208

"Catalina" drame en cinq actes, en sept tableaux, dont un prologue
en société avec M. Auguste Maquet Théâtre-Historique. - 14 octobre
1848. "Distribution" on title-page, pp. 2-172. Théatre complet de
Alex. Dumas Tome XV Paris Calmann Lévy, éditeur ancienne maison
Michel Lévy frères, 1874. 12mo. "Théatre complet" in 25 volumes.

There was one parody of the play and I doubt whether it was ever
published :
"Catilina", un Pot pourri, par Romain Duclacoit (Jules Lantin).

"MOCQUET"   1849

During 1849 Dumas had worked almost unceasingly not only on
"Le vicomte de Bragelonne" but also on "Le collier de la reine" and
"Les mille et un fantômes". Towards the end of that year he was
very upset by his need to bring the first mentioned work to a close
for Porthos' death in the chapter 'La mort d'un Titan', and he abruptly stopped writing to go to Villers-Cotterets to be once again
among his boyhood friends. From there, on 19th December, he wrote
to Perrée, an editor of 'Le Siècle', apologising for the delay in
sending the final few feuilletons of the romance. However, he included
in his letter an account of a poacher he had known in his youth named
Mocquet who had been befriended by General Dumas. Conceivably this
could have been a sop to the subscribers to 'Le Siècle' for the interruption in the serial story, and with the one exception known to me,
and described below, this particular anecdote would seem to have been
printed only in that journal, there to remain buried until it was
translated and published as a supplement to a few very early American
translations of the romance.

The matter does not, however, end here for in 1864 Dumas wrote
an article entitled 'Le pays natal' for 'Le journal littéraire' in
which he gave a variation of the story of the Mocquet family.
Original separate edition from that published in 'Le Siècle'. Semaine
littéraire du Courrier des Etats-Unis. Receuil Choisi de romans,
feuilletons, ouvrages historiques et dramatiques, en prose et en vers,
des auteurs modernes les plus renommés. XVIII série - Volume 4. New-
York, F. Gaillardet, Bureau du Courrier des Etats-Unis, 1847 (sic).
"La vicomte de Bragelonne", (Suite des "Trois Mousquetaires" et de
"Vingt ans après".) Par Alexandre Dumas. 8vo., pp. (3)-289, Fin de
la sixième partie; (291)-839, Septième partie to the end of the work;
all in double columns. Followed by "Mocquet", pp. (841)-849 in double
columns, and dated 'Villers-Cotterets, 19 décembre 1849'.

"LA JEUNESSE DES MOUSQUETAIRES"   1849

Drawn by Dumas and Maquet from "Les trois mousquetaires" it is
curious that it was written four years later than the drama "Les mousquetaires" which was based on "Vinst ans après. In the prologue
Dumas has developed at greater length the young vicomte de Bragelonne's
courtship, with its accompanying tragedy. The epilogue deals with the
trial and (unseen) execution of Milady.

Parran, in his limited bibliography of Dumas, wrote : 'Un des
plus grands succès des auteurs et de l'acteur Mélingue, dans le rôle
d'Artagnan'.

Original edition.
"Le jeunesse des mousquetaires", pièce en quatorze tableaux, par MM.
Alexandre Dumas et A. Maquet. Représentée pour la première fois, à
Paris, sur le Théâtre-Historique, le 17 février 1849. Paris, Dufour
et Mulat, 1849, large 8vo., pp. 76 in double columns; 8 vignettes.
Buff wrappers repeating the title-page, except 'par M. Alexandre Dumas'
only.

"La jeunesse des mousquetaires" Pièce en 14 tableaux, par MM. Alexandre Dumas et Auguste Maquet. Représentée pour la première fois
sur le Théâtre-Historique, le 17 fevrier 1849. Caption title. Woodcut at head of title. Buff wrappers repeating caption title, except
'par M. Alexandre Dumas' only. Paris, Dufour et Mulat, 1849, large
8vo., pp. 76 in double columns. Frontispiece etching of Mme. Bonacieux; extra illustrated with 8 coloured plates of actors in the
principal roles (the illustrations are from the 'Galerie dramatique.
Théatre Historique!).
(The Bibliothèque de l'Arsenal holds another copy of this edition,
apparently a prompt copy annotated by a producer, with positions for
actors and stage furniture pasted in; it does not contain any illustrations.)

"La jeunesse des mousquetaires", pièce en quatorze tableaux, par MM.
Alex. Dumas et Aug. Maquet, Représentée pour la premiere fois, à
Paris, sur le Théâtre-Historique, le 17 février 1849. (Vignette)
Bruxelles, J.-A. Lelong, libraire des théâtres royaux, 1850, 18mo.,
pp. 'Personnages de la pièce' on verso of title-page, (3)-223. Yellow
wrappers : Répertoire de la scène française. 18ᵐᵉ' année. No. 12.

"La jeunesse des mousquetaires". Pièce en 14 tableaux; par MM. Alexandre Dumas et Auguste Maquet. Représentée pour la première fois sur
le Théâtre-Historique, le 17 février 1849. (Paris), n.d. (185),
large 8vo., pp. 76 in double columns. Caption title. Woodcut at
head of title. Engraved frontispiece of Mme. Bonacieux and 7 illustrations. Imprimerie Dondey-Dupré.

"La jeunesse des mousquetaires", drame en cinq actes, en douze tab-
leaux, avec prologue et épilogue, par Alex. Dumas et Aug. Maquet.
Nouvelle édition. Paris, Michel Lévy frères, 1864, 12mo., pp. 200.
(Théâtre-Historique, 17 février 1849; Porte-Saint-Martin, 26 novembre
1863.)
Reprinted, same format and pagination, (1866) and (1868).

Ibid   Paris, Michel Lévy frères, n.d. (187), folio,
pp. 56 in double columns. Caption title. Woodcut at head of title.

"La jeunesse des mousquetaires" drame en cinq actes, en douze tableaux
avec prologue et épilogue en société avec M. Auguste Maquet Théâtre-
Historique. - 17 fevrier 1849. "Distribution" on title-page and
page 2, pp. 2-200. Théatre complet de Alex. Dumas Tome XIV Paris
Calmann Lévy, éditeur ancienne maison Michel Lévy frères, 1874.
12mo. "Théatre complet" in 25 volumes.

"La jeunesse des mousquetaires". Drame en cinq actes, en douze tableaux avec prologue et épilogue par MM. Alexandre Dumas et Auguste
Maquet. Représentée pour la première fois, à Paris, sur le Théâtre-
Historique, le 17 février 1849, et repris sur le théâtre de la Porte-
Saint-Martin, le 26 novembre 1863. Paris, Calmann-Lévy, n.d. (188),
folio, pp. 56 in double columns. Caption title. Woodcut at head of
title.

210

"La jeunesse des mousquetaires" drame en cinq actes, en douze tableaus
avec prologue et épilogue en société avec Alexandre Dumas Théâtre-
historique. - 17 février 1849. "Distribution" on title-page and
page 2, pp. 2-200. Théatre de Auguste Maquet Paris Calmann Lévy,
éditeur rue Auber 3, et boulevard des Italiens, 15 a la librairie
nouvelle 1893 12mo. Theatre in 4 volumes.

"LES MILLE ET UN FANTOMES"   1849

This work comprises a collection of stories, all more or less
connected with the supernatural and occult, which originally included
"Les mariages du père Olifus", "Le testament de M. de Chauvelin" and
"La femme au collier de velours"; these three comparatively lengthy
stories are dealt with separately in this Bibliography. Thus this
leaves, in addition to the collection of stories now known as "Les
mille et un fantômes", in actual fact the chapters beginning with
'Une journée à Fontenay-aux-roses' (this bearing an alternative title
in some editions), with the shorter stories "Un diner chez Rossini",
which includes "Les deux étudiants de Bologne", "Les gentilhommes de
la Sierra-Morena" which has its latter part "Histoire de Don Bernardo
de Zuniga".

Despite Glinel and Parran who have credited Paul Bocage with
collaboration in the work it is much more likely that Paul Lacroix
('le bibliophile Jacob') had suggested to Dumas the available sources
from which he could draw his plots.

The work was dedicated to his friend and patron the duc de
Montpennier who, with other members of the Orléans family, had been
driven into exile in the previous year. It goes without saying that
this dedication was included only in the pirated editions, although
Dumas had bravely announced it in his journal 'Le Mois'. The work
also included a letter to Véron (and this was included in the editions
published in France) in whose journal 'Le Constitutionnel' it appeared
as a serial during 1849 and, possibly, into the very early weeks of
1850. It should be noted that in the pirated editions the whole
series is almost invariably issued under the general title of "Les
mille et un fantômes".

Original edition.
"Les mille et un fantômes", par Alexandre Dumas. Bruxelles, Meline,
Cans et Cie., 1849, 18mo., 3 volumes. Pagination : (1)-8 introductory letter to Véron, (9)-11 dedication to the duc de Montpensier,
verso blank, (13)-237 "Une journée a Fontenay-aux-Roses"; (1)-78 "Une
journée a Fontenay-aux-Roses" (suite), (79)-144 "Un diner chez Rossini",
followed by (145)-243 "Les gentilhommes de la Sierra-Morena"; (1)-326
"Les mariages du père Olifus". There are no tables of contents.

Ibid   La Haye, chez les héritiers Doorman, 1849, 3
volumes, same format and pagination as the preceding edition.

"Les mille et un fantômes" par Alexandre Dumas. Bruxelles, Livourne,
Meline, Cans et compagnie; Leipzig, J.P. Meline, 1849, 3 volumes,
same format and pagination as the preceding editions.

Ibid   Bruxelles, Livourne, Meline, Cans et compagnie;
Leipzig, J.P. Meline, 1849, 18mo., 4 volumes, Pagination : Volume
(1)-7 introductory letters to Véron, (9)-11 dedication to the duc de

Montpensier, (13)-180 "Une journée à Fontenay-aux-Roses"; Volume 2, (1)-76 "Une journée à Fontenay-aux-Roses" (suite), (77)-164 "Un diner chez Rossini"; Volume 3, (1)-26 "Un diner chex Rossini" (suite), (27)-149 "Les mariages du père Olifus"; Volume 4, pp. (1)-149, "Les mariages du père Olifus" (suite). Blue wrappers.

Ibid   Bruxelles, Ch. Muquardt, 1849, 18mo., 6 volumes, pp. 160, 157, 161, 156, 147 and 182, with 2 blank pages.

Ibid   (Vignette) Bruxelles et Leipzig, C. Muquardt (Volumes 4-6, Ch. Muquardt), 1849, 6 volumes, same format and pagination as the preceding edition.

"Les mille et un fantômes" par Alexandre Dumas. Bruxelles, Librairie de Tarride, 1849, 16mo., 8 volumes, pp. 140, 148, 136, 145, 136, 140, 135 and 141. Contents : Volume 1, "Une journée à Fontenay-aux-Roses; Volume 2, "Une journée à Fontenay-aux-Roses" (suite) ending on page 111, and followed by "Un diner chez Rossini" and "Les deux étudiants de Bologne"; Volume 3, "Les deux étudiants de Bologne" (suite) and followed by "Les gentilhommes de la Sierra-Morena" and "L'histoire merveilleuse de Don Dernardo de Zuniga", the remainder of the volume containing "Les mariages du père Olifus"; Volume 4, "Les mariages du père Olifus" (suite); Volume 5, "Les mariages du pere Olifus" (suite) ending on page 95, verso blank, (97)-136 "La testament de M. de Chauvelin"; Volume 6, "Le testament de M. de Chauvelin" (suite); Volumes 7 and 8, "La femme au collier de velours". Yellow wrappers. La nouveauté littéraire, chez Tarride.

"Les mille et un fantômes", par Alexandre Dumas. Bruxelles, Librairie Allemande, Française et Etrangère de Mayer et Flateau, 1849, 8 volumes, same format and pagination as the preceding edition.

Ibid   Paris, Alexandre Cadot, éditeur, 32 rue de la Harpe, 1849, 8vo., 2 volumes, pp. 318 and 309 each with an additional unnumbered page table of contents. Sceaux, impr. E. Dépée.

"Les mille et un fantômes" par Alexandre Dumas. Bruxelles, Alphonse Lebègue, 1849-1850, 18mo., 6 volumes. Pagination : Volumes 1-4 (1849), 160, 157, 161 and 156; Volume 5 (1850 - which could be a misprint), 147; Volume 6 (1849), 182. There are variant spellings of the publisher's first name - 'Alph', 'Alphonse' and 'Alp'. There are no separate titles to the component stories, but chapter-heads are given.

Ibid   Publiés par Dufour et Mulat. Edition illustrée par Andrieux et Ed. Coppin. (Vignette) Paris - 1852 chez Marescq et Cie., libraires ... . 4to., pp. (1)-3 'A M. ***' signed : Alexandre Dumas, (3)-96 all in double columns and comprising only "Une journée à Fontenay-aux-Roses".
Reprinted, same format and pagination, 1854.

"Les mille et un fantômes", par Alexandre Dumas. Paris, Vialat et Cie., 1854, same format, pagination and illustrations as the preceding edition. Impr. S. Raçon et Cie.

"Le Siècle. Oeuvres complètes d'Alexandre Dumas Quinzième série. "Les mille et un fantômes". Paris, au bureau du Siècle, n.d. (1859), 4to., pp. (225)-271, including table of contents, all in double columns.

"Les mille et un fantômes". Par Alexandre Dumas. Paris, Impr. de

Gaittet, 1861, same format, pagination and illustrations as the
Marescq et Cie., 1852, edition.

"Les mille et un fantômes" par Alexandre Dumas. Paris, Michel Lévy
frères, 1861, 12mo., pp. 237.
Several times reprinted, same format and pagination, by both Michel
Lévy frères and Calmann-Lévy.

Ibid   Paris, Michel Lévy frères, 1861, 4to., pp. 72 in
double columns Caption title. Woodcut at head of title.

Ibid   Edition illustrée par Andrieux et Ed. Coppin
Paris Calmann-Lévy, éditeur ancienne maison Michel Lévy frères,
1889, 4to., pp. 96 in double columns.
Several times reprinted, same format and pagination.

Alexandre Dumas "La peinture chez les anciens". ... "Les deux
étudiants" par Alexandre Dumas. Publiée par Dufour et Mulat. Edition
illustrée par J.-A. Beaucé, etc. (Paris), Marescq et Cie., n.d.
(1856), 4to., pp. 16 in double columns. Woodcut at head of title and
1 illustration. Impr. Simon Raçon et cie.

"Jacquot sans-oreilles" par Alexandre Dumas. Paris, Michel Lévy
frères, 1873, 12mo., pp. xxviii, 229 and unnumbered page table of
contents. "Les deux étudiants" completes the volume, pp. (167)-229.
Several times reprinted, same format and pagination, by both Michel
Lévy frères and Calmann-Lévy.

"Les mariages du père Olifus" par Alexandre Dumas. Paris, Alexandre
Cadot, éditeur, ... , 1849, 8vo., 5 volumes of which Volume 1 comprises
pp. 326 and unnumbered page table of contents, and consists of "Un
diner chez Rossini" and "Les gentilhommes de la Sierra-Morena".

Alexandre Dumas illustré par Ed. Coppin. "Don Bernardo de Zuniga".
Publie par Dufour et Mulat. (Vignette) Paris, Marescq et Cie.,
Editeurs, Librairie centrale des publications illustrées a 20 centimes,
1855, 4to., pp. 16 in double columns, and unnumbered page table of
contents; 5 illustrations. Yellow wrappers. Impr. Simon Raçon et
cie.

Alexandre Dumas. "La peinture chez les ancienne". ... "Don Bernardo
de Zuniga" par Alexandre Dumas. Publiée par Dufour et Mulat. Edition
illustrée par J.-A. Beaucé, etc., (Paris), Marescq et Cie., n.d.
(1856), 4to., pp. 16 in double columns; 5 illustrations. Woodcut at
head of title. Impr. S. Raçon et cie.

"Jane" par Alexandre Dumas. Paris, Michel Lévy frères, 1862, 12mo.,
pp. 324 and unnumbered page table of contents. The volume is completed by, inter alia, "Don Bernardo de Zuniga", pp. (269)-324.
Several times reprinted, same format and pagination, by both Michel
Lévy frères and Calmann-Lévy.

Alexandre Dumas "Le capitaine Paul" "Murat" "Le Kent" "Pierre le
cruel" "Don Bernardo de Zuniga" edition illustrée par les principaux
artistes Paris, Calmann Lévy, éditeur ancienne maison Michel Lévy
frères, 1887, 4to., pp. 16 in double columns. Brown covers with :
'Illustrées par J.-A. Beaucé et les principaux artistes; Alexandre
Dumas oeuvres illustrées'.
Reprinted, same format and pagination, (1890), 1897.

"Les mariages du père Olifus" par Alexandre Dumas. Paris, Alexandre Cadot, éditeur, ... , 1849, 8vo., 5 volumes of which Volume 1 comprises pp. 326 and unnumbered page table of contents, and consists of "Un diner chez Rossini" and "Les gentilhommes de la Sierra-Morena".

"LES MARIAGES DU PERE OLIFUS"   1849

This work, originally part of "Les mille et un fantômes, and with a plot unusual for Dumas (and no collaborator has been suggested) tells of the surprising adventures of a much-married Dutch sailor. In some of the later chapters Olifus visits the Philippine Islands and calls on a M. la Géronnière, a planter in the interior. This gentleman, more than surprised to find himself referred to in the romance, wrote to Dumas and offered him the story of his own experiences which were, in fact, published in 'Le Mousquetaire" between 2nd September and 31st October, 1855.

The work first appeared serially in 'Le Constitutionnel' during 1849 and during its publication in that journal Dumas learned of the sudden death of his old friend James Rousseau, the third collaborator in his first play "La chasse et l'amour". Dumas immediately wrote a 'memoir' of him which was sent to 'Le Constitutionnel' and duly appeared as Chapters XIII and XIV of the romance. These two chapters continued to be published in the editions published in volume form.

Original edition.
"Les mille et un fantômes", par Alexandre Dumas. Bruxelles, Meline, Cans et Cie., 1849, 18mo., 3 volumes; the third volume consists solely of "Les mariages du père Olifus", pp. (1)-326. There is no table of contents.

Ibid   La Haye, chez les héritiers Doorman, 1849, 3 volumes, same format and pagination as the preceding edition.

"Les mille et un fantômes" par Alexandre Dumas. Bruxelles, Livourne, Meline, Cans et compagnie; Leipzig, J.P. Meline, 1849, 3 volumes, same format and pagination as the preceding editions.

Ibid   Bruxelles, Livourne, Meline Cans et compagnie; Leipzig, J.P. Meline, 1849, 18mo., 4 volumes. "Les mariages du père Olifus" occupies pp. (27)-149 of Volume 3 and the whole of Volume 4, pp. (1)-149. Blue wrappers.

Ibid   Bruxelles, Ch. Muquardt, 1849, 18mo., 6 volumes. "Les mariages du père Olifus" is included in the final volumes.

Ibid   (Vignette) Bruxelles et Leipzig, C. Muquardt (volumes 4-6, Ch. Muquardt), 1849, 6 volumes, same format and pagination as the preceding edition.

"Les mille et un fantômes" par Alexandre Dumas. Bruxelles, Librairie de Tarride, 16mo., 8 volumes. "Les mariages du père Olifus" completes Volume 3 ending on page 136, occupies the whole of Volume 4 (pp. 145), and ends on page 95 of Volume 5. Yellow wrappers. La nouveauté littéraire, chez Tarride.

"Les mille et un fantômes", par Alexandre Dumas. Bruxelles, Librairie Allemande, Française et Etrangère de Mayer et Flateau, 1849, 8 volumes, same format and pagination as the preceding edition.

"Les mariages du père Olifus" par Alexandre Dumas. Paris, Alexandre
Cadot, éditeur, 32, rue de la Harpe, 1849, 5 volumes. Pagination :
326 and unnumbered page table of contents; 303, verso table of contents; 305, verso blank, and unnumbered page table of contents; 297,
verso blank, and unnumbered page table of contents; 327, verso table
of contents. Volume 1 comprises "Un diner chez Rossini" and "Les
gentilhommes de la Sierra-Morena"; "Les mariages du père Olifus"
starts with Volume 2 and ends on page 142 of Volume 4, being followed
by "Le testament de M. de Chauvelin". Yellow wrappers. Sceaux.
Imprimerie de E. Dépée.

"Les mille et un fantômes" par Alexandre Dumas. Bruxelles, Alphonse
Lebègue, 1849-1850, 18mo., 6 volumes. Pagination : Volume 1-4
(1849), 160, 157, 161 and 156; Volume 5 (1850 - which could be a misprint), 182; Volume 6, (1849), 182. There are variant spellings of
the publisher's first name - 'Alph', 'Alphonse' and 'Alp'. There are
no separate titles to the component stories, but chapter headings are
given.

Alexandre Dumas. "Les mariages du père Olifus". Paris, Michel Lévy
frères, 1855, 4to., pp. 96 in double columns, including table of contents. Caption title. Woodcut at head of title. Buff wrappers
repeating woodcut. Oeuvres complètes d'Alexandre Dumas. Musée littéraire du siècle.

"Les mariages du père Olifus". Par Alexandre Dumas. Publiés par
Dufour et Mulat. Edition illustrée par J.-A. Beaucé, Ed. Coppin,
etc. (Vignette) Paris, Marescq et cie., 1856, 4to., 2 parties en 1
volume, pp. 96 in double columns.

Ibid   Paris, Impr. de Gaittet, 1861, same format and
pagination as the preceding edition; illustrated.

"Les mariages du père Olifus" par Alexandre Dumas. Paris, Michel
Lévy frères, 1861, 12mo., pp. 264. There is no table of contents.
Several times reprinted, same format and pagination, by both Michel
Lévy frères and Calmann-Lévy.

Ibid   No place, publisher or date (c 186), 4to., pp.
(173)-224; illustrated.

Ibid   Edition illustrée par J.-A. Beaucé, Ed. Coppin,
etc. (Vignette) Paris, Calmann-Lévy, éditeur ancienne maison Michel
Lévy frères, 1887, 4to., pp. 96 in double columns.

Alexandre Dumas. "Les mariages du père Olifus". Edition illustrée
par J.-A. Beaucé, Ed. Coppin, etc. Paris, Calmann-Lévy, n.d. (1897),
4to., pp. 96 in double columns. Alexandre Dumas Oeuvres illustrées.

"JAMES ROUSSEAU"   1849

Rousseau was one of the three collaborators in "La chasse et
l'amour", and an old friend of Dumas.

As has been written in the introductory paragraphs to "Les
mariages du père Olifus" Dumas, on hearing of his death, wrote a
'memoir' of him which was sent to 'Le Constitutionnel' and was duly
published as Chapters XIII and XIV of that romance, and subsequently
incorporated under the same chapter numbers in the editions published
in volume form - the chapter titles being 'Intercalation' and 'James

Rousseau' respectively. It should be noted that at least in the original Meline, Cans et Cie., 1849, edition of "Les mille et un fantômes", of which "Les mariages du père Olifus" occupies the whole of Volume 3 these two chapters are combined into one.

James Rousseau is also referred to in Dumas' "Mémoires", Chapters CIV, CV, CXXXVII and CCLXI.

"LE TESTAMENT DE M. DE CHAUVELIN"   1849

This is one of the series of stores comprising "Les mille et une fantômes". The setting is the year 1774, the last year of Louis XV's reign, and the death of that king is vividly described. The story is woven around the death of de Chauvelin who was a friend and favourite of Louis; it is possible that he did die in the king's presence, but whether he fell dead at the king's feet at a card party given in Dubarry's rooms is pure conjecture. Dumas has asserted that he heard the story from an old antiquary, Villenave, who in his youth was a member of de Chauvelin's household, and an account of him prefaces the work. Dumas certainly had no collaborator.

The work appeared serially in 'Le Constitutionnel' during 1849 and possibly into the very early weeks of 1850.

Original editon.
"Les mille et un fantômes" par Alexandre Dumas. Bruxelles, Librairie de Tarride, 1849, 16mo., 8 volumes. "Le testament de M. de Chauvelin" occupies pp. (97)-136 of Volume 5 and the whole of Volume 6, pp. 140. Yellow wrappers. La nouveauté littéraire, chez Tarride.

"Les mille et un fantômes", par Alexandre Dumas. Bruxelles, Librairie Allemande, Française et Etrangère de Mayer et Flateau, 1849, 8 volumes, same format and pagination as the preceding edition.

"Les mille et un fantômes". "Le testament de Monsieur de Chauvelin" par Alexandre Dumas. Bruxelles, Meline, Cans et cie., 1849, 18mo., 2 volumes, pp. 2 preliminary leaves, 168. There is no table of contents.

Semeine littéraire du Courrier des Etats-Unis. "Le testament de M. de Chauvelin", par Alexandre Dumas. New-York, F. Gaillardet (P. Arpin), 1849, 8vo., pp. (337)-380 in double columns.

"Les mariages du père Olifus" par Alexandre Dumas. Paris, Alexandre Cadot, éditeur, 32, rue de la Harpe, 1849, 5 volumes. The work ends on page 142 of Volume 4 and is followed by "Le testament de M. de Chauvelin", pp. (143)-297, being continued into Volume 5 and ending on page 327, verso table of contents. Yellow wrappers. Sceaux. Imprimerie de E. Dépee.

"Les mille et un fantômes" par Alexandre Dumas. Bruxelles, Alphonse Lebègue, 1849-1850, 18mo., 6 volumes. Pagination : Volumes 1-4 (1849), 160, 157, 161 and 156; Volume 5 (1850 - which could be a misprint), 182; Volume 6 (1849), 182. There are variant spellings of the publisher's first name - 'Alph', 'Alphonse' and 'Alp'. There are no separate titles to the component stories, but chapter headings are given.

"Les mille et un fantômes". "Le testament de Monsieur de Chauvelin" par Alexandre Dumas. Bruxelles, Meline, Cans et cie., 1850, 24mo., pp. 2 preliminary leaves, 212. There are no tables of contents.

Ibid   La Haye, chez les héritiers Doorman, 1850, same
format and pagination as the preceding edition.

"Le testament de M. de Chauvelin". Followed by "Un diner chez Rossini"
and "Les gentilhommes de la Sierra-Morena". Par Alexandre Dumas.
Paris, Impr. de Walder, n.d. (1855), 4to., pp. 273-304, 305-314 and
315-327 respectively in double columns. Illustrated.

"Le testament de M. de Chauvelin" par Alexandre Dumas. Paris,
Michel Lévy frères, 1861, 12mo., pp. 273.
Several times reprinted, same format and pagination, by both Michel
Lévy frères and Calmann-Lévy.

Ibid   Paris, Michel Lévy frères, 1861, 4to., pp. 72 in
double columns; illustrated.

Ibid   Paris, Calmann-Lévy, n.d. (c 189), same format
and pagination as the preceding edition. Caption title. Woodcut at
head of title. Musée littéraire contemporain.

"LA FEMME AU COLLIER DE VELOURS"   1849

        This is the last story in the collection "Les mille et un fan-
tômes" and, once again, it was Dumas working alone. Dumas has stated
that it was Charles Nodier who related the germ idea of the work to
him and this is probably correct. The original source must have been
German with, conceivably, some French version of it; Dumas has used
for his main character Hoffmann, the German writer of fantasies.
Washington Irving used the theme in his "Tales of a Traveller" - that
entitled "The Adventures of a German Student" which Pétrus Borel un-
ashamedly published in translation in 'La Sylphide' under the title
of "Gottfried Wolfgang", the name of the hero in Irving's story.

        The scene of the main part of the work is laid in Paris in 1793,
and Dubarry's death is quite terrifyingly described. There is an
introduction touching on Nodier at the Bibliothèque de l'Arsenal, and
concluding with his death in 1844. The story ran serially in 'Le
Constitutionnel' during 1849 and possibly into the very early weeks of
1850.

Original edition.
"Les mille et un fantômes" par Alexandre Dumas. Bruxelles, Librairie
de Tarride, 1849, 16mo., 8 volumes, the final two volumes with pp. 135
and 141 being filled entirely with "La femme au collier de velours".
Yellow wrappers. La nouveauté littéraire, chez Tarride.

"Les mille et un fantômes", par Alexandre Dumas. Bruxelles, Librairie
Allemande, Française et Etrangère de Mayer et Flateau, 1849, 8 volumes,
same format and pagination as the preceding edition.

Semaine littéraire du Courrier des Etats-Unis. New York, Paul Arpin,
1849. "La femme au collier de velours", par Alexandre Dumas. 8vo.,
pp. (387)-452 in double columns.

"Les mille et un fantômes" par Alexandre Dumas. Bruxelles, Alphonse
Lebègue, 1849-1850, 18mo., 6 volumes. Pagination : Volumes 1-4
(1849), 160, 157, 161 and 156; Volume 5 (1850 - which could be a misprint), 147; Volume 6 (1849), 182. There are variant spellings of the

publisher's first name - 'Alph', 'Alphonse' and 'Alp'. There are no separate titles to the component series, but chapter headings are given.

"Les mille et un fantômes". "La femme au collier de velours" par Alexandre Dumas. Bruxelles, Livourne, Meline, Cans et compagnie; Leipzig, J.P. Meline, 1850, 12mo., pp. 320. Beige wrappers.

Ibid   La Haye, chez les héritiers Doorman, 1850, same format and pagination as the preceding edition.

"La femme au collier de velours", par Alexandre Dumas. Bruxelles, Meline, Cans et cie.; Leipzig, J.P. Meline, 1850, same format and pagination as the preceding editions.
(It should be noted that an error on page 28 of the above three editions is corrected on page 38 in a footnote; this would certainly point them to being printed from the serial issue in 'Le Constitutionnel' since no such correction had to be made in the Alexandre Cadot, 1850, edition.)

"La femme au collier du velours" par Alexandre Dumas. Paris, Alexandre Cadot, éditeur, 32, rue de la Harpe, 1850, 8vo., 2 volumes, pp. 326 and 333, each with an additional unnumbered page table of contents. Yellow wrappers. Sceaux. Imprimerie de E. Dépée.

"La femme au collier de velours". "Le capitaine Marion". "La Junon". "Le Kent". Par Alexandre Dumas. Publiés par Dufour et Mulat. Dessins par J.-A. Beaucé, Ed. Coppin, Lancelot, etc. (Vignette) Paris, Marescq et Cie., 1857, large 8vo., "La femme ... ... ", pp. 96 in double columns.

"La femme au collier de velours" par Alexandre Dumas. Paris, Michel Lévy frères, 1861, 12mo., pp. 234.
Several times reprinted, same format and pagination, by both Michel Lévy frères and Calmann-Lévy.

Alexandre Dumas. "La femme au collier de velours". "Le capitaine Marion". "La Junon". Dessins par J.-A. Beaucé, Ed. Coppin, Lancelot, etc. Paris, Calmann-Lévy, 1884, 4to., "La femme ... ... ", pp. 96 in double columns. Musée littéraire contemporain.
Reprinted, same format and pagination, 1897.

"La femme au collier de velours" par Alexandre Dumas Dessins par J.-A. Beaucé, Ed. Coppin, Lancelot, etc. (Vignette) Paris, Calmann Lévy, editeur, ancienne maison Michel Lévy frères, 1889, 4to., pp. 96 in double columns.

"La femme au collier de velours" par Alexandre Dumas. Illustrations par Alphonse de Neuville. In : 'L'Univers illustré', journal hebdominaire, Paris, folio, 21 mars - 23 mai 1896 (39e année), Nos. 2139-2148, pp. 229-232, 249-252, 269-272, 289-292, 309-312, 329-332, 349-352, 369-372, 389-392, and 409-411; printed in three columns with a woodcut at the head of each number.

"LE CHEVALIER D'HARMENTAL"   (Drama)   1849

    In collaboration with Maquet this play was drawn from the romance of the same name. To quote Parran : 'Ce drame, très bien charpente, présente, comme le roman dont il est tiré, un vif intérèt'.

218

Original edition.
"Le chevalier d'Harmental" drame en cinq actes et dix tableaux, avec
prologue, par Alexandre Dumas et Auguste Maquet. Musique de M. Varney. Représenté pour la première fois, à Paris, sur le Théâtre-
Historique, le 26 juillet 1849. Paris, Alexandre Cadot, 1849, large
8vo., pp. (1)-48 in double columns. Yellow wrappers.

"Le chevalier d'Harmental", drame en cinq actes, dix tableaux et un
prologue, par MM. Alex. Dumas et Auguste Maquet. Musique de M.
Varney. Représenté pour la première fois, à Paris, sur le Théâtre
Historique, le 23 (sic) juillet 1849. Bruxelles, J.-A. Lelong, 1849,
12mo., pp. 154.

"Le chevalier d'Harmental" drame en cinq actes, en dix tableaux et
un prologue en société avec M. Auguste Maquet Théâtre-Historique. -
26 juillet 1849. "Distribution" on title-page, pp. 174-340. Théatre
complet de Alex. Dumas Tome XV Paris Calmann Lévy, éditeur ancienne
maison Michel Lévy frères, 1874. 12mo. "Théatre complet" in 25 volumes.

An opera was drawn from the play :
"Le chevalier d'Harmental" opéra-comique en cinq actes d'après Alexandre Dumas et Auguste Maquet poème de Paul Ferrier musique de André
Messager Paris, Calmann-Lévy, éditeur, 1896, 12mo., verso of title-
page 'Personnages', (1)-94; half-title, "Le chevalier d'Harmental"
opéra-comique en cinq actes représenté pour la première fois, à
Paris, au Théâtre national de l'Opéra-Comique, le 5 mai 1896.

"LA REGENCE"
"LOUIS QUINZE"   1849
"LOUIS QUINZE ET SA COUR"

      These works can usefully be treated together, for "Louis quinze
... " is, in fact, a continuation of "La Régence". They comprise a
further instalment of Dumas' series of historical works. In their
compilation he was setting himself out to raise interest in, and to
popularise, French history. There can be little doubt that Dumas
worked alone, using contemporary memoirs and similar works of
reference.

"LA REGENCE"

Original edition.
"La Régence", par Alexandre Dumas. Paris, Alexandre Cadot, 1849,
8vo., 2 volumes, pp. 349 and 301.

"La Régence" par Alexandre Dumas. Bruxelles, Alphonse Lebègue, 1849,
24mo., 2 volumes, pp. 144 and 132. Green wrappers. Muséum littéraire.

Ibid   Bruxelles, Livourne, Meline, Cans et compagnie,
1849, 18mo., 2 volumes, pp. 273 (misprint for 173) and 150. Blue
wrappers.

Ibid   Bruxelles, Livourne, Meline, Cans et compagnie;
Leipzig, J.P. Meline, 1849, 16mo., 2 volumes, pp. 271 and 234.

"La Régence", par Alexandre Dumas. La Haye, chez les héritiers
Doorman, 1849, 2 volumes, same format and pagination as the preceding
edition.

Ibid   Bruxelles, Leipzig, Librairie de Ch. Muquardt,
1849, 24mo., 2 volumes, pp. 144 and 132.

"La Régence" par Alexandre Dumas. Paris, Michel Lévy frères, 1866,
12mo., pp. 301, verso blank, (303)-307 table of contents.
Several times reprinted, same format and pagination, by both Michel
Lévy frères and Calmann-Lévy.

Ibid   Paris, Calmann-Lévy, n.d. (c 189), 4to. Musée
littéraire contemporain.

"LOUIS QUINZE"
Ouvrage entièrement inédite. "Louis quinze" par Alexandre Dumas.
Paris, Alexandre Cadot, 1849, 8vo., 5 volumes, pp. 327, 312, 334, 320,
all including additional unnumbered page table of contents, and 296
with no table of contents.

"Louis quinze" par Alexandre Dumas. Bruxelles, Livourne, Meline,
Cans et cie.; Leipzig, J.P. Meline, 1849-1850, 18mo., 5 volumes.
Pagination : Volumes 1 and 2 (1849), 170 and 160; Volumes 3-5
(1850), 134, 155 and 145. 'Pièces justificatives' occupy pp. (112)-
145 of Volume 5.

Ibid   Bruxelles, Livourne, Meline, Cans et compagnie;
Leipzig, J.P. Meline, 1849-1850, 24mo., 4 volumes. Pagination :
Volumes 1 and 2 (1849), 263 and 249; Volumes 3 and 4 (1850), 336 and
332. 'Pièces justificatives' occupy pp. 281-332 of Volume 4.

"Louis quinze", par Alexandre Dumas. La Haye, chez les héritiers
Doorman, same years of publication, format and pagination as the
preceding edition.

"Louis quinze" par Alexandre Dumas. Bruxelles, Leipzig, Librairie
de Ch. Muquardt, 1849-1850, 24mo., 5 volumes. Pagination : Volumes
1 and 2 (1849), 170 and 160; Volumes 3-5 (1850), 134, 155 and 145.
'Pièces justificatives' occupy pp. (112)-145 of Volume 5.

Ibid   Bruxelles, Alp. Lebègue (Volume 1) and Alph.
Lebègue (Volumes 2-5), 1849-1850, 24mo. Pagination : Volume 1 (1849),
144; Volumes 2-5 (1850), 132, 148, 143 and 132. 'Pièces justificatives'
occupy pp. 53-132 of Volume 5. Museum littéraire.

Ibid   Bruxelles, Kiessling et compagnie, 1849-1850;
same years of publication, format and pagination as the preceding
edition.
(There are two recorded copies of this work - Bruxelles, Alp. Lebègue
(Volume 1), Alph. Lebègue (Volumes 2, 3 and 5), Kiessling et compagnie
(Volume 4), all with the 'A.L.' monogram on the title-page; same years
of publication, format and pagination as the preceding.)

"La Régence et Louis quinze" par M. Alexandre Dumas Paris, éditeurs
: MM. Dufour et Mulat, ... , 1850. 4to. Paged continuously : "La
Régence", pp. (1)-140; "Louis quinze", pp. (141)-456, (457)-459 table
of contents "La Régence", 460-466 table of contents "Louis XV",
unnumbered page 'classement des gravures'. Frontispiece and 14 full-
page illustrations. Typographie de bureau, 14, rue Gaillon Tiré sur
presses mécaniques par Aristide.
Reprinted, same format, pagination and illustrations, 1857.

"La Régence et Louis XV", par Alexandre Dumas. Paris, Dufour, Mulat
et Boulanger, 1854, 4to., pp. 438 and tables of contents; 16 illustrations.
Reprinted, same format, pagination and illustrations, 1857.

"La Régence et Louis quinze" par Alexandre Dumas. Paris, Malmanayde et de Riberolles, libraires, 1855, 4to., 2 volumes paged continuously : Volume 1 ends at page 233 and Volume 2 at page 456, with the tables of contents ending on page 466; additional unnumbered page 'classement des gravures'. Volume 1 has 9 plates and Volume 2, 6.

"Louis XV et sa cour" par Alexandre Dumas. Paris, Michel Lévy frères, 1866, 12mo., 2 volumes, pp. 296 and 308, with table of contents printed at the head of each chapter.
Several times reprinted, same format and pagination, by both Michel Lévy frères and Calmann-Lévy.

Ibid   Paris, Calmann-Lévy, n.d. (c 189), 4to. Musée littéraire contemporain.

"LA GUERRE DES FEMMES"   (Drama)   1849
      Written by Dumas in collaboration with Maquet this play was drawn from the romance of the same name. Dumas, by some clever altering, built up a most effective finale for the stage version without in any significant way varying from the end of the romance.

Original edition.
"La guerre des femmes" drame en cinq actes et dix tableaux. Par Alexandre Dumas et Auguste Maquet. Musique de M. Varney. Décors peints par MM. Ernest Ciceri et Lechevallier; costumes déssinés par M. Giraud et exécutés par M. Ferdinand et mademoiselle Philis; Machines de M. Adolphe Pierrard. Représenté pour la première fois, a Paris, sur le Théatre-Historique, le 1er octobre 1849. Caption title. Yellow wrappers repeating caption title. Paris, Alexandre Cadot, 1849, large 8vo., pp. 57 (the last page misnumbered 35) in double columns.

Ibid   Buff wrappers. La France dramatique au dix-neuvième siècle choix de pièces modernes. "La guerre des femmes". Paris, Tresse, Successeur de J.-N. Barba, 1872, large 8vo., pp. 57 (correctly numbered) in double columns.

"La guerre des femmes" drame en cinq actes, en dix tableaux en société avec M. Auguste Maquet Théâtre-Historique. - ler. octobre 1849. "Distribution" on title-page, pp. 2-196. Théatre complet de Alex. Dumas Tome XVI Paris Calmann Levy, éditeur ancienne maison Michel Lévy frères, 1874. 12mo. "Théatre complet" in 25 volumes.

"LE CONNETABLE DE BOURBON OU L'ITALIE AU
SEIZIEME SIECLE"   1849
      Although this play is signed by Grangé and de Montépin Dumas is known to have shared in its writing.

Original (and only) edition.
"Le connétable de Bourbon ou l'Italie au XVIe siècle", drame a grand spectacle, en cinq actes et douze tableaux par E. Grangé et X. de Montepin. Mise en scène de M. Cormon; Ballets de M.E. Lerouge; Musique du drame de M. Adolphe Vaillard; celle du Ballet de M. Auguste Morel. ... représenté pour la première fois, a Paris, sur le théatre de la Porte-Saint-Martin, le 20 octobre 1849. Caption title, followed

by 'Distribution' : 'personnages' 'acteurs'. Yellow wrappers repeating caption title. Paris, Alexandre Cadot, éditeur .... 1849, large 8vo., pp. (1)-31 in double columns. Imprimerie de E. Dépée, a Sceaux.

"LA TESTAMENT DE CESAR"   1849

Glinel, in his "Le théâtre inconnu d'Alexandre Dumas père" should be quoted here at some length. He wrote : 'Une lettre du 7 novembre 1849 adressée à Dumas par Jules Lacroix, à propos des répétitions de ce drame, et une lettre de Dumas aux sociétaires, du 9 du même mois, ne laissent aucun doute sur la collaboration de celui-ci au "Testament de César". Dans cette dernière lettre, Dumas demands à être nommé le premier comme le plus ancien. Que se passa-t-il ensuite? Toujours est-il que Jules Lacroix fut seul nommé au théâtre comme il figure seul en tête de la brochure. Voici enfin une preuve décisive de la collaboration de Dumas : à la suite d'un exemplaire imprimé du "Testament de César", se trouve un manuscrit d'Alexandre Dumas, formant ensemble le no. 4712 du catalogue de la bibliothèque du baron de Stassart, léguée à l'Académie royale de Belgique. Or, ce manuscrit n'est autre chose que le premier acte, en prose, du "Testament de César", que Jules Lacroix a mis ensuite en vers avec sa précision et son élégance habituelles ... '.

Original edition.
"Le testament de César" Drame en cinq actes et en vers suivi d'un épilogue par Jules Lacroix Représenté pour la première fois à la Comédie française le 10 novembre 1849. Paris, Firmin Didot frères, libraires imprimeurs de l'institut, rue Jacob, 56. Tresse, Palais-National, 2; Michel Lévy, rue Vivienne, 1849, 8vo., second half-title (unnumbered) with on verso : 'personnages' 'acteurs', pp. (3)-180. Green wrappers repeating title-page.

The play is now included in the three volume edition of Jules Lacroix's plays. Paris, Calmann-Lévy, first published in 1875.

"LE COMTE HERMANN"   1849

Parran has written : 'Ce drame est une des compositions les plus importantes de Dumas, une de celles auxquelles il attachait le plus de prix. L'oeuvre fut ailleurs remarquablement interprétée par Mélingue, Laferrière et Rouvière'.

Dumas would appear to have had no collaborator in the writing of the play, which has often been spoken of as the counterpart to his "Antony". As well as writing a preface to it he wrote 'Un dernier mot à mes lecteurs', defying his critics to prove that the play was a translation, or the imitation, of a German drama. The epilogue is, in fact, a long monologue intended only for readers of the play and not for use on the stage.

Original edition.
"Le comte Hermann" drame en cinq actes, par M. Alexandre Dumas, représenté pour la première fois, a Paris, sur le Théâtre-Historique, le 22 novembre 1849. Caption title. Yellow wrappers : 2me série du magasin théâtral Pièces nouvelles jouées sur tous les théâtres

de Paris. Théatre Historique. "Le comte Hermann". Paris, Marchant, n.d. (1849), large 8vo., pp. (1)-2 'Préface' unsigned, 43 in double columns, followed on the remainder of page 43 and the whole of page 44 'Un dernier mot à mes lecteurs Alex. Dumas. 1er décembre 1849'. ("Le comte Hermann", drame en cinq actes, de M. Alexandre Dumas. 'Préface'. Paris, Impr. de Firmin-Didot frères, n.d. (1849), 8vo., pp. 4; published in the journal 'L'Ordre', 20 novembre 1849.)

"Le comte Hermann", drame en cinq actes, par M. Alexandre Dumas, Représenté, pour la premiere fois, à Paris, sur le Théâtre-Historique, le 22 novembre 1849. (Vignette) Bruxelles, J.-A. Lelong, 1849, 18mo., pp. 151; 153-156 'Un dernier mot à mes lecteurs. Alex. Dumas, 1er décembre 1849'.

Théatre Français publié par G. Schultz. Onzième série. I. livraison. "Le comte Hermann", par M. Alexandre Dumas. Bielefeld. Velhagen & Klasing, 1850, 24mo., pp. (3)-130.
Ibid   Deuxième édition. 1864, same format and pagination.

"Le comte Hermann" drame en cinq actes par M. Alexandre Dumas représenté pour la première fois, à Paris, sur le Théatre-historique, le 22 novembre 1849. Paris, Barbré, n.d. (185), 4to., pp. 16 in treble columns, and including 'Un dernier mot à mes lecteurs'. Caption title. Woodcut at head of title. Magasin théatral illustré.

"Le comte Hermann", drame en cinq actes, par M. Alexandre Dumas, Représenté pour la première fois, à Paris, sur le Théâtre-Historique, le 22 novembre 1849. Paris, Impr. de Walder, n.d. (1856), same format and pagination as the preceding edition. Caption title. Woodcut at head of title.

"Le comte Hermann" drame en cinq actes et un épilogue Théâtre-Historique. - 22 novembre 1849. Pp. (197)-201 'Préface' signed : Alex. Dumas. 21 novembre 1849, followed by "Distribution", 201-317, 317-320 'Un dernier mot a mes lecteurs' signed : Alex. Dumas. 1er décembre 1849. Théatre complet de Alex. Dumas Tome XVI Paris Calmann Lévy, éditeur ancienne maison Michel Lévy frères, 1874. 12mo. "Théatre complet" in 25 volumes.

"LE CACHEMIRE VERT"   1849
     This comedy was written in collaboration with Eugène Nus.

Original edition.
"Le cachemire vert" comédie en un acte, par MM. Alexandre Dumas et Eugène Nus, représentée, pour la première fois, a Paris, sur le théâtre du Gymnase-Dramatique, le 15 décembre 1849. Caption title. Yellow wrappers : 2me série du magasin théatral pièces nouvelles jouées sur tous les théatres de Paris. Théatre du Gymnase-Dramatique.
"Le cachemire vert", Comédie en un acte, de MM. Alexandre Dumas et Eugène Nus. (Vignette) Paris, Marchant, n.d. (1849), large 8vo., pp. 13 in double columns.

Ibid   Paris, Impr. de Dondey-Dupré, n.d. (1850), same format and pagination as the preceding edition. Caption title.

"Le cachemire vert", comédie en un acte, par MM. Alex. Dumas et Nus. Représentée, pour la première fois, à Paris, sur le théâtre Gymnase-

Dramatique, le 15 décembre 1849. Bruxelles, J.-A. Lelong, libraire des théâtres royaux, 1850, 12mo., pp. 47.

Repertoire du Théâtre français à Berlin. No. 393. (Deuxième Série No. 143.) "Le cachemire vert", comédie en un acte, par MM. Alex. Dumas et Eug. Nus. Berlin, Ad. Mt. Scheslinger, Libraire et Editeur de Musique, 1853, 8vo., pp. 27. Imprimé chez I.W. Krause.

"Le cachemire vert" comédie en un acte, par MM. Alexandre Dumas et Eugène Nus, représentée, pour la première fois, a Paris, sur le théatre du Gymnase-Dramatique, le 15 décembre 1849. Paris, Impr. de C. Bonnet, n.d. (1861), large 8vo., pp. 11 in double columns.

"Le cachemire vert" comédie en un acte, en prose en société avec M. Eugène Nus Gymnase-Dramatique. - 15 décembre 1849. "Distribution" on title-page, pp. (269)-307. Théatre complet de Alex. Dumas Tome XI Paris Calmann Lévy, éditeur ancienne maison Michel Lévy frères, 1874. 12mo. "Théatre complet" in 25 volumes.

"MEMOIRES DE J.-F. TALMA"   1849-1850

Talma died in 1826 and Dumas has stated that some twenty years after the great tragedian's death his papers, which had been passed to a certain M. Pastoret for preparation for publication in memoir form, were still awaiting attention. It was then that Pastoret suggested to Talma's two sons that Dumas would be the most appropriate person to carry out the work. Dumas was duly approached and agreed, but through pressure of other work he brought his material up to only 1799, and it was never completed.

The oddity is that these 'memoirs' have escaped the attention of almost all of French 19th century authorities - Glinel simply notes that they have been attributed to Dumas by Victor Fournel. It is highly probable that in their compilation Dumas worked alone. It should be noted here that prior to the publication of Dumas' work there appeared, in 1836, "Etudes sur l'art théatral" suivies d'anecdotes inédites sur Talma, et de la correspondance de Ducis avec cet artiste, Depuis 1792, jusqu'en 1815; par madame veuve Talma, née Vanhove, maintenant comtesse de Chalot. A Paris, chez Henri Feret, libraire, ..." Dumas may well have used the very early parts of this work in his own compilation.

Original edition.
"Mémoires de J.-F. Talma" écrits par lui-même. Et receuillis et mis en ordre sur les papiers de sa famille par Alexandre Dumas. Paris, Hippolyte Souverain, 1849-1850, 8vo., 4 volumes. Pagination : Volumes 1 and 2 (1849), 314 and 297; Volumes 3 and 4 (1850), 316 and 316.

Ibid   Bruxelles, Alph. Lebègue et Sacré fils, 1850, 24mo., 3 volumes, pp. 127, 112 and 116.

"Mémoires de Talma" par Alexandre Dumas. Bruxelles, Kiessling et compagnie, 1850, same format and pagination as the preceding edition.

Ibid   Bruxelles et Leipzig, Kiessling et compagnie. Vienne, A la librairie de J.F. Gress, 1850, same format and pagination as the preceding editions.

Ibid   Bruxelles, Gand et Leipzig, Librairie de Ch.

Muquardt, 1850, same format and pagination as the preceding editions. Vignettes on title-pages.

"LE COLLIER DE LA REINE" 1849-1850

In so far as the period is concerned this work is the second in Dumas' 'Revolutionary' series, all intended by him to be known collectively as "Les mémoires d'un médecin" but of which only the first, "Joseph Balsamo", is now usually thus entitled. The work, its title is self-explanatory, is followed in turn by "Ange Pitou" and "La comtesse de Charny". The actual period is 1784-1786. It was written in collaboration with Maquet and is generally regarded as the last of the great romances in which the two worked in association.

The prologue is based on La Harpe's "Prophétie de Cazotte", incidentally also used in Bulwer Lytton's "Zanoni".

The work first appeared serially in 'La Presse' in 1849-1850.

Original edition.
There is a curiosity here in that two separate editions were published in the United States as follows :
Semaine Littéraire du Courrier des Etats-Unis. Receuil Choisi de romans, feuilletons, ouvrages historiques et dramatiques, en prose et en vers des auteurs modernes les plus renommés. XVII série; 1849. New-York; F. Gaillardet, 1849, large 8vo., pp. (3)-316 in double columns. At head of page 3 : "Le collier de la reine".

Semaine Littéraire du Courrier des Etats-Unit. "Le collier de la reine", par Alexandre Dumas. Episode des "Mémoires d'un médecin". (New York) Paul Arpin, Bureau du Courrier des Etats-Unit, 1849, large 8vo., pp. (3)-316 in double columns. (XVII série.)
Unless there is some error in the dating it can only be assumed that the publishers regarded the work as complete with the publishing of the final 1849 feuilleton, or that they did not bother to issue in the following year an additional volume.

"Mémoires d'un médecin", par Alexandre Dumas. "Le collier". Bruxelles, Librairie de Tarride, 1849-1850, 18mo., 9 volumes. Pagination : Volumes 1-6 (1849), 138, 136, 127, 152, 143 and 143; Volumes 7-9 (1850), 155, 153 and 157. Yellow wrappers. La Nouveauté littéraire.

"Le collier de la reine". Par Alexandre Dumas. 1849-1850, 12mo., 6 volumes. Volumes 1-4 - Leipzig, Brockhaus & Avenarius. 1849. Pp. 147, 160, 156 and 142. Volumes 5-6 - Leipzig, F.A. Brockhaus. 1850. Pp. 150 and 179. At the end of Volume 6 : 'Fin du tome dix-septième et du "Collier de la reine".' Imprimerie de F.A. Brockhaus.

"Mémoires d'un médecin", par Alexandre Dumas. "Le collier". Bruxelles, librairie allemande, française et étrangère de Mayer et Flateau, 1849-1850, 18mo., 9 volumes, same years of publication, format and pagination as the Bruxelles, Librairie de Tarride, 1849-1850, edition.

"Les mémoires d'un médecin. Le collier". Par Alexandre Dumas. Bruxelles, Alphonse Lebègue, 1849-1850, 18mo., 7 volumes. Pagination : Volumes 1-5 (1849), 131, 140, 160, 98 and 142; Volumes 6-7 (1850), 112 and 106. Green wrappers.

"Le collier de la reine", deuxième série des "Mémoires d'un médecin" par Alexandre Dumas. Bruxelles, Livourne, Meline, Cans et compagnie;

Leipzig, J.P. Meline, 1849-1850, 12mo., 6 volumes. Pagination :
Volumes 1-3 (1849), 268, 262 and 272; Volumes 4-6 (1850), 271, 262
and 191.

Ibid   La Haye, chez les héritiers Doorman, same years
of publication, format and pagination as the preceding edition.

"Le collier de la reine" par Alexandre Dumas. Berlin, Librairie
B. Behr, 1849-1850, 12mo., 6 volumes. Pagination : Volume 1-3
(1849),147, 160 and 156; Volumes 4-6 (1850), 142, 150 and 179.

"Le collier de la reine", deuxième série des "Mémoires d'un médecin"
par Alexandre Dumas. Bruxelles, Livourne, Meline, Cans et compagnie;
Leipzig, J.P. Meline, 1849-1850, 18mo., 7 volumes. Pagination :
Volumes 1-3 (1849), 176, 168 and 170; Volumes 4-7 (1850), 164, 169,
176 and 187.

"Le collier de la reine" par Alexandre Dumas. Paris, Alexandre
Cadot, 32, rue de la Harpe, 1849-1850, 8vo., 11 volumes. Pagination
: Volumes 1-6 (1849), 'Avant-propos' signed : Alexandre Dumas 29
novembre 1848, (1)-17, (18)-310 and unnumbered page table of contents,
309, 301, 299 all with verso blank and unnumbered page table of contents, 318 and unnumbered page table of contents, 303, verso blank,
and unnumbered page table of contents; Volumes 7-11 (1850), 310 and
unnumbered page table of contents, 309, 287, 303 and 275 all with
verso blank and unnumbered page table of contents. Yellow wrappers.
Sceaux - Imprimerie de E. Dépée.

Ibid   Paris, Michel Lévy frères, 1853-1854, 12mo., 3
volumes.

"Le collier de la reine" par Alexandre Dumas. Paris, Michel Lévy
frères, 1855, 4to., pp. 226 in double columns, including table of
contents. Caption title. Woodcut at head of title. Musée littéraire
du siècle.

"Mémoires d'un médecin Le collier de la reine", par Alexandre Dumas.
Paris, Dufour, Mulat et Boulanger, 1856, large 8vo., pp. 596 in double
columns, including table of contents; 40 illustrations.

"Le collier de la reine". Par M. Alexandre Dumas. In : 'L'Echo
des feuilletons'. Dixième année. Paris, Dufour, Mulat et Boulanger,
1857, 4to., pp. (441)-574 in double columns; illustrated.

"Mémoires d'un médecin. Le collier de la reine" par Alexandre Dumas.
Paris, Legrand, Pomey et Crouzet, n.d. (1857), large 8vo., pp. (6),
535, including table of contents; frontispiece and 40 full-page
illustrations.

"Le collier de la reine", par Alexandre Dumas. Paris, Morris et
cie., n.d. (c 1857), 4to., pp. 226 in double columns. Caption title.
Woodcut at head of title.

"Le collier de la reine" par Alexandre Dumas. In : 'Journal du
jeudi', No. 160, 10 novembre 1861, to No. 202, 6 avril 1862. Treble
columns. Engraving at head of each number.

"Mémoires d'un médecin. Le collier de la reine", par Alexandre Dumas.
Paris, Dufour et Mulat, 1863, large 8vo., pp. 596 in double columns,
including table of contents; 40 illustrations.

"Mémoires d'un médecin. Le collier de la reine" par Alexandre Dumas.
Paris, Dufour, Boulanger et Legrand, 1863, large 8vo., pp. 595 and

unnumbered page table of contents and 'classement des gravures'; 40
illustrations.

"Le collier de la reine" par Alexandre Dumas. Paris, Michel Lévy
frères, 1863, 12mo., 3 volumes. Pagination : (i)-iv 'Avant-propos',
(1)-281, verso blank (283)-284 table of contents; 283, verso blank,
(284)-285 table of contents; 304, (305)-306 table of contents.
Frequently reprinted, same format but with varying paginations, by
both Michel Lévy frères and Calmann-Lévy.

Ibid   Paris, Calmann-Lévy, n.d. (188), 4to. Musée
littéraire contemporain.

There was one play drawn from the romance :
"Le collier de la reine" drame en cinq actes treize tableaux tiré
du roman d'Alexandre Dumas par Pierre Decourcelle Paris, Calmann-
Lévy, 1896, 12mo., pp. 3 unnumbered 'Personnages', 'Tableaux', (1)-
223.

"LA TULIPE NOIRE"   1850

     Dumas has most successfully accomplished in this work what must
be regarded as a most difficult thing to do - that of centring the
interest of the story not in a human being, or beings, but on an
inanimate object. Rosa's and van Baerle's troubles and dangers are
involved, but the real concern of the book is as to whether a really
black tulip can be raised and whether the credit for doing this is to
be given to the true producer. The period is 1672-1673, beginning
with the fate of the brothers de Witt and ending with the Haarlem
Floral Festivel. Again, the work is pure Dumas despite suggestions
to the contrary. De Flotow, the composer, has said that the original
idea of the plot was given to Dumas by his friend King William III
of Holland on the occasion of his coronation in 1849, but I consider
that this is doubtful for the reason that Dumas would almost certainly
not have failed to have written an introduction to the book giving
the circumstances of how it came to be written.

     The story was not published serially previous to its publication
in volume form.

Original edition.
"La tulipe noire" par Alexandre Dumas. Paris Baudry, libraire-
éditeur ... . 34, rue Coquilliere. N.d. (1850), 8vo., 3 volumes.
Pagination : Each volume has a half-title listing works published
by Baudry; 313, verso blank, and unnumbered page table of contents;
304 and unnumbered page table of contents; 316 and unnumbered page
table of contents. Yellow wrappers repeating the title-pages. Corbeil, typ. et lith. de CRETE.
(It is worth noting that there are at least two versions of the
advertisements printed on the versos of the half-titles; the advertise-
ents in Volume 3 of my copy includes : "D'Artagnan capitaine des
mousquetaires. Sa vie, ses aventures, sa mort glorieuse", complete
in 2 volumes, but with no author's name given.)

"La tulipe noire", par Alexandre Dumas. Bruxelles, Librairie du
Panthéon, 1850, 18mo., 2 volumes, pp. 142 and 221. Yellow wrappers.
La nouveauté littéraire.

"La tulipe noire" par Alexandre Dumas. Bruxelles, Librairie Tarride, 1850, same format and pagination as the preceding edition.

"La tulipe noire", par Alexandre Dumas. Bruxelles, Meline, Cans et comp., 1850, 12mo., 2 volumes, pp. 261 and 248.

"La tulipe noire" par Alexandre Dumas. Bruxelles, Livourne, Meline, Cans et compagnie; Leipzig, J.P. Meline, 1850, same format and pagination as the preceding edition. Grey wrappers.

Ibid   Bruxelles, Alphonse Lebègue, 1850, 18mo., 2 volumes, pp. 156 and 168. Green wrappers. Muséum littéraire.

"La tulipe noire". Par Alexandre Dumas. Bruxelles, Ch. Muquardt, 1850, same format and pagination as the preceding edition.

Ibid   New-York, Bureau du Courrier des Etats-Unis, 1850. 8vo., pp. 96 in double columns; "La tulipe noire" ends on page 89, and is followed by "Idylle moderne", pp. 90-93, signed : Alexandre Dumas, and "Pan Twardowski", pp. 94-96, by Louis Viardot. Caption title.

Semaine Littéraire du Courrier des Etats-Unis. "La rulipe noire", par Alexandre Dumas. New-York, F. Gaillardet, 1850. Volume 5 part 3, 8vo., pp. (257)-345 in double columns, and followed by "Idylle moderne", pp. (346)-349 comprising six chapters with at the end the initials 'A.D.'.

"La tulipe noire" par Alexandre Dumas. Paris, Michel Lévy frères, n.d. (185), 4to., pp. 64 in double columns. Caption title. Woodcut at head of title. Musée littéraire du siècle. Paris - Impr. Ve Dondey-Dupré.

"La tulipe noire", par Alexandre Dumas. Paris, Michel Lévy frères, 1860, 12mo., pp. 307, verso table of contents.
Frequently reprinted, same format and pagination, by both Michel Lévy frères and Calmann-Lévy.

Ibid   Paris, Calmann-Lèvy, n.d. (188), 4to. Musée littéraire contemporain.

Ibid   Illustrations par Charles Morel. Paris, Calmann-Levy, n.d. (1900), 4to., pp. 224. Le monde illustré.

NOTE : Chapter XXV in editions published in France is entitled 'Le président van Systems', but in the Belgian pirated editions this particular chapter has the title 'Le président van Herysen'.

"TROIS ENTR'ACTES POUR 'L'AMOUR MEDECIN'"   1850

These entr'actes were written in one evening for a performance on the anniversary of Molière's birth, and reference should be made here to Gautier's "Histoire de l'art dramatique en France ... ... " (6me. série), pp. 142-145. '... Non content d'avoir joué Molière tel qu'il est, M. Arsène Houssaye (le nouveau directeur du théâtre de la République) a voulu nous le faire voir dans le milieu où il s'est produit. Sur sa requête, Alexandre Dumas lui a improvisé un public de 1665, et une comédie en trois entr'actes pleine de détails charmants et de traits de moeurs finement sentis, qui vous représentent la société de l'époque et le monde théâtral d'alors. ... Une particularité assez bizarre, c'est que plusieurs personnes, à qui le petit répertoire de Molière n'est pas familier, ont acceuilli par des 'chut!' ls scène de l'Opérateur et des Trivelins, qu'elles croyaient intercalée par Alexandre Dumas, qui a eu, du reste, plusieurs fois dans la soirée le périlleux honneur de voir sa prose confondue avec celle du grand maître.' The play ran for only three nights.

The work was not published separately. It was, however, included in the 25 and 15 volumes "Théatre complet de Alex. Dumas". "Trois entr'actes pour 'L'amour médecin'" Théâtre-Français (sic). - 15 janvier 1850 (Jour anniversaire de la naissance de Molière) "Distribution" on title-page, pp. (321)-359. Théatre complet de Alex. Dumas Tome XVI Paris Calmann Lévy, éditeur ancienne maison Michel Lévy frères, 1874. 12mo. "Théatre complet" in 25 volumes.

It formed part of Volume X of the 15 volume edition.

"URBAIN GRANDIER"   (Drama)   1850

Through his "Crimes célèbres" Dumas was thoroughly familiar with Urbain Grandier's history, and in the play he gave free rein to his imagination. Gautier in his "L'art dramatique en France ... ..." was a little over-enthusiastic when he wrote : 'Voici, sans contredit, le plus beau drame et le plus pompeux spectacle que le Théâtre-Historique nous ait offert depuis son ouverture; ... MM. Dumas et Maquet viennent d'ajouter à leur couronne dramatique : perle désignée dans leur éblouissant écrin, sous l'étiquette d' "Urbain Grandier". ... Nous nous bornerons à dire qu'au point de vue de la pièce amusante, Alexandre Dumas n'a rien fait de mieux réussi qu' "Urbain Grandier", depuis et y compris la "Tour de Nesle".'

Original edition.
"Urbain Grandier" drame en cinq actes, avec prologue, par MM. Alexandre Dumas et Auguste Maquet, représenté, pour la première fois, a Paris, sur le Théatre-Historique, le 30 mars 1850. Caption title. Yellow wrappers : 2me· série du magasin théatral pièces nouvelles, jouées sur tous les théatres de Paris. Théatre Historique. "Urbain Grandier", Drame en cinq actes et treize tableaux, de MM. Alexandre Dumas et Auguste Maquet. (Vignette) Paris. Administration de la librairie théatrale, Ancienne Maison Marchant, 1850, large 8vo., pp. 44 in double columns.

"Urbain Grandier", drame en cinq actes et treize tableaux, dont un prologue, par MM. A. Dumas et A. Maquet. Mise en scène de M.A. Vizentini. Représenté, pour la première fois, à Paris, sur le Théâtre-Historique, le 30 mars 1850; à Bruxelles, sur le Théâtre-Royal de la Monnaie, en juin 1852. Bruxelles, J.-A. Lelong, 1852, 18mo., pp. 160. Répertoire de la scène française, 20e année, no. 25.

"Urbain Grandier" drame en cinq actes, avec prologue, par MM. Alexandre Dumas et Auguste Maquet, représenté, pour la première fois, à Paris, sur le Théatre-historique, le 30 mars 1850. Paris, Imprimerie Dondey-Dupré, n.d. (c 1855), large 8vo., pp. 44 in double columns. Caption title.

"Urbain Grandier" drame en cinq actes et un prologue treize tableaux en société avec M. Auguste Maquet Théâtre-Historique. - 30 mars 1850. "Distribution" on title-page, pp. 2-136. Théatre complet de Alex. Dumas Tome XVII Paris Calmann Lévy, éditeur ancienne maison Michel Lévy frères, 1874. 12mo. "Théatre complet" in 25 volumes.

"L'AUBERGE DE SCHAWASBACH"
"LE VINGT-QUATRE FEVRIER"   1850

This depressing little play was written by Dumas in imitation of the German play by Zacharie Werner. In the original edition under its first title the murder, which was Werner's finale, was altered to a sort of renunciation, but in the later versions published under its second title the German original is followed. As will be seen the play was published under its second title in the Calmann-Lévy "Théâtre complet".

Original edition.
"L'Auberge de Schawasbach" pièce en un acte, par M. Alexandre Dumas, représentée, pour la première fois, a Paris, sur le théatre de la Gaité, le 30 mars 1850. Caption title. Yellow wrappers : Magasin théatral pièces nouvelles jouées sur tous les théatres de Paris. Théatre de la Gaité. "L'Auberge de Schawasbach", Pièce en un acte, de M. Alex. Dumas. (Vignette) Paris. Administration de librairie théatrale, Ancienne Maison Marchant, 1850, large 8vo., pp. 12 in double columns.

Ibid   (Paris), Imprimerie de Dondey-Dupré, n.d. (c 1851), same format and pagination as the preceding edition. Caption title.

"Le vingt-quatre février" drame en un acte imité de la pièce allemande de Z. Werner Gaité. - 30 mars 1850. "Distribution" on title-page, pp. (137)-174. Théatre complet de Alex. Dumas Tome XVII Paris Calmann Lévy, éditeur ancienne maison Michel Lévy frères, 1874. 12mo. "Théatre complet" in 25 volumes.

"LES CHEVALIERS DU LANSQUENET"   1850

Gustave Simon in his "Histoire d'une Collaboration Alexandre Dumas et Auguste Maquet Documents inédits ... ", (Paris, Editions George Crès & Cie., MCMXIX), on pp. 129-133 quotes the text of a letter from Dumas to Maquet written in December, 1850, in which he says : ' ... Maintenant j'ai un tiers dans "Les Lansquenets", je ne sais pas ce que cela fera; j'ai un tiers dans "Pauline" qui ne m'a pris ni travail d'exécution, ni travail de mis en scène. ... '. It is obvious, therefore, that during 1850 Dumas was working in association with Grangé and de Montépin.

Original (and only) edition.
"Les chevaliers du Lansquenet", drame en cinq actes et dix tableaux, précédé de : "Les derniers 100 louis", prologue en un acte, par MM. E. Grangé et X. de Montépin, représenté, pour la première fois, a Paris, sur le théatre de l'Ambigu-Comique, le 4 mai 1850. Caption title followed by 'personnages' 'acteurs', large 8vo., pp. (1)-48 in double columns. Yellow wrappers. Magasin théatral Pièces nouvelles jouées sur tous les théatres de Paris. Théatre de l'Ambigu-Comique, "Les chevaliers du Lansquenet", Drame en 5 actes et 10 tableaux, précédé d'un prologue en 1 acte, de MM. E. Grangé et X. de Montépin. Paris. Administration de librairie théatrale, ... Ancienne Maison Marchant, 1850.

"PAULINE"   (Drama)   1850

In his "Histoire d'une Collaboration Alexandre Dumas et Auguste

Maquet Documents inédits ... " Gustave Simon quotes on pp. 130-131
the text of a letter Dumas wrote to Maquet in December, 1850, in which
he writes : ' ... Aujourd'hui, vous me cites que je travaille en
collaboration. Combien de fois, mon ami, vous ai-je dit de lire
"Pauline" et de voir s'il n'y aurait pas une pièce avec "Pauline",
pourquoi voulais-je essayer de faire une pièce avec des décors et
sans mon nom avec "Le Corricolo"?'

Vapereau in his "Dictionnaire universel des contemporaines"
(Paris, Hachette, 1858), in the article dealing with Xavier de Montépin, confirms Dumas' collaboration in the writing of this play and
states that the play was also performed at the Ambigu-Comique in 1850.

Original edition.
"Pauline" drame en cinq actes et huit tableaux, précédé de "La chasse
au tigre" prologue en un acte tiré du roman de M. A. Dumas par MM.
E. Grangé et X. de Montépin Représenté pour la première fois, à Paris,
sur le Théâtre Historique, le 1er juin 1850. Paris, Librairie théât-
rals, 1850, large 8vo., pp. 38 in double columns. Caption title.
(Magasin théâtral.) Paris, Typographie Dondey-Dupré.

Ibid   Bruxelles, J.-A. Lelong, Imprimeur-Editeur Libraire des théâtres royaux Rue des Pierres, 46 Le soir au Théâtre
Royal, 1850.

"MONTEVIDEO, OU UNE NOUVELLE TROIE"   1850

     Dumas had met and talked with General Pacheco y Obez when he was
on a mission to France trying to enlist support for the saving of
Montevideo from being overwhelmed by forces from Buenos Ayres, and
he subsequently wrote of the heroic struggle during the city's
eight years siege. The work ends with an appeal, and something in
the nature of a diatribe against England and Austria. The work comprises six chapters in all, of which the first two were initially
published in the final two numbers of "Le Mois"; later Dumas quoted
from it in his translation of Garibaldi's memoirs. It also crops
up in his "Parisiens et Provinciaux", as well as in the article "Comment je mis Garibaldi" published in "L'Indépendant. L"Indipendente".
It must have been started towards the end of 1849 and finished in the
early months of 1850.

Original (and only) edition.
"Montevideo, ou une nouvelle Troie", par Alexandre Dumas. Paris,
Imprimerie centrale de Napoléon Chaix et Cie., 12mo., pp. 174.
Dedicated 'Aux Héroique Défenseurs de Montevideo'. Signed : Alex-
andre Dumas.

"LA CHASSE AU CHASTRE"   (Drama)   1850

     This 'fantasy' was based on the story of that name, and it has
been stated that Maquet collaborated. However, if reference is made
to Goizet's "Histoire anecdotique de la collaboration au théâtre"
(Paris, au Bureau du Dictionnaire des Théatres, 1867), it can be read
on page 160 that this play is one of the six which Maquet expressly
asked Goizet to delete from those in which he had any share of the
writing.

As will be seen the original edition consisted of three acts
and eight tableaux. The Calmann-Lévy 25 and 15 volume editions of
Dumas' "Théatre complet" print the work in three acts and seven tableaux, the seventh and eighth of the original having been telescoped
into one.

Original edition.
"La chasse au chastre" fantaisie en trois actes et huit tableaux,
par M. Alexandre Dumas, représentée pour la première fois, a Paris,
sur le Théatre-Historique, le 3 août 1850. Caption title. Yellow
wrappers : Magasin théatral Pièces nouvelles jouées sur tous les
théatres de Paris. Théatre Historique. "La chasse au chastre",
Fantaisie en trois actes et huit tableaux, par M. Alexandre Dumas.
(Vignette) Paris. Administration de librairie théatrale, Ancienne
Maison Marchant, 1850, large 8vo., pp. 24 in double columns.

"La chasse au chastre" fantaisie en trois actes, en sept tableaux
Théâtre Historique. - 3 août 1850. "Distribution" on title-page,
pp. (175)-248. Théatre complet de Alex. Dumas Tome XVII Paris Calmann Lévy, éditeur ancienne maison Michel Lévy frères, 1874. 12mo.
"Théâtre complet" in 25 volumes.

"LES FRERES CORSES"   (Drama)   1850
Signed by Grangé and de Montépin alone this play was based on
Dumas' romance of the same name. Whilst André Maurel in his "Les
trois Dumas" (Paris A la librairie illustrée, n.d. (1896), lists it
on page 154 among Dumas' plays I doubt very much whether Dumas had any
more than a very small hand in its writing. It still remains a mystery as to why Dumas did not himself draw a play from his romance, and
it is not inappropriate to mention here that there are several English
versions, and a great many adaptations and parodies, which were performed not only in Britain but also in the United States.

Original edition.
"Les frères corses" drame fantastique en trois actes et cinq tableaux,
tiré du roman de M. Alexandre Dumas. Par MM. E. Grangé et X. de
Montépin, représenté pour la première fois, à Paris, sur le Théatre-
Historique, le 10 août 1850. Caption title followed by 'personnages'
'acteurs', large 8vo., pp. (1)-26 in double columns. Yellow wrappers
repeating caption title. Paris, Administration de librairie théatrale,
... Ancienne Maison Marchant, 1850. Paris, Imprimerie Dondey-Dupré.

Ibid   Paris, Typographie Dondey-Dupré, n.d. (c 1851),
same format and pagination as the preceding edition.

"LA COLOMBE"
"HISTOIRE D'UNE COLOMBE"   1850
The first draft of this story, written in the form of letters
and Dumas' only attempt to use such a form in a romance (vide "De
Paris à Cadix"), was possibly by the comtesse Dash who may have
brought it to him for revision. According to the date of the letters
the period covered by the work is 5th May, 1637, to 10th September,
1638. They deal with the imagined fate of Antoine, comte de Moret,
the illegitimate son of Henri IV, who was believed to have been

killed during the battle of Castelnaudary in 1632 although his body
was never found. Dumas was later to write a romance around this
subject entitled "Le comte de Moret".

I have not been able to trace any serial issue of the work
before its publication in volume form, although there may well have
been one.

Original edition.
"La colombe", par Alexandre Dumas. Bruxelles, Librairie du Panthéon,
1850, 18mo., pp. 128. Yellow wrappers. La nouveauté littéraire.

"La colombe" par Alexandre Dumas. Bruxelles, Alphonse Lebègue, 1850,
18mo., pp. (5)-112.

"Ange Pitou", par Alexandre Dumas. Edition autorisée pour la Belgique
et l'étranger, interdite pour la France. Bruxelles, Meline, Cans et
Cie., 1851, 18mo., 5 volumes. The last volume comprises 287 pages
and is completed by "La colombe", pp. 161-287.

Ibid   La Haye, chez les héritiers Doorman, 1851, same
format and pagination as the preceding edition.

"Histoire d'une colombe" par Alexandre Dumas. Paris, Alexandre Cadot,
éditeur, 32, rue de la Harpe, 1851, 8vo., 2 volumes. Pagination :
Volume 1, 1851, 303, verso blank, and 8 pages of publisher's advertisements; Volume 2, dated 1852 on title-page but 1851 on wrapper, 319.
"Histoire d'une colombe" ends on page 57 of Volume 2, verso blank, and
is followed by "Chateaubriand" pp. (59)-235, verso blank, and "Le roi
Pépin" pp. (237)-319. There are no tables of contents. Yellow
wrappers. Sceaux, impr. de E. Dépée.

"Histoire d'une colombe", par Alexandre Dumas. Edition autorisée
pour la Belgique et l'étranger, interdite pour la France. Bruxelles,
Meline, Cans et Cie., 1852, 16mo., pp. 236.

Ibid   La Haye, chez les héritiers Doorman, 1852, same
format and pagination as the preceding edition.

"Histoire d'une colombe" par Alexandre Dumas. Bruxelles, Livourne,
Meline, Cans et cie.; Leipzig, J.P. Meline, 1852, same format and
pagination as the preceding editions. Blue wrappers.

Semaine Littéraire du Courrier des Etats-Unis. Receuil Choisi de
romans, feuilletons, ouvrages historiques et dramatiques, en prose
et en vers des auteurs modernes les plus renommés. Vol. 5, part 4,
1853. New-York : F. Gaillardet, 1853. "La colombe". Par Alexandre
Dumas. Large 8vo., pp. (1)-34 in double columns.

"La colombe" was published in "Le Monte-Cristo" starting with No. 69
dated 26th August and running through to No. 80 dated 3rd October,
1862, in double columns.

"La colombe" "Maître Adam le Calabrais" par Alexandre Dumas. Paris,
Michel Lévy frères, 1863, 12mo., pp. 304 and unnumbered page table of
contents. "La colombe" occupies pp. (1)-136.
Several times reprinted, same format and pagination, by both Michel
Lévy frères and Calmann-Lévy.

"La colombe" par Alexandre Dumas Paris, Calmann-Lévy, n.d. (c 187),
4to., pp. (1)-26 in double columns. Caption title. Woodcut at head
of title.

Ibid   Paris, Calmann-Lévy, n.d. (188), same format and
pagination as the preceding edition. Musée littéraire contemporain.

"LE TROU DE L'ENFER"   1850-1851

    This story is, in fact, the first part of the work published
under the collective title of "Dieu dispose", and was first published
included in that collective title in : 'L'Evenément' (Impr. de
Serrière. Paris - Primes de L'Evenément, 1850-1851, folio), a comparatively little known journal which offered it as a bonus to its
subscribers. The work was originally divided into four parts entitled respectively : "Le trou de l'enfer" and "Le château double"
forming together the present "Le trou de l'enfer", and "Les coulisses
d'une révolution" and "Mine et contre-mine" to be published as "Dieu
dispose". But these divisions are not shown in the first editions to
be published in France under the separate titles, but only in the
edition of "Dieu dispose" published by Meline, Cans et compagnie and
J.P. Meline in 1851. It is well, therefore, to treat the complete
work as two separate entities under their respective titles.

    "Le trou de l'enfer" is, in a disagreeable way, an impressive
story concerned with secret societies in Germany during the Napoleonic
suppression and includes one of Dumas' most ignoble characters, Samuel
Gelb. The work opens about mid-1810, and closes with Napoleon on the
way to his Russian campaign nearly two years later. It is almost
certainly Dumas working alone.

Original edition.
"Dieu dispose" par Alexandre Dumas. Bruxelles, Livourne, Meline,
Cans et compagnie; Leipzig, J.P. Meline, 1851, 18mo., 6 volumes,
comprising : Première partie. "Le trou de l'enfer", pp. (3)-13
'prologue', (14)-231; Seconde partie. "Le château double", pp. (3)-
248; Seconde partie. "Le château double" (suite), pp. (1)-110.
The remaining sequence of the omnibus title will be found under "Dieu
dispose".

Semaine Littéraire du Courrier des Etats-Unis. "Dieu dispose" par
Alexandre Dumas. New-York, Bureau du Courrier des Etats-Unis, 1851,
large 8vo., pp. 340 in double columns, of which "Le trou de l'enfer"
and "Le château double" occupy pp. (3)-51 and (52)-125 respectively.

"Le trou de l'enfer" par Alexandre Dumas Paris Alexandre Cadot,
éditeur, 32, rue de la Harpe, 1851, 8vo., 4 volumes, pp. 320, 320,
324 and 354, each with an additional unnumbered page table of contents.
"Le trou de l'enfer" ends on page 164 of Volume 4, and is followed
by "Chronique de Charlemagne". Yellow wrappers. Sceaux, impr. E.
Depée.
Both Parran and Glinel say 1850-1851 for the years of publication,
but the Bibliothèque Nationale copy is dated 1851 and I have never
traced copies with an earlier date.
Reprinted, same format and pagination, with Volumes 1-3 dated 1852,
and Volume 4, 1853.

"Le trou de l'enfer", par Alexandre Dumas. Publié par Dufour et
Mulat. Edition illustrée par J.-A. Beaucé et Lancelot. Paris,
Marescq et Cie., 1855, 4to., pp. 154 in double columns, and unnumbered
page table of contents; 10 illustrations.

"Le trou de l'enfer" par Alexandre Dumas publié par Dufour et Mulat Edition illustrée par J.-A. Beaucé et Lancelot. (Vignette) (Paris), Lécrivain et Toubon, 1860, 4to., pp. 154 in double columns, and 2 unnumbered pages table of contents and 'placement des gravures'; 10 illustrations.
Reprinted, same format, pagination and illustrations, 1861.

"Le trou de l'enfer" par Alexandre Dumas; Paris Michel Lévy frères, libraires-éditeurs, 1862, 12mo., pp. 363. There is no table of contents.
Frequently reprinted, same format and pagination, by both Michel Lévy frères and Calmann-Lévy.

Alexandre Dumas "Le trou de l'enfer" Edition illustrée par J.-A. Beaucé et Lancelot. Paris, Calmann-Lévy, 1897, 4to., pp. 154 in double columns, and unnumbered page table of contents. Caption title. Woodcut at head of title. Oeuvres illustrées.

"Le trou de l'enfer" par Alexandre Dumas Paris Calmann-Lévy, n.d. (c 189), 4to. Caption title. Woodcut at head of title. Musée littéraire contemporain.

"DIEU DISPOSE"   1850-1851

As explained under "Le trou de l'enfer" this work is, in reality, the second portion published in its entirety first under the collective title "Dieu dispose" in the journal 'L'Evenément'. It comprises the third and fourth parts entitled respectively : "Les coulisses d'une révolution" and "Mine et contre-mine".

The period is now 1829-1830 and the writing, compared with the earlier parts, is markedly inferior; it would seem that Dumas was working on a roughly outlined draft prepared by someone else, but the collaborator cannot be identified. It is a story of revenge and a good deal more - the 'Tugenbund' is still present, as is the malevolent and unsavoury Samuel Gelb, but it is all too long drawn out.

Original edition.
The following three entries comprise those editions which include both "Le trou de l'enfer" and "Dieu dispose", but which do not divide he two works into their components parts : "Dieu dispose", par Alexandre Dumas. Bruxelles, Lebègue, (Volume 1 'Alp. Lebègue', Volume 2 'Alph. Lebègue', Volumes 3-6 'Alphonse Lebègue', Volumes 7-8 'Alph. Lebègue'), 1850-1851, 18mo., 8 volumes. Pagination : Volumes 1-3 (1850), 160, 156 and 166; Volumes 4-8 (1851), 160, 176, 160, 178 and 154.

Ibid   Bruxelles, Kiessling et compagnie, same years of publication, format, number of volumes and pagination as the preceding edition.

Ibid   Bruxelles, Livourne, Meline, Cans et Cie.; Leipzig, J.P. Meline, 1850-1851, 18mo., 8 volumes. Pagination : Volume 1 (1850), 159; Volumes 2-8 (1851), 152, 166, 157, 160, 151, 172 and 171. Blue wrappers. Bibliothèque Littéraire.

"Dieu dispose" par Alexandre Dumas. Bruxelles, Livourne, Meline,

Cans et compagnie; Leipzig, J.P. Meline, 1851, 18mo., 6 volumes, comprising : Troisième partie (Volume 3). "Les coulisses d'une révolution", pp. (113)-264; Troisième partie (Volume 4). "Les coulisses d'une révolution" (suite), pp. (1)-264; Troisième partie (Volume 5). "Les coulisses d'une révolution" (suite), pp. (1)-47, verso blank; Quatrième partie "Mine et contre-mine", pp. (51)-260; Quatrième partie. (Volume 6). "Mine et contre-mine" (suite), pp. (1)-288.

"Dieu dispose", par Alexandre Dumas. La Haye, chez les héritiers Doorman, 1851, same number of volumes, format and pagination as the preceding edition.

Semaine Littéraire du Courrier des Etats-Unis. "Dieu dispose" par Alexandre Dumas. New-York, Bureau du Courrier des Etats-Unit, 1851, 8vo., pp. 340 in double columns, of which "Les coulisses d'une révolution" and "Mine et contre-mine" occupy pp. (126)-228 and (229)-340 respectively.

(The entries for the Meline, Cans et compagnie; J.P. Meline, and Semaine Littéraire ... editions should be read in conjunction with the same publishers' entries under "Le trou de l'enfer".)

"Dieu dispose" par Alexandre Dumas Paris Alexandre Cadot, éditeur, 32, rue de la Harpe, 1851, 8vo., 6 volumes, pp. 318, 325, 301, 318, 325 and 280; Volume 6 is completed by "Le prix de pigeons" par Alexandre Dumas fils, pp. (281)-351. Each volume has an additional unnumbered page table of contents. Yellow wrappers. Sceaux, impr. E. Dépée.

"Dieu dispose" par Alexandre Dumas Paris Michel Lévy frères, libraires-éditeurs, 1862, 12mo., 2 volumes, pp. 371, verso unnumbered page table of contents, and 365, verso blank, 2 unnumbered pages table of contents.
Frequently reprinted, same format and pagination, by both Michel Lévy frères and Calmann-Lévy.

Ibid   Paris, Calmann-Lévy, 1897, 4to. Caption title. Woodcut at head of title. Musée littéraire contemporain.

"ANGE PITOU"   1850-1851

    The third of the great Revolutionary romances, and the sequel to "Le collier de la reine", this was to be succeeded by "La comtesse de Charny". It first appeared serially in 'La Presse' from 17th June, 1850, to 26th June, 1851, and was contracted for just prior to Dumas' rupture with Maquet; the latter may have helped with the first outline of the work, but that could be all. In the romance Dumas drew upon his boyhood memories and made Ange Pitou a native of his own district near Villers-Cotterets. (The historical Ange Pitou was a Royalist agent and street-singer who lived from 1767 to 1846.) The work centres around the fall of the Bastille and covers the period July, 1789, to early October of the same year. The whole of the work is in Dumas' best style; it was abruptly brought to an end, Dumas giving as a reason the imposition of a prohibitive stamp duty on journals publishing works in feuilleton form.

Original edition.
"Mémoires d'un médecin", par Alexandre Dumas. "Ange Pitou". Bruxelles, Librairie du Panthéon, 1851, 18mo., 7 volumes.

Pagination : 128, 145, 133, 136, 136, 153 and 256. Yellow wrappers.
La nouveauté littéraire. "Mémoires d'un médecin", par Al. Dumas.
"Ange Pitou". Bruxelles, Librairie du Panthéon, 1851.

"Ange Pitou", par Alexandre Dumas. Edition autorisée pour la Belgique et l'étranger, interdite pour la France. Bruxelles, Meline,
Cans et Cie., 1851, 18mo., 5 volumes. Pagination : 255, 270, 254,
255 and 287. "Ange Pitou" ends on page 157 of Volume 5, the volume
being completed by "La colombe", pp. 161-287.

Ibid   La Haye, chez les héritiers Doorman, 1851, same
number of volumes, format and pagination as the preceding edition.

"Ange Pitou" par Alexandre Dumas. Bruxelles, Livourne, Meline, Cans
et compagnie; Leipzig, J.P. Meline, 1851, same number of volumes,
format and pagination as the preceding editions.

"Mémoires d'un médecin. Ange Pitou". Par Alexandre Dumas. Auteur
de "Monte-Christo", des "Trois mousquetaires", etc. Bruxelles, Alp.
Lebègue, 1851, 24mo., 6 volumes. Pagination : 111, 127, 128, 127,
137 and 125; "Ange Pitou" ends on page 43 of Volume 6, which is completed by "Chateaubriand", pp. (45)-125.

"Mémoires d'un médecin. Ange Pitou". Par Alexandre Dumas. Auteur
de "Monte-Christo", des "Trois mousquetaires", &. Edition autorisée
pour la Belgique et l'étranger, interdite pour la France. Bruxelles
et Leipzig, Kiessling, Schnée et compagnie, 1851, same number of
volumes, format and pagination as the preceding edition. Pp. (45)-
125 of Volume 6 comprising a 'necrology' of François-René Chateaubriand.

"Ange Pitou", par Alexandre Dumas. Bruxelles, Librairie de Ch.
Muquardt, 1851, 24mo., 6 volumes, pp. 157, 148, 166, 143, 176 and 163.

"Ange Pitou", par Alexandre Dumas. Paris, Alexander Cadot, éditeur,
32, rue de la Harpe, 1851, 8vo., 8volumes. Pagination : 320 including table of contents; 322, 315 each with an additional unnumbered
page table of contents; 304 including table of contents; 326, 306,
305 and 334 each with an additional unnumbered page table of contents.
Yellow wrappers. Sceaux, impr. de E. Dépée.

"Ange Pitou" par Alexandre Dumas. Berlin, 1851. Librairie B. Behr,
24mo., 5 volumes (Tomes 14-18), pp. 166, 164, 156, 160 and 83; each
volume has 2 title-pages followed by 4 unnumbered pages. The work
is described as "Mémoires d'un médecin" Serie 3.

Semaine Littéraire du Courrier des Etats-Unis. "Ange Pitou" (Troisième épisode des "Mémoires d'un médecin".) Par Alexandre Dumas. Caption title. (New-York, F. Gaillardet, 1846 (sic).) 8vo., pp. (1)-246
in double columns.
It is clear that the publisher contined with the '1846' dating from
his publishing of "Joseph Balsamo" in that year; the date should
obviously have been corrected to '1851'.

Le Siècle. "Ange Pitou" par Alexandre Dumas. Paris, Bureaux du
Siècle, 1853, 4to., pp. 177 in double columns, and unnumbered page
table of contents.

"Ange Pitou" par Alexandre Dumas. Paris, Michel Lévy frères, 1854,
12mo., 2 volumes, pp. 342 and 338 each with 2 additional pages table
of contents.
Frequently reprinted, same format but with varying paginations, by
both Michel Lévy frères and Calmann-Lévy.

"Mémoires d'un médecin Ange Pitou" par Alexandre Dumas Paris Dufour,
Mulat et Boulanger, éditeurs (se réservent le droit de reproduction
et de traduction a l'étranger) 21 quai Malaquais 1856, large 8vo.,
pp. (1)-489, verso blank, (491)-493 table of contents, and unnumbered
page 'classement des gravures'; frontispiece and 27 full-page illustrations.
Reprinted, same format and pagination but with 24 illustrations,
1861.

"Mémoires d'un médecin. Ange Pitou" par Alexandre Dumas. Paris,
Dufour et Mulat, 1857, large 8vo., pp. (1)-489, verso blank, (491)-
493 table of contents, and unnumbered page 'classement des gravures';
frontispiece and 26 full-page illustrations.

"Ange Pitou" par Alexandre Dumas. In : 'Journal du jeudi', No.
203, 10 avril 1862, to No. 235, 21 juillet 1862. Treble columns.
Engraving at head of each number.

"Mémoires d'un médecin. Ange Pitou" par Alexandre Dumas. Paris,
Legrand, Troussel et Pomey, n.d. (c 186), same format and pagination
as the Dufour, Mulat et Boulanger, 1856, edition, but with frontispiece and 26 full-page illustrations.

"Ange Pitou" par Alexandre Dumas. Paris, Calmann-Lévy, n.d. (c 187),
4to., pp. 177 in double columns, page 178 table of contents. Caption
title. Oeuvres complètes d'Alexandre Dumas.

Ibid   Paris, Calmann-Lévy, n.d. (c 189), 4to., 2 volumes. Musée littéraire contemporain.

"Ange Pitou", par Alexandre Dumas. Paris, Calmann-Lévy, n.d.
(c 189), 8vo., pp. 677.

"LOUIS XVI"
"LOUIS XVI ET LA REVOLUTION"   1850 -
"HISTOIRE DE LOUIS XVI ET DE MARIE-ANTOINETTE"

     The above are the same work published under differing titles
and are a further addition to Dumas' series of historical works de--
signed to popularise French history. This is Dumas writing alone.

Original edition.
"Louis XVI" par Alexandre Dumas. Paris, Alexandre Cadot, éditeur,
32, rue de la Harpe, 1850-1851, 8vo., 5 volumes, pp. 317, 312, 304,
304 and 407. There are no tables of contents. Yellow wrappers.
Impr. Bonaventure et Ducessois.

"Louis XVI", par Alexandre Dumas. Bruxelles, Meline, Cans et Cie.,
1850-1851, 16mo., 5 volumes. Pagination : Volumes 1 and 2 (1850),
239 and 226; Volumes 3-5 (1851), 215, 267 and 242.

Ibid   La Haye, chez les héritiers Doorman, 1850-1851,
same years of publication, format and pagination as the preceding
edition.

Ibid   Bruxelles, Livourne, Meline, Cans et Cie.; Leipzig,
J.P. Meline, 1850-1851, same years of publication, format and pagination as the preceding editions.

(The four following editions are emasculated versions, and for purposes

of comparison end with Chapter 2, Volume 2, of "Histoire de Louis
XVI et de Marie-Antoinette" in the Dufour et Mulat, 1852, edition
referred to below.)

"Louis seize" par Alexandre Dumas. Bruxelles, Alph. Lebègue, 1850-
1851, 18mo., 5 volumes. Pagination : Volumes 1 and 2 (1850), 134
and 124; Volumes 3-5 (1851), 120, 118 and 158. Muséum littéraire.
Green wrappers - Volumes 1 and 2 with the imprint 'Alphonse Lebègue'
and Volumes 3-5 with 'Alph. Lebègue'.

Ibid   1850-1851, Volumes 1 and 2, Bruxelles, Alph.
Lebègue, 1850, and Volumes 3-5, Bruxelles et Leipzig, Kiessling et
compagnie, 1851; same format and pagination as the preceding edition.

Ibid   Bruxelles et Leipzig, Kiessling et compagnie,
1850-1851, same years of publication, format and pagination as the
preceding editions.

Ibid   (Vignette) Bruxelles, Librairie de Ch. Muquardt,
même maison a Leipzig et a Gand. 1851, same format and pagination
as the preceding editions.

"Histoire de Louis XVI et de Marie-Antionette" par M. Alex. Dumas
Paris Dufour et Mulat, libraires-éditeurs quai Malaquais, 21 1852,
large 8vo., 3 volumes. Pagination : Volume 1, (1)-416, (417)-422
table of contents, frontispiece and 13 plates; Volume 2, (1)-424,
(425)-432 table of contents, frontispiece and 15 plates; Volume 3,
(1)-390, (391)-394 table of contents, (395)-396 'classement des
gravures' for the 3 volumes, frontispiece and 9 plates. The text
proper ends on page 319 of Volume 3, verso blank, 'pièces justificatives' pp. (321)-390. Lagny. - typographie de Vialat et Cie.
The engravings are by Philippoteaux, and this is the first illustrated
edition of the work.
Reprinted, same format, pagination and illustrations, 1852, 1853.

"Louis XVI et la révolution" par Alexandre Dumas. Paris, Michel Lévy
frères, 1866, 12mo., 2 volumes, pp. 324 and 326.
Quite frequently reprinted, same format but with varying paginations,
by both Michel Lévy frères and Calmann-Lévy.

"CHATEAUBRIAND"   1851
     The vicomte de Chateaubriand died in 1848 and had been a close
friend of Dumas. Together with François Villemain, the then Minister
of Public Instruction, he had been a witness at Dumas' marriage to
Ida Ferrier on 1st February, 1840. This is Dumas' personal 'memoir'
of him.

Original edition.
"Histoire d'une colombe" par Alexandre Dumas. Paris, Alexandre Cadot,
editeur, 1851, 8vo., 2 volumes. "Histoire d'une colombe" ends on
page 57 of Volume 2, verso blank, and is followed by "Chateaubriand",
pp. (59)-235, verso blank, and "Le roi Pépin", pp. (237)-319. There
are no tables of contents.

"Chateaubriand" par Alexandre Dumas. It was used to complete the
sixth and final volume of "Mémoires d'un médecin. Ange Pitou", Bruxelles, Alp. Lebègue, 1851, 24mo., pp. (5)-80.

Ibid   Edition autorisée pour la Belgique et l'étranger,

interdite pour la France. Bruxelles et Leipzig, Kiessling, Schnée
et cie., 1851, 16mo., pp. (5)-80.

"Notice sur M. de Chateaubriand" signed : Alex. Dumas. In :
'L'Echo des feuilletons receuil de nouvelles, légendes, anecdotes,
épisodes, ... Extraits de la presse contemporaine.' Directeurs :
MM. Dufour, Mulat et Boulanger. Tome dixième. Paris, chez les
éditeurs, 1857, 8vo., pp. (225)-250 in double columns. Woodcut at
head of title and preceded by steel engraving of Chateaubriand.

"Les morts vont vite" par Alexandre Dumas Paris Michel Lévy frères,
libraires-éditeurs, 1861, 12mo., 2 volumes. "Chateaubriand" occupies
pp. (1)-92 of Volume 1.
Several times reprinted, same format and pagination, by both Michel
Lévy frères and Calmann-Lévy.

Ibid   Paris, Michel Lévy frères, n.d. (187), 4to.
Musée littéraire contemporain.

"LA BARRIERE CLICHY"   1851

     Lecomte has written in his "Alexandre Dumas 1802-1870 Sa Vie
intime Ses oeuvres" that this drama was written 'en société avec
Auguste Maquet et Paul Meurice', but he has overlooked the fact that
according to Goizet in his "Histoire anecdotique de la collaboration
au théâtre" this was one of the six plays from which Maquet wished
to have his name deleted as having had anything to do with the writing.

     The play opens just before Napoleon's banishment to Elba and
ends with his return from that island. There is a slight link with
his earlier play "Napoléon Bonaparte" by the inclusion here of the
old soldier, Lorrain. In a brief postscript to the published version
referring to his political beliefs Dumas has written : 'Je nie avoir
jamais fait une pièce politique à un autre point de vue que les idées
republicaines.' It may be noted that the title of the play as included in the Lévy editions of the "Théatre complet" is "La barrière
de Clichy".

Original edition.
"La barrière Clichy" drame militaire en 5 actes et 14 tableaux, par
M. Alexandre Dumas, Mise en scène de M. Albert, Musique de M. Fessy,
Ballet de M. Laurent, Décorations de MM. Wagner, Cicéri, Cheret,
Duflocq, Moynet et Sacchetti. Représenté, pour la première fois, a
Paris, sur le Théâtre National (Ancien Cirque) le 21 avril 1851.
Paris, Librairie théatrale, 1851, 8vo., pp. 48 in double columns.
Caption title. Pink wrappers with vignette. Magasin théatral.
Pièces nouvelles jouées sur tous les théatres de Paris.

Ibid   Paris, Imprimerie de madame veuve Dondey-Dupré,
n.d. (1851), same format and pagination as the preceding edition.

"La barrière de Clichy drame militaire en cinq actes, en quatorze
tableaux Théâtre-National (ancien Cirque). - 21 avril 1851. "Distribution" on title-page and page 2, pp. 2-149; post-scriptum, pp.
149-150 signed : Alex. Dumas. Théatre complet de Alex. Dumas
Tome XVIII Paris Calmann Lévy, éditeur ancienne maison Michel Lévy
frères, 1874. 12mo. "Théâtre complet" in 25 volumes.

Note : "Analyse de la pièce de 'La barrière Clichy', drame militaire

... par M. A. Dumas ... ." Angers, Impr. de Cosnier et Lacheze,
n.d. (1852), 4to., pp. 4. Théâtre d'Angers.

"LE DRAME DE QUATRE-VINGT-TREIZE   :   SCENES DE LA VIE
REVOLUTIONNAIRE"   1851

This work is, in fact, a continuation of Dumas' "Louis XVI"
(and alternative titles) since it is a narrative of the years 1789-
1793. Just as with the preceding works it is Dumas working alone.

Original edition.
"Le drame de quatre-vingt-treize, scènes de la vie révolutionnaire",
par Alexandre Dumas. Paris, Hippolyte Souverain, 1851, 8vo., 7 volumes, pp. 302, 300, 320, 302, 308, 311 and 308. Yellow wrappers.

"Le drame de quatre-vingt-treize. Scènes de la vie révolutionnaire",
par Alexandre Dumas. Bruxelles, Alp. Lebègue (with the exception of
Volumes 4 and 5 which have the imprint 'Alphonse Lebègue'), 1851,
18mo., 5 volumes, pp. 125, 162, 155, 128 and 200; each volume has the
half-title : 'Scènes de la vie révolutionnaire'. Green wrappers.
Muséum littéraire with the imprint 'Alph. Lebègue'.

"Le drame de quatre-vingt-treize. Scènes de la vie révolutionnaire"
par Alexandre Dumas. Bruxelles, Livourne, Meline, Cans et Cie.;
Leipzig, J.P. Meline, 1851, 16mo., 3 volumes, pp. 245, 240 and 268;
each volume has the half-title : 'Scènes de la vie révolutionnaire'.

"Le drame de quatre-vingt-treize. Scènes de la vie révolutionnaire",
par Alexandre Dumas. Bruxelles et Leipzig, Kiessling et Compagnie,
1851, 18mo., 5 volumes, pp. 125, 162, 155, 128 and 200.

"Le drame de quatre-vingt-treize - Scènes de la vie révolutionnaire",
par Alexandre Dumas. Bruxelles, Librairie de Ch. Muquardt, même
maison a Leipzig et Gand. 1851, 5 volumes, same format and pagination
as the preceding edition.

(It is quite possible that Dufour et Mulat may have published in 1852
an illustrated edition of this work as "L'histoire de deux siècles"
which includes the full text of "Le drame de quatre-vingt-treize. ...".)

"Le drame de quatre-vingt-treize" par Alexandre Dumas. Paris, Michel
Lévy frères, 1866-1867, 12mo., 3 volumes, pp. 300, 282 and 311.
Often reprinted, same format and pagination, by both Michel Lévy
frères and Calmann-Lévy.

"LE VAMPIRE"   1851

It may be recalled that the first play that Dumas saw performed
when he arrived in Paris in his youth was "Le vampire", written by
Charles Nodier, Carmouche et Jouffroy, and which was published by
Barba in 1820. It was in all probability based on Doctor Polidori's
"The Vampyre". The version that Dumas saw must have impressed him,
for after all those years he wrote a version of his own which suffers
from precisely the same defect as that which he pointed out with
regard to the version by Nodier and his friends - the repetition of
a similar tragedy in different acts.

No earlier edition of the play can be traced before its publication by Lévy in the "Théâtre complet". It may be added that Glinel

has insisted that its first performance was on 30th December and not on 20th of that month.

Original edition.
"Le vampire" drame fantastique en cinq actes, en dix tableaux en société avec M. Auguste Maquet Ambigu-Comique. - 20 décembre 1851. "Distribution" on title-page, pp. (151)-287. Théatre complet de Alex. Dumas Tome XVIII Paris Calmann Lévy, éditeur ancienne maison Michel Lévy frères, 1874. 12mo. "Théatre complet" in 25 volumes.

The play was published in Volume XI of the Lévy "Théatre complet" in 15 volumes.

"OLYMPE DE CLEVES"   1851-1852

This fine romance is less well-known than it deserves. It was the last romance that Dumas wrote before he left for Brussels in December, 1851. The period of the story is 1727-1729, covering the early years of Louis XV's reign after the death of the Regent d'Orléans, and it deals with the lives of some strolling players who became involved with members of the Court and thus introducing some of the intrigues revolving around the first love affairs of the young king.

It was first published serially in 'Le Siècle' from 16th October, 1851, to 19th February, 1852.

Original edition.
"Olympe de Clèves" par Alexandre Dumas. Bruxelles, Librairie du Panthéon, 1851-1852, 18mo., 9 volumes. Pagination : Volumes 1 and 2 (1851), 126 and 125; Volumes 3-9 (1852), 140, 151, 135, 142, 128, 151 and 151. Yellow wrappers. La Nouveauté littéraire. Reprinted, same number of volumes, format and pagination, 1854.

Ibid   Bruxelles, Alphonse Lebègue, 1851-1852, 18mo., 7 volumes. Pagination : Volumes 1-4 (1851), 160, 158, 160 and 160; Volumes 5-7 (1852), 160, 163 and 192, followed by pp. 193-200 being Dumas' note 'au lecteur'. Green wrappers. Muséum littéraire.

Ibid   Bruxelles, Librairie de Ch. Muquardt, and, Alphonse Lebègue, 1851-1852, 18mo., 7 volumes. Same pagination as the preceding edition with Volume 1 (1851) having the imprint 'Librairie de Ch. Muquardt', and Volumes 2-4 (1851) and 5-7 (1852) having the imprint 'Alphonse Lebègue'.

Ibid   Bruxelles et Leipzig, Kiessling et Compie.; Vienne, A la librairie de J.F. Gresse, 1851-1852, 7 volumes, same years of publication, format and pagination as the two preceding editions. Brown wrappers.

Ibid   Bruxelles, Meline, Cans et Cie., 1852, 24mo., 8 volumes, pp. 159, 157, 119, 152, 147, 140, 129 and 132.

"Olympe de Clèves", par Alexandre Dumas. La Haye, chez les héritiers Doorman, 1852, same format and pagination as the preceding edition.

"Olympe de Clèves" par Alexandre Dumas. Bruxelles, Livourne, Meline, Cans et compagnie; Leipzig, J.P. Meline, 1852, 18mo., 5 volumes, pp. 246, 288, 254, 313 and 276. Volume 5 has an epilogue 'Au lecteur', pp. 277-284.

242

Ibid   Bruxelles, Librairie de C. Muquardt, même maison
à Gand et Leipzig, 1852, 14mo., 8 volumes, pp. 159, 157, 119, 152,
147, 140, 129 and 132.

Ibid   Paris, Alexandre Cadot, éditeur, 37, rue Serpente,
1852, 8vo., 9 volumes, pp. 332, 319, 307, 319, 309, 327, 314, 314 and
319; each volume has an additional unnumbered page table of contents.
Yellow wrappers. Sceaux, impr. de E. Dépée.
(Parran raises the interesting point here in his work covering the
original editions of Dumas that : 'Dans cet ouvrage, comme la
plupart de ceux destinés aux cabinets de lecture, il y a sur les
titres des erreurs de date et de tomaison.' This has not been my
experience, although it is worth recording that Talvart et Place
give the pagination of the 9 volumes which they record as having been
published in 1852 as follows - 332 and additional page table of contents, 320 including table of contents, 308 including table of contents, 320 including table of contents, 309 and additional page table
of contents, 328 including table of contents, 314, 314 and additional
page table of contents for each volume, and 320 including table of
contents.)

Ibid   Paris, Impr. de Walder, n.d. (c 185), 4to., pp.
(179)-402 in double columns.

Ibid   Paris, Michel Lévy frères, 1856, 12mo., 3 volumes,
pp. 284, 276 and 261.
Often reprinted, same format but with varying paginations, by both
Michel Lévy frères and Calmann-Lévy.

Journal du dimanche. "Olympe de Clèves". No. 645, 3 janvier 1864,
through to No. 692, 16 juin 1864, with final 'Au lecteur' on pp.
123-124, in treble columns, signed : Alexandre Dumas. 4to.; woodcut at head of each issue.

"Olympe de Clèves" par Alexandre Dumas. Paris, Calmann-Lévy, n.d.
(c 189), 4to., 3 volumes. Musée littéraire contemporain.

"CONSCIENCE"
"CONSCIENCE L'INNOCENT"
"DIEU ET DIABLE"   1852
"LE BIEN ET LE MAL"

     This work, one of Dumas' own favourites, concerns the adventures
of a conscript and covers the period starting in 1810 to 1815, ending
with Napoleon's passage through Villers-Cotterets on his way to Water-
loo. It will be recalled that Dumas was an eye-witness of this event.

     It was Dumas' intention on arriving in Brussels in December,
1851, to continue his Revolutionary romances with "La comtesse de
Charny". In this, however, he was held up by his inability to get in
that city a copy of Michelet's "Histoire de la Révolution". To fill
in the time until a copy came from Paris a friend lent him to read
Hendrik Conscience's "Le conscrit". Dumas was particularly taken by
one chapter in that book dealing with the blindness of the hero, and
he wrote to the young Flemish author asking his permission to use this
incident in a story he was considering writing. Permission was readily
granted and the result was that Dumas' work, in due course, was entitled "Conscience" and "Conscience l'innocent"; it was also published

under the alternative titles of "Dieu et diable" and "Le bien et le
mal". The romance first appeared in 'Le Pays' with omissions, owing
to political considerations, concerning Napoleon. These were restored
when the work was published in volume form.

Original edition.
"Conscience l'innocent" par Alexandre Dumas. Bruxelles, Livourne,
Meline, Cans et Cie.; Leipzig, J.P. Meline, 1852, 18mo., 3 volumes,
pp. (1)-4 Dumas' letter to Meline, (5) dedication to Michelet :
' A Michelet l'historien, A Michelet le philosophe, A Michelet le
poëte! Lisez ce livre, mon cher Michelet, et vous jugerez si je
vous ai lu. Seulement, n'en reprenez pas ce qui est à vous, venant
de vous, - le reste ne vaudrait pas la peine de vous être offert.
Alex. Dumas.', verso blank, (7)-294, 268 and 269. Yellow wrappers,
the backs of all of which announce "Mémoires d'Alexandre Dumas" in
'12 à 15 volumes.'

"Conscience l'innocent", par Alexandre Dumas. La Haye, chez les
héritiers Doorman, 1852, same number of volumes, format and pagination
as the preceding edition.

"Conscience l'innocent" par Alexandre Dumas. Bruxelles, Livourne,
Meline, Cans et Cie.; Leipzig, J.P. Meline, 1852, 24mo., 4 volumes,
pp. 134, 140, 125 and 144. Blue wrappers.

"Dieu et diable" par Alexandre Dumas. Bruxelles, Alphonse Lebègue,
1852, 18mo., 3 volumes, pp. 164, 144 and 212. At the head of the
opening chapter in each of the three volumes is printed : 'Dieu et
diable. Dieu! Conscience l'innocent'. Blue wrappers. Muséum
littéraire.

Ibid   Bruxelles et Leipzig, Kiessling et compagnie,
1852, same number of volumes, format and pagination as the preceding
editions.

Ibid   Bruxelles et Leipzig, Kiessling et Compagnie;
Vienne, A la librairie de J.F. Gress, 1852, same number of volumes,
format and pagination as the two preceding editions.

"La bien et le mal", par Alexandre Dumas. Bruxelles, Imprimerie de
V. Manche, 1852, 18mo., 4 volumes, pp. 117, 128, 164 and 163. Buff
wrappers. Nouveauté littéraire.

"Conscience l'innocent" par Alexandre Dumas. Bruxelles, Gand et
Leipzig, Librairie de C. Muquardt, 1852, 24mo., 4 volumes, pp. 134,
140, 125 and 144. Impr. de G. Stapleaux.

"Conscience" par Alexandre Dumas. Paris, Alexandre Cadot, éditeur,
37, rue Serpente, 1852, 8vo., 5 volumes, pp. 303, 329, 301, 286 and
226; Volume 5 is completed by "Le pendu de la piroche" pp. (227)-274,
and "Les trois chants du bossu" pp. (275)-332, both by Alexandre Dumas,
fils. Each volume has an additional unnumbered page table of contents.
Yellow wrappers. Sceaux, impr. de E. Dépée.
(Talvart et Place give a different pagination from the above : Volume 1, pp. 304 including table of contents, Volumes 2-5, pp. 329, 301,
286 and 332 each with an additional unnumbered page table of contents;
the pagination of the two works by Dumas fils remains the same.)

Semaine Littéraire du Courrier des Etats-Unis. "Dieu et diable" par
Alexandre Dumas. New-York : Charles Lassalle, Editeur, 1853, 8vo.,

244

pp. - première partie, "Conscience l'innocent" (3)-70; deuxième partie "L'invasion" (71)-160 in double columns.

"Conscience", par Alexandre cumas. Paris, Impr. de Walder, 1855, 4to., pp. 100 in double columns.

Ibid   Paris, Impr. de J. Voisvenel, n.d. (c 1856), same format and pagination as the preceding edition.

"Conscience" par Alexandre Dumas. Paris, Librairie théatrale, 1857, same format and pagination as the two preceding editions.

Alexandre Dumas. "Conscience l'innocent". Paris, Michel Lévy frères, 1861, same format and pagination as the three preceding editions, the volume being completed by "Marianna", pp. (101)-138.

"Conscience l'innocent" par Alexandre Dumas. Paris, Michel Lévy frères, 1861, 12mo., 2 volumes, pp. 254 and (255)-256 table of contents, and 280 and (281)-282 table of contents. "Conscience ... " finishes on page 231 of Volume 2, verso blank, "Marianna" pp. (233)-280.
Often reprinted, same format and pagination, by both Michel Lévy frères and Calmann-Lévy.

Ibid   Paris, Calmann-Lévy, n.d. (c 188), 4to., pp. 100 in double columns, the volume being completed by "Marianna", pp. (101)-138. Caption title. Woodcut at head of title. Musée littéraire contemporain.

"BENVENUTO CELLINI"   (Drama)   1852

    Lecomte has written that this drama was written 'par Paul Meurice (avec Alexandre Dumas)' even although it was signed by Meurice alone. Glinel has stated that it was based on Dumas' "Ascanio" in the writing of which Meurice participated only very slightly. In any event, Dumas protested most strongly against the play's production, but despite his opposition it was produced, and according to Gautier it was a brilliant success with Mélingue in the title-rôle.

Original edition.
"Benvenuto Cellini", drame en cinq actes et huit tableaux, par M. Paul Meurice, musique de M. Adolphe de Groot. (Paris, Porte-Saint-Martin, 1er avril 1852.) Paris, Michel Lévy frères, 1852, 12mo., pp. vii, 88. The wrapper has : Bibliothèque dramatique. Théâtre moderne.

Ibid   Paris, Michel Lévy frères, n.d. (c 1862), folio. Bound with it .s "Frisette", comédie vaudeville en un acte, par MM. Labiche et Lefranc. Théâtre contemporain illustré; 11e et 12e livraison.
Reprinted, 1863, 1864 and 1866.

Théatre de Paul Meurice I "Benvenuto Cellini" Paris Calmann Lévy, éditeur, n.d. (1892), 8vo., pp. (i)-ii 'Préface générale du théatre' dated 'Février 1891', unnumbered page 'A mon frère', verso 'personnages' 'acteurs qui ont créé les rôles', (3)-132, (133)-134 'Note de la première édition' dated 'Conciergerie. - Avril 1852'; half-title : "Benvenuto Cellini" drame représenté pour la première fois sur le théatre de la Porte-Saint-Martin Le 1er avril 1852 direction

de M. Marc Fournier. Brown wrappers. Paris. - May & Motteroz, L.-
Imp. ... .

"Benvenuto Cellini", Paris, Calmann-Lévy, n.d. (c 189), 12mo., pp.
11-435. (Théâtre de Paul Meurice. I.) The wrapper states : "Benvenuto Cellini", drame. Nouvelle édition.

An opera was drawn from the work :
"Ascanio" opéra en cinq actes, sept tableaux d'après le drame "Benvenuto Cellini" de Paul Meurice poème de Louis Gallet musique de
Camille Saint-Saëns Paris Calmann Lévy, éditeur ancienne maison
Michel Lévy frères, 1890, 12mo., unnumbered page 'divertissement
réglé par M. Hansen costumes dessinés par M. Bianchini décors :
... ', pp. (vi)-vii 'chant', (viii)-ix 'divertissement troisième
acte divertissement mythologique réglé par M. Hansen', (x)-xi
'figuration', verso (unnumbered) 'personnages', (1)-92. Half-title
: "Ascanio" opéra Représenté pour la première fois, à Paris, a
l'Académie National de Musique, le 21 mars 1890. Orange wrappers
repeating title-page. Imprimerie Chaix, rue Bergère, 20, Paris.

"Ascanio" opéra en cinq actes, six tableaux d'après le drame "Benvenuto Cellini" de Paul Meurice poème de Louis Gallet musique de
Camille Saint-Saëns Paris, Calmann-Lévy, éditeurs, n.d. (c 189),
12mo., verso of title-page : 'Personnages', pp. (1)-88.

"Ascanio" Opéra en 5 Actes et 7 Tableaux d'après le drame "Benvenuto
Cellini" de Paul Meurice Poème de Louis Gallet musique de C. Saint-
Saëns Partition Chant et Piano réduite par l'Auteur (Edition conforme
au manuscrit original) (Monogram) Paris Durand et Schoenewerk,
éditeurs 4, place de la Madeleine, 4 Propriété pour tous les pays. -
Déposé selon les traités internationaux. Droits de représentation,
de traduction et d'exécution réservés. N.d. (c 189), 4to. Unnumbered
page with coin showing the head of François I and 'Benvenuto fecit',
verso - Mise en scène spécialement réglée par M.P. Gailhard; unnumbered
page : Académie nationale de musique Direction de MM. Ritt et Gailhard. (Paris, Mars 1890) "Ascanio" Opéra en 5 Actes et 7 Tableaux
'Personnages'. 'Rôles'. 'Interprètes'. with information as to the
place and time of the action of the opera, and names of the Chef
d'Orchestre, etc.; verso and following page (unnumbered) 'Index', verso
blank, pp. 1-391 comprising the music and libretto. Half-title :
"Ascanio" followed by woodcut. Title-page printed in red and black.
Imp. Delanchy.

Note : The actual number of 'personnages' differ for each work;
"Benvenuto Cellini" has a cast of eleven male characters and five fe-
male, while "Ascanio" has a cast of eight males and four females with,
of course, 'choeurs'; it may be worth adding that according to each
work the action of "Benvenuto Cellini" takes place in Paris in 1540
while that of "Ascanio", despite its adaptation, takes place in Paris
in 1539.

"UN GIL BLAS EN CALIFORNIE"
"IMPRESSIONS DE VOYAGE. UN AN SUR LES BORDS DU
SAN-JOAQUIN ET DU SACRAMENTO"   1852
"CALIFORNIE. UN AN SUR LES BORDS DU SAN-JOAQUIN
ET DU SACRAMENTO"

From whom Dumas obtained the material for this work, which was
written in 1851, remains a mystery. It may safely be assumed that he

had met in Paris some returned traveller from California and had listened to the account of his adventures there. It should be remembered, too, that at that time a good deal was being published in the press relative to the Californian gold-rush and, indeed, Dumas had devoted space to it in his journal 'Le Mois'.

There would appear to have been no serial publication and the introductory letter to his publisher Cadot, dated 20th July, 1852, would seem to bear this out. The work opens in May, 1849, and ends in October, 1850, shortly after the great fire of San Francisco. As will be seen there are annoying variations in dates in connection with the Cadot editions.

Original edition.
"Un Gil Blas en Californie" par Alexandre Dumas. Paris Alexandre Cadot, éditeur, 37, rue Serpente, 1852, 8vo., 2 volumes, pp. (1)-55, verso blank, letter 'Mon cher éditeur' dated : 'Montmorency, 20 juillet 1851' and signed 'Tout à vous, Alexandre Dumas', (57)-317, verso blank, unnumbered page table of contents, and (1)-295, verso table of contents. Yellow wrappers. Imprimerie de E. Dépée, a Sceaux.

Ibid   Paris, Alexandre Cadot, ... , 1852, 8vo., 2 volumes, pp. 317 and table of contents, and 296 including table of contents - this is according to Talvart et Place.

Ibid   Paris, same publishers, format and pagination as the original edition but the year of publication of Volume 1 is 1855, and of Volume 2, 1853. Yellow wrappers but with the date of Volume 2, 1854; the versos of both half-titles list works by Dumas published by Cadot.

Ibid   Paris, same publishers, format and pagination as the preceding; Volume 1 dated 1855 and Volume 2, 1854.

Ibid   Paris, same publishers, format and pagination as the preceding, but Volume 1 carrying a portrait of Dumas engraved by Rajon 'sur chine colant' - this according to Talvart et Place.

Ibid   Paris, same publishers, format and pagination as the preceding, but Volume 1 dated 1854 and Volume 2, 1853, the yellow wrappers of both being dated 1855.

"Impressions de voyage. Un an sur les bords du San-Joaquin et du Sacramento". Rédigé sur les récits d'un émigrant, par Alexandre Dumas. Bruxelles, Alphonse Lebègue, 1852, 18mo., 6 volumes each of 144 pages. The work includes, pp. (5)-26 of Volume 1, 'En guise de préface, Au rédacteur en chef de la partie littéraire du Siècle', starts 'Mon cher Desnoyers' and is dated : 'Montmorency, 20 juillet 1851'. Green wrappers. Muséum Littéraire.
(There should be interpolated here the curious fact that, very possibly before the publication of the above, Alphonse Lebègue published in 1852 under the same title and in the same format, an edition in 2 volumes comprising pp. 144 and 149; the "Impressions de voyage ... ... " ended on page 121 of Volume 2, verso blank, pp. (123)-149 being occupied by "Adrienne Lecouvreur" par Elie Berthet. There was a second issue of 2 volumes, pp. 144 and 144, and this time the "Impressions de voyage ... ... " ended on page 86 of Volume 2, the remainder being filled by "La comtesse de Broko", pp. (87)-144. Both editions have green wrappers. Muséum Littéraire.)

"Californie. Un an sur les bords du San-Joaquin et du Sacramento".
Impressions de voyage rédigées sur les récits d'un émigrant par
Alexandre Dumas. Bruxelles, Livourne, Meline, Cans et cie.; Leipzig,
J.P. Meline, 1852, 18mo., 2 volumes, each consisting of 265 pages
and with an additional page table of contents.

"Californie. Un an sur les bords du San-Joaquin et du Sacramento".
Impressions de voyage. Rédigées sur les récits d'un émigrant par
Alexandre Dumas. Bruxelles, Livourne, Meline, Cans et Cie.; Leipzig,
J.-P. Meline, 1852, 8vo., pp. 265. There is no table of contents.

Ibid   La Haye, chez les héritiers Doorman, 1852, same
format and pagination as the preceding edition.

"Californie. Un an sur les bords du San-Joaquin et du Sacramento" :
impressions de voyage, rédigées sur les récits d'un émigrant, par
Alexandre Dumas ... . Bruxelles, Livourne, Meline, Cans et compagnie;
Leipzig, J.P. Meline, 1852, 24mo., 2 volumes, pp. 122 and 131.
(This, the only copy I have traced, may either be incomplete as to
the number of volumes or, like the Lebègue editions referred to above,
be a curiosity published earlier than the other Meline, Cans editions.)

"Impressions de voyage. Un an sur les bords du San-Joaquin et du
Sacramento". Rédigé sur les récits d'un émigrant, par Alexandre
Dumas. Bruxelles et Leipzig, Kiessling et compagnie; Vienne, A la
librairie de J.F. Gresse, 1852, 18mo., 2 volumes, pp. 144 and 144.
(This is obviously a reprint of one of the Lebègue curiosities
referred to above.)

"Un Gil Blas en Californie" par Alexandre Dumas. Paris, Michel Lévy
frères, 1861, 12mo., pp. (1)-31, Dumas' letter 'Mon cher éditeur'
dated : 'Montmorency, 20 juillet 1851' and signed : 'Tout à vous,
Alex. Dumas', verso blank, (33)-323, verso table of contents.
Often reprinted, same format and pagination, by both Michel Lévy frères
and Calmann-Lévy.

Ibid   Paris, Calmann-Lévy, 1878, 4to., pp. (1)-6 Dumas'
letter as described in the previous entry, 6-51, including table of
contents, all in double columns. Caption title. Woodcut at head of
title repeated on green wrappers : Alexandre Dumas "Impressions de
voyage Un Gil Blas en Californie." Musée littéraire contemporain.

"LES DRAMES DE LA MER"
"HISTOIRE NAUTIQUE. EPISODES DE LA MER"
"SCENES NAUTIQUES. EPISODES DE LA MER"   1852
("BONTEKOE" : "LE CAPITAINE MARION" : "LA JUNON" :
"LE KENT")

    The four sub-titles, which covered records of courage, were re-
written by Dumas working from his reading of their details. They
comprise the adventures of the Dutch captain, Bontekoe, in the early
XVlth century drawn from the ship's master's own narrative; the murder
of Caption Marion du Fresne in northern New Zealand in 1772, founded
on Croizet's "Nouveau voyage a la mer du Sud ... "; the wrecking of
the 'Juno' in 1792 and the burning of the East Indiaman the 'Kent' in
1825; the two last are among the great maritime tragedies, and all are
vividly retold.

Original edition.
"Les drames de la mer" par Alexandre Dumas. Paris, Alexandre Cadot,
1852, according to Parran and Glinel, but I am very doubtful. Vicaire,
together with the copy held by the Bibliotheque Nationale copy, give
clearly :
"Les drames de la mer" par Alexandre Dumas. Paris, Alexandre Cadot,
éditeur, 37, rue Serpente, 8vo., 2 volumes. Pagination : Volume 1,
'Esquisses biographiques I Bontekoe' (unnumbered), chapitre premier.
1619. (unnumbered), (5)-163, verso blank,'Esquisses biographiques
II Le capitaine Marion 1772' chapitre premier. 'La baie de meurtrier'
(unnumbered), (169)-296, and unnumbered page table of contents; Volume
2, 'Episodes de la mer La Junon 1795', second half-title, 'La Junon',
(5)-214. 'Episodes de la mer. Le Kent' (unnumbered), (217)-323, verso
table of contents. Yellow wrappers. Sceaux, Imp. par E. Dépée.
(Vicaire states that the work was recorded in the "Bibliographie de
la France" : 6 novembre 1852. And, incidentally, Talvart et Place
follow Parran and Glinel and give the paginations : 296 and table
of contents, and 324 including table of contents.)

Ibid   Paris, Michel Lévy frères, 1860, 12mo., pp. 'Bontekoe 1619', (1)-86; 'Le capitaine Marion', (87)-147; verso blank,
'La Junon 1795', (149)-247, verso blank, 'Le Kent', (249)-302, (303)-
304 table of contents.
Often reprinted, same format and pagination, by both Michel Lévy
frères and Calmann-Lévy.

Editions under individual titles in the order of years of publication.
"Histoire nautique. Episodes de la mer" par Alexandre Dumas. Bruxelles, Alphonse Lebègue, 1852, 18mo., pp. 158. Contents and pagination : 'Bontekoe 1619', (5)-116. "Le roi Pépin", (117)-158. Blue
wrappers. Muséum littéraire.

"Scènes nautiques. Episodes de la mer. Naufrages" par Alexandre
Dumas. Bruxelles, Alphonse Lebègue, 1852, 18mo., pp. 149. Contents
and pagination : 'La Junon', (5)-79, 'Le Kent', (80)-121, blank.
The volume is completed by "Adrienne le couvreur" par Elie Berthet,
pp. (123)-149. Blue wrappers. Muséum littéraire.

"Scènes nautiques. Episodes de la mer. Naufrages". Par Alexandre
Dumas. Bruxelles, Ch. Muquardt, 1852, same format and pagination as
the preceding edition.

"Histoire nautique. Episodes de la mer" par Alexandre Dumas. Bruxelles et Leipzig, Kiessling et compagnie; Vienne, A la librairie de
J.F. Gresse, 1852, 18mo., pp. 158. Same contents and pagination as
the first Bruxelles, Lebègue, 1852, edition.

"Scènes nautiques. Episodes de la mer. Naufrages" par Alexandre
Dumas. Bruxelles et Leipzig, Kiessling et compagnie, 1852, 18mo.,
pp. 149. Contents and pagination : 'La Junon, 1795', (5)-79, 'Le
Kent', 80-121 (including sub-heading : 'La Cambria', 91-101, 'Le
major MacGregor', 101-115, and 'L'explosion', 115-121, blank. The
volume is completed by "Adrienne Lecouvreur" par Elie Berthet.

"Le page du duc de Savoie (épisode des guerres du XVe siècle)" par
Alexandre Dumas Paris Dufour, Mulat et Boulanger, éditeurs ... 1857,
4to., pp. (1)-382, (383)-384 table of contents. "Le page du duc de
Savoie ... " ends on page 365, and is followed by "Les drames de la
mer Le Kent" pp. (366)-382; 12 steel engravings including the frontispiece. Yellow wrappers repeating the title-page except : par M.
Alexandre Dumas.

"Le capitaine Marion", par Alexandre Dumas. Paris, Marescq et cie., 1857, large 8vo., pp. 16 in double columns.

Ibid   Paris, Impr. de Gaittet, n.d. (1861), same format and pagination as the preceding edition.

Ibid   Paris, S. Raçon et Cie., n.d. (c 1861), same format and pagination as the preceding editions; 1 plate.

"La Junon 1795", par Alexandre Dumas. Paris, Marescq et cie., 1857, large 8vo., pp. 32 in double columns; illustrated.

"Le Kent", par Alexandre Dumas. Paris, Marescq et cie., 1857, large 8vo., pp. 16 in double columns; illustrated.

"La femme au collier de velours". "Le capitaine Marion". "La Junon". "Le Kent". Par Alexandre Dumas. Publiés par Dufour et Mulat. Dessins par J.-A. Beaucé, Ed. Coppin, Lancelot, etc. (Vignette) Paris, Marescq et Cie., 1857, large 8vo., 4 parties en 1 volume. Paginations for "La capitaine Marion", "La Junon" and "Le Kent" are 16, 32 and 16 respectively, all in double columns.

"Impressions de voyage. Journal de Madam Giovanni en Australie, aux îles Marquises, à Tahiti, à la Nouvelle-Calédonie, en Californie et au Mexique" par Alexandre Dumas. (Vignette) Paris, Dufour, Mulat et Boulanger, 1858, large 8vo., pp. 224 including 2 pages table of contents and 'Classement des gravures'; 7 plates. The "Journal de Madame Giovanni ... ... " ends on page 210 and is followed by "Les drames de la mer. Le capitaine Marion" pp. 211-221, and which is not illustrated.

"La Junon 1795", par Alexandre Dumas. Paris, Impr., Simon Raçon et Cie., n.d. (c 1859), large 8vo., pp. 32 in double columns; illustrated. Episodes de la mer.

"Le Kent" par Alexandre Dumas. Paris, S. Raçon et Cie., n.d. (c 1859), large 8vo., pp. 16 in double columns; 1 illustration. Episodes de la mer.

Romans historiques, aventures, anecdotes, mystères par Alexandre Dumas. "Les drames de la mer Le capitaine Marion". Paris, Dufour, Boulanger et Legrand ... , 1863, large 8vo., pp. (211)-221, verso blank, table of contents (223)-224, covering this work together with "El Salteador" and "Journal de Madame Giovanni" with which it is bound; illustrated. Lagny, Imprimerie de A. Varigault.

Romans historiques, aventures, anecdotes, mystères par Alexandre Dumas. "Les drames de la mer. Le Kent". Paris, Boulanger et Legrand ... , 1864, same format and pagination as the Paris, Dufour, Mulat et Boulanger, 1857, edition; 12 steel engravings. Lagny, Imprimerie de A. Varigault.

Alexandre Dumas. "La femme au collier de velours". "Le capitaine Marion". "La Junon". Dessins par J.-A. Beaucé, Ed. Coppin, Lancelot, etc. Paris, Calmann-Lévy, 1884, the three in one volume. "La capitaine Marion", pp. 16 in double columns; 1 full-page and 3 half-page illustrations. (The full-page illustration of 'Le capitaine Kock' is a duplicate of one of the half-page illustrations - 'Le capitaine Cook'.) "La Junon", pp. 32 in double columns, 3 full-page and 8 half-page illustrations. Musée littéraire contemporain. Reprinted, same format, pagination and illustrations, 1897.

Alexandre Dumas "Le capitaine Paul" "Murat" "Le Kent" "Pierre le cruel" "Don Bernardo de Zuniga" édition illustrée par les principaux artistes Paris, Calmann-Lévy, éditeur ancienne maison Michel Lévy frères, 1887, 4to., pp. 16 in double columns. Brown wrappers with 'Illustrés par J.-A. Beaucé et les principaux artistes.' Alexandre Dumas oeuvres illustrées.
Reprinted, same format, pagination and illustrations, n.d. (c 1890), 1897.

"Un drame de la mer". ("Le Kent"), from "Les drames de la mer" par Alexandre Dumas. With explanatory notes ... by A.C. Clapin. London, Hachette et Cie., 1888, 8vo., pp. 57.

"Le capitaine Marion" par Alexandre Dumas Paris Calmann-Lévy, 1889, 4to., pp. 16 in double columns. Caption title; illustrated.

"La Junon 1795" par Alexandre Dumas Paris Calmann-Lévy, 1889, 4to., pp. 16 in double columns. Caption title; illustrated.

Alexandre Dumas. "Le capitaine Marion" "La Junon". Dessins par J.-A. Beaucé, Ed. Coppin, Lancelot, etc. Paris, Calmann-Lévy, 1897, 4to., pp. 16 and 32 in double columns respectively. Alexandre Dumas oeuvres illustrées.

"ISAAC LAQUEDEM" 1852-1853

As early as 1832 Dumas has stated that he sold to the publisher Charpentier a romance to be completed in eight volumes built around the legend of the Wandering Jew. Later, feeling that the subject was too big for so few volumes he repaid the advance and cancelled the contract. Some twenty years later, in exile in Brussels, he started what he justifiably claimed would be his greatest work and which would consist of eighteen or more volumes.

The paper which had contracted to publish the serial issue of the work, 'Le Constitutionnel', had just been sold into Jewish ownership, and that part of the opening narrative relating to biblical matters was seized upon by the ultra-clerical press which bitterly attacked the new ownership. Frightened by the uproar the new proprietor of the paper mutilated Dumas' 'copy' by omitting a number of chapters and publishing a garbled version of others. Dumas was furious and abruptly stopped writing. It was commonly stated at the time that the censorship had interfered in the work's publication and, indeed, Dumas even stated as such in a letter dated 10th August, 1864, which was included in the preface to his drame "Les mohicans de Paris", but this assumption is untenable.

The serial issue in 'Le Constitutionnel' ran from 10th December, 1852, to 8th January, 1853; this omits almost all of seventeen chapters with a few sentences inserted to bridge the gaps. When the work was published in volume form all the omissions were restored. The prologue (Chapters 1-6) describes the arrival of an unknown pilgrim in Rome at Easter, 1469; the introduction (Chapters 7-9) describes Jerusalem from David's time to the coming of the Romans, and thus constitutes a sort of double prologue; the remainder, which completes the first part (and is all that was written) is devoted to Christ's life and to the few months immediately preceding Nero's accession as emperor. This is Dumas writing alone and at his very best. Blaze de Bury saw the plan of the entire work and in his book "Alexandre Dumas sa vie, son temps, son oeuvre" (Paris, Calmann-Lévy, 1885) devotes pp. 285-310 to an outline of it.

Original edition.
"Isaac Laquedem" par Alexandre Dumas. Bruxelles, Alphonse Lebègue, 1852-1853, 18mo., 5 volumes. Pagination : Volume 1 (1852), (1)-126 'prologue' (although not so headed), 127-192 'introduction' 'Jerusalem' (divided into three parts); Volumes 2-5 (1853), 189, 200, 138 and 104, followed by 8 pages of publisher's advertisements. Volume 5 ends : 'Fin du cinquième volume et de la première partie'.

Ibid   Bruxelles, Librairie de Ch. Muquardt, même maison a Leipzig et a Gand, 1852-1853, 18mo., 5 volumes, Volume 1 (1852), Volumes 2-5 (1853), same pagination as the preceding edition. Green wrappers.

Ibid   Bruxelles et Leipzig, Kiessling et compagnie, same years of publication, format and pagination as the preceding editions.

Ibid   Bruxelles, Livourne, Meline, Cans et cie.; Leipzig, P. Meline, 1853, 18mo., 4 volumes, pp. 282, 296, 316 and 288. Volume 4 ends : 'Fin du quatrième volume et de la première partie'.

Ibid   Paris, A la librairie théatrale, 1853, 8vo., 5 volumes, pp. 320, 297, 307, 323 and 316 : 'fin du cinquième volume et de la première partie'. Yellow wrappers.

Semaine Littéraire du Courrier des Etats-Unis. "Isaac Laquedem" par Alexandre Dumas. New-York, Bureau du Courrier des Etats-Unis, 1853, 8vo., pp. - 'Prologue' (5)-40, 'Introduction' (41)-48 in double columns, ending with Chapter II 'Avec Salomon, Jerusalem a épuisé son ère ... .'

"Isaac Laquedem" par Alexandre Dumas Paris Calmann-Lévy, éditeur ancienne maison Michel Lévy frères ... a la librairie nouvelle 1878, 12mo., 2 volumes, pp. 322 and unnumbered page table of contents, and 335, verso blank, (337)-338 table of contents. At the end of Volume 2 is printed : 'La publication de cet ouvrage, qui parut dans 'Le Constitutionnel' vers 1853, ayant été interdite sous l'Empire, Alexandre Dumas attendait un temps propice pour continuer son travail; mais, comme on sait, la mort vint le surprendre pendant la guerre de 1870, et l'oeuvre importante qu'il avait conçue est malheureusement restée inachevée'.
Reprinted, same format and pagination, 1889.

"LE DERNIER ROI DES FRANCAIS ... "
"HISTOIRE DE LA VIE POLITIQUE ET PRIVEE DE LOUIS-PHILIPPE" 1852-1853
"HISTOIRE DE DIX-HUT ANS, DEPUIS L'AVENEMENT DE LOUIS-
PHILIPPE JUSQU'A LA REVOLUTION DE 1848"

The first two of the above titles are one and the same work, whilst the third comprises the major portion of its two predecessors. I feel, therefore, that the three varying titles may be dealt with together.

This is an important work dealing with the entire career of Louis-Philippe from his birth to his death. It will be remembered

that Dumas as a young man was employed in secretarial work in the
office of the duc d'Orléans, as he then was, and later became on very
friendly terms not only with the future king but also with the young
duc de Montpensier. Dumas has, however, shown a restraint and fair-
ness in describing so many of the events he has recorded.

Original edition (as "Le dernier roi ... ".)
"Le dernier roi" par Alexandre Dumas. Paris, Hippolyte Souverain,
éditeur, rue des Beaux-Arts, 5, 1852, 8vo., 8 volumes. Pagination :
300 and additional unnumbered page table of contents; 300 including
table of contents; 306 and additional unnumbered page table of contents; 304 including table of contents. With Volume 5 the title of
the work was altered to "Le dernier roi des français, 1771-1851",
the pagination being : 315 and additional unnumbered page table of
contents; 304 including table of contents; 302 and 306 each with an
additional unnumbered page table of contents. Yellow wrappers. Lagny,
impr. de Vialat et Cie.

"Le dernier roi des français (Louis-Philippe) 1772 (sic)-1851". Par
Alexandre Dumas. Bruxelles, Alphonse Lebègue, 1852, 18mo., 7 volumes,
pp. 156, 148, 156, 159, 148, 156 and 196. "Le dernier roi ... " ends
on page 157 of Volume 7, verso blank, pp. (159)-196 being occupied by
'Décrets du président de la République sur la vente des biens de la
famille d'Orléans' and 'Mémoire à consulter'. It should be noted that
the half-titles of each volume print the correct dates : 1771-1851.

Ibid   Bruxelles, Librairie de Ch. Muquardt, 1852, same
number of volumes, format and pagination as the preceding edition.

Original edition (as "Histoire de la vie politique ... ".)
"Histoire de la vie politique et privée de Louis-Philippe" par M. A.
Dumas. Paris Dufour et Mulat libraires-éditeurs 21, quai Malaquais
1852, large 8vo., 2 volumes. Pagination : Volume 1, 320, frontispiece 'Philippe égalité sa femme leurs enfants, Mme de Genlis leur
gouvernante' and 9 engravings; Volume 2, 299, 'Pièces justificatives'
(300)-311, verso 'classement des gravures' for the two volumes, frontispiece 'Louis Philippe Marie Amélie et Madame Adelaide' and 9 engravings. The engravings are by de Riffaut, Philippoteaux, Charpentier
and Gabe. Lagny. - typographie de Vialat et Cie.
The work was first issued in 40 parts, and was reprinted in volume
form, same format, pagination and illustrations, n.d. (185).

Ibid   Arrangée a l'usage des écoles et maisons d'éducation par Mme. A. Brée. Avec une gravure. Leipzig, Librairie de
Baumgartner, 1853, 8vo., pp. 354 of which (344)-354 comprise the
vocabulary. The engraving is a portrait of Louis-Philippe by M.
Lämmel.

"Histoire de la vie politique et privée de Louis-Philippe. Depuis
son avènement jusqu'à la révolution de 1848" par Alexandre Dumas.
Illustrée de magnifiques gravures sur acier. (Vignette) Paris, P.-
H. Krabbe, 1853, large 8vo., 2 volumes, pp. 320 and 311; pp. 297-299
of Volume 2 are entitled 'Voici maintenant le jugement que porte la
presse anglaise sur Louis-Philippe', and pp. 300-311 consist of 'Pièces
justificatives'. Each volume has 5 plates.

Original edition (as "Histoire de dix-huits ans, depuis l'avènement
de Louis-Philippe ... ".)
"Histoire de dix-huit ans, depuis l'avènement de Louis-Philippe jusqu'à

la révolution de 1848", par Alexandre Dumas., Illustrée de magnifiques
gravures sur acier. (Vignette) Paris, P.-H. Krabbe, 1853, large 8vo.,
pp. 381 and 396; 'Pièces justificatives' occupy pp. 321-381 of Volume
1 and pp. 313-396 of Volume 2. There are altogether 16 engravings in
the two volumes.
Reprinted, same number of volumes, format and pagination as the preceding edition, 1854.

It should be noted that none of these titles were ever published by
either Michel Lévy frères or Calmann-Lévy.

"HISTOIRE DE DEUX SIECLES OU LA COUR, L'EGLISE ET LE
PEUPLE DEPUIS 1700 JUSQU'A NOS JOURS ... "

This is a curious hybrid of a work, and the only satisfactory
way of dealing with it is to set out at length the varying titles and
contents of the edition starting with the 1852, and then the 1852-
1854 editions. The first collected edition, in part 'original',
comprises : 'La splendeur et les misères de Louis XIV. - Le Régent,
sa politique, ses ministres, sa famille, ses roués; Louis XV, ses
amours; Madam de Mailly, Madame de Vintimille, Madame de Lauraguais,
Madame de Châteauroux, Madame de Pompadour, le parc aux cerfs; Madame
du Barry. - Les Jésuites, le franc-maçonnerie et son origine. - Les
philosophes. - Louis XVI, Marie-Antoinette. - Vie privée du roi et de
la reine, pamphlets du temps, la Révolution, les cordeliers, les
Jacobins et leurs clubs. - Philippe-Egalité. - Le duc de Chartres,
suivi de la vie privée et publique de Louis-Philippe 1er.'
This material was published under the collective title :
"Histoire de deux siècles, ou la cour, l'église et le peuple depuis
1650 jusqu'à nos jours" comprenant "la splendeur et les misères de
Louis XIV, suivi de la vie privée et politique de Louis-Philippe 1er.",
par M. A. Dumas. Paris, Dufour et Mulat, 1852, large 8vo., 2 volumes,
pp. 438 and unnumbered page 'classement des gravures', and 422; in all
there were 30 engravings.

A 10 volume large 8vo. edition appeared between 1852 and 1854 from
Dufour et Mulat, but this did not contain 'La splendeur et les misères
de Louis XIV', Volume 1 beginning with 'La Régence et Louis XV' followed by 'Louis XVI et la Révolution' and including 'Le drame de quatre-
vingt-treize, scènes de la vie révolutionnaire' and then following
with 'La vie privée et politique de Louis Philippe 1er.". Information
is then given that Paul Lacroix completed the account of the 1848
Revolution and the proclamation of the Empire and the Napoleonic
dynasty. Volumes 1-4 are dated 1852, Volumes 5-7, 1853, and Volumes
8-10, 1854.

This was succeeded by :

"Histoire de deux siècles ou la cour, l'église et le peuple depuis
1700 jusqu'à nos jours ... " par M. A. Dumas "Et terminée par la
Révolution de 1848, la proclamation de l'Empire et la Dynastie Nap-
oléonienne" Par M. Paul Lacroix (Bibliophile Jacob) ... Paris,
Dufour, Mulat et Boulanger, 1854, large 8vo., 10 volumes, pagination
: Volume 1, 432, (433)-438 table of contents, 'classement des gravures' (unnumbered), frontispiece and 15 engravings; Volume 2, 416,
(417)-422 table of contents, frontispiece and 11 engravings; Volume 3,
424, (425)-432 table of contents, frontispiece and 15 engravings;

Volume 4, 390, (391)-394 table of contents, 'classement des gravures volumes 1-3' (unnumbered), frontispiece and 9 engravings, 'Pièces justificatives' occupying pp. (321)-390; Volumes 5, 320, frontispiece and 9 engravings; Volume 6, 311, verso 'classement des gravures volumes 5-6' (unnumbered), frontispiece and 9 engravings, 'Pièces justificatives' occupying pp. (300)-311; Volume 7, 394, (395)-400 table of contents, frontispiece and 3 engravings; Volume 8, 392, (393)-400 table of contents, frontispiece and 3 engravings; Volume 9, 392, (393)-400 table of contents, frontispiece and 9 engravings; Volume 10, 396, (397)-404 table of contents, frontispiece and 9 engravings.

Ibid   Paris, Legrand, Troussel et Pomey, n.d. (185), large 8vo., 10 volumes, the same pagination as the preceding edition but with the following number of engravings in each volume : 14, 13, 15, 9, 9, 9, 6, 3, 9 and 9.

Ibid   Paris, Legrand et Crouzet, n.d. (c 186), 10 volumes, same format, pagination and illustrations as the preceding edition.

"LA COMTESSE DE CHARNY"   1852-1855

In this, the final work in the Revolutionary romances, Dumas is again working alone and gives rather more history than in the previous three works in the series. He drew considerably on Michelet's "Histoire de la Révolution". The period is October, 1789, to January, 1793, and closes, historically, with the king's execution on 21st January of that year, although the fictional narrative continues after that date into 1794. Dumas has stated that he had written the first two volumes before he left Paris for Brussels, that a further twelve were written during his stay in the latter city, and the final five after 1853 the last one being in September, 1854. As with other of his long romances Dumas found this work difficult to finish off, and he has written that Cadot had continually to worry him for the final volume - in point of fact Cadot had more than once announced the final part only to find that more manuscript arrived.

There were no serial publication of the work. Dumas had by now made arrangements with his Belgian publishers to simultaneously receive copies of his manuscripts as and when he sent the originals to Paris.

Original edition.
"La comtesse de Charny" par Alexandre Dumas. Bruxelles, Meline, Cans et cie., 1852-1854, 18mo., 14 volumes. Pagination : Volumes 1-6 (1852), 273, 268, 270, 266, 265 and 270; Volumes 7-8 (1853), 275 and 261; Volumes 9-14 (1854), 258, 266, 253, 245, 278 and 232. There are no tables of contents.

Ibid   Bruxelles, Livourne, Meline, Cans et cie.; Leipzig, J.P. Meline, 1852-1854, 18mo., 14 volumes, same years of publication of individual volumes and the same pagination as the preceding edition.

Ibid   Paris, Alexandre Cadot, éditeur, 37, rue Serpente, 1852-1855, 8vo., 19 volumes. Pagination : Volumes 1-6 (1852), 305 and unnumbered page table of contents, 299 and 2 unnumbered page tables of contents, 299 and unnumbered page table of contents; 320 including table of contents, 316 and unnumbered page table of contents, 312 including table of contents; Volumes 7-12 (1853), 301, 302, 308 each with an additional unnumbered page table of contents, 320 including table of contents, 302 and unnumbered page table of contents, 304 including table of contents; Volumes 13-19 (1855), 320, 311, 307, 307 each with an additional unnumbered page table of contents, 315 and 2 unnumbered pages table of contents, 317 and unnumbered page table of contents, 304 including table of contents. Yellow wrappers. Sceaux, impr. E. Dépée.

"Mémoires d'un médecin. La comtesse de Charny", suite d' "Ange Pitou", par Alexandre Dumas. Bruxelles, Alphonse Lebègue, imprimeur-éditeur, 1852-1855, 24mo., 14 volumes. Pagination : Volumes 1-6 (1852), 118, 132, 124, 119, 128 and 131; Volumes 7-9 (1853), 132, 126 and 134; Volume 10 (1854), 132; Volumes 11-14 (1855), 127, 122, 120 and 107. The title-page of Volume 14, only, bears the additional : 'Edition autorisée pour la Belgique et l'étranger, interdite pour la France'.

"La comtesse de Charny" par Alexandre Dumas. Bruxelles, Librairie de C. Muquardt (and Alph. Lebègue), 1852-1855, 18mo., 14 volumes. Pagination : Volumes 1-10 (Librairie de C. Muquardt) - Volumes 1-5 (1852), 143, 143, 156, 153 and 152; Volumes 6-10 (1853), 152, 157, 146, 136 and 146; Volumes 11-14 ("Mémoires d'un médecin. La comtess de Charny" suite d' "Ange Pitou", par Alexandre Dumas. Bruxelles, Alph. Lebègue, 1853) - 127, 122, 120 and 107. As with the preceding Alphonse Lebegue edition only Volume 14 bears the additional : 'Edition autorisée pour la Belgique et l'étranger, interdite pour la France' on the title-page.

"Mémoires d'un médecin. La comtesse de Charny" par Alexandre Dumas. Edition autorisée pour la Belgique et l'étranger, interdite pour le France. Bruxelles, Leipzig, Kiessling et cie. and Kiessling, Schnée et cie., 1852-1855, 24mo., 14 volumes. Pagination : Volumes 1-5 (1852), 118, 132, 124, 119 and 128; Volumes 6-9 (1853), 131, 132, 126 and 134 (all published by Kiessling et cie.); Volume 10 (1854), 132; Volumes 11-14 (1855), 127, 122, 120 and 107 (all published by Kiessling, Schnée et cie.)

Semaine Littéraire du Courrier des Etats-Unit. "La comtesse de Charny", par Alexandre Dumas. 4e épisode des "Mémoires d'un médecin". New-York; Bureau du Courrier des Etats-Unis, 1853, 4to., pp. 448 in double columns.

"Mémoires d'un médecin La comtesse de Charny" par Alexandre Dumas Paris Dufour, Mulat et Boulanger, éditeurs (se réservent le droit de reproduction et de traduction à l'étranger) 21 quai Malaquais 1856, large 8vo., 4 volumes. Volumes 1-2 paged continuously (1)-272, 273-542; (543)-544 table of contents; Volumes 3-4 paged continuously (1)-320, 321-630, (631)-633 table of contents, verso blank, (635)-636 'classement des gravures'; frontispiece to each volume and 64 full-page illustrations.

"La comtesse de Charny", par Alexandre Dumas. Paris, Librairie théatrale, 1857, folio, pp. 340 in double columns.

"Mémoires d'un médecin. La comtesse de Charny" par Alexandre Dumas. Paris, Dufour, Mulat et Boulanger, 1858, same format, number of volumes, pagination and illustrations as the 1856 edition. Reprinted, 1861.

"La comtesse de Charny" par Alexandre Dumas. Paris, Michel Lévy

frères, 1861, 12mo., 6 volumes. Pagination : 318, (319)-320 table of contents; 312, no table of contents; 323, verso table of contents; 314, (315)-316 table of contents; 315, verso blank, (317)-318 table of contents; 306, (307)-308 table of contents.
Frequently reprinted, same format but with varying paginations, by both Michel Lévy frères and Calmann-Lévy.

"Mémoires d'un médecin. La comtesse de Charny" par Alexandre Dumas. Paris, Boulanger et Legrand, 1861, large 8vo., 2 volumes, same pagination and illustrations as the Dufour, Mulat et Boulanger, 1856, edition.

"La comtesse de Charny" par Alexandre Dumas. Paris, Michel Lévy frères, 1861, 4to., pp. 364 in double columns. Caption title. Woodcut at head of title. Musée littéraire contemporain.
Reprinted, Calmann-Lévy, 188 , and subsequently, same format and pagination.

"La comtesse de Charny" par Alexandre Dumas. In : 'Journal du jeudi', no. 236, 3 août 1862, through to No. 332, 31 mai 1863. Treble columns. Engraving at head of each number.

"Mémoires d'un médecin. La comtesse de Charny" par Alexandre Dumas. Paris, Legrand, Pomey et Creuzot, n.d. (c 1865), large 8vo., 2 volumes, same pagination and illustrations as the Dufour, Mulat et Boulanger editions referred to above.

"La comtesse de Charny" par Alexandre Dumas. Illustrations de Janet-Lange, et divers gravées sur bois. Bordeaux, Bureau des Publications Illustrées, n.d. (c 1880), 4to., pp. 768 in double columns. (Comprises 95 livraisons.)

Ibid   Paris, Calmann-Lévy, éditeurs ancienne maison Michel Lévy frères, A la librairie nouvelle, 1896, large 8vo., pp. (3)-763 in double columns, verso blank, (765)-767 table of contents. Frontispiece portrait of Dumas; illustrated.

"MES MEMOIRES"   1852 -
"SOUVENIRS DE 1830 A 1842"   1854 - 1855

    These two works must be dove-tailed under the one bibliographical heading.

    The "Mémoires" are quite delightful and it is unfortunate that they take the reader no further than about 1832. The first 213 chapters were published in 'La Presse' and the remainder appeared, erratically, in 'Le Mousquetaire' from its first issue as a specimen number on 12th November, 1853 (actual publication started on the 21st of that month), until 13th May, 1855; the remaining chapters were subsequently published under the misleading title of "Souvenirs de 1830 à 1842" - they do not, in fact, extend nearly as far as the latter year. Dumas' promise to continue writing his memoirs was never carried out.

    The late Monsieur Paul van der Perre in an article in the 'Bulletin du Bibliophile', août-septembre, 1931, pp. 355-361, entitled 'Mémoires d'Alexandre Dumas", stated that the Meline, Cans edition of 1852-1856 without strictly meriting the title 'originale' has priority over the Paris, Cadot, edition more because of the importance of its

text than because of the dates of publication. And attention should
be drawn here to the letter dated 23rd December, 1851, which is printed
in Volume 1 of the Meline, Cans edition, from Dumas to Meline; it
contains the following passage : 'Le journal 'La Presse' publie en
ce moment "Mes Mémoires", mais vous devez comprendre combien ces
mémoires d'un auteur républicain, fils d'un général républicain, sub-
issent de coupures en ce moment. Par bonheur, mon excellent mémoire
me permet de rétablir ici ce que l'on coupe à Paris. Je vous offre,
mon cher Meline, de revoir moi-même les épreuves de votre réimpression
et de faire de votre édition complète qui paraitra a l'étranger ... .'

From the serial issue in 'La Presse' and the 1852-1854 Cadot
edition three quite lengthy portions were extracted and included in
Dumas' "Souvenirs dramatiques" under the chapter titles : 'La littérature et les hommes d'état', 'Le "Louis XI" de Mély-Janin et le "Louis
XI" de Casimir Delavigne', and 'Dix ans de la vie d'une femme, ou la
moralité de M. Scribe'. Again, from the continuation of the work in
'Le Mousquetaire' were extracted a number of chapters dealing with
the early life and struggles of the actor Mélingue to be published as
a separate work under the title of "Une vie d'artiste".

All reprintings after the original issues of both "Mes mémoires"
and the "Souvenirs de 1830 à 1842" have been combined into one work
bearing the former of these titles.

As a footnote it may be mentioned that the back wrapper of the
Cadot, 1852-1854, edition, Volume 1, advertises "Sous l'ébenier" by
Dumas as 'sous presse', which can only be a printer's error. On the
back wrapper of Volume 8 "La comtesse de Charny" is advertised as not
having been published as a serial, and in the same place of Volume 8
the same work is stated to be previously unpublished (sic) but now
complete and for sale in 15 volumes - as will be known the complete
Cadot edition comprised 19 volumes.

"MES MEMOIRES" : Original edition to be published in Belgium.
"Mémoires d'Alex. Dumas" Bruxelles. Meline, Cans et compagnie, 1852-
1856, 12mo.; première série volumes 1-15; deuxième série volumes 1-11;
26 volumes.
Pagination : première série, Volumes 1-13 (1852), (1)-4 'préface des
éditeurs belges' signed : Meline, Cans et compagnie, éditeurs,
'Dédicace. Ces mémoires sont dédiés a l'honorable comte d'Orsay,
mon frère d'art, mon ami de coeur. Alexandre Dumas' (unnumbered),
verso blank, (8)-261, 280, 278, 272, 257, 246, 263, 254, 258, 263,
262, 245 and 266; Volumes 14-15 (1853), 300 and 334.
Pagination : deuxième série, Volumes 1-3 (1853), 257, 234 (Note. Au
rédacteur du journal 'La Presse') (235)-260) and 273, verso blank,
(Note. Au rédacteur du journal 'La Presse') (275)-287; Volumes 4-8
(1854), 286, 291, 280 (Note.) (281)-286, 301 and 288; Volumes 9-11
(1856), 245, 262 and 270. Blue wrappers.

Ibid   Bruxelles, Livourne, Meline, Cans et compagnie;
Leipzig, J.P. Meline, 1852-1856, 12mo., same years of publication for
all volumes and the same pagination.
There are no tables of contents in either issue.

"Les mémoires d'Alexandre Dumas". Bruxelles, Alphonse Lebègue, 1852,
18mo., volumes 1-14. Pagination : 176, 152, 160, 172, 164, 160,
175, 160, 164, 160, 168, 164, 144 and 135, verso blank, (1)-15 pub-

lisher's catalogue dated 'Septembre - 1852'; Volume 3 has the date
'1853' which must be regarded as a misprint, and at the foot of page
135 of Volume 14 is printed : 'Fin des deux premières parties'.
"Mémoires d'Alexandre Dumas". Bruxelles, Alphonse Lebègue (with the
exception of Volume 27 which has 'Alph. Lebègue'), 1853-1856, 18mo.,
volumes 15-29. Pagination : Volumes 15-22 (1853), 146, 204, 177,
177 (Note. Au rédacteur du journal 'La Presse', (i)-xvi signed :
Alexandre Dumas, Bruxelles, 13 mars 1853), 183 (Note. Au rédacteur
du journal 'La Presse' signed : Alexandre Dumas, 7 septembre 1853),
160, 165 and 182; Volumes 23-26 (1854), 168 (Note. Correction concerning M. Fulchiron, (i)-v), 168, 185 and 192. Volumes 27-28 (1855),
163 and 188; Volume 29 (1856), 150. There are no tables of contents.
On the title-pages of Volumes 19-29 is : 'Edition complète, autorisée
par l'auteur'. Blue wrappers. Muséum littéraire.
(The Lebègue printing has some eight feuilletons less that the material
which appeared in both 'Le Mousquetaire' and in the Cadot, 1854-1855,
edition of "Souvenirs de 1830 à 1842", but one more chapter than the
standard Lévy issue.)

"Les mémoires d'Alexandre Dumas", Bruxelles et Leipzig, Kiessling et
compie. Volumes 1-15; "Mémoires d'Alexandre Dumas", Bruxelles et
Leipzig, Kiessling et compagnie. Volumes 16-29. 1852-1856, 18mo.
Pagination : Volumes 1-14 (1852), 176, 152, 160, 172, 164, 160, 175,
160, 164, 160, 168, 164, 144 and 135 (Volume 4 is mis-dated 1851);
Volumes 15-21 (1853), 146, 204, 177, 177 (with xiv pages of 'Notes'),
183 (with xii pages of 'Notes'), 160 and 165; Volumes 22-26 (1854),
182, 168, 185 and 192; Volumes 27-28 (1855), 185 and 192; Volume 29
(1856), 150. There are no tables of contents. (Each volume carries
on its title-page the monogram 'A.L.' which links the edition with
that of Alphonse Lebègue.)

Original edition to be published in France (and the United States).
"Mes mémoires", par Alexandre Dumas. Paris, Alexandre Cadot, éditeur,
37, rue Serpente, 1852-1854, 8vo., 22 volumes. Pagination : Volumes
1-14 (1852), 324, 314, 319, 308, 330, 308, 344, 318, 328, 304, 328,
328, 328 and 334; Volumes 15-22 (1854), 312, 332, 213, 293, 298 (Note
au rédacteur du journal 'La Presse' (i)-xviii), 311, 301 and 311.
There are no tables of contents. Yellow wrappers. Fontainebleau,
impr. E. Jacquin.

Ibid   Paris, Alexandre Cadot, ... , 1854-1855, 8vo.,
22 volumes; Volumes 1-18 (1854) and Volumes 19-22 (1855), same pagination as the preceding edition. Yellow wrappers.
(I may mention here that I have seen a copy of the Cadot edition, same
pagination as the preceding with the following years of publication :
Volumes 1-6, 1855; Volumes 7-10, 1854; Volumes 11-18, 1855; Volumes
19-20, 1854; and Volumes 21-22, 1855. Unless there are misprints in
the dating there could be a Cadot edition dated entirely '1855'.)

"Mémoires d'Alexandre Dumas". 'Ces mémoires sont dédiés à l'honorable
Comte d'Orsay, mon frère d'art, mon ami de coeur. Alexandre Dumas'.
New-York, Bureau du Courrier des Etats-Unis, 1852, 8vo., 2 volumes,
pp. (4)-387; half-title; (6)-236, all in double columns.
(I have traced only one copy of this American edition, and I do not
know whether further volume(s) had been published to complete the
work.)

"Mes mémoires" par Alexandre Dumas. Paris, Michel Lévy frères, 1863,

12mo., 10 volumes. Pagination : 315, verso blank, (317)-320 table
of contents; 315, verso blank, (317)-320 table of contents; 311,
verso blank, (313)-316 table of contents; 319, verso blank, (321)-324
table of contents; 313, verso blank, (315)-318 table of contents; 288,
(289)-310 note dated 13 mars 1853, (311)-314 table of contents; 310,
(311)-320 Note A dated 7 septembre 1853 and Note B dealing with letters
from Béranger, (321)-324 table of contents; 312, (313)-316 table of
contents; 316, (317)-320 table of contents; 315, verso blank, (317)-
319 table of contents.
Several times reprinted, same format but with slightly varying paginations, by both Michel Lévy frères and Calmann-Lévy.

"Mes mémoires" par Alexandre Dumas Paris Michel Lévy frères, n.d.
(c 1865), 4to. Pagination : première série (1)-381, verso blank,
(383)-386 table of contents; deuxième série (1)-498, (499)-504 table
of contents, all in double columns. Woodcut at head of each 'série'.
Poissy - typ. et stér. de Aug. Bouret. Musée littéraire contemporain.

"Mémoires d'Alexandre Dumas" Paris, impr. de Serrière, n.d. (186),
4to., same pagination as the preceding edition.

"Mes mémoires", par Alexandre Dumas. Poissy, Impr. de A. Bouret, n.d.
(1866), 4to., same pagination as the preceding editions.

"SOUVENIRS DE 1830 A 1842"

Original edition.
"Souvenirs de 1830 à 1842" par Alexandre Dumas. Paris, Alexandre
Cadot, éditeur, 37, rue de Serpente, 1854-1855, 8vo., 8 volumes. Pagination : Volumes 1-4 (1854), 303, (i)-vii correction with regard
to M. Fulchiron and headed 'Note', 299, 320 and 303 (pp. 277-303 comprising matter concerning F. Gaillardet); Volumes 5-8 (1855), 304,
320, 315 and 308. There are no tables of contents. Yellow wrappers.
Fontainebleau, impr. E. Jacquin.

Ibid   Paris, Alexandre Cadot, ... , 1855-1858, 8vo.
Volumes 1-6 (1855), Volumes 7-8 (1858), same pagination as the preceding edition.

Ibid   Paris, Alexandre Cadot, ... , 1857-1858, 8vo.
Volume 1-4 (1857), Volumes 5-8 (1858), same pagination as the preceding editions.

"LA MAISON DE SAVOIE DEPUIS 1555, JUSQU'A 1850"   1852-1856

     This work was originally issued in parts and was ultimately bound
into four volumes, the first volume carrying the title : "La maison
de Savoie depuis 1555 jusqu'à 1850" roman historique par Alexandre
Dumas Edition illustrée d'environs 200 dessins Vol. 1. Turin,
publié par C. Perrin éditeur rue de la Vierge aux Anges, 3 1852;
the remaining three volumes being more simply entitled : "La maison
de Savoie" roman historique par Alexandre Dumas Edition illustrée
d'environs 200 dessins, then volume number and year of publication.
The work is illustrated with superb coloured lithographs, Volume 1
having as a frontispiece a coloured lithograph of Dumas after Giraud
with a facsimile signature. The number of illustrations differ in
some copies.

Volumes 1 and 2 comprise the actual first edition of "Le page du duc de Savoie" although, as will be seen, it is here entitled "Emmanuel Philibert ... ... " with an additional 60 pages of mainly historical matter, obviously by Dumas, following the epilogue and divided into 4 chapters : 'un mot à nos lecteurs', 'Victor Amédée 1er.', "Régence de madame royale Christine de France' and 'Régence de madame royale Christine de France' (suite). Again as will be seen, Volume 3 consists of "Mémoires de Jeanne d'Albert du Luynes ... ... ", which is with certain reservations "La dame de volupté" and including some of the early chapters of "Les deux reines" - these are numbered XXX-XXXVI and are Chapters I-II of the standard Lévy edition of that work. The contents of the rest of Volume 3 and the whole of Volume 4 are set out below.

Original (and only) edition. Volume 1 :
The title-page described as above, large 8vo., half-title : "La maison de Savoie depuis 1555 jusqu'à 1850", verso of title : 'L'Editeur déclare de vouloir jouir du privilége accordé par la loi du février 1826 et de celui de la propriété littéraire conformément aux Traités avec les Puissances étrangères, soit le texte, soit pour la traduction de cet ouvrage.' imprimé avec les presses mécaniques de l'établissement de Joseph Favale et comp., a'Turin. Pp. : Première partie "Emmanual Philibert ou la France et Italie au XVI siècle", (1)-214, fin de la première partie. Deuxième partie "Emmanual Philibert ou la France et l'Italie au XVI siècle", (215)-513, fin de la deuxième partie et du premier volume. Verso 'classement des planches du 1er volume' (unnumbered), 2 unnumbered pages 'table des matières première partie' "Emmanual Philibert ou la France et l'Italie au XVI siècle" and verso 'table des matières deuxième partie' ... .

"La maison de Savoie" roman historique par Alexandre Dumas Edition illustrée d'environ 200 dessins Vol. II. Turin, publié par C. Perrin éditeur rue de la Vierge aux Anges, 3 1854. Half-title : "La maison de Savoie", verso of title as in Volume 1. Troisième partie "Emmanuel Philibert ou la France et l'Italie au XVI siècle", pp. (5)-273, "Emmanuel Philibert ... ... " ending on page 212 and followed by 'Un mot à nos lecteurs' - 'Charles Emmanuel surnommé le grand', (213)-247, 'Victor Amédée Ier.', (248)-256, 'Régence de madame royale Christine de France' (257)-264, 'Régence de madame royale Christine de France' (suite), (265)-273, fin de la troisième partie et du second volume. Verso 'classement des planches du 2me volume' (unnumbered), 2 unnumbered pages 'table des matières troisième partie' "Emmanuel Philibert".

Ibid Edition illustrée d'environ 200 dessins Vol. III. Turin, publié par C. Perrin éditeur 1855. Half-title : "La maison de Savoie", followed by coloured lithograph of Victor Amédée II, verso of title as in Volume 1. Pp. : 'Avis à mes lecteurs' (5)-12, "Maison de Savoie" "Mémoires de Jeanne d'Albert de Luynes comtesse de Verrue surnommé dame de volupté" (13)-339, verso blank, coloured lithograph of Charles Emmanuel III, "Charles Emmanuel III ou La France et l'Italie depuis 1730 jusqu'à 1773" (341)-548, fin du troisième volume. Unnumbered page 'table des matières', verso blank, 2 unnumbered pages 'classement des gravures du 3me volume'.

Ibid Vol. IV. Turin, publié par C. Perrin éditeur 1856. Half-title : "La maison de Savoie", verso of title as in Volume 1, Pp. : "Victor Amédée III, ou la France et l'Italie depuis

1773 jusqu'en 1796" (5)-286, "Charles Emmanuel IV, ou la France et
l'Italie depuis 1796 jusqu'en 1802" (287)-460, "Victor Emmanuel I,
ou la France et l'Italie depuis 1814 jusqu'en 1821" (461)-552, "Charles
Felix, ou la France et L'Italie depuis 1821 jusqu'en 1831" (553)-570,
"Charles Albert, ou la France l'Italie depuis 1831 jusqu'en 1849"
(571)-666, fin du quatrième volume. 'Table des matiéres' and 'classement des gravures' occupy the 6 following unnumbered pages.

Note : "La page du duc de Savoie" and "La dame de Volupte ... " are
covered fully under their individual titles when they were later published in their separate editions.

"LE PASTEUR D'ASHBOURN"   1853

This is one of Dumas' weaker works. It is based to an extent on
a story by the German Auguste Lafontaine which had been translated into
French by de Montolieu under the title of "Nouveaux tableaux de famille,
ou La vie d'un pauvre ministre de village et de ses enfants". Dumas
transferred the scene of the action to Derbyshire in England, and by
far the most interesting part is the lengthy epilogue describing Dumas'
visit to England in 1850 with the intention of being present at Louis-
Philippe's funeral, telling how it having been very plainly hinted
to him that the Orléans family would not welcome his presence so that
he stayed instead at Holland House and later at Newstead where, he
says, he obtained the material for his story. It is, perhaps, worth
noting here that despite the setting of the story it has never been
published in English translation. The work was first published serially in 'Le Pays'.

Original edition.
"La pasteur d'Ashbourne" par Alexandre Dumas. Paris, Alexandre Cadot,
éditeur, 37, rue Serpente, 1853, 8vo., 8 volumes. Pagination : 297
and 2 pages of publisher's advertisements; 315 and 1 page of publisher's advertisements, 307, 328 and 1 page of publisher's advertisements,
318, 302, 317 and 302, all with an additional unnumbered page table
of contents. Yellow wrappers. Fontainebleau, impr. E. Jacquin.
(Talvart et Place give the different following paginations : 297
and 3 pages containing table of contents and advertisements; 315 and
2 pages containing table of contents and advertisements; 308 including
table of contents; 328 and 2 pages containing table of contents and
advertisements; 318, 302, 317 and 302 each with an additional page
table of contents.)

Ibid   Bruxelles, Livourne, Meline, Cans et cie.; Leipzig,
J.P. Meline, 1853, 16mo., 4 volumes, pp. 328, 291, 317 and 336. Brown
wrappers.

Ibid   Bruxelles, Alphonse Lebègue, 1853, 18mo., 6 volumes, pp. 136, 140, 127, 137, 149 and 144.

Ibid   Bruxelles, Librairie de Ch. Muquardt, Même maison
a Leipzig et a Gand, 1853, 18mo., 6 volumes, same pagination as the
preceding edition.

Ibid   Edition autorisée pour la Belgique et l'étranger,
interdite pour la France. Bruxelles et Leipzig, Kiessling et compagnie,
1853, 6 volumes, same format and pagination as the preceding editions.

"Le pasteur d'Ashbourne", par Alexandre Dumas. Edition autorisée pour la Belgique et l'étranger, interdite pour la France. Bruxelles, et Leipzig, Kiessling, Schnée et Cie.; Bâle, J.G. Neukirch, 1853, 6 volumes, same format and pagination as the preceding editions.

"Le pasteur d'Ashbourne" par Alexandre Dumas. Paris, Michel Lévy frères, n.d. (c 185), 4to., pp. 170 in double columns, and additional unnumbered page table of contents.

Ibid Paris, Michel Lévy frères, 1860, 12mo., 2 volumes, pp. 318, (319)-320 table of contents, and 306, (307)-308 table of contents.
Not very frequently reprinted, same format and pagination, by both Michel Lévy frères and Calmann-Lévy.

Ibid Paris, Calmann-Lévy, n.d. (c 188), 4to., pp. 170 in double columns, and additional unnumbered page table of contents. Caption title. Woodcut at head of title. Musée littéraire contemporain.

"UN MOT SUR LA POESIE EN BELGIQUE" 1853

This is an article that first appeared in the issues dated 5th and 14th July, and 2nd August, 1853, of 'Le Pays', and seemingly reprinted at some later date in the 'Revue de Paris'. It was never included in any of the collections of Dumas' miscellaneous writing or "Causeries", for a 'causerie' it undoubtedly was.

Dumas writes of the work he has accomplished since his arrival in Brussels, of earlier visits and the friends he then made, of the 'pirating' of his works, of his meeting with Meline; and goes on to write, inter alia, of Belgian authors and particularly of Belgian poets, quoting from various works of theirs.

"LE MOUSQUETAIRE" JOURNAL DE M. ALEXANDRE DUMAS 1853-1857

"Le Mousquetaire" was Dumas' most important journal. It was published daily, and included a number of hitherto unpublished works, namely, "El Salteador", "Histoire des mes bêtes" (in part), "La jeunesse de Pierrot", "Marie Dorval", "Mes mémoires" and "Les mohicans de Paris" (both in part), the plays "L'Orestie" and "Romulus", and "Une vie d'artiste", as well as any number of his 'causeries' and a number of amusing adaptations from 'Saphir' the Austrian humourist, a good many of which were never reprinted. Additionally, contributions from Dumas' numerous friends were published - and this was the reason for the journal's ultimate demise for, while in its earlier days Dumas was a regular contributor, as time went on his contributions became fewer and fewer and the pages were left to be filled by others. Without work by him the journal could not possibly continue as a financial success. As a matter of interest some of the contributors were Lamartine, George Sand, Dumas fils, Méry, Janin, and Gérard de Nerval whose "Pandora" started to appear in October, 1854; translations of Gogol, Poe and Mayne Reid were also published.

"Le Mousquetaire" journal de M. Alexandre Dumas. Bureaux : Rue Laffitte, N° 1, à la Maison d'Or. Prix du numéro du jour, 10 c. - Un numéro ancien, 20 c. Prix de l'abonnement Paris : 1 mois .. 3 fr. 3 mois .. 9 fr. .. 6 mois .. 18 fr. .. 1 an .. 36 fr. Départements : 1 mois .. 4 fr. 3 mois .. 12 fr. 6 mois .. 24 fr. 1 an ..

48 fr. Tous les articles sont signés. - La Critique est indépendente
du Rédacteur en chef et reste sous la responsabilité de l'Ecrivain qui
la signe. Le Journal ne reçoit pas de Réclames des Théâtres ni des
Libraires. Il paie ses Loges et il achète ses Livres.

The first number, a specimen copy, was published on 12th November,
1853, with an introduction signed : Alexandre Dumas 31 octobre
1853, but actual publication started on 21st November, continuing
until 7th February, 1857. The sheets measured 48 x 34 cms., and each
number consisted of 4 pages each of 3 columns. There were a number
of errors in the dating and numbering of issues, but a complete colla-
tion of the journal could never be accomplished within the compass of
this Bibliography.
The journal was revived for a short time in 1866, and the bibliographical reference with regard to "Les Nouvelles" should be consulted
concerning this 'deuxième série'.

The following parody of "Le Mousquetaire" was published :

"Le moustiquaire" journal de MM. Dumasnoir et Cie. Paraissant le
Jeudi et le Dimanche. Bureaux : rue Richelieu, No. 27. Tous les
articles sont signés. - La critique est illimitée; le rédacteur en
chef n'en répond pas. Le Journal ne paie pas ses Loges et n'achète
pas les Livres dont il rende compte. Prix de l'abonnement. Paris :
6 mois. 5 fr. 1 an. 10 fr. Prix de l'abonnement. Départements :
6 mois. 6 fr. 1 an. 12 fr.

There were 36 numbers published comprising, in all, 150 pages. Each
issue consisted of 4 pages varying in size; the first 9 numbers
measured 48 x 34 cms, nos. 10 to 33 inclusive measured 40 x 27 cms.,
and the final nos. 34 to 36 measured 44 x 30 cms. The date of the
first issue was Jeudi, 2 février, 1854, and the last 16 avril, 1854.
The first number was introduced by an article 'Pourquoi le moustiquaire' signed : Anténor DUMASNOIR.

"LE ROI DE BOHEME ... ..."
"LA JEUNESSE DE PIERROT"   1854

    This children's fairy story when it was first published in 'Le
Mousquetaire' between 10th and 19th December, 1853, was entitled "Le
roi de Bohème, conte de fée, renfermant la première partie de la vie
et des aventures de Pierrot", which would point to a sequel but no
such sequel was ever written. In his brief introduction Dumas credits
the story to Aramis who, he wrote, told it for the amusement of the
duchesse de Longueville's children.

Original edition.
Publications du mousquetaire. "La jeunesse de Pierrot" (Vignette
showing Aramis holding up Pierrot, drawn by C. Perrichon after Eustache
Lorsay) par Aramis Paris a la librairie nouvelle 15, boulevard des
Italiens. 1854. 18mo., half-title "La jeunesse de Pierrot conte de
fée". (Verso Paris. - imprimerie de Mme Ve Dondey-Dupre, Rue Saint-
Louis, 46, au Marais), pp. (v)-vii 'Mes chers enfants ... ... Alex.
Dumas', verso blank, (1)-150 and additional unnumbered page table of
contents. Blue wrappers repeating title-page.
(It has been stated that Coulon-Pineau were the original publishers;
the name appears nowhere on the work, but oddly "La jeunesse de

264

Pierrot" does appear among the publications advertised by Coulon-Pineau in their edition of Dumas' "Saphir pierre précieuse montee": prix: 75 centimes.)

Collection Hetzel. "L'homme aux contes" par Alexandre Dumas. Edition autorisée pour la Belgique et l'étranger, interdite pour la France. Bruxelles, Meline, Cans et compagnie, 1857, 18mo., pp. (5)-9 'préface', (11)-208 and unnumbered page table of contents. "La jeunesse de Pierrot" occupies pp. (103)-208. Green wrappers.

Ibid   Bruxelles, Office de la publicité, 1857, same format and pagination as the preceding edition.

Ibid   Edition interdite pour la France. Leipzig, A. Dürr, 1857, same format and pagination as the preceding editions. Reprinted, same format and pagination, 1861.

Publications du mousquetaire "La jeunesse de Pierrot" (Vignette showing Aramis holding up Pierrot) Par Aramis Paris A la librairie nouvelle 15, Boulevard des Italiens, 1854, same format and pagination as the original edition. Buff wrapper with, in red, "La jeunesse de Pierrot" par Alex. Dumas. Paris Adolphe Delaye, Libraire, 4-6 rue Voltaire, 1858.

"Le père Gigogne" contes pour les enfants par Alexandre Dumas Paris Michel Lévy frères, 1860, 12mo., 2 volumes, pp. 311, verso unnumbered page table of contents, and 315, verso unnumbered page table of contents. "Le jeunesse de Pierrot" occupies pp. (1)-151 of Volume 2. Several times reprinted, same format and pagination, by both Michel Lévy frères and Calmann-Lévy.

Ibid   Paris, Impr. de E. Blot, 1860, 4to.

"ROMULUS"   1854

        Dumas has written that the main idea of this comedy was obtained from a story by the German, Auguste Lafontaine. On 15th January, 1854, in a 'causerie' in 'Le Mousquetaire' he reported on the play's first performance and wrote his review in the form of a brief version of it. The full text of the play was published in that journal between 22nd and 27th January, 1854. There was no collaborator.

Original edition in volume form.
"Romulus" comédie en un acte, en prose par M. Alexandre Dumas Paris a la librairie théatrale ... 1854 8vo., verso of title-page 'distribution de la piece', pp. (5)-59; half-title "Romulus" comédie Représentée pour la premiere fois, à Paris, au Théâtre-Français le 13 janvier 1854. Verso : Paris. - typographie de Mme Ve Dondey-Dupré. Green wrappers repeating title-page.

"Romulus" comédie en un acte et en prose par Alexandre Dumas. Représentée à Paris, au Théatre Français, en janvier 1854. (Vignette) Bruxelles, Imprimerie de J.-A. Lelong, Libraire des théatres royaux, 1854, 18mo., pp. 64. Blue wrappers with : Répertoire de la scène française, 22me année.

"Romulus" comédie en un acte, en prose par M. Alexandre Dumas. Paris, Barbré, n.d. (1863), folio, pp. 8 in double columns. Caption title. Woodcut at head of title. Le magasin théâtral.

"Romulus" comédie en un acte, en prose Théâtre-Français. - 13 janvier

1854. "Distribution" on title-page, pp. (1)-56. Théatre complet de Alex. Dumas Tome XIX   Paris Calmann Lévy, éditeur ancienne maison Michel Lévy frères, 1874. 12mo. "Théatre complet" in 25 volumes.

"LA JEUNESSE DE LOUIS XIV"   1854

Arsène Houssaye in his "Confessions" has written that Dumas, in 1853 and back from his exile in Brussels, came to his office with the offer of two comedies - the above-named and "La jeunesse de Louis XV". It was agreed that a week should be given for the writing of each play and the two manuscripts were, in due course, promptly delivered. Both plays were, however, immediately stopped by the censor. The staging of "La jeunesse de Louis XIV" was transferred to the Théâtre Vaudeville de Bruxelles where it was first performed with tremendous success on 20th January, 1854. It was not for years allowed to be acted in France. In 'causeries' published in 'Le Mousquetaire' on 8th December, 1853, and 29th March, 1855, Dumas refers to the play, and there was also a notice regarding the Brussels performance in the number for 20th February, 1854.

In so far as "La jeunesse de Louis XV" is concerned reference should be made to the bibliographical entry under "Le verrou de la reine".

Original edition.
"La jeunesse de Louis XIV" comédie en cinq actes en prose, par Alex. Dumas. Interdite a Paris par la censure. Bruxelles et Leipzig, Kiessling, Schnée et compagnie, libraires, rue villa-Hermosa, 1. 1854. 24mo., pp. 'acte premier' with on verso : 'personnages' (both unnumbered), (7)-306, and 2 unnumbered pages of publishers' advertisements; half-title : "La jeunesse de Louis XIV" comédie. Verso : 'Avis. Cette comédie, ayant été déposée selon le voeu de la loi belge, ne peut être ni reproduite, ni représentée sans l'autorisation des propriétaires'. Bruxelles. - Imprimerie de A. Labroue et Cie. Yellow wrappers. Bibliothèque diamant. "La jeunesse de Louis XIV" comedie en cinq actes et en prose par Alex. Dumas. Interdite a Paris par la censure. Propriété des éditeurs. Bruxelles et Leipzig, Kiessling, Schnée et Cie, libraires, ... 1854.

"La jeunesse de Louis XIV", comédie en cinq actes en prose, par Alex. Dumas. Interdite à Paris par la censure. Bruxelles, Librairie de J.B. Tarride, éditeur, 1854, same format and pagination as the preceding, with the similar 'avis' on the verso of the half-title.

"La jeunesse de Louis XIV". Comédie en cinq actes, en prose par Alexandre Dumas. Nouvelle édition seule conforme à la représentation. Représentée pour la première fois, a Paris, sur le théatre de l'Odéon, le 14 mars 1874. Paris, Michel Lévy frères, 1874, 12mo., pp. 156. Reprinted, same format and pagination, 1878. Brown wrappers.

"La jeunesse de Louis XIV" comédie en cinq actes, en prose Vaudeville (Bruxelles). - 20 janvier 1854. 'A mon ami Noel Parfait ancien représentant du peuple Souvenir d'exil Alex. Dumas'. "Distribution" on title-page, pp. 58-226. Théatre complet de Alex. Dumas Tome XIX Paris Calmann Lévy, éditeur ancienne maison Michel Lévy frères, 1874. 12mo. "Théatre complet" in 25 volumes.

"La jeunesse de Louis XIV"; comédie en cinq actes, par Alexandre Dumas. Nouvelle édition. Paris, Calmann-Lévy, 1878, 4to., pp. 42 in double columns. Caption title. Woodcut at head of title. 'Distribution de la pièce' on title-page. Portrait of Dumas on the wrapper, and : 'Représentée pour la première fois, à Paris, sur le théâtre de l'Odéon, le 14 mars 1874, et reprise sur le théâtre de l'Ambigu, le 5 octobre 1878'.

"La jeunesse de Louis XIV" comédie en cinq actes par Alexandre Dumas Représentée pour la première fois, a Paris, sur le théatre de l'Odéon, le 14 mars 1874, et reprise sur le théatre de l'Ambigu, le 5 octobre 1878. (Paris, Calmann-Lévy), n.d. (188), same format and pagination as the preceding edition. 'Distribution de la pièce' on title-page. Caption title. Woodcut at head of title.

"UNE VIE D'ARTISTE"
"AVENTURES ET TRIBULATIONS D'UN COMEDIEN"   1854

This account of the struggles and early difficulties of the actor Etienne Mélingue was printed in the first place as part of Dumas' "Mémoires", and was later republished in serial form in 'Le Mousquetaire' between December, 1853, and March, 1854. The work's particular interest lies in the fact that Mélingue was to become in due course one of the best interpreters of leading characters in some of Dumas' plays, notably Buridan, d'Artagnan, Chicot, Dantès and Grandier. The difference in title of the French and Belgian editions may be noted.

Original edition in volume form.
"Une vie artiste" par Alexandre Dumas. Paris, Alexandre Cadot, éditeur, 37, rue Serpente, 1854, 8vo., 2 volumes, pp. 312, (313)-315 table of contents, and 319, (321)-323 table of contents. Yellow wrappers. Sceaux, impr. E. Dépée.

Collection Hetzel. "Aventures et tribulations d'un comédien", par Alex. Dumas. Bruxelles, Alph. Lebègue, 1854, 24mo., pp. 293, (295)-300 table of contents.

"Aventures et tribulations d'un comédien" par Alex. Dumas. Collection Hetzel. Bruxelles et Leipzig, Kiessling, Schnée et Cie., 1854, 24mo., pp. (5)-13 'Avant-propos', (15)-293, (295)-300 table of contents. Yellow wrappers : Bibliothèque diamant. Autorisé pour le Belgique et l'etranger. Interdite pour la France.

Collection Hetzel. "Aventures et tribulations d'un comédien" par Alexandre Dumas. Bruxelles, Meline, Cans et Cie., 1855, same format and pagination as the preceding edition.

"Un vie d'artiste", par Alexandre Dumas. Paris, S. Raçon et Cie., n.d. (c 1857), large 8vo., pp. 96 in double columns; 7 illustrations. Caption title.

Alexandre Dumas. "Une vie d'artiste" (Mélingue). "Chronique de Charlemagne". "Praxède". "Pierre le cruel". Edition illustrée par J.-A. Beaucé et Ed. Coppin. Paris, Marescq et cie., 1857, large 8vo., pp. 96, 32, 16 and 16 respectively, all in double columns.

Collection Hetzel. "Aventures et tribulations d'un comédien" par Alexandre Dumas. Nouvelle édition. Leipzig, Alph. Dürr, 1860, 24mo., pp. (5)-15 'Avant-propos', (15)-293, (295)-300 table of contents. Typ. de Vᵉ J. van Buggenhoudt, Bruxelles.

"Une vie d'artiste" par Alexandre Dumas. Paris, Michel Lévy frères,
1860, 12mo., pp. (1)-10 'Avant-propos', (11)-308, (309)-312 table of
contents.
Often reprinted, same format and pagination, by both Michel Lévy
frères and Calmann-Lévy.

Alexandre Dumas "Une vie d'artiste" édition illustrée par J.-A.
Beaucé et Ed Coppin (Vignette) Paris Calmann-Lévy, éditeur ancienne
maison Michel Lévy frères, 1889, 4to., pp. (1)-96 in double columns.
Reprinted, same format and pagination, 1897. Oeuvres illustrées
d'Alexandre Dumas.

"Une vie d'artiste" par Alexandre Dumas. Paris, Calmann-Lévy, 1895,
4to., pp. (1)-96 in double columns. Caption title. Woodcut at head
of title repeated on buff wrappers. Musée littéraire contemporain.

"L'OEUVRE DE NOTRE-DAME-DES-SEPT-DOULEURS"   1854

This is Dumas' 'causerie' published in 'Le Mousquetaire' for
8th and 9th January, 1854, dealing with Abbé Moret's charitable work,
and was written to enlist sympathy for it.

Original and only edition in volume form.
Publications du Mousquetaire. "L'oeuvre de Notre-Dame-des-Sept-
Douleurs" signed : Alex. Dumas. Paris, Impr. de E. Brière, n.d.
(1854), 8vo., pp. 8. Extrait des nos. 49 et 50, 8-9 janvier 1854,
du "Mousquetaire".

"EL SALTEADOR"
"LE GENTILHOMME DE LA MONTAGNE"   (Romance)   1854

This romance concerns the youth of the future Emperor Charles V
and the period is 1497-1519; it actually opens in June, 1519, and
closes with Charles receiving news of his election to the crown but,
throughout, the story reverts to earlier events. Again it is Dumas
working alone but undoubtedly the writing shows signs of haste. It
would seem that the work was wanted urgently for publication in 'Le
Mousquetaire', where it did in fact appear between 5th February and
28th March, 1854.

In 1860 Dumas drew from the work the play "Le gentilhomme de la
montagne", and the result was a very clear improvement on the romance.
As will be seen Calmann-Lévy, in 1878, published "El Salteador", as
it was originally issued, under the play's title and it is under the
title of "Le gentilhomme de la montagne" that it has been republished
in subsequent years.

Original edition.
"El Salteador" par Alexandre Dumas. Paris, Alexandre Cadot, éditeur,
37, rue Serpente, 1854, 8vo., 3 volumes, pp. 313, 299 and 333, each
with an additional unnumbered page table of contents. "El Salteador"
ends on page 268 of Volume 3, being followed by "Les étoiles commis
voyageurs", pp. 269-333; Volume 3 includes at the end an 8 page list
of Cadot's publications, including works by Dumas, and dated :
octobre 1849. Sceaux, impr. E. Depée.

"El Salteador", roman de cape et d'épée, par Alex. Dumas. Collection

Hetzel. Bruxelles, Alphonse Lebègue, 1854, 12mo., 2 volumes, pp. 225 and 196. There are no tables of contents.

Collection Hetzel. "El Salteador", roman de cape et d'épée, par Alex. Dumas. Bruxelles et Leipzig, Kiessling, Schnée et Cie, 1854, 2 volumes, same format and pagination as the preceding edition.

"El Salteador" par Alexandre Dumas. Bruxelles, Alphonse Lebègue, 1854, 18mo., 3 volumes, pp. 159, 152 and 110. Volume 3 is completed, with separate pagination, by "Ferréda" par Clément Michaels, fils, pp. (1)-27. Blue wrappers. Muséum littéraire.

Ibid   Bruxelles, Librairie de Ch. Muquardt. Même maison a Leipzig et a Gand. 1854. 3 volumes, same format and pagination as the preceding edition, but in this case Volume 3 is completed, again with separate pagination, by "Ferréda", par Clément Michaels, Fils, pp. (1)-27, and "La vierge des Bataves", par Clément Michaels, Fils. (Année 79), pp. (29)-40.

Alexandre Dumas illustré. "El Salteador". Paris, Dufour, Mulat et Boulanger, 1857, large 8vo., pp. 128 in double columns; 4 illustrations. There is no table of contents.

"El Salteador", par Alexandre Dumas. Paris, Michel Lévy frères, 1861, 4to., pp. 48 in double columns. Caption title.

Romans historiques, aventures, anecdotes, mystères par Alexandre Dumas. "El Salteador". Paris, Dufour, Boulanger et Legrand ... , 1863, large 8vo., pp. 128 in double columns; illustrated. There is no table of contents. Lagny, Imprimerie de A. Varigault.

"Le (sic) Salteador" par Alexandre Dumas. Paris, Michel Lévy frères, 1863, 12mo., pp. 319, verso unnumbered page table of contents. Several times reprinted with the title error, same format and pagination, by both Michel Lévy frères and Calmann-Lévy.

"Les compagnons de Jéhu" par Alexandre Dumas Edition illustrée par A. de Neuville (Vignette) Paris Calmann-Lévy, éditeurs, n.d. (1878), 4to., published in 2 parts. Pagination : part 1, 254, (255)-256 table of contents; part 2 (illustrée par A. de Neuville et Lix), 99, verso blank, "Le gentilhomme de la montagne", (1)-130, (131)-132 table of contents for Volume 2. Both works are printed in double columns. Green wrappers with vignettes. Alexandre Dumas oeuvres illustrées. Reprinted, same format and pagination, n.d. (1884).

Ibid   Paris, Calmann Lévy, éditeur ancienne maison Michel Lévy frères, n.d. (1889), 4to., pp. (1)-130 in double columns, (131)-132 table of contents.

"SAPHIR PIERRE PRECIEUSE MONTEE"   1854

     Moritz Gottlieb Saphir was born in Hungary in 1795. His grand-father was called Israel Israel, and when the Jews were ordered by Emperor Joseph II to adopt family names he was asked by what name he wished to be known. He did not know and the magistrate who was interviewing him, noticing he was wearing a signet ring with a sapphire, suggested that he should call himself simply 'Saphir'. This he did. Moritz Gottlieb was first sent to Prague to study the Talmud, and from there he went to Vienna. He began to write satirical criticisms and pamphlets and two of the latter, in 1828, created a sensation. He travelled considerably throughout Europe and in Brussels formed a friendship with Dumas who, subsequently, in the drawing-rooms of Prince Napoleon and Princess Mathilde, told so many anecdotes about him that many people came to believe that Saphir was somebody Dumas had created out of his own imagination. He died in 1858 in Baden.

This book is a collection of some of Saphir's articles reshaped by Dumas, and of them the following were first published in 'Le Mousquetaire' : 'Le Livre de la Vie et son Censeur', 5th-8th February; 'Réflexions mondaines d'un Hanneton', 9th February; 'L'homme et les Années de la vie', 11th February; 'Histoire merveilleuse d'un homme qui passe en revue les feuilles de son Album', 12th-19th, and 22nd-23rd February; 'L'Homme d'expérience', 14th February; and 'Les Etoiles commis-voyageurs', 24th-28th February and 1st-3rd March, all in 1854. "Saphir pierre précieuse montée" was never included in the Lévy collected edition of Dumas' works, but two of the articles, 'L'Homme d'expérience' and 'Les étoiles commis-voyageurs' were published in some of Dumas' volumes of "Causeries", and the latter may be referred to under its own title in this Bibliography.

Original (and only) edition.
Bibliothèque du mousquetaire "Saphir pierre précieuse montée" par Alexandre Dumas Paris Coulon-Pineau, libraire successeur de Charpentier Palais-Royal, galérie d'Orléans, 16. 1854. 8vo., ('Quelques mots au Lecteur') (1)-4, (5)-193, verso blank, 'Comment je fis connaissance avec mon ami Saphir', (195)-240, signed : E. Deschanel. Pour copie conforme : AL. DUMAS, (241)-242 table of contents, and 6 pages of publisher's advertisements which include "Histoires cavalières", par D.-L. Eïmann, avec une Préface par Alexandre Dumas, and "La Jeunesse de Pierrot", par Aramis. (Livre pour enfants). Half-title : "Saphir", verso "Ouvrages phonétiques" Par Adrien Feline. Buff wrappers repeating title-page, but with decorated border and "Saphir" printed in blue to resemble sapphires. Imprimerie MAULDE et RENOU, rue de Rivoli, 114.

"LES ETOILES COMMIS VOYAGEURS"   1854
        This work which is not, as may be imagined from its title, a children's story but a satire which originated from Saphir the Viennese humourist whose acquaintance Dumas made when he was living in Brussels. It first appeared in 'Le Mousquetaire' between 24th February and 3rd March, 1854.

Original edition in volume form.
"El Salteador" par Alexandre Dumas. Paris, Alexandre Cadot, éditeur, 37, rue Serpente, 1854, 8vo., 3 volumes, of which Volume 3 consists of pp. 333 with an additional unnumbered page table of contents. "El Salteador" ends on page 268 of this volume and is followed by "Les étoiles commis voyageurs", pp. 269-333, unnumbered page table of contents, and an 8 page list of Cadot's publications. Sceaux, impr. E. Dépée.

Bibliothèque du mousquetaire "Saphir pierre précieuse montée" par Alexandre Dumas Paris Coulon-Pineau, libraire successeur de Charpentier ... . 1854. 8vo., pp. (1)-240, (241)-242 table of contents, and 6 pages of publisher's advertisements. "Les étoiles commis-voyageurs" occupies pp. (83)-123.

Alexandre Dumas illustré. "Maître Adam le calabrais", Paris, Dufour,
Mulat et Boulanger, éditeurs ... , 1857, large 8vo., pp. (1)-56,
followed by "Les étoiles commis voyageurs", pp. (57)-64, both in
double columns. Caption title. Woodcut at head of first page; 2
full-page illustrations.

Collection Hetzel. "Causeries" par Alexandre Dumas. Edition autorisée pour la Belgique et l'étranger, interdite pour la France. Bruxelles, Meline, Cans et compagnie, 1857, 24mo., pp. 221 and unnumbered
page table of contents. Dumas' 'Avant-propos' pp. (5)-10, and the
contents include "Les étoiles commis-voyageurs".

Collection Hetzel. "Causeries", par Alexandre Dumas. Edition autorisée pour la Belgique et l'étranger, interdite pour la France. Bruxelles, Office de publicité, 1857, same format and pagination as the
preceding edition. Typ. de J. Vanbuggenhoudt.

Collection Hetzel. "Causeries" par Alexandre Dumas. Bruxelles,
Meline, Cans et Cie., 1857, 24mo., 3 volumes (the wrapper of Volume
3 dated '1858'), pp. 229, 221 and 205, each with an additional unnumbered page table of contents. Volume 2 contains "Les étoiles commis
voyageurs".

Collection Hetzel. "Causeries", par Alexandre Dumas. Edition
autorisée pour la Belgique et l'étranger, interdite pour la France.
Bruxelles, Office de publicité, 1857, 32mo., 4 volumes, pp. 221, 225,
229 and 205, each with an additional unnumbered page table of contents.
Volume 1 contains "Les étoiles commis-voyageurs".

Ibid   Leipzig, A. Dürr, 1857, 4 volumes, same format,
pagination and contents as the preceding edition.

"Causeries" par Alexandre Dumas Paris Michel Lévy frères, 1860,
12mo., 2 volumes, pp. 270, verso table of contents, and 286 and
unnumbered page table of contents. "Les étoiles commis voyageurs"
occupies pp. (139)-174 of Volume 1.
Several times reprinted, same format and pagination, by both Michel
Lévy frères and Calmann-Lévy.

Ibid   Coulommiers, impr. de A. Moussin, n.d. (1861),
4to., pp. 88 in double columns. Caption title. Woodcut at head of
title.

Romans historiques, aventures, anecdotes, mystères par Alexandre
Dumas. "Les étoiles commis voyageurs". Paris, Boulanger et Legrand
... , 1864, large 8vo., pp. (57)-64; illustrated. Lagny, Imprimerie
de A. Varigault.

"CATHERINE BLUM"   1854

     It was during the period of his stay in Brussels that Dumas
expanded the style of writing which he had developed with the Pitou
episodes in "Ange Pitou" and subsequently in "La comtesse de Charny",
and this further development took him to his boyhood days at Villers-
Cotterets and his boyhood memories. "Catherine Blum" was one of the
results.

     Despite the suggestion that the original idea for the work came
from Iffland's play "Die Jaeger" this is Dumas working quite along.
The period is 1829-1830 and the story concerns Vatrin, one of the

forest-keepers at Villers-Cotterets and a friend of both General Dumas himself in his youth. It is an eminently human story of a simple household with its own threatening tragedy. It includes, moreover, another example of detection as exemplified by d'Artagnan in his report to Louis XIII on the Guiches-de Wardes duel. The sequel to "Catherine Blum" may be found in "Bernard, histoire pour les chasseurs" which, curiously, was written twenty years earlier. Dumas, in 1858, drew a five act play from his romance which he entitled "Les gardes-forestiers". The romance was first published serially in 'La Pays'.

Original edition.
"Catherine Blum" par Alexandre Dumas. Paris, Alexandre Cadot, éditeur, 37, rue Serpente, 8vo., 2 volumes, pp. 318 and 319, each with an additional unnumbered page table of contents. Yellow wrappers. Sceaux, impr. E. Dépée.

"Catherine Blum", par Alexandre Dumas. Bruxelles, Alphonse Lebègue, 1854, 18mo., 2 volumes, pp. 175 and 160.

"Catherine Blum" par Alexandre Dumas. Bruxelles, Livourne, Meline, Cans et Ce.; Leipzig, P. Meline, 1854, 16mo., 2 volumes, pp. 222 and 246.

Ibid   Bruxelles, Librairie de Ch. Muquardt, 1854, 18mo., 2 volumes, pp. 175 and 160.

Ibid   Bruxelle_ et Leipzig, Kiessing, Schnée et Ce., 1854, 2 volumes, same format and pagination as the preceding edition.

Semaine Littéraire du Courrier des Etats-Unis. "Cathering Blum" souvenir de jeunesse, par Alexandre Dumas. New-York, Charles Lassalle, Editeur, 1854, large 8vo., pp. 88 in double columns. (Bound with the work is "La dernière bohemienne" and "Hahmed le derviche", neither of which, of course, is by Dumas.)

"Catherine Blum", par Alexandre Dumas. Paris, Impr. de Walder, n.d. (1855), 4to., pp. 54 in double columns. Caption title.

"Catherine Blum" par Alexandre Dumas. Paris, Michel Lévy frères, 1860, 12mo., pp. 269, verso blank, unnumbered page table of contents. Often reprinted, same format and pagination, by both Michel Lévy frères and Calmann-Lévy.

Ibid   Paris, Calmann-Lévy, n.d. (c 188), 4to., pp. 54 in double columns. Caption title. Woodcut at head of title.

"LE MARBRIER"   1854

       Audebrand has said that Paul Bocage collaborated in this play, and Dumas has confirmed that he did receive some slight help. Parigot in his book "Alexandre Dumas père" wrote : ' ... "Le marbrier" est un drame significatif. Tout y est concentré, remassé et intime. L'invention romanesque en est presque absente, hormis cet Américain, qui, demandant pour son fils le main d'une jeune fille, s'éprend pour son propre comte. C'est bien un ouvrier de la famille, mais de qualité plus littéraire, qui enlèvera, haut de main, les trois actes de "La Princesse Georges" ou de "Francillon".' Dumas refers to the play in 'causeries' in 'Le Mousquetaire' dated 24th and 31st May, 17th June and 25th September, 1854.

Original edition .
"Le marbrier" drame en trois actes par Alexandre Dumas musique de
M. Montaubry Représenté pour la première fois, à Paris, sur le
théâtre du Vaudeville, le 22 mai 1854. Paris Michel Lévy frères,
libraires-éditeurs ... 1854. 12mo., verso of title-page 'distribution
de la pièce' (unnumbered), pp. (3)-48, followed by 20 pages of the
publishers' catalogue. Green wrappers : Bibliothèque dramatique
Théâtre moderne "Le Marbrier" drame en 3 actes par Alexandre Dumas
Prix : 1 franc.

"Le marbrier". Drame en trois actes, par Alexandre Dumas. ... Paris,
Michel Lévy frères, n.d. (1855), folio, pp. 14 in double columns.
Caption title. Woodcut at head of title. Théâtre contemporain
illustré. 175e livraison.
Reprinted, same format and pagination, n.d. (1868).

"Le marbrier" drame en trois actes Vaudeville. - 22 mai 1854.
"Distribution" on title-page, pp. (227)-280. Théâtre complet de Alex.
Dumas Tome XIX Paris Calmann Lévy, éditeur ancienne maison Michel
Lévy frères, 1874. 12mo. "Théâtre complet" in 25 volumes.

"LE PAGE DU DUC DE SAVOIE"   1854

        As I have already pointed out earlier this historical romance
originally comprised part of Dumas' work published under the general
title of "La maison de Savoie", and issued by Perrin of Turin.

        "Le page du duc de Savoie" covers the period of Henri II's reign
from May, 1555, to July, 1559, with a short continuation concerning
the Duke and Duchess of Savoy up to mid-January, 1562, and an epilogue
which brings the work to an end in 1580. With the exception of the
band of adventurers involved in the story, and the page himself, most
of the characters are historical. The work runs parallel to "Les deux
Diane" but is in no way its sequel. Dumas had no collaborator in its
writing.

        There is one remarkable thing to be pointed out about this work.
As Dumas originally wrote it under contract with Perrin this publisher
was astounded, and very probably shocked, to read in the final manuscript pages that Dumas had made the House of Savoy descended from an
illegitimate child and, furthermore, a changeling. This had to be
altered, and as a result Dumas rewrote the final several thousand
words and thus suppressing the original ending. It had been first
intended to entitle the romance "Leone-Leona", and Dumas refers to it
under this title in 'Le Mousquetaire' in the issue for 1st February,
1854. The change of the title may possibly have been due to the fact
that George Sand had written a work some good few years earlier under
the nearly similar title of "Leone Leone". After its publication by
Perrin the romance appeared in serial form in 'Le Constitutionnel'.

Original edition.
"Le page du duc de Savoie" par Alexandre Dumas. Collection Hetzel.
Bruxelles et Leipzig, Kiessling, Schnée et cie, 1854, 24mo., 5 volumes.
Pagination : 212, 212 ('première partie' ending on page 112), each
with 2 additional unnumbered pages table of contents, 222 with an
additional unnumbered page table of contents, 212 ('deuxième partie'
ending on page 129) and 2 additional unnumbered pages table of contents,

and 228 with an additional unnumbered page table of contents. The title-pages of Volumes 3-5 state : Edition autorisée pour la Belgique et l'étranger, interdite pour la France. Yellow wrappers. Bibliothèque diamant, with each wrapper bearing the words : Edition autorisée pour la Belgique et l'étranger, interdite pour la France.

"Le page du duc de Savoie" par Alexandre Dumas. Bruxelles, Alphonse Lebègue, 1854, 5 volumes, same format and pagination as the preceding edition.

Ibid   Paris, Alexandre Cadot, éditeur, 37, rue Serpente, 1855, (the Bibliothèque Nationale copy stamped '1854' on the title-pages), 8vo., 8 volumes. Pagination : 318, 302, each with an additional unnumbered page table of contents, 307, verso table of contents, 314 and additional unnumbered page table of contents, 311, 311, each with verso table of contents, 325 and additional unnumbered page table of contents, 319, verso table of contents. "Le page du duc de Savoie" ends on page 149 of Volume 8, verso blank, and is followed by "Causeries", pp. (151)-319; following the table of contents of Volume 8 are 4 pages of publisher's advertisements. Included in the 10 "Causeries", which are all reprinted from 'Le Mousquetaire' in the issue for 28th, 29th, 30th and 31st October, 5th November, 7th October, 23rd September, 4th August, 25th October, 9th November, all of 1854 and reprinted in that order, were 4 devoted to "La dame au volubilis" which resulted in Madame Clémence Badère's pamphlet "Le soleil Alexandre Dumas", Paris, Dentu, ... , 1855, 8vo., pp. (5)-84. Fontainebleau, impr. E. Jacquin.

"Le page du duc de Savoie" (épisode des guerres du XVe siècle)" par Alexandre Dumas Paris Dufour, Mulat et Boulanger, éditeurs, ... 1857, 4to., pp. (1)-382, (383)-384 table of contents. "Le page du duc de Savoie" ends on page 365 and is followed by "Les drames de la mer Le Kent", pp. (366)-382; 12 steel engravings including the frontispiece. Yellow wrappers repeating the title-page except 'par M. Alexandre Dumas.

Collection Hetzel. "Le page du duc de Savoie" par Alexandre Dumas. Nouvelle édition. Leipzig, Alph. Dürr, 24mo., 5 volumes, same pagination as the Kiessling, Schnée et cie., and Alphonse Lebègue, editions referred to above.

"Le page du duc de Savoie" par Alexandre Dumas. Paris, Michel Lévy frères, 1862, 12mo., 2 volumes, pp. 317, verso blank, (319)-320 table of contents, and 290, (291)-292 table of contents. Often reprinted, same format and pagination, by both Michel Lévy frères and Calmann-Lévy.

Romans historiques, aventures, anecdotes, mystères par Alexandre Dumas. "Le page du duc de Savoie". Paris, Boulanger et Legrand ..., 1864, same format, pagination and illustrations as the Dufour, Mulat et Boulanger, 1857, edition. Lagny, Imprimerie de A. Varigault.

"Le page du duc de Savoie" par Alexandre Dumas, Paris, Michel Lévy frères, 1865, 4to., pp. 167 in double columns, and additional unnumbered page table of contents. Caption title. Woodcut at head of title. Reprinted, same format and pagination, 1866.

Ibid   Paris, Calmann-Lévy, n.d. (c 188), same format and pagination as the preceding edition. Caption title. Woodcut at head of title. Musee littéraire contemporain.

"LA CONSCIENCE"   (Drama)   1854

     Gilnel in his "Alexandre Dumas et son oeuvre" wrote : 'Ce drame est tiré d'une trilogie de l'allemand A.W. Iffland : "Le crime par ambition". MM. Michel Lévy frères qui, le 4 mai 1846, avient passé un traité avec Lockroy et exerçaient les droits de celui-ci, prétendirent que leur cédant avait collaboré à la "Conscience"; ils furent déboutés de leur demande par jugement du tribunal de la Seine (1re Chambre) du 3 mai 1855'. Judging from the report of the above-mentioned action in 'Le Mousquetaire' for 16th May, 1855, it would seem that Lockroy's participation consisted simply of minor alterations during rehearsals.

     All editions of the play carry the dedication to Victor Hugo, whose reply may be read in "Les contemplations", pièce XV, le livre cinquième. The play was a brilliant success, and was re-staged in 1869 at the Odéon with even greater success.

Original edition.
"La conscience" drame en cinq actes et en six tableaux par Alexandre Dumas Paris librairie d'Alphonse Taride galerie de l'Odéon 1854 L'éditeur se réserve le droit de traduction et de reproduction. 12mo., pp. (5)-7 'dédicace' signed : A. Dumas, and 'préface' signed : A. Dumas. Paris, 7 novembre 1854. Verso (unnumbered) 'personnages', (9)-108. Yellow wrappers repeating title-page. Verso of half-title : typographie de Ch. Lahure, Imprimeur du Sénat et de la Cour de Cassation, rue de Vaugirard, 9. In later editions the preface is printed at the end as a 'postscript', and differs as to the first third with the remainder being identical.

Ibid   Paris, librairie Alphonse Taride, ..., 1855, 4to., pp. 30 in double columns. Caption title.

"La conscience", drame en cinq actes et en six tableaux, par Alexandre Dumas. Représenté pour la première fois, à Paris, sur le théatre impérial de l'Odéon, le 4 novembre 1854. Paris, Simon Raçon et Cie., n.d. (1857), 4to., same pagination as the preceding edition. Oeuvres diverses.

Ibid   (Paris), Alphonse Taride, n.d. (1858), 4to., and has bound in with it "Positif et négatif", comédie en un acte, par Félix Henneguy, pp. 28 and 3 respectively in double columns. Caption title. Woodcut at head of title. Musée théatral illustré. 4e et 5e livraisons.

Ibid   (Paris), Michel Lévy frères, n.d. (1863), 4to., and has bound in with it "Chasse-croisé", comédie en un acte, par MM. N. Fournier et Meyer, pp. 28 and 7 respectively in double columns. Caption title. Woodcut at head of title. Théâtre contemporain illustré. 671e et 672e livraisons.

"La conscience" drame en six actes Odéon. - 4 novembre 1854. 'A Victor Hugo' ... signed : Alex. Dumas, and "Distribution" on title-page, pp. 2-114, 'post-scriptum' 114-116 signed : Alex. Dumas. Paris, 7 novembre 1854. Théâtre complet de Alex. Dumas Tome XX Paris Calmann Lévy, éditeur ancienne maison Michel Lévy frères, 1874. 12mo. "Théâtre complet" in 25 volumes.

There was one parody of the play :
"L'Inconscience", par Edouard Jaloux. This was a play in two parts, and was published as a feuilleton in March, 1856, in 'L'Ere nouvelle théatrale'.

"LE CAPITAINE RICHARD"   1854

This is Dumas, once again, working with no collaborator. He has claimed that the main episode was told to him by Schlegel, the German littérateur, possibly in the form of an anecdote. The period covered is 1809-1815 and, therefore, deals with the final part of Napoleon's career, the chapters covering the Russian campaign and the retreat of the Grand Army being very good indeed. It is, again, the story of twins with a remarkable resemblance to each other. The curious thing is that history and romance are not well-blended - there is a section of pure history then one of romance, and either could be lifted from the other without injury. But both are admirable in their own right. The work was first published serially in 'Le Monde Illustré', circa 1854.

Original edition.
"Le capitaine Richard" par Alexandre Dumas. Edition autorisée pour la Belgique et l'Etranger, interdite pour la France. Bruxelles, Livourne, Meline, Cans et Compie.; Leipzig, P. Meline, 1854, 16mo., 2 volumes, pp. 248 and 248. There are no tables of contents. Buff wrappers with the title : "Le capitaine Richard (scènes militaires)" and the Leipzig member of the publishers 'J.P. Meline'.

Collection Hetzel. "Le capitaine Richard", par Alexandre Dumas. Edition autorisée pour la Belgique et l'étranger, interdite pour la France. Bruxelles, Alph. Lebègue, 1855, 18mo., 2 volumes, pp. 211 and 206, each with an additional unnumbered page table of contents. Yellow wrappers. Bibliothèque diamante.

Collection Hetzel. "Le capitaine Richard" par Alexandre Dumas. Edition autorisée pour la Belgique et l'étranger, interdite pour la France. Bruxelles et Leipzig, Kiessling, Schnée et Compie., 1855, 2 volumes, same format and pagination as the preceding edition.

Collection Hetzel. "Le capitaine Richard", par Alexandre Dumas. Edition autorisée pour la Belgique et l'étranger, interdite pour la France. Bruxelles et Leipzig, Kiessling, Schnée et Cie.; Bâle, J.G. Neukirch, 1855, 2 volumes, same format and pagination as the preceding editions.

"Le capitaine Richard" par Alexandre Dumas. Paris, Alexandre Cadot, éditeur, 37, rue Serpente, 1858, 8vo., 3 volumes. Pagination : 326 and additional unnumbered page table of contents, 309, verso blank, and unnumbered page table of contents, and 351, verso table of contents. "Le capitaine Richard" ends on page 247 of Volume 3, verso blank, and is followed by "Une chasse aux éléphants", pp. (249)-351. Yellow wrappers. Fontainebleau, impr. E. Jacquin.

"Le capitaine Richard", par Alexandre Dumas. Paris, Dufour, Mulat et Boulanger, 1858, large 8vo., pp. 142 in double columns, and additional unnumbered page table of contents; illustrated.

"Le capitaine Richard" par Alexandre Dumas, Paris, Michel Lévy frères, 1860, 12mo., pp. 306 and additional unnumbered page table of contents. Fairly frequently reprinted, same format and pagination, by both Michel Lévy frères and Calmann-Lévy.

Romans historiques, aventures, anecdotes, mystères par Alexandre Dumas. "Le capitaine Richard". Paris, Dufour, Mulat, Boulanger et Legrand ... , 1862, large 8vo., pp. 142 in double columns and additional unnumbered page table of contents; illustrated. Lagny, Imprimerie de A. Varigault.

"Le capitaine Richard", par Alexandre Dumas. Paris, Legrand et Crouzet, n.d. (c 1863), same format and pagination as the preceding edition; illustrated.

Ibid   Paris, Legrand, Troussel et Pomey, n.d. (186), same format and pagination as the preceding editions; illustrated.

"Le capitaine Richard" par Alexandre Dumas. Paris, Calmann-Levy, n.d. (188), 4to. Musée littéraire contemporain.

"VIE ET AVENTURES DE CATHERINE CHARLOTTE DE GRAMONT DE GRIMALDI, DUCHESSE DE VALENTINOIS, PRINCESSE DE MONACO"   1854 "LA PRINCESSE DE MONACO - VIE ET AVENTURES"

The usually accredited author of the above work, a mixture of memoirs, gossip, and the description of more or less colourful events, is comtesse Dash. Probably Dumas did some editing and revision of it. What he did do was insufficient for him to consider including it among his collected works (this much is obvious from the preface), although his publishers for fairly apparent reasons did. It was originally published in 'Le Mousquetaire' under the first of the above titles between 1st January and 18th September, 1854.

Original edition.
"Vie et aventures de la princesse de Monaco" receuillies par Alexandre Dumas. Paris, Alexandre Cadot, éditeur, 37, rue Serpente, 1854, 8vo., 6 volumes. Pagination : 317, 310, 309, 301, each with an additional unnumbered page table of contents, 302, with 2 additional unnumbered pages table of contents and publisher's advertisements, and 320, including table of contents. Yellow wrappers. Fontainebleau, impr. E. Jacquin.

Ibid   Paris, Alexandre Cadot, ... , 1855, 12mo., 2 volumes, pp. (3)-14 'Introduction' signed : Alexandre Dumas, (17)-392, and additional unnumbered page table of contents, and 391, with 2 additional unnumbered pages table of contents. The title-page of Volume 1 has in addition : "Vie et aventures de Catherine-Charlotte de Gramont duchesse de Valentinois, princesse de Monaco". Yellow wrappers.
Reprinted, same format and pagination, 1857.

"La princesse de Monaco - vie et aventures" receuillies par Alexandre Dumas Paris Michel Lévy frères, libraires éditeurs ... 1865, 12mo., 2 volumes, pp. (1)-12 'préface' signed : Alexandre Dumas, (13)-323, verso table of contents, and 316, (317)-319 'Appendice Attestation de Magdeleine Blondeau, première femme de chambre de madame la princesse de Monaco', verso table of contents.

Ibid   Nouvelle édition. Paris, Calmann-Lévy, 1887, 2 volumes, same format and pagination as the preceding edition.
Reprinted, same format and pagination, n.d. (189).

"CAUSERIES"   1854 -

These series of articles published in volume form appeared for the most part initially in 'Le Mousquetaire' and 'Le Monte-Cristo', or as additional material to complète one or other of Dumas' major works. As one exception to this, "Causeries d'un voyageur" were first published in 'Le Pays' in the issues of that journal for 7th, 8th, and 9th July, 1854.

Original editions.
"Causeries d'un voyageur", par M. Alexandre Dumas ... . Paris, Impr. de Morris, n.d. (1854), 4to., pp. 30.

"Le page du duc de Savoie" par Alexandre Dumas. Paris, Alexandre Cadot, éditeur, 37, rue Serpente, 1855, 8vo., 8 volumes. "Le page du duc de Savoie" ends on page 149 of Volume 8, verso blank, and is followed by "Causeries", pp. (151)-319, verso table of contents and 4 pages of publisher's advertisements; there were 10 causeries in all and were those that appeared in 'Le Mousquetaire' in the issues for 28th, 29th, 30th, 31st October; 5th November; 7th October; 23rd September; 4th August; 25th October; and 9th November, all in 1854, and reprinted in that order.

"Ingénue" par Alexandre Dumas. Paris, Alexandre Cadot, ... , 1853-1855, 8vo., 7 volumes. "Ingénue" ends on page 183 of Volume 7 (1855), verso blank, and is followed by "Causeries d'un voyageur", pp. (205)-314. There is no table of contents.

"Les mohicans de Paris" par Alexandre Dumas. Paris, Alexandre Cadot, ... , 1854-1855, 8vo., 19 volumes. "Les mohicans de Paris" ends on page 142 of Volume 19 (1855) and is followed by "Causeries" : 'Etudes sur le coeur et le talent des poëtes; Diane de Lys, talent ou la Dame aux Perles ; Suzanne, d'Ange ; Le Demi-monde ; Le Demi-monde (suite)'. pp. (143)-309 and an additional unnumbered page table of contents.

Collection Hetzel. "Causeries" par Alexandre Dumas. Edition autorisée pour la Belgique et l'étranger, interdite pour la France. Bruxelles, Meline, Cans et Cie., 1857, 24mo., 3 volumes (not numbered and the wrapper of Volume 3 dated '1858'). Pagination and contents :
Volume 1, 229 and additional unnumbered page table of contents; 'Ah! qu'on est fier d'être français. A ceux qui veulent se mettre au théatre. Eugène Sue, sa vie et ses oeuvres. Etat civil du comte de Monte-Cristo. Les petits cadeaux de mon ami Delaporte. Une voyage à la lune. Ce qui'on voit chez madame tussaud'.
Volume 2, 221 and additional unnumbered page table of contents; 'Les trois dames. Les rois du lundi. Une chasse aux éléphants. L'homme d'expérience. Les étoiles commis voyageurs. La dernière année de Marie Dorval'.
Volume 3, 205 and additional unnumbered page table of contents; 'Un dernier mot sur Béranger. Désir et possession. Les courses d'Epsom. Une mère. Un fait personnel. Le curé de Boulogne. A propos d'un petit malheur'. Green wrappers.

Collection Hetzel. "Causeries", par Alexandre Dumas. Edition autorisée pour la Belgique et l'étranger, interdite pour la France. Bruxelles, Office de publicité; Leipzig, Alphonse Dürr, 1857, 24mo., 4 volumes. Pagination and contents :
Volume 1, 221 and additional unnumbered page table of contents; 'Les trois dames. Les rois du lundi. Une chasse aux éléphants. L'homme d'expérience. Les étoiles commis-voyageurs. La dernière année de Marie Dorval'.
Volume 2, 225 and additional unnumbered page table of contents; 'Le lion d'Aurés. Poëtes, peintres et musiciens. Béranger, sa vie et ses oeuvres. Un plan d'économie. La figurine de César. Une fabrique de vases étrusques à Bourg-en-Bresse'.
Volume 3, 229 and additional unnumbered page table of contents; 'Ah! qu'on fier d'être français. A ceux qui veulent se mettre

au théâtre. Eugène Sue, sa vie et ses oeuvres. Etat-civil
du comte de Monte-Cristo. Les petits cadeaux de mon ami
Delaporte. Une voyage à la lune. Ce qu'on voit chez madame
Tussaud'.
Volume 4, 205 and additional unnumbered page table of contents; 'Un
dernier mot sur Béranger. Désir et possession. Les courses
d'Epsom. Une mère. Un fait personnel. Le curé de Boulogne.
A propos d'un petit malheur'.
(There seem to have been binders' errors. The volume numbers given
above are those quoted by Talvart et Place, but according to the
Bibliothèque Nationale Volume 1 is numbered Volume 4, Volume 2 is
numbered Volume 3, Volume 3 is numbered Volume 1, and Volume 4 is
numbered Volume 2; the contents of each of the volumes are the same.)

Collection Hetzel. "Causeries" par Alexandre Dumas. Edition autorisée pour la Belgique et l'Etranger, interdite pour la France. Leipzig, Alph. Dürr, 1857, 24mo., pp. 225 and additional unnumbered page
table of contents. Contents : 'Le lion d'Aurès. Poëtes, peintres
et musiciens. Béranger: sa vie et ses oeuvres. Un plan d'économie.
La figurine de César. Une fabrique de vases étrusques à Bourg en
Bresse'.

Collection Hetzel. "Causeries" par Alexandre Dumas. Edition autorisée pour la Belgique et l'Etranger, interdite pour la France. Leipzig, Alph. Dürr, 1857, 24mo., pp. 229 and additional unnumbered page
table of contents. Contents : 'Ah! qu'on est fier d'être français.
A ceux qui veulent se mettre au théâtre. Eugène Sue, sa vie et ses
oeuvres. L'état civil du comte de Monte-Cristo. Les petits cadeaux
de mon ami Delaporte. Une voyage à la lune. Ce qu'on voit chez madame
Tussaud'.

"Le capitaine Richard" par Alexandre Dumas. Paris, Alexandre Cadot,
... , 1858, 8vo., 3 volumes. "Le capitaine Richard" ends on page 247
of Volume 3, verso blank, and is followed by "Une chasse aux éléphants", pp. (249)-351, with an additional unnumbered page table of
contents.

"Les louves de Machecoul" par Alexandre Dumas. Paris, Alexandre
Cadot, ... , 1859, 8vo., 10 volumes. "Les louves de Machecoul" ends
on page 86 of Volume 10 and is followed by, inter alia, "Une chasse
aux éléphants", pp. (137)-256.

"Causeries" par Alexandre Dumas Paris Michel Lévy frères, libraires-
éditeurs, ... , 1860, 12mo., 2 volumes, pp. 279, verso table of contents, and 286 with an additional unnumbered page table of contents.
Contents : Volume 1, 'Les trois dames. Les rois du lundi. Une
chasse aux éléphants. L'homme d'expérience. Les
étoiles commis voyageurs. Un plan d'économie. La
figurine de César. Une fabrique de vases étrusques à
Bourg en Bresse. Etat civil du comte de Monte-Cristo'.
Volume 2, 'Ah! qu'on est fier d'être français. A ceux
qui veulent se mettre au théatre. Les petits cadeaux de
mon ami Delaporte. Une voyage à la lune. Ce qu'on
voit chez madame Tussaud. Le lion d'Aurès. Les courses
d'Epsom. Une visite à Garibaldi'.
Often reprinted, same format and pagination, by both Michel Lévy
frères and Calmann-Lévy.

Ibid   Paris, Michel Lévy frères, 1861, 4to., pp. 88 in double columns. Caption title. Woodcut at head of title. Musée littéraire contemporain.

"Causerie à propos de ma tête et de ma main".
"Causerie sur les poëtes, les leporides, les microphytes et les microzoaires".
"A propos de Cléopatre et des nuits de Rome".
"Madame Monaco : histoire de brigands".
"La chasse".
These 5 causeries were all published in 'Le journal illustré' during 1864 and apparently none have been reprinted. The first appeared in Nos. 8 and 9 of the journal, the second in Nos. 11, 12 and 13, and the third in No. 14, the fourth in No. 16, and the fifth is Nos. 34 and 35.

"Deux causeries, par Alexandre Dumas, à Lille". Programme des soirées du 24 et du 26 février 1866. Lille, impr. de Danel, n.d. (1866), 12mo., pp. 8. Autobiographie.

Ibid   Lille, impr. de Danel, n.d. (1866), 12mo., pp. 15.

"L'homme d'expérience" par Alexandre Dumas. Published in : 'L'Univers illustré', journal hebdomadaire, Paris, 23 mai 1896 (39e année), folio, No. 2148, page 412 occupying a single column.

"INGENUE"   1854-1855

   This work is not quite up to the standard of the great Revolutionary romances. It opens on 24th August, 1788, and ends with the death of Marat on 13th July, 1793.

   Paul Lacroix, who was a leading authority on Restif de la Bretonne, suggested to Dumas as the subject of a romance the incident between Restif and his daughter brought about by the latter's choice of husband and which prompted the scurrilous story by Restif himself entitled "Ingénue Saxancourt". While Dumas' romance was in serial form it was brought to the attention of two young men, nephews of the original Ingénue and by now a very old woman, who took legal steps to stop publication. In the event the whole matter was settled amicably out of court when it was realised that Ingénue as presented by Dumas bore no resemblance to her depiction by Restif - the only stipulation was that all issues of the book when it was published should have appended copies of the letters exchanged between the nephews and Dumas. A 'causerie' and the letters were published in 'Le Mousquetaire' on 25th October, 1854, and 14th Janaury and 14th March, 1855.

   The romance was first published as a serial in 'Le Siècle' from 30th August to 12th September, 1854. Both Parran and Glinel give the year of publication in volume form as 1854, which is unlikely, but both the Bibliothèque Nationale and the Bibliothèque de l'Arsenal have copies dated 1853-1855; it can only be surmised, therefore, that through a printer's error there is a misdating of the first two Cadot volumes, which should read '1854'. It will be noted that the editions published in Bruxelles, Leipzig, and Basle are all dated 1854-1855.

Original edition.
"Ingénue" par Alexandre Dumas. Paris Alexandre Cadot, éditeur, 37, rue Serpente, 1853 (sic)-1855, 8vo., 7 volumes. Pagination : Volumes 1 and 2 (1853), 307, and 307 followed by 4 pages of publisher's adver-

tisements; Volumes 3-7 (1855), 302, 362 each with 1 page of publisher's advertisements, 328, 309, verso blank, and 1 page of publisher's advertisements, and 314 and 1 page of publisher's advertisements. There are no tables of contents. "Ingénue" ends on page 183 of Volume 7, verso blank, and is followed by "Causeries d'un voyageur", pp. (205)-314. Yellow wrappers. Fontainebleau, imprimerie de E. Jacquin. (There are slight variations in the numbers of pages of Cadot's advertisements in the Bibliothèque Nationale and Bibliothèque de l'Arsenal copies. These may well persist in other copies of the Cadot edition.)

"Ingénue". Par Alex. Dumas. Edition autorisée pour la Belgique et l'étranger, interdite pour la France. Bruxelles, Alph. Lebègue, 1854-1855, 24mo., 5 volumes. Pagination : Volumes 1-4 (1854), 211, 204, 207 and 211; Volume 5 (1855), 191, and (i)-vii, 'Note" by the publishers. "Ingénue" ends on page 112 of Volume 5 and is followed by "Blanche de Beaulieu", pp. (113)-189. The pagination in all volumes includes table of contents.

"Ingénue" par Alex. Dumas. Bruxelles et Leipzig, Kiessling, Schnée et Compie., 1854-1855, same years of publication for each of the 5 volumes, same format and pagination. Bibliothèque diamandaux.

Ibid   Bruxelles et Leipzig, Kiessling, Schnée et Cie.; Bâle, J.G. Neukirch, 1854-1855, same years of publication for each of the 5 volumes, same format and pagination as the preceding editions.

Semaine Littéraire du Courrier des Etats-Unis. "Ingénue", par M. Alexandre Dumas. New-York, Charles Lasalle, 1855, 8vo., pp. (3)-234 in double columns. Caption title.

"Ingénue" par Alexandre Dumas. Paris, Michel Lévy frères, 1860, 12mo., 2 volumes, pp. 319, verso table of contents, and 330 and additional unnumbered page table of contents. Several times reprinted, same format and pagination, by both Michel Lévy frères and Calmann-Lévy.

Ibid   Paris, Michel Lévy frères, n.d. (186), 4to., pp. 164 in double columns; page 155 comprises a note from the publishers, and includes the 4 letters exchanged between Dumas and the grandsons of Restif de la Bretonne; page 156 table of contents.

Ibid   Paris, Calmann-Lévy, 1883, same format and pagination as the preceding edition. Caption title. Woodcut at head of title. Musée littéraire contemporain.

"LES MOHICANS DE PARIS"   1854-1855
"SALVATOR LE COMMISSIONAIRE"   1855-1859

        Considered as one work only, and it was first published as a serial under the first of the above titles to be divided into the two separate titles when issued in volume form, this is Dumas' longest work, amounting to more than a million words. The period of the story is from 1827 to 1830, although on occasions it goes back to earlier years. The canvas is enormous and includes characters from all classes of society in Paris of the period - old officers from Napoleon's days, the duc de Reichstadt, detectives (the famous Monsieur Jackal), police spies, convicts, students, and scores of others. It can be taken that Paul Bocage collaborated in the writing, and the irregularity of the publishing dates indicates its erratic appearance. As a cohesive whole the work certainly suffered from interruptions in its writing.

281

The work's first appearance serially was in 'Le Mousquetaire'
on the following dates : 1854, 25th-31st May, 1st-15th June, 17th-
30th June, 1st-31st July, 1st-31st August, 1st-4th September, 23rd-
30th September, 3rd-7th October, 10th-12th October, 14th-15th October,
18th-21st October, 24th-27th and 31st October, 1st-3rd November, 8th-
11th November, 14th-17th November, 20th and 22nd-24th November, 7th-
11th December, 14th-18th December, 21st-25th and 30th-31st December;
1855, 1st-5th January, 9th-13th January, 18th-22nd January, 27th-31st
January (the number for 27th January being Chapter viii of Volume 15
forms the start of what is now known as "Salvator le commissionaire"),
1st, 2nd and 6th-13th February, 26th-30th April, 1st and 5th-9th May,
12th-16th May, 20th-24th May, 27th-30th May, 1st-5th June, 7th-9th
June, 16th-21st June, 23rd-28th June, 1st-5th July, 8th-12th July,
15th-20th July, 24th-26th and 28th and 29th July, 1st August, 3rd-
6th August, 9th-14th August, 20th-21st August, 23rd-25th and 29th-30th
August; 1856, 11th-25th February, 4th-5th and 7th-9th March, 11th,
12th, 14th-16th, 18th, 19th, 21st, 22nd and 24th-26th March (and in
point of fact this last number is just about the half-way mark in
"Salvator ..."). The serial issue then continued appearing in 'Le
Monte-Cristo' on the following dates : 23rd April, 1857, to 22nd
July, 1858, and from 21st April to 28th July, 1859 (and it must be
remembered that in these particular years this journal was published
weekly).

There was a further serial issue : "Les Mohicans de Paris",
par Alexandre Dumas, 'Journal du dimanche', 17th October, 1861,
commencing with No. 414, to 29th June, 1862, No. 487, and followed by
"Les Mohicans de Paris. Salvator" (deuxième partie) starting on 3rd
July, 1862, No. 488, to 30th April, 1863, the final number being 574,
4to., in treble columns with woodcut at head of each issue. Caption
title.

Original edition.
"Les Mohicans de Paris", par Alex. Dumas. Collection Hetzel. Bruxelles, Alp. Lebègue et cie., 1854-1855, 24mo., 10 volumes. Pagination
: Volumes 1-6 (1854), 215, 210, 202, 209, 219 and 217; Volumes 7-10
(1855), 211, 213, 219 and 202. Each volume has an additional unnumbered page table of contents. Volume 10 ends : 'Fin de la première
partie'. Yellow wrappers. Bibliothèque diamant. Edition autorisée
pour la Belgique et l'étranger, interdite pour la France. The publisher's name on the wrappers is spelt 'Alph. Lebègue'.

Ibid Collection Hetzel. Bruxelles et Leipzig, Kiessling, Schnée et Compie., 1854-1855, 10 volumes, same years of publication, format and pagination as the preceding edition. Yellow
wrappers. Bibliothèque diamant. Edition autorisée pour la Belgique
et l'étranger, interdite pour la France.

"Les Mohicans de Paris" par Alexandre Dumas. Paris, Alexandre Cadot,
éditeur, 37, rue Serpente, 1854-1855, 8vo., 19 volumes, pp. 303, 301,
303, 319, 311, 303, 314, 308, 320, 304, 304, 320, 312 (all including
table of contents), 310, 322, 313, 313, 306 and 309 (all with an
additional unnumbered page table of contents). Yellow wrappers.
Fontainebleau, Impr. de E. Jacquin.

"Les Mohicans de Paris. Salvator" par Alexandre Dumas. Collection
Hetzel. Edition autorisée pour la Belgique et l'étranger, interdite
pour la France. Bruxelles, Alph. Lebègue, 1855-1859, 24mo., 13 volumes. Pagination : Volumes 1-5 (1855), 212, 202, 206, 201 and 204;

Volumes 6 and 7 (1856), 158 and 160; Volumes 8-12 (1858), 206, 180,
195, 190 and 188; Volume 13 (1859), 164, all with an additional unnumbered page table of contents.

"Les Mohicans de Paris. Salvator". Par Alexandre Dumas. Edition
autorisée pour la Belgique et l'étranger, interdite pour la France.
Collection Hetzel. Bruxelles et Leipzig, Kiessling, Schnée et Compie;
Leipzig, Alphonse Dürr, 1855-1859, 24mo., 13 volumes. Volumes 1-7
were published by Kiessling, Schnee et Compie., and Volumes 8-13 by
Alphonse Dürr, the years of publication being - Volumes 1-5 (1855),
Volumes 6-7 (1856), Volumes 8-12 (1858), and Volume 13 (1859), with
the same pagination as the preceding edition.

"Les Mohicans de Paris. Salvator le commissionaire" par Alexandre
Dumas. Paris, Alexandre Cadot, éditeur, 37 rue Serpente, 1856-1859,
8vo., 14 volumes. Pagination : 322, 314 each with an additional
unnumbered page table of contents, 324 including table of contents,
329, 317, 309, 309 each with an additional unnumbered page table of
contents, 312 including table of contents, 322, 305 each with an
additional unnumbered page table of contents, 320 including table of
contents, 310, 325 each with an additional unnumbered page table of
contents, and 328 including table of contents. "Salvator le commissionaire" is followed in Volume 14 by "La frégate 'L'Espérance'."

"Les mohicans de Paris", par Alex. Dumas. Collection Hetzel. Edition
autorisée pour la Belgique et l'étranger, interdite pour la France.
Bruxelles, Alph. Lebègue, 1857, 24mo., 10 volumes, same pagination
as the Lebègue 1854-1855 edition.

"Les mohicans de Paris" par Alexandre Dumas. Paris, Dufour, Mulat
et Boulanger, 1857-1860, large 8vo., 4 volumes. Pagination : Volumes
1 and 2 (1857), 477 and 408, each with 3 additional unnumbered page
table of contents, verso of page (411) of Volume 2 'classement des
gravures', and each volume with a frontispiece and 14 plates; Volumes
3 and 4 (1860) are entitled "Romans historiques, aventures, mystères"
par Alexandre Dumas, and paged respectively 338 and 336, each with 2
additional unnumbered pages table of contents, and each having 11
plates.
Volumes 1 and 2 were reprinted, same format, pagination, frontispiece
and plates, 1860. Lagny. - Typographie de A. Varigault et Cie.

"Les mohicans de Paris. Salvator", par Alexandre Dumas. Bruxelles,
Meline, Cans et Cie., 1858-1859, 24mo., 13 volumes.

Semaine Littéraire du Courrier des Etats-Unis. "Les mohicans de Paris"
par Alexandre Dumas. New-York, Charles Lassalle, Editeur, 1860-1861,
large 8vo., 2 volumes. Pagination : Volume 1 (1860), 4-611, and
Volume 2 (1861), 4-465, both in double columns, Volume 2 being completed by "Une nuit étrange" par Wilkie Collins, pp. (467)-476. Volume 104, Nos. 1 and (2).

Romans historiques, aventures, anecdotes, mystères par Alexandre
Dumas. "Les mohicans de Paris". Paris Dufour, Boulanger et Legrand
... , 1862, large 8vo., 4 volumes. Pagination : (1)-477, (478)-480
table of contents; (1)-408, (409)-411 table of contents; (1)-338,
(339)-340 table of contents; (1)-336, (337)-338 table of contents;
illustrated. Imprimerie de A. Varigault.

"Les mohicans de Paris" par Alexandre Dumas. Paris, Michel Lévy
frères, 1862, 12mo., 4 volumes. Pagination : 312, (313)-314 table

of contents; 298, (299)-300 table of contents; 308, (309)-310 table of contents; 285, verso blank, (287)-288 table of contents. Frequently reprinted, same format and pagination, by both Michel Lévy frères and Calmann-Lévy.

"Salvator" suite et fin des "Mohicans de Paris" par Alexandre Dumas. Paris, Michel lévy frères, 1862-1863, 12mo., 5 volumes. Pagination : 299, verso table of contents; 301, verso blank, (303)-304 table of contents; 290, (291)-292 table of contents; 282, (283)-284 table of contents; 255, verso table of contents. "Salvator" ends on page 196 of Volume 5 and is followed by "Monseigneur Gaston Phoebus chronique dans laquelle est racontée l'histoire du démon familier du sire de Corasse", pp. (197)-255. Frequently reprinted, same format and pagination, by both Michel Lévy frères and Calmann-Lévy.

"Salvator" - suite et fin des "Mohicans de Paris" - par Alexandre Dumas. Saint-Germain (no publisher or printer stated), n.d. (c 186), 4to., pp. 346 in double columns. Caption title. Woodcut at head of title.

"Les mohicans de Paris" par Alexandre Dumas. Paris, Dufour, Boulanger et Legrand, 1863, large 8vo., 4 volumes, same pagination and illustrations as the Dufour, Mulat et Boulanger, 1857-1860, edition.

"Les mohicans de Paris" par Alexandre Dumas. Paris, Calmann-Lévy, n.d. (188), 4to. Caption title. Woodcut at head of title.

"Salvator le commissionaire" par Alexandre Dumas. Paris, Calmann-Lévy, n.d. (188), 4to. Caption title. Woodcut at head of title. Both of the above in Musée littéraire contemporain.

"LA DERNIERE ANNEE DE MARIE DORVAL"   1855

The actress Marie Dorval had been Dumas' friend for many years, and was the original Adèle d'Hervey in "Antony". In May, 1849, she had died in rather tragic circumstances and some years later Dumas wrote a tribute to her which was first published in 'Le Mousquetaire' between 17th and 31st July, 1855. This tribute was republished as a brochure, the proceeds from its sale and from the sale also of Dumas' original holograph manuscript, going towards the maintenance of her grave, the cost of a monument over it, and for the assistance of her dependants. The work was dedicated to George Sand.

Original edition.
Alexandre Dumas "La dernière année de Marie Dorval" Paris Librairie nouvelle boulevard des Italiens, 15, en face de la maison dorée 1855 18mo., pp. (5) "La dernière année de Marie Dorval" 'A George Sand' - 96; verso of half-title : Paris. - Typ. de Mme .Ve Dondey-Dupré, rue Saint-Louis, 46. Pink wrappers repeating the title-page with the added words under Marie Dorval : '50 centimes pour son tombeau'. (According to Parran the brochure includes a portrait, but neither my copy nor any others that I have seen shows any sign of its inclusion.)

Collection Hetzel. "Causeries" par Alexandre Dumas. Bruxelles, Meline, Cans et compagnie, 1857, 24mo., pp. 221 and additional unnumbered page table of contents, includes "La dernière année de Marie Dorval".

Collection Hetzel. "Causeries", par Alexandre Dumas. Edition autorisée pour la Belgique et l'étranger, interdite pour la France. Bruxelles, Office de publicité, 1857, same format, pagination and contents
as the preceding edition.

Collection Hetzel. "Causeries", par Alexandre Dumas. Edition autorisée pour la Belgique et l'étranger, interdite pour la France. Bruxelles, Office de publicité, 1857, 32mo., 4 volumes, pp. 221, 225, 229
and 205, each with an additional unnumbered page table of contents.
(According to the Bibliothèque Nationale "La dernière année de Marie
Dorval" is included in Volume 4, but Talvart et Place say in Volume
1.)

"Les morts vont vite" par Alexandre Dumas Paris Michel Lévy frères,
1861, 12mo., 2 volumes, pp. 322 and 294, each with an additional
unnumbered page table of contents. "La dernière année de Marie Dorval"
occupies pp. (241)-294 of Volume 2.
Reprinted, same format and pagination, by both Michel Lévy frères and
Calmann-Lévy.

"MLLE. ISABELLE CONSTANT"   1855
     This is purely and simply an appreciation of Mademoiselle Con-
stant the actress.

Original (and only) edition.
Nouvelle galerie des artistes dramatiques vivants contenant 40 portraits en pied des principaux artistes dramatiques de Paris ... peints
et gravés sur acier par Ch. Geoffroy chaque portrait est accompagné
d'une notice biographique et d'une appréciation sur le vie d'artiste.
Paris A la librairie théatrale, Boulevard Saint-Martin, 12. N.d.
(1855), 4to.; "Mlle. Isabelle Constant", signed : Alex. Dumas, 4
unnumbered pages, with a steel engraving of Mlle. Constant in the play
"César Borgia".

"MARIE GIOVANNI. JOURNAL DE VOYAGE D'UNE PARISIENNE"
"TAITI - MARQUISES - CALIFORNIE. JOURNAL DE MADAME
GIOVANNI ... "   1855
"IMPRESSIONS DE VOYAGE. JOURNAL DE MADAME GIOVANNI"
"JOURNAL DE MADAME GIOVANNI"

     This is the narrative of the travels of a Frenchwoman, married
to an Italian merchant, to New Zealand, Australia, the Pacific Islands,
California and Mexico, between 1843 and 1853. 'Marie Giovanni' is
purely and simply the narrator's assumed name, and it has never been
established definitely who she was. Her notes, which were doubtless
added to in her conversations with Dumas, were edited by him and the
work was first published serially in 'Le Siècle' in 1855. The first
feuilleton was so misprinted, seemingly no proofs were submitted, that
Dumas printed the correct text in 'Le Mousquetaire' for 4th and 5th
April, 1855, with the threat that he would continue doing so with
every other faulty issue. It can be presumed that accurate printing
followed in 'Le Siècle' for no more feuilletones were published by
Dumas in his own journal. Dumas later reprinted the work in a rather
abridged version in 'Le Monte-Cristo' between 17th November, 1859, and
26th January, 1860.

It should be noted that the Cadot, 1856, edition ends abruptly in the middle of the journey through Mexico. The work has never been included in the Lévy editions of Dumas' collected works.

Original edition.
Collection Hetzel. "Marie Giovanni journal de voyage d'une paris-ienne", rédigé par Alexandre Dumas. Edition autorisée pour la Bel-gique et l'étranger, interdite pour la France. Bruxelles, Alph. Lebègue, 1855, 18mo., 4 volumes, pp. 217, 210, 211 and 193, each with an additional unnumbered page table of contents.

Ibid   Bruxelles et Leipzig, Kiessling, Schnée et Cie., 1855, 18mo., 4 volumes, 217, 210, each with an additional unnumbered page table of contents, 212 including table of contents, and 193 with an additional unnumbered page table of contents. Impr. A. Lebègue.

Ibid   Bruxelles et Leipzig, Kiessling, Schnée et Compie., 1855-1856, 18mo., 4 volumes. Volumes 1-3 (1855) and Volume 4 (1856), same pagination as the preceding edition. Yellow wrappers, Volume 4 having the year '1855'.

"Taïti - Marquises - Californie Journal de Madame Giovanni" rédigé et publié par Alexandre Dumas Paris Alexandre Cadot, éditeur, 37, rue Serpente, 1856, 8vo., 4 volumes. Pagination : 318, 310, 318 and 311, each with an additional unnumbered page table of contents. Yellow wrappers. Fontainebleau, impr. E. Jacquin.

"Impressions de voyage. Journal de Madame Giovanni en Australie, aux îles Marquises, á Tahiti, á la Nouvelle-Calédonie, en Californie et au Mexique", par Alexandre Dumas. (Vignette) Paris, Dufour, Mulat et Boulanger, 1858, large 8vo., pp. 224 including 2 pages table of contents and 'classement des gravures'; 7 plates engraved by Philipp-oteaux, Pannemayer, Fouget, etc. The "Journal" ends on page 210 and is followed by "Les drames de la mer. Le capitaine Marion", pp. 211-221, and which is not illustrated.

"Journal de madame Giovanni", roman historique par Alexandre Dumas. Paris, Legrand et Crouzet, n.d. (1858), same format, pagination and illustrations as the preceding edition.

"Marie Giovanni. Journal de voyage d'une parisienne", rédigé par Alexandre Dumas. Edition autorisée pour la Belgique et l'Etranger, interdite pour la France. Bruxelles, Alph. Lebègue, 1861-1863, 24mo., 5 volumes. Pagination : Volumes 1 and 2 (1861), 281 and 277; Vol-ume 3 (1863 and probably a misprint), 270; Volumes 4 and 5 (1862), 229 and 170, each volume having an additional unnumbered page table of contents.

Romans historiques, aventures, anecdotes, mystères par Alexandre Dumas. "Le journal de Madame Giovanni". Paris, Dufour, Boulanger et Legrand ... , large 8vo., pp. (1)-210. There is no table of contents; illustrated. Lagny, Imprimerie de A. Varigault.

"Impressions de voyage. Journal de Madame Giovanni en Australie, en Californie, aux îles Marquises, à Taïti, à la Nouvelle-Calédonie, et au Mexiquë", rédigé et publié par Alexandre Dumas. Paris, Impr. de Voisvenel, n.d. (c 1865), large folio, pp. 16 in double columns.

Ibid   Paris, Legrand, Troussel et Pomey, n.d. (c 1868), same format, pagination and illustrations as the Dufour, Mulat et Boulanger, 1858, edition.

"MADAME EMILE de GIRARDIN"   1855

On the 29th June, 1855, Madame de Girardin, née Delphine Gay, died, and on 3rd July 'Le Mousquetaire' was published with a black border on its front page and with an obituary by Dumas. This obituary, accompanied by articles about her and a portrait, was later issued as a pamphlet by Serriers, Paris, 1856, (29 juin), 18mo.

"EUGENE-AUGUSTE COLBRUN"
"MON AMI COLBRUN"   1855

This is the laudatory article on the actor who was one of Dumas' friends and who was engaged at the Théâtre-Historique, his first part being Friquet in "La reine Margot". The article first appeared as a 'causerie' in the issue of 'Le Mousquetaire' for 27th November, 1854. When it was republished in "Propos d'art et de cuisine" it was quite considerably enlarged.
"Nouvelle galerie des artistes dramatiques vivants", par Ch. Geoffroy. Paris, Librairie théâtrale, 1855, 4to., 2 volumds, 82 portraits. "Eugène-Auguste Colbrun" was one of the articles included.

"Les louves de Machecoul" par Alexandre Dumas. Paris, Alexandre Cadot, éditeur, 37, rue Serpente, 1859, 8vo., 10 volumes. "Les louves de Machecoul" ends on page 86 of Volume 10 and is followed by, inter alia, "Eugène-Auguste Colbrun", pp. (257)-315, verso blank, and additional unnumbered page table of contents. Yellow wrappers. Fontainebleau, impr. de E. Jacquin.

"Propos d'art et de cuisine" par Alexandre Dumas. Paris Calmann-Lévy, éditeur ancienne maison Michel Lévy frères ... 1877, 12mo., pp. 304 and additional unnumbered page table of contents. "Mon ami Colbrun" occupies pp. (169)-197.

"LE LIEVRE DE MON GRAND-PERE"   1855

In the introduction to this delightful children's story Dumas writes that the 'véritable père' of the work was de Cherville. It may be pointed out that the original holograph manuscript is entirely in Dumas' writing.

Original edition.
"Le lièvre de mon grand-père". Par M. Alexandre Dumas. In : 'L'Echo des feuilletons receuil de nouvelles, légendes, anecdotes, épisodes, ... '. Paris chez les éditeurs, 1855, large 8vo., pp. (488)-493 'Causerie en manière d'explication', 493-524, in double columns.

Collection Hetzel. "Le lièvre de mon grand-père" par Alexandre Dumas. Edition autorisée pour la Belgique et l'étranger, interdite pour la France. Bruxelles, Alph. Lebègue, 1856, 24mo., pp. (v)-xxxiii 'Explication en manière de causerie - Alex. Dumas'; blank, half-title, blank, (37)-172, with 2 additional unnumbered pages table of contents. Yellow wrappers.

Ibid   Bruxelles, Meline, Cans et Cie., 1856, same format and pagination as the preceding edition.

Bibliothèque choisi. Vol. LXIII. "Le lièvre de mon grand-père" par Alexandre Dumas. Suivi de "Les eaux du Taunus" par Victor Hérault.

Paris, 1856. Leipzig, chez Wolfgang Gerhard, 24mo., pp. 159. "Le lièvre de mon grand-père" ends on page 130, and 'Les eaux du Taunus" occupies pp. 131-159.

"Le lièvre de mon grand-père" par Alexandre Dumas. Paris, Alexandre Cadot, éditeur, 37, rue Serpente, 1857, 8vo., pp. (1)-44 'Causerie en manière d'explication', (45)-309, verso blank, and additional unnumbered page table of contents. At the end of page 309 is printed : Samedi 22 février 1856, à une heure trois quarts du matin. Yellow wrappers. Fontainebleau, Imp. de E. Jacquin.

"Le père Gigogne" contes pour les enfants par Alexandre Dumas Paris Michel Lévy frères, libraires-éditeurs 1860, 12mo., 2 volumes, pp. 311 and 315, each with verso table of contents. "Le lièvre de mon grand-père" occupies pp. (1)-183 of Volume 1.
Several times reprinted, same format and pagination, by both Michel Lévy frères and Calmann-Lévy.

Ibid   Paris, Michel Lévy frères, 1860, 4to., pp. 157 in double columns. Caption title. Woodcut at head of title. "Le lièvre de mon grand-père" is included. Musée littéraire contemporain.
Reprinted, same format and pagination, Calmann-Lévy, 189 .

"LES GRANDS HOMMES EN ROBE DE CHAMBRE : CESAR"   1855

     This is one of the works in the series devoted to historical narrative about famous men. The title indicated its period - BC 102-44. It was first published serially in 'La Presse' and then subsequently between 31st August and 19th December, 1855, in 'Le Mousquetaire'.

Original edition.
Collection Hetzel. "Les grand hommes en robe de chambre" par Alexandre Dumas. "César". Edition autorisée pour la Belgique et l'Etranger, interdite pour la France. Bruxelles, Alph. Lebègue, 1855, 24mo., 4 volumes, pp. 204, 202, 204 and 212.

Ibid   Bruxelles et Leipzig, Kiessling, Schnée et Compie., 1855, 4 volumes, same format and pagination as the preceding edition. Bruxelles, Imp. A. Lebègue.

"César" par Alexandre Dumas. Paris Alexandre Cadot, éditeur, 37, rue Serpente, 1856, 7 volumes, pp. 317, 301, 326, 326, 322, 313 and 333, each with an additional unnumbered page table of contents. "César" ends on page 248 of Volume 7 and is followed by "Le tueur de lions", par J. Gérard, pp. 251-333. Yellow wrappers. Fontainebleau, impr. E. Jacquin.

"Les grand hommes en robe de chambre César" par Alexandre Dumas Paris Michel Lévy frères, libraires-éditeurs 1866, 12mo., 2 volumes, pp. 298 and 304. There are no tables of contents.
Reprinted, same format and pagination, by both Michel Lévy frères and Calmann-Lévy.

"LES GRAND HOMMES EN ROBE DE CHAMBRE : HENRI IV,   1855-1856
LOUIS XIII, ET RICHELIEU"

     The period of this lively work of historical narrative, which was drawn mainly from contemporary memoirs and similar material, is

1553-1643. "Henri IV" first appeared in 'Le Mousquetaire' fairly regularly between 4th January and 26th February, 1855, whilst that portion relating to Louis XIII and Richelieu was published more irregularly in that journal between 26th April, 1855, and 30th March, 1856. Parran refers to a one volume edition of "Louis XIII et Richelieu" published by Michel Lévy frères in 1860, but I have never been able to trace a copy.

Original editions.
Collection Hetzel. "Les grands hommes en robe de chambre" par Alexandre Dumas. "Henri IV". Edition autorisée pour la Belgique et l'Etranger, interdite pour la France. Bruxelles, Alph. Lebègue, 1855, 24mo., pp. (v)-vi 'préface', (7)-249.

Ibid   Bruxelles et Leipzig, Kiessling, Schnée et compie., 1855, same format and pagination as the preceding edition. Yellow wrappers. Bruxelles, Imp. d'Al. Lebègue.

"Les grands hommes en robe de chambre Henri IV" par Alexandre Dumas Paris Alexandre Cadot, éditeur, 37, rue Serpente, 1855, 8vo., 2 volumes, pp. 322 and 330, each with an additional unnumbered page table of contents. Yellow wrappers. Fontainebleau, impr. E. Jacquin.

Collection Hetzel. "Les grands hommes en robe de chambre" par Alexandre Dumas. "Louis XIII et Richelieu". Edition autorisée pour la Belgique et l'Etranger, interdite pour la France. Bruxelles et Leipzig, Kiessling, Schnée et compie., 1855-1856, 3 volumes. Pagination : Volume 1 (1855), 219; Volumes 2 and 3 (1856), 235 and 201.

"Les grands hommes en robe de chambre. Richelieu" par Alexandre Dumas. Paris Alexandre Cadot, éditeur, 37, rue Serpente, 1856, 8vo., 5 volumes. Pagination : 320, including table of contents, 306, 315, 326 and 347, each with an additional unnumbered page table of contents. Yellow wrappers. Fontainebleau, impr. E. Jacquin.

"Les grands nommes en robe de chambre. Henri IV". Par Alexandre Dumas. Paris, Charlieu, 1857, 18mo., pp. 267.

"Les grands hommes en robe de chambre Henri IV Louis XIII et Richelieu" par Alexandre Dumas Paris Michel Lévy frères, 1866, 12mo., 2 volumes paged continuously. Pagination : 2 unnumbered pages 'avant-propos', 307. "Henri IV", 2 unnumbered pages 'avant-propos', (3)-222; "Louis XIII et Richelieu", (223)-307. There are no table of contents.
Several times reprinted, same format but with varying pagination, by both Michel Lévy frères and Calmann-Lévy.

"ABD-el-HAMID-BEY. JOURNAL D'UN VOYAGE EN ARABIE"
"PELERINAGE DE HADJI-ABD-el-HAMID-BEY (du COURET) MEDINE   1856
ET LE MECQUE"

     This work, which was first published at irregular intervals in 'Le Mousquetaire' between 26th December, 1854, and 14th December, 1855, was announced as 'publié par Alexandre Dumas'. The final instalment in that journal ended with : Fin de la première partie. The work related the experiences of the traveller du Couret. It was never included in the Lévy collected edition of Dumas' works.

Original edition.
Collection Hetzel. "Abd-El-Hamid-Bey. Journal d'un voyage en Arabie".
Rédigé par Alexandre Dumas. Edition autorisée pour la Belgique et
l'étranger, interdite pour la France. Bruxelles, Alphonse Lebègue,
1856, 18mo., 4 volumes, pp. 199, 198, 200 and 211, each with an addi-
tional unnumbered page table of contents. Yellow wrappers.
Ibid   Bruxelles et Leipzig, Kiessling, Schnée et Compie.,
1856, 4 volumes, same format and pagination as the preceding edition.
Yellow wrappers. (The title of Volume 1 is wrongly spelt "Ald-el-
Hamid-Bey".)

"Pélerinage de Hadji-Abd-el-Hamid-Bey (du Couret) Médine et le Mecque"
publié par Alexandre Dumas Paris Alexandre Cadot, éditeur, 37, rue
Serpente, 1856-1857, 8vo., 6 volumes. Pagination : Volumes 1-5
(1856), pp. viii 'Le Caire', journal de deux voyageurs, par MM.
Arnaud et Wayssières, 325 and 4 pages of publisher's advertisements,
319, 314, 299 and 317; Volume 6 (1857), 323. Each volume has an
additional unnumbered page table of contents. Fontainebleau, impr.
E. Jacquin.
Talvart et Place give the following pagination : 325 and table of
contents, 320 including table of contents, 314 and table of contents,
300 including table of contents, 317 and table of contents, and 324
including table of contents.
The Cadot edition includes chapters previously omitted from the serial
issue. Quérard, wrongly gives the years of publication by Cadot as
1855-1856.

"LE TUEUR DE LIONS"
"LA CHASSE AU LION"   1856
"LE LION D'AURES"

     Dumas knew Jules Gérard well, and admired men of his adventurous
type. Four articles first appeared in 'Le Mousquetaire' on 24th,
25th, 27th and 30th November, 1853 - the first under the title of "Le
tueur de lions" and the final three with the title of "La chasse au
lion", to be reissued in the final volume of the Cadot, 1856, 7 volume edition of "César" under the first of the above titles. They
were ultimately included in some editions of Dumas' "Causeries" (which
see) under the collective title of "Le lion d'Aurès".

"L'ORESTIE"   1856

     In the writing of this play Dumas drew upon Aeschylus, Sophocles
and Euripides, but principally from the first of these. No one except
de Mirecourt has ever suggested a collaborator and, in point of fact,
Dumas in 'Le Mousquetaire' challenged anyone to prove that any single
line in the tragedy was not his. The complete text was first published in 'Le Mousquetaire' between 1st and 24th February, 1856.

Original edition.
"L'Orestie" tragédie en trois actes et en vers Imitée de l'antique
par Alexandre Dumas. Paris, a la librairie théatrale, 1856, 12mo.,
pp. 107, and (1) which carries the postscript : 'Merci aux artistes
qui, après m'avoir fait un succès, m'ont forcé de venir recevoir les
applaudissements qui leur étaient dus. - Alex. Dumas. 5 janvier 1856'.
Half-title : "L'Orestie" tragédie Représentee pour la première fois,

à Paris, sur le théâtre de la Porte-Saint-Martin, le 5 janvier 1856.
Verso of title : 'distribution de la pièce', followed by an unnumbered page with : 'au peuple. Alex. Dumas', verso blank. Green wrappers repeating the title-page- Typ. Morris et comp.

Ibid   Deuxième édition. Same publishers, 1856, same format and pagination as the preceding edition. Green wrappers.

"L'Orestie" tragédie en trois actes, imitée de l'antique Porte-Saint-Martin. - 5 janvier 1856. 'Au peuple' : Alex. Dumas, and "Distribution" on title-page, pp. 118-187. Théatre complet de Alex. Dumas Tome XX Paris Calmann Levy, éditeur ancienne maison Michel Lévy frères, 1874. 12mo. "Théatre complet" in 25 volumes.

"SAMSON"   1856

     Lecomte in his "Alexandre Dumas 1802-1870 Sa Vie intime. Ses Oeuvres" refers to the opera "Samson" which was written in collaboration with Edouard Duprez, and implies that the manuscript is entirely lost. This is not altogether true because portions of it were sung in 1856 at the Ecole spéciale de chant, and subsequently printed.

Original (and only) edition.
Ecole spéciale de chant. Première séance de l'année 1856. Exécution de fragments de l'opéra (inédit) de "Samson", poëme de MM. Alex. Dumas et Ed. Duprez. Vaugirard, Impr. Choisnet, 1856, 8vo., pp. 8.

"MON ODYSSEE AU THEATRE-FRANCAIS"   1856

     In 1856 a number of distinguished writers were invited to contribute to a book which was to be entitled "Paris et les Parisiens au XIXe siècle". Dumas' contribution was to be on the subject of 'Le Théâtre-Français', and he duly wrote an extremely readable account of his association with that theatre from his early manhood until 1854. As will be seen the article was later published under a different title.

Original edition.
"Paris et les Parisiens au XIXe siècle moeurs, arts et monuments". Texte par MM. Alexandre Dumas, Théophile Gautier, ... Illustrations par MM. Eugène Lami, Gavarni et Rouargue. (Vignette) Paris, Morizot, 1856, large 8vo., pp. 461 and additional unnumbered page table of contents; 25 illustrations.
Dumas' contribution : "Mon Odyssée au Théâtre-Français" occupies pp. 317-402 and is divided as follows : 'Talma' pp. 317-320; 'Firmin' pp. 320-329; 'M. Lafon' pp. 330-338; 'Mademoiselle Mars' pp. 338-348; 'Mademoiselle Louise Despréaux' pp. 348-360; 'Le garçon d'accessoires et le pompier' pp. 361-365; 'Les vieux lustres et le lustre neuf' pp. 365-371; 'Le cheval incitatus' pp. 371-382; 'Mademoiselle de Belle-Isle' pp. 382-391; 'Un mariage sous Louis XV' pp. 391-398; 'Les demoiselles de Saint-Cyr' pp. 398-402. There are no illustrations to Dumas' contribution.

"Souvenirs dramatiques" par Alexandre Dumas Paris Michel Lévy frères, libraires-éditeurs ... 1868, 12mo., 2 volumes, pp. 421, verso blank, unnumbered page table of contents, and 436 with additional unnumbered page table of contents. "Mon odyssée à la Comedie-Française" occupies pp. (185)-292 of Volume 1.

"LA TOUR SAINT-JACQUES-1a-BOUCHERIE"   1856

This historical drama was in part inspired by "Isabel de Bavière", and was written in association with Xavier de Montépin.

Original edition.
"La tour St.-Jacques-la-boucherie" drame historique en cinq actes et neuf tableaux par MM. Alexandre Dumas et X. de Montépin Mise en scène de M. St.-Ernest - Musique de M. Fessy - Décors de MM. Maynet, Laroque, Daran et Sachetti. Représenté pour la première fois, à Paris, sur le théatre Impérial du Cirque, le 15 novembre 1856. Caption title. Yellow wrappers. Magasin théatral "Le tour St-Jacques-la-boucherie" drame historique en cinq actes et neuf tableaux par MM. Alexandre Dumas et X. de Montépin représenté .... Paris, Librairie théatrale, 1856, 8vo., pp. 32 in double columns.

"La tour Saint-Jacques-la-boucherie" drame historique en cinq actes et neuf tableaux par MM. Alexandre Dumas et X. de Montépin. Représenté pour la première fois, a Paris, sur le théatre Impérial du Cirque, le 15 novembre 1856. Paris, a la librairie théatrale, n.d. (1857), 4to., pp. 16 in treble columns. Caption title. Woodcut at head of title. Théatre contemporain. Magasin théatral illustré.

"La tour Saint-Jacques" drame en cinq actes, en neuf tableaux en société avec M. X. de Montépin Théâtre impérial du Cirque. - 15 novembre 1856. "Distribution", pp. (190)-191, 191-334. Théatre complet de Alex. Dumas Tome XX Paris Calmann Lévy, éditeur, ancienne maison Michel Lévy frères, 1874. 12mo. "Théatre complet" in 25 volumes.

There was one unpublished parody of the drama :
"La cour Saint-Jacques-la-Boucherie", 1 acte et 3 tableaux, par G. Bondon. Parodie aux Délassements-Comiques, le 20 décembre 1856.

"MEMOIRES D'UN JEUNE CADET"
"UN CADET DE FAMILLE"   (1856)

This work, published under the above two titles, is a translation by Victor Perceval of Edward John Trelawney's "Adventures of a younger son". It was first published at irregular intervals in 'Le Mousquetaire' between 3rd August, 1855, and 9th February, 1856.

Original edition.
Panthéon Populaire Illustré. Alexandre Dumas illustré par Gustave Doré. "Mémoires d'un jeune cadet". Paris, Typographie Henri Plon, n.d. (1856), 4to., pp. (1)-120 in double columns. Caption title. Woodcut at head of title.
This edition of the work is followed by "Un courtisan" (imité de l'anglais), pp. (121)-128 in double columns; there are no illustrations to the second work.

"Un cadet de famille" traduit par Victor Perceval publié par Alexandre Dumas Paris Michel Lévy frères, éditeurs, 1860, 12mo., 3 volumes, pp. (1)-2 'Mon cher Editeur ... ' signed : A. Dumas. 20 août 1856, (3)-316, 297, and 187.
Occasionally reprinted, same format and pagination, by both Michel Lévy frères and Calmann-Lévy.

"UN COURTISAN"   1856

In the issues of 'Le Mousquetaire' for 21st to 26th August, and
1st September, 1855, Victor Perceval had this story published as
'imité de l'anglais'. The work was subsequently bound in with "Un
cadet de Famille" in the Lévy collected edition of Dumas' works and,
also, bound in with the alternative title "Mémoires d'un jeune cadet".

Original edition.
Panthéon Populaire Illustré. Alexandre Dumas illustré par Gustave
Doré. "Un courtisan". (imité de l'anglais) follows immediately
after "Mémoires d'un jeune cadet". Paris, Typographie Henri Plon,
n.d. (1856), 4to., pp. (121)-128 in double columns. It is not illustrated.

"Un cadet de famille" traduit par Victor Perceval publié par Alexandre Dumas Paris Michel Lévy frères, éditeurs, 1860, 12mo., 3
volumes. "Un cadet de famille" ends on page 187 of Volume 3, verso
blank, and is followed by "Un courtisan" (imité de l'anglais), pp.
(189)-246.
Occasionally reprinted, same format and pagination, by both Michel
Lévy frères and Calmann-Lévy.

"MADAME DU DEFFAND"
"LE SECRETAIRE DE LA MARQUISE DU DEFFAND"
"MEMOIRES D'UNE AVEUGLE, MADAME DU DEFFAND"   1856-1857
"LES CONFESSIONS DE LA MARQUISE"

This biographical romance covers the life of Horace Walpole's
famous correspondent the marquise du Deffand, and spans the years
1696-1780. It is highly probable that the comtesse Dash had considerably more to do with the writing than did Dumas who, in all like-
lihood, offered suggestions and possibly rewrote part of it. The
work was first published serially, and very irregularly and incom-
pletely, under the title of "Le secrétaire de la marquise du Deffand"
in 'Le Mousquetaire' between 6th June and 3rd December, 1855, this
particular part of the work ending with Chapter XLI of "Mémoires d'une
aveugle, madame du Deffand". The complete edition published by Cadot
has this particular Chapter numbered XIII in Volume 3. As will be
seen Michel Lévy frères and Calmann-Lévy published the work in two
parts.

Original edition.
"Madame du Deffand" publié par Alexandre Dumas Paris Alexandre
Cadot, éditeur, 37, rue Serpente, 1856-1857, 8vo., 8 volumes. Pagination : Volume 1-2 (1856), 327 and 319; Volumes 3-8 (1857), 317 and
8 pages of publisher's advertisements, 303, 323, 313, 307 and 313.
Each volume has an additional unnumbered page table of contents.
Yellow wrappers. Fontainebleau, impr. E. Jacquin.
(Talvart et Place give different paginations as follows : 328 and
320, both including table of contents, 317 and additional page table
of contents, 304 and 324, both including table of contents, 313 and
additional page table of contents, 308 including table of contents, and
313 with additional page table of contents.)

"Le secrétaire de la marquise du Deffand" publié par Alexandre Dumas.
Paris, 1856-1858. Leipzig, chez Wolfgang Gerhard, 24mo., 8 volumes.

Pagination : Volumes 1-2 (1856), 156 and 139; Volumes 3-8 (1858), 160, 160, 160, 160, 160 and 146. Blue wrappers. Impr. Giesecke et Devrient, Leipzig. Volumes 24, 25, and 243-247 of the Bibliothèque choisie.

Publié par Alexandre Dumas. "Madame du Deffand". Paris, Alexandre Cadot, ... , 1858, 12mo., 3 volumes, pp. 395, 360 and 337.

"Mémoires d'une aveugle - madame du Deffand" publiés par Alexandre Dumas. Paris, Michel Lévy frères, 1862, 12mo., 2 volumes, pp. 303 and 301.
Several times reprinted, same format and pagination, by both Michel Lévy frères and Calmann-Lévy.

"Les confessions de la marquise" Suite et fin des "Mémoires d'une aveugle" publiées par Alexandre Dumas. Paris, Michel Lévy frères, 1862, 12mo., 2 volumes, pp. 262 and 267.
Several times reprinted, same format and pagination, by both Michel Lévy frères and Calmann-Lévy.

"Mémoires d'une aveugle - madame du Deffand" publiées par Alexandre Dumas. Paris, Michel Lévy frères, 1864, 4to., pp. 107 in double columns. Caption title. Woodcut at head of title. Musée littéraire contemporain.

"Les confessions de la marquise" Suite et fin des "Mémoires d'une aveugle" publiées par Alexandre Dumas. Paris, Michel Lévy frères, 1864, 4to., pp. 91 in double columns. Caption title. Woodcut at head of title. Musée littéraire contemporain.

"MEMOIRES DE JEANNE D'ALBERT DE LUYNES COMTESSE DE VERRUE SURNOMME DAME DE VOLUPTE"
"LA DAME DE VOLUPTE (COMTESSE DE VERRUE)"   1856-1857
"LA COMTESSE DE VERRUE"
"LA DAME DE VOLUPTE; MEMOIRES DE MADEMOISELLE DE LUYNES"

        Reference to "La maison de Savoie depuis 1555 jusqu'à 1850" will show that this work was first included in the third volume of that romantic history, and first published in 1855. There are considerable variations between the version published in that work and those editions subsequently issued in separate volume form. There is little doubt that it is mainly the work of the comtesse Dash with a good deal of editing by Dumas. The period covered is 1670-1700. So far as I am aware the work was never published serially.

Original edition (in separate volume form).
"La dame de volupté (comtesse de Verrue)" par Alexandre Dumas. Edition autorisée pour la Belgique et l'étranger, interdite pour la France. Bruxelles, Alphonse Lebègue, 1856-1857, 18mo., 3 volumes, pp. Volume 1 (1856), 221; Volume 2 and 3 (1857), 240 and 206.

"La comtesse de Verrue" par Alexandre Dumas. Edition autorisée pour la Belgique et l'étranger, interdite pour la France. Bruxelles et Leipzig, Aug. Schnée et Compie., 1856-1857, same years of publication, format and pagination as the preceding edition. It should be noted that the title-pages of Volumes 2 and 3 read as follows : "La Dame de Volupté (Comtesse de Verrue)", par Alexandre Dumas. Edition autorisée pour la Belgique et l'Etranger, interdite pour la France. Bruxelles et Leipzig, A. Schnée et Compie.; Bruxelles, Kiessling et

Compie. The half-titles of the 3 volumes are uniformly : "La dame
de volupté (Comtesse de Verrue)".

"La dame de volupté mémoires de Mlle de Luynes" publiées par Alexandre Dumas. Paris Michel Lévy frères, libraires-éditeurs, 1863,
12mo., 2 volumes, pp. 284 and 332. There are no tables of contents.
Frequently reprinted, same format and pagination, by both Michel Lévy
frères and Calmann-Lévy.

"La dame de volupté" publiée par Alexandre Dumas Paris, Calmann-
Lévy, n.d. (c 187), 4to., pp. (1)-3 'Avant-propos' signed : Alex.
Dumas, 3-104 in double columns. Caption title. Woodcut at head of
title.

"LE VERROU DE LA REINE"   1857

     In 1853, following the writing of "La jeunesse de Louis XIV"
(which, as has been noted, was censored in France and first produced
in Belgium), Dumas wrote "La jeunesse de Louis XV" which was also
interdicted by the censorship. After considerable modification and
abridgement, being reduced in the process from five acts to three and
from sixty-six scenes to forty-eight, the play was ultimately renamed
"Le verrou de la reine". It is Dumas writing alone, and the play is
curiously reminiscent of "Mademoiselle de Belle-Isle".

Original edition.
"Le verrou de la reine" comédie en trois actes par Alexandre Dumas.
Représentée sur le théâtre du Gymnase, le 15 décembre 1856. Paris,
Michel Lévy frères, n.d. (1857), 12mo., pp. 148-236.

"Le verrou de la reine" comédie en trois actes Gymnase-Dramatique.
- 15 décembre 1856. "Distribution" on title-page, pp. 2-90. Théâtre
complet de Alex. Dumas Tome XXI Paris Calmann Lévy, éditeur
ancienne maison Michel Lévy frères, 1874. 12mo. "Théâtre complet"
in 25 volumes.

"L'INVITATION A LA VALSE"   1857

     Audebrand in his "Alexandre Dumas à la maison d'or souvenirs de
la vie littéraire" and Lecomte in his "Alexandre Dumas 1802-1870 Sa
Vie intime Ses Oeuvres" both state that Paul Meurice collaborated in
the writing of this most attractive play. Meurice may have supplied
the idea of the plot, but the writing of the play is pure Dumas.

     In his "Causeries", under the individual title of 'Les courses
d'Epsom', Dumas has written that he started the play during a dull
Sunday in London, but was interrupted at the seventh or eighth scene.
The occasion was one of his two visits when he had come to watch the
English elections, which could only have been in early 1857 for Parlia-
ment was dissolved that year on 21st March to reassemble on 1st April;
the Sunday was thus 29th March. It is curious, therefore, that at the
unveiling of Doré's statue of Dumas in Paris 'The Times' correspondent
should report (in the issue for 5th April, 1883) Edmond About as saying
in his address : '... It was in March, 1858, at Marseille. ...
(Dumas) took me into his room after the first performance of his "Les
gardes forestiers" and said to me 'I will patch up a little scene for
Montigny, the plot's in my head.' On waking I found a roll of paper

addressed to Montigny which contained the thing he had promised, which was simply a masterpiece - "L'Invitation à la valse".' About, manifestly, must have been mistaken for Glinel has stated that he had seen the original manuscript, with annotations all written in Dumas' hand - at the start 'Fait pour ma chère petite enfant Isabelle, à laquelle ce manuscrit appartient. 10 avril 1857'*, and on the final page : 'Non corrige et tel qu'il doit être offert à un bibliophile, pour lequel les fautes sont des preuves d'authenticité. Alex. Dumas'. In any event "Les gardes forestiers" was first performed in March, 1858.

After its performances at the Théâtre du Gymnase the play was also performed 47 times during 1857-1858 at the Théâtre-Français.
*This was Isabelle Constant the actress.

Original edition.
"L'invitation a la valse" comédie en un acte et en prose par Alexandre Dumas Représenté (sic) pour la première fois, à Paris, sur le théâtre du GYMNASE, le 18 juin 1857. Paris Beck, libraire-éditeur rue des Grands-Augustins, 20 1837 Droits de représentation, de reproduction et de traduction réservés. 12mo., verso of title-page 'personnages' 'acteurs', pp. (3)-48. Buff wrappers repeating the title-page but headed 'théâtre du Gymnase' and with the correct date '1857'. Lagnie. - Imprimerie de VIALAT.

Répertoire du Théâtre Français à Berlin. No. 403. Deuxième série. No. 153. "L'invitation à la valse". Comédie en un acte et en prose par Alexandre Dumas. Représentée ... . Berlin, chez Ad. Mt. Schlesinger, Libraire et Editeur de Musique, 1858, 8vo., pp. 35.

"L'invitation à la valse" comédie en un acte et en prose par Alexandre Dumas. Deuxième édition. ... . Paris, Beck, 1867, same format and pagination as the Beck original edition. Pale yellow wrappers.

"L'invitation a la valse" comédie en un acte Gymnase-Dramatique. - 3 août 1857. "Distribution" on title-page, pp. (91)-146. Théâtre complet de Alex. Dumas Tome XXI Paris Calmann Lévy, éditeur ancienne maison Michel Lévy frères, 1874. 12mo. "Théatre complet" in 25 volumes.

"L'invitation à la valse", comédie en un acte, en prose, par Alexandre Dumas. Représentée pour la première fois, à Paris, sur le théâtre du Gymnase, le 18 juin 1857. Paris, Barbré, 1887, 12mo., pp. 48.

"LES COMPAGNONS DE JEHU"   (Drama)   1857

As will be seen this play was signed by Charles Gabet alone, but Lecomte states that Dumas assisted in its writing. In the issue of 'Le Monte-Cristo' for 23rd April, 1857, Dumas wrote that he had given Hostein permission to have a drama drawn from his romance of the same name by whatever person he thought fit; at the time of writing Dumas did not know who this person would be. Considering the date of its first performance the play could only have been drawn from either the serial issue in 'Journal pour tous' or from one or the other of the pirated editions - a curious example of a play drawn from an author's romance before that romance appeared in volume form in his own country. Needless to say it was never included in Dumas' collected theatre.

Original (and only) edition.
"Les compagnons de Jéhu" drame en cinq actes et quinze tablezux Tiré
du roman populaire de M. Alexandre Dumas Par M. Charles Gabet Musique
de M. Focsey, chef d'orchestre - Décors de M. Louis Cheret - Machines
de M. Florentin Génisson - Costumes de M. Ferdinand et de Mademoiselle
Philis. Représenté pour la première fois, a Paris, sur le théatre de
la Gaité, le 2 juillet 1857. 4to., pp. (1)-23 in treble columns.
Caption title. Woodcut at head of title. Magasin théatral illustré
a la librairie théatrale, n.d. (1857). Paris - Imprimerie Walder.

"LA REVUE NOCTURNE"   1857
     This is a free imitation of a ballad by the German, Sedlitz, and
consists of 22 verses each of 4 lines rhyming alternately. It was
first published in the issue of 'Le Monte-Cristo' for 16th July, 1857,
but because of a printer's error the last verse was omitted. This was
corrected in the next issue of the journal for 23rd July by printing
the omitted lines. The first 21 verses were again published in "Propos
d'art et de cuisine", and since the full version was only printed
elsewhere in a little-known Italian publication it is useful to give
the final verse here.

                    'Voila la funèbre revue
                    Qu'à l'heure de minuit, dit-on,
                    Rêvant à sa grandue déchue,
                    Passe l'autre Napoléon.'

     The Italian publication in which the whole ballad was published
in French was :
"LA SIRENA"; augurio pel cap d'anno per cura di Vincenzo Torelli.
(Napoli, stamperia del Fibrano, 1861), Anno XV, pp. 33-36.

"Propos d'art et de cuisine" par Alexandre Dumas Paris Calmann-
Lévy, éditeur ancienne maison Michel Lévy frères ... 1877, 12mo.,
pp. 304 and additional unnumbered page table of contents. "La revue
nocturne" occupies pp. (253)-257, with introductory and concluding
paragraphs to the poem proper.

"LES COMPAGNONS DE JEHU"   (Romance)   1857
     In June, 1856, Dumas' friend Jules Simon asked him to contribute
a romance to run as a serial in the 'Journal pour tous'. For some
time Dumas had been considering writing a work which would start with
the arrest of Louis XVI and Marie-Antoinette at Varennes on the night
of 21st June, 1791, and which would be entitled "René d'Argonne", and
it is useful here to refer to Dumas' later work "Le volontaire de '92".
Simon agreed and a contract was signed, the serial to start within the
fortnight.
     With Paul Bocage the actor Dumas visited Varennes and subsequently
went to see his son at Saint-Assise. Somehow Dumas could not make
the proposed romance take shape and Dumas, fils, who was then working
on "La question d'argent", suggested dropping it for the time being
and substituting something else. Dumas hesitated, but when his son
outlined for him two characters, Roland de Montrevel and Sir John
Tanlay, and then with the use of Charles Nodier's "Souvenirs de la
Révolution" for the background, he had soon shaped his plot. The
result was "Les compagnons de Jéhu", which Simon accepted. It has been

suggested that de Cherville was a collaborator, and if this is so then
any help would appear to have been insignificant; a brief draft may
have been made by Bocage, but it could not have been more than that.

The period is that of the early years of the Consulate. The
work opens with an historical note on Avignon, and the story really
begins in 1799 at the time of Napoleon's return from Egypt. It ends
with the battle of Marengo in 1800. Prefaced to the work as 'Un mot
au lecteur' is a considerable part of an article entitled 'La figurine
de César'. The work ran as a serial in the 'Journal pour tous' during
1857, the last instalment appearing on 4th April of that year.

Original edition.
Collection Hetzel. "Les compagnons de Jéhu" par Alexandre Dumas.
Edition autorisée pour la Belgique et l'étranger, interdite pour la
France. Bruxelles, Alph. Lebègue, 1857, 24mo., 5 volumes, pp. 200,
192, 200, 214 and 226, each with an additional unnumbered page table
of contents. 'Avant-propos - La ville d'Avignon' occupies pp. (5)-
64 of Volume 1. Yellow wrappers.

Ibid   Bruxelles et Leipzig, Aug. Schnée et compie.,
1857, 5 volumes, same format and pagination as the preceding edition.
Yellow wrappers.

Semaine Littéraire du Courrier des Etats-Unis. "Les compagnons de
Jéhu" par Alexandre Dumas. New-York, Charles Lassalle, Editeur,
1857, large 8vo., pp. 2, 4-224 in double columns.

According to Talvart et Place the first edition to be published in
France was :
"Les compagnons de Jéhu" par Alexandre Dumas Paris Alexandre Cadot,
1857, 8vo., 7 volumes. Pagination : 301, and additional page table
of contents; 304, 312, both including table of contents; 334, 325,
310 and 325, all with an additional page table of contents.

But both the Bibliothèque Nationale and the Bibliothèque de l'Arsenal
possess copies as follows :
"Les compagnons de Jehu" par Alexandre Dumas Paris Alexandre Cadot,
éditeur, 37, rue Serpente, 1857, 8vo., 7 volumes. Pagination :
Volume 1 (1858) (sic), 'Avant-propos', pp. (1)-69, verso blank, (71)-
301 and 8 pages of publisher's advertisements; Volume 2 (1858) (sic),
303; Volumes 3-7 (1857), 311, 334, 325, 310 and 325, each volume
having an additional unnumbered page table of contents. Yellow
wrappers. Fontainebleau, impr. E. Jacquin.
This anomaly would point to the fact that there was very possibly a
second edition printed in 1858, and that the Nationale and Arsenal
copies are composites.

"Les compagnons de Jehu" par Alexandre Dumas Paris Dufour, Mulat
et Boulanger, éditeurs 6, rue de Beaune, près le Pont-Royal (ancien
Hôtel de Nesle) 1859, large 8vo., pp. (1)-12 'Avant-propos', 13-283,
284-287 'Causerie', unnumbered page table of contents and 'Classement
des gravures'; frontispiece and 8 illustrations. Yellow wrappers
repeating the title-page. Lagny - Imprimerie de Vialat.

Alexandre Dumas "Les compagnons de Jéhu" Paris Librairie nouvelle
A. Bourdilliat et Ce., 1859, 12mo., 2 volumes, pp. (i)-xxvii 'Avant-
propos', verso blank, (29)-380, and 395. There are no tables of contents. Grey wrappers.

Romans historiques, aventures, anecdotes, mystères par Alexandre
Dumas. "Les compagnons de Jehu". Paris Dufour, Boulanger et Legrand
... , 1863, same format pagination and illustrations as the Dufour,
Mulat et Boulanger, 1859, edition. Lagny, Imprimerie de A. Varigault.

"Les compagnons de Jéhu" par Alexandre Dumas Paris Michel Lévy
frères, 1864, 12mo., 3 volumes, pp. 280 and additional unnumbered
page table of contents, 297, verso blank, and additional unnumbered
page table of contents, and 243 verso table of contents.
Frequently reprinted, same format but with occasional variations in
pagination, by both Michel Lévy frères and Calmann-Lévy.

"Les compagnons de Jéhu" par Alexandre Dumas. Paris, Legrand et
Crouzet, n.d. (c 1865), large 8vo., pp. 287, and additional unnumbered
page table of contents; illustrated.

Ibid   Paris, Legrand, Troussel et Pomey, n.d. (c 1868),
same format, pagination and illustrations as the preceding edition.

Ibid   Paris, Michel Lévy frères, n.d. (c 1868), 4to.,
published in two parts. Pagination : Part 1, 254, (255)-256 table
of contents; Part 2, 90, 91-92 'Un mot au lecteur' in which Dumas
writes how, on his son's advice, after reading Nodier's "Souvenirs de
la Révolution", he had given up the idea of writing the romance "Réne
d'Argonne" and written the present work instead; all in double columns.
Caption titles. Woodcuts at head of titles. Musée littéraire contemporain.

"Les compagnons de Jéhu" par Alexandre Dumas Edition illustrée par
A. de Neuville (Vignette) Paris Calmann-Lévy, éditeurs, n.d. (1878),
4to., published in two parts. Pagination : Part 1, 254, (255)-256
table of contents; Part 2 (illustrée par A. de Neuville et Lix), 90,
followed by 'Un mot au lecteur' (see the preceding entry) 91-92, followed by "Un gentilhomme de la montagne", pp. (1)-130, (131)-132 table
of contents for the whole of Part 2. Both works are printed in double
columns. Green wrappers with vignettes. Alexandre Dumas oeuvres
illustrés.
Reprinted, same format, illustrations and pagination, n.d. (1884).

"Les compagnons de Jéhu" par Alexandre Dumas Edition illustrée par
A. de Neuville (Vignette) Paris Calmann Lévy, éditeur ancienne
maison Michel Lévy frères, 1890, 4to., pp. (1)-254 in double columns,
2 unnumbered pages table of contents; (1889), (1)-81, followed by 'Un
mot au lecteur' signed : Alex. Dumas, pp. 82-89, both in double
columns.

"LE MENEUR DE LOUPS"   1857

     This is one of Dumas' best minor works and is built around a
popular legend of his boyhood days in Villers-Cotterets, and much
elaborated by him. Dumas developed the legend into an acute and
merciless study of the corruption of a man's character by envy. To
my knowledge the work was never published as a feuilleton before its
issue in volume form, but it was printed in 'Le Monte-Cristo' between
26th January and 12th April, 1860.

Original edition.
Collection Hetzel. "Le meneur de loups", par Alexandre Dumas. Bruxelles, Office de la publicité, 1857, 24mo., 2 volumes, pp. 227 and 217,
each with an additional unnumbered page table of contents.

"Le meneur de loups" par Alexandre Dumas. Paris, Alexandre Cadot, éditeur, 37, rue Serpente, 1857, 8vo., 3 volumes, pp. 313, 329 and 318, each with an additional unnumbered page table of contents. Yellow wrappers. Fontainebleau, impr. E. Jacquin.

Collection Hetzel. "Le meneur de loups" par Alexandre Dumas. Edition autorisée pour la Belgique et l'Etranger, interdite pour la France. Bruxelles et Leipzig, A. Schnée et Compie.; Bruxelles, Kiessling et Compie., 1857, 24mo., 2 volumes, pp. 227 and 217, each with an additional unnumbered page table of contents. Yellow wrappers. Bruxelles. Alphonse Lebègue, imprimeur.

"Le meneur de loups" roman par Alexandre Dumas. Paris 1857. Halle, a l'expédition de la bibliothèque choisie (W. Schmidt), 24mo., 3 volumes, pp. 160, 160 and 156. "Le meneur de loups" ends on page 109 of Volume 3 and is followed by "Les héritiers : Page de la vie d'un homme qui a été mort" par Philibert Audebrand, pp. (113)-156.

"Le meneur de loups" par Alexandre Dumas Paris Michel Lévy frères, 1860, 12mo., pp. 311, verso table of contents. Fairly frequently reprinted, same format and pagination, by both Michel Lévy frères and Calmann-Lévy.

Ibid   Paris, Calmann-Lévy, n.d. (c 188), 4to. Musée littéraire contemporain.

"CHARLES LE TEMERAIRE"   1857

    It would seem probable that this piece of pictoresque history, for the work has no plot, may well have been written a number of years earlier than 1857 because of its similarity of treatment with his books of "Chroniques" and "Jehanne la Pucelle". It is Dumas working alone. The work covers the life of the last duc de Bourgogne, the son of Philippe le Bon, from 1435 to 1477; there is a prologue dealing with the Battle of Poitiers and also a final chapter devoted to the end of his great rival, Louis XI, in 1483.

Original edition.
Collection Hetzel. "Charles le téméraire" par Alexandre Dumas. Edition autorisée pour la Belgique et l'étranger, interdite pour la France. Bruxelles, Meline, Cans et compagnie, 1857, 24mo., 2 volumes, pp. 234 and 225, each with an additional unnumbered page table of contents. Green wrappers.

Ibid   La Haye, chez les héritiers Doorman, 1857, 2 volumes, same format and pagination as the preceding edition.

"Charles le téméraire", par Alexandre Dumas. Edition autorisée pour la Belgique et l'étranger, interdite pour la France. Bruxelles, A L'Office de la publicité, 1857, 24mo., 2 volumes, pp. 238 and 228, the unnumbered pages tables of contents preceding the actual text.

Collection Hetzel. "Charles le téméraire" par Alexandre Dumas. Edition autorisée pour la Belgique et l'étranger, interdite pour la France. Leipzig, Alph. Dürr, 1857, 2 volumes, same format and pagination as the preceding edition.

"Charles le téméraire" par Alexandre Dumas Paris Michel Lévy frères, libraires-éditeurs, 1860, 12mo., 2 volumes, pp. 324 and 310, each with an additional unnumbered page table of contents.

(Both Parran and Glinel state that the first edition to be published in France, by Michel Lévy frères, is dated '1859'. I have never found a copy so dated.) Occasionally reprinted, same format and pagination, by both Michel Lévy frères and Calmann-Lévy.

Ibid   Paris, Michel Lévy frères, 1860, 4to., pp. 83 in double columns. Caption title. Woodcut at head of title. Musée littéraire contemporain.

"L'HOMME AUX CONTES"   1857

'L'homme aux contes' was Dumas' friend Gérard de Nerval who died in 1855, and two years later Dumas put the tales on paper. They were all published in 'Le Monte-Cristo' between 1857 and 1860. Not all of them could be included, obviously, in the pirated editions and it is, perhaps, best to set out in full for comparative purposes the stories as they were finally collected in the Lévy editions.

1. "Le soldat de plomb et la danseuse de papier".
2. "Petit-Jean et gros-Jean".
3. "Le roi des taupes et sa fille".
4. "La reine des neiges".
5. "Les deux frères".
6. "Le vaillant petit tailleur".
7. "Les mains géantes".
8. "La chèvre, le tailleur et ses trois fils".
9. "Saint Népomucène et le savetier".

It is highly probable that the sources for most of them were either Danish or German and, in point of fact, Nos. 1, 2 and 4 were from Hans Andersen and Nos. 6 and 8 from the brothers Grimm. It can be accepted that they were modified for French children.

Original edition.
Collection Hetzel. "L'homme aux contes", par Alexandre Dumas. "Le soldat de plomb et la danseuse de papier". "Petit-Jean et gros-Jean". "Le roi des taupes et sa fille". "La jeunesse de Pierrot". Edition autorisée pour la Belgique et l'étranger, interdite pour la France. Bruxelles, Office de publicité, 1857, 24mo., pp. 208 and additional unnumbered page table of contents. The edition includes 'préface', pp. (5)-9.

Ibid   Bruxelles, Meline, Cans et compagnie, 1857, same format and pagination as the preceding edition. Green wrappers.

Ibid   Edition interdite pour la France. Leipzig, A. Dürr, 1857, same format and pagination as the preceding editions.

Ibid   Nouvelle édition. Interdite pour la France. Leipzig, A. Dürr, 1861, same format and pagination as the preceding editions.

"L'homme aux contes" par Alexandre Dumas. Calmann Lévy, éditeur ancienne maison Michel Lévy frères ... , 1876, 12mo., pp. (i)-v (unsigned), verso blank, (7)-309, verso blank, additional unnumbered page table of contents.
Several times reprinted, same format and pagination.

"LE MONTE-CRISTO"   1857-1862

With "Le Mousquetaire" this is the other of Dumas' most important
journals and it was for some years a considerable success for, as will
be seen, he put a great deal of his own work into it. And even when
he was away in Russia he kept it regularly supplied with material.
It was in the number for 22nd April, 1858, that Dumas published his
'prospectus' for a tour of the eastern Mediterranean which was first
postponed by his journey through Russia and the Caucasus, and postponed again in 1860, to be finally stopped effectually by his co-
operation with Garibaldi and the events and fortunes associated with
him.

Some of his best 'causeries' are to be found in the journal. It
published the continuation of "Les mohicans de Paris", and the complete
serial issues of, among other works, "Madame de Chamblay" ("Ainsi
soit-il!"), "La route de Varennes", "Impressions de voyage : en
Russie", "La maison de glace", "Black", "Le chasseur de Sauvagine",
"Une colombe", "Une odyssée en 1860", and "Le volontaire de '92".

"Le Monte-Cristo" journal hebdomodaire de romans, d'histoire, de
voyages et de poésie, publié et rédigé par Alexandre Dumas, seul.
Bureaux de vente et d'abonnement a Paris, rue Notre-Dame-des Victoires,
No. 11. Les lettres non affranchies seront refusées. Prix d'abonnement : Paris : Un an 8 fr. Six mois : 4 fr. 50 Départements :
Un an : 10 fr. Six mois : 5 fr. 50 Paris, Imprimerie de E. Brière
et ce., etc.
The dates of issue were : 23 avril 1857 - 10 mai 1860, 4to., in
double columns, comprising 160 numbers.

To be followed :
"Le Monte-Cristo", seul receuil des oeuvres inédites d'Alexandre
Dumas. 5e année, 1er janvier - 10 octobre 1862. Paris, au bureau
du journal, rue Notre-Dame-des-Victoires, No. 11. L'abonnement était
de 11 fr.par an pour Paris, et de 15 fr. pour les départements. 4to.,
in double columns, published on Tuesdays and Fridays, and comprising
81 numbers.

"BLACK"   1858

As its title shows, Black the spaniel, is a prominent character
in this quite delightful story. In so far as period matters, and
that is very little, it is from 1793 to 1842. De Cherville may have
had some hand in the original draft outline, but the writing is
obviously Dumas alone. With regard to the Tahiti portion Dumas very
probably obtained material and hints from Madame Giovanni. The work
was originally published as a serial in 'Le Constitutionnel' in 1857-
1858, the last number being dated 13 février 1858. It was reprinted
in 'Le Monte-Cristo' from 16th February to 3rd May, 1860.

Original edition.
Collection Hetzel. "Black", par Alexandre Dumas. Edition autorisée
pour la Belgique et l'étranger, interdite pour la France. Bruxelles,
Office de publicité, 1858, 24mo., 3 volumes, pp. 188, 222 and 200,
each with an additional unnumbered page table of contents. Typ. de
Buggenhoudt.

Ibid   Bruxelles, Meline, Cans et Cie., 1858, 3 volumes,
same format and pagination as the preceding edition.

302

Ibid   La Haye, les héritiers Doorman, 1858, 24mo., 3
volumes, pp. 186, 220 and 195, each with 2 additional unnumbered pages
table of contents. Green wrappers.
(It is interesting to note here that at the end of Volume 3, following
the table of contents, is printed : 'Collection Hetzel. Avis import-
and. Beaucoup des ouvrages publiés dans la collection Hetzel sont
plus complètes que les mêmes ouvrages publiés en France. Ils sont
imprimés sur les manuscrits originaux en Belgique et m'ont point à
subir les retranchements qu'exige souvent la législation française'.)

Collection Hetzel. "Black" par Alexandre Dumas. Edition autorisée
pour la Belgique et l'étranger, interdite pour la France. Leipzig,
Alph. Dürr, 1858, 24mo., 3 volumes, pp. 188, 222 and 200, each with
an additional unnumbered page table of contents.

"Black" par Alexandre Dumas. Paris Alexandre Cadot, éditeur, 37,
rue Serpente, 1858, 8vo., 4 volumes. Pagination - 317, 304, 305 and
330, each with an additional unnumbered page table of contents.
Yellow wrappers. Fontainebleau, impr. E. Jacquin.

"Black" par Alexandre Dumas. Paris, 1858. Naumbourg, à l'expédition
de la Bibliothèque choisi (L. Garcke), 24mo., 4 volumes, pp. 160,
160, 160 and 136. "Black" ends on page 89 of Volume 4 and is followed
by : "Encore un rêve. Histoire de deux bagues et d'un médaillon"
par L.J. Stahl, pp. (91)-136. Volumes 254, 255, 257 and 258 de la
Bibliothèque choisie. Naumbourg, imprimerie de Louis Garcke.

Semaine Littéraire du Courrier des Etats-Unis. "Black" par Alexandre
Dumas New-York, Charles Lassalle, 1858, 8vo., pp. (3)-156 in double
columns, followed by "Un duel de dix-neuf ans", pp. (157)-160 in
double columns and unsigned; it is not by Dumas.

"Black", par Alexandre Dumas. Paris, Dufour, Mulat et Boulanger,
1859, large 8vo., pp. 220; frontispiece and 6 plates.

"Black" par Alexandre Dumas Paris Michel Lévy frères libraires-
éditeurs, 1860, 12mo., pp. 316, (317)-319 table of contents.
Often reprinted, same format and pagination, by both Michel Lévy
frères and Calmann-Lévy.

Romans historiques, aventures, anecdotes, mystères par Alexandre
Dumas. "Black". Paris, Dufour, Boulanger et Legrand ... , 1862,
large 8vo., pp. (1)-218, (219)-220 table of contents; illustrated.
Lagny, Imprimerie de A. Varigault.

"Black" par Alexandre Dumas. Paris, Michel Lévy frères, 1864, 4to.,
pp. 88 in double columns. Caption title. Woodcut at head of title
repeated on yellow wrappers. Musée littéraire contemporain.

"L'HOROSCOPE"   1858

      The period of this seemingly unfinished work is 1559, the opening
year of the reign of François II. The early chapters are concerned
with the horoscopes of the three most powerful men in France of the
time : the duc de Guise, the prince de Condé, and the connétable
de Montmorency. Not one of these ever came near to being fulfilled
in the romance, and so far as it progresses it deals chiefly with
prominent people at François' court. It is Dumas working along, and
he could conceivably have got the idea for the work from Soulié's
short story "Les quatre Henri". What interrupted the work is not

known, but it was at least more or less satisfactorily rounded off for publication as a complete work.

Original edition.
Collection Hetzel. "L'horoscope" par Alex. Dumas. Edition autorisée pour la Belgique et l'Etranger, interdite pour la France. Bruxelles, Office de Publicité, Leipzig, Alphonse Dürr, libraire-éditeur, 1858, 24mo., 3 volumes, pp. 193 and additional unnumbered page table of contents; 208 (pp. 207 and 208 being table of contents); 233 and additional unnumbered page table of contents. "L'horoscope" ends on page 101 of Volume 3 and is followed by "Aventures de Lyderic, comte de Flandre", pp. (105)-233. Bruxelles, Impr. Guyot.

Ibid   Bruxelles, Meline, Cans et Cie., 1858, 3 volumes, pp. 193, 205 and 233, each with additional unnumbered pages table of contents. The pagination of "L'horoscope" and "Aventures de Lyderic ... ... " are the same as in the preceding edition. Green wrappers.

Ibid   Leipzig, Alphonse Dürr, libraire-éditeur, 1858, 3 volumes, same format and pagination as the original edition. On verso of half-titles : Déposé aux termes de la loi.

"L'horoscope" par Alexandre Dumas Paris Alexandre Cadot, éditeur, 37, rue Serpente, 1858, 8vo., 2 volumes, pp. 325 and 318, each with an additional unnumbered page table of contents. Yellow wrappers. Fontainebleau, impr. E. Jacquin.

Semaine Littéraire du Courrier des Etats-Unis. "L'Horoscope" par Alexandre Dumas New-York Charles Lassalle, Editeur, 1859, large 8vo., pp. (1), 3-119 in double columns. Vol. 90, Nos. 1-5.

"L'horoscope" par Alexandre Dumas Paris Michel Lévy frères, libraires-éditeurs, 1860, 12mo., pp. 283, verso table of contents. Several times reprinted, same format and pagination, by both Michel Lévy frères and Calmann-Lévy.

Ibid   Paris, Michel Lévy frères, 1861, 4to., pp. 74 in double columns. Caption title. Woodcut at head of title. Musée littéraire contemporain.

"L'HONNEUR EST SATISFAIT"   1858

    The original holograph manuscript of this play has the following note on it written by Dumas : 'J'offre à M. Isnard ce premier manuscrit d'une pièce faite à la Blancarde en deux jours'. Lecomte has has suggested that it was written in collaboration with Paul Bocage, but I find this as difficult to accept as Glinel's quite remarkable statement that it is a translation from the German. Neither holds water.

Original edition.
"L'honneur est satisfait" comédie en un acte et en prose par Alexandre Dumas Paris A la librairie théatrale 14, rue Grammont 1858 Représentation, reproduction et traduction réservées. 8vo., 'personnages' on verso of title-page, pp. (1)-48. Half-title : "L'honneur est satisfait" comédie en un acte et en prose Représentée pour la première fois à Paris, sur le théâtre du Gymnase, le 19 juin 1858. Pale cream wrappers repeating the title-page. Paris. - imprimerie de J. Claye, rue Saint-Benoit, 7.

"L'honneur est satisfait" comédie en un acte Gymnase-Dramatique. -
19 juin 1858. "Distribution" on title-page, pp. (1)-50. Théatre
complet de Alex. Dumas Tome XXIII Paris Calmann Lévy, éditeur
ancienne maison Michel Lévy frères, 1874. 12mo. "Théatre complet"
in 25 volumes.

"CLEOPATRE, REINE D'EGYPTE"
"JEANNE D'ARC"
"LUCRECE"   1858
"SAPPHO"

These four articles, published in the work described below,
were not reprinted and are not to be found in Dumas' collected works.
Their writing is Dumas alone.

In so far as "Cléopatre, reine d'Egypte" is concerned Dumas drew
for the first half on his "César", but more particularly on the other
figure in the series "Les grands hommes en robe de chambre : Octave
Auguste", published in 'Le Monte-Cristo' between 23rd April and 6th
August, 1857, and which was never completed to be published in Volume
form, breaking off with the disaster to Antony's army in Parthia. The
second half is fresh material which was possibly intended for the un-
completed "Octave Auguste".

With regard to "Jeanne d'Arc" Dumas has to an extent drawn on
"Jehanne le Pucelle", but he reveals a more human person. "Lucrèce"
has no connexion with his "Crimes célèbres". It is concerned with
Rome at the time of Tarquin. "Sappho" was first published in 'Le
Monte-Cristo' in the issue for 7th January, 1858, and includes four
poems by Dumas with the titles : 'Les vers menaçants d'Alcée',
'Chant d'Alcée à Bacchus', 'Traduction de Sappho' and 'Invocation de
Sappho à Venus', the first two being translations from Alcaeus, the
third earlier renderings by Boileau and Delille (of which Dumas
disapproved), and the fourth a translation from Sappho.

Original (and only) edition.
"Les étoiles du monde   galerie historique des femmes les plus
célèbres de tous les temps et de tous les pays   texte par Messieurs
d'Araquy, Dufayl, Alexandre Dumas, de Genrupt, Arsène Houssaye, Miss
Clarke   dessins de G. Staal   Gravés par les premiers Artistes anglais.
(Vignette) Paris   Garnier frères, éditeurs   6, rue des Saints-Pères -
Palais-Royal, 215   1858   Traduction reservée. 4to., pp. (i)-xiii
'introduction' signed : d'Araquy, verso blank, (xv)-xvi 'La femme',
poem signed : Hector de Charlieu, (1)-340, and additional unnumbered
page table of contents. Dumas' contributions : "Cléopatre, reine
d'Egypte", pp. (81)-98; "Jeanne d'Arc", pp. (115)-138; "Lucrèce", pp.
(219)-234; "Sappho", pp. (287)-300. Engraved frontispiece, and engraved portraits accompany the first three contributions by Dumas.
Illustrated boards and spine. Paris. Henri Plon, imprimeur.

"LA ROUTE DE VARENNES"   1858

When Dumas signed a contract with Jules Simon to write a romance
to be entitled "René d'Argonne" (which was not, in fact, written
under that title but instead, and ultimately, "Un volontaire de '92"),
and which was to start with the arrest of Louis XVI and Marie-
Antoinette in Varennes, he asked for a fortnight in which to visit

that town. He and Paul Bocage left Paris on 19th July, 1856, travelled
by rail to Châlons, and on the following day he started his investiga-
tions. Dumas wished to follow the royal flight closely for he had
always suspected the accuracy of historians with regard to the fatal
journey and its following tragedy. The result, as he expected, showed
numerous errors. But he made one slip himself in mistaking one
authority for another, with the result that he had to pay small damages
to a descendant of the person referred to.*

His account of the flight, comparing the earlier accounts with
the topography of the land, first appeared serially in 'Le Monte-
Cristo' from 28th January to 22nd April, 1858.

Original edition.
Collection Hetzel. "La route de Varennes", par Alexandre Dumas.
Edition autorisée pour la Belgique et l'étranger, interdite pour la
France. Bruxelles, J. Rozez, 1858, 24mo., pp. (5)-10 'avant-propos',
(11)-216.

Collection Hetzel. "La route de Varennes" par Alex. Dumas. Edition
autorisée pour la Belgique et l'étranger, interdite pour la France.
Bruxelles, Meline, Cans et compagnie, 1858, same format and pagination
as the preceding edition. Green wrappers.

Collection Hetzel. "La route de Varennes" par Alex. Dumas. Edition
autorisée pour la Belgique et l'Etranger, interdite pour la France.
Leipzig, Alphonse Dürr, 1858, same format and pagination as the
preceding editions. On verso of half-title : Déposé aux termes de
la loi.

"La route de Varennes" par Alexandre Dumas Paris Michel Lévy frères,
libraires-éditeurs, 1860, 12mo., pp. (1)-8 'avant-propos', (9)-279.
Reprinted, same format and pagination, by both Michel Lévy frères and
Calmann-Lévy.

* 'Note à consulter pour M. Alexandre Dumas contre M. Bigault de
Préfontaine', Paris, Impr. Edouard Blot, n.d. (1865), 4to., pp. 8.

"LA RETRAITE ILLUMINEE"   1858

This article was first published in the Auxerre journal 'L'Yonne'
in the issue for 12th August, 1857, and reprinted in 'Le Monte-Cristo'
for 20th August of the same year. 'Sommeville' is the pseudonym of
Charles Le Père, a previous Minister of the Interior.

Original edition .
"La retraite illuminée" par Alexandre Dumas, avec divers appendices
sur la fête Auxerroise par MM. Joseph Bard et Sommeville. (Vignette) Auxerre, Ch. Gallot, imprimeur, libraire-éditeur. MDCCCLVIII.
18mo. Pagination : unnumbered page 'dédicace Aux Artistes de
l'Illumination auxerroise, Leur Concitoyen, C. Gallot', verso blank,
(7)-11 'Mon cher Gallot, ...', signed : SOMMEVILLE, verso blank,
(13)-46 'Retraite illuminée. Causerie avec mes lectures' signed :
Alex. Dumas, (47)-68 'Ce qu'il y a dans une bouteille de migraine.
Impressions de voyages, par un parisien qui n'est pas Alexandre Dumas',
signed : SOMMEVILLE, (69)-83 'Origines des retraites illuminées',
signed : SOMMEVILLE. 21 juillet 1855, verso blank, (85)-88 'Fête
d'Auxerre', signed : Le chevalier Joseph BARD (de la Côte-d'Or).
Title-page in red and black. Verso of half-title : Tiré à 75
exemplaires.

306

"Propos d'art et de cuisine" par Alexandre Dumas Paris Calmann-Lévy, éditeur ancienne maison Michel Lévy frères ... , 1877, 12mo., pp. 304 and additional unnumbered page table of contents. "La retraite illuminée" occupies pp. (1)-28. Reprinted, same format and pagination, 1894.

"La retraite illuminée" par Alexandre Dumas avec divers appendices sur la fête Auxerroise par MM. Joseph BARD et SOMMEVILLE 2e. édition (Vignette, differing from the 1858 edition) Auxerre Albert Hslloy, imprimeur, libraire-éditeur MDCCCLXXXIX. Same format, contents and pagination as the original edition. Title-page in red and black. Buff wrappers repeating the title-page except that the date is printed : 1889. Limited edition with the number of copies not stated.

"LES LOUVES DE MACHECOUL"   1858
     This story of La Vendée includes a rather lengthy section dealing with the adventures and ultimate capture of the duchesse de Berri, of which Dumas had considerable knowledge. It opens with the troubles in La Vendée in 1795 and the succeeding years, but quickly passes to the main story starting in 1831 and ending in 1843. De Cherville is generally considered to have helped in the writing of the work, and this supposition is probably justifiable. As will be seen it concludes with a 'Note' on Deutz, extracted from Dumas' memoirs. The work first appeared serially during 1858 in the 'Journal pour tous'.

Original edition.
Collection Hetzel. "Les louves de Machecoul", par Alex. Dumas. Edition autorisée pour la Belgique et l'étranger, interdite pour la France. Bruxelles, Office de publicité, 1858, 24mo., 8 volumes. Pagination : 208, 186 and additional unnumbered page table of contents, 202, 198, 194, 194, 180 and 194. "Les louves de Machecoul" ends on page 173 of Volume 8 and is followed by 'Note' on Hyacinthe-Simon Deutz (Extrait des "Mémoires d'Alex. Dumas"), pp. (174)-194 and 2 pages table of contents.

Ibid   Edition autorisée pour la Belgique et l'étranger, interdite pour la France. Bruxelles, Meline, Cans et compagnie, 1858, 24mo., 8 volumes. Pagination : 205 and 2 unnumbered pages table of contents and 16 pages of publishers' catalogue; 186 and additional unnumbered page table of contents and 16 pages of publishers' catalogue; 199, 195, 192, 192, 177 and 194, each with 2 unnumbered pages table of contents. "Les louves de Machecoul" ends on page 173 of volume 8 and is followed by 'Note' on Hyacinthe-Simon Deutz (Extrait des "Mémoires d'Alex. Dumas"), pp. (174)-194.

Collection Hetzel. "Les louves de Machecoul" par Alex. Dumas. Edition autorisée pour la Belgique et l'Etranger, interdite pour la France. Leipzig, Alphonse Dürr, 1858, 8 volumes, same format and pagination as the Bruxelles, Office de publicité, edition referred to above.

"Les louves de Machecoul" par Alexandre Dumas. Paris Alexandre Cadot, éditeur, 37, rue Serpente, 1859, 8vo., 10 volumes. Pagination : 333, verso blank, unnumbered page table of contents; 326 and additional unnumbered page table of contents; 317, 315, 305, 321, 329, each with verso blank and additional unnumbered page table of contents;

307, verso unnumbered page table of contents; 317 and 315, each with verso blank and additional unnumbered page table of contents. "Les louves de Machecoul" ends on page 86 of Volume 10 and is followed by 'Note' on Hyacinthe-Simon Deutz, pp. (99)-136, "Une chasse aux éléphants", pp. (137)-256, "Eugène-Auguste Colbrun", pp. (257)-315. Yellow wrappers. Fontainebleau, impr. E. Jacquin.

Semaine Littéraire du Courrier des Etats-Unis. "Les louves de Machecoul épisode de la guerre de la Vendée en 1832" par Alexandre Dumas. New-York, Charles Lassalle, Editeur, 1859, large 8vo., pp. 638 (misprint for 368) in double columns. "Les louves de Machecoul ..." ends on page 363 and is followed by "Une maison de la rue Thibautode" (par E. Frank), pp. (364)-368.

Romans historiques. "Les louves de Machecoul". Par Alexandre Dumas. Paris, En Vente Librairie Charles Tallandier, n.d. (1860), large 8vo., pp. (1)-463, verso blank, (465)-467 table of contents; illustrated.

"Les Louves de Machecoul". Par Alexandre Dumas. Paris, Dufour, Mulat et Boulanger, 1860, same format, pagination and illustrations as the preceding edition.

"Les louves de Machecoul" par Alexandre Dumas Paris Michel Lévy frères, libraires-éditeurs, 1860, 12mo., 3 volumes. Pagination : 317, verso blank, (319)-320 table of contents; 320 (321)-322 table of contents; 316, (317)-318 table of contents.
Frequently reprinted, same format but with varying paginations, by both Michel Lévy frères and Calmann-Lévy.

Collection Hetzel. "Les louves de Machecoul" par Alex. Dumas. Nouvelle édition interdite pour la France. Leipzig, Alphonse Dürr, 1861, 8 volumes, same format and pagination as the Alphonse Dürr, 1858, edition.

"Les louves de Machecoul" par Alexandre Dumas. Paris, Michel Lévy frères, 1861, 4to., pp. 208 in double columns. Caption title. Woodcut at head of title. Musée littéraire contemporain.

Romans historiques, aventures, anecdotes, mystères par Alexandre Dumas. "Les louves de Machecoul". Paris Dufour, Boulanger et Legrand ... , 1862, large 8vo., pp. (1)-463, verso blank, (465)-467 table of contents; illustrated. Lagny, Imprimerie de A. Varigault.

"LE CHASSEUR DE SAUVAGINE"   1858

It can be accepted that de Cherville was responsible for the first rough draft of this work which has the Normandy coast as its setting. The period is 1818-1841. In the rewriting it is pure Dumas and, perhaps as a matter of slight interest, the book was a great favourite of Dante Gabriel Rossetti. It opens with an introduction in which Dumas describes himself and his friends, de Cherville among them, seeing Victor Hugo off at Antwerp for his journey to Jersey on 1st August, 1852. The work was published serially in the 'Echo des feuilletons' during 1858, and was reissued in 'Le Monte-Cristo' from 6th October to 17th November, 1859.

Original edition.
Collection Hetzel. "Le chasseur de Sauvagine" par Alexandre Dumas.

Edition autorisée pour la Belgique et l'étranger, interdite pour la France. Bruxelles, Meline, Cans et Cie., 1858, 18mo., 2 volumes, pp. 180 and 187, each with an additional unnumbered page table of contents.

Ibid   La Haye, Les héritiers Doorman, 1858, 2 volumes, same format and pagination as the preceding edition.

Collection Hetzel. "Le chasseur de Sauvagine" par Alex. Dumas. Edition autorisée pour la Belgique et l'Etranger, interdite pour la France. Leipzig, Alphonse Dürr, 1858, 18mo., 2 volumes, pp. 182 and 190. On verso of half-titles : Déposé aux termes de la loi.

"Le chasseur de Sauvagine" par Alexandre Dumas. Paris, Alexandre Cadot, éditeur, 37, rue Serpente, 1858, 8vo., 2 volumes, pp. (1)-29 'Avent-propos' signed : Alex. Dumas, 15 novembre 1857, (31)-317, and 317, each with an additional unnumbered page table of contents. Fontainebleau, impr. E. Jacquin.

Semaine Littéraire du Courrier des Etats-Unit. "Le chasseur de Sauvagine" par Alexandre Dumas. New-York, Charles Lassalle, Editeur, 1858, 8vo., pp. (3)-80 in double columns.

"Le chasseur de Sauvagine". Par M. Alexandre Dumas. In : 'L'Echo des feuilletons receuil de nouvelles, légendes, anecdotes, épisodes, ...' Paris, chez les éditeurs, 1858, large 8vo., pp. (193)-282 in double columns.

Collection Hetzel. "Le chasseur de Sauvagine" par Alex. Dumas. Nouvelle édition interdite pour la France. Leipzig, Alph. Dürr, 1861, 18mo., 2 volumes, pp. 180 and 189, each with an additional page table of contents.

"Le chasseur de Sauvagine" par Alexandre Dumas Paris Michel Lévy frères, libraires-éditeurs, 1861, 12mo., pp. (1)-14 'avant-propos', (15)-286 and unnumbered page table of contents.
Several times reprinted, same format and pagination, by both Michel Lévy frères and Calmann-Lévy.

"LE PERCE-NEIGE"	c 1858
"LE CHASSE-NEIGE" "L'OURAGAN"	1859
"LE FAISEUR DE CERCUEILS"	1859
"UN COUP DE FEU"	1859

All of these short stories were adapted from Pouschkine, and all other than "Le perce-neige" were first published in 'Le Monte-Cristo' in the issues for 30th September, 7th, 14th and 21st October, and 4th November, 1858, having been forwarded by Dumas from Russia. It may well be that "Le perce-neige" was also published in that journal.

Original editions.
Collection Hetzel. "La duchesse de Lauzun" par la comtesse Dash. Edition autorisée pour la Belgique et l'Etranger, interdite pour la France. Leipzig, Alphonse Dürr, 18mo., 8 volumes. Volume 8, n.d. (c 1858) is concluded by "Le perce-neige". Nouvelle de Pouschkine, traduite par Alex. Dumas, pp. (137)-184.

Collection Hetzel. "La maison de glace" de Lagetchnikoff traduit par Alex. Dumas. Edition autorisée pour la Belgique et l'Etranger, interdite pour la France. Leipzig, Alp. Dürr, 1859, 24mo., 4 volumes. The pagination of Volume 4 is 170, pp. (169)-170 being table of contents. "La maison de glace" ends on page 72 and is followed by three stories by Pouschkine 'traduites par Alex. Dumas' : "Un coup de feu", pp. (75)-101; "Le faiseur de cercueils", pp. (105)-129; "L'ouragan", pp. (133)-168.

"Jane" par Alexandre Dumas Paris Michel Lévy frères, libraires-éditeurs, 1862, 12mo. "Jane" ends on page 198, and is followed by "Un coup de fer", pp. (199)-235, verso blank, "Le faiseur de cercueils", pp. (237)-268; "Don Bernardo de Zuniga", pp. (269)-324, and additional unnumbered page table of contents.
Several times reprinted, same format and pagination, by both Michel Lévy frères and Calmann-Lévy.

"La boule de neige" par Alexandre Dumas Paris Michel Lévy frères, libraires-éditeurs, 1862, 12mo. "La boule de neige" ends on page 258, and is followed by "Le chasse-neige", pp. (259)-291, verso unnumbered page table of contents.
Several times reprinted, same format and pagination, by both Michel Lévy frères and Calmann-Lévy.

"AINSI SOIT-IL!"
"MADAME DE CHAMBLAY"   (Romance)   1858-1862

This work is contemporary, covering the period 1836 to 1856 but is mainly concerned with the final decade. It has a certain resemblance in style to some of Dumas' earlier works, notably "Pauline". Originally published under the first of the above titles it was later changed to "Madame de Chamblay" owing to another author having used the former title. There is no doubt that Madame de Chamblay existed - indeed, Dumas has admitted this to be so.

At the end of the final volumes of the complete pirated and French editions there is printed the date of completion : Alex. Dumas. Naples, 19 juin 1861. This is important when the years of publication of the various editions are considered. Serial issue started in 'Le Monte-Cristo' on 19th November, 1857, and continued with interruptions until 8th July, 1858, when it abruptly stopped, presumably because of Dumas' absence in Russia. This break occurs at what is now the end of Chapter XIX of Volume 1 in the Lévy editions, and would be the end of the final volume in the Brussels editions referred to below. As is known 'Le Monte-Cristo' ceased publication in May, 1860, to be resumed with the issue for 1st January, 1862, and the romance was continued in that number, to appear regularly until its completion in the issue for 22nd April of the same year.

Original (incomplete) editions.
Collection Hetzel. "Ainsi soit-il!" par Alexandre Dumas. Edition autorisée pour la Belgique et l'étranger, interdite pour la France. Bruxelles, Office de publicité, 1858, 24mo., 2 volumes.

Collection Hetzel. "Ainsi soit-il!" par Alex. Dumas. Edition autorisée pour la Belgique et l'Etranger, interdite pour la France. Paris, Jung-Treuttel ... , 1861, 24mo., 4 volumes, pp. 191, 186, 170 and 152. "Ainsi soit-il!" ends on page 107 of Volume 4, and is followed by "Une séance de magnétisme, pp. 111-125, and "Etude de Tête d'après la Bosse", pp. 129-152. On the page facing the title-page : Déposé aux termes de la loi. Bruxelles - Typ. de Ve J. van Buggenhoudt.

Original (complete) edition.
"Ainsi soit-il!" par Alexandre Dumas. Paris, 1858 and 1862, 18mo.,
4 volumes :
Volume 1, Paris, 1858. Naumbourg, a l'expédition de la bibliothèque
choisie (L. Garcke), pp. (5)-160.
Volume 2, Paris, 1862. Naumbourg, chez G. Paetz, libraire-éditeur,
pp. (5)-160.
Volume 3, Paris, 1862. Naumbourg, chez G. Paetz, ... , pp. (5)-160.
Volume 4, Paris, 1862. Naumbourg, chez G. Paetz, ... , pp. (5)-167.
"Ainsi soit-il!" ends on page 115 of Volume 4, verso blank, and is
followed by "Les deux coups de feu récit du Bas-Anjou" par Th. Pavie,
pp. (119)-167. Blue wrappers. Naumbourg, Imprimerie de G. Paetz.
Bibliothèque choisie. Vols. CCLXIX, CCLXX, CCCCXXV and CCCCXXVI.
(I have seen a copy of Volume 2 more correctly dated '1858'.)

"Ainsi soit-il!" par Alexandre Dumas. Paris, Alexandre Cadot,
éditeur, 37, rue Serpente, n.d. (1862), 8vo., 5 volumes. Pagination
: 317, verso blank, and additional unnumbered page table of contents,
and 15 pages of publisher's advertisements; 312, and additional
unnumbered page table of contents; 311, 301 and 333, with no tables
of contents. "Ainsi soit-il!" ends on page 231 of Volume 5, verso
blank, and is followed by "Un épisode de la traite des négres" par
Paul Duplessis, pp. (233)-333. Yellow wrappers. Fontainebleau,
impr. E. Jacquin, et Sceaux, impr. E. Dépée.

"Madame de Chamblay" par Alexandre Dumas Paris Michel Lévy frères,
libraires-éditeurs, ... , 1862, 12mo., 2 volumes, pp. 268 and 289.
There are no tables of contents.
Several times reprinted, same format and pagination, by both Michel
Lévy frères and Calmann-Lévy.

Ibid   Paris, Michel Lévy frères, 1865, 4to., pp. 117 in
double columns. Caption title. Woodcut at head of title. Musée
littéraire contemporain.
Reprinted, same format and pagination, 1873.

"HISTOIRE D'UN CHIEN ET DE ONZE POULES"   1858
"HISTOIRE DE MES BETES"   1867

     The work under the second of the above titles consists, to all
intents and purposes, of a series of rather disconnected 'causeries'
dealing not only with animals and birds but also with hunting and
other experiences.

     The original 'Le Mousquetaire' foreshadowed the works' first
appearance when, in the issues of that journal for 29th and 30th
October, 1st to 25th, and 28th and 29th November, 1855, "Histoire
de mes bêtes" - 'Causerie avec mes lectures à propos d'un chien,
de deux coqs et de onze poules' was published. The issue for 29th
November concluded with what is now the end of Chapter XXVIII. Further
portions appeared in 'Le Mousquetaire' (deuxième série) between 18th
November and 11th December, 1866. The above parts of the work were
reissued in Dumas' journal 'Dartagnan!". The editions of the work to
be published in volume form must be divided into two parts :

Original edition (comprising the 'Le Mousquetaire', 1855,
'causeries').
"Histoire d'un chien et de onze poules" par Alexandre Dumas. Paris,

1858. Naumbourg, a l'expédition de la bibliothèque choisie (L. Garcke). 24mo., 2 volumes, pp. 160 and 160. Pale blue wrappers. La bibliothèque choisie. Nos. 256 and 276.

Collection Hetzel. "Histoire de mes bêtes" par Alexandre Dumas. Bruxelles, Meline, Cans et Cie., 1858, 16mo.

Ibid   Bruxelles, Meline, Cans et Cie., 1858, 24mo., 2
volumes.

Ibid   La Haye, les héritiers Doorman, 1858, 24mo., 2
volumes.

Ibid   Leipzig, Alph. Dürr, 1858, 24mo., 2 volumes.

Original (complete) edition.
"Histoire de mes bêtes" par Alexandre Dumas Paris Michel Lévy frères, libraires-éditeurs, ... , 1867, 12mo., pp. 329, verso blank, (331)-333 table of contents.

Ibid   Deuxième édition Paris Michel Lévy frères, libraires éditeurs ... , 1868, same format and pagination as the preceding edition.
Several times reprinted, same format and pagination, by both Michel Lévy frères and Calmann-Lévy.

"Histoire de mes bêtes" par Alexandre Dumas édition illustrée d'un beau portrait de l'auteur de 11 dessins hors texte par Adrien Marie et de nombreuses vignettes dans la texte Paris Calmann Lévy, éditeur ancienne maison Michel Lévy frères rue Auber, 3, et boulevard des Italiens, 15 a la librairie nouvelle Droits de reproduction et de traduction réservés n.d. (1877), large 8vo., verso of title-page : Il a été tiré de cet ouvrage 25 exemplaires sur papier de Hollande, numérotés 10 exemplaires sur papier de Chine, numérotés (unnumbered page - illustration), (1)-396, (397)-399 table of contents. Yellow wrappers repeating title-page and with vignette. Paris. - Imprimerie J. Cathy, 3, rue Auber.
This edition was reprinted, same format and pagination, yellow wrappers repeating the title-page but with a different vignette, n.d. (1878).

"MEMOIRES D'UN POLICEMAN"   1859

This work is a translation by Victor Perceval from the English of "Stories of a detective" by C. Water (a pseudonym). As will be seen the title-page clearly states : Publiés par Alexandre Dumas, and yet it has been credited to him when his only apparent connexion was a brief recommendation to Cadot in which he wrote that if 'Le Mousquetaire' was still being published he would have printed the book there. It is, perhaps, worth quoting the letter to Cadot.

'Mon cher Cadot,
     Lisez donc les quelques pages que je vous envoie. Je viens de les faires traduires de l'anglais, et elles me semblent une histoire curieuse de la police de nos voisins.

     Si 'Le Mousquetaire' n'était pas mort en ce moment et n'attendait pas le résurrection éternelle je les eusse gardées pour moi.

                          Tout à vous.
                          Alexandre Dumas.'
This letter was published on the leaf following the title-page.

Original edition.
Traduction de Victor Perceval. "Mémoires d'un policeman" publiés
par Alexandre Dumas Paris Alexandre Cadot, éditeur, 37, rue Serpente,
1859, (dépôt - 1858), 8vo., 2 volumes, pp. 325 and 325, each with an
additional unnumbered page table of contents. Yellow wrappers.
Fontainebleau, impr. E. Jacquin.

Publiés par Alexandre Dumas. "Mémoires d'un policeman". Traduits
par Victor Perceval. Paris, Alexandre Cadot, éditeur, 37, rue
Serpente, n.d. (1859), 8vo., pp. 325 and additional unnumbered page
table of contents. Fontainebleau, impr. E. Jacquin.

Ibid   Deuxième édition. Paris, Alexandre Cadot, ... ,
n.d. (1859), same format and pagination as the preceding edition.

The work was reprinted at least five more times, the last being :
Publiés par Alexandre Dumas "Mémoires d'un policeman" traduits par
Victor Perceval cinquième édition Paris Degorge-Cadot, éditeur,
37, rue Serpente, 37. N.d. (c 187), 12mo., pp. (7)-335, verso table
of contents; the title-page is followed by an unnumbered page : 'Mon
cher Cadot, ... Alexandre Dumas'.

"LES BALEINIERS VOYAGE AUX TERRES ANTIPODIQUES"   1859
     Doctor Félix Maynard served as a surgeon for a number of years
on whaling-ships and kept lengthy notes of his travels. He became
friendly with Dumas and contributed a number of articles to 'Le Mousquetaire' during 1855. As its title implies this work covers his
experiences almost entirely in the seas neighbouring New Zealand.
Dumas edited the work, and his own narrative skill can be seen in the
resulting book. The period is approximately 1837-1838 and 1845-1846.
It first appeared as a serial in 'La France' during 1855, and was
there entitled : "Terres Antipodiques".

Original edition.
Docteur Maynard "Les baleiniers voyage aux terres antipodiques"
publié par Alexandre Dumas Paris Alexandre Cadot, éditeur, 37, rue
Serpente, 1859, 8vo., 3 volumes, pp. 316, 318 and 333, each with an
additional unnumbered page table of contents. Yellow wrappers.
Fontainebleau, impr. E. Jacquin.

"Les baleiniers voyage aux terres antipodiques journal du docteur
Maynard" publié par Alexandre Dumas Paris Michel Lévy frères,
libraires-éditeurs, 1860. 12mo., 2 volumes, pp. 312 and additional
unnumbered page table of contents, and 309, verso blank, and additional
unnumbered page table of contents.
Reprinted, same format and pagination, by both Michel Lévy frères and
Calmann-Lévy.

Ibid   Paris, Michel Lévy frères, 1864, 4to., pp. 98 in
double columns. Caption title. Woodcut at head of title. Musée
littéraire contemporain.

"HISTOIRE D'UN CABANON ET D'UN CHALET"
"MONSIEUR COUMBES"   1859
"LE FILS DE FORCAT - MONSIEUR COUMBES"
     From internal evidence it is probable that de Cherville supplied

the idea for this work, which has for its setting the neighbourhood
of Marseilles around 1831.   It is a good example of the novel of
character as opposed to the novel of mere interest, or perhaps rather
it is a judicious blending of both.   It is a little surprising that
Dumas did not adapt it for the stage.

Original edition.
Collection Hetzel. "Histoire d'un cabanon et d'un chalet", par Alex.
Dumas. Edition autorisée pour la Belgique et l'étranger, interdite
pour la France. Bruxelles, Meline, Cans et Cie., n.d. (1859), 18mo.,
2 volumes, pp. 190 and 180, both including table of contents.

Ibid   La Haye, chez les héritiers Doorman, n.d. (1859),
2 volumes, same format and pagination as the preceding edition.

Collection Hetzel "Histoire d'un cabanon et d'un chalet" par Alex.
Dumas Edition autorisée pour la Belgique et l'Etranger, interdite
pour la France Bruxelles, Office de publicité; Leipzig, Alphonse
Dürr, n.d. (1859), 18mo., 2 volumes, pp. 188, and (189)-190 table of
contents, and 177, verso blank, (179)-180 table of contents, followed
by 8 pages of advertisements 'Collection Hetzel' and 3 pages of
advertisements 'Collection Meline, Cans et Ce'. Verso of half-titles
: Déposé aux termes de la loi. Green wrappers repeating title-pages
except with the wording : Edition interdite pour la France.

Ibid   Leipzig, Alphonse Dürr, n.d. (1859), same format,
pagination, wrappers, etc., as the preceding edition.

"Histoire d'un cabanon et d'un chalet", par Alexandre Dumas. Edition
autorisée pour la Belgique et l'étranger, interdite pour la France.
Paris, Naumbourg, à l'expédition de la Bibliothèque choisie (G.
Paetz), 1860, 18mo., 2 volumes, pp. 160 and 145. Bibliothèque choisie,
Nos. 325 and 326.

Alexandre Dumas "Monsieur Coumbes" Paris Librairie nouvelle ...
A. Bourdilliat et Ce, éditeurs La traduction et la reproduction sont
reservées 1860. 12mo., pp. 314, (315)-316 table of contents. Paris
- Imp. de la Librairie Nouvelle. A. Bourdilliat.

Ibid   Deuxième édition. Paris Librairie nouvelle ...
A. Bourdilliat et Ce., 1860, same format and pagination as the
preceding edition.

"Le fils de forçat - Monsieur Coumbes" - par Alexandre Dumas
Paris Michel Lévy frères, libraires-éditeurs, 1864, 12mo., pp. 314,
(315)-316 table of contents.
Frequently reprinted, same format and pagination, by both Michel
Lévy frères and Calmann-Lévy.

"LE MEDECIN DE JAVA"
"L'ILE DE FEU"   1859

     As the first of these alternative titles shows the scene of this
work is set in Java; the period is the middle of the 19th century.
Dumas adopted an unusual style here, one which is reminiscent of his
other stories with a supernatural atmosphere such as "Les mille et un
fantômes" and, perhaps more particularly, "Les mariages du père Olifus". He had a collaborator and it may safely be assumed that it was
his old friend Joseph Méry, himself the author of works dealing with
Java, and who would therefore be able to provide the local 'colour'.

The variation of titles between those editions published in Belgium, and subsequently in France and Germany, should be remarked. Moreover, the texts differ considerably. There are approximately 25,000 more word in the Belgian printings - pages and sometimes paragraphs being omitted from the editions published in France. But in spite of this the general plot of the work remains substantially the same in the French texts.

Original edition.
Collection Hetzel. "Le médecin de Java" par Alexandre Dumas. Edition autorisée pour la Belgique et l'Etranger, interdite pour la France. Bruxelles, Meline, Cans et cie., 1859, 8vo., 3 volumes, pp. 213, verso blank, unnumbered page table of contents; 218 and additional unnumbered page table of contents; 198 and additional unnumbered page table of contents.
(There are slight omissions in the second Volume of this edition.)

"Le médecin de Java" par Alexandre Dumas Bruxelles Collection Hetzel Meline, Cans et compagnie, n.d. (1860), 3 volumes, same format and pagination as the preceding edition.

Collection Hetzel. "Le médecin de Java", par Alexandre Dumas. Leipzig, Alph. Dürr, n.d. (1860), 3 volumes, same format and pagination as the preceding editions.

"L'Ile de feu" roman fantastique par Alexandre Dumas. Paris, 1869. Naumbourg s/S chez G. Paetz, libraire-éditeur, 24mo., 4 volumes, pp. 160, 160, 160 and 142. Pale blue wrappers. Bibliothèque choisie, Nos. 989-992.

L'ile de feu" par Alexandre Dumas Paris Michel Lévy frères, libraires-éditeurs, 1870, 12mo., 2 volumes, pp. 285, verso blank, unnumbered page table of contents, and 254, and additional unnumbered page table of contents.
Occasionally reprinted, same format and pagination, by both Michel Lévy frères and Calmann-Lévy.

"LA MAISON DE GLACE"   1859
This grim story of hatred, vindictiveness and treachery was, as Dumas has stated in 'Le Monte-Cristo' adapted from a work by I.L. Lazhechnikov. It is concerned with the times of the Empress Anne, and starts in 1739. The work was first published in 'Le Monte-Cristo' from 15th July, 1858, to 24th February, 1859, Dumas forwarding the instalments from Russia.

Original edition.
"La maison de glace de Lagetchnikoff" par Alexandre Dumas. Edition autorisée pour la Belgique et l'étranger, interdite pour la France. Bruxelles, J. Rozez, 1859, 24mo., 4 volumes, pp. 190, 192, 196 and 170. Collection Hetzel.

Collection Hetzel. "La maison de glace de Lagetchnikoff" trad. par Alex. Dumas Edition autorisée pour la Belgique et l'Etranger, interdite pour la France Leipzig Alphonse Dürr, 1859, 32mo., 4 volumes, pp. 190, 190 (each with an additional unnumbered page table of contents), 194, (195)-196 table of contents, and 168, (169)-170 table of contents. "La maison de glace ... " ends on page 72 of Volume 4 and

is followed by three stories by Pouschkine 'nouvelles traduites' :
"Un coup de feu", pp. (75)-101; "Le faiseur de cerceuils", pp. (105)-
129; "L'ouragan", pp. (133)-168.   Bruxelles, Imp. de Guyot, successeur
de Stapleaux.

"La maison de glace" par Alexandre Dumas Paris Michel Lévy frères,
libraires-éditeurs, 1860, 12mo., 2 volumes, pp. 324, (325)-326 table
of contents, and 278, (279)-280 table of contents.
Often reprinted, same format and pagination, by both Michel Lévy
frères and Calmann-Lévy.

Ibid   Paris, Michel Lévy frères, n.d. (c 186), 4to.,
pp. 156 in double columns. Caption title. Woodcut at head of title,
repeated on brown wrappers. Musée littéraire contemporain.
Reprinted, Calmann-Lévy, 1894, same format and pagination, both with
an additional unnumbered page table of contents.

"LE CAUCASE"   1859

On 7th November, 1858, Dumas left those Russian territories
described in his "Impressions de voyage - en Russie". In his own
words : 'Avec ce dernier échantillon de la race kalmouke, je disais
adieu à la Russie de Rourik et d'Ivan le Terrible. En entrant à Kis-
ler, j'allais saluer la Russie de Pierre 1er, de Catherine II et de
l'empereur Nicolas. Si vous désirez, chers lecteurs, connaître la
suite de notre voyage de Kislar à Poti, nous vous renvoyons à notre
livre institulé "Le Caucase".'

In the next part of his travels he visited among other places
Derbend, Baku, Tiflis and Poti, and from this last he went on to
Trebizond and Constantinople, finally arriving in Marseilles towards
the middle of March, 1859 - he had been away from France for all of
ten months. For reasons best known to himself Dumas completed the
writing with regard to the Caucasian part of his travels much earlier
than the concluding part of his previous wanderings to the north. The
explanation probably is that he wrote much about his travels in the
Caucasus while he was actually travelling and, in any event, he was
delayed for some time in Poti before continuing to Constantinople.

As will be seen "Le Caucase" opens with a fairly lengthy sketch
entitled : "Le Caucase depuis Prométhée jusqu'à Chamyl". Then
follows the account of his own experiences. The first number of his
journal comprised the introductory matter just referred to, pp. (1)-8
and signed : Alexandre Dumas. Tiflis 1er décembre 1858. "Le
Caucase" was completed in 30 parts, each consisting of 8 pages printed
in double columns, and appearing daily from 16th April to 15th May,
1859, inclusive, being numbered 1-30. (The statement in the 'Gazetiers
et Gazettes' for 1860 that '50 numbers had appeared of which 30 were
occupied with the account of Dumas' journey into the country of
Schamyl' is incorrect, and no other such similar statement has never
been made.)

It has been frequently asserted that Nos. 14, 20 and 21 were
confiscated by a court order because they contained material copied
from a work by one, Edouard Merlieux. However the journal has precisely the same text as that published in the standard Lévy editions.

The journal was duly published in monthly form.

316

Original edition.
"La Caucase" journal de voyages et romans paraissant tous les jours.
En vente, à la librairie théatrale, boulevard Saint-Martin, 12, Paris,
Charlieu, éditeur, n.d. (1859), 30.4 x 21.5 cms., in double columns.
At the head of page : 15 centimes le Numéro. Vignette covering the
top half of the page and consisting of a wood cut of mountain scenery
(the vignettes on all 30 issues are identical). En vente chez Dela-
vier, rue Notre-Dame-les-Victoires, 11. 'Nous commençons notre publication par le voyage d'Alexandre Dumas au Caucase. Cet ouvrage,
entièrement inédit, sera complet en trente numéros pour laquels on
peut s'abonner à l'avance.' Publié à 5 francs l'ouvrage complet.
Typ. de H.S. Dondey-Dupré.

"Le Caucase. Voyage d'Alexandre Dumas". Woodcut of troika with Dumas
and travelling companion in snow-covered forest country. Paris, A la
librairie théatrale, Charlieu, éditeur; Typographie H.S. Dondey-Dupré,
n.d. (1859), 4to., pp. 240, in 30 parts, with the same woodcut at the
head of each part. Buff wrappers repeating the woodcut.

Collection Hetzel. "Le Caucase. Nouvelles impressions de voyage"
par Alex. Dumas. Bruxelles, Livourne, Meline, Cans et cie.; Leipzig,
J.P. Meline, 1859, 18mo., 3 volumes. Pagination : (v)-xlix 'Introduction. Coup d'oeil général sur le Caucase', (51)-316, including
table of contents, 310 and 296.

Ibid   Par Alexandre Dumas. Bruxelles, Office de publicité; Leipzig, Alph. Dürr, 1859, 3 volumes, same format and pagination as the preceding edition.

Collection Hetzel. "Le Caucase. Nouvelles impressions de voyage"
par Alex. Dumas. Leipzig, Alphonse Dürr, 1859, 3 volumes, same format
and pagination as the preceding editions. Imprimerie de E. Guyot.

"Le Caucase depuis Prométhée jusqu'à Chamyll" par Alexandre Dumas.
Paris, 1859. Naumbourg, A l'expédition de la Bibliothèque choisie
(G. Paetz), 1859, 18mo., 7 volumes, pp. 160, 160, 160, 160, 160, 160
and 141. Dumas' work ends on page 129 of Volume 7 which is completed
by "Histoire d'une mère", conte d'Andersen traduite librement du dandis
par D. Soldi, pp. (131)-141. Pale blue wrappers. La Bibliothèque
choisie. Vols. CCLXXXXIII, CCLXXXXIV, CCCI-CCCV.

"Impressions de voyage - le Caucase" par Alexandre Dumas Paris
Michel Lévy frères, libraires-éditeurs, 1864, 12mo., 3 volumes. Pagination : (1)-45 'Introduction coup d'oeil général sur le Caucase',
verso blank, (47)-306, (307)-308 table of contents; 303, verso table
of contents; 290, (291)-292 table of contents.
Several times reprinted, same format and pagination, by both Michel
Lévy frères and Calmann-Lévy.

"L'ART ET LES ARTISTES CONTEMPORAINS AU SALON DE 1859"   1859

    This book comprises notes on works by Gérome, Giraud, Isabey,
Jadin, Millet, Nanteuil and others, together with critical comments.
Calmann-Lévy also published the work but did not include it in the
collected edition of Dumas' works.

Original edition.
Alexandre Dumas "L'art et les artistes contemporains au salon de
1859" Paris Librairie nouvelle, boulevard des Italiens, 15; A.

Bourdilliat et Ce., éditeurs. La traduction et la reproduction sont reservées. 1859. 12mo., pp. (1)-180, and 'Index', pp. (181)-188. Grey wrappers. Paris - Imp. de la Librairie Nouvelle. A. Bourdilliat. "L'art et les artistes contemporains au salon de 1859", par Alexandre Dumas. Paris, Calmann-Lévy, n.d. (c 188), 12mo.

"LA FREGATE 'L'ESPERANCE'"   1859
"LA PRINCESSE FLORA"

This is a Russian story adapted from Marlinsky (A. Bestuzhev) in which Dumas apparently kept very closely to the original. The period is 1829-1831. It was first published serially in 'Le Monte-Cristo' during 1859 under the first title given above.

Original edition.
Collection Hetzel. "La frégate 'L'Espérance'." Par Alexandre Dumas. Edition autorisée pour la Belgique et l'étranger, interdite pour la France. Bruxelles, Office de publicité; Leipzig, A. Dürr, 1859, 24mo., pp. 231, and additional unnumbered page table of contents. Green wrappers. Imprimerie de E. Guyot.

"Les mohicans de Paris. Salvator le commissionaire" par Alexandre Dumas. Paris, Alexandre Cadot, éditeur, ... , 1856-(1859), 8vo., 14 volumes. "Les mohicans de Paris. ... " ends on page 250 of Volume 14 (1859) and is followed by "La frégate 'L'Espérance'", pp. (251)- 327, verso table of contents. Yellow wrappers. Fontainebleau, impr. E. Jacquin.

"La princesse Flora" par Alexandre Dumas Paris Michel Lévy frères., libraires-éditeurs, 1862, 12mo., pp. 253, verso blank, and additional unnumbered page table of contents.
Often reprinted, same format and pagination, by both Michel Lévy frères and Calmann-Lévy.

Ibid   Paris, Michel Lévy frères, n.d. (186), 4to. Caption title. Woodcut at head of title. Musée littéraire contemporain.

"MARIANNA"   1859

This story is regarded as a model of its kind, and it is certainly one of the best short stories that Dumas ever wrote. The original idea may well have come from some anecdote told to him during his Russian travels. It could have been published first in a periodical in France. It was reprinted in 'Le Monte-Cristo' in the issues numbered 65-68 and dated 12th to 22nd August, 1862.

Original edition.
Collection Hetzel. "Herminie" & "Marianna" par Alexandre Dumas. Edition autorisée pour la Belgique et l'étranger, interdite pour la France. Bruxelles, Meline, Cans et compagnie, 1859, 24mo., pp. 174, additional unnumbered page table of contents, and 16 pages of publishers' advertisements. "Marianna" occupies pp. 97-174. Typ. J. Nys.

Ibid   La Haye, les héritiers Doorman, 1859, 24mo., pp. 174 and additional unnumbered page table of contents. "Marianna" occupies pp. (100)-174.

318

Ibid   Leipzig, Alph. Dürr, 1859, 24mo., pp. 174 and
additional unnumbered page table of contents. "Marianna" occupies
pp. 97-174.

Alexandre Dumas "Conscience l'innocent". Paris, Michel Lévy frères,
1861, 4to., pp. 138 in double columns. "Conscience ... " ends on
page 100, and is followed by "Marianna", pp. (101)-138.

"Conscience l'innocent" par Alexandre Dumas. Paris, Michel Lévy
frères, 1861, 12mo., 2 volumes, pp. 254, (255)-256 table of contents,
and 280, (281).282 table of contents. "Conscience ..." ends on page
231 of Volume 2, verso blank, "Marianna", pp. (233)-280.
Often reprinted, same format and pagination, by both Michel Lévy
frères and Calmann-Lévy.

Ibid   Paris, Calmann-Lévy, n.d. (188), 4to., pp. 138
in double columns of which "Marianna" occupies pp. (101)-138. Caption
title. Woodcut at head of title. Musee littéraire contemporain.

"JANE"   1859
        "Jane" was another of the several satisfactory literary results
of Dumas' Russian travels. It deals with the experiences of some
Russian sailors who were cast ashore in Holland in consequence of the
blockading fleets of Britain and Russia being off that country's
coast in 1812. The work is, again, adapted from Marlinsky (A. Bestuzhev). The odd thing is that the caption of each page of, at least,
the Bruxelles, Meline, Cans edition is 'Elim', the christian name of
the main character in the story, and this could possibly point to a
serial issue of the work under that title before volume publication
when its name was changed for one reason or another.

Original edition.
Collection Hetzel. "Jane" par Alexandre Dumas. Edition autorisée
pour la Belgique et l'étranger, interdite pour la France. Bruxelles,
J. Rozez, 1859, 24mo., pp. 174 and additional unnumbered page table
of contents. Typ. J. Nys.

Ibid   Bruxelles, Meline, Cans et Cie., 1859, same format
and pagination as the preceding edition.

Ibid   La Haye, les héritiers Doorman, 1859, same format
and pagination as the preceding editions.

Ibid   Leipzig, Alph. Dürr, 1859, same format and pagination as the preceding editions. Typ. et Lith. de J. Nys.

"Jane" nouvelle par Alexandre Dumas. Paris, 1860. Naumbourg, chez
G. Paetz, libraire-éditeur. 18mo., pp. 146 of which "Jane" occupies
pp. (5)-126, being followed by "Une tache sur l'hermine" par comte
de Legurat, pp. (127)-146. Grey wrappers. Bibliothèque choisie;
collection des meilleurs romans français. No. 355.

"Jane" par Alexandre Dumas Paris Michel Lévy frères, libraires-
éditeurs, 1862, 12mo., pp. 324 and additional unnumbered page table
of contents. "Jane" ends on page 198, and is followed by "Un coup de
feu", pp. (199)-235, verso blank, "Le faiseur de cerceuils", pp. (237)-
268, and "Don Bernardo de Zuniga", pp. (269)-324.
Several times reprinted, same format and pagination, by both Michel
Lévy frères and Calmann-Lévy.

319

"CONTES POUR LES GRANDS ET LES PETITS ENFANTS"
"CONTES POUR LES ENFANTS"   1859

As is obvious from the titles these works comprise a collection
of Dumas' stories for children.

Original edition.
Collection Hetzel. "Contes pour les grands et les petits enfants"
par Alexandre Dumas. Bruxelles, Office de publicité; Leipzig, Alphonse
Dürr, 1859, 24mo., 2 volumes, pp. 192 and 202.

Contents : Volume 1; "Les deux frères", "Le vaillant petit tailleur",
             "L'homme sans larmes", "Les mains géantes", "Le sifflet
             enchanté".
             Volume 2; "Blanche de neige", "La chèvre, le tailleur et
             ses trois fils", "Le roi des quilles", "La reine des
             neiges".

Ibid   Bruxelles, Meline, Cans et cie., n.d. (1859),
24mo., 2 volumes, same format and pagination as the preceding edition.

"Contes pour les enfants" par Alexandre Dumas. Paris, 1859 et 1860.
Naumbourg, a l'expédition de la bibliothèque choisie (G. Paetz),
24mo., 2 volumes, Volume 1, 1859; Volume 2, 1860.

Contents : Volume 1; "Les deux frères", "Les mains géantes", "La
             reine des neige", "La balle ambitieuese et le sabot phil-
             osophe".
             Volume 2; "La balle ambitieuese et le sabot philosophe"
             (suite), "Le roi des quilles", "Le sifflet enchanté",
             "La petite sirène".

Each volume has an additional unnumbered page table of contents. Pale
blue wrappers. La Bibliothèque choisie. Nos. 327 and 328.

"LE SIFFLET ENCHANTE"   1859

This is one of Dumas' delightful children's stories. It was
first published in the issue of 'Le Monte-Cristo' for 20th October,
1859.

Original edition.
Collection Hdtzel. "Contes pour les grands et les petits enfants"
par Alexandre Dumas. Bruxelles, Office de publicité; Leipzig, Alphonse
Dürr, 1859, 24mo., 2 volumes, pp. 192 and 202. "Le sifflet enchanté"
is included in Volume 1.

Ibid   Bruxelles, Meline, Cans et cie., n.d.(1859), 24mo.,
2 volumes, same format and pagination as the preceding edition.

"Contes pour les enfants" par Alexandre Dumas. Paris, 1859 et 1860.
Naumbourg, a l'expédition de la bibliothèque choisie (G. Paetz), 24mo.,
2 volumes, Volume 1, 1859; Volume 2, 1860. "Le sifflet enchanté" is
included in Volume 2. Pale blue wrappers. La Bibliothèque choisie.
Nos. 327 and 328.

"La père Gigogne" contes pour les enfants par Alexandre Dumas Paris
Michel Lévy frères, libraires-éditeurs, 1860, 12mo., 2 volumes. "Le
sifflet enchanté" occupies pp. (233)-246 of Volume 2.
Several times reprinted, same format and pagination, by both Michel
Lévy frères and Calmann-Lévy.

Ibid   Paris, Michel Lévy frères, 1860, 4to., pp. 157 in
double columns. Caption title. Woodcut at head of title. "Le sifflet
enchante" is included. Musée littéraire contemporain.
Reprinted, same format and pagination, Calmann-Lévy, n.d. (189).

"AMMALAT-BEG"   1859
"SULTANETTA"

        Once again here is a story from Marlinsky (A. Bestuzhev) which
Dumas adapted. The story is centred in Dagestan in and around 1828,
and Dumas has written that the original manuscript was found among
Malinsky's papers after his death in battle and passed on to him.
The work was written by Dumas, or at any rate completed, in Tiflis in
December, 1858. The only conceivable reason for Michel Lévy frères
changing the original title to "Sultanetta" when it was first published by them was that a Russian general named Yermoloff had published
a French translation of the original manuscript in 1835 as "Ammalat-
Bey", the publishers being Pougin et Lacointe of Paris. A comparison
of the texts illustrates Dumas' great improvements on the original.
"Ammalat-Beg" was first published serially in 'Le Moniteur Universel'
during 1858.

Original edition.
Collection Hetzel. "Ammalat-Beg", par Alexandre Dumas. Edition
autorisée pour la Belgique et l'étranger, interdite pour la France.
Bruxelles, J. Rozez, 1859, 24mo., 2 volumes, pp. (5)-9 'Avant-propos',
verso blank, (10)-144, and 197.

Ibid   Bruxelles, Meline, Cans et compagnie, 1859, 2
volumes, same format and pagination as the preceding edition. Green
wrappers.

Ibid   Leipzig, Alph. Dürr, 1859, 2 volumes, same format
and pagination as the preceding editions. Typ. & Lith. de J. Nys.
Bruxelles.

"Ammalet-Beg" par Alexandre Dumas. Paris, Alexandre Cadot, éditeur,
37, rue Serpente, n.d. (1859), 8vo., 2 volumes, pp. 326 and additional
unnumbered page table of contents, and 352 including table of contents.
Yellow wrappers. Fontainebleau, impr. E. Jacquin.

"Sultanetta" par Alexandre Dumas Paris Michel Lévy frères, libraires
éditeurs, 1862, 12mo., pp. (1)-3 'Avant-propos', verso blank, (5)-320.
There is no table of contents.
Several times reprinted, same format and pagination, by both Michel
Lévy frères and Calmann-Lévy.

"MOULLAH-NOUR"   1859
"LA BOULE DE NEIGE"

        The scene of this adaptation from Marlinsky (A. Bestuzhev) is
this time the fortress town of Derbend, and concerns the bandit whose
name provides the original title of the work. Dumas seems to have
been the first to introduce the story to French readers. I can advance
no reason for the change of title by Michel Lévy frères and, as with
"Ammalat-Beg" it presumably was published serially before volume publication, possibly in 'Le Moniteur Universel'.

Original edition.
Collection Hetzel. "Moullah-Nour" par Alexandre Dumas. Edition
interdite pour la France. Bruxelles, Meline, Cans et compagnie, n.d.
(1859), 24mo., 2 volumes, pp. 181 and 152, each with an additional
unnumbered page table of contents; following the table of contents of
Volume 2 there are 11 pages of publishers' advertisements. Green
wrappers.

Collection Hetzel. "Moullah-Nour", par Alexandre Dumas. Edition
autorisée pour la Belgique et l'étranger, interdite pour la France.
Leipzig, Alph. Dürr, 1859, 24mo., 2 volumes, same format and pagination as the preceding edition. Bruxelles - Typ. et Lith. de J. Nys.

"La boule de neige" par Alexandre Dumas Paris Michel Lévy frères,
libraires-éditeurs, 1862, 12mo., pp. 291, verso table of contents.
"La boule de neige" ends on page 258 and is followed by "Le chasse-
neige", pp. (259)-291.
Several times reprinted, same format and pagination, by both Michel
Lévy frères and Calmann-Lévy.

Ibid   Paris, Michel Lévy frères, n.d. (186), 4to.
Musée littéraire contemporain.

"LETTRES DE SAINT-PETERSBOURG (SUR LE SERVAGE EN RUSSIE)"
"DE PARIS A ASTRAKHAN"   1859-1862
"IMPRESSIONS DE VOYAGE. EN RUSSIE"

        This, the first portion of Dumas' account of his travels in
Russia which had as its sequel "Le Caucase, journal de voyages et
romans", is of particular interest for these days if only for the
unusual route that he followed. Daniel Dunglas Home, the spiritualist,
was going to Moscow to be married and asked Dumas to be his best man.
Dumas accepted. After staying in Saint-Petersbourg for about six
weeks he went to Finland, from there to Moscow and down the Volga
through Nijni-Novgorod to the Caspian Sea, finally crossing the Steppes
through Astrakhan, and leaving Kislar to reach the Caucasus on 7th
November, 1858. The journey was so hazardous that at times he had a
Cossack escort to take him from one military post to another.

        In addition to the narrative of his journey a great deal of
historical matter is given, as well as material on Russia's social
problems particularly regarding the emancipation of the serfs, agri-
cultural neglect, labour difficulties and problems of education.
He met old friends and fellow-countrymen and women, and introduced
to his readers in France Russian novelists and poets, not only assess-
ing the value of their work but also in the case of the latter giving
verse translations into French of a number of their poems. It is
relevant here to quote some of Dumas' comments from his book :
'Russia is one of the elementary forces, she encroaches but to destroy';
'Russians have an instinctive dislike of foreigners'; 'Russia has few
lawyers; in this country of absolute rule where the defence of the
accused is non-existent, where there is no public debate, lawyers are
not only rare but little more than useless'; and, 'justice has bandages
over its eyes'.

Serial issue.
From the start of his journey Dumas sent the earlier portions of his
"Impressions" (which were modified slightly at a later reprinting) by

every mail to his journal 'Le Monte-Cristo' where they appeared in each current number running from 17th June, 1858, to 28th April, 1859; these concluded with the end of Chapter XXV, or what is now Chapter XLIII of the standard edition of the book. The contributions then abruptly stopped. According to Dumas the following chapters, which are now XLIV to LXVII, appeared in 'Le Constitutionnel'. It would seem that these later parts of the work were written at some subsequent date, possibly when he was in Naples for that would account for their appearance only in 1862. In any event, when 'Le Monte-Cristo' resumed publication in that year the rest of his account of his journey appeared in it, first as feuilletons dated 28th March, and 1st, 4th and 8th April (which incidentally are not reprinted in the volume text), and which were followed by what now form Chapters LXVIII to LXIX, appearing between 11th April and 27th May, 1862, to be followed again by four more feuilletons dated 3rd, 6th, 10th and 13th June, bringing the number of chapters to LXXII, and completing the Russian travels as distinct from those in the Caucasus.

Various editions.
These must be divided into those which reprint Dumas' contributions to 'Le Monte-Cristo' and those which reprint, without the feuilletons referred to above, the story of his travels up to the completion of the writing of the work in mid-1862. In its first and incomplete form the various editions of the work were published in the following order :

Collection Hetzel. "Lettres de Saint-Pétersbourg (sur le servage en Russie)", par Alexandre Dumas. Edition autorisée pour la Belgique et l'étranger, interdite pour la France. Bruxelles, J. Rozez, 1859, 16mo., pp. 232.

This 'Collection Hetzel' edition was published nearly simultaneously by the following, all in 16mo., pp. 232, and all in green wrappers :

"Lettres de Saint-Pétersbourg" par Alexandre Dumas. Edition autorisée pour la Belgique et l'étranger, interdite pour la France. Bruxelles, Meline, Cans et cie., 1859.

Ibid   Bruxelles, Livourne, Meline, Cans et cie.; Leipzig, J.P. Meline, 1859.

Ibid   La Haye, les héritiers Doorman, 1859.

"Lettres de Saint-Pétersbourg", par Alexandre Dumas. Edition autorisée pour la Belgique et l'Etranger, interdite pour la France. Leipzig, Alph. Dürr, 1859.
(The above work was never issued as a separate title in France, but was always included in the complete edition of the work.)

Alexandre Dumas. "De Paris à Astrakhan nouvelles impressions de voyage". Première (- Troisième) série. Paris, librairie nouvelle, boulevard des Italiens, 15, A. Bourdilliat et Cie, éditeurs, 1860, 8vo., 3 volumes, pp. 318, 313 and 306, each with an additional unnumbered page table of contents. Impr. Bourdilliat.

There then followed the publication of the full work but in the case of those editions published outside France (except Canada in the present century) "Lettres de Saint-Pétersbourg (sur le servage en Russie)", referred to above, was not included.

Collection Hetzel. "De Paris à Astrakhan. Nouvelles impressions de voyage" par Alex. Dumas. Edition autorisée pour la Belgique et l'étranger, interdite pour la France. 8 volumes. Volumes 1-5, Bruxelles, Meline, Cans et compagnie, 1858-1859, 24mo. Pagination - Volumes 1-3 (1858), 190, and additional unnumbered page table of contents, 190 and 196; Volumes 4 and 5 (1859), 195 and 188. Volumes 6-8, Leipzig, Jung-Treuttel, 1862, 24mo., pp. 187, 199 and 195. Green wrappers.

Ibid   La Haye, les héritiers Doorman; Leipzig, Jung-Treuttel, same years, same number of volumes, format and pagination as the preceding edition.

Collection Hetzel. "De Paris à Astrakhan nouvelles impressions de voyage" par Alex. Dumas. Edition autorisée pour la Belgique et l'Etranger, interdite pour la France. Leipzig, Alphonse Dürr, Jung-Treuttel, 1858-1862, 24mo., same years of publication and pagination as the preceding editions.

"Impressions de voyage en Russie, etc." par Alexandre Dumas. "Aux bains de Louèche" par Charles Durier. Paris, 1858-1862. Naumbourg, a l'expedition de la Bibliothèque choisie, (L. Garcke) volumes 1-4, (G. Paetz) volumes 5-9, 24mo. Pagination : Volumes 1-3 (1858), 160, 160 and 160; Volumes 4-6 (1859), 160, 160 and 148 (pp. 108-148 being filled with Durier's "Aux bains de Louèche"); Volumes 7-9 (1862), 160, 178 and 176. All : Imprimées chez G. Paetz. Bibliothèque choisie. Vols. 277-280, 295-296, and 485-487.

"Impressions de voyage : en Russie" par Alexandre Dumas (and including "Lettres sur le servage en Russie") Paris Michel Lévy frères, libraires-éditeurs, 1865-1866, 12mo., 4 volumes. Pagination : (1)-8 'explications préliminaires', (9)-304, and additional unnumbered page table of contents; 340, and additional unnumbered page table of contents; 309, verso blank, and additional unnumbered page table of contents; 271, verso table of contents, pp. (119)-120 comprise an introduction signed : Alex. Dumas. Saint-Pétersbourg 19 septembre (1er octobre) 1858., followed by "Lettres sur le servage en Russie", pp. 121-271.
Reprinted, Calmann-Lévy, same number of volumes, format and pagination, 1876, 1884, 1885 and 1893.

"JACQUOT SANS-OREILLES"   1860

     This Russian story is a highly successful attempt to reconstruct a picture of that country in the final years of the 18th century, and the early years of the 19th, when the power of the great Muscovite nobles was still to a great extent unchecked. Thoroughly Slav as it is in its scenes and characters there has never been any suggestion of an original work on which Dumas could have drawn. It is very probable that it was constructed from a good deal of general information that Dumas obtained during his travels in that country. There does not appear to have been any serial publication, and it is more than a little curious that so powerful a work was not published in France until after Dumas' death.

Original edition.
Collection Hetzel. "Jacquot sans-oreilles", par Alexandre Dumas.

324

Edition interdite pour la France. Bruxelles, Meline, Cans et cie.,
n.d. (1860), 24mo., pp. 182, and additional unnumbered page table of
contents. Impr. E. Guyot.

Collection Hetzel. "Jacquot sans-oreilles", par Alex. Dumas. Edition
interdite pour la France. La Haye, chez les héritiers Doorman, n.d.
(1860), same format and pagination as the preceding edition. Green
wrappers.

"Jacquot sans-oreilles" par Alex. Dumas. Edition interdite pour la
France. Leipzig, Alphonse Dürr, n.d. (1860), same format and pagination as the preceding editions. Bruxelles - Imp. de E. Guyot, succ.
de Stapleaux.

"Jacquot sans-oreilles" nouvelle russe par Alexandre Dumas. Paris,
1869 - Naumbourg, s/S chez G. Paetz, libraire-éditeur, 18mo., pp. 131.
Pale blue wrappers. Bibliothèque choisie. Vol. CMLXX.

"Jacquot sans-oreilles" par Alexandre Dumas Paris Michel Lévy
frères, libraires-éditeurs, 1873, 12mo., pp. (i)-xxviii 'avant-propos'.
(1)-166, followed by "Les deux étudiants", pp. (167)-229, verso blank,
and additional unnumbered page table of contents.
A second edition, same format and pagination, was published by Michel
Lévy frères in the same year.
Thereafter, occasionally reprinted, same format and pagination, by
Calmann-Lévy.

"UNE AVENTURE D'AMOUR"   1860

      Reputedly this work covers an affair of Dumas', and if this is
so it is important from the biographical point of view. It is well
related and covers the years 1836 and 1856. It was first published in
'Le Monte-Cristo' between 13th October, 1859, and 12th January, 1860.

Original edition.
Collection Hetzel. "Une aventure d'amour" par Alexandre Dumas. Edition interdite pour la France. Bruxelles, Livourne, Meline, Cans et
cie.; Leipzig, J.P. Meline, n.d. (1860), 24mo., pp. 223.

Collection Hetzel. "Une aventure d'amour", par Alexandre Dumas.
Edition interdite pour la France. Bruxelles, Office de publicite;
Leipzig, Alphonse Dürr, n.d. (1860), same format and pagination as
the preceding edition.

"Une aventure d'amour" par Alexandre Dumas Paris Michel Lévy frères,
libraires-éditeurs, 1862, 12mo., pp. 274, and additional unnumbered
page table of contents. "Une aventure d'amour" ends on page 189,
verso blank, and is followed by "Herminie", pp. (191)-274.
Frequently reprinted, same format and pagination, by both Michel Lévy
frères and Calmann-Lévy.

"LE PERE LA RUINE"   1860

      Dealing largely with fishermen on or beside the River Marne the
period of this work is 1794 to 1834, but more particularly in the
last few of these years. It can be taken as certain that de Cherville
collaborated to an extent in its writing; the final chapters, however,
are pure Dumas. De Cherville, himself, wrote an article many years

after Dumas' death entitled 'Les pêcheurs à la ligne' in which he gave away, perhaps unconsciously, the story of his collaboration in "Le père la ruine". He tells how he lived for twenty years by the rivers Marne and Seine, and sketches their fishermen in such a way as to leave no doubt that he must be given for, at the very least, the original idea for Dumas' story. The work first appeared serially in 'Le Siècle' during 1860.

Original edition.
Collection Hetzel. "Le père la ruine" par Alexandre Dumas. Edition interdite pour la France. Bruxelles, Meline, Cans et Cie., n.d. (1860), 24mo., 2 volumes, pp. 192 and 207, each with an additional unnumbered page table of contents.

Ibid Leipzig, Alph. Dürr, n.d. (1860), 2 volumes, same format and pagination as the preceding edition.

"Le père la ruine". Roman. Par Alexandre Dumas. Paris, 1860. Naumbourg, chez G. Paetz, Libraire-éditeur. 18mo. 3 volumes, pp. 160, 160 and 159. "Le père la ruine" ends on page 55 of Volume 3, the remainder of the volume being filled by "Ludovic" par G. Vattier. Pale blue wrappers. La Bibliothèque choisie. Nos. 345-347.

"La père la ruine" par Alexandre Dumas Paris Michel Lévy frères, libraires-éditeurs, 1860, 12mo., pp. 317, verso blank, (319)-320 table of contents.
Several times reprinted, same format and pagination, by both Michel Lévy frères and Calmann-Lévy.

Ibid Paris, Michel Lévy frères, 1862, 4to., pp. 62 in double columns. Caption title. Woodcut at head of title. Musée littéraire contemporain.

"LE ROMAN D'ELVIRE"   1860

This comic opera is the third work of this type to be written by Dumas. The first was, of course, "Piquillo" and the second was "La Bacchante" (which was developed from an earlier draft entitled "Thais") which although produced at the Théâtre de l'Opéra-comique on 4th November, 1858, was never published, the original libretto and score having been destroyed in a fire at the Salle Favart.

"Le roman d'Elvire" is virtually the same work as "Un conte de fées" involving, to all intents and purposes, a change of title and with few important alterations.

Original edition.
"Le roman d'Elvire" opéra comique en trois actes par Alexandre Dumas & A. de Leuven musique d'Ambroise Thomas de l'Institut Mise en scène de M.E. Mocker Paris Michel Lévy frères, libraires-éditeurs rue Vivienne, 2 bis 1860 Tous droits réservés 12mo., 'personnages' on verso of title-page, pp. (1)-97. Half-title : "Le roman d'Elvire" opéra comique Représenté pour la première fois, à Paris, sur le théâtre impérial de l'Opéra-Comique, le 4 février 1860. Pale green wrappers. Paris. - imprimerie de J. Claye.

"Le roman d'Elvire", Opéra comique en 3 actes, Paroles de MM. Alexandre Dumas et de Leuven, Musique de Ambroise Thomas de l'Institut.

Représenté pour la 1er fois à Paris sur le théâtre de l'Opéra Comique, le 4 février 1860. Grand partition Parties d'Orch^e. Paris, G. Brandes et S. Dufour ... , n.d. (1860), small folio, pp. 477 comprising the full musical score.

"Le roman d'Elvire" opéra-comique en trois actes en société avec M. Adolphe de Leuven musique d'Ambroise Thomas Opéra-Comique. - 4 février 1860. "Distribution" on title-page, pp. (51)-142. Théatre complet de Alex. Dumas Tome XXII Paris Calmann-Levy, éditeur ancienne maison Michel Lévy frères, 1874. 12mo. "Théatre complet" in 25 volumes.

"L'ENVERS D'UNE CONSPIRATION"
("LE FILS DE DONALD LE NOIR")   1860

It is apparent from the original holograph manuscript of this play that it was Dumas' intention to entitle it "Le fils de Donald le Noir". The first four acts were so headed, but the fifth act was headed "L'envers d'une conspiration", and it was under this latter title that the play was both performed and published. It has often been suggested that Lockroy collaborated, but any such collaboration could have been only minimal.

Original edition.
"L'envers d'une conspiration" comédie en cinq actes, en prose par Alexandre Dumas Paris Michel Lévy frères, libraires-éditeurs ... 1860, 12mo., 'personnages' on verso of title-page, pp. (1)-132. Half-title : "L'envers d'une conspiration" comédie Représentée, pour la première fois, à Paris, sur le Théâtre du Vaudeville, le 4 juin 1860. Pale green wrappers. Paris - imprimerie de Edouard Blot ... Ancienne maison Dondey- Dupré.

"L'envers d'une conspiration" comédie en cinq actes, en prose par Alexandre Dumas représentée, pour la première fois, a Paris, sur le théâtre du Vaudeville, le 4 juin 1860. Caption title. Woodcut at head of title. (Paris) Michel Lévy frères, n.d. (1862), 4to., pp. 29 in double columns. Théâtre contemporain illustré. 593e livraison.

"L'envers d'une conspiration" comédie en cinq actes Vaudeville. - 4 juin 1860. "Distribution" on title-page, pp. 144-248. Théatre complet de Alex. Dumas Tome XXII Paris Calmann-Levy, éditeur ancienne maison Michel Lévy frères, 1874. 12mo. "Théatre complet" in 25 volumes.

"LE GENTILHOMME DE LA MONTAGNE"   (Drama)   1860

Dumas drew this play from his romance "El Salteador" and improved upon it, particularly in so far as the drawing of the distinctive characteristics of each of the bandits are concerned. But it is by no means one of his best dramatic works. Again Lockroy has been put forward as a collaborator, but this is very doubtful.

Original edition.
"Le gentilhomme de la montagne" drame en cinq actes et huit tableaux par Alexandre Dumas musique de Amédée Artus; décors de MM. Cambon, Thierry, Poisson et Daran ballet de M. Honoré, costumes dessinés par M. Giraud Paris Michel Lévy frères, libraires-éditeurs rue

Vivienne, 2 bis 1860 Tous droits réservés 12mo., 'personnages' on
verso of title-page, pp. (1)-144. Half-title : "Le gentilhomme
de la montagne" drame Représenté, pour la première fois, á Paris,
sur le théâtre de la Porte-Saint-Martin, le 12 juin 1860. Pale green
wrappers. Paris. - imprimerie de Edouard Blot, 46, rue Saint-Louis.
(Ancienne maison Dondey-Dupré.)

"Le gentilhomme de la montagne" drame en cinq actes et huit tableaux
par Alexandre Dumas représenté, pour la première fois, a Paris, sur
le théâtre de la Porte-Saint-Martin, le 12 juin 1860. Caption title.
Woodcut at head of title. (Paris) Michel Lévy frères, n.d. (1862),
4to., pp. 31 in double columns. Théâtre contemporain illustré. 513^e
livraison.

"Le gentilhomme de la montagne" drame en cinq actes, en huit tableaux
avec prologue Porte-Saint-Martin. - 12 juin 1860. "Distribution" on
title-page, pp. (2)-120. Théatre complet de Alex. Dumas Tome XXIII
Paris, Calmann Levy, éditeur ancienne maison Michel Lévy frères,
1874. 12mo. "Théatre complet" in 25 volumes.

"LES MEMOIRES D'HORACE"   1860

     The remarkable thing about this work is that, to my knowledge,
it was never published in volume form. Its only publication was as a
serial, where it appeared with a great deal of irregularity in 'Le
Siècle' from 16th February to 19th July, 1860. Dumas more or less
suggested in the final feuilleton that it was to be continued, but
apparently it never was. The work covers the period 65-29 BC in
ancient Rome, and Dumas, to add to the obscurity surrounding it,
states that it was derived from a manuscript found in the Vatican
Library. He may have had some assistance in the writing, but his own
style is very apparent throughout.

"LA MARQUISE D'ESCOMAN"   1860
"LES DRAMES GALANTS LA MARQUISE D'ESCOMAN"

     There is a good deal of evidence from its style that Dumas had
assistance in the writing of this work, but no name has ever been
suggested. The period is 1831-1840, and the book deals with the
world of society when Dumas was in his thirties. It was first published serially in 'Le Constitutionnel' during 1860, commencing with
the issue for 13th April.

Original edition.
Collection Hetzel. "La marquise d'Escoman" par Alexandre Dumas.
Edition interdite pour la France. Bruxelles, Meline, Cans et compagnie, n.d. (1860), 18mo., 5 volumes, pp. 189, 199, 178, 181 and 133,
each with an additional unnumbered page table of contents; Volume
5 has 8 pages of publishers' advertisements following the table of
contents. On the verso of the half-titles : Déposé aux termes de
la loi.

Alexandre Dumas "Les drames galants La marquise d'Escoman" Paris
Librairie nouvelle A. Bourdilliat et cie., boulevard des Italiens,
15. 1860. 12mo., 2 volumes, pp. 281 and 291, each with an additional
unnumbered page table of contents. Buff wrappers. Impr. A. Bourdilliat.

"Les drames galants - la marquise d'Escoman" par Alexandre Dumas Paris Michel Lévy frères, libraires-éditeurs, 1860, 12mo., 2 volumes, pp. 281, verso table of contents, and 291, verso table of contents. Frequently reprinted, same format and pagination, by both Michel Lévy frères and Calmann-Lévy.

"LA DAME DE MONSOREAU" (Drama) 1860

As its title shows this play was drawn from Dumas' romance of the same name, but there are very clear differences - one of the most notable being that Chicot is made to become to all intents and purposes Diane's brother. Moreover, it is Chicot pretending to be Bussy who fights magnificently at the end to ensure the latter's safety and the happiness of Diane and her lover.

In a letter written in December, 1850, Dumas suggested to Maquet that a play could be drawn from the romance, but it was not until ten years later that the play was produced, and the history of its vicissitudes may be read in Gustave Simon's "Histoire d'un collaboration Alexandre Dumas et Auguste Maquet documents inédits portraits et facsimiles" Paris, Editions Georges Crès & Cie., MCMXIX.

Original edition.
"La dame de Monsoreau" drame en cinq actes et dix tableaux Précédé de 'L'étang de Beauge' prologue par Alexandre Dumas & Auguste Maquet Paris Michel Lévy frères, libraires-éditeurs 2 bis, rue Vivienne, 2 bis 1860 Tous droits réservés 12mo., 'personnages' on verso of title-page, pp. (1)-16 'prologue', (17)-196. Half-title : "La dame de Monsoreau" drame Représenté, pour la première fois, à Paris, sur le théâtre de l'Ambigu-Comique, le 19 novembre 1860. Pale green wrappers with the date '1861'. Paris. - Imprimerie de Edouard Blot, rue Saint-Louis, 46.

"La dame de Monsoreau", drame en 5 actes et 10 tableaux, précédé de 'L'étang de Beaugé', prologue, par Alexandre Dumas et Auguste Maquet, Représenté pour la première fois, à Paris, sur le théatre de l'Ambigu-comique le 19 novembre 1860. (Paris) Michel Lévy frères, n.d. (1863), 4to., pp. 40 in double columns. Caption title. Woodcut at head of title. Théâtre contemporain illustré.
Reprinted, same format and pagination, (1868), 1869, and by Calmann-Lévy, n.d. (1885).

"La dame de Monsoreau" drame en cinq actes, en dix tableaux précédé de 'L'étang de Beaugé' prologue en société avec M. Auguste Maquet Ambigu-Comique. - 19 novembre 1860. "Distribution" on title-page, pp. 122-292. Théatre complet de Alex. Dumas Tome XXIII Paris Calmann lévy, éditeur ancienne maison Michel Lévy frères, 1874. 12mo. "Théatre complet" in 25 volumes.

"La dame de Monsoreau", opéra en cinq actes, huit tableaux, tiré par Auguste Maquet du roman d'Alexandre Dumas et Auguste Maquet. Musique de Gaston Salvayre. Paris, Calmann-Lévy, 12mo., pp. 104. (This opera was first presented in Paris on 30th January, 1888.)

Théâtre Nationale de l'Opéra. "La Dame de Monsoreau" grand opéra en Cinq actes et 7 tableaux tiré par M.A. Maquet du Drame d'Alexandre Dumas et A. Maquet. Musique de G. Salvayre. Paris, Chouden père et fils. Partition Piano et Chant transcrite par L. Roques, n.d. (1888), 4to., pp. ii-iii, 427.

"La dame de Monsoreau" drame en cinq actes, en dix tableaux précédé de 'L'étang de Beaugé' prologue en société avec Alexandre Dumas Ambigu-Comique. - 19 novembre 1860. "Distribution" on title-page, pp. 190-360. Théatre de Auguste Maquet Tome IV Paris Calmann-Lévy, éditeurs 3, rue Auber, 3 (n.d.), 1893. 12mo. "Théatre" in 4 volumes.

"L'ARABIE HEUREUSE" ... ... "   1860

This work is, in fact, a continuation of du Couret's travelling experiences which were first published serially in 'Le Mousquetaire' under the title "Pèlerinage de Hadji-el-Hamid-Bey ... " during 1854 and 1855. The opening words of the first sentence are : '... Au retour de mon pèlerinage à la Mecque, ... '. Quérard has stated that the work was first published serially in 'Le Siècle', and this may well be so.

Original edition.
"L'Arabie heureuse souvenirs de voyages en Afrique et en Asie par Hadji-Abd-el-Hamid-Bey" publiés par Alexandre Dumas Paris Michel Lévy frères ... , 1860, 12mo., 3 volumes, pp. 300, 322, each with an additional unnumbered page table of contents, and 313, verso blank, additional unnumbered page table of contents.
Reprinted, same format and pagination, by both Michel Lévy frères and Calmann-Lévy.

Ibid   Paris, Michel Lévy frères, 1861, 4to., pp. 134 in double columns. Caption title. Woodcut at head of title.

"LA VIE AU DESERT"   1860

This is a translation of R. Gordon-Cumming's book "A lion hunter in South Africa", to which Dumas wrote a preface. Three-quarters of this preface had previously been published as a 'causerie' in the issue for 7th May, 1857, of 'Le Monte-Cristo'.

Original edition.
"La vie au désert cinq ans de chasse dans l'intérieur de l'Afrique meridionale" par Gordon Cumming publié par Alexandre Dumas Paris, Michel Lévy frères, ... , 1860, 12mo., 2 volumes, pp. (1)-16 'avant-propos' signed : Alexandre Dumas, (17)-21 'préface' signed : R. Gordon-Cumming, verso blank, (23)-284, (285)-288 table of contents, and 272, (273)-275 table of contents.
Occasionally reprinted, same format and pagination, by both Michel Lévy frères and Calmann-Lévy.

"La vie au désert. Cinq ans de chasse dans l'intérieur de l'Afrique méridionale", par Gordon Cumming. Publié par Alexandre Dumas. (Vignette) Paris, Impr. de Blot, n.d. (1860), 4to., pp. 132 in double columns.

"LE PERE GIGOGNE"   1860

As its title indicates this work comprises a collection of children's stories, some from the Danish and some from the German. "La jeunesse de Pierrot" is dealt with separately in this Bibliography,

as are "Le lièvre de mon grand-père" and "Le sifflet enchanté".
"Blanche de neige", "Pierre et son oie", "La petite sirène" and "Le
roi des quilles" were all published earlier in 'Le Monte-Cristo'.

Original edition.
"Le père Gigogne contes pour les enfants" par Alexandre Dumas Paris
Michel Lévy frères, libraires-éditeurs, 1860, 12mo., 2 volumes, pp.
311, verso table of contents, and 315, verso table of contents.

Contents : Volume 1; "Le lièvre de mon grand-père", "La petite
sirène", and "Le roi des quilles".
Volume 2; "La jeunesse de Pierrot", "Pierre et son oie",
"Blanche de neige", "Le sifflet enchanté", "L'homme sans
larmes", and "Tiny la vaniteuse".

Ibid   Paris, Michel Lévy frères, 1860, 4to., pp. ⁷ in
double columns. Caption title. Woodcut at head of title. Mus(
littéraire contemporain.

"Le roi des quilles" par Alexandre Dumas. Illustrations par Mlle.
Sain. Published in : 'L'Univers illustré', journal hebdomadaire,
Paris, folio, 19-26 septembre 1896 (39ᵉ année), Nos. 2165 and 2166,
pp. 752, 769-772 in three columns; two woodcuts.

"MEMOIRES DE GARIBALDI"
"MEMOIRES DE JOSEPH GARIBALDI"   1860

    Early in 1860 Dumas, knowing Garibaldi only by repute, travelled
to Turin expressly to meet the future dictator. There developed a
firm friendship between the two men with the result that Dumas was
given permission by Garibaldi to translate and publish the Italian's
account of his life up to the siege of Rome. Dumas' work is of
particular importance because when Garibaldi later published his own
text he suppressed or modified parts of what he had written earlier.
The result of this was that Dumas was accused of having altered the
original material. This is quite untenable and can be proved by the
existence of two other versions which were made from Garibaldi's original manuscript and which support Dumas' text - one is by an American,
Dwight, which was published in New York in 1882, and the other by a
German, Melena, whose version was translated into English and published
in 1887. The period of Dumas' original version to be published in
France was from 1807 to 1849, but the Belgian and Naumbourg texts
carry events to 1860. The work appeared serially in 'Le Siècle', and
Dumas spoke of issuing it also in his own Italian paper "L'Indépendant.
L'Indipendente".

Original (French) edition.
"Mémoires de Garibaldi" Traduits sur le manuscrit original par Alexandre Dumas Paris Michel Lévy frères, libraires-éditeurs ... 1860,
12mo., 2 volumes, pp. (1)-26 'Un mot au lecteur' signed : Alex.
Dumas, (27)-309, verso blank, (311)-312 table of contents, and 265,
verso blank, (267)-268 table of contents.
Reprinted in 'deuxième' and troisième' editions by Michel Lévy frères
in 1861 and 1866, same number of volumes, format and pagination.

Ibid   Paris, Calmann-Lévy, 1882, 1887 and 1889, same
number of volumes, format and pagination as the preceding edition.

331

"Mémoires de Joseph Garibaldi" publiés par Alexandre Dumas. Paris, chez tous les libraires, 1860, 4to., pp. 156 in double columns. Caption title. Typ. Renou et Maulde.

Ibid   Paris, Michel Lévy frères ... , 1860 and 1861, 4to.; Volume 1 (1860), pp. (1)-5 'Un mot au lecteur' signed : Alex. Dumas, (5)-96; Volume 2 (1861), 98, including table of contents for both volumes; double columns. Caption titles. Woodcuts at heads of title repeated on paper wrappers. Volume 1, yellow wrappers, and Volume 2, pink wrappers. Musée littéraire contemporain.

Original editions (other than those published in France).
"Mémoires de Joseph Garibaldi" publiés par Alexandre Dumas. Paris, 1860-61. Naumbourg, chez G. Paetz, libraire-éditeur. 24mo., 5 volumes. Pagination : Volumes 1-3 (1860), 160, 160 and 137; Volumes 4 and 5 (1861), 160 and 160. "Mémoires de Joseph Garibaldi" end on page 98 of Volume 5, the remainder being filled by "La vallée de Chaumoni" par X. Marmier. Pale blue wrappers.
It should be noted here that from page 65 onwards of Volume 4, and the whole of Volume 5, there is published material additional to the Lévy editions - the Chapters thus comprised were written by Dumas and describe Garibaldi's life to the time of his retirement to Caprera in November, 1860, after Victor-Emmanuel's entry into Naples.

Ibid   2me. édition. Paris, 1860-1861. Naumbourg, chez G. Paetz, libraire-éditeur, 24mo., 5 volumes. Volumes 1 and 2 were published in 1860 and the remainder in 1861. Same pagination as the preceding edition. Pale blue wrappers.

"Mémoires de Garibaldi" par Alexandre Dumas précédés d'un discours sur Garibaldi par Victor Hugo et d'une introduction par George Sand ... Seule édition complète, interdite pour la France. Bruxelles, Meline, Cans et Ce., n.d. (1861), 12mo., 3 volumes, pp. 212, 214, both including 2 pages table of contents, and 220, including 1 page table of contents and followed by 12 pages of publishers' advertisements.
Reprinted, 3 volumes, same format and pagination as the preceding edition, 1865.

"Mémoires de Garibaldi" traduits sur le manuscrit original par Alexandre Dumas avec une introduction par George Sand (Vignette - woodcut portrait of Garibaldi down to his waist) Bruxelles Office de publicité, montagne de la cour, 39 - édition Hetzel - n.d. (1861), 4to., pp. (I)-II 'Garibaldi et Victor Hugo', II-V 'Discours de M. Victor Hugo', VI-VIII 'Second discours de M. Victor Hugo', (1)-7 'introduction' signed : George Sand. Nohant, 26 mai 1860, verso blank, (9)-184, all in double columns. There is no table of contents. The final page is completed by Garibaldi's 'order of the day', signed : J. Garibaldi Naples, 8 novembre 1860. Green board covers repeating the title-page.

"JOURNAL DU JEUDI"   1860

The 1st May, 1860, saw the first issue of this journal :

"Journal du jeudi" : 'Littérature, histoire, voyages. Editeur, A. Dugit. Rédacteurs, Alexandre Dumas, Alexandre Dumas fils, Emile Souvestre.'

332

I am the first to admit that I do not know the journal's ultimate fate. In all probability its life was very brief, for on the 9th of that month Dumas left Marseilles for Sicily with the intention of visiting the eastern Mediterranean.

"L'INDEPENDANT - L'INDIPENDENTE"   1860 -

The future publication of this daily paper, its text being partly in French and partly in Italian, was announced in the following prospectus :

"L'Indépendant", journal franco-italien d'Alexandre Dumas. Marseille, typogr. de Barlatier-Feissat et Demouchy, n.d. (1860), 4to., pp. 3. Prospectus signed : A. Dumas. 7 août 1860, et précédé d'une lettre d'envoi signée : Félix Valmont.

There would appear to be some mystery as to when publication actually started and to what extent, and for how long, Dumas actively participated with contributions to it. Benjamin Pifteau has said that the paper continued to be published after Dumas left Italy in 1864 and that he continued to send material from Paris. I can verify the first fact because the last known issue was dated 12th July, 1875, when apparently the paper expired, the National Library in Florence receiving under its prescriptive rights no further copies after that date.

The paper was first published in Sicily and later in Naples, and was founded in its interests of Dumas' friend Garibaldi, although Dumas from time to time criticised, and even opposed, some of Garibaldi's actions.

According to the Biblioteca e Archivo Museo del Risorgimento in Milan the first issue was dated as follows : "L'Independente". Giornale politico letterario. (Fondato da A. Dumas.) Messina, 8 agosto 1860; Anno I, no. 1.
But the Biblioteca Nazionale 'Vittorio Emmanuele III' in Naples has the following run of the paper :
Anno I, no. 1 (11/10/60) - no 176 (15/5/1861) ultimo pubblicato.
Anno II, no 1 (15/5/1852) - Anno VIII, no 113 (23/5/1868) ultimo pubblicato.
This latter Library has further numbers running from January, 1869, to the end of December, 1874, but these would not, unless very improbably, have any contributions by Dumas, even posthumous ones.

"LE PRISONNIER DE BASTILLE"   1861

There is a great deal of confusion surrounding this play, all resulting from the lengthy controversy over a period of ten years, off and on, between Dumas and Maquet. Simon in his "Histoire d'une collaboration Alexandre Dumas et Auguste Maquet documents inédits ... " mentions more than half a dozen plays drawn, or reputedly drawn, from "Le vicomte de Bragelonne". Dumas refers particularly to "Marchiala, ou la fin des mousquetaires" and this, after considerable altering and cutting, may have become in the end "Le prisonnier de la Bastille". But this is all supposition. One thing is clear and that is that Dumas absolutely refused to have the play included in his 'collected theatre', giving as his reason that it was produced during his absence in Italy and so seriously altered by the manager of the theatre at which it was produced that he would not give his sanction until it was printed as he had written it.

Original edition.
"Le prisonnier de la Bastille. Fin des mousquetaires". Drame en cinq
actes et neuf tableaux, par Alexandre Dumas. Musique de M. Groot.
Décors de MM. Cambon, Chérot, Chanet, Daran, Poisson et Fromont. Représenté pour la première fois, à Paris, sur le Théâtre Impérial du
Cirque, le 22 mars 1861. Paris, Michel Lévy frères, n.d. (1861),
4to., pp. 23 in double columns. Caption title. Woodcut at head of
title. Théâtre contemporain illustré.
Reprinted, same format and pagination, (1865), (1867), and bound with
it "La petite voisine", comédie-vaudeville en un acte, par M. Jules
Delahaye. Théâtre contemporain illustré. Livraisons 713 et 714.

Ibid   Paris, Calmann-Lévy, n.d. (188), same format and
pagination as the preceding edition.

"UNE NUIT A FLORENCE"   1861

      Dealing with the murder of the Duke Alexandre de Medicis by his
cousin Lorenzo this romance was taken by Dumas from his not too
successful play "Lorenzino". The period is the year 1537, although
towards the end it is extended slightly to 1547. The work shows
hasty writing, and it was very probably written to fulfil some contract for a romance to be published serially. Dialogue from "Lorenzino" is included, and stage directions have been replaced by connec-
tive material. The original holograph manuscript is autographed at
the end of the introduction : A M. Parfait pour remettre à M.
Lockroy.

Original edition.
Collection Hetzel. "Une nuit à Florence sous Alexandre de Médecis"
par Alexandre Dumas. Bruxelles, Meline, Cans et cie., n.d. (1861),
16mo., pp. 201, and additional unnumbered page table of contents.

"Une nuit à Florence sous Alexandre de Médicis" par Alexandre Dumas.
Leipzig. Collection Hetzel. Alph. Dürr, Libraire-Editeur, n.d. (1861),
same format and pagination as the preceding edition. Typ. J. Nys,
Bruxelles.

Ibid   Paris, Michel Lévy frères, 1861, 12mo., pp. (1)-
31 'Quelques mots sur l'Italie', verso blank, (33)-260, and additional
unnumbered page table of contents.
Reprinted by both Michel Lévy frères and Calmann-Lévy, same format
and pagination.

Ibid   Paris, Calmann-Lévy, 1880, 4to., pp. (1)-5
'Quelques mots sur l'Italie", 5-33, including table of contents, in
double columns. Caption title. Woodcut at head of title repeated
on pale pink wrappers. Musée littéraire contemporain.

"UNE ODYSSEE EN 1860"   1861
"LES GARIBALDIENS; REVOLUTION DE SICILE ET DE NAPLES"

      Dumas' intention when he sailed on 9th May, 1860, from Marseilles
in his yacht 'Emma' was to fulfill a lifelong wish to visit the shores
of the eastern Mediterranean. When he arrived at Genoa he learned
of Garibaldi's departure for Sicily with the 'Thousand'. Dumas
immediately sailed south to place his money, his boat and himself at

334

the dictator's disposal. His original intention of writing another
"Impressions de voyage" never, of course, came about. Instead what
was ultimately published after the period of devoting himself and his
energies in the service of the General and to the cause of a united
Italy could properly be called the work of the first modern war
correspondent.

While the first appearance of the shortened version of the work
under the title of "Les Garibaldiens" was its serial issue in 'La
Presse', the original issue of the full text under the title of "Une
Odyssée en 1860" was published in 'Le Monte-Cristo' from 1st January
to 3rd October, 1862, unless as is highly probable it had previously
been published in "L'Indépendant - l'Independente". Included in
'Le Monte-Cristo' is material in the form of four 'causeries' which
together were entitled in the original manuscript "Comment je mis
Garibaldi". It should be noted that the text as printed in 'Le Monte-
Cristo' has never been published in volume form.

Original edition (of the serial issue in 'La Presse').
"Les Garibaldiens - révolution de Sicile et de Naples" par Alexandre
Dumas Paris Michel Lévy frères, libraires-éditeurs ... , 1861, 12mo.,
pp. facsimile of letter from Garibaldi facing page (1), - 374, (375)-
376 table of contents.
Several times reprinted, same format but with varying paginations, by
both Michel Lévy frères and Calmann-Lévy.

"LE PAPE DEVANT LES EVANGILES, ... "   1861
The theory has been advanced that this work was the reason for
Dumas having been proscribed by Pope Pius IX from landing at Civita
Vecchia from his yacht 'Emma'. This would infer that there is an
earlier edition of the book than that published in 1861 and which could
only have been privately printed and clandestinely distributed as a
pamphlet for propaganda purposes. But the oddity of the matter is
that not one of all the Italian national, municipal or university
libraries consulted possesses a copy of it, and this raises the question as to whether the religious authorities seized all the copies
they could lay their hands on and destroyed them. If Dumas' dates are
right the work could not have been published in any early issues of
'L'Indépendant - L'Independente'. There are certainly quite a number of copies of the 1861 edition extant, not only held in Italy but
elsewhere, published both in French and Italian. The available
evidence would seem to point to the edition comprising 96 pages being
the earlier publication of the two.

Original edition.
"Le Pape devant les Evangiles, l'histoire et la raison humaine" par
Alexandre Dumas. Réponse à Sa Grandeur Monseigneur (Felix) Dupanloup
Evêque d'Orléans. Naples, De Androsio, 1861, 25 x 16 cms., pp.
xxxvi, 96.
The last lines of page 96 are as follows : 'Après quoi Sire, vous
ferez ce que faisait Charlemagne, qui / scellait ses ordonnances avec
le prommeau de son épée, et les / fesait respecter avec la pointe.
/ ALEX. DUMAS.'

"Le Pape devant les Evangiles, l'histoire et la raison humaine" par
Alexandre Dumas. Réponse à Sa Grandeur Monseigneur (Felix) Dupanloup

Evêque d'Orléans. (Précédé :) Lettre à M. le Vicomte de la Guérronnière par Monseigneur l'Evêque d'Orléans. (Segue :) A. Dumas. Son Eminence Monseigneur le Cardinal Antonelli. (In copertina :) Propaganda italienne. Naples, De Androsio, 1861, 27 x 16 cms., pp. xxxvi, 118. The letter addressed to Cardinal Antonelli is dated : 26 mars 1861.

"Le Pape devant les Evangiles, l'histoire et la raison humaine : réponse à Monseigneur Dupanloup", Napoli, Museo de Famiglia, 1861, 8vo., pp. 115.

Propaganda italianna. "Il Papa innazi il Vangelo, la storia e la ragione umana", par Alessandro Dumas. Risposta a Sua Grandezza Monsignor Dupanloup. Napoli, Tipografia di Francesca Giannini, 1861, 8vo., pp. 115.

"BRIC-A-BRAC"   1861

    This work comprises, purely and simply, a collection of articles and 'causeries' from various sources. A good many of them can be found in 'Le Mousquetaire' and 'Le Monte-Cristo', but there is one important exception :

"Jacques Fosse le sauvateur", par Alexandre Dumas. Paris, Impr. de Dubuisson, 1858, large 8vo., pp. 15. The above is the original edition of the work. "Désir et possession" was later published in 'L'Univers illustré', journal hebdomadaire, Paris, 23 mai 1896 (39e année), folio, No. 2148, page 412 in double columns.

Original edition. "Bric-à-brac" par Alexandre Dumas Paris Michel Lévy frères, libraires-éditeurs, 1861, 12mo., 2 volumes, pp. 304 and 304, each with an additional unnumbered page table of contents.

Contents :   Volume 1; "Deux infanticides", "Poëtes, peintres et musiciens", "Désir et possession", "Une mère", "Le curé de Boulogne", "Un fait personnel", "Comment j'ai fait jouer a Marseille le drame des forestiers", "Heures de prison", "Jacques Fosse", "Le château de Pierrefonds", "Le lotus blanc et la rose mousseuse".
             Volume 2; "La rétraite illuminée", "Causerie culinaire", "Romulus et Pizarre", "Le cimitière Clamart", "De la sculpture et des sculptures", "Les gorilles", "Le triomphe de la paix", "Le Carmel", "Mon ami Colbrun", "Cas de conscience", "Un poëte anacréontique", "La revue nocturne", "Une séance de magnetisme", "Etude de tête d'après la Bosse".

Subsequent issues by both Michel Lévy frères and Calmann-Lévy were of the first volume only, same format but with varying pagination.

"Bric-à-brac" par Alexandre Dumas. Paris, Michel Lévy frères, 1865, 4to., pp. 93, including table of contents, in double columns. Caption title. Woodcut at head of title repeated on the pink wrappers. The contents are exactly the same as the Michel Lévy frères, 1861, 2 volume, edition referred to above. Musée littéraire contemporain.

"LES MORTS VONT VITE"   1861
     Whilst this work consists of personal memories of some of Dumas'
friends there is related as well much of interest with regard to himself.

Original edition.
"Les morts vont vite" par Alexandre Dumas Paris Michel Lévy frères,
libraires-éditeurs, 1861, 12mo., 2 volumes, pp. 322 and 294, each
with an additional unnumbered page table of contents.

Contents :   Volume 1; "Chateaubriand", "M. le duc et madame la
              duchesse d'Orléans", "Hégésippe Moreau", "Béranger".
              Volume 2; "Eugène Sue", "Alfred de Musset", "Achille
              Devéria. - Lefèvre Deumier", "La dernière année de Marie
              Dorval".

With the exception of "Chateaubriand" all of the above were published
either in 'Le Mousquetaire' or 'Le Monte-Cristo'.
Several times reprinted in 2 volumes, same format and pagination,
by both Michel Lévy frères and Calmann-Lévy.

Ibid   Paris, Michel Lévy frères, (187), 4to. Musée littéraire
contemporain.

"LE FLEAU DE NAPLES"   1862
     This excellent piece of journalism can be credited to the early
part of Dumas' residence in Naples when he was among those friends of
Garibaldi who were living in that city from late in 1860 onwards.

Original edition.
"Le capitaine Pamphile" par Alexandre Dumas Paris Michel Lévy
frères, libraires-éditeurs, 1862, 12mo., unnumbered page 'Note de
l'éditeur', pp. (3)-297, verso blank, (299)-300 table of contents.
"Le capitaine Pamphile" ends on page 273, verso blank, and is followed
by "Le fleau de Naples", pp. (275)-297.
Frequently reprinted, same format and pagination, by both Michel Lévy
frères and Calmann-Lévy.

"MASANIELLO"   1862
     An article with this title was published in the issues of 'Le
Monte-Cristo', Nos. 52-58, running from 27th June to 18th July, 1862.
It is a detailed account of the revolt led at Naples by a man of that
name who lived between 1623 and 1647. It has never been reprinted.

     It may be mentioned here that a work entitled "Masaniello" or,
among alternative titles, "Masaniello; or, the fisherman of Naples"
has frequently been published in the United States with Dumas given as
the author. It is not by him, but curiously it does include as an
interpolated story, the second and third chapters of Dumas' "Cherubino
et Celestini", that is to say "Antonio" and "Maria", of his "Souvenirs
d'Antony".

"IVANHOE"   1862
     Although this work is described as Dumas' translation the intro-

duction to it gives a good indication that he did probably little more than actually direct the work of translating, and probably in parts improving the rendering. As early as circa 1822 Dumas wrote a 'Mélodrame en 3 actes et'a grand spectacle' based on Scott's novel; it was probably his first attempt at playwriting done alone. It was never performed or published, and the manuscript is held by the Bibliothèque Municipale de Dieppe having been presented to that Library by Dumas, fils. Victor Perceval also had the work published as having been translated by him, which would not have precluded Dumas from having given his help.

Original edition.
"Ivanhoe" par Walter Scott traduit par Alexandre Dumas Paris Michel Lévy frères, libraires-éditeurs, 1862, 12mo., 2 volumes, pp. (1)-7 'Préface Comment je traduisis le roman d'Ivanhoe' signed : Alex. Dumas, verso blank, (13)-305, and 207. There are no tables of contents.
Several times reprinted, same format and pagination, by both Michel Lévy frères and Calmann-Lévy.

Alexandre Dumas "Ivanhoe" de Walter Scott. Paris, Michel Lévy frères, 1864, 4to., pp. 160 in double columns. Caption title. Woodcut at head of title. Musée littéraire contemporain.

"I BORBONI DI NAPOLI"
"LES BOURBONS DE NAPLES"   1862-1863

While he was living in Naples Dumas was fortunate enough to have access to the private royal archives there. These included not only letters written by outstanding people living during the period of Ferdinand I, including the Hamiltons, Nelson, Caraccioli, Ruffo and others, but also the copies of every pamphlet, scurrilous or otherwise, which Ferdinand had kept for his own amusement when, under his orders, all other copies had had to be burned.

In the writing of the resulting history, which covers the period 1734 to approximately 1815, he had no collaborator. In so far as that part of this important work which was published in French in the issues of 'Le Monte-Cristo' from 22nd July to 12th September, 1862, is concerned this covers roughly the first 2 volumes of the Italian version.

Original edition.
"I Borboni di Napoli" par Alessandro Dumas. Questa storia, pubblicata pe' soli lettori dell'INDEPENDENTE, è stata scritta su documenti nuovi, inediti e sconosciuti, scoperti dall'autore negli archivi segreti della polizia, e degli affari esteri di Napoli. Documenti appoggio dei primi quatro volumi. (1734-1800), Napoli, 1862-1863, 8vo., 10 volumes.
Running titles to all volumes except No. 5 : "Supplemento dell' Tndependente"; in the centre of the title-page of this volume is printed : Documenti in appoggio dei primi quatro volumi. (1734-1800). Volumes 1-5 are dated 1862, with the imprint : Napoli, Tipografia Universale, Toledo, 329.
Volume 6, with the same imprint, is dated 1863 and with : V. 5 printed on the title-page.
Volumes 7-10 are dated 1863; Volumes 7-9 with the imprint : Napoli,

Stabilimento Tipografico del Plebiscito Chiaia 63, Volume 7 having :
V. 6 on the title-page, Volume 8 with : V. 7, and Volume 9 with :
V. 8.
Volume 10 has the imprint : Napoli, Dall Stamperia di Salvatore de
Marco, Vico S. Niccolo alla Carita No. 14.

Pagination : Volumes 1 and 2, "Carlo III e Ferdinando I", 360 and
368.
Volumes 3 and 4, "Ferdinando I", 365 and 346; at the
bottom of the final page of Volume 4 is printed : Fine
del IV volume e della part prime. There are no indexes
or tables of contents for Volumes 1-4.
Volume 5, "Regni di Carlo III e di Ferdinando I", 350,
the last 2 of which are 'Indice' beginning with "Ferdinando VI e Carlo III, re di Spagna" (Bulau, estratto
dalle memorie del barone di Gleischer) for page 1, and
ending with : Morte di Lord Orazio Nelson, for page
333.
Volume 6, "Regni di Giuseppe Napoleone a Napoli e di
Ferdinando I in Sicilia", 359. There is no index or
table of contents.
Volume 7, "Regni di Gioacchino Murat in Napoli e di
Ferdinando I in Sicilie", 358. There is no index or
table of contents.
Volume 8, "Gioacchino Murat in Russia", 360; at the
start of the text for Volume 8 is the following :
Capitolo I. "Regno di Murat a Napoli di Ferdinando I
a Palermo". There are no other chapter headings, and
no index or table of contents.
Volume 9, "Gioacchino Murat alla Grande Armata ed a
Napoli. 1 principe Francesco vicario generale in
Sicilia", 351; on the first page of the text is :
Capitolo I. "Regni di Murat a Napoli. Regno di Murat
a Napoli. Regno di Ferdinando in Sicilia". There are
no other chapter headings. On the verso of page 351
(which is unnumbered) is the heading : Titoli de'
volumi della storia de'Borboni di Napoli finora pubbli-
cati, and under it is a list of the first 9 volumes.
Volume 10, "Morte di Murat", 304. 'Capo primo' begins
the text on page 5, 'Capitolo secondo' on page 47,
'Capo quarto' on page 147 (there are no pages missing),
and 'Capo quinto' on page 187. There is no index or
table of contents.

There are no illustrations in any of the volumes.
That there was a second edition is apparent, but there are varying
dates : one particular edition is dated 1862-1864 and another 1862-
1865, Volumes 3 and 10 of the latter are stated to be : 2nd edition.
It should be added here that the work as a whole was first published
serially in "L'Independant - L'Indipendente".

"LE VOLONTAIRE DE '92"
("RENE D'ARGONNE. "LES MEMOIRES D'UN VOLONTAIRE   1862 -
DE '93; RENE BESSON".)

    The introductory paragraphs to "Les compagnons de Jéhu" refer to
the romance which it was intended to be entitled "René d'Argonne".

The period was to be 1791 and succeeding years, opening with the arrival of Louis XVI and his family at Varennes in their attempted flight. The years went by and finally Dumas, at the end of 1861 when writing a prospectus for the revival of the journal 'Le Monte-Cristo' referred to a work entitled "Les volontaires de 1792" as being completed in four volumes.

The work first began to appear in that journal in the issue for 25th April, 1862, and continued to be published until the last number but one, that for 3rd October of the same year which, nevertheless, stated that the work would be continued in the next issue. At this point the romance consisted of a quite lengthy introduction and 37 feuilletons, with a total of 48 chapters. There was then a long hiatus, and the work continued in the revived 'Le Mousquetaire', this time under the title of "Les mémoires d'un volontaire de '93: René Besson", 17 feuilletons being published between 23rd February and 11th March, 1867. The 17th feuilleton had at its end the word : Fin.

The story was again published in the journal 'Dartagnan', 25 feuilletons being printed in the issues from 30th April to 4th July, 1868, and comprising the introduction and the first 21 chapters, abruptly ending with the collapse of that journal. Dumas, in announcing its publication in the 'Dartagnan', had said that it would consist of 8 volumes. No edition published either in or outside France is known, although Chincholle who knew Dumas well in his later years had stated that it was almost ready for publication in book form.
(It is, perhaps, interesting to mention here as a footnote that translations of the work were published in the United States in the 19th Century under the misleading title of "Love and liberty. A thrilling narrative of the French revolution of 1792". My own copy of the rare T.B. Peterson and brothers, 1874, edition containes 17 chapters of text additional to that published in 'Le Monte-Cristo' and ends with the fall of Robespierre; it is more of a picturesque history than a romance in this particular translation.)

"LES DEUX REINES"   1864

The two queens which give the title to this romance are Marie-Louise and Marie-Anna de Neuberg, the successive wives of Charles II, King of Spain and 'le dernier roi de la maison de Charles-Quint'. The work is a continuation of "La dame de volupté" and deals with the subsequent course of events in the comtesse de Verrue's life at Charles' court. The work ends with his death in 1700, and can be considered as going back to 1681. Again it is mainly the work of the comtesse Dash, with editing by Dumas.

Original edition.
"Les deux reines" suite et fin des mémoires de Mlle de Luynes publiés par Alexandre Dumas Paris Michel Lévy frères, libraires-éditeurs, 1864, 12mo., 2 volumes, pp. 333 and 329. There are no tables of contents.
Often reprinted, same format and pagination, by both Michel Lévy frères and Calmann-Lévy.

"Les deux reines" suite et fin de la dame de volupté publiée par Alexandre Dumas Paris, Calmann-Lévy, n.d. (c 187), 4to., pp. (1)-127 in double columns. Caption title. Woodcut at head of title.

"LA VEILLEE ALLEMANDE" 1864

There were considerable difficulties concerning the production of this play, which were only finally resolved by the omission from the playbills of Dumas' name as a collaborator in its writing. The song in the first scene is Dumas' "Marguerite au rouet" which was first published in Chapter V of "Le Speronare".

Original (and only) edition.
"La veillée allemande" drame en un acte par Bernard Lopez Représenté pour la première fois, à Paris, sur le théâtre de Belleville, le 21 novembre 1863. Paris E. Dentu, éditeur libraire de la société des gens de lettres Palais-Royal, 17 et 19, galerie d'Orléans Et à la librairie centrale, 24, boulevard des Italiens. 1864. Tous droits réservés 12mo., pp. (5)-36, verso of title-page 'personnages' 'acteurs'. Orange wrappers repeating the title-page with the caption : Bibliothèque au théâtre moderne. Coulommiers - Typographie A. Moussin.

"LES MOHICANS DE PARIS" (Drama) 1864

This play was rewritten and completely reconstructed three times before it was finally accepted by the censorship. Why the censor should interfere is a matter for speculation, but it could have been on account of Dumas' republican sympathies. When it was rewritten a fourth time Dumas, in exasperation, wrote to Napoleon III and his letter forms the preface to the original published edition. (The manuscript of this letter is held by the Bibliothèque de l'Arsenal.) Lecomte wrote : '"Les Mohicans" furent rendus, avec des modifications qui ne les empêchèrent pas de réussir brillament.' Paul Bocage has been stated to have helped with the writing of the play, very possibly because he helped to an extent in the writing of the romance from which it was drawn.

Original edition.
"Les mohicans de Paris" drame en cinq actes, en neuf tableaux avec prologue par Alexandre Dumas Paris Michel Lévy frères, libraires éditeurs rue Vivienne, 2 bis, et boulevard des Italiens, 15 a la librairie nouvelle 1864 Tous droits réservés 12mo., pp. (i)-vii preface comprising the letter to Napoleon III, verso blank, unnumbered page 'distribution', 2-28 'prologue', 28-162. Half-title : "Les mohicans de Paris" drame Représenté, pour la première fois, à Paris, sur le théâtre de la Gaité, le 20 août 1864. Yellow wrappers repeating the title-page, but with the date M DCCC LXIV. Poissy. - typ. et stér. de Aug. Bouret.

Ibid Paris, Michel Lévy frères, n.d. (1864), 4to., pp. 45 in double columns, and Dumas' post-scriptum comprising the letter to Napoleon III part of page 45 and pp. 46-47. Caption title. Woodcut at head of title.
Reprinted, same format and pagination, (1865).

"Les mohicans de Paris" drame en cinq actes, en neuf tableaux avec prologue Gaieté (sic). - 20 août 1864. Preface comprising the letter to Napoleon III, pp. (i)-vii, verso blank, unnumbered page 'Distribu-tion', pp. 2-28 'prologue', 28-162. Théâtre complet de Alex. Dumas Tome XXIV Paris, Calmann-Lévy, éditeur ancienne maison Michel Lévy frères, 1874. 12mo. "Théâtre complet" in 25 volumes.

341

"LA SAN-FELICE"   (Romance)   1864-1865
"EMMA LYONNA"

    As was the case when he was in Russia Dumas, during the time he
lived in Naples between 1860 and 1864, was absorbed by the local
history as well as the social and political conditions there. It
naturally followed that considerable material was provided for his
journal 'L'Indépendant - L'Indipendente'. Furthermore he had at
hand all the background material that he needed for his romance "La
San-Felice", as it was first called, and which later because of its
length was divided into two - the first portion retaining the original
title and the second being given that of "Emma Lyonna".

    The period concerned is 1798-1800, and the story revolves around
the King and Queen of Naples and the Two Sicilies, Lord Nelson, Sir
William and Lady Hamilton, Admiral Caraccioli, various conspirators,
and the inevitable hangers-on of a decadent monarchy and a corrupt
court. The central and tragic figure is 'La San-Felice' who was
considerably idealised by Dumas in his story. The work first appeared
serially in 'La Presse', and was also published in an Italian translation in "L'Indépendant - L'Independente'.

Original edition.
"La San-Felice" par Alexandre Dumas Paris Michel Lévy frères,
libraires-éditeurs, 1864-1865, 12mo., 9 volumes. Pagination : Volumes 1-6 (1864), 320 including table of contents, 318 and additional
unnumbered page table of contents, 324 including table of contents,
313 and additional unnumbered page table of contents, 320 and 324
both including table of contents; Volumes 7-9 (1865), 318 and 313
both with an additional unnumbered page table of contents, and 324
including table of contents, the final volume being dated : Saint-
Gratien, 15, septembre 1864. Orange wrappers. Part of the Bibliothèque Nouvelle.

"La San-Felice". Roman des moeurs par Alexandre Dumas. Paris, 1864-
1865. Naumbourg, chez G. Paetz, libraire-éditeur. 24mo., 17 volumes.
Pagination : Volumes 1-10 (1864), all of 160 pages each; Volumes 11-
17 (1865), all of 160 pages each with the exception of Volume 17 which
has 140 pages. Pale blue wrappers. La Bibliothèque choisie. Volumes
1-4, nos. 685-688; volumes 5-6, nos. 689-690; volumes 7-8, nos. 707-
708; volumes 9-10, nos. 717-718; volumes 11-14, nos. 722-725; volumes
15-17, nos. 780-782.

"La San-Felice" par Alexandre Dumas Deuxième édition Paris Michel
Lévy frères, libraires éditeurs, 1865, 9 volumes, 12mo., same pagination as the original Michel Lévy edition.

Journal du dimanche. "La San- Felice". No. 807. 23 juillet, 1865
('Note préliminaire'), then No. 808, 27 juillet, 1865, through to
No. 915, 5 août, 1866, in treble columns. 4to. Woodcut at head of
each issue, and 'Alexandre Dumas'.

"La San-Felice" par Alexandre Dumas. Paris, Legrand, Troussel et
Pomey, 1872, large 8vo., 4 volumes. Pagination : Volume 1, 2 preliminary leaves, 390 including 2 pages table of contents; Volume 2,
2 preliminary leaves, 372 including 1 page table of contents; Volume
3, 2 preliminary leaves, 382 including 2 pages table of contents; Volume 4, 399, of which page (397) is the table of contents and (398)-399
give 'classement des gravures' for the 4 volumes. The illustrations,

after Philippoteaux, total 64, and are included in each volume as follows : 17, 13, 16 and 18 respectively.

"Le San-Felice" par Alexandre Dumas Paris Calmann Lévy, éditeur ancienne maison Michel Lévy frères, 1876, 12mo., 4 volumes. Pagination : 319 verso table of contents, 318 and additional unnumbered page table of contents; 323 verso table of contents; 350 and additional unnumbered page table of contents.

"Emma Lyonna" par Alexandre Dumas Paris Calmann Lévy, éditeur ancienne maison Michel Lévy frères, 1876, 12mo., 5 volumes. Pagination : 280 and (281)-282 table of contents; 318 and additional unnumbered page table of contents; 313 verso blank and additional unnumbered page table of contents; 322, (323)-324 table of contents.
Occasionally reprinted under the above two titles, same number of volumes, same format and pagination, by Calmann-Lévy.

"La San-Felice", par Alexandre Dumas. Paris, Legrant et Crouzet, n.d. (1883), same number of volumes, same format, pagination and with identical illustrations as the Legrand, Troussel et Pomey, 1872, edition.

"CAUSERIE SUR EUGENE DELACROIX ET SES OEUVRES" 1865

Delacroix died in 1863 and an exhibition of some of his works was held late in the following year. This 'causerie' is the text of the speech that Dumas made at that exhibition. It would, from the nature of things, have been published in one or other of the Paris journals during December, 1864.

Original (and only) edition.
"Causerie sur Eugène Delacroix et ses oeuvres faite par Alexandre Dumas le 10 décembre 1864 dans le salle d'exposition des oeuvres d'Eugène Delacroix". Paris, 1865. Naumbourg, chez G. Paetz, libraire-éditeur. 24mo., pp., half-title "Causerie sur E. Delacroix et ses oeuvres", title-page, (5)-120 text of the speech, (121) additional similar half-title, verso blank, (123)-147 text, followed by 6 leaves of publisher's advertisements. La Bibliothèque choisie. No. 777.

"SOUVENIRS D'UNE FAVORITE" 1865

It is quite incorrect to describe, as has been done, this work as a sequel to "La San-Felice" and "Emma Lyonna". It is purely and simply a picturesquely written account of the career of Emma, Lady Hamilton, the wife of the British Ambassador in Naples. The period is roughly 1765 to 1815, and without any doubt this is Dumas working alone. As a subterfuge Dumas described it as a manuscript which Lady Hamilton had herself written and given to a priest before her death.

Original edition.
"Souvenirs d'une favorite" par Alexandre Dumas Paris Michel Lévy frères, libraires éditeurs, 1865, 12mo., 4 volumes, pp. 318, 320, 320, and 300. "Souvenirs d'une favorite" ends on page 272 and is followed by 'Notes', pp. (273)-300. There are no tables of contents.
Several times reprinted, same format and pagination, by both Michel Lévy frères and Calmann-Lévy.

"Souvenirs d'une favorite" par Alexandre Dumas. Paris, 1865. Naumbourg s/S chez G. Paetz, libraire-éditeur. 24mo. 8 volumes, pp. 162, 152, 153, 152, 153, 148, 150 and 124. Pale blue wrappers. La Bibliothèque choisie. Nos. 829-836.

"Souvenirs d'une favorite", par Alexandre Dumas. Paris, Impr. de C. Towne, n.d. (1865), 4to., pp. 303 in double columns. Feuilleton de 'L'Avenir national'.

"BOUTS-RIMES"   1865

Both Ferry in his "Dernières années d'Alexandre Dumas" and Pifteau in "Alexandre Dumas en manches de chemise" refer at some length to this work. Some years previous to 1864 a number of seemingly impossible rhyming words were given to Méry as a test for his skill in writing verse. On 1st November, 1864, Dumas suggested to readers of 'Le petit journal' that they should engage in a competition using these words, and prizes were offered for the best verses. In the event 378 verses were submitted which were printed in volume form with an introduction by Dumas. (The words were : femme - Catilina - âme - fouina - jongle - citoyen - ongle - paien - mirabelle - Mirabeau - belle - flambeau - Orestie - Gabrio (a pet-name for the comtesse Dash among her friends) - répartie - agio - figue - faisan - ligue - Parmesan - noisette - pâté - grisette - bâté.) It was Dumas who provided the words.

Original (and only) edition.
"Bouts-rimés" publiés par Alexandre Dumas Paris librairie du petit journal 21, boulevard Montmartre 21 1865 Pp., blank leaf after the title-page, (i)-x 'quelques mots nécessaires' signed : Paris, le 9 mars 1865. Alexandre DUMAS. 1-378. Yellow wrappers repeating the title-page. Poissy. - typ. et stér. de A. Bouret.

"LES GARDES FORESTIERS"   1865
"LES FORESTIERS"

This play was drawn from his romance "Catherine Blum". It keeps very close to the original and, indeed, in many instances large parts of the original dialogue remain unaltered. It was first performed in Marseilles at the Grand-Théâtre on 23rd March, 1858, and Dumas gives an amusing account of the first production there in the article 'Comment j'ai fait jouer à Marseille le drame des forestiers' in "Bric-à-brac" (which see).

The play must not be confused with "Le garde forestier" which was produced thirteen years earlier under the names of de Leuven and Brunswick, but in the composition of which Dumas shared. As will be seen it was published in Dumas' 'collected theatre' under the title of "Les forestiers".

Original edition.
"Les gardes forestiers" drame en cinq actes actes par Alexandre Dumas représenté, pour la première fois (sic), a Paris, sur le Grand-Théatre-Parisien, le 28 mai 1865 musique de M. Borssal, décors de M. Victor Simon. Paris, Michel Lévy frères, n.d. (1865), 4to., pp. 36 in double columns. Caption title. Woodcut at head of title. Théâtre contemporain illustré.
Reprinted, same format and pagination, n.d. (1866).

"Les forestiers" drame en cinq actes Grand-Théâtre (Marseille.) –
23 mars 1858. "Distribution" on title-page, pp. (147)-274. Théatre
complet de Alex. Dumas Tome XXI Paris, Calmann-Lévy, éditeur ancienne maison Michel Lévy fréres, 1874. 12mo. "Théatre complet" in
25 volumes.

"UN PAYS INCONNU"   1865

Dumas wrote a brief introduction to this work with his tongue in
his cheek. He refers to his stay in the United States (which, of
course, he never visited) and mentions meeting in New York a traveller
named Middleton Payne who had returned from Brazil where a tribe descended from the Aztecs had been discovered at a place called Géral-
Milco. Furthermore, Dumas says that he wrote the book from Payne's
manuscript notes. If that gentleman did exist it is much more probable that "Un pays inconnu" is a translation which Dumas revised and
edited.

Original edition.
"Un pays inconnu" publié par Alexandre Dumas Paris Michel Lévy
frères, libraires éditeurs librairie nouvelle. 1865, 12mo., pp. (1)-2
Dumas' unsigned foreword, 3-320. There is no table of contents.
Occasionally reprinted, same format and pagination, by both Michel
Lévy frères and Calmann-Lévy.

"LE COMTE DE MORET"   1865-1866

This romance hinges on the war in Piedmont and the imaginary
career of Antoine, comte de Moret, the illegitimate son of Henri IV
who was believed to have been killed during the battle of Castelnaudary
in 1632, although his body was never found. A legend persisted that,
seriously wounded, he had escaped to die as an aged hermit in Anjou
during the reign of Lous XIV. Dumas' story opens on 5th December,
1628, and ends in 1630.

In 1850 Dumas had already written what was in fact to be the
sequel to this work and which was entitled "La colombe", related in
the form of letters and dealing with the fate of that remarkable man.
The period covered by "La colombe", according to the dating of the
letters comprising the work, was 5th May, 1637, to 10th September,
1638, although their contents covered events both at, as well as after,
the battle of Castelnaudary.

Between 17th October, 1865, and 23rd March, 1866, with only
occasional lapses, "Le comte de Moret" was published serially in Jules
Noriac's daily journal 'Les nouvelles'. Copies of the journal were
lodged with the Bibliothèque Nationale, but the 'run' in that Library
is incomplete and lacks those issues dated 18th and 21st October, 1st,
2nd, 3rd and 27th November, 1865, and 1st March, 1866, in all of which
issues the romance appeared.

The romance is Dumas working entirely alone, and why it has never
been published in volume form until comparatively recently in France
under the titles of "Le comte de Moret" and "Le sphinx rouge" (it was
never issued in pirated editions in Belgium, Holland or Germany) remains a mystery. For what it is worth it has been stated that the work
fell off in quality towards its ending, when it consisted rather more

of historical matter and quotations from memoirs than of pure romance.
Be that as it might be the work contains some excellent writing.

"LES NOUVELLES"
"LE MOUSQUETAIRE"   (Deuxième série.)   1865-1867

   The first of the above journals was, according to Vapereau in
his "Dictionnaire universel des contemporains", Paris, Hachette,
founded by Jules Noriac, and commenced publication on 20th September,
1865. The importance of this period of the journal's history lies in
the fact that Dumas contributed to it his "Le comte de Moret".

   Apparently the periodical ran into difficulties, possibly financial, and in the spring of 1866 Dumas took it over as 'rédacteur en
chef'. On the 18th November of the same year he renamed it 'Le
Mousquetaire', the original series of which had ended with the issue
dated 7th February, 1857. The revived 'Le Mousquetaire' continued to
be published up to 25th April, 1867. In it was published part of the
unfortunate "Le volontaire de '92" under a different title, and a part
also of Dumas' "Histoire des mes bêtes".

"PROJET D'UN NOUVEAU THEATRE HISTORIQUE", addressed :
'A mes amis connus et inconnus de la France et de   1866
l'étranger' and : 'A mes bons amis des faubourgs'.

   Times were difficult for Dumas and he launched an appeal for funds
to help him to found a new Théâtre Historique for the production of
his own plays. His efforts achieved very little and the theatre never
materialised. The full text of his appeal may be read in Gabriel
Ferry's "Les dernières années d'Alexandre Dumas 1864-1870", Paris,
Calmann Lévy, 1883, pp. 54-56, and in L.-Henry Lecomte's "Alexandre
Dumas 1802-1870 Sa Vie intime. Ses Oeuvres", Paris, Tallandier,
(1902), pp. 178-180.

   There were three issues of the appeal as follows : "Projet d'un
nouveau Théâtre Historique" : 'A mes amis connus et inconnus ... ',
signed : Alexandre Dumas 24 février 1866. Lille, Impr. de Danel,
n.d. (1866), 4to., pp. 3.

Ibid   'A mes bons amis des faubourgs', signed : Alexandre Dumas with the same date, Lille, Impr. de Danel, n.d. (1866),
4to., pp. 3.

Ibid   'A mes bons amis des faubourgs", signed : Alexandre Dumas with the same date, Lille, Impr. de Danel, n.d. (1866),
large 8vo., pp. 2.

"GABRIEL LAMBERT"   (Drama)   1866
"GABRIEL LE FAUSSAIRE"

   This play was drawn from the romance of the same name and must
have been extremely difficult to write. Lambert in the romance was,
of course, a vulgar adventurer. The idea of writing the play orig-
inated from Amédée de Jallais, a playwright of some experience, when
he brought to Dumas a 'scenario' taken from the romance. Dumas found
this so well done that he decided to write the play in collaboration
with de Jallais. However, the antipathy aroused by the principal

character, which was played by Lacressonnière, doomed it; there was only a single amusing scene in the play, one introduced by Dumas in which a vagrant steals a clock with superb audacity in the presence of its owner. The play had a short run, but it was revived under the title of "Gabriel le faussaire" on 23rd September, 1868, at the Théâtre Beaumarchais where it was more kindly received.

Original edition.
"Gabriel Lambert" drame en cinq actes et un prologue par Alexandre Dumas & Amédée de Jallais Paris Michel Lévy frères, libraires éditeurs rue Vivienne, 2 bis, et boulevard des Italiens, 15 a la librairie nouvelle 1866 Tous droits réservés. 12mo., verso of title-page 'personnages', pp. (1)-38 'prologue', (39)-132. Half-title : "Gabriel Lambert" drame Représenté pour la première fois, à Paris, sur le théâtre de l'AMBIGU-COMIQUE, le 16 mars 1866. Brown wrappers : "Gabriel Lambert" drame en six actes dont un prologue par Alex. Dumas & A. de Jallais Paris Michel Lévy frères, ... MDCCCLXVI. Imprimerie L. Toinon et Cie, à Saint-Germain.

"Gabriel Lambert" drame en cinq actes et un prologue par Alexandre Dumas et Amédée de Jallais représenté pour la première fois, à Paris, sur le théâtre de l'Ambigu-Comique, le 16 mars 1866. Paris, Michel Lévy frères, n.d. (1866), 4to., pp. 25 in double columns. Caption title. Woodcut at head of title. Théâtre contemporain illustré.

"Gabriel Lambert" drame en cinq actes et un prologue en société avec M. Amédée de Jallais Ambigu-Comique. - 16 mars 1866. "Distribution" on title-page, pp. (163)-299. Théâtre complet de Alex. Dumas Tome XXIV Paris, Calmann-Lévy, éditeur ancienne maison Michel Lévy frères, 1874. 12mo. "Théâtre complet" in 25 volumes.

"LES HOMMES DE FER"
'PEPIN; CHRONIQUE DU ROI PEPIN'
'CHARLEMAGNE; CHRONIQUE DE CHARLEMAGNE'   1867
'LE SIRE DE GIAC; LA MAIN DROITE DU SIRE DE GIAC'
'GUELFES ET GIBELINS'

Of these four short works the first two are purely and simply, as their titles indicate, 'chronicle' stories; "Le sire de Giac; ... ... ' is an historical romance; while the final work is an historical study including in its last half a translation from Dante.

Original edition.
"Les hommes de fer" par Alexandre Dumas Paris Michel Lévy frères, éditeurs, ... , 1867, 12mo., pp. 305, verso blank, and an additional unnumbered page table of contents. Pagination : 'Pépin' (1)-58; 'Charlemagne' (59)-180; 'Le sire de Giac' (181)-241, verso blank; 'Guelfes et Gibelins' (243)-305.
Reprinted, same format and pagination, by both Michel Lévy frères and Calmann-Lévy.

"LA TERREUR PRUSSIENNE"   1867

As early as 1848 Dumas, during his candidature for the Chamber of Deputies, had warned France with quite remarkable prescience of the danger of Prussian invasion. In mid-1866 there occurred the 'Seven

Weeks' War' in which Prussia defeated Austria and in July of that year occupied Frankfurt. In Paris there had appeared a new anti-Prussian paper called 'La Situation' and its proprietor commissioned from Dumas a romance based on the events in the war. Dumas went to Frankfurt in the autumn of 1866 and visited battlefields, his book being written with the precise intention of once more awakening his countrymen to the menace on their doorstep. Fortunately he did not live to know of the defeats of 1870-1871.

'La Situation' stipulated that there should be sixty feuilletons, each of four hundred lines. Dumas made only one request, which was granted, and that was that he should be allowed to use his own characters. To fill in the required space he included hunting stores related by the hero of the romance, the tragic action of which takes place between 7th June, 1866, and 5th June, 1867.

The first appearance of the work was thus : Alexandre Dumas. "La Terreur Prussienne. Episode de la guerre en 1866". Paris, Bibliothèque de la Situation, Journal Politique, 1867, 4to., pp. (3), 192 in double columns.

Original edition.
"La terreur prussienne à Frankfort Episode de la guerre en 1866". Par Alexandre Dumas. Paris. 1868. Naumbourg s/S., chez G. Paetz, Libraire-Editeur, 24mo., 4 volumes, pp. 160, 160, 160 and 173 (the last page being unnumbered). Bibliothèque choisie. Nos. 916-919.

"La terreur prussienne" par Alexandre Dumas Paris Michel Lévy frères, éditeurs ... ... , 1868, 12mo., 2 volumes, pp. 296 and additional unnumbered page table of contents, and 292, (293)-294 table of contents.
Several times reprinted, same format and pagination, by both Michel Lévy frères and Calmann-Lévy.

"L'ECOLE DES BEAUX-ARTS"   1867

The title of this article is self-explanatory. It should, perhaps, be mentioned that in the opening pages of the work noted below there are reproduced facsimile autographs of the contributors and Dumas' autograph is naturally included.

Original edition.
"Paris guide" par les principaux écrivains et artistes de la France. Paris, Librairie internationale; Bruxelles, Leipzig, Livourne, A. Lacroix, Verboeckhoven et cie., 1867, 8vo., 2 volumes, pp. xx, xlv, 902, (1)-27 'index', and xxiv, (903)-2140, both with maps and plates. "L'école des beaux-arts" par Alexandre Dumas is included in Volume 1, pp. 855-876.
A second edition was published in the same year.

"PROJET D'UNE ECOLE NATIONALE DE PEINTURE, DE SCULPTURE
ET DE LITTERATURE"   c 1867

The nature of this pamphlet is again self-explanatory.

It was published under the above title, carries no title-page but with a caption title, n.d. (c 1867), 8vo., pp. 3, signed : Lundi,

11 heures du soir. Alexandre Dumas. The pamphlet has plain rose-
coloured wrappers.

"PARISIENS ET PROVINCIAUX"   1867

 The period of this work, which deals largely with hunting and
family life, is 1840. De Cherville had a small share in the writing
of the earlier portions of it, but Dumas completed it himself. Pifteau in his "Alexandre Dumas en manches de chemise" is quite wrong in
stating that all of the earlier part was written by de Cherville.
The work was written in 1864 when it was published serially in 'La
Presse'.

Original edition.
"Parisiens et provinciaux" par Alexandre Dumas. Paris, 1867. Tes-
chen, chez Charles Prochaska, Libr.-Editeur, 24mo., 4 volumes, pp.
160, 160, 160 and 142.

"Parisiens et provinciaux" par Alexandre Dumas Paris Michel Lévy
frères, libraires éditeurs ... , 1868, 12mo. 2 volumes, pp. 288, (289)-
290 (wrongly numbered 326) table of contents, and 274, (275)-276 table
of contents.
Reprinted, same format and pagination, Calmann-Lévy, c 188 .

"LES FOUS DU DOCTEUR MIRAGLIA"   1867

 This work may well have been originally published in 'L'Indépendant - L'Indipendente' but it was certainly published as an article,
in three parts, in 'La Presse' on 6th, 7th and 8th June, 1863.

 It was dedicated to Dr. A. Castle the phrenologist who, some ten
years earlier, had written a pamphlet entitled "Phrenological examination of the character of Alexandre Dumas". "Les fous du docteur Miraglia" first describes the appearances of Dr. Miraglia's patients,
then goes on to give a description of the skulls of four criminals
and an account of their crimes. There is finally described their
performances in the play "Le Bourgeois de Gand", by Romand, which
Miraglia had arranged for them to perform in Dumas' presence.

Original edition.
"Jacques Ortis" - "Les fous du docteur Miraglia" - par Alexandre
Dumas Paris Michel Lévy frères, libraires-éditeurs ... , 1867, 12mo.,
pp. 306 and an additional unnumbered page table of contents. "Jacques
Ortis" ends on page 260, being followed by "Les fous du docteur Mira-
glia", pp. (261)-306.
Reprinted, same format and pagination, Calmann-Lévy, 1885, 1897.

"LES BLANCS ET LES BLEUS"   (Romance)
"LA HUITIEME CROISADE"   1867-1868

 On 18th November, 1866, the journal 'Les Nouvelles' changed its
title to 'Le Mousquetaire' (deuxième série) after Dumas had acquired
control, and on 21st November, 1866, there was published his 'avant-
propos' to a work "Les bleus et les blancs : Roman national" in 6
volumes, as it was then entitled. In the issue for 13th January, 1867,
the romance started publication and it continued to appear with a

broken sequence of only four separate issues until 22nd February, 1867. This did not finally consist of the announced 6 volumes, but is nevertheless a complete story in itself with the sub-title : "Les prussiens sur le Rhin", its period being 1793. Ultimately two additional sections entitled : "Le 13 vendémiaire" and "Le 18 fructidor" were written, with a final supplementary one called : "La huitième croisade"; the first two of these covered the years 1795-1797, and the last that of the campaign from Acre to Aboukir, 1799. These three additional portions were published serially in 'La petite presse'. In an introductory footnote to "La huitième croisade" Dumas wrote that he intended to write a further section which would carry on the history of the Empire to 1815, but this was never written.

The whole work, now known as "Les blancs et les bleus", is complementary to "Les compagnons de Jéhu" and was dedicated in Dumas' 'avant-propos' as follows : 'Ce livre est dédié à mon illustre ami et collaborateur Charles Nodier. J'ai did 'collaborateur' parce que l'on se donnerait la peine d'en chercher un autre, et que ce serait peine perdue!'

Original edition.
"Les blancs et les bleus" par Alexandre Dumas Paris Michel Lévy frères, libraires éditeurs ... , 1867-1868, 12mo., 3 volumes. Pagination : Volume 1 (1867), (1)-4 'avant-propos', (5)-302, (303)-305 table of contents; Volumes 2-3 (1868), ("Le 13 vendémiaire") 199, verso blank, ("Le 18 fructidor") (201)-319, verso blank, (321)-323 table of contents, and ("Le 18 fructidor" - suite), 124, ("La huitième croisade") (125)-260, (261)-263 table of contents.
Occasionally reprinted, same format and pagination, Calmann-Lévy.

"LES TAUREAUX ESPAGNOLS AU HAVRE"   (1868)
The title of this pamphlet is self-explanatory.

Original (and only) edition.
"Les taureaux espagnols au Havre", par Alexandre Dumas. Première, deuxième et troisième courses. Programme de la quatrième. Prix 25 cent. Chez tous les libraires du Havre, n.d. (1868), 24mo., pp. 47. The wrapper forms the title-page.

"ARTICLES SUR L'EXPOSITION AU HAVRE"   1868
An International Marine Exhibition was held at Le Havre during 1868, and Dumas gave there a series of lectures which, according to Ferry, mostly dealt with Dumas' Russian travels and experiences. These lectures appeared in the Paris newspapers, but seemingly have not been collected and published in volume form. One 'causerie' is, however, known from the following :

"Havre-de-Grâce : Exposition Maritime Internationale au Havre pour 1868". Programme officiel ... No. 7. 8vo. This contains 'Causerie sur le compagnie transatlantique'.

"SOUVENIRS DRAMATIQUES"   1868
This book consists of a collection of articles previously contri-

buted to various journals, among them 'Le Mousquetaire' and 'Le Monte-Cristo'.

Original edition.
"Souvenirs dramatiques" par Alexandre Dumas Paris Michel Lévy frères, libraires éditeurs ... , 1868, 12mo., 2 volumes, pp. 421, verso blank, and additional unnumbered page table of contents, and 436 and additional unnumbered page table of contents.

Vol. 1 : 'Les mystères. Le théatre des anciens et le notre. William Shakespeare. De la subvention des théatres. Corneille et le Cid. Pichat et son léonidas La littérature et les hommes d'état. Mon Odyssée a la comédie-française. Les trois Phédre. Action et réaction. Le baron Taylor.'
Vol. 2 : 'L'Oedipe de Sophocle et l'Oedipe de Voltaire. Othello. La camaraderie, les collaborateurs et M. Scribe. Le Louis XI de Mély-Janin et le Louis XI de Casimir Delavigne. De la critique littéraire. Les auteurs dramatiques au conseil d'état. Dix ans de la vie d'une femme, ou la moralité de M. Scribe. A propos de Mauprat. Henri V et Charles II. De la nécessité d'un second théatre-français L'Ulysse de Ponsard.'
Reprinted, same format and pagination, Calmann-Lévy, 1881.

"MADAME DE CHAMBLAY"   (Drama)   1868
        Only some of the plot of the romance of the same name from which Dumas drew this play was used, and on his own admission he found the writing of the dénouement difficult; the ending is certainly rather weak and melodramatic. No collaborator has ever been suggested. The play was first performed at the Salle Ventadour on 4th June, 1868.

Original edition.
"Madame de Chamblay" drame en cinq actes par Alexandre Dumas Paris Michel Lévy frères, éditeurs rue Vivienne, 2 bis, et boulevard des Italiens, 15 A la librairie nouvelle 1869 Droits de reproduction, de traduction et de représentation réservés. 12mo., 6 unnumbered pages 'Un mot sur la pièce et sur les artistes', unnumbered page 'préface' "Aristide" tragédie en une scène verso unnumbered page 'personnages', pp. (1)-96. Half-title : "Madame de Chamblay" drame Représenté sur le théâtre de la Porte-Saint-Martin le 31 octobre 1868. Green wrappers repeating the title-page but dated 'MDCCCLXIX'. Clichy - Impr. M. Loignon, Paul Dupont et Cie., rue du Bac-dernières, 12.

"Madame de Chamblay" drame en cinq actes par Alexandre Dumas représenté pour la première fois (sic), à Paris, sur le théatre de la Porte-Saint-Martin, le 31 octobre 1868. Paris, Michel Lévy frères, n.d. (1869), 4to., pp. (1)-2 'Un mot sur le pièce et sur les artistes' signed : Alexandre Dumas, (3)-19 in double columns. Caption title. Woodcut at head of title. Théâtre contemporain illustré.

"Madame de Chamblay" drame en cinq actes Salle Ventadour. - 4 juin 1868 Porte-Saint-Martin. - 31 octobre 1868. Pp. (1)-5 'Un mot sur la pièce et sur les artistes' signed : Alex. Dumas. Unnumbered page 'preface' "Aristide" tragédie en une scène, and "Distribution", pp. 7-91. Théatre complet de Alex. Dumas Tome XXV Paris, Calmann-Lévy, éditeur ancienne maison Michel Lévy frères, 1874. 12mo. "Théâtre complet" in 25 volumes.

"Madame de Chamblay", drame en cinq actes, en prose, par Alexandre Dumas. Paris, Calmann-Lévy, 1881, 12mo., pp. 91, and omitting 'Un mot sur la pièce et sur les artistes'.
(Apparently the play was revived in this year.)

"CAROLINE DE BRUNSWICK REINE D'ANGLETERRE SA VIE, - SON PROCES, - SA MORT"   1868

The title of this work is self-explanatory.

Original (and only) edition.
"Caroline de Brunswick reine d'Angleterre sa vie, - son procès. - sa mort" par Alexandre Dumas. I. Paris, 1868. Naumbourg s/S., chez G. Paetz, libraire-éditeur. 24mo., pp. 147 (1). Pale blue wrappers. Illustrated.
At the bottom of page 147 is printed : 'Note de l'éditeur. La suite de cet ouvrage n'est pas encore délivrée par M. Alexandre Dumas'.

"DARTAGNAN" journal d'Alexandre Dumas   1868

This latest venture of Dumas as the owner of a journal started publication on 4th February, 1868, and continued in existence until 4th July of that year, comprising in all 66 numbers. It was published every Tuesday, Thursday and Saturday. In it appeared once again "Histoire de mes bêtes", some of which had already been published in the first 'Le Mousquetaire' and reprinted in 'Les Nouvelles'. There was also reprinted "Un volontaire de '92", of which 48 chapters had been published in 'Le Monte-Cristo' during 1862. Again, a number of 'causeries' was included, probably the most important of which dealt with the sinking of the 'Vengeur' on the so-called 'glorious First of June'. It is of some interest that Dumas' daughter, Madame Petel, contributed to the journal.

"Dartagnan" journal d'Alexandre Dumas Rédacteur en Chef : Alexandre DUMAS Administrateur : Alfred MERCIER Le Sécretaire de la Rédaction : Georges LE BARROIS Abonnements : Paris et Départements Trois mois ... 4 fr. Six mois ... 8 fr. Un an ... 15 fr. Etranger, port en sus. Le Numéro : 10 centimes. Ecrire pour tout ce qui concerne la rédaction, à M. Alexandre DUMAS, 107, boulevard Malesherbes. Typographie Alcan-Lévy, boulevard de Clichy.

"THEATRE-JOURNAL"   1868-1869

After 'Dartagnan' had ceased publication Dumas, on the day following its final number, started the final journal under his own control. It has been stated that he was, in fact, 'rédacteur en chef' of the 'Théâtre-Journal' from 4th February, 1868, and this could very well be true. The 'Théâtre-Journal' was published only on Sundays, and ran from 5th July, 1868, to 14th March, 1869, in all 36 numbers.

"LES BLANCS ET LES BLEUS"   (Drama)   (1869)

This play was drawn from the first part only of Dumas' romance of the same name. He had no collaborator in its writing, and it was the last play to be written, performed and published during Dumas' life-time. It was apparently successful, and Gabriel Ferry in his "Les dernières années d'Alexandre Dumas 1864-1870" wrote interestingly on its production at the Châtelet : 'Comme le Châtelet ne possédait pas une troupe d'ensemble suffisante pour jouer un drame de l'impor-tance de "Les blancs et les bleus", on alla chercher des interprètes au dehors. Laray fut engagé spécialement pour remplir le rôle de Pichegru. Taillade fut demandé à l'Odéon pour tenir le personnage de Saint-Just.' ... .'

Original edition.
"Les blancs et les bleus" drame en cinq actes, en onze tableaux par Alexandre Dumas représenté pour la première fois, à Paris, sur le théatre du Chatelet, le 10 mars 1869. Paris, Michel Lévy frères, n.d. (1869), 4to., pp. 28 in double columns. Caption title. Woodcut at head of title. Théâtre complet d'Alexandre Dumas.
Reprinted, same format and pagination, n.d. (1874).

"Les blancs et les bleus" drame en cinq actes, en onze tableaux Châtelet. - 10 mars 1869. "Distribution" on title-page and part page 94, pp. 94-192. Théatre complet de Alex. Dumas Tome XXV Paris, Calmann-Lévy, éditeur ancienne maison Michel Lévy frères, 1874. 12mo. "Théatre complet" in 25 volumes.

"CAUSERIE SUR L'ITALIE"   1869
        This work consists of a guide to places and things worth seeing in Italy. It is, perhaps, worth mentioning that an article entitled 'Charlotte Dreyfus et Alexandre Dumas' was published in 'Les matinées Espagnoles' in the issue for 30th March, 1874.

Original (and only) edition.
"Causerie sur l'Italie" par M. Alexandre Dumas. 'A Madame Charlotte Dreyfus'. Paris, Impr. de Schiller, 1869, 8vo., pp. 15.

"CREATION ET REDEMPTION"   1870
("LE DOCTEUR MUSTERIEUX" "LA FILLE DU MARQUIS")
        This long work, again divided into parts for the convenience of publication in the editions issued in France, was Dumas' final great effort in the writing of a romance. It is concerned with the adven-tures of a doctor and a young girl during several of the Revolutionary years - the period for "Le docteur mystérieux" is 1785-1793, and for "La fille du marquis" 1793-1794. It is undoubtedly Dumas working alone, and Chincholle in his "Alexandre Dumas aujourd'hui" emphasises this by stating that Dumas himself searched out all the necessary references.
        The work must have been maturing in Dumas' brain over a consider-able period, for in an article entitled 'De la critique et surtout les critiques' included in the speciman number of 'Le Mousquetaire' dated 12th November, 1853, he wrote that he had agreed with the owners of 'La Revue de Paris' for its publication of the work in serial form. There was then a very long lapse. Chincholle says that Dumas was dictating it to a secretary in 1867, and goes on to add that it was intended to be published in 'Le Siècle'; indeed, Dumas had previously announced it for publication in his 'Dartagnan'. That it was published

serially would seem to be indicated by the original edition, as well as that published in the United States, described below.

Original edition.
"Création et rédemption" roman par Alexandre Dumas. Paris, 1870. Naumbourg s/S., chez G. Paetz, Libraire-éditeur. 24mo., 8 volumes, pp. 160, 158 and 1 leaf of publisher's advertisements, 160, 160, 160, 160, 160, and 138 and 3 leaves of publisher's advertisements. La Bibliothèque choisie. Nos. 1061-1068.

"Création et rédemption" par Alexandre Dumas New-York Charles Lassalle, éditeur, ... , 1870, 4to., pp. 378 in double columns. Semaine littéraire. Volume 35, nos. 1-12, 23 juillet - 8 octobre, 1870.

"Création et rédemption Le docteur mystérieux" par Alexandre Dumas Paris Michel Lévy frères, libraires éditeurs ... , 1872, 12mo., 2 volumes, pp. 319, verso blank, and additional unnumbered page table of contents, and 311, verso table of contents.

"Création et rédemption La fille du marquis" par Alexandre Dumas Paris Michel Lévy frères, libraires éditeurs ... , 1872, 12mo., 2 volumes, pp. 274 and additional unnumbered page table of contents, and 281, verso blank, and additional unnumbered page table of contents. Several times reprinted, same format and pagination, by both Michel Lévy frères and Calmann-Lévy.

"INTRIGUES GALANTES A LA COUR ITALIENNE"   1870

According to Lorenz in his "Catalogue général de la librairie française" the author of this book was one Paul Fuchs, and it was : 'signé du pseudonyme d'Alexandre Dumas'. The work deals with the period of Victor-Emmanuel with which Dumas was very familiar and, moreover, opens with the description of a hunt - a subject beloved by Dumas. I disagree with Lorenz.

Original (and only) edition.
"Intrigues galantes à la cour Italienne" Roman par Alexandre Dumas Propriété de l'Editeur Wurzbourg F.A. Julien libraire-éditeur, 1870, 24mo., pp. 288, in 7 chapters. Verso of title-page : Imprimerie Bieling (Dietz), Nurembourg.
The chapters are entitled : 1. 'Une chasse royale'. 2. 'Bianca di Rissoli'. 3. 'La signora Bianca d'Alighieri'. 4. 'Heureux amants'. 5. 'Une mission secrète'. 6. 'La bataille de Mentana ou "Rome ou la mort!"'. 7. 'Rétribution'.

"LE ROMAN DE VIOLETTE"   1870

There is some quite considerable element of doubt as to whether this work was, in fact, written by Dumas. As will be seen it is stated on the title-page as an 'oeuvre posthume d'une célébrite masquée'; the very word posthumous is the main reason for having doubts as to its being attributable to Dumas who, as will be well-known, died in December, 1870. In the months immediately previous to his death Dumas did not write, and if it was written at some earlier period why was its publication delayed to the few weeks following his death?

354

But if the style of writing, which is light and flowing and quite typical of Dumas, is considered then a reasonably convincing case can be made for it having been written by him, conceivably in the late 1830's and then thrown aside. Furthermore, the writer's references to 'mes chers lecteurs et chères lectrices', as well as the illusions to mythology, and mythological goddesses and persons, give additional strength to the fact that the work could have come from his pen. If he did write it there may exist somewhere letters from him to the publisher, or other persons, referring to the work and how and why it should be published under a pseudonym.

Original (and only) edition.
"Le roman de Violette" oeuvre posthume d'une célébrite masquée (Vignette) Lisbonne chez Antonio da Boa-Vista 1870 16mo., pp. (1)-2 'avant-propos', (3)-195. Title-page printed in black and red. Halftitle : "Le roman de Violette". No printer's name is given. Half leather red binding, which may not have been the original. Printed on hand-made paper.

"LE CAPITAINE RHINO"
"LE LION PERE DE FAMILLE"
"UNE CHASSE AU TIGRE"   1872

This book contains these three stories issued under the general title of the first. The first two were translated and puplished in 1868 in 'Dartagnan', having been previously published, anonymously, in the 'Temple Bar Magazine'.

Original edition.
"Le capitaine Rhino" publié par Alexandre Dumas Paris Michel Lévy frères, libraires éditeurs ... , 1872, 12mo., pp. (i)-iv 'Avant-propos' signed : A.D., "Le capitaine Rhino" (5)-128; "Le lion père de famille" (129)-177; "Une chasse au tigre" (179)-223, verso table of contents.
Several times reprinted, same format and pagination, by both Michel Lévy frères and Calmann-Lévy.

"LE PRINCE DE VOLEURS"   1872
"ROBIN HOOD LE PROSCRIT"   1873

These two works comprise a slightly abridged version of Pierce Egan the younger's long novel "Robin Hood and Little John; or, the Merry Men of Sherwood Forest". Scott's "Ivanhoe" had made Robin Hood's name familiar in France as well as in England, and this may explain why Dumas published a translation of this particular work. As with "Ivanhoe" Victor Perceval had the work published as having been translated by himself, and it is highly likely that the version 'publié par Alexandre Dumas' is Perceval's.

Original edition.
"Le prince des voleurs" publié par Alexandre Dumas Paris Michel Lévy frères, libraires éditeurs ... , 1872, 12mo., 2 volumes, pp. (1)-5 unsigned 'préface', verso blank, (7)-293, and 275. There are no tables of contents.

"Robin Hood le proscrit" publié par Alexandre Dumas Paris Michel

Lévy frères, éditeurs ... , 1873, 12mo., 2 volumes, pp. 262 and 273.
There are no tables of contents.
Both works several times reprinted, same format and pagination, by
both Michel Lévy frères and Calmann-Lévy.

"GRAND DICTIONNAIRE DE CUISINE" 1873

Dumas, an expert and practical cook, was always interested in
the various national dishes of the countries he visited or in which
he travelled. It had been his wish for many years to compile a work
dealing with food and its preparation, and reference may be made here
to, among other similar articles, the 'causerie culinaire' which he
wrote for his journal 'Le Monte-Cristo'. As is known he was under contract with Lévy for the publishing of the general run of his works,
but for this immense book he reserved his own right of publication.
The pity of it is that because of the intervention of the Franco-
Prussian War his work could not be published until more than two years
after his death.

Reference will be found later in this Bibliography to his "Petit
dictionnaire de cuisine".

Original edition .
"Grand dictionnaire de cuisine" par Alexandre Dumas (Vignette)
Paris Alphonse Lemerre, éditeur 27-39, passage Choiseul, 27-29
M DCCC LXXII (title-page printed in black and red). Demy quarto.
Pagination : half-title "Alexandre Dumas et le grand dictionnaire
de cuisine", verso blank, (iii)-vi 'Alexandre Dumas et le grand dictionnaire de cuisine' signed : L.T., lithograph portrait of D.-J.
Vuillemot, unnumbered page 'A M. D.-J. Vuillemot' signed : A. Lemerre, verso blank, (1)-33 'Quelques mots au lecteur' signed : Alexandre Dumas, 34-35 'Une cuisine modèle', (36)-97 consisting of letter
'A Jules Janin' signed : Alexandre Dumas, (98)-103 'Calendrier gas-
tronomique par Grimod de la Reynière', (104)-106 'Encore un mot au
public' signed : A.D., (107)-1087 comprising the dictionary proper
starting with 'Abaisse' and ending with 'Vespétro', 1087-1126 comprising the section dealing with 'Vins' and 'Vinaigre', 1126-(1138)
completing the dictionary proper, (1139)-1155 comprising 'Menus'. verso
: imprimé par J. Claye pour A. Lemerre, éditeur a Paris. Les portraits ont été gravés par Rajon et imprimés par SALMON. Unnumbered
page 'Annexe au grand dictionnaire de cuisine', verso blank, 3-11
'Annexe au grand dictionnaire de cuisine' Maison Alexandre BORNIBUS
60, boulevard de la Villete, a Paris. 'Etude sur la moutarde' Par
Alexandre Dumas. 'Réponse à une lettre anonyme adressée aux gourmandes
de tous les pays' signed : Alexandre DUMAS. Page 12 'Annexe' consisting of an advertisement by Maison Potel et Chabot boulevard des
Italiens, 25, et rue Vivienne, 28. Frontispiece : lithograph portrait of Dumas. The work was published at 20 francs. Additionally,
there were editions of 50 numbered copies on 'papier de Hollande'
published at 40 francs, and of 5 copies - the latter being presented
to Rajon.

"PROPOS D'ART ET DE CUISINE" 1877

This is another collection of Dumas' articles and 'causeries'.

356

Original edition.
"Propos d'art et de cuisine" par Alexandre Dumas Paris Calmann Lévy,
éditeur ancienne maison Michel Lévy frères ... , 1877, 12mo., pp. 304,
and additional unnumbered page table of contents.

Contents : 1 'La retraite illuminée'. 2 'Causerie culinaire'.
3 ' "Romulus" et "Pizarre" '. 4 'Le cimitière Clamart'.
5 'De la sculpture et des sculpteurs'. 6 'Les gorilles'.
7 'Le triomphe de la paix'. (Par Eugène Delacroix).
8 'Le Carmel'. 9 'Mon ami Colbrun'. 10 'Cas de conscience'. 11 'Un poëte anacréontique'. 12 'La revue
nocturne'. 13 'Une séance de magnétisme'. 14 'Etude de
tête d'après la Bosse'.
Reprinted, same format and pagination, Calmann-Lévy, 1894.

Of the above, nos. 1, 2, 8, 11 and 12 were first printed in 'Le Monte-
Cristo'; no. 6 in "Bric-a-brac"; nos. 3, 4, 7, 9, 10 and 14 in 'Le
Mousquetaire', as was also no. 5 but over the name of Dumas fils;
no. 13 comprises the second of two articles which were printed originally in 'La Presse' (this latter on 16th September, 1847) and reprinted in 'La Revue de Paris' in October and November, 1947 - the
first article was never reprinted.
Earlier printings of two of the articles were as follows :

"Les quarante-cinq" par Alexandre Dumas. Bruxelles, Livourne,
Meline, Cans et compagnie; Leipzig, J.P. Meline, 1847, 18mo., 6 volumes, the final volume pp. 225. "Les quarante-cinq" ends on page 108,
and is followed by "Une amazone", pp. 109-192, and "Une séance de
magnétisme chez M. Alexandre Dumas", pp. 193-225.

Ibid   La Haye, chez les héritiers Doorman, 1847, same
format and pagination as the preceding edition.

Collection Hetzel. "Ainsi soit-il!" par Alex. Dumas. Edition
autorisée pour la Belgique et l'Etranger, interdite pour la France.
Paris, Jung-Treuttel ... , 1861, 24mo., 4 volumes. "Ainsi soit-il!"
ends on page 107 of Volume 4, and is followed by "Une séance de magnétisme", pp. 111-125, and by "Etude de Tête d'après la Bosse". pp.
129-152. On page facing the title-page : Déposé aux termes de la
loi. Bruxelles - Typ. de Ve J. van Buggenhoudt.

"JOSEPH BALSAMO"   (Drama)   1878

    In his letter to Napoleon III which is printed as an introduction
to his play "Les Mohicans de Paris" Dumas refers to this drama, and
also to the play he was drawing from the romance "Olympe de Clèves"
which he never finished. Lecomte, in his "Alexandre Dumas 1802-1870
Sa Vie intime Ses Oeuvres" has written : 'Enfin l'on peut, très
raisonnablement, attribuer à Dumas père une certaine part dans "Joseph
Balsamo", drame en 5 actes et 8 tableaux, représenté à l'Odéon, le 18
mars 1878, sous le nom et pars les soins de Dumas fils ... '.

    The play was never published, but excerpts from it can be read
in "Alexandre Dumas père et la Franc-Maçonnerie" par Côte-Darly
(Mme. A. Lantoine) Paris Collection du 'Symbolisme', 1924.

"LA SAN-FELICE"   (Drama)   1881

    This entry is self-explanatory.

Original edition.
"La San-Felice", drame en cinq actes et sept tableaux, tiré du roman
d'Alexandre Dumas, par M. Maurice Drack (pseudonyme d'Auguste Poite-
vin). Représenté pour la première fois, à Paris, au Théâtre du
Château-d'eau, le 11 novembre 1881. Paris, Calmann-Lévy, ancienne
maison Michel Lévy frères, n.d. (1881), 4to., pp. 34 in double columns.
Caption title. Woodcut at head of title.
Reprinted, same format and pagination, (c 1882).

"PETIT DICTIONNAIRE DE CUISINE"   1882

     As can be seen this briefer version, in smaller format, of the
"Grand dictionnaire de cuisine" is quite considerably curtailed, and
was clearly published for active use in the kitchen - in other words
a cook's working copy. All introductory articles are omitted with the
exception of 'Encore un mot au public' with a revised title. The
dictionary proper is not so comprehensive and fewer menus are listed.

Original (and only) edition.
"Petit dictionnaire de cuisine" par Alexandre Dumas (Vignette)
Paris Alphonse Lemerre, éditeur 27-31, passage Choiseul, 27-31
M D CCC LXXXII 8vo. Pagination : half-title "Petit dictionnaire
de cuisine", (i)-iii 'Un mot au public' signed : Alexandre Dumas,
verso blank, (1)-785 comprising the dictionary proper starting with
'Abaisse' and ending with 'Vespétro', 785-800 comprising the section
dealing with 'Vins' et 'Vinnaigre', 800-808 completing the dictionary
proper, (809)-819 comprising 'Menus'. Decorated grey boards. "Dictionnaire de Cuisine" par Alexandre Dumas revu et complété par J.
VUILLEMOT, Elève de Carême Ancien Cuisinier, Propriétaire de l'Hôtel
de la Cloche, à Compiègne, etc. Paris Alphonse Lemerre, éditeur
27-31, passage Choisseul, 27-31 Spine : A. Dumas Dictionnaire de
cuisine Paris A. Lemerre éditeur. Paris. - Typ. Ch. Unsinger, 83,
rue du Bac.

"VOYAGE EN BOURBONNAIS"   1884

     This is the reprint of an 'Extrait de la 'Revue Bourbonnaise' '
published in that review's issues for February, March and April, 1884.

Original (and only) edition.
Alexandre Dumas "Voyage en Bourbonnais une visite a Achille Allier"
(Vignette) Moulins imprimerie de C. Desrosiers. 1884. Pp. (1)-2
consist of an introductory note signed : A.R. Moulins, 10 février
1884, with a footnote on page (1) : 'Alexandre Dumas "Impressions
de voyage. Le midi de la France", Tome I, P. 64-96 Nouv. édit. Calmann-Levy, éditeur, (Vignette) 3-39. The work is divided into 5 sections entitled : 'Moulins', 'Souvigny', 'Bourbon-l'Archambault',
'Saint-Menoux' and 'La Palice'. There is one full-page illustration
of the Chapelle Neuve de Souvigny and several vignettes. Blue wrappers
repeating the title-page. Moulins. - Imprimerie C. Desrosiers.

"LA FIN DE MURAT"   (Drama)   1890

     This entry is self-explanatory.

Original (and only) edition.
Jean Berleux. "La fin de Murat" en trois tableaux D'après Alexandre
Dumas Paris Paul Ollendorff éditeur ... 1890. 8vo., pp. unnumbered
'préface' signed : J.B., verso of the final page of the preface
'personnages', (9)-60, with : 'Villers-le-Sec, octobre, 1889.' Frontispiece drawing of Joachim Murat. Printed on 'papier Hollande'. Green
wrappers.

The following works can only, because of their varied nature, be
placed in a section devoted to 'miscellanea'. Their titles and contents speak for themselves.

'Le monde dramatique' Tome premier 1835 Illustrated title-page
followed by second title-page 'Le monde dramatique' (Vignette)
'revue des spectacles anciens et modernes'. 8vo., pp. (i)-iv 'Introduction' signed : Frédéric Soulié, (v)-vi 'Prospectus' signed :
L'Editeur, 1-408, followed by 3 pages 'table générale' and 6 unnumbered leaves 'classement des gravures'. Pp. 57-59 "Mystères" (Vignette) "Histoire de l'ancien Théatre Français - Les confrères de la
passion" signed : Alexandre Dumas.

"Contes et nouvelles". Par Alexandre Dumas. (Vignette) Bruxelles.
Meline, Cans et compagnie, 1838, 16mo., pp. 259, verso blank, and
additional unnumbered page table of contents. Contents : "La main
droite du sire du Giac. Scenes historiques. 1425-1426", pp. (5)-54;
"Pascal Bruno. Roman historique", pp. (55)-199; verso blank; "M. le
baron Taylor", pp. (201)-241; verso blank; "Une visite a Nimes", pp.
(243)-253; verso blank; A M. Alexandre Dumas. 'Les arènes de Nimes' ",
pp. (255)-259, signed : J. Reboul. Yellow wrappers repeating the
title-page.

'La Sylphide. Modes, littérature, beaux-arts'. Deuxième série. Tome
IV. (Vignette) Paris. Aux bureaux de la sylphide, 1841, 4to. In-
cludes "Obéissance. A Mme. E^{XXX} de H^{XXX}." Signed : Alex. Dumas.
This is a poem consisting of three verses each of 5 lines.

"L'histoire et la poésie" signed : Alexandre Dumas. Published in
'L'ane d'or'. Egrin littéraire. (Extrait de 'La revue pittoresque',
1844.) Pp. 2-4 in four columns.

'Nouveau Tableau de Paris' - Balzac, Dumas, Soulié, Gozlan, Monnier,
... . Illustré par Gavarni, Daumier, D'Aubigny, Traviés, H. Monnier.
Paris, Marescq et Cie., 1845, 8vo., pp. 416. 15 places hors-texte.

"Fragments des oeuvres d'Alexandre Dumas", choisis a l'usage de la
jeunesse. Par Miss Mary Russell Mitford. (Portrait of Dumas) Londres. Pierre Rolandi, libraire. ... 1846. 8vo., pp. (i)-ii 'Préface',
(iii)-iv 'Advertisement' (in English) signed : Mary Russell Mitford
... Oct. 10th 1846, (v)-xiii 'M. Alexandre Dumas. Notice biographique', verso blank, 'Fragments choisis des oeuvres d'Alexandre Dumas'
(unnumbered), (1)-480, (481)-483 table of contents. 'Ces fragments
sont choisis dans quelques-uns des romans historiques de l'auteur, et
dans ces "Impressions de voyage", où il donne l'essor à sa brillante
imagination'.

"Eau de mélisse des Carmes déchaussés de la rue de Vaugirard. Mono-
graphie historique et médicale par Boyer, propriétaire de l'Eau de
mélisse des Carmes, seul successeur des Carmes déchaussés de la rue

de Vaugirard". Paris, 14, rue Taranne, et chez tous les libraires,
1859, 18mo., pp. 82 and additional unnumbered page table of contents.
Typ. Cosson et comp.
(According to Vicaire, who states that he learned from Boyer's son-in-
law, Renouard-Larivière, that Dumas was the writer of this publicity
brochure.)

Collection Hetzel "La cuisinière poétique" par M. Charles Monselet
avec le concours de MM. Méry, A. Dumas, Th. de Banville, Th. Gautier,
... ... etc. Bruxelles, Meline, Cans et compagnie, n.d. (c 1859),
24mo., pp. (5)-7 'Invitation a la table', signed : Charles Monselet,
8-196, (197)-199 table of contents. Dumas' contribution was : "Le
poulet roti", pp. 187-190, signed : Alex. Dumas. Green wrappers.
Bruxelles. - typ de Ve J. van Buggenhoudt.

"Petites nouvelles de M. Alexandre Dumas père" et "Causerie a
propos de la dame aux camélias" de M. Alexandre Dumas fils. Paris,
1868. Naumbourg s/S., chez G. Paetz, libraire-éditeur. 24mo. Pagination : half-title "Petites nouvelles et causerie a propos de la
dame aux camélias", "Le dévouement des pauvres petite histoire en
quatre ou cinq chapitres". Par Alexandre Dumas père. (Verso blank),
(7)-38; "L'armoire d'acajou". Par Alexandre Dumas père. (Verso
blank), (41)-63, verso blank. "Le vengeur" par Alexandre Dumas père.
(Verso blank). (67)-86. "Un monsieur qui croit aux rêves" par Alexandre Dumas père. (Verso blank), (89)-92; "Un billet a vue" par
Alexandre Dumas père. (Verso blank), (95)-104; "Les chiens enragés"
par Alexandre Dumas père. (Verso blank), (107)-118; "Les petites
incurables" par Alexandre Dumas père. (Verso blank), (121)-133;
verso blank, "Causerie d'Alexandre fils a propos de la dame aux
camélias", (verso blank), (137)-160. There is no table of contents.
La Bibliothèque choisie. No. 938.

"La vie des bois et du désert Récits de chasse et de pêche" par
Bénédict-Henry Révoil avec deux histoires inédits par Alexandre Dumas
père. (Vignette) Tours Alfred Mame et fils, éditeurs, MDCCCLXXIV,
large 8vo. unnumbered page 'Préface' signed : Bénédict-Henry Revoil
- Paris, 1re septembre 1873, pp. (7)-223, verso blank, (225)-233 "Deux
histoires inédites d'Alexandre Dumas père - La chasse dans le nord de
l'Europe", and (234)-236 "Une chasse a l'ours en Russie", unnumbered
page table of contents. Yellow wrappers repeating title-page. Tours,
impre. Mame.

Petite Collection Rose. Alexandre Dumas. "Contes d'un voyageur".
(Vignette) Paris, Librairie A. Lemerre, n.d. (188), 24mo., pp. (i)-ii
'Notice'; (1)-57 "Alcide Jollivet"; (58)-73 "Comment Saint-Eloi fut
guéri de la Vanité"; (74)-99 "Le bifteck d'ours"; (100)-117 "Le Lazza-
rone et l'Anglais". There is no table of contents. Printed on pink
paper.

Lectures littéraires "Pages choisies des Grands Ecrivains Alexandre
Dumas" Avec une Introduction par Hippolyte Parigot Paris Librairie
Calmann-Lévy, 1897, 8vo., pp. (i)-xxxiii 'Introduction' signed :
Hippolyte Parigot Paris, le 12 janvier 1897, verso blank, (1)-87
première partie 'Mémoires et souvenirs', verso blank, (89)-170 deux-
ième partie 'Impressions de voyage', (171)-303 troisième partie
'Romans', verso blank, (305)-382 quatrième partie 'Théatre', (383)-
384 table of contents.

DETAILED LISTS OF DUMAS' THEATRICAL
WORKS PUBLISHED IN VOLUME SERIES

Oeuvres complètes de Alex. Dumas. Théatre. Paris, Charpentier, libraire-éditeur, rue Montesquieu, N° 4. 1834-1836. 8vo., 6 volumes, frontispieces by Célestin Nanteuil 'tiré sur Chine' to the first 4 volumes. EVERAT, Imprimeur, rue du Cadran, N° 16.

Tome 1 : "Comment je devins Auteur dramatique", pp. (i)-xlvii, signed : Alex. DUMAS. 20 décembre 1833; "Henri III et sa cour"; "Antony"; pp. (1)-325, and additional unnumbered page table of contents.

Tome 2 : "Christine"; "Charles VII"; pp. (1)-384, and additional unnumbered page table of contents, followed by 3 unnumbered pages 'extrait du catalogue de Charpentier. Ouvrages de Mme. Desbordes-Valmore Préface des Poésies de Madame Desbordes-Valmore, Par M. Alex. Dumas' signed : 'Alex. Dumas.'

Tome 3 : "Teresa"; "Richard Darlington"; pp. (1)-490, and additional unnumbered page table of contents.

Tome 4 : "La tour de Nesle" (en participation avec M. F. Gaillardet); "Angèle"; pp. (1)-416, and additional unnumbered page table of contents.

Tome 5 : "Catherine Howard"; "Napoléon"; pp. (1)-500, and additional unnumbered page table of contents.

Tome 6 : "Don Juan de Marana"; "Kean"; pp. (1)-443, and additional unnumbered page table of contents, followed by 16 unnumbered pages catalogue of the 'librairie Charpentier'. The final volume : Imprimé par Mme. Poussin.

Théatre complet d'Alexandre Dumas. Nouvelle édition revue et corrigée par l'auteur. Paris. Librairie de Charles Gosselin, 9, rue Saint-Germain-des-Prés. Tresse, libraire, successeur de Barba, Palais-Royal. MDCCCXLI. 12mo., 3 volumes. Imprimerie de V° Dondey-Dupré, 46, rue Saint-Louis.

Première série : "Henri III et sa cour"; "Stockholm, Fontainebleau et Rome" (the play throughout being entitled "Christine"); "Napoléon Bonaparte"; "Antony"; "Charles VII chez ses grands vassaux"; "Le mari de la veuve"; pp. (1)-425, and additional unnumbered page table of contents.

Deuxième série : "Richard Darlington"; "Teresa"; "La tour de Nesle" (par MM. Gaillardet et ***); "Angèle"; "Catherine Howard"; pp. (1)-509, and additional unnumbered page table of contents.

Troisième série : "Don Juan de Marana"; "Kean"; "Caligula"; "Paul Jones"; "L'Alchimiste"; "Mademoiselle de Belle-Isle"; pp. (1)-558, and additional unnumbered page table of contents.

Reprinted, 3 volumes, same format and pagination, 1843.

Théâtre de Alex. Dumas. Oeuvres nouvelles. Paris, Passard, libraire-éditeur, 9, rue des Grands-Augustins, 1846, 8vo., 4 volumes. Corbeil, impr. Crété.

Tome 1 : "Mademoiselle de Belle-Isle"; "Halifax"; drame en prose et comédie en prose mêlée de chant; pp. 327.

Tome 2 : "Paul Jones"; "L'Alchimiste"; drames en prose et en vers; pp. 315.

Tome 3 : "Le laird de Dumbiky"; "Le mari de la veuve"; drame et comédie en prose; pp. 338.

Tome 4 : "Lorenzino"; "Caligula"; drame en prose et tragédie précédée d'un prologue; pp. 348.

Théatre complet de Alex. Dumas. Paris, Michel Lévy frères, libraires-éditeurs, rue Vivienne, 2 bis, et boulevard des Italiens, 15, à la librairie nouvelle, 1863-1874, 12mo. 15 volumes. Poissy, typ. Bouret et typ. S. Lejay et Cie.

Première série   : "Comment je devins auteur dramatique"; "La chasse et l'amour"; "La noce et l'enterrement"; "Henri III et sa cour"; "Christine"; "Napoléon Bonaparte".

Deuxième série   : "Antony"; "Charles VII chez ses grands vassaux"; "Richard Darlington"; "Teresa"; "Le mari de la veuve".

Troisième série   : "La tour de Nesle"; "Angèle"; "Catherine Howard"; "Don Juan de Marana".

Quatrième série   : "Kean"; "Piquillo"; "Caligula"; "Paul Jones"; "L'Alchimiste".

Cinquième série   : "Mademoiselle de Belle-Isle"; "Un mariage sous Louis XV"; "Lorenzino"; "Halifax"; "Les demoiselles de Saint-Cyr".

Sixième série   : "Louise Bernard"; "Le laird de Dumbiky"; "Une fille du Régent"; "La reine Margot".

Septième serie   : "Intrigue et amour"; "Le chevalier de Maison-Rouge"; "Hamlet"; "Le cachemire vert".

Huitième série   : "Monte-Cristo" (1re partie); "Monte-Cristo" (2e partie); "Le comte de Morcerf" (3e partie de "Monte-Cristo"); "Villefort" (4e partie de "Monte-Cristo").

Neuvième série   : "Catilina"; "La jeunesse des mousquetaires"; "Les mousquetaires".

Dixième série   : "Le chevalier d'Harmental"; "La guerre des femmes"; "Le comte Hermann"; "Trois entr'actes pour "L'amour médecin" ".

Onzième série   : "Urbain Grandier"; "Le vingt-quatre février"; "La chasse au chastre".

Douzième série   : "Romulus"; "La jeunesse de Louis XIV"; "Le marbrier"; "La conscience"; "L'Orestie".

Treizième série   : "La tour Saint-Jacques"; "Le verrou de la reine"; "L'invitation à la valse"; "Les forestiers"; "L'honneur est satisfait".

Quatorzième série : "Le roman d'Elvire"; "L'envers d'une conspiration"; "Le gentilhomme de la montagne"; "La dame de Monsoreau".

Quinzième série   : "Les Mohicans de Paris"; "Gabriel Lambert"; "Madame de Chamblay"; "Les blancs et les bleus".

WORKS TO WHICH DUMAS CONTRIBUTED PREFACES

ANQUETIL   :   "Bianca capello ou Venise et Florence au XVIe
                siècle" avec une préface par Alexandre Dumas Brux-
                elles librairie de Ch. Muquardt, ... Même maison
                à Leipzig et à Gand. 1853, 18mo., 6 volumes. 'Prèface
                de M. Alexandre Dumas. Comment j'aurais dû faire le
                roman de BIANCA CAPELLO, et comment c'est M. ANQUETIL
                qui l'a fait', pp. (i)-xxiv of Volume 1 and signed :
                'Bruxelles, ce quatre août 1853. Alexandre Dumas'.
                Buff wrappers.

BEAUVOIR, Roger de   :   Profile et charges à la plume. "Les soupeurs
                de mon temps". Paris, Achille Faure, 1868, 8vo., pp.
                (iii)-xxxi 'Préface' by Dumas, (3)-243, and additional
                unnumbered page table of contents. Yellow wrappers.

BERTRAND, Léon   :   "Tonton, tontaine, tonton". Préface par Alexandre
                Dumas. Dessins de Martinus. Paris, E. Dentu, 1864,
                8vo., pp. (iii)-xi 'Avant-propos' signed : Alexandre
                Dumas, Naples, ce 15 janvier 1864, (1)-287, and addi-
                tional unnumbered page table of contents. Woodcuts at
                chapter-heads.

CHADEUIL, Gustave   :   "Les amours d'un idiot" Préface par Alexandre
                Dumas. Paris Librairie centrale ... 1870, 12mo.,
                pp. (i)-vi 'Préface' signed : Alexandre Dumas Paris,
                30 octobre 1869, (9)-302. Yellow wrappers.

CHARPILLON   :   "Dictionnaire historique de toutes les communes du
                département de l'Eure. Histoire - Géographie Statis-
                tique" Par M. Charpillon, ancien juge de paix. Avec
                le collaboration de M. l'abbé Caresme. Précédé d'une
                préface d'Alex. Dumas père. Cet ouvrage est publié
                sous le patronage du Conseil général et de M. le Préfet
                de l'Eure. Tome II. (Vignette) Les Andelys, chez
                Delcroix, libraire-éditeur, ... , 1879, 4to., pp. (i)-
                iv 'Préface d'Alexandre Dumas A mon ami Charpillon,
                Juge de Paix à Gisors, auteur du Dictionnaire histor-
                ique du département de l'Eure' signed : Alexandre
                Dumas. Paris, le 22 décembre 1867;' 1-1005 in double
                columns, followed by a map of the département de l'Eure.

CHINCHOLLE, Charles   :   "Dans l'ombre", avec une préface d'Alexandre
                Dumas. Paris, Librairie internationale A. Lacroix,
                Verboeckhoven et Ce, Editeurs ... même maison a Brux-
                elles, a Leipzig, et a Livourne, 1871, 12mo., pp. (vii)-
                xiv 'Préface', (16)-283, verso blank, (285)-286 table
                of contents.

CHINCHOLLE, Charles   :   "Le lendemain de l'amour" avec une préface
                d'Alexandre Dumas. Paris, Calmann-Lévy, 1880, 12mo.,
                verso of title-page : A la mémoire d'Alexandre Dumas,
                pp. (1)-8, 'Préface' signed : Alexandre Dumas, (9)-
                304, (305)-306 table of contents.

364

DEMOUGEOT, Edouard : "Jacques Burke, ou l'or et la mort" drame en
cinq actes. Musique nouvelle de M. Blangy, représenté
pour la première fois, a Paris, sur le Théatre Beaumarchais, le 1er janvier 1865. Aved une préface par M.
Alexandre Dumas. Paris, Michel Lévy frères, n.d.
(1865), 4to., preface consisting of 11 lines signed :
Alexandre Dumas, on the first page of the play, pp.
(2)-21 in double columns.

DESBORDES VALMORE : "Les pleurs" Poésies Nouvelles par Madame
Desbordes Valmore (Vignette) Paris, chez Charpentier,
libraire, Palais-Royal M DCCC XXXIII, 8vo., pp. (i)-
viii signed : Alex. Dumas, (5)-389, verso blank,
and 2 additional unnumbered pages table of contents;
steel engraving frontispiece.

DESBORDES VALMORE, Marceline : "Les Pleurs", poésies nouvelles,
Bruxelles, E. Laurent, 1833, 24mo., pp. (5)-13 'Préface de Alex. Dumas', (14)-219.

EIMANN, D.-L. : "Histoire des cavalières" avec une préface par
Alexandre Dumas. Paris Librairie Charpentier ... .
1854, 8vo., pp. (5)-8 'Au lecteur' signed : Alexandre
Dumas, (9)-184, and additional unnumbered page table
of contents. Yellow wrappers.

FRAMINET, Claude Inventeur du Diamant Américain : "Le diamant et
ses imitations" Préface par Alexandre Dumas. Paris,
En vente chez M. J. Madre, libraire, n.d. (1868), 8vo.,
pp. (i)-xxi 'Préface', verso blank, (1)-42. Green
wrappers.

GERARD, Jules : "Mes dernières chasses - Le tueur de lions" précédée
d'une notice sur Jules Gérard par Alexandre Dumas.
Paris, Calmann-Lévy, 1877, 8vo., pp. (1)-31 Dumas'
'Notice', 242.
Reprinted, same format and pagination, 1882, 1889.

GRISIER, A. : "Les armes et le duel" par A. Grisier professeur
de LL. AA. RR. les princes fils du roi, a l'école
royale polytechnique, au collége royal Henri IV, et au
conservatoire royale de musique, ouvrage agrée par
S.M. l'Empereur de Russie. Préface anecdotique par
Alexandre Dumas. Notice sur l'auteur par Roger de
Beauvoir. - Epitre en vers de Méry. Lettre du comte
Ludovic d'Horbourg. Dessins par E. de Beaumont. A
Paris, chez Garnier frères, libraires, 10, rue Richelieu, 215, Palais-Royal, même maison A Rio-Janeiro,
69, rue d'Ouvidor. 1847. Large 8vo., 2 engravings
following the title-page, 3 unnumbered pages : 'A
Sa Majesté Nicolas 1er Empereur de toutes les Russies
... ... ' signed : A. Grisier, Professeur d'Armes
... ... , verso blank, 1 unnumbered page consisting
of letter addressed to Grisier dated 'Paris, le 12
août 1842' signed : Kisseleff Ambassade impériale de
Russie, verso blank, pp. (7)-9 'Avertissement', signed

: A. Grisier. Paris, septembre 1846, verso blank.
(11)-54 'Préface en forme de causerie, ou causerie en
forme de préface' signed : Alexandre DUMAS, (55)-72
'Notice sur Grisier', Par M. Roger de Beauvoir',
signed : Roger de Beauvoir. De la Folie-Bellanger,
près Grosbois, 4 août 1846, (73)-79 letter to de
Beauvoir signed : E. Grisier, verso blank, (81)-89
'Le duel avant-propos', verso blank, (91)-556,
unnumbered page 'A mes lecteurs' signed : A. Grisier,
verso blank, (559)-565 'A M. Grisier, après la lecture
de son manuscrit' signed : Méry. Paris, Novembre
1846, verso blank, 567-572 'lettre a M. Grisier'
signed : Comte Lud. d'Horbourg. Courbevoie, 6
décembre, followed by 'Note de l'Editeur', (573)-583
'table des matières', verso blank, followed by 8
unnumbered pages of drawings of fencing positions.
Imprimerie Dondey-Dupré, rue St-Louis, 46, au Marais.
Reprinted, same format, pagination and illustrations,
1847.

GRISIER, (A) : "Les armes et le duel" par A. Grisier Chevalier
de la Légion d'honneur, décoré de la médaille d'or
et d'honneur de Suède professeur d'armes De la
maison civile et militaire de S.M. l'Empereur, des cent-
gardes, du lycée Napoléon et du Conservatoire impérial
de musique ouvrage agréé par S.M. l'Empereur de
Russie préface anecdotique par Alexandre Dumas notice
sur l'auteur, par Roger de Beauvoir. - épître en vers
de Méry. - lettres du comte d'H*** et du comte d'I***
dessins par E. de Beaumont portrait de Grisier par E.
Lassalle troisième édition revue, corrigée et augmentée Paris chez E. Dentu, éditeur libraire de la
société des gens de lettres 13 et 17, galérie d'Orléans
(Palais-Royal) et chez l'auteur, rue du Faubourg-
Montmartre, 1864. Large 8vo., 3 unnumbered pages
'dédicace de la première édition A sa Majesté Nicolas
Ier Empereur de toutes les Russies ... ... ' signed :
A. Grisier, professeur d'armes ... ... , verso blank,
1 unnumbered page consisting of letter address to
Grisier dated 'Paris, le 12 août 1842' signed :
Kisseleff Ambassade impériale de Russie, verso blank,
followed by portrait engraving of Grisier entitled 'Le
Chevalier de St Georges', (11)-13 'avertissement de la
première édition' signed : A. Grisier. Paris,
septembre 1846, verso blank, (15)-58 'préface en forme
de causerie ou causerie en forme de préface' signed
: Alexandre DUMAS, (59)-76 'Notice sur Grisier' Par
M. Roger de Beauvoir, signed : Roger de Beauvoir.
De la Folie-Bellanger, près Grosbois, le 4 août 1846,
(77)-83 letter to de Beauvoir signed : E. Grisier,
verso blank, (85)-93 'Le duel avant-propos', verso
blank, (95)-572, unnumbered page 'A mes lecteurs'
signed : A. Grisier, verso blank, (575)-581 'A M.
Grisier apres la lecture de son manuscrit' signed :
Méry. Paris, Novembre, 1846, verso blank, 583-588
letter to Grisier signed : Comte L. d'H***. Courbevoie, 6 décembre, 589-596 letter to Grisier signed :

Comte D'I***. Paris, 15 janvier 1862, (597)-607 'table des matières'. Woodcuts facing pages 56 and 72; fencing positions facing pages 228, 230, 232, 234, 236, 238, 240 and 242. Lagay, imprimerie de A. Varigault.

HADJI-ABD-el-HAMID-BEY : "Voyage au pays des Niam-Niams ou hommes a queue" avec le portrait d'un Niam-Niam, et une notice biographique sur l'auteur par Alexandre Dumas, par Hadji-Abd-el-Hamid-Bey Paris, P. Martinon, libraire, ... , 1854, 8vo., pp. (7)-20 introduction signed : Alex. Dumas, (21)-102, unnumbered page table of contents, verso blank, and additional unnumbered page detailed table of contents; portrait of a Niam-Niam following the title-page and facing Dumas' introduction Green wrappers, front wrapper repeating the title-page, and back wrapper repeating the portrait of a Niam-Niam.

LANGLE, Caliste de : "Les coeurs vaillants" - Louise de Kéristan - Rose Legère - Jeanne de Nelglas. Paris, E. Dentu ... 1869, 8vo., pp. (i)-iv 'préface' signed : Alex. Djmas, (1)-278, and 3 additional unnumbered pages table of contents. Brown wrappers.

LAROCHE, Benjamin : "Oeuvres dramatiques de Shakspeare (sic)" Traduction nouvelle par Benjamin Laroche, précédée d'une introduction sur le génie de Shakspeare (sic), par Alexandre Dumas Tome premier Paris, Marchant, Editeur du magasin théatral ... , 1839, 4to., pp. (iii) viii 'Introduction' signed : Alexandre Dumas, (1)-700 and additional unnumbered page table of contents. (The first of only two volumes.)

MAYNARD, Félix : Publié par Alexandre Dumas "Impressions de voyage De Paris a Sébastopol" par le Dr Félix Maynard Paris Librairie nouvelle boulevard des Italiens, 15, en face de la maison dorée. 1855, 16mo., pp. (i)-viii 'préface' signed : Alex. DUMAS. Paris, le 8 juillet 1855, (1)-5 'avant-propos', verso blank, (7)-308. Bibliothèque nouvelle. Paris. - Typ. de Mme Ve Dondey-Dupré, rue Saint-Louis, 46.

MEURICE, Paul : Nouvelle bibliothèque dramatique Paul Meurice (Vignette) "Les deux Diane" drame en cinq actes et huit tableaux représenté pour la première fois a Paris sur le théatre de l'Ambigu, le 8 mars 1865. Paris, Librairie internationale ... A. Lacroix, Verboeckhoven et Ce éditeurs, n.d. (1865), 4to., pp. (3)-32 in double columns; on the verso of the front wrapper, immediately above 'personnages' is printed a letter from Dumas to Meurice.

(There has been so much bibliographical confusion with regard to both the romance of the same name and the play that it is essential for clarification to quote the relevant part of Dumas' letter which comprised what is, in fact, a preface to the first (1865) edition.)

'Mon cher Meurice,

....

Vous fites sous mon nom les "Deux Diane".

L'ouvrage eut du succès, autant, plus peut-être, que si je l'eusse fait moi-même.

Mais, au moment où je vendis mes livres à Lévy, je previns Parfait et Lévy que le roman des "Deux Diane", vous appartenant en entier, devait disparaître de ma collection. Absent depuis cinq ans bientôt de la France, je n'ai pu rappeler cette circonstance au souvenir de mes deux amis; de sorte que le livre a été réimprimé comme étant de moi, quoiqu'il soit de vous.

Aujourd'hui que votre intention est de faire un drame de ce livre, je dois déclarer sur l'honneur que je ne suis pour rien dans sa composition, et que même, pour mettre ma conscience à couvert, et peut-être aussi pour me ménager des regrets le jour où je devrais vous le rendre, je ne l'ai jamais lu.

Seulement je puis affirmer qu'à toute personne qui m'a fait compliment sur les "Deux Diane" j'ai raconté la petite anecdote que je consigne ici comme un fait ayant valeur de renonciation à toute propriété sur ce livre, une fois révolu le traité de Lévy, qui l'a réimprimé par erreur.

Je desiré, mon bon et cher Paul, que cette lettre soit rendue publique. .... Quant au drame, faites ce que vous voudrez. Je renonce à tout droit sur lui, n'y ayant aucun droit.

Quant au livre, il me ferait plaisir qu'à la nouvelle édition de Lévy fera des "Deux Diane", il mit votre nom près du mien, jusqu'au moment où la propriété vous reviendra, laissant la place à votre nom seul. ....

                              Alexandre Dumas.'
Reprinted, 12mo., 1865, and 4to., (187).

REBOUL, Jean : "Poésies" par Jean Revoul, de Nîmes. Précédées d'une préface par M. Alexandre Dumas. Et d'une lettre à l'éditeur, par M. Alphonse de Lamartine. Paris, Librairie de Charles Gosselin et Cie., MDCCCXXXVI, 8vo., pp. (i)-iv Lettre à l'éditeur, signed : Lamartine, (v)-xvi 'Une visite à Nîmes' par M. Alexandre Dumas. "Les arènes de Nîmes", poem, 1-368, (369)-371 table of contents. Yellow wrappers.

There were two intervening editions of the book before the following was published :

"Poésies" par Jean Revoul de Nîmes précédées d'une préface par M. A. Dumas et d'une lettre a l'éditeur par M. de Lamartine. Quatrième édition revue et corrigée. Paris, Librairie de Charles Gosselin et Cⁱᵉ., MDCCCXXXVII, 12mo., pp. (1)-4 Lettre a l'éditeur signed : Lamartine, (5)-15 'Une visite a Nîmes' par M. Alexandre Dumas, (16)-21 'A. M. Alexandre Dumas' signed : J. Reboul. (23)-332, (333)-335 table of contents.

368

REVOIL, Bénédict Henry : "Vive la chasse" par Bénédict Henry Révoil préface par Alexandre Dumas Paris Librairie Achille Faure ... 1867, 12mo., pp. (i)-ii 'préface' signed : Alexandre Dumas, (1)-299, verso blank, and additional unnumbered page table of contents.

"Histoire physiologique et anecdote des chiens de toutes les races" par Bénédict-Henry Révoil préface et post-face par Alexandre Dumas (Vignette) Paris, E. Dentu ... 1867, 8vo., pp. (i)-vii 'Préface' signed : Alexandre Dumas, (1)-388, (389)-394 'Post-face - Une anecdote de chien" signed : Alexandre Dumas, and additional unnumbered page table of contents.

VAYSSIERES, A. : Collection Hetzel. "Souvenirs d'un voyage en Abyssinie" par A. Vayssières, avec un avant-propos d'Alexandre Dumas. Edition autorisée pour la Belgique et l'étranger, interdite pour la France. Bruxelles, Meline, Cans et cie., 1857, 2 volumes, pp. 222 and 206, each with an additional unnumbered page table of contents. 'Avant-propos d'un ami de l'auteur' signed : Alex. Dumas occupies pp. (5)-19 of Volume 1. Green wrappers.

"Notice sur la ville de Louviers et son arrondissement" (extrait du "Dictionnaire historique de l'Eure", de MM. Charpillon et l'abbé Caresme), précédée d'une préface d'Alexandre Dumas. Les Andelys, Delcroix, 1881, 8vo., pp. i-iv 'Préface' signed : Alexandre Dumas Paris, Le 22 décembre 1867, 23 in double columns.

"La ville d'Evreux et son arrondissement" (extrait du "Dictionnaire historique du département de l'Eure") précédée d'une préface d'Alexandre Dumas père. Les Andelys, Delcroix, 1881, 8vo., pp. i-iv 'Préface' signed : Alexandre Dumas Paris, le 22 décembre 1867, 148, and map; illustrated.

"La ville de Vernon et son canton" (extrait du "Dictionnaire historique du département de l'Eure") précédée d'une préface de A. Dumas. Les Andelys, Delcroix, 1881, 8vo., pp. i-iv 'Préface' signed : Alexandre Dumas Paris, le 22 décembre 1867, 11, and map; illustrated.
The preface to the three above-mentioned works is identical.

GENERAL INDEX

374

386

AUTHOR INDEX TO WORKS TO WHICH
DUMAS CONTRIBUTED PREFACES

TITLE INDEX TO WORKS TO WHICH
DUMAS CONTRIBUTED PREFACES